D1473926

Dear Laura —
A Whitley legacy
Seasons Greetings 2012
Love Always — Gail

There Are No Letters Like Yours

The Correspondence of Isabelle de Charrière and Constant d'Hermenches

Isabelle de Charrière

Translated and with an introduction and annotations
by Janet Whatley *and* Malcolm Whatley

University of Nebraska Press
Lincoln and London

Publication of this volume was assisted by financial support from the University
Committee on Research and Scholarship of the Graduate College and the Dean's
Fund of the University of Vermont, from the Foundation for the Production and
Translation of Dutch Literature, and from Pro Helvetia.
Translations of the letters are based on Isabelle de Charrière, *Oeuvres Complètes*
© 2000 by the University of Nebraska Press
Manufactured in the United States of America

Library of Congress Cataloging-in-Publication Data

Charrière, Isabelle de, 1740–1805
There are no letters like yours : the correspondence of Isabelle
de Charrière and Constant d'Hermenches / Isabelle de Charrière ;
Translated and with an introduction and annotations by Janet Whatley
and Malcolm Whatley.
   p.   cm. – (European women writers series)
   Includes bibliographical references and index.
   ISBN 0-8032-1714-5 (cloth: alk. paper)
1. Charrière Isabelle de, 1740–1805—Correspondence. 2. Constant
de Rebecque, David-Louis-Constant de, 1722–1785—Correspondence.
3. Authors, Swiss—18th century—Correspondence. I. Constant de
Rebecque, David-Louis-Constant de, 1722–1785. II. Whatley, Janet,
1938– . III. Whatley, Malcolm, 1935– . IV. Title. V. Series.
PQ1963.C55Z484   2000
848'.509—dc21
[B]   99-30004
                                                         CIP

CONTENTS

MAPS AND ILLUSTRATIONS

ACKNOWLEDGMENTS

In the long process of making this book, we have received support of many kinds from many sources. We are grateful for the interest and attention of our friends and colleagues. Joan Hinde Stewart and Jacqueline Letzter have, from the outset, offered their insights and expertise with an engaged enthusiasm for our work and have greatly contributed to our pleasure in doing it. We also want particularly to thank Veronica Richel and Grant Crichfield, who have read portions of the manuscript and made useful suggestions.

The staff members of Bailey-Howe Library at the University of Vermont have provided the unstinting help for which they are well known; Connell Gallagher, the director of Special Collections, has always been willing to track down and gain access for us to rare eighteenth-century volumes.

Some members of the team of specialists who assembled the great critical edition of Isabelle de Charrière's *Oeuvres complètes* have given us invaluable advice and encouragement. Cecil Courtney has cheered us on from the beginning of our enterprise and has given us some important leads. Simone and Pierre Dubois, to whom all readers of Isabelle de Charrière owe so much, welcomed us to their home in the Hague in the summer of 1998; in our long conversation and subsequent correspondence, they have helped us fine-tune our ideas on the complicated epistolary relationship contained in this book.

The staff of the University of Nebraska Press has helped make this labor-intensive project a joy to work on. From the warm welcome they gave our proposal to their care with the seemingly infinite detail of page preparation, they have been unfailingly responsive, considerate, and insightful. We consider ourselves fortunate to have worked with them.

At the University of Vermont, the Department of Romance Languages and the Dean's Fund of the College of Arts and Sciences subsidized research travel to Utrecht and Castle Zuylen, from which much of this correspondence was written. The Dean's Fund and the University Committee on Research and Scholarship have provided grants to help defray the costs of publication; funding has also been provided by the Foundation for the Production and Translation of Dutch Literature and by Pro Helvetia. We thank them all.

Some of the material in the Introduction to this volume first appeared in an essay by Janet Whatley, "Letters to a Libertine: The Correspondence of Belle de Zuylen and Constant d'Hermenches," in *Women Writers in Pre-Revolutionary France: Strategies in Emancipation*, ed. Colette Winn and Donna Kuizenga (New York: Garland, 1997), 335–348; Garland Publishing has kindly granted permission to use that material here in its modified and expanded form.

INTRODUCTION

In 1760 the twenty-year-old Belle de Zuylen sent a clandestine letter to a military officer, David-Louis Constant d'Hermenches. With that she launched a correspondence of some sixteen years that is one of the richest of a whole age of great letter writing. Through some happy accidents of history and personality, this epistolary dialogue has come down to us almost entire; it gives us intimate access to the workings of two minds of extraordinary vigor and scope, as well as to the life of eighteenth-century Europe.

One of the correspondents, Belle de Zuylen, was to become better known to posterity by her married name—Isabelle de Charrière. In her own time she was only moderately famous as a writer of novellas; but the years have shown her to be an author of rare insight and subtlety, whose subjects range from the intricate ambiguities of courtship and marriage to the wrenching dislocations of the French Revolution.

David-Louis Constant d'Hermenches was known in his own time as a man of the world with considerable standing in the aristocratic salons; as a courageous soldier; as a fine amateur actor and musician; as a writer of occasional pamphlets and verse; as an activist, along with Voltaire, in causes of justice; and as something of a womanizer. Today he is known chiefly through this correspondence with Belle de Zuylen; the keenness of his intellect and the verve of his personal style survive mainly in his letters to her.

Isabella Agneta Elisabeth van Tuyll van Serooskerken—known familiarly to her contemporaries as Belle de Zuylen—was born in 1740. The period of her youth and early maturity coincided with the last decades of the Dutch Republic, in which the princes of the House of Orange were the hereditary Stadholders—the chief magistrates of the state. Her father, Diederik Jacob, Baron van Tuyll van Serooskerken, belonged to a highly respected family of the ancient Dutch nobility, and he had connections with some of the most powerful people in the Netherlands. Known as a man of steady, imperturbable temperament and unassailable integrity, he was entrusted—in a country where much of the land is below sea level—with the inspection of dikes and public works. His wife, Helena Jacoba, née de Vicq, was from a wealthy merchant family of Amsterdam that had amassed a fortune in the East Indies. While she was of a more impetuous nature than her husband, they seem to have been a devoted and happy couple. Belle was the eldest of the five children who survived to adulthood; the others were Willem René, Diederik Jacob (Ditie, her favorite), Johanna Maria (Mitie), and Vincent Maximiliaan. For her brothers, especially Ditie and Vincent, Belle was a comrade, confidant, and mentor (she was always giving them reading assignments). She was fond of her sister, Mitie, but was frequently exasperated with her. It was with her paternal cousin Anna Elisabeth (Annebetje) that she had the most sisterly relationship of her life.

The Tuyll family had two chief residences, both of which are still standing: a handsome gray stone town house by a canal in Utrecht—the Kromme Nieuwe Gracht—where they spent the winter months; and the ancestral chateau at Zuylen, a few miles away on the River Vecht, where they spent the summers and where Belle was born. Castle Zuylen, with its moat and medieval turrets, its serpentine wall, its orchards and formal gardens, attracts a steady flow of visitors today—not only for its association with a famous writer but for its intrinsic beauty of architecture and setting. Belle's father had parts of the chateau remodeled; the main entrance is of an unostentatious elegance that comports with what we know of his character. Today one can walk through the very corridors and trace the very garden paths where Belle and her father paced up and down, arm in arm, pursuing their arguments and shaping their consensus about her future. The rows of ancestral portraits that loomed over the dining room, and whose presence Belle was to satirize and exorcize in one of her first literary works, loom there still.

Like most aristocratic children of their time, the young Tuylls were educated by tutors and governesses. One of them deserves special mention: Jeanne-Louise Prevost joined the Tuyll household when Belle was eight years old. Two years later Mlle Prevost took Belle to spend a year in her native city of Geneva, with a brief visit to Paris and Versailles. French was the international language of the European upper classes, and it was already in use in Belle's family along with their native Dutch. By her own report, Belle's eagerness to perfect her French dates from that trip to Geneva. It became her primary language of expression, and in it she developed a wonderfully lucid and supple style. The Dutch language appears in her letters to her family, but mainly in isolated words and phrases.

Mlle Prevost left the Tuyll household when Belle was thirteen. She remained warmly attached to her former pupil, and over the next five years wrote to her frequently. None of Belle's answers have survived, but Mlle Prevost's letters are a valuable document of Belle's early adolescence. She is clearly aware of Belle's great gifts, and is full of admiration for the wide reading, the variety of talents that Belle is developing—painting, harpsichord, needlework; but she also sees tendencies in Belle that require some vigilance and self-discipline. She warns Belle about her penchant for melancholy; she suggests that she reflect a little on the tears of wounded vanity that flow too easily; she urges her to take measures to combat the "vapors." Mlle Prevost saw rather clearly the particular mixture of fragility and robustness in the young girl who had been her charge. She gives advice much like what the adult Isabelle de Charrière herself will often give: "Compare yourself only with what you should be; otherwise you could be too easily satisfied."[1]

1. Letter 29, *O.C.* 1: 61.

Belle de Zuylen did not marry until she was thirty. The status of an un-married adult woman had its awkwardness and discomforts, but she had a full decade for independent personal development. Her need for intellectual nourishment and discipline was the requirement of her nature that she ex-pressed the most often and the most earnestly. "Not for a throne," she said, "would I give up the things that occupy me in my room" (97).[2] She im-mersed herself in the French classical writers: Montaigne, Pascal, Molière, Racine, La Fontaine, La Rochefoucauld, Fénelon, and that model of all letter-writers, Mme de Sévigné. By the age of eighteen she had read Mon-tesquieu's *De l'esprit des lois,* and she was reading the works of Voltaire, Rousseau, and the whole community of philosophes as they were coming off the press.

The language and literary culture of France exercised a powerful pull on her, but the culture of French high society and the political culture of France attracted her not at all. She could be merciless on the subject of French artificiality, and she lamented the efforts of Hollanders who laboriously affected a foreign style they could never internalize or master. The age of the French classical writers she adored was also the most violent period of French military aggression against Holland. The French influence on Dutch culture that she welcomed was that which had come with the in-flux of French Protestants at the time of the Revocation of the Edict of Nantes in 1685. La Fontaine's fables had spread through Holland in the book crates of the exiles who sought refuge in the land of Erasmus and Spinoza—the land where Descartes and Pierre Bayle had been free to write, and where the publishing houses of Amsterdam, Utrecht, and the Hague were pouring forth the critical and subversive texts from which the En-lightenment rose.[3] "I would like the whole world to be my country," she wrote (395). She reflected on what she perceived as anomalies in her temperament and situation. "It is truly an astonishing thing that I am called Dutch and Tuyll" (210). But in a sense, it is her very "Dutchness"—that Dutch humanist heritage—that makes of her a cosmopolite; it is part of the context of her love for the language and literature of England, and for her readings of the philosophers of the Scottish Enlightenment.

Belle chafed under the constraints on behavior and resented the rounds of social appearances imposed by her membership in the aristocracy, yet she took immense pride in the integrity that was the hallmark of her family. "Of all the Tuylls of my acquaintance there is not one miser, not one deceiver, not one coward, not one woman of easy virtue, not a one who would com-mit a base act for any self-interest whatsoever—no one, in fact, who is not

2. Numbers in parentheses following quotations refer to pages in this volume.
3. In 1788, in her *Observations et conjectures politiques,* she wrote: "To whom does France owe that pleasing influence she exerts ... if it is not to her refugees, scattered throughout the Protestant countries?... Thanks to French tutors, Dutch and German children learn La Fontaine by heart as soon as they are old enough to speak" (*O.C.* 10: 79).

beneficent and capable of generous acts" (201). While Belle was expected to meet the standards of behavior and decorum for a young woman of her class, her parents helped her maintain a domain of autonomy and independence in which she pursued her own studies.

Belle's was a vital and vigorous private mental life, but that was not all that she wished for. She wanted a husband and children, and she wanted the status and independence of a married woman. As she advanced through her twenties, she came to feel that such prospects were eluding her. The distinction of her family and her own personal grace and beauty ought to have made her the most marriageable of young women—and indeed, there was an international list of noblemen courting her, sometimes through royal intermediaries (Frederick the Great was interested in her prospects, and her name was suggested to the young prince of Orange). Yet nothing was happening. She was not quite rich enough for the most avid fortune-hunters, and she was far too headstrong—too outspoken, too witty, too irreverent—for a titled suitor looking for the placidity of an arranged marriage. She had a freedom of manner, a way of moving through a room, that made people talk. "That one, a demoiselle!" exclaimed an ambassador's wife (145). As Belle told James Boswell, who wooed her with with a comic ambivalence, "I lack the subaltern talents."⁴ She was, she noted ruefully, regarded as a "marvel"; there was more of her than she knew what to do with or than anyone else knew what to do with. But in fact what she valued above all was her practical sense: "What makes me and my mind such great friends is its excellence for everyday use" (97). She intended to master some hard essential things: physics, for which one must have mathematics: "I don't like half-knowledge" (58). She warded off melancholy, boredom, and the disheartening contemplation of a series of uninspiring suitors with a vigorous self-imposed intellectual discipline of mathematics and music, poetry and history—and the beginnings of her own writing.

Her first published work, *Le Noble* (1762), is from this period of her young womanhood, and it probably did not improve her marital prospects. It is a high-spirited satire of the pretentions of the nobility, in which the rebellious aristocratic heroine elopes with her plebeian lover by leaping out of the ancestral chateau onto a platform that she builds by throwing the family portraits out the window.

At about the same time she also wrote and circulated a provocative literary self-portrait: "Portrait de Zélide."

> Compassionate by temperament, liberal and generous by inclination, only on principle is Zélide charitable. When she is gentle and easygoing, be grateful to her: it's an effort. When she is civil and polite for very long with people she doesn't care about, redouble your admiration: that's a martyrdom. By nature, her vanity is limitless: knowledge

---

4. *O.C.* 1: 124.

and scorn of mankind had soon enough made her vain, but still, she goes too far with it to please even herself. She has quite concluded that glory is worth nothing at the cost of happiness, but still would she take measures for the sake of glory. When will the enlightenment of her mind command the inclination of her heart? Then will Zélide cease to be a coquette. Sad contradiction! Zélide, who would not without good reason strike a dog or crush the lowest insect, would perhaps at certain moments make a man unhappy, and that simply to amuse herself—to procure for herself a kind of glory that flatters her reason not at all and touches her vanity only for an instant. But the charm of it is brief; the aspect of such a success restores her to herself; no sooner has she recognized her intention than she despises it, abhors it, and wants to renounce it forever.

You ask me perhaps, is Zélide beautiful?... pretty?... passable? I do not know; that depends on whether one loves her or whether she wants to make herself loved. She has a beautiful bosom; she knows it, and makes rather much of it at the expense of modesty. Her hands are not white; she knows that too, and makes a joke of it—but she could do without that pretext for a joke.

Affectionate to excess, and no less scrupulous, she can be made happy neither by love nor without love. Friendship has no holier nor more worthy temple than Zélide. Seeing that she is too sensitive to be happy, she has almost given up on happiness; she attaches herself to virtue, she avoids regrets, and seeks diversions. Pleasures are rare for her, but they are keen; she seizes them and savors them ardently. Knowing the vanity of plans and the uncertainty of the future, she would above all make the passing moment happy.

Do you not perceive it? Zélide is somewhat sensual. Her imagination can be merry even when her heart is afflicted. Sensations too keen and powerful for her machine, and an excessive vitality without a satisfactory object—these are the sources of all her ills. With less susceptible organs, Zélide would have had the soul of a great man; with less mind and reason, she would have been only a weak woman.[5]

The vividness and mobility of expression, the touch of arrogance, the sensual richness—the painter Quentin de La Tour despaired, he said, at capturing it all on canvas; nonetheless he left us a ravishing portrait in pastels of Belle de Zuylen in the prime of her youth.

David-Louis, Baron de Constant de Rebecque, Seigneur d'Hermenches et de Villars-Mendraz, was born in 1722 to a family of the French nobility who, as Protestants, had emigrated to Switzerland in the sixteenth century and had settled near Lausanne. His father, Samuel de Constant, had had a

5. *O.C.* 10: 37.

distinguished military career in the service of Holland—in a letter to the duc de Richelieu, Voltaire would describe d'Hermenches as the son of "the very devil of a general." At the age of fourteen, d'Hermenches was commissioned as an officer in the regiment that his father owned. In 1744 he marrepried Louise de Seigneux, seven years older than he; they had a son and a daughter. In 1745, when his father was a general in the War of the Austrian Succession, d'Hermenches was made his adjutant. The black headband that he wore later on covered the disfigurement from a wound he received fighting against the French at the Battle of Fontenoy in 1745.

D'Hermenches had a talented amateur's bent for writing, and tried his hand at poems and plays. While he did not take himself very seriously as a writer, he was quite seriously engaged in the intellectual life of his time. When Voltaire moved to Lausanne in 1755, there sprang up between the two of them a camaraderie based largely on their love of the theater, but extending to their commitment to justice and to an engaged debate on the role of religion in human affairs. Most of the Constant clan in Lausanne became involved in producing and acting Voltaire's plays, which were put on at a private theater at the estate of d'Hermenches' sister. D'Hermenches himself triumphed as the amorous and despotic sultan; he created the role of Orosmane in Voltaire's *Zaïre*.

He was also involved in one of the great Enlightenment-era causes that Voltaire pursued so famously; he played a significant role in the celebrated Calas case (of which more later), in which Voltaire led a movement that succeeded in reversing the verdict of a *parlement* that had executed an innocent man. Shortly afterwards Voltaire published a pamphlet on deism, d'Hermenches published a rebuttal, and the two exchanged letters about it.

In the late 1740s d'Hermenches had gone to the Hague as a colonel in a Swiss regiment in the service of Holland. His wife had moved there with him, but the couple were gradually becoming estranged. Her health seems to have required a more retired life, and she had returned to their estate near Lausanne. It was as a married man who had been living alone in the Hague that Constant d'Hermenches met Belle de Zuylen in 1760.

With his black headband and his mordant wit, d'Hermenches cut a dashing figure in the society of the Hague. By the testimony of at least one acquaintance, Edward Gibbon, he was regarded as abrasive and arrogant.[6] He could also be charming, and, as his letters show, he wanted to be able to think of himself as generous. He had quite a reputation as a libertine, but in his own credible accounts of his affairs with women he appears more scrupulous than unprincipled. He cared a great deal about what people thought of him, and he meditated at length about what he thought of himself.

6. See *Le Journal de Gibbon à Lausanne* 165.

His niece Rosalie de Constant—whose reputation as a "devilishly intelligent" child had once reached Belle (451)—left a literary portrait of him
that can be set next to the "Portrait de Zélide":

> He possessed along with a handsome physique a great deal of wit and
> all the resources to achieve success. Great ambition and great amour-
> propre left him few moments of repose. He wanted to ally all kinds of
> pleasures with all kinds of business; philosophy with sensuality; the
> most extreme economy with ostentatious display and magnificence; his
> wife with his mistresses. He wanted to be, in turn, courtier, author,
> military officer, farmer, scholar—even a pious one—, although always
> an epicurean. He laid claim to everything; he had every ambition: he
> wanted to dominate in society, govern his friends, crush his enemies,
> triumph over all his rivals. Sometimes he succeeded; but many things
> escaped him, and the end of his life was less happy than the beginning.[7]

The occasion of the meeting between Belle and d'Hermenches was a ball
given at the Hague on February 28, 1760 by the Duke of Brunswick-Wolfenbüttel, to mark the marriage of the sister of the Stadholder Willem V,
prince of Orange. "I have never bothered about etiquette," she wrote later,
"and whenever I have encountered what might be called a physiognomy, I
have always had a passion for getting it to speak" (94). "Do you remember
when you and I met? You reproached me for something or other from our
second word; at our third, we were friends for life. You knew me at once;
you saw into me" (263). That moment of instant mutual recognition was
enough to make her write her first letter to him, in March 1760—a nervous
testing of the waters, in which she both invites and discourages a correspondence. She expects no response, she says. "Burn this" is the refrain of
her early letters—but she tells him exactly how to route a letter back to her.

Two years passed before Belle's next letter to him. They had the occasion
to see each other again in June 1762 at another ball at the Hague, this one
given by the British ambassador to celebrate the birthday of King
George III. She wrote to d'Hermenches from Utrecht shortly afterwards,
and from then on their correspondence can be traced almost continuously
until its end, fourteen years later.

The risks of a clandestine correspondence between a highborn Dutch virgin and an older married man of the world are obvious. But Belle de Zuylen
rather enjoyed playing with fire and quibbling with d'Hermenches over

7. The original French of this passage, from Rosalie de Constant's *Souvenirs*, is given in
Philippe Godet, *Madame de Charrière et ses amis, d'après de nombreux documents inédits
(1740–1805)* 1: 38.

whether theirs was a *liaison dangereuse* (his term for what he said it was not). They were sophisticated readers of the great epistolary novels of their time—Richardson's *Clarissa*, Rousseau's *La Nouvelle Héloïse*—and were well versed in their literary and moral conventions. (That *summa* of epistolary and libertine traditions, *Les Liaisons dangereuses* of Choderlos de Laclos, was not published until 1782, six years after the end of their correspondence.)

In those novels, the heroine who writes letters—and especially letters to a libertine—teeters on the rim of an abyss. But Belle is not Clarissa or Julie or Mme de Tourvel. While she is not unaware that conventional wisdom would ascribe danger to her correspondence with d'Hermenches, and while she may for a time enjoy—even dramatize—a sense of risk, she intends to take from this experience what she wants and no more. She has behind her an unshakeable self-respect, grounded in her love and pride in her family, and in the probity (a key word in her discourse) that she regards as the essential element of the Tuyll heritage. And while she resorts to elaborate casuistry to excuse her concealment of the correspondence, she is never willing to put at risk her parents' trust and love and never willing to claim her own happiness at the price of theirs.

However tempting the comparison might be, d'Hermenches is not a Lovelace or a Valmont. While he says that he has the instincts of a conqueror, he seems not to possess those of a destroyer. The account he gives in these letters of his relationships with women—especially the most vulnerable ones—suggest that he is a man of considerable scruples and generosity. His dealings with Belle are based an an epistolary contract that is at least implicit in their early letters. We do not know what they said directly to each other or what Belle is referring to in her first letter by "what you offered at the concert"; what does ensue is a chaste attachment of depth, scope, and duration.

D'Hermenches says:

> ... no one senses better than I do all her worth; no one could be more useful to her; I am not a dangerous connection for her.... I have had many misfortunes in my life, lovely Agnes, but you make me forget them all; you reconcile me with life, with human society. (8–9)

To which she replies:

> I hear it incessantly repeated, even by those who admire you, that you are the most dangerous of men, and that one cannot be too much on one's guard with you. (10)
>
> ... It vexes me, I admit, to have to give up the most charming letters in the world, and the pleasure of writing without constraint to a man who would understand me so well—on whom nothing would be lost.... A correspondence like yours ... would flatter me and instruct me. (11)

... You tell me that I make you forget your misfortunes—that I reconcile you with the human race. If what you say is sincere, I regret having to renounce the pleasure of rendering you such a great service. (13)

Thus they envision the potential of their correspondence: he, with all his worldly experience, will be for her an ideal reader, the witness to all the range and subtlety of her personality—the one on whom nothing will be lost (and indeed she fears that what she has to offer *will* be lost). She, in turn, will be for him a fresh source of moral inspiration; she will understand him (he later says) as nobody else does. She will regenerate him, cure his misanthropy, serve as his moral compass, help him redeem his losses.

What they had envisioned, of course, is not absolutely realized; some things *are* lost on d'Hermenches. Nevertheless, their correspondence gave them a medium in which to shape their inner lives in words as she passed from girlhood to maturity and as he lived out a decade and a half of his middle age. Both of them used these letters to reflect on their own characters, on their sense of their own possibilities, on their awareness of their own latent powers and unused talents—and on their own fallibilities and vulnerabilities. D'Hermenches felt that his military career was stagnating; Belle was watching her twenties go by without bringing her the marriage that, she felt sure, was the precondition of her independence and proper use of her energies. Both of them felt trapped in their personae as well as their circumstances: the middle-aged man cast in the role of the arrogant rake, the misanthropic Don Juan; the young woman in that of the arrogant, impudent *bel esprit* or *femme savante*. Each sought from the other a more complete kind of recognition and comprehension.

Both d'Hermenches and Belle found the society of the Hague—the society of high-ranking diplomats and officers and their wives—stuffy and pretentious. They found it resentful of genius and quick to judge—particularly to judge *them*—on the basis of petty prejudices. "The ladies of the Hague," wrote Belle, "tear me to shreds" (7). And yet, that same society was their realm of public life. Both of them reflected at length on what it means to come to terms with the world that one must live in. Thus, many of their letters that seem to be mere gossip about long-forgotten Dutch socialites are in fact meditations on the nature of friendship, on the formations and limits of loyalty, on one's expectations in human intercourse. For these two, gossip is hardly ever merely gossip.

Belle used the correspondence with Constant d'Hermenches to explore realms of experience that might otherwise have been closed to her. She could speak of her own desires, her own sensuality, her need to deploy her mental energies, her hopes for what she could give and receive in marriage and motherhood. She also learned how to be a friend to a complicated older man—how to let him air his disappointments and resentments; how to help him think about the shape of his life as well as her own; how to choose among the many kinds of advice he gave her. Throughout the sixteen years of their letters, d'Hermenches never stopped telling her of the profound sense of refreshment, clarity, and moral grounding he found in his epistolary friendship with her. "Write me," he says, "one of your good long letters that are a whole course of instruction for me" (185).

The early part of their correspondence is clandestine and accident-prone—letters slip out of Belle's pockets and fall into her mother's hands—but its content is not particularly private: they talk about each other's literary efforts, and the nature of friendship versus love; about d'Hermenches' collaboration with Voltaire on behalf of the Calas family; about Belle's transparently anonymous novella.

After a couple of years of this, in the summer of 1764, d'Hermenches comes to the kermess at Utrecht bringing his friend, the marquis de Bellegarde, a Catholic nobleman from Savoie. Suddenly there is a plan: Belle should marry the marquis. Bellegarde, while attractive enough, was middle-aged, heavily in debt, a casual womanizer, not excessively bright, and totally devoid of initiative. Belle leapt into the project with abandon. This marriage, she thought, would give her liberty, an establishment of her own, a pleasant, easy-going man to make a life with, and children to raise and educate. At the same time it would place her in a social circle of which d'Hermenches was a part. D'Hermenches, who is normally not given to Rousseauistic effusions, imagines himself as neighbor and guest, forming with them "a trio of perfect intimacy such as no poet, I think, has ever yet dared imagine" (112). This project will, of course, be a fiasco. But while it lasts—and it goes on for years—it is an objective around which the relationship between Belle and d'Hermenches can form and re-form itself.

Almost immediately, Belle writes d'Hermenches a letter—the famous Letter 107—that redefines their relationship. She begins by owning up to the fact that their correspondence—like all correspondences—has indeed been constructed according to rules devised to achieve certain objectives. She then proceeds to rewrite the rules. With a new candor she lays out the ways in which a marriage must provide for the emotional needs of the parties—the erotic needs, certainly, but the whole range of other temperamental needs as well. "My senses are like my heart and my mind, avid to be pleased.... The most imperceptible odor delights or disturbs me; the very air that I breathe—now a little softer, now a little finer—works on me with all the variations that it undergoes itself. So you may judge of the rest; you may judge of my desires and distastes" (88–89). The letter is a display—a celebration even—of her own capacity for desire: not a desire for anyone in particular but a more general sexual energy—a component of her total personal energy, hers to use and bestow and create with. If she had no parents, she says, she could imagine herself as a Ninon de Lenclos—a free-living *femme de lettres* who openly takes lovers. But she *does* have parents, and her authentic and spontaneous concern for their feelings closes off that route. There remains marriage: what are its true and proper obligations? What reciprocity of attentive comprehension and forgiveness should be expected between husband and wife? As she will do over and over again in her fiction, she reimagines and redesigns the marriage contract. She does not expect her acute and delicate sensuality to be satisfied in every nuance; but she does hope that the terrain of the feelings and the senses need not be a minefield, that the marital relationship need not be a punitive one, that an impulse or an error need not be a catastrophe.

This liberal and humane kind of marriage is what she can imagine having with the marquis. But family difficulties lie ahead: the marquis is Catholic while Belle's family is Protestant. Memories of the wars of the Reformation—memories at the heart of Dutch identity—are still fresh. The reporting on the progress of the elaborate plots to obtain the consent of Belle's parents involves the reader in the very fabric of eighteenth-century family life.

D'Hermenches offers to write to her father to introduce Bellegarde as a suitor; but Belle, trusting no one as she does herself, writes the letter for him—the formal letter of one man to another recommending the disposition of a marriageable daughter. It is a masterful performance of ventriloquism. Belle is bent on controlling her own circulation, to the point of occasionally being appalled at her talent for plotting.

The long and complicated betrothal negotiations produce an intense spate of writing. Keeping herself awake all night with coffee, Belle pours out her heart in some truly astonishing letters—forty-four of them between July and November 1764. They are a strange kind of indirect loveletter, in which a passion for d'Hermenches is deflected onto the slightly absurd figure of Bellegarde. As the familiarity between the two correspondents deepens, Belle increasingly taps d'Hermenches' experience as a man of the world to make it part of what she knows or can imagine. Thus she embarks on long, leisurely speculations: "It seems to me that if I were a libertine, it would be in the style of the Marquis rather than in yours; you seek conquests, I would only seek pleasures" (100). And she goes on to compare and contrast various motives and styles of conquests, as she explores masculine prerogatives and subterfuges. D'Hermenches, drawn in by her candor and curiosity, begins to tell tales from his amatory history. Her imagination takes fire, and she begins to picture herself as one in a series of a libertine's conquests—in fact, she momentarily views herself in a whole range of roles that she cannot and would not want to live out in her own life. If the marriage to the marquis falls through, she wonders, will she become d'Hermenches' mistress?

That is not what happens. D'Hermenches' response to her feverish speculations is to defuse them. This relationship is not an amorous enterprise for him—he needs her more as a friend than as a mistress, and he needs more to be her friend than to be her lover. While Belle may briefly imagine herself as a fallen woman, she has the luxury of doing so with impunity because she has been deeply rooted in Tuyll probity and self-respect and in the solidity (she would say, at times, stolidity) of that Dutch culture that so exasperates her and to which she owes so much. And it is because of her confidence in his relationship to their correspondence that she is able to give him—and now us—such full access to her mind and to the range of her desires.

She refuses to let herself be dissipated and frittered away—either by society balls or by an addictive correspondence. "I cannot bear to neglect the things I do—to be learning nothing, to do only a single thing for a single person. A certain pride and an ardent desire for growth, for knowledge, for perfection, make me revolt against that state" (183).

Great friend though he is, great witness and sympathizer, there are limits to d'Hermenches' understanding of her: "Now tell me, for the love of God, what is there left for you to learn?... You already know only too much" (185). He has always mistrusted her love of mathematics, which, he says, "shrinks the imagination" (55); and he has always been uneasy with her investment in the dailiness of the things that surround her. He undervalues her touch on the ordinary, the quotidian. He likes imagining for her a brilliant role in French society—a notion she scorns. He fears for her a stoical resignation to obscure and modest circumstances that will limit and embitter her.

Their correspondence enters a period when the subject is no longer the blaze of passion. The negotiations over the marriage are stuck on two points: the dowry and the difference of religions. Bellegarde's estates are encumbered and he needs capital to pay off his mortgages. Belle's father pays her sister Mitie's dowry annually in an amount that is the interest on one hundred thousand florins. Bellegarde wants to be given a hundred thousand florins outright as dowry, not taking into account that in Mitie's case, the capital is not alienated from the Tuyll family estate. The difference in religion is more important. Van Tuyll cannot bring himself to give his daughter in marriage to a Catholic, but he commits himself to providing her dowry and receiving her husband if they wait until she achieves her majority at the age of twenty-five—provided that the legitimacy of Belle's children and their right to inherit the Bellegarde estates can be guaranteed. It turns out that this will require a dispensation from Rome.

Misgivings—or at any rate, grounds for misgivings—begin to occur to Belle. Rumors reach her that she cannot ignore and with which she directly confronts d'Hermenches several times: does the marquis have syphilis? Is this future she is trying to craft—a future of a sane marital happiness, friendship, and healthy intelligent children—poisoned at its physical base? And does the marquis even want her—in particular, does he want the whole being that she is? Over the course of the letters, we can observe Belle alternately perceiving and obscuring the possibility that, while d'Hermenches may be the person on whom nothing is lost, the marquis is the person on whom *everything* would be lost. D'Hermenches repeatedly urges Belle to keep her letters to Bellegarde short: "Don't metaphysicalize with a man who, I swear to you, never turns a page" (317).

The dowry, the dispensation, the question of Bellegarde's health—the whole dilatory nature of the proceedings work heavily on Belle, and she comes more and more to realize the depth of her unwillingness to cause her parents unhappiness. She decides to go for a half-year sojourn in England—the land of freedom, eccentricity, and *humour.* Her letters are now reports of English high society, and she finds she is describing not only its liberty but its coarseness. She watches Garrick perform, has Shakespeare explained to her, attends a session of Parliament, and talks to David Hume about roast beef and plum pudding; one evening she finds herself the target of a casual seduction scheme at the home of an aristocratic hostess.

She returns to Holland in May 1767, and by the following January it becomes clear that the Church will not give a dispensation on any terms that Belle can accept, and that prospects for a marriage to Bellegarde are at an end.

The correspondence is no longer clandestine, and it opens out into broader, more public channels. Constant d'Hermenches has, all along, been writing to her not only about her psyche and his, but also of his ambitions and frustrations as a career army officer. No less than Belle, he has been giving himself over to late-night confessions. We listen to him trying to figure out which of his prospects are now played out forever; to imagine what possibilities there are for new ventures; to decide what bids for recognition and glory are worth the candle. He finds in her the only friend who seems to understand his relationship to his métier. When he has the chance to leave the service of Holland as a staff officer and become a line officer in France, it is Belle that he consults about the implications of his choice. Once in France, he writes to her describing his life in the service of a newly revitalized French military system and the honors that begin to come his way.

In the spring of 1768 the French military presence on Corsica was increased, and d'Hermenches was transferred there. It was not the posting he would have most preferred, and indeed, at the time he was sent there it was not clear how the prospective belligerents were going to align themselves. Nevertheless, he did see prospects in the assignment for advancing his career. Again, it is Belle more than anyone else who understands the significance of these events to him: "You speak to me of my lot," he says, "in the same way I was thinking about it.... No one has written to me as you have about this expedition" (403). He receives this new assignment at the very moment that Belle is undertaking the translation of an influential work by an erstwhile suitor, James Boswell: his *Account of Corsica, the Journal of a Tour to that Island; and Memoirs of Pascal Paoli* (London, 1768). Shortly thereafter she abandons simultaneously both the translation and the idea—only briefly entertained with much seriousness—of marrying Boswell; but the work has fired her interest in the cause of Corsican independence that d'Hermenches is being sent to suppress. His letters give reports of the evolving diplomatic and political relationships among the key players on the island. He sends firsthand accounts of field conditions and battles, extracts from which Belle gets published in Dutch gazettes. Their letters to each other form a debate—by no means outdated today—on the rights and wrongs of colonial wars, and on the status of "advanced" nations bringing "enlightened" government to "backward" ones as mitigation for their domineering geopolitical strategies.

His letters from Corsica also show what that kind of war can do to and for a man: how it can focus his energies and his hopes for recognition; how it can both harden and bruise him; and how it can leave a long hangover, in which the returning soldier can neither recognize his old life nor find his place in a new one.

At about the time when d'Hermenches is returning from Corsica in 1768, Belle's family is devastated by the death of her mother. She died of a fever to which she was probably susceptible in the aftermath of a smallpox inoculation that Belle had strongly urged. When d'Hermenches is again established on the continent, his natural daughter Sophie, who was born in 1753, is living with him.

The correspondence has been going on for nearly a decade. Belle begins to speak of a pervasive weariness as she tries to take care of a family of bereaved and grumpy men, and as various marriage plans weave and unravel themselves. D'Hermenches is no longer her prime and unique confidant; there are more and more letters to her brother Ditie—who is not witty or ironic or even especially verbal. To Ditie she can write about the modest, scrupulous man she is falling in love with: her brothers' tutor, Charles-Emmanuel de Charrière, a quiet Swiss country gentleman. In her letters to d'Hermenches she writes hints and fragments of what's going on, and as he begins to guess who the "friend" is that she is apparently becoming attached to, he is disappointed and disapproving. "That's just the sort of notion someone like you would take into her head" (473). "I think that Charrière is an excellent man, but what pleasure, what amenity could you ever find in this?" (478). He reiterates an old anxiety of his: that she will, out of a kind of idealism and selective optimism, do something irrevocable that will not result in lasting happiness—either for her or for her husband. But d'Hermenches ascribed to Belle a bent toward a brilliance of life-style that she never had, while the difference between her own and Charrière's temperaments was certainly something that she was taking into account.

Belle's father also has misgivings about the alliance. As to fortune and rank, she is clearly marrying below the expectations of the aristocracy of Europe—the prince of Orange is reported to have asked later, "Could one ever have thought that the daughter of Monsieur van Zuylen would marry Monsieur de Charrière?"[8] But Diederik van Tuyll was, in this as in many things, ultimately more interested in what would make his daughter happy than in what society would think about it, and so when Belle persuaded him that this would indeed make her happy, he gave his consent.

Strange as it may seem, Charrière himself expressed doubts similar to those of d'Hermenches; it was only with difficulty that he could be persuaded by Belle that a marriage to him could make her happy for long.

Among the people who were giving Belle their opinions about her marriage prospects in late 1770 was also her dear and intimate friend, her cousin Annebetje. She offered an interpretation of d'Hermenches' behavior—his down-valuing of a marriage with Charrière, his conduct with respect to other suitors, and his way of dealing with his wife and seeking a divorce. She suggested that these may all have been motivated by an interest in marrying her himself. We don't know in what spirit Annebetje made the comment, but Belle was horrified.

In 1771 she did marry Charrière. Shortly afterwards she received a deeply upsetting letter from Ditie, who was in Lausanne where d'Hermenches was living. There were rumors; we know neither their source nor how widespread they were, and even in his letter he reported that he had sought corroboration but found none. He had heard that d'Hermenches had adduced evidence from Belle's letters of her love for him, and that his love for her had played a role in his decision to seek a divorce. She was appalled at this echoing of Annebetje's comments. We don't know whether this matter was cleared up or simply smoothed over, but Ditie later visited in d'Hermenches' home, and d'Hermenches came to visit the Charrières after they settled in Colombier.

The waning of their relationship has its own beauty of cadence, its own poignancy. Belle distances herself from the rash young girl she once was; the tone of her letters becomes graver and more matronly—and somewhat dismissive of the exuberant thrust-and-parry of their old exchanges. She cannot, she says, talk or write as she used to do. "I would divert you as an old man of eighty could divert a lass of twenty" (517). But we detect a nostalgia for their entente when she writes, "There are no letters like yours" (502). There are more letters from d'Hermenches than from Belle in these last years. His need of her letters—"the very breath of life to me"—seems stronger than ever (490). He will deeply miss her ardent attention; she will miss his trenchant vitality—that "salt that is yours alone" (520).

He wrote to her only once after he remarried in 1776. So far as is known, she never answered.

_____

8. *O.C.* 1: 578, n. 1.

The correspondence between Belle de Zuylen and Constant d'Hermenches is a structured work of literature in its own right: a joint creation with an extraordinary literary cohesiveness, with dense, complex interweavings of word and theme. Each relentlessly works through and builds on the implications of the other's criticism or metaphor or joke.

They fully exploit a certain code of the period—to be found in many correspondences—that invokes the license of the epistolary genre. They use the little markers that on the surface signal randomness or incoherence but are in fact conventions of epistolary writing that claim permission to trace and record subtle, unexpected associations of thought. They speak of their own *extravagance* and *étourderie* (distractedness), of the "rhapsody" or the "nonsense" they have just written; they discuss each other's "idleness" or "singularity." "Here I am, pen in hand," writes Belle; "that pen will move to the bidding of a crazed head. Don't expect me to be rational; don't imagine for a minute that I'm writing to please you; I'm writing because I can do nothing else." (80). She is given to ending her letters with "I'm nodding off," "I'm falling asleep"—letting him know that she is sharing with him the very last, most intimate moments of her day—all of which produces the odd effect of making her letter a sort of pillow talk.

At the same time, they have the most alert and wakeful of intellects. When Belle is laying out a moral position (for instance, on Catholic-Protestant marriages), she does it with an intricate precision that amuses and exasperates d'Hermenches. Their code word for this, throughout their letters, is *métaphysique*: "I blame you," he says, "for having put too much metaphysics into this business" (137). To which she answers: "Here is one of my metaphysical scruples" (145).

Either of them could have written a treatise on the properties of the distinctively epistolary relationship. They were familiar with—and refer to—the great correspondences of the past and present: Abelard and Héloïse, Madame de Sévigné, Lady Mary Wortley Montagu, Voltaire. They reflect on the kind of relationships the letter fosters or diminishes, and on the paradoxes of presence and separation. There are moments for her when she feels that this "blaze of correspondence" has become an obsession, an addiction; that it is drawing all vitality into itself and away from the rest of her life—from her studies and her friendships. She reminds d'Hermenches that he is receiving an idealized version of her; even the letters that purport to be complete and utterly frank self-revelations are bound to be artifacts. D'Hermenches is too gallant ever to suggest that he has anything better to do than to write to her; he tells her many times over that time spent writing to her is not time lost but time redeemed. But he too knows that a friendship by letter is a very imperfect predictor of a friendship in life, and he goes on at length about what a dreadful husband he would be for her. Just before a meeting in the Hague in December 1764—a meeting that follows closely upon their most intense exchange of letters—he writes both to reassure her and to disabuse her concerning the amorous danger of their encounter:

> Your imagination is everything; that is what carries the fire; your senses count for nothing, as you will see when we meet. If I make bold to kiss your hand in a corridor, or to press it while we are dancing, I will merely seem pitiful to you. The finest letters most often produce the coolest meetings, just as the most tender rendezvous are followed by the most laconic love-notes. (215)

And when they do meet, she herself—with a touch of chagrin—has to acknowledge the discrepancy:

> As I said, I don't know how to talk to you the way I know how to write to you. It's a man I see before me—a man I haven't spoken to ten times in my life. . . . Well then, let us write. (219)

Of the two correspondents, Belle has the more perfect control of her literary medium. Regardless of how complex her prose becomes as she follows all the the convolutions of her thought, she is almost never less than lucid. D'Hermenches' prose is often—but not always—of a pungent directness. In his late-night confessional mode, as he tries to reconcile himself with himself and himself with society, the syntax begins to slide off the table (the punctuation was never stably on it), and the reader begins to suspect that these letters are fueled by something more spirituous than Belle's coffee. Even in his most sober mode, there is a quirkiness to d'Hermenches' use of language—he seems to be reassembling it. Like Belle, he is a beneficiary of the festive play of language that was fostered by *précieux* salon society, and that was deepened and expanded by the great writers of French classicism. But he uses that language in a way that is eccentric—that is, literally to say, off center. He will choose a word that is off to the side of the expected usage in order to achieve a rhetorical effect or to achieve a finer precision; he will use words in their rarer rather than their commoner meanings. Early on, Belle writes, "What makes your prose preferable to your poetry, I think, is that these vivid, striking thoughts—slightly strange and sometimes even bizarre—, which work so well in your essays and letters, do not accommodate themselves well to the constraints of verse" (36). In her last letter to him, she says of his, "I need still to recognize in them *you,* and find in them that salt that is yours alone—that mixture of gaiety and acerbity that gives all your descriptions such piquancy" (520). He can drive the translator to distraction, but the more one rereads him the more one realizes that what had seemed to be an uncontrolled ramble is in fact a close-knit exposition. As these two writers move in on our consciousness, d'Hermenches becomes more than a foil for his more famous correspondent. He has created himself for future readers no less than she has.

D'Hermenches was to achieve the rank of major general (*maréchal de camp*), and he was elected to the Académie de Dijon—the same academy that had awarded the literary prize that made Rousseau famous. The young widow whom d'Hermenches married after his divorce, Marie Taisne de Remonval, died only three years after their marriage and left him with another young son. Constant d'Hermenches died in Paris in 1785 and was buried the next day in the Cimetière des Etrangers.

While we know little about the later life of d'Hermenches, of Isabelle de Charrière's we know a great deal.

To her contemporaries, the marriage of the beautiful and brilliant Belle de Zuylen seemed a notable comedown. Her marriage took her to the small town of Colombier, near Neuchâtel, where Charles-Emmanuel de Charrière lived with his aged father and two unmarried sisters. Charrière was a man of great kindness and intelligence, who helped his wife in every way he could. Isabelle de Charrière tried for a time to be a family woman only, to be satisfied with whist games and little parties and short journeys. She wanted children; she had none, although she went from spa to spa seeking a cure for her infertility. There seems to have been other kinds of sadness: Charrière's gentle letters to her speak of his distress at some fundamental incompatibility between them such as d'Hermenches had warned her about. She continually complained of ill health. It appears that she had a brief, unhappy affair with a much younger man. But whatever may have been missing in their marriage, Charrière seems to have helped her find the steadiness and repose to write.

In 1784 she published the epistolary novella *Lettres neuchâteloises*. Then came in swift succession the works that have been the cornerstone of her reputation as a writer: *Lettres de Mistriss Henley* (1784), *Lettres écrites de Lausanne* (1785), and its popular sequel *Caliste* (1787). Among their themes are the maturing relationship of a courting couple, the economic and sexual vulnerability of working-class women, the difficulties of marriage between well-meaning but ill-matched partners, the facts of social and emotional life to be conveyed to an adolescent daughter, the tragedy of a "fallen" woman who is profoundly virtuous and of the man who loves her but lacks the courage to marry her. These short works are suggestive and open-ended: the characters are sometimes still struggling to find some resolution even on the last page. With the exception of *Caliste,* which people loved, these novels violated too many fictional conventions to win Isabelle de Charrière more than a modest success in her own time, but with their unsparing lucidity they speak to today's reader with an immediacy one finds in very few novels of the eighteenth century.

If we read them after an immersion in the correspondence of Belle de Zuylen and Constant d'Hermenches, the letters come to seem a sort of writer's notebook. When she set down the talk in the bedrooms, corridors, and gardens of Zuylen; when she recounted her debates with her father, or dwelt on a domestic detail—an abandoned corset, a beloved dog—she was assembling and storing the components of her very particular fictional world, in which crises will crystallize around the apparently trivial: a dress dropped in the mud, a cat sleeping on the wrong chair.

Her novels probably owe something of their remarkable sexual frankness to the fact that for a decade she was able to say who she thought she was to an experienced, unshockable listener. In her letters she articulated her refusal to equate all virtue with chastity; in her novels she wove that refusal into the lives and the discourse of her characters. D'Hermenches had given her a certain window on the world of men—their desires, ambitions, and disappointments—her novels evince an extraordinary understanding of the ways in which men as well as women pay for their passions, their actions, and their failures to act.

Isabelle de Charrière composed *Caliste* during a stay of a year and a half in Paris (1786–87), where she frequented the political and philosophical salons, and met a number of the future makers and victims of the French Revolution. There, when she was forty-six, she found herself face to face in a Paris drawing-room with the gifted, lonely, and restless son of d'Hermenches' widowed brother Juste. Between Benjamin Constant and Isabelle de Charrière there passed a current of instantaneous mutual recognition, which resulted in an immensely difficult but lifelong friendship. Another brilliant correspondence sprang up. This time, however, it was she who watched a much younger man struggle to discover what to do with his gifts, while he delighted in finding in her an intellectual partner with whom he could talk "on all subjects, with an inexhaustible ardor."[9] The French Revolution began shortly after the beginning of their friendship. The two of them followed the early events as partners in sympathy for what the Revolution might accomplish: an end to the abuses of feudalism. But as the Revolution went on, Isabelle de Charrière was more and more repelled by its violence and by the dogmatism of the Revolutionary regimes, while Constant was more and more drawn by the possibilities of a new political order. Then he met and fell in love with Germaine de Staël, who was his own age. Her energy, her taste, her personal and literary style were those of a new generation: more florid, more expansive, far removed from the classical restraint that had informed eighteenth-century expressions of wit and feeling—and the letters of Belle and d'Hermenches. Mme de Staël admired Isabelle de Charrière's work (*Caliste* was an important influence on her *Corinne*, as it was on Benjamin Constant's masterpiece *Adolphe*), but Isabelle de Charrière disliked the style of the new generation. In particular, she disliked Germaine de Staël, and she felt keenly the loss of Benjamin's passionate attention. Their friendship was severely strained, but was not utterly

9. Benjamin Constant recounts his meeting with Isabelle de Charrière in *Ma Vie* (1807–1811). See the edition by C. P. Courtney, *Ma Vie (Le Cahier rouge)* 20–22.

broken—he remained for her a trusted reader and critic of the work of her later years, and it was to him that she wrote the last letter of her life.

The 1790s were for her a whole new period of productivity: as well as novels, she produced plays, essays, poems, music, and operas. From her haven in Switzerland she watched the unfolding of events of the Revolution and befriended some *émigré* families seeking refuge from the Terror. Their situation revealed to her a new kind of subject. She was intrigued by the situation of these uprooted, wandering aristocrats, who were waiting to learn whether their world had vanished forever. She had little sympathy with those of the refugees who refused to face the end of the Ancien Régime, who refused to learn anything new; she admired those who responded with lucidity and courage to their situation, and who yet preserved a certain moral style and an ethos of courtesy and generosity that she thought to be precious gifts of an aristocratic upbringing like that of her own family. She wrote epistolary dialogues between royalists and revolutionaries, such as *Lettres trouvées dans des porte-feuilles d'émigrés* (1793), hoping against hope that the lines of communication might be kept open. She began to inquire into the transformations of personal lives and expectations wrought by the Revolution. "Whom does one write for, from now on?" begins *Trois Femmes* (1795), one of her finest works of the period. Persistently she asked in these late works: whom does one educate and how and for what? —and then she provided enigmatic, provocative fables (such as *Sainte-Anne*) to probe around in these questions.

Just before the end of her turbulent century, in 1799, she wrote to her nephew Willem René a superb letter that is a summing-up of her reflections on the Revolution. It is also a proposal to help a young nobleman reconceive the gifts of education and sensibility that his family and class had given him, and put them to use in the new world that was painfully coming into being.

Isabelle de Charrière died on December 26, 1805, at the age of sixty-five.

This translation is based on the critical edition of Isabelle de Charrière's *Oeuvres complètes* published by G. A. van Oorschot (Amsterdam, 1979–84). The letters are identified here both by date and by the numbers assigned to them in that edition as they appear chronologically with the entire (extant) correspondence of Isabelle de Charrière. (The reader will notice that this collection of 267 letters begins with Letter 59 and ends with Letter 464.) The Oorschot critical edition is also the chief source of those of our notes that identify people in the family and social circles of Belle de Zuylen and Constant d'Hermenches and for the chronologies and annotated roster; Frederick Pottle's *Boswell in Holland* and *James Boswell: The Earlier Years* provide complementary information. C. P. Courtney's authoritative *Isabelle de Charrière (Belle de Zuylen): A Biography* has been indispensable.

CHRONOLOGY

1722 NOVEMBER 17: Birth of David-Louis, Baron de Constant de Rebecque, in Lausanne, later to become Seigneur d'Hermenches et de Villars-Mendraz.

1736 Becomes an officer in his father's regiment, the Constant Regiment.

1740 OCTOBER 20: Birth of Isabella Agneta Elisabeth van Tuyll van Serooskerken in the chateau of Zuylen, near Utrecht.

1743 D'Hermenches becomes his father's adjutant.

1744 D'Hermenches marries Louise de Seigneux, seven years his senior.

1745 D'Hermenches serves in the forces of the United Provinces against France in the War of the Austrian Succession. He is wounded in the forehead at the Battle of Fontenoy.

1750 D'Hermenches' son, Guillaume-Anne Constant de Villars, is born in the Hague.

1750 Belle goes to Switzerland and France with her Swiss governess, Jeanne-Louise Prevost. She returns in 1751.

1753 Mlle Prevost leaves Holland for reasons of health.
D'Hermenches' illegitimate daughter, Sophie-Jeanne-Louise Joly Dufey, is born in Savoie.

1755 D'Hermenches' daughter, Constance-Louise, is born in Lausanne. D'Hermenches' friendship with Voltaire begins.

1756 Beginning of the involvement of the Constant clan of Lausanne in producing and acting the plays of Voltaire at a private theater belonging to d'Hermenches' sister.

1759 Belle's oldest brother, Reinout Gerard, drowns in the Vecht River.

1760 D'Hermenches and Belle meet at the duke of Brunswick's ball at the Hague on FEBRUARY 28. In MARCH she writes her first letter to him.

1762 JULY: They meet again at the Hague at a ball given by the British ambassador. D'Hermenches goes to visit his son in England, where two letters from Belle reach him; the correspondence resumes.
AUGUST: *Le Noble,* Belle's first published fiction, comes out in *Le Journal étranger.* She has also been composing poems and literary portraits that circulate among her friends.

1762–63 Winter: D'Hermenches is on leave at Hermenches, his estate near Lausanne. He is involved in the Calas case, travels, and spends some time in Paris.

1763 A separate and anonymous edition of *Le Noble* is withdrawn from commerce by Belle's parents. She writes her self-portrait, *Portrait de Zélide,* and it circulates among her friends.
APRIL: Her sister, Johanna Maria (Mitie), marries Cornelis de Perponcher de Sedlnitzky.
AUGUST: James Boswell arrives in Utrecht. He is warmly received by the Tuyll family and becomes a friend of Belle.
NOVEMBER: D'Hermenches considers leaving the Dutch service and consults Belle about it.

1764 D'Hermenches is back at the Hague, after more than a year's absence.

1764 JUNE: Boswell begins his grand tour of Europe and begins his correspondence with Belle.
JULY: D'Hermenches and Belle meet again at the Utrecht kermess; he introduces her to his friend the marquis de Bellegarde. They begin planning to arrange a marriage between Belle and the marquis.
AUGUST: Belle ghostwrites a letter for d'Hermenches to send to her father, proposing Bellegarde as a husband. Belle's father refuses to give his consent for his dependent daughter to marry a Catholic but assures her that her choosing to do so after she reaches her majority will not harm her financial position. She declares to d'Hermenches that both she and Bellegarde are free at this point, but she makes it clear that she intends to take up the marriage plans again in a year.
SEPTEMBER: Belle stays with Mme Hasselaer at her home, Westerhout, at Wijk aan Zee. There she meets another suitor, Baron van Pallandt, and begins a tense correspondence with him, of which only her letters survive.
NOVEMBER: D'Hermenches is reviewing his options: stay in Holland and hope to get his own regiment, accept the post of chamberlain of the emperor in Brussels, serve France as an officer in a Swiss regiment. He asks for Voltaire's help. Voltaire writes on his behalf to the sister of the duc de Choiseul, French Minister of War.
DECEMBER: Belle and d'Hermenches see each other at social events at the Hague. He is offered a position in the French military, retaining his rank as colonel. He sells his company to Gabriel Golofkine and leaves the Hague on DECEMBER 25 to join the Eptingen Regiment in France. Belle and d'Hermenches will not see each other again until after she is married.

1765 FEBRUARY: D'Hermenches is in Paris.
MARCH: He takes up his post with the Eptingen Regiment in Lille.

DECEMBER: He is in Landrecies.

APRIL: Bellegarde sends Belle's father an inventory of his assets.

JULY: Bellegarde comes to Utrecht. There are a number of slightly awkward meetings between him and Belle.

AUGUST: M. van Tuyll writes to Bellegarde about the necessity of a papal dispensation to guarantee the legitimacy of prospective heirs.

OCTOBER: Belle reaches her majority.

DECEMBER: Belle's favorite cousin, Anna Elisabeth (Annebetje), marries the count of Athlone.

1766 JANUARY: Boswell writes a long letter to M. van Tuyll proposing to marry Belle under certain specified conditions.

MARCH: Belle meets Bellegarde at the Hague. Belle announces to d'Hermenches that her parents are giving her a dowry of one hundred thousand florins.

APRIL: D'Hermenches is called to Lille to receive the crown prince of Brunswick.

MAY: Bellegarde is received at Zuylen by Belle's father.

JULY: First extant letter to Belle from Charles-Emmanuel de Charrière.

AUGUST: Maurice Quentin de la Tour does Belle's portrait in pastels. D'Hermenches receives signs of favor from the duc de Choiseul, who suggests that he should receive the *Croix de Mérite*; he frequents the country house of the duc d'Orléans (Villers-Cotterêts).

DECEMBER: Belle leaves for England.

1767 JANUARY–MAY: Belle spends half a year in England.

D'Hermenches is in his new garrison in Mézières in Champagne.

JULY–AUGUST: He takes part in the Grand Manoeuvers at Compiègne.

In late summer he is at Chantilly, in the Condé circle, then moves to winter quarters at Besançon.

OCTOBER: Belle resumes a correspondence with Boswell, who is practicing law in Edinburgh.

1768 JANUARY: All prospects for a papal dispensation are exhausted. The Bellegarde courtship is ended.

FEBRUARY: More letters with Boswell. His *Account of Corsica* is about to be published, and Belle discusses translating it into French.

MARCH: *Account of Corsica* has become an immense and influential success.

D'Hermenches writes from Paris that he will be leaving for Corsica with the Eptingen Regiment.

JUNE: Belle drops the translation of *An Account of Corsica* as well as all idea of marrying Boswell.

JULY: D'Hermenches writes from Saint-Florent in Corsica.

AUGUST: The Corsican War begins. D'Hermenches asks Belle to publish a letter of his describing one of his battles. SEPTEMBER: the letter appears in the *Gazette d'Utrecht*.

NOVEMBER: D'Hermenches is on leave in France.

DECEMBER: Belle's mother dies following a smallpox inoculation.

1769 APRIL: D'Hermenches returns to Corsica.

MAY: He is involved in a decisive French victory in the battle on the Golo River. Corsica is subdued.

AUGUST: D'Hermenches is given command of another Swiss regiment in the service of France, the Jenner Regiment.

SEPTEMBER: He returns to France.

OCTOBER: He is promoted to brigadier.

DECEMBER: He is posted to Huningue in Alsace.

1770 There begins the last round of negotiations with the two suitors, the German Count of Wittgenstein and Lord Wemyss.

JULY: D'Hermenches suspects that Belle is in love with Charrière. He disapproves.

OCTOBER: Belle's father, after early misgivings, accepts Charrière.

1771 FEBRUARY: Belle de Zuylen and Charles-Emmanuel de Charrière are married.

The couple spend five months in Utrecht because of Belle's ill health, and then two months in Paris. Belle's brother Ditie tells her of rumors that d'Hermenches has been discussing her indiscreetly.

SEPTEMBER: Isabelle and Charles-Emmanuel de Charrière arrive at their house, Le Pontet, in Colombier, near Neuchâtel.

1772 JANUARY: D'Hermenches visits the Charrières at Colombier.

JULY: D'Hermenches' divorce from his wife, Louise de Seigneux, is final.

SEPTEMBER: Mme d'Hermenches—Louise de Seigneux—dies.

1773 APRIL or MAY: Isabelle consults doctors and tries various cures for infertility and "vapors."

MAY: Ditie dies of tuberculosis in Naples. Isabelle learns of it in JUNE.

JULY: Isabelle meets her father and other family members at Spa and stays until late SEPTEMBER. Then she spends several weeks with her father in Utrecht and Zuylen.

1774 Summer: She and her husband visit her father at Zuylen. They will return in the summers of 1775 and 1776.

1775 JULY: Last extant letter from Isabelle de Charrière to Constant d'Hermenches.

1776 SEPTEMBER 1: Belle's father, Diederik Jacob van Tuyll, dies.

OCTOBER: Cornelis de Perponcher drowns in the Vecht, leaving Mitie with five children.

NOVEMBER: D'Hermenches marries a thirty-three-year-old widow, Marie-Catherine-Philippine Taisne de Remonval.

DECEMBER 12: The last extant letter in the correspondence, in which d'Hermenches invites Isabelle de Charrière and her husband to come and visit him and his new wife.

David-Louis Constant d'Hermenches (unknown artist).
Musée des Suisses à l'Etranger, Château de Penthes, Genève.

Portrait of Isabelle Agneta Tuyll de Serooskerken (Belle de Zuylen)
by Maurice-Quentin de la Tour, © Musée d'art et d'histoire, Genève,
inv. no. 1915–91, photo by Yves Siza, MAH.

THE LETTERS

In February of 1760, Isabella Agneta Elisabeth van Tuyll van Serooskerken and her family attended a ball given at the Hague by the Duke of Brunswick-Wolfenbüttel, commanding officer of the military forces in Holland, to mark the marriage of the sister of the Stadholder Willem V. On that evening she met for the first time David-Louis Constant de Rebecque, Seigneur d'Hermenches et de Villars-Mendraz. Belle de Zuylen and Constant d'Hermenches had never been formally introduced, but when she caught sight of the arresting figure—he was in full uniform and wearing his distinctive black headband—she took measures to remedy that. "You took no notice of me, but I saw you," she wrote later. "I spoke to you first—'Monsieur, you're not dancing?'" After that evening she left the Hague for Utrecht quite suddenly. Her first letter to him is yet another initiative on her part, acknowledging the offer of his friendship that he had evidently made to her.

59. *To Constant d'Hermenches, March 22, 1760*[1]

Utrecht

I will not dissemble, Monsieur; ever rash and imprudent, I will let myself be guided by the trust that some people immediately inspire, and of which you spoke to me one day. This guide may not be very sure, but it is so persuasive that one can be pardoned for following it. If you were ever to make me repent my credulity, I would have reason to hate you, and you may be sure that I would not fail to do so.

The music you would like to send me will be most welcome; I shall learn it with great pleasure.

I was distressed at not going to the opera, and at leaving without saying goodbye to you; it is to make up for that omission that I am writing this letter. I entreat you, Monsieur, to continue to maintain for me the offer that you made to me at the concert, though I cannot hope to hold it altogether in suspension. I will confess to you that it had occurred to me to make use of it by way of a correspondence that would have been tolerable for a friend and very pleasant for me. But I saw so many dangers in that, and realized that if

---

1. The numbers by which the letters are identified are those assigned to them in the critical edition (*O.C.*), which contains practically all of Belle de Zuylen's extant correspondence. In this volume, the header on a page identifies the last letter received before the page begins. Since the letters were often written over periods of days, they sometimes have internal datelines. Unfortunately Belle and d'Hermenches were not consistent about whether these dates corresponded to the preceding or the following material, and only sometimes does the context make it clear.

this exchange were discovered it would cause such terrible indignation that I have entirely given up the idea. We will see whether the friend's friendship can be sustained without anything to nourish it; I am inclined to doubt it—and whatever he says, I have a better opinion of his intellect than of his heart.

This letter requires no answer, and I expect none. If, however, you really want to reply, address the envelope to Mme Geelvinck at the house of the late Mme de Delen; but do not wait long, for the Widow is leaving in a week.[2]

Please send me the music quite openly, by way of my sister, as you said. Let us avoid any air of mystery: nothing is more inimical to secrecy.

I dare not recommend it to you, this secrecy—it would be offensive. But keep in mind that neither my parents nor the public would forgive me for this recklessness if they came to know of it, and be prudent as well as discreet, I implore you.

Will you not find it matter for strange reflections that in spite of all these fears I still find pleasure in sending you all this silliness? Burn it quickly, Monsieur, and forget it; my fears seem to lend it more meaning than it can claim; that displeases me.

Agnes Isabelle de T de S.[3]

If you answer me, do not forget your sacred and solemn promise to be sincere.

ᑕᏡ *No answer to that first letter has been preserved. Belle and d'Hermenches had another opportunity to see each other on June 4, 1762, at a ball given at the Hague by the British ambassador, Sir Joseph Yorke, to celebrate the birthday of King George III.*

The complications of conducting a clandestine correspondence figure in these next several letters, and the participants named in this one were to have continuing roles to play. Cornelis de Perponcher de Sedlnitzky (1733–76), a councillor in the Court of Justice of Holland, was courting Belle's sister, Mitie, at this time; he married her in 1763. Count Anthony Bentinck van Rhoon (1734–68) was the husband of Belle's cousin Maria Catharina, née van Tuyll; he was governor of the city of Woerden.

2. Catharina Geelvinck (1738–92), née Hasselaer, was a close friend and near contemporary of Belle's who figures prominently in the correspondence, from here to the very end. Her family were rich Amsterdam merchants who moved in the same circles as Belle's mother's family. She was a wife at eighteen, a mother at nineteen, and a widow at twenty—Belle and d'Hermenches often refer to her simply as "the Widow." She was a great beauty, and she enthralled the men of her circle.
3. D'Hermenches invariably addresses Belle as "Agnes," though she seems not to have gone by that name anywhere except in her correspondence with him.

61. *To Constant d'Hermenches, July 23-24, 1762*

After all, why should I constrain myself, and refuse you something that is essentially innocent, that you've seemed ardently to desire, and which for that very reason I find pleasure in granting you? You have sworn to me that I was running no risk—that there would be no more danger in speaking to you or in writing to you than there would be in simply thinking. Very well, then; I want to believe you—even though in these circumstances your word would not appear to be an altogether sure guarantee. I will adopt, Monsieur, the opinion of you that you have prescribed for me. You may laugh at my credulity, but do not punish me for it—it does you too much honor; and remember the friendship that you so solemnly swore to me. When I absolutely refused to write to you, I did not know that a severe congestion would put you at death's door, and might prevent me from seeing you ever again.

Besides that, I did not know how to go about it in complete safety. My father and my mother watch over me very closely because they love me a great deal; and because I love them very much as well, I am in despair when I cause them grief or anxiety. The conduit through which I am getting this letter to you leaves me nothing to fear on that score; and as for what is called "decorum," since it is founded only on opinion, I see no great evil in violating it when doing so neither alarms virtue nor disturbs good order.

Little by little, this apologia—which I thought I needed to address both to myself and to you, Monsieur—has become very long, and yet I find that nothing less will do; I could even wish it longer, to justify my indulgence— and who knows whether this letter will ever be sent?

Here, then, is the story that I spoke of, and that you have so insistently requested. You will remember, perhaps, that after our first meeting, also, I left the Hague without saying goodbye to you, and I was sorry; whether out of vanity or friendship—or both—I would have liked to carry away with me the assurance of your esteem and your remembrance. To console myself, and to compel you to think about me, I began writing to you the night before my departure. For various reasons, I was unable to finish; I slipped the letter into my portfolio and forgot that it was there. Several days after my return to Utrecht, when I was at the ball, I went to fetch something from it during supper, and all my letters fell out without my seeing it happen. I had already returned to the ballroom when a young man picked them up; my mother asked him for them immediately, and they were given to her. Someone came to tell me about it; I remembered that something could have been found that would cause me trouble, and I was seized by an indescribable anxiety—which I hid as well as I could. In a bantering tone, I asked to have my letters back; I tried to seem cheerful and calm, but with no success. My mother, whether out of suspicion or simply out of curiosity, refused to give them back to me. When I got home, my chambermaid and I (she is devoted to me) racked our brains to find a way to get them back. We could find none that didn't expose me to more risks than the ones I was trying to avoid.

I spent the night in mortal fear, and the next day everything I had dreaded did in fact take place. I won't recount to you our conversation, although it is still vivid in my mind—there are scenes that cannot be erased. To imagine this one, you have only to picture a father and a mother whose morals and ideas of decorum are very rigid; whose daughter and her reputation are infinitely dear to them; and who found in that sign of recklessness a thousand reasons to fear, both for the present and the future. On the other side, there was the most affectionate daughter in the world, and she was in fact a little guilty—even guiltier than they thought, for I did not confess that I had sent yet another letter. From what I had said, they believed that my intention to write had been only a moment's whim, and that it had not recurred. Sincere and scrupulous as I am in the matter of probity, the need to deceive my parents was not the least of my sufferings. I succeeded without much difficulty, but I was almost sorry at my success: when our heart is touched, it is all the more painful to deceive the people who love us. But on that occasion the truth, without doing any good, would have done so much harm that I resisted the inclination to tell it. They asked me whom the letter was addressed to. I absolutely refused to reply, and they did not press me; but was it difficult to guess? I had spoken a great deal about you; I had hardly spoken of anyone else.

So consider, Monsieur, whether I could have given you any other greeting at the theater, or whether I was wrong in refusing to write.

That this episode has left so little distrust in my parents' minds increases my scruples all the more; I showed sincere regret for having been about to do something that would distress them. To reassure them, I pretended to find in such a correspondence many more risks and more impropriety than I really saw in it; is that not a tacit promise?—And if an explicit promise is sacred and inviolable, isn't it at least a little base not to honor this one—especially since my parents rely (or pretend to rely) on the idea that their trust is more likely than anything else to restrain a scrupulous and generous person?

This present letter may be excusable—it's merely explaining to you my conduct—but it seems to me that other letters would not be. I see what one might answer—but even so, would it not be more honorable of me not to write? I could tell you that you would lose nothing by it, and that my letters would hardly give pleasure to a man accustomed to those of Monsieur de Voltaire and his like; but whether that were true or not, you would find in such a speech more affectation than modesty. Besides, it would almost oblige you to answer me; and I would just as soon you did not. —If, however, you wish to anyway, answer me not by the post, but by the boat that comes directly to Utrecht and that leaves Thursdays and Saturdays. I know by experience that they open the letters at the post. The address on the envelope of your letter must be to Monsieur de Perponcher; he is too much a gentleman to lack discretion, and he respects me too much to have scruples about obliging me in this way. You will not have the same fears as you did regarding my friend, and there will be no need of a receipt.

Agnes is much obliged to you for the charming verses. I couldn't send you the little trifles that I've written and that I write every day for my own amusement; I rarely keep a copy. You can ask my cousin Anthony and my friends in Amsterdam for some when you see them.

The first proof of friendship that you must give me is to burn this letter. An accident or a moment's distraction can do as much harm as a deliberate treachery; the safest thing is to burn it. If I did not entreat you out of prudence I would do so out of vanity: I would be annoyed if you read it a second time. It was written with innumerable interruptions, and I doubt that I have ever written anything worse; you will hardly be able to reproach me for having whetted a taste for what I am refusing you.

My eyes are drooping with sleepiness; I must stop. Farewell, Monsieur

The night of July 23, 1762

After next Friday I will no longer expect your letters. I don't know whether Monsieur Perponcher is staying any longer in Utrecht. His address is in the Zaale Straat. There is no need to write, and if you do not write I will certainly not draw any conclusions that might be unfavorable to you or unpleasant for me; but in the name of God, if you write, forget none of the precautions that I advise—no blunders, no carelessness. I shall never forget how I spent the days between the episode I have recounted to you and my receipt of your letter. Your distrust of my friend made you delay longer than I expected; since I did not suspect your fears, I imagined all kinds of accidents and anticipated all sorts of unpleasantness. I do not exhort you to discretion; I judge, Monsieur, of your feelings by my own, and I count on your friendship.

CR *Belle learned that her letter was forwarded to England, where d'Hermenches was visiting his twelve-year-old son, Guillaume-Anne Constant de Villars, who was at school there.*

62. *To Constant d'Hermenches, July 27, 1762*

My God! how I regret having written you! My letter, which was sent to England, will only seem insipid to you; first, because it is long and badly written—and you may be very busy with all sorts of pleasanter things; and then because of my detailed instructions on how to get an answer to me— which will seem ridiculous now that they are pointless. With only the ladies of the Hague to choose from, a man can't afford to be too particular, but things may be different in London, and there my letter may well make you think that it would have been no crime for me to forget your request and stand by my refusal.

My cousin Bentinck wanted to write to me; I had asked him to give me news of you. All of a sudden, he imagined that his letters were not good enough and that I would judge them too critically; and that is why, Monsieur, I was unaware of your departure; once again I am very sorry. If—in spite of the distance, the joy of seeing your son again, and the pleasure of conversing with sages—you have the time and inclination to write to me, address your letter to the Councillor Perponcher at the Hague and it will be sure to reach me. As for my cousin Anthony Bentinck, I don't want him to know a word of all this.

Here are some verses I have just sent him, which you are free to find quite bad, since I do not offer them as good:

> Bien chimérique, honneur frivole!
> Combien tu sais nous éblouir!
> Aux autels d'une vaine idole
> Notre bonheur même s'immole,
> Notre raison va s'asservir.
> Heureux le mortel assez sage
> Pour dédaigner de se faire applaudir,
> Qu'après la gloire on ne voit point courir,
> Et qui du plus brillant suffrage
> Croirait trop payer l'avantage
> S'il l'achetait d'un moment de plaisir.[1]

Farewell, d'Hermenches. To be consistent with my reasoning and my virtues of the other day, I must converse with you no longer; if it were only my reputation that forbade it, I would not do such violence to my feelings, and you would have as many of my letters as you could wish.

Addressed as they were to Bentinck, the verses were made the more passable by their aptness: I had reproached him for a kind of humble vanity that was preventing him from doing something that he wanted to do; that led to these reflections on vanity in general.

Will you be put out if we go to Mme Hasselaer's while you are in London?[2] In any case, it's not my doing; I have told you what I know about it.

---

1. Illusory treasure, frivolous honor! / How well you know how to dazzle us! / At the altars of an empty idol, / Our very happiness is immolated, / Our reason is enslaved.

Happy the mortal wise enough / To disdain the world's applause, / Who is never seen pursuing glory, / And who would reckon the most brilliant praise / Far too dearly bought / Were the price one moment of pleasure.

2. Mme Hasselaer (1734–1809) was another of Belle's friends who figure frequently in the correspondence. Her father and the Widow's were brothers. She was born Susanna Hasselaer—her married name and maiden name are the same because she married a cousin.

It seems to me, Monsieur, that I cannot stop using a defensive tone with you—I must be extraordinarily afraid of seeming guilty to you. Still, I have scarcely been susceptible to your threat of confounding me with the majority of women. Someone who scorns them for their sentiments as much as you seem to do, and who, knowing me a only little, would pass such a judgment—such a person would not deserve to have me disabuse him, and would not offend me at all. By the way, the ladies of the Hague tear me to shreds; you may judge whether I'm greatly distressed by it.

This page is the product of idleness; I'm not at home, I am alone, I have no books, and so meanwhile I am finishing this. I have not yet told you how proud I am that you approve of "The Sparrows."[3] Our Muses are to be commended for singing only of friendship.

63. From Constant d'Hermenches, August 7, 1762

London

What exquisite pleasure and surprise! I have never felt so flattered . . . two letters! And from whom? From the person who fills my thoughts the most, and on whom I counted the least. I will begin by admitting to you, Mademoiselle, that I had judged you unworthy of my feelings for you; your last journey to the Hague had made me conclude that you were as frivolous as you were charming and witty; many little things confirmed this judgment, and I found it a pity that someone as gifted as you should pursue things to wonder at rather than substantial impressions.

What a sudden transition! All my attention is drawn toward the marvels of your heart—there is no doubt it is excellent. You remember my entreaties, my woes; you want to dispel the clouds that made me misjudge you. I would adore you even if you were ugly and sullen!

I can tell you without exaggerating that you write better than anyone I know in the whole world, not excepting Voltaire—so I will take care not to compete with you in that arena. In any case, it is not because of your wit that I attach myself to you: it is because you are good. I want to pay you homage by truth, by simplicity; all the ornaments that wit might add would only detract from feelings such as mine. If I had any wit, it is not on you that I would exercise it—it must serve only to impress fools or address dunces.

Do you imagine that, thinking as I do, I can altogether acquiesce in what you said about regretting having sent me an ill-written letter? —and about distrusting me because of persons with whom I may correspond! I could answer by saying that you have invested a great deal of wit in making the case

3. A poem of Belle's, probably "Heureux moineaux" [Happy sparrows]; it has been preserved only by a copy made by Boswell. See *O.C.* 10: 334–35.

that you are not as witty as you would like to be; that's like Jupiter complaining that his thunder isn't loud enough ...

But let's proceed to how this is affecting me. I believed you to be quite insensitive to my unhappiness at no longer seeing you, and very busy with new things; I thought that I had been shelved in your memory rather as certain books—books that one had wanted to acquire at any price and then has merely skimmed—get shelved in a library. I said, that's a pity: no one senses better than I do all her worth; no one could be more useful to her; I am not a dangerous connection for her—and yet she simply drops me! She has made me feel how happy one would be to be noticed by her, and then she forgets me ... I must seek out some diversion, since I cannot in turn forget her.

Content enough with what I saw day by day, yet barely affected by a thousand new discoveries, I returned to London after a journey through the provinces. There I find two letters, penned by an enchanting hand ... my eyes tell me what my heart dares not believe. Ten years ago, I would have recounted to you the welcome I gave them, and yet ten years ago I would not have felt so keenly all their worth. I am still in ecstasy; could it be meant for me alone, I ask myself, all this spontaneity, all this trust? When one writes so well, so nobly, with such ease, can it be that one has not yielded more than once to the temptation to make oneself admired? Agnes is a prodigy, compounded of perfections that I had never known! Why must she be confined to the ordinary sphere of her sex—she who has of her sex only its beauty? May she have happiness and pleasures in proportion to the luminous rays of her genius! Criticism must blanch before the superiority of her talents! She has no rivals among men or women. May affectation—that rust that corrodes all the gifts of nature—never debase so much grace and true beauty!

What am I doing in this isle? I have fulfilled the duty that brought me here; what curiosity can make me stay, when I am separated from the rarest production of humanity? Come, let us pack our bags, take our leave, break all engagements. Ye elements, be propitious! I write these words, and I embark on the same ship that is to take them to you ...

So now I'm in Holland, even as you're reading this. But why must we pass through the hands of a Monsieur Perponcher? The more intimate the things I have to say, the less do I like to have them pass through generous hands; mercenary and anonymous confidants are always better—this I know by experience. A bought discretion is safer than a promised one—surely you understand? Someone who shares in a secret out of self-interest will conceal it, just as a person who keeps one out of generosity is tempted to claim credit for it. I would prefer that you simply have someone who puts your letters in the post, and who receives mine; you would be sheltered from conjectures and obligations, and from the need to manipulate.

The episode of the portfolio made me shudder. My God, am I worth it—your being put through such an ordeal? —But can it really be Agnes' mother who would use force to read things that fall out of her daughter's pockets, and who has to be begged to give them back? There are no relationships that authorize such plundering; I have never permitted myself such a thing even in moments when passion might excuse everything.

I have had many misfortunes in my life, lovely Agnes, but you make me forget them all; you reconcile me with life, with human society; if only I could reciprocate in some way all the good you do me! —You see how I write to you—in haste, in the torrent of first sensations. One would need to study and choose his words to answer you as one should; you couch things miraculously.

I will be at the Hague very shortly; if you are staying with Mme Hasse-laer, I can go there. I can pass by Utrecht, I can meet at the Widow's; we can write every day. They never open letters at the post—and besides, our language is indecipherable in these climes, believe me.

You are very kind to thank me for my naughty reply to your charming poem "The Sparrows"; I wanted to answer in the requisite form, but I was still too sick; you will certainly have grasped my objections better than I could have expressed them. You have a singular talent for poetry; I especially admire how thoroughly you possess its language and rules. Everything that Anthony has shown me of yours is full of reflections and felicitous phrases ... I cannot get used to seeing your handwriting in his hands; it's like a canary playing up to a hoot-owl.

I hope I will have the happiness of talking to you more freely about all these things; you will be able to judge of my devotion and esteem by my openness.

You have said that there was a question of a marriage for you. Please be good enough to inform me of everything that concerns you; describe to me the state of your soul, your wishes, your pleasures. You have too much spirit and imagination not to need counsel.

Who are these ladies of the Hague who tear you to shreds? I have heard no such thing; I have seen altogether unanimous approbation of your genius, your bearing, your graces. Perhaps you have given short-sighted people the occasion to suspect you of a pretention to being an intellectual; that is a pitfall, when indeed one has a great deal of intellect together with a great deal of honesty. There's a charlatanism[1] for people of wit just as there is for fools: the former hide what they have too much of, the latter make it seem

---

1. This is the first in a long exchange of comments on what they call *charlatanerie*. It becomes clear that they are not chiefly referring to an intention to deceive and swindle but rather are touching the older use of the word based on the spiel of a vendor of medicines at fairs and markets, which then came to mean a mountebank or carnival performer. Their concern is with the priority given to the presentation rather than the content of one's actions. Where they say "charlatan" we might say "huckster" or "ad-man."

that they have what they don't—and in that consists the equilibrium of Society.

Farewell, adorable Agnes; in truth, all the words of devotion, respect, passion, are too feeble to express everything that I feel for you. I am, until the last breath of my life, the most zealous of your friends and the most submissive of your servants.

CR *Belle and her parents had been visiting Mme Hasselaer at Westerhout, her country house at Beverwijk near Wijk aan Zee in northern Holland. Westerhout will be the scene of several episodes treated in the correspondence. D'Hermenches stopped off there on his way from England, but since Belle had not received his letter, she was disconcerted by his appearing.*

64. *To Constant d'Hermenches, September 9, 1762*

Zuylen

If I had received your letter sooner, Monsieur, my gratitude would have made me risk everything to secure you a better welcome at Mme Hasselaer's; but I had not received it, and I was not even sure that I was one of the reasons for your journey. The anxiety visible in my parents' faces and the excessive attention with which they watched over me made me regard your visit as a misfortune rather than as a pleasure—or, rather, what would have been a pure pleasure in other circumstances was, in these, mingled with pain. After the whist party, when I saw that you really did not want to have supper with us, I was in despair at having offended you; above all, I feared that you might leave the next day without my having the opportunity to set things straight. Fortunately I did see you again, and I made reparations as much as I could and should; I made my apologies to you and you seemed to receive them.

It is in order to complete that regaining of your esteem that I write today; after this, I hope that I will write no more, and that I shall know how to sacrifice an amusement for the sake of prudence and scrupulousness. Many reasons forbid me to write, beyond those I have already recounted. I hear it incessantly repeated, even by those who admire you, that you are the most dangerous of men, and that one cannot be too much on one's guard with you. Besides its being a kind of temerity on my part to prefer my prejudice in your favor to the judgment of the whole world, that very judgment would guarantee the loss of my reputation if an accident or an imprudence made anyone suspect a correspondence between us.

But even aside from public opinion, I see well enough by your letter that this correspondence would not be suitable. The two letters for which you thank me were perhaps already too much, but my motive for writing them was innocent; I only wanted to give you some pleasure and to justify myself. Your esteem was precious to me, and I wanted you to think of me as something other than a completely frivolous person, full of vanity and coquetry, unworthy and incapable of friendship. But by no means did I wish that the possibility of seeing me again would make you leave England ... A friend that I might want to keep would not be so very zealous—he does not express himself as you do; nor could I take everything you say merely as conventional politeness. It seems to me, Monsieur, that either you are, or else you pretend to be, more than a friend ... and I would want neither to sustain a folly nor to be the dupe of a deception. Not only would it be shameful, it would be very risky for me; you have too much art, too many talents; that wit that you seem to disdain, you use with too much advantage. If it is true that you were so preoccupied with me—with my forgetting you—even in England; if it is true that my letters gave you so much joy that they quite precipitated your return; then how do you expect me to regard you as a man who can give me only useful advice, or as a connection that would have nothing dangerous about it? And if it all amounts merely to pretty things said simply for the pleasure of saying them, then what becomes of that truth, that simplicity, all those sentiments on which I should base my so great trust? You see, Monsieur, that I would have to be very blind or very coquettish to consent to this proposal of frequent letters and intimate liaison. It vexes me, I admit, to have to give up the most charming letters in the world, and the pleasure of writing without constraint to a man who would understand me so well—on whom nothing would be lost. Unfortunately there are only a very few things that amuse me; a correspondence like yours *would* amuse me—it would flatter me and instruct me—and thus the sacrifice of it is difficult.

It is, in fact, such a noble sacrifice that I dare not be entirely sure I will be capable of it; I will try my best, however, and to begin with I will not give you any address for answering me. Your objections to trusting the discretion of friends are very well founded. I will *buy* someone's discretion to get this letter to you, and any others that I may write you later to show you something or to inform you of some interesting change in my situation. When I want to ask your advice I will give you a safe address.

Permit me to say nothing to you yet about my marrying; that may still be a long way off. I have not yet made any commitment, and I am not on the point of making up my mind.

I was much amused by the canary playing up to the hoot-owl; at least that owl will do no harm, which is better than

A cat with smooth insinuating ways[1]

1. From La Fontaine's *Fables* (1685): "Le Chat, la Belette, et le petit Lapin" [The cat, the weasel, and the little rabbit]. There is a pun: the word used for the owl by d'Hermenches and Belle is *chat-huant*—literally "hooting cat."

in whom the canary might fail to recognize the cat-tribe's malice: imprudently romping with him, it could forget the danger and realize it only after it was too late. The canary acts as you say: it is drawn to kindness, and prefers it to wit. You should applaud it for that conduct. You must admit that when you were making that pretty comparison, and took it ill that the hoot-owl should have some of my writing, you had strayed very far from your fine system.

You say that I have invested a great deal of wit in persuading people that I did not have much of it; you invest much too much in proving that you scorn it, and that you'd prefer to have none of it.

I am very glad, Monsieur, that you are pleased with my style and my verses; doubtless there must be some truth in your praises. What you say to me about the pretention to wit is very judicious; I will make the best use of it I can. It isn't really a deliberate pretention: when I am amused I say almost at random whatever comes into my head, and that's not always appropriate. When I'm bored I am unfortunately frank enough to yawn and fall asleep, which is humiliating and unkind. People say that I disdain all ordinary conversation, and that I think that my intellect is superior to everyone else's. People also take it amiss that I want to know more than most women; they do not know that, being subject to a black melancholy, I have no health—nor, so to speak, life—except by continual occupation of my mind. By no means do I believe that a great deal of knowledge makes a woman more estimable, but I cannot do without learning things; it is a necessity under which I am placed by my upbringing and my way of life. Besides, why should I do violence to an innocent taste? So long as I am not at all vain, and do not neglect my duties, what can people reproach me for? Perhaps someone could prove to me that learning is incompatible with our duties; in that case, I ask forgiveness ... But people do me too much honor or too much injury in believing me to be very enlightened; at the very most I have taken a few steps in that direction.

You said to me that evening at Mme Hasselaer's that your letter was no longer worth anything; did you mean that I had destroyed your favorable opinion of me? That I had caused your esteem to vanish, and had extinguished your friendship? I hope not, Monsieur. It may well be that my conduct is inconsistent and heedless, but that, at any rate, is my whole crime.

You say that before you received my letters, you believed yourself to be shelved in my memory like books in a library books that one had wanted to acquire at any price, but then had barely skimmed. That will never be your fate; but you are for me like those rare and precious things that one has been foolish enough to want to acquire and keep at any price, even though one can make no use of them. I have sought too hard to be noticed and then esteemed by you, since we can gain very little by it: we can neither see each other nor write to each other. *That* is what you must find ridiculous; *that* is what you should reproach me with—but only as a folly and an imprudence.

I have done nothing, it seems to me, that might make me unworthy of your esteem, and I would be very sorry to lose it a second time. I want to continue to count for something in your thoughts; I hope that you will always take an interest in me, that you will always be my friend. What does it matter if your friendship is useless?... but perhaps it will be useful to me from time to time. I am very grateful for what you have done in order to see me, although I am sorry you have been to so much trouble, especially since you have had so little success. Your praises flatter me; your good opinion of my heart pleases me.

I was touched by the passage in your letter where you tell me that I make you forget your misfortunes—that I reconcile you with the human race. If what you say is sincere, I regret having to renounce the pleasure of rendering you such a great service. But if to the advantages of fortune, health, superior talents, you join virtue, humanity, true philosophy—you will not need my help to forget your misfortunes, or to love life and humanity. May you henceforth have only happy moments!

Do not count on my letters, Monsieur, for a very long time. Anthony will sometimes be able to give you news of me. That is my conclusion, and the only prudent decision. I will also be able to receive news of you through my cousin—but no more writing. Farewell.

65. *From Constant d'Hermenches, September 14 or 21, 1762*

Tuesday, at the Hague

Monsieur Perponcher asks me so kindly and so naturally whether I have nothing to send you by way of him, that I think I can do it without your blaming me. —Sublime, almost divine being! —I hesitated, however, all day yesterday, and if he had not come into my room this morning to ask me if my package was ready, I would still be caught in this dilemma—caught between an ardent desire and the fear of displeasing the person who pleases me the most in the whole world, and for whom I have the most respect. I told him that I was having copies made of some verses that I had received, and that if they were ready, I would take the liberty of sending them to you through him; he told me that Obdam is also about to send you something;[1] he gave me his address. Finally, he removed all my scruples about using such a channel, and I confess that the idea of binding myself and being obliged to someone who will soon be a family connection of yours utterly persuaded me.

But my God, what shall I say to you? You make a crime out of the most natural feeling I have ever experienced in my life. Just what are those ex-

---

1. Count Jacob van Wassenaer van Obdam (1724–79), a friend of both Belle and d'Hermenches, will figure in several ways later on. He will briefly be one of Belle's suitors.

pressions that bring down on me such harshness from you? You find too much fire, too much force in the exact account I have given you of the emotions your letters have aroused in me. Truly, Mademoiselle, you are unjust—however philosophical, however moderate you may be. Here is my answer: if ever you were to have the happiness of receiving something similar—I don't say from a man you love, but from a woman, and even a woman who would have only your ordinary respect—then pleasure, and admiration, and gratitude would arouse in you emotions like mine.

It seems to you that I am, or that I feign to be, more than a friend. I feign nothing, Mademoiselle; but if preferring you to everything that I know, prizing you for your true worth, feeling that one will be attached to you for life, regretting all the moments that one does not see you, being greedy for the moments when one might meet you—if all that goes beyond what is permissible for being your friend, then I acknowledge myself unworthy of that honor. That blaze of my friendship, which frightens you so, is only in proportion to the thing that is loved. I would be an ordinary friend if you were an ordinary person; and without metaphysicalizing over the word, I think I must tell you that I know of no difference between the true friend and the true lover; the price to be paid in both cases is *to love;* circumstances and situations dictate the terms of payment. Madame de Sévigné surely loved her daughter as much as Abelard could love Héloïse;[2] the touchstone of true feeling is to give everything that one can give, according to one's principles or estate, and to sacrifice everything to the happiness and the well-being of the beloved. That is my idea of perfection in friendship, as in love, and I would have found no being worthy of it had I not known you. If our principles were in accord, if you found that I deserved your entire trust, it would be up to you to limit both my rights and the demonstrations of this sentiment that I have offered you under the name of pure and respectful friendship, which I will sustain until my last breath. And as for that commonplace that you use: *How do you expect me to regard you as a man who can give me useful counsels, who would be in no way dangerous?* etc. ... Admit that I need not respond. Must one turn for useful advice to someone luke-warm—someone who has more precious interests elsewhere? Do you believe that such a person would go to the trouble it would take to know your interests; would risk all by arguing with you; would persevere to sound the depths of your thoughts? I appeal to your good faith for the answer to that. I know very well that I have never consulted such friends—the world is teeming with them—except on the color of the clothes I wanted to

---

2. The letters of Marie de Rabutin-Chantal, marquise de Sévigné (1626–96) have been considered masterpieces of epistolary art; many of them were addressed to her daughter. The correspondence of the twelfth-century lovers Abelard and Héloïse was much admired in the eighteenth century; hence the subtitle of Rousseau's popular 1761 novel *Julie, ou La Nouvelle Héloïse.*

buy, and that I have always lived to regret their flimsy and superficial advice.

Voltaire says somewhere: "Of friends—of friends one has none except one's mistress." And as for me, I tell you this: for a friend—for a useful friend—one has none except him who, while bearing in his heart the makings of an impassioned lover, also has that strength and that self-denial that keeps him within the limits of veneration and friendship. It is thus that Madame Guyon[3] wanted to love God; but Madame Guyon was mad; she de ceived herself; she conceived God to be most perfect being available to her senses. Do not take this as a sacrilege—I loathe such things. Please understand me: our hearts require a being such as ourselves, who can understand us, and whose language we know. Therein lies the error of the mystics, and that is what leads them to sacrilege, then to delirium, and then to crime. As for myself, I have proposed it to Agnes to regard me as someone who loves her completely; who knows both the impulsion and the constraints in that word *completely*, and to whom she can, in consequence, give all her trust. By that, I do not mean to eliminate all precautions, all the restrictions, that prudence dictates; I subscribe to all of them; she knows it, she has seen it. But may she never so insult me as to say that she would trust me more, would have more respect for me, if I were a trivial friend!

I am writing in big letters because our Councillor is supposed to believe that this is a literary work and not a letter; I write hastily because I have spent a long time deliberating whether I would base my response on yours, or follow the impulse of feeling; you see which choice I made, and I have too little time to reread and edit; so please fill in the gaps for me.

I must tell you that never in my life was I as embarrassed and ill at ease as I was in that visit to Beverwijk. I had gone there persuaded that you would be there without your parents—I had been told so positively. I believed for certain that you had received my letter; and I had to believe that you were expecting me, since you had not written to me *not* to come; it was solely a sacrifice that I made to your peace of mind not to have supper with you the first evening—for, what consideration did I owe people who were conducting themselves so improperly toward me? It was for propriety's sake that I stayed the second day, and I was glad I did. You certainly did everything you properly could to console me, and I will never forget that evidence of the beauty of your character.

How could you even bring up the term "respect" between the two of us? I am bound to respect the most reprehensible thing you might ever have done; you are so far above everyone else in the world, that what would be despic-

---

3. Jeanne-Marie Bouvier de la Motte, Mme Guyon du Chesnoy (1648–1717), French mystic associated with the Quietist movement. Her influence caused considerable public turbulence; she was the catalyst of a struggle between two powerful men of the church, Bossuet and Fénelon.

able in you would adorn and do honor to another! At the same time I want to show you my good faith.

Agnes, I have been so unworthy as to suspect you of showing some favor to that handsome flutist[4]—to believe that perhaps you would have preferred that I not come to trouble your Society; and I was furious that your parents should fear my presence on your behalf while they were quite willing to have people believe that you received his attentions.

I wrote to you twenty times during that short stay. I was much disturbed; but I have never varied in my profound veneration for you. Thus, never take that tone with me, it mortally wounds me.

But tell me, I beg you, in what sense is it said that I am dangerous? I see prejudices against me that grieve me: many people avoid me; others, who would be my natural companions, fail to seek me out. I'm not talking about those whom jealousy or petty-mindedness would set against me, but people capable of judging and of feeling. Do they say that I am false or malicious?

I beg you to take as literal everything that I have said to you concerning your mind and your style. I can exaggerate nothing in this respect; I protest that I am utterly astonished at the aptness and the vivacity of your thoughts. You justify very well your taste for the occupations that are not the ordinary ones of your sex, but let me make one annotation: You are in no way permitted to be bored, nor to yawn. To begin with, a mind like yours must find occupation even in the smallest things; moreover, it is for this that the mind has been given to us, that we may work through difficult things. Vanquishing boredom, conforming to the tone of the people around us, is such a thing; and when all is said and done, a distracted and bemused air is what goes with a little head that cannot hold all that it may take in, not a good head that disdains trifles.

After innumerable difficulties, I have received the verses that you gave to Obdam; they are charming, and truly you are a poet; the ones you wrote on friendship are very good—the ideas are sound. The verses should begin only when you are no longer talking of "Sparrows." (There, you see how frank I am.)

Would you like me to send you an act of a tragedy? I had begun writing it purely as a joke on some people—I wanted to make them think it was by Voltaire, and they did; others did too. People are strongly urging me to finish the piece; I sense all the pitfalls, and the difficulty; and I will only undertake it when I am all alone in my forests at Hermenches. If you are willing not to make fun of me, and to give me your opinion, I will send it to the address of Monsieur Perponcher—provided that you prepare him and that you give me the order to do so.

I assure you, Mademoiselle, that it would be a great cheat for you not to write to me; it costs so little, and I feel so keenly its value that not to write

---

4. Someone named Sardi. Belle will misread *fluteur* as *flateur* [*sic*]—"flutist" as "flatterer."

would be burying your talents and your genius to absolutely no profit.

I am at your feet.

Tuesday

Here are some pamphlets that I am adding to fatten the packet; I have put in a few things of my own; among others *Beaux Génies*, etc., and I have arranged them as you find them.[5]

I implore you to see me only as one who wants to do everything to please you; and so that I may not lose those privileges that a cool friendship, it seems, will allow me to hope for from you, cut and prune away pitilessly everything that you find excessive; but never suspect me of falsity. I will be simply a good old fellow of a friend rather than lose you.

> Oui, mon coeur s'arrêtant sur un penchant si doux
> Veut à ce sentiment se borner avec vous.[6]

Ah! if I had time, I would ask you what you mean by *virtue* in those marvelous words that conclude your letter; I am not lacking in it, if what you mean by it is humanity, beneficence, the forgetting of injuries, fidelity in my commitments, gratitude, respect for true merit; and it is often those very sentiments which sadden me and disturb my daily well-being.

66. *To Constant d'Hermenches, September 15 or 22, 1762*

Wednesday

If you are my friend as you claim to be—generous, capable of sacrifices—give up this correspondence without a murmur. It is only for good reasons, Monsieur, that I ever resolve to give up a thing that could give me pleasure, and I rarely change a firm resolution. Word has come to me in the last few days that people are saying there is a well-established commerce of letters between us. I do not suspect you of a betrayal; I have confidence in my sister's suitor[1]—it is obvious that this kind of talk is only a conjecture that public malice spreads and credits, but I do not want to justify calumny, and validate what hatred invents against me.

I thank you for the brochures; I am very pleased to have them. I have not yet been able to read them; I have scarcely finished your letter. I am writing this on a first impulse.

---

5. The pamphlets are brochures that deal with the Calas case, which will be discussed in subsequent letters; the other texts are poems by d'Hermenches that have not been found.
6. "Yes, my heart, halting at so sweet an affection, / Will, with you, content itself with this feeling." These verses, apparently by d'Hermenches, are a direct response to "The Sparrows," in which the *doux penchant* that ties the poet to a faithful friend is preferred over any imaginable lover.
1. Councillor Perponcher, who has been carrying their letters.

It is very possible, I assure you, that the Councillor will never become my relative. The handsome musician you mention is agreeable; perhaps he singled me out—but he praised me little, and I have had no reason to think him a flatterer.[2] Besides, my parents would be as fearful about him as about you.

In the name of God, Monsieur, burn my letters and do not ask me for more; my friends must be able to defend me truthfully against scandal-mongering.

67. *To Constant d'Hermenches, September 25–30, 1762*

Another woman would perhaps not have undertaken to defend Sardi, but I thought you were too fair-minded to get annoyed with him or with me, and that you would esteem me all the more for being true and just on all occasions.

Mme Hasselaer had reasons for not being glad to see you just then at Beverwijk—reasons that you were unaware of and that have nothing to do with me; if you knew them you would find it easier to excuse her.

I beg you, Monsieur, do not see in my resolution not to write you either ill-humor or mistrust; see in it only what is there: scrupulousness and reason. I could have ceased to answer as of today, but I loathe anything resembling severity or disdain. Once more, burn my letters. Even supposing that it might cost you something, it seems to me that you owe me a sacrifice that is so necessary to my peace of mind.

68. *From Constant d'Hermenches, October 5, 1762*

The Hague

I have rarely in my life experienced as palpable a grief as that caused by the verdict you pronounce on me, and by the suspicion understandably aroused in you by a remark based on I know not what. I want to believe that you are not accusing me of a betrayal; but admit it that for no other reason could you with so little pain make this resolution that so wounds me. However, not only am I innocent of the crime of indiscretion, I have acted and spoken as was necessary to destroy a conjecture that you yourself have perhaps given rise to; at any rate it is Anthony who must have said at some time that he believed you had written me.

Obdam read at a dinner the verses that you gave him; people found them very charming. (They are in praise of him, and rather scornful of me.) I have a copy of them; someone asked to read them; it would have been affectation to refuse, so I showed them. And there is exactly everything that I know about this.

---

2. The idea of Sardi as flatterer comes in by mistake: see Letter 65, n. 4.

But this doubt fills me with despair. A betrayed secret is like a theft; it always leaves a cloud over those who might be suspected, until the culprit is discovered. I beg you to do your utmost to bring that about.

Furthermore, let me tell you that I find your fears a little exaggerated on all these counts. They cannot damage your reputation because your conduct and your sentiments are known; so what are you afraid of? Whom must you so avoid displeasing? You are not in the dreadful situation of fearing you will miss out on a good marriage; your mind, your birth, your face, your fortune still promise you a brilliant destiny. Woe to those who will not know how to render you justice; woe to you if you attach your happiness to their opinion! It is only your parents' scowls that alert the attention of strangers—what do they want? I fail to understand it. When it is a question of *me*, who would prevent you from saying: "I think well of this man; he has never said anything to me but what was wise and reasonable; why should I flee him? I have never written to him, but if I had, I would not blame myself for it." Would you be excommunicated, disinherited for this? On the contrary, I think that such a tone would dispel much of the exaggerated importance that people attach to every little thing you do.

Here I am rambling on telling you all these things; it is impossible that they haven't often occurred to you. I will obey you, but you must know that it is the cruelest sacrifice you could demand. I will burn your letters, but I will not conceal from you that I will copy everything that bears the character of your genius and of the sublime tenor of your mind. These are fragments that are too rare—that do to much honor to the human mind—to be annihilated; written in my hand and in the form of scraps, they can never be dangerous in my portfolio. Alas! what a cruel bereavement! what a pity that a thing so innocent in itself—even good—can be condemned! For after all, who would not call someone a madman who would leave precious stones buried underground, and treasures with which he could adorn himself and enrich his friends? For that is how it is with everything you think, and with your magical style; all those things that you do not put into circulation are so many thefts committed against the perfection of the mind and the human heart—I'm saying this badly, but I'm saying what I think.

Ah, why not write me one more time? I'm heading post-haste for Switzerland; I am fleeing almost with horror a country where I no longer have the hope of seeing you, and where you have been troubled on my account; I hate myself for it. I implore you to reassure me and tell me what you think about all this. Once again, I cannot keep from telling you that although you are very young, you are not such a child as to take so tragically things that are innocent in themselves and that are made culpable only by the secrecy to which you are driven by so much surveillance.

If you have something to confide in me or to tell me that concerns you, won't you do it? My address is simply "Lausanne, Switzerland." One does not become guilty of the crime of correspondence merely by asking a casual question of someone to whom one has already written.

I would be very sorry if the good Councillor were not to become your relative, because if your sister were at the Hague I might hope to see you there more often.

I cannot leave you without entreating you once more to honor me with a word here; humanity itself demands that you dispel a little of the gloom that your last letter spread over my spirit, and I append a request that you tell me Mme Hasselaer's reasons. If you deign to be ever so slightly one of my friends, you will deign to tell me; it is important to me, and you can be very sure that I will not abuse your confidence—is this not true?—you who deign to honor me with your esteem, which I will repay through the course of my life, with the most sincere respect, the most profound veneration, the warmest and truest admiration, and my most tender devotion—which I take the liberty of very humbly putting at the feet of the incomparable Agnes.

ᘉ *The brochures that were enclosed with Letter 65 dealt with the epochal Calas Affair—the Protestant Jean Calas had been broken on the wheel for a crime he didn't commit. The brochures, the affair, and d'Hermenches' role in it come up often in the letters, and their context needs to be understood.*[1]

In the 1700s Protestantism was outlawed in France: Protestants were not to have churches or attend Protestant worship services. For attending a Protestant assembly, one could be—and many were—condemned to the galleys for life. To practice law or medicine, to function as a clerk or even a grocer, one needed a parish priest to attest to one's good standing as a practicing Catholic. Children of parents not married by a priest were illegitimate and could not inherit: the property of such a person was confiscated, and anyone successfully denouncing such an illegal inheritance was rewarded with a portion of what was seized. The actual situation of Protestants in France varied considerably: the official laws were enforced and honored more or less sedulously in different parts of the country, and many priests would marry and baptize just about anybody. Since Protestants regarded such Catholic rituals as empty and meaningless, most of them were content to go through the motions to keep their civil records in order.

But in the southern regions around Languedoc, traditions of bitter antagonism predominated. There was an annual festive commemoration in Toulouse of the so-called "Délivrance": on May 17, 1562, armed stand-offs between Catholics and Protestants had culminated when some four thousand Protestants were killed after having laid down their weapons under the the terms of a truce—thus was the city "delivered" from the menace of heresy. Feelings were running high in the early 1760s in anticipation of the bicentenary of the Délivrance.

1. What we say here is based almost entirely on Edna Nixon, *Voltaire and the Calas Case.*

The Huguenot Jean Calas was a moderately successful fabrics merchant in Toulouse. Fine ladies and distinguished clergymen were among his customers; his wife, née Rose Cabibel, was the second cousin of a marquise, and his family had dined in fine houses—though they lived in quarters above their shop and warehouse. His third son, Pierre, was in business with him; his second son, Louis, had converted to Catholicism and was receiving a stipend from him; his two daughters, Rosine and Nanette, lived with him; his youngest son, the fifteen-year-old Donat, was apprenticed to a manufacturer in Nîmes.

In the fall of 1761 Jean's ambitious eldest son, Marc-Antoine, would have been practicing law—as one of his Huguenot friends was doing—were he not having trouble getting his parish priest to give him the attestation he needed. On the evening of October 13, 1761, after eating dinner with his family and a visting friend, one Gaubert Lavaysse, he went downstairs to the storehouse; a couple of hours later, his brother Pierre found him hanged.

In eighteenth-century France, the public hangman took the body of a suicide, stripped it naked, dragged it face-down through the streets to give the crowd opportunity to do to it what crowds like that do, and then hanged it on a gibbet. The suicide's property was confiscated.

The Calas family, in their shock and distress, took Marc-Antoine's body down and told the chief magistrate who came to investigate on the scene that they had found it on the floor. But, given the clear evidence of rope burns and strangulation, that left one looking for a murderer. It took the magistrate, David de Baudrigue, no time at all to find one: clearly Marc-Antoine had wanted to convert to Catholicism and his Calvinist father had hanged him for it! (The parents of converts to Catholicism were forced to pay out money under various rubrics, and it was widely believed among Catholics—at least in the south—that Huguenots were enjoined by their church, and by the pronouncements of Calvin himself, to kill any of their children who converted.) David de Baudrigue immediately arrrested Jean, his wife, their son, the visitor Lavaysse, and the family's long-time Catholic domestic, Jeanne Viguier, for murder and conspiracy.

The Capitoulat—a sort of combination of city council and magistrates' court—did not believe the Calases when they told of Marc-Antoine's suicide. By November 19 the Capitoulat had decided that the evidence and confessions they desired would be obtained by subjecting the three Calases to "the Question ordinary"—one was stretched by a system of weights and pulleys—and "the Question extraordinary"—a couple of gallons of water were forced into one by a program of suffocations and releases. The other two accused were to be "presented" to the instruments of torture. The sentences were not carried out because, while it was proper enough for the Capitoulat to prescribe the Question, only a Parlement—a regional supreme court of which there were thirteen in France—had the legal option of "presenting." The

Capitoulat's sentence was therefore found to be irregular—une sentence baroque—*and the case was transferred up from the Magistrates to the Parlement of Toulouse.*

The accusers' evidence consisted largely in reports that there had been talk of conjectures that Marc-Antoine was considering converting. On March 9, 1762, the Parlement of Toulouse sentenced Jean Calas to be subjected to the Question, ordinary and extraordinary; then to do abject penance before the church of Saint-Etienne; then to be tied to a scaffold and have all the bones of his limbs and his pelvis broken with iron rods; then to be bound face upward on a wheel where, formally, he was to live "for as long as it pleases God to give him life"—but if that was as long as two hours, the executioner had the option of strangling him. They postponed their decision on the other accused: they had simply not been able to get evidence or confessions out of anybody, but they expected that on the tenth of March, they would be able to get what they needed from Jean. They didn't. The Archives Nationales report that "Calas to his last moment maintained his innocence and took God as his witness." The priest who was with him is reported to have said, "Our own martyrs died in this way."

The Parlement then tried to make the whole business go away. On March 18 Pierre was banished for life, Mme Calas and Gaubert Lavaysse were released "for lack of proof," and Jeanne Viguier was acquitted. The president of the Parlement got the secretary of state to issue lettres de cachet *under which the two Calas daughters were confined in separate convents to keep them from causing any trouble.*

But the business would not go away. By a week or so after the execution, one Dominique Audibert, a merchant from Marseilles, was in the Protestant city of Geneva. His report of the essential facts of the case reached Voltaire, who had two estates, each within a short ride of Geneva—Ferney on the French side of the frontier and les Délices on the Swiss side. Voltaire was immediately galvanized by the case; he had no doubt that an atrocious crime had been committed, but he was not sure whether a fanatically Protestant father or a rabidly oppressive Catholic Parlement had committed it. (He applied the term l'infâme *impartially to fanatically religious intolerance of either persuasion.) His doubt was resolved when he was able to interview Donat Calas, who had made his way to Geneva to seek refuge. By early April, a small activist group had been formed at les Délices that included ministers, businessmen, a lawyer or two, and at least one banker. They mounted what would become an international campaign of legal pleas, letters, publications, and personal appeals to bring pressure on the French monarchy for justice. From what d'Hermenches writes to Belle, it appears he was part of that group and of that campaign.*

The goal was to get the verdict of the Parlement reversed, and to obtain restitution in some form for the Calas family. There would be four steps in this program: first, to get the matter before the King's Council—a body in-

cluding the Chancellor and about half-a-dozen others; second, to get the King's Council to place the case before the Grand Council, the highest court of the land, which comprised a couple of hundred representatives of departments of the monarchy as well as of the various parlements. *If the Grand Council found that procedures had been irregular (they had no power to review procedurally proper findings of lower courts) they could decide—step three—to retry the case themselves; then they would collect the records of the case as well as new testimony, and arrive at a new verdict— step four.*

Commerce in influence was a part of all four steps, but step one consisted in little else; so Voltaire quickly wrote letters to most of his influential friends. Those included Mme de Pompadour, who became one of Mme Calas's champions; the duc de Richelieu, a marshall of France; Guillaume de Lamoignon, the chancellor of France; the duc de Choiseul, Louis XV's powerful minister. He had also written up a version of Donat's account of things and had had it published, along with other tracts on the case.

The committee engaged the services of three prominent lawyers in Paris who had connections with the King's Council; the lawyers produced at least seven mémoires *that were published. Maître Elie de Beaumont got fifteen members of the Paris bar to cosign one of his, which was published with an anonymous introduction that praised Voltaire for his efforts. Some or all of these must have been in the packet that d'Hermenches sent with Letter 65.*

References to all this will appear here and there in the letters that follow.

69. To Constant d'Hermenches, October 9–10, 1762

I believe you, Monsieur, I believe you: you have surely said nothing amiss; you did not want to injure me, who have never done you any harm. You did not want to punish me for having singled you out; for that, one would need to be exceedingly malicious as well as foolish. For if you had hoped to involve me in a liaison with you, would you have put the public in a position to say to me: this man who urgently asks for your friendship is completely unworthy of it; he is indiscreet, he is treacherous—and is so specifically with respect to you? That would have been to create an insuperable obstacle to what you were seeking, and would have caused you to be scorned and hated by a person whose confidence and esteem you desired. I felt from the beginning that if you were base enough to boast, you would at least wait until you had some reason to do so ... Finally, I have persuaded myself that even if I were to doubt your honor, your probity, I should not in this case doubt your discretion. Here is my judgment, strictly laid out: simply following my prejudice, I would have said that it was impossible for you to commit a base act; but the meannesses of men cure one of the disposition to judge blindly in their favor, and after having lived for a while, one rarely says "it is impossible." You will agree with this, I am sure, and you will be pleased with me when I assure you that far from deciding to believe you guilty on a mere appearance, I would need the strongest proofs; and since I do not see even appearances against you, I have no suspicions.

At the Hague they believe I am in correspondence with everyone on earth. They saw that I pleased you; they do not like me. And that, along with what Monsieur Bentinck must have said, is enough to give rise to all this talk. I would be surprised, however, at that imprudence on the part of my cousin. As for the verses, it was completely natural to show them around, and they seemed more apt to make a good effect than a bad, since I was sending them completely openly, without any secrecy, and Obdam could not fail to pass them around. Let me repeat, I do not suspect you, I do not accuse you.

Let us not go to the trouble of discovering who wanted to slander me; resentment is painful to a good heart. In general I disdain my enemies, and I hardly bother to know who they are so I won't have to hate them or despise them.

There is some truth in what you say about my parents; I could, I think, justify them in part, but that would take too long. To tell you that they love me very much should suffice to engage you to respect them in your judgments. It would be impossible for me to change their ideas, and they will never change their conduct so long as their principles do not change. Their intentions are pure, and they are firm—as indeed they should be—in doing what appears right to them. If they are sometimes excessive, I must nonetheless submit to their will, at least as much as is necessary to their peace of mind and their satisfaction ... I would not pardon myself for causing them grief during the little time I may have left to be dependent upon them.

Supposing that I need not be afraid of failing to make an advantageous and honorable marriage, still I must be careful not to disturb the tranquillity of my future lot by any imprudent acts; a jealous husband is surely the worst of all overseers. It is true that I'm not so childish as to take innocent things as tragic; it is also true that I don't think I should allow my happiness to depend on the opinion of the fools who make up three quarters of the public; but I am and I must be scrupulous where my duty and the serenity of my life are concerned. I do not want either to disquiet my parents or to disquiet my husband; nor do I want to give them grounds for tormenting me.

If someone other than you read my letters, or if you read them yourself without any prejudice, I would seem very frail and inconsistent. I incessantly give the strongest reasons for not writing, and yet I write. A stranger would tear them up out of impatience, and would find that you had very little judgment and taste to ask for a correspondence which signifies nothing—letters that, so far, speak only of letters. That is what comes, Monsieur, of your being eloquent enough to make me break my resolution, but not so eloquent as to make me change it. I am being drawn in by the pleasure of writing to you, the chagrin of distressing you; I argue for silence, but

I do not know how to keep it. I promise, Monsieur, to write you in Lausanne when I have something interesting to tell you—permitting myself more or less according to circumstances. I will count on your good faith and your discretion, and if I want to know something concerning you, I will inform you of the means for getting it to me. If my letters are rare, bear in mind that I am convinced of the validity of the reasons I have put forth so many times, but that I neither suspect nor fear anything on your part.

Saturday evening, October 9

It seems to me that I can, without risk or indiscretion, answer you regarding Mme Hasselaer. Her uncle and aunt have some prejudice against you; she is considerate of them, loves and respects them, and she was afraid that they might be angry were you to meet each other at her house a second time with their daughter,[1] especially because the first time people said that you had come on account of Mme Geelvinck and that you were in love with her. I am sure that at another time she would have received you with pleasure and politeness. So be a friend of hers as before; she is very agreeable; pardon a little ill humour—and never say a word about any of this.

The brochures on the Calas family made me shed tears of indignation and pity. I applaud, Monsieur, your motives and your work; only—permit me to say it—I do not much like the editorial preface. If, in listening to and consoling the widow and orphan, I had taken a few moments intended for writing verses, I would have thought—whether I were famous or not—that I had only fulfilled an essential obligation, and it seems to me that public praise of a thing of so little merit would not flatter me. I could give several reasons for this sentiment, but I think that you understand them without my stating them.

I will end here because I have already written a great deal and I do not wish to say anything that might commit you to answering me. Farewell, Monsieur, I wish you a happy journey. The expression is very common, but no matter. I wish you also calm days and a tranquil heart, content with others and above all content with yourself. Without this last item there is, I think, no complete happiness, and with it no unbearable ills. —But I don't know why I take it into my head to tell you things that you know very well, and to take a tone that is almost moralizing.

So burn this letter as well; I have promised that you will receive others from time to time—perhaps very rarely. That will be when I think I am obliged by the interest you take in me, and when the rights of friendship win out over the laws of propriety.

Let us say nothing to Monsieur Bentinck; if he thinks that I have written to you and has said so, he probably thought that there was no harm in it. —But still, I have a lingering doubt.

---

1. Recall that Mme Hasselaer's uncle is the father of the Widow, Mme Geelvinck.

70. *From Constant d'Hermenches, October 14, 1762*

You come at just the right moment, Mademoiselle, to calm my anxiety. I admit to you that upon reflection I did not fear an unjust judgment on your part; the affinity of soul that—as if by inspiration—formed a bond between us protects us, I think, from the common hazards of other liaisons. We know without saying it that it would be a dishonor for me to boast, just as it would be for you to sacrifice me to the spite of others. The sense of everything that I owe you is so innate within me that I would never need to prescribe rules for my conduct; the very words *discretion, baseness, unworthiness* cause me real grief; they have no place in our discourse, and I will not conceal from you that that entire page of your letter, which is exactly right and very well expressed, caused me an almost physical pain, so foreign is it to my nature ever to be in the situation of discussing such matters with you. But I was sorry for the distress that this could cause you; I was humiliated and furious at the very appearance of a justification. You respond in a manner that fills me with respect and gratitude, and which would make me adore your mind and character even more, if such a thing were possible.

I hope that the alarm that you have had has been dispelled. After all, what does it matter that some people, through vague conjectures, have ventured to claim that you have a correspondence with someone whom you never see? At worst, malice might chalk it up to your being a wit; but better this form of ridicule than another: to whom in the Seven Provinces could wit be ascribed if not to you? So come to terms with this, and believe that there are people who envy you, people who are intimidated—and perhaps not a single enemy among them. If you suddenly became stupid, you would see how people would love you!

I come to the defense of the editor's preface because it was my doing; I could tell you that I defend it because Monsieur Chais[1] had had the same idea as I. I understand you very well—but if we cut out all praise for those who have done only what they ought, whom would we praise? You have forgotten on one page what you were saying on the other: that the meannesses of men cure one of the disposition to judge them favorably; your own generous and compassionate heart makes you find generous actions unworthy of praise, because for you they would be merely natural. But do you not see people every day—good Christians, very humane folk—who avert their gaze from unhappy wretches; who exhibit their pity more to forestall importunity than to learn the circumstances of the misfortune and remedy it? I see that every day ... and even with the best of hearts it is immensely difficult to resist the contagion of example. In this particular case, Monsieur de Voltaire is truly praiseworthy, because he was in no way called upon to help that Protestant family. The Genevans refused them refuge; he risked the displeasure of the French Ministry—which lavishes favors on him—by

1. Pastor of the Walloon Church at the Hague.

bringing to light what comes of the spirit of intolerance, and by attacking the probity and the justice of a *parlement*. For the sake of helping people whose own party abandoned them, he would make for himself a thousand powerful enemies.

I found Calas the son, who was hiding in a Swiss village—terrified that the French resident consul there would have him arrested—because his father, unjustly, had been broken on the wheel. I sent him to Voltaire, who gave him refuge on French soil in spite of this consul; he gave him money and recommendations; he persuaded the mother to go and demand vengeance. He is using his pen on their behalf.[2] Do you really think—beautiful, virtuous Agnes—that such actions do not deserve to be celebrated, if only to give courage to good but timid hearts? Voltaire wrote me at the time, with real bitterness: "A man of influence, to whom I had written a heart-rending letter about the abominable Calas episode, answered me: 'What does it matter if we have broken one man on the wheel, when we are losing Martinique?'"[3]

For a week now I have not been out of doors because of illness; I have plenty of time to reflect here, distanced from any objects of interest, and to feel what a small thing life is. Ah! if ever I were summoned to live in your company! I think that it is the only place in the world that could please me. These people here, who move around like automata and whose egotism makes them even more stupid than the good God created them, fill me with disgust for my species. In no country are there so many as at the Hague; I long to leave—I never see you here, and it is in Lausanne that you give me some hope of hearing from you; I will be there in two weeks.

I respect the secrecy in which you cloak the marriage prospects that can be glimpsed in several of your remarks, but you must admit that it is painful to be ignorant of what is preoccupying and probably troubling someone whom one cares about immensely.

Mme Hasselaer had told Golofkine of her fear of displeasing the burgomaster if she were to give me a cordial welcome;[4] I must admit that I would never have suspected that that good Widow should be the reason why I was received anywhere with mistrust. Indeed, I am much to be pitied if the best I deserve is that people should shun me.

You fill me with the deepest veneration by what you tell me about your parents, and in truth, Mademoiselle, every word from you adds to my admiration for the beauty of your soul and the sublimity of your mind. Believe

2. The account given in Nixon, *The Calas Case* 133–34, does not mention d'Hermenches, but it is not inconsistent with his account.

3. This letter, dated April 14, 1762, is in *Voltaire's Correspondence* 48: 194–95.

4. "The burgomaster" is Mme Hasselaer's uncle and the father of the Widow. He is suspicious of d'Hermenches' intentions toward his daughter. "Golofkine" is d'Hermenches' fellow-officer, Gabriel-Marie-Ernest Golofkine, colonel in the Swiss Guards; he will figure significantly in future events.

that all my feelings for you are commensurate with them; I put myself very humbly at your feet.

The Hague, October 14

I do not leave until a week from now.

71. *To Constant d'Hermenches, October 18–19, 1762*

There is a tone of chagrin in your letter which causes me real pain. I am very sorry, Monsieur, that you are ill, and even sorrier that you are having some disagreeable reflections. I would like not to have been obliged to enlarge on a subject that was very unpleasant for both of us; but now all that is finished—and forever, I hope.

The idea of taking revenge on Mme Hasselaer undoubtedly occurred to you only on account of that ill humor against your whole species that you complain about, and I am persuaded that a moment's reflection will drive it from your heart forever. What would be the meaning of this humanity on which one prides oneself, this admiration for a just and kind soul, if one thought seriously of taking revenge for a mere discourtesy—one, moreover, that comes neither from hatred nor from scorn? I would be appalled if a visit that I more or less brought upon her were to cause the slightest vexation for Mme Hasselaer at the same time she is heaping tokens of friendship and consideration on me. You cannot possibly blame me or find me importunate or tyrannical, Monsieur, when I request of you on behalf of my parents and friends a conduct that you would be glad you had maintained even toward people of no concern to you—a conduct to which your heart and your principles undoubtedly dispose you.

Your defense of the editor's preface is very just and very satisfying. Monsieur de Voltaire has done more than I realized. The response of that *man of influence* is abominable. One could make many reflections on the folly and cruelty of these political men who would sacrifice everything to what they call the glory and the well-being of the state, and who have no concern for the happiness of those who compose it. They should see that the only glory for a king is in the happiness of his subjects, and that the good of the state lies only in the well-being of individuals. I think I would prefer to make the inhabitants of a village happy than to reign over a world of pitiful wretches.

Let me not answer just yet concerning any marriage prospects that I might have; I appreciate, Monsieur, the motives for your curiosity, but I would not render you any service in hastening to satisfy it, since I have nothing to tell you that would give you any great pleasure. I have already told you that I am free and that nothing is certain. Please believe, however, that there is not the least mistrust of your discretion in the silence that I still wish to preserve.

Farewell, Monsieur; do not expect a letter from me in Lausanne for some time, and remember that I am well known in Switzerland; people there know that we know each other, thus prudence is as necessary there as here. I beg you to believe that I feel all the gratitude, all the esteem—in short, all the sentiments on my part that you so deserve.

I reproach myself for having mentioned, without thinking about it, *discretion* and *mistrust*.

Tuesday, the 19th

You must know that if I didn't ask you for the tragedy you have begun, it is not out of indifference to what you are doing, but because that would give rise to too many letters; our literary wit would lead us too far; besides, I would not like to be a judge.

If I were writing to someone other than you, Monsieur, I would burn my letter because of the item on politicians, which seems to me fairly pedantic.

I am afraid that this may arrive too late at the Hague. You were to leave Wednesday; it all depends on the arrival of the post and the moment of your departure.

72. *To Constant d'Hermenches, October 23 – November 6, 1762*[1]

I want to amuse myself for a few moments, Monsieur, by answering your letter; I don't know as yet whether I will make you wait for it a long time, or whether I will send it right away. In spite of the kindheartedness you find in me, I must confess to you that I am not too worried about what would become of your thoughts if I forbade their coming to me; they will go their own way whenever you wish, just as they did before we met. If I were not afraid of seeming affected and prudish, I would say some more very true things about that.

You are not the first to regret that I am not a man; I have regretted it myself very often. Not that it is by any means certain that I would be such an admirable man, but I would probably be a less misplaced creature than I seem to be at present; my situation would give me more liberty to pursue my interests; a more robust body would better serve an active mind ... We have to believe that nature is wise, and try our best to fulfill the role that she has assigned us, whatever it may be; we have no choice in the matter. Someone wrote me the other day, "I beg you, don't become an agreeable man." I think that such a thing would be permitted me, but only on condition that it should in no wise prevent my being an estimable woman.

I would be delighted to see your draft of a tragedy, but as for giving you my opinion—that is something I ought not to venture. One must know a man to his depths to be able to criticize his work without imprudence; it is often the weak point of the strongest people, and the reef on which friend-

1. This letter answers one from d'Hermenches that has not been found.

ship founders. I do not pique myself on being a good judge; but just as I am easy-going about what people do to amuse themselves and their friends, so am I exacting as to what they do expressly to attract public admiration. There, intention is no substitute for merit; one must render oneself worthy of the admiration one is striving for. A man of wit is no less a man of wit for having been unable to write a fine tragedy, but I absolutely do not want him to have a mediocre one performed. It is on this footing that I would give you my opinion, Monsieur, and if I had promised to be completely frank, I would be merciless toward anything I saw as a defect. You can surely see how imprudent this would be, knowing you as little as I do; and if I were either to praise you or blame you unfairly, who knows whether I might not put you in an awkward position? If, for example, Voltaire had consulted me on *Tancrède*,[2] I would perhaps have approved that he have it performed, but I would certainly have advised him not to have it printed, and not to let us make the comparison between it and his good plays. I don't know Monsieur La Sarraz[3] well enough to be able to to evaluate his judgment; couldn't you ask the opinion of some man of taste who does not himself write tragedies, who wouldn't know that it is by you, and who would not have been told that it's by Voltaire? That wouldn't be difficult, and it would be the safest thing.

I don't approve of any kind of revenge regarding Mme Hasselaer, whom I am fond of—as she deserves that I be—and who has never disparaged you; she was a little less glad to see you at her home than you would have wished—that's all. That last evening—and especially when she spoke to you from the window when I refused to say a word—did she not show considerable good humor? Perhaps if her husband were not hellbent on obtaining a position that her uncle has at his disposal, she would have received you more warmly. Can we really demand that people forget all their own interests, merely to please us?

As for my parents—you would not be settling any scores by winning their respect; it would not be a mortification for them to find you worthy of esteem, since they have never decided that you were not. Of all the men in the world, my father is the most reserved in his judgments; you were not even mentioned in the episode of the intercepted papers; he has never spoken ill of you, never advised me to be on my guard against you. He knew you only slightly before Mr. Yorke's ball; then he listened to you with pleasure, recounted your conversation to me the next day, and seemed, I thought, happy to find some merit in a man whom his daughter thought highly of. My mother—as well as I—made fun of somebody the other day for going to the trouble of reviving an old tale that put you in an un-

2. This tragedy of Voltaire's was performed in Paris in 1759.
3. Henri de La Sarraz, an officer in the Swiss Guards and a friend of d'Hermenches who will figure often and variously in the letters.

favorable light, and she did not find it amiss that I was called your Don Quixote. It does not require your presence for both of them to keep a constant eye on me; they believe, I think, that I am attractive enough to please, and scatterbrained enough to commit indiscretions—and clearly they are not so wrong, since here I am writing to you. If you were as virtuous as Cato, a commerce of letters that decorum condemns would still displease them, and if you want to be worthy in their eyes of perfect respect, you must begin by leaving off urging their daughter to fail in her duty.

It is time, Monsieur, to finish this letter. I will give it to Perponcher, who is just leaving; I do not want an envelope addressed to you in my handwriting to be seen at the post, nor to make myself unnecessarily dependent on yet someone else's discretion.

Your praises, Monsieur, would make me vain, if I could become so, but I know myself too well—I am too unsparing of myself ever to be vain. When we examine ourselves carefully and in good faith, we find ample reason to maintain a sort of humility, in spite of the most flattering praise.

Do not be annoyed at what I said about the tragedy; I should have explained myself better on that point. Whether or not it would be imprudent to commit myself to telling you my opinion, I am sure I would do it if we were together; if you wished it even a little, I would forget what one might fear from an author's vanity, and I would resolve to risk having to criticize a little in return for the pleasure of admiring a great deal in a manner that would not be suspect. What I have said on this subject at the beginning of my letter is not at all intended to be offensive; the more I value your friendship, the less I would want to risk giving you the least reason to be vexed with me for a judgment which, again, might not be just. I do not want to give you any such cause except when I cannot do otherwise.

As I told you, the Councillor was on the point of leaving; so no more letters. Do not think of sending me any through some other channel. Miss Aston will be able to give you news of me from time to time in her half-English jargon; I don't know whether you would rather see my writing in her hands or in Anthony's. People tell me that she was highly thought of in Lausanne. I'm not surprised, she deserves it in all respects.

Burn this letter too, you will not regret it; it seems written only to be burned. I was rereading yours the other day before putting them in safekeeping against the treacheries of fortune, and I saw that on the first reading I had misread "flatterer" for "flutist," in reference to Sardi;[4] my answer is probably all awry. This correction will seem to you of little interest, if, as is very apparent, you have forgotten all about it. Finish your tragedy if you think it is good. I advise you to have it judged by someone impartial; apparently the outline is completely done.

Farewell, Monsieur; believe that nothing that concerns you is indifferent

4. She read his "fluteur" as "flateur" [*sic*].

to me, and that your satisfaction in both the greatest and the smallest things is the object of my sincerest wishes.

Perponcher's success[5] is still in doubt.

CR During the winter of 1762–63 d'Hermenches was away from the Hague. He spent a good deal of that time at his estate near Lausanne, but from Voltaire's correspondence with him we learn that he also traveled. He made a trip to Paris, and was active on behalf of victims of the unrest associated with the Calas case. In a letter of October 19, 1762, Voltaire commends d'Hermenches for his efforts to "arrange protectors in Holland for those whom this fatal affair of the Calas family may force to change countries."[6]

Belle continues to write, but from late October on she keeps her letters, using them rather as a personal journal. In late June of 1763 she sends him the whole packet.

73. *To Constant d'Hermenches, November 27–29, 1762*

I have a desire to say some disagreeable things to you; perhaps they will seem less unpleasant than a very long silence that might suggest that I am forgetting you. If I send you this some day, you will see that I have not gone for very long without thinking of you. It is Monsieur de Lassay[1] who reminds me of you just now; I have been entertaining myself by reading his letters. How admirable in his loves is this Lassay! He always loves to distraction; when the object of his love dies or leaves him, he thinks he is alone on the face of the earth; he has lost everything in losing the one person for whom he lived; everything is a burden to him; he has only to die, and the death he longs for cannot fail to come at any moment. But instead of death, there comes another mistress—altogether as charming as the late one, altogether as different from all other women—who is going to grant him yet once more the inexpressible happiness of loving and being loved. And his generous love begins to hope once again that the husband will always be jealous, and that the woman, ever unfaithful, will do nothing to obtain peace and find repose in her own home. After her, another: the same protestations, the same vows; and so on for fifty years, I think. And still he says that he is very delicate in his tastes; that it is very easy to have a flirtation with him, but very difficult to inspire in him a passion. After so many letters to so many different mistresses—who are all the most beautiful and the

---

5. The success of his suit for Mitie's hand.
6. *Voltaire's Correspondence* 50: 187.
1. The marquis de Lassay was known for his amorous adventures; he published his memoirs, *Recueil de différentes choses*, in 1727.

most passionate in the world—and other letters that he inscribes "To a woman I had loved," "To a young girl I had loved," he claims that he has loved only three times in his life, and he seems to find his heart still brand-new.

How much better, I thought while reading these memoirs, how much better to flee love and prefer friendship, less jealous, less anxious! You may say that the one kind of love is the same as the other; but in receiving letters from a friend, one reflects much less bitterly that these same expressions may have been used before than one does when receiving letters from a lover. I would be very much afraid, if I loved a man as agreeable, as witty, as sought-after as the Marquis de Lassay, that when his letters by some chance came to be printed I would find myself merely the twentieth marvel, the twentieth sole person to deserve his love.

Good night, I'm going to bed, I'm sick, I'm coming down with a cold, I'm sad, I'm stupid. You will perhaps find that my reflections accord with all that.

November 27

Someone said to me the other day that Mlle de Marquette the elder was marrying a Swiss officer, and that you had arranged this marriage. At first I was angry with you; I found it very bad that you would cold-bloodedly cause a perjury, and have an eternal love promised to a person who can inspire only distaste and aversion. "What a pernicious philosophy these philosophes have!" I said to myself. "They think that a small fortune is not too dearly bought by taking on a companion who is disagreeable, deformed, almost monstrous, to whom neither the eyes nor the heart could become accustomed. Is that the law of nature and of reason? These people who speak of virtue and who pride themselves on it," I went on, "what poor moralists they are! They think they are rendering a service to a friend when they induce him to make a commitment that he will neither be able to keep nor want to keep. Without any scruple, they create an unhappy wife, a guilty husband, a ridiculous and hateful union. If one is carried away by passion, this might be excusable; but how can one, cold-sober, arrange an evil! Oh! how little effect Julie and Emile have on their admirer!" [2] —That's what I was thinking yesterday; today I have almost forgiven you. I was told that the gallant was almost sixty; perhaps he can no longer love what is lovable, and thus will not hate his partner.

I hope so for his sake, for her sake, for your honor, for your conscience; for I want to believe that you have one, and that you feel some of these same regrets that so torment me whenever I have the least thing to reproach myself with. Truly, simply for my own peace of mind, I must not do the smallest ill to my neighbor, for it amounts to doing a terrible thing to my-

2. Julie is the heroine of Rousseau's novel *Julie, ou La Nouvelle Héloïse* (1761); Emile is the central character of his *Emile, ou De l'éducation* (1762).

self. I cannot forget the wrongs I have done, I cannot mitigate or set aside the feeling of them. You can count on it, I will never do you any wrongs, since they make me suffer so much; and it will be easy for me not to commit any, since I will always be your truest friend.

What will you say, d'Hermenches, if I continue to rhapsodize on everything that comes into my head? Just now I have taken from a corner of my desk a confession of faith written when I was fifteen; one can readily see from the handwriting, the style, and the spelling that this is the work of someone very young. I have reread it; I'm almost tempted to send it to you. That will set us on the path of discussing religion as well. Don't you tremble at the thought of this correspondence continuing? Aren't you afraid that instead of the wit for which I am reproached, I may weary you with childishness, with stupidities of all kinds? Wouldn't you say: "Don't be so much at ease! I prefer your pretentions"?

74. *To Constant d'Hermenches, late November or early December 1762*

Perponcher's fate is still uncertain; they want my sister to decide, and she can't make up her mind. There have never been more tactful parents, a more gentlemanly lover, nor a more indecisive girl. They have all been making me their confidante; I would like to help make them all happy, but the future is so unclear, and even what is plausible is so uncertain, that I hesitate to give the least advice.

75. *To Constant d'Hermenches, December 29, 1762*

I have only this one scrap of paper in my room; I won't leave my fire to go look for others; I will fill it lazily with whatever my pen wants to write, and then, d'Hermenches, it will be for you. I take pleasure in it, I prepare some pleasure for you, no one is the worse for it; why should it be a crime? Wretched, blind victims of opinion, we dare not use the innocent pleasures that come our way to sweeten this life, subject to so many ills; since we cannot avoid the latter, let us at least seize the former. —That is my policy for the moment.

I think that the decision concerning the Councillor will be pronounced in a few days. If it is favorable, I think I will entrust him with this package; if it is not, he will be so sad that I will not dare ask him anything, and in that case too he could not get for me the answer I would wish from you without fresh maneuvers. Let us write without its costing too much; I can always throw everything into the fire.

You may already know about the sad event that has put our whole family in mourning, and has filled our house in particular with grief and consterna-

tion.[1] We have seen a healthy, happy man lose, in a single instant, awareness, feeling, hearing, power of speech. A single instant has made him pass
before our very eyes from the peak of health to the most pitiable state, and
all the efforts of skill, all the wishes and care of tenderness were unable to
pull him out of it. What would his wife and children not have given for a
word—a single word! —a glance that seemed to recognize them when his
eyes, already dimmed, opened upon them; a movement of the hand that they
tried to believe was voluntary—these were so precious to them. We have
seen terrible scenes, which have wrenched my heart. I have witnessed it all,
for neither am able nor do I want to spare myself. I have seen my uncle
dying, and I think I see him still. This suffocation, this anguish in a kind of
death that is said to be gentle, have struck me hard. I have reflected with
surprise on what it costs to die. Why, I said, does God's goodness not make
easy a thing that is in nature, that we must all undergo? Why do we not die
as we are born? It occurred to me that our first fathers simply ceased to live,
and that if we were abstemious, temperate in everything—if we lived like
Rousseau's savages[2]—we would perhaps die without death-throes and without pain, simply because a long use weakens and finally extinguishes our
organs and our faculties. Our machine would perhaps simply wind down; it
would not fall apart.

76. *To Constant d'Hermenches, January 9, 1763*

I think that Rousseau said the same thing, I don't know where; at least it
seems to me that I haven't imagined it, and this could all be very banal for
you. Never mind, haven't you deliberately exposed yourself to everything
that a girl—young, half blue-stocking, half-philosopher, something of a *bel
esprit*—might want to tell you? You could hardly feel deceived or dare complain—what else were you ever led to expect?

I have seen the verses that you wrote for Mme Pater;[1] although they contain some charming ideas, I am not as pleased with them as I am with your
prose. You will say that it's because the prose is for me. Indeed that difference may count for something in my judgment: accustomed as I am to
seeing your praises addressed to me, I may regard with some ill humor
those addressed to another. But if it is this sentiment that blinds me, it goes

1. The sad event was the death of her father's brother, Jan Maximiliaan van Tuyll van Serooskerken, on December 18, 1762. He was the father of all of Belle's paternal cousins, whose
guardian her father becomes.
2. The "state of nature" and the process of dying are discussed in Rousseau's *Discours sur
l'origine et les fondements de l'inégalité parmi les hommes* (1755).
1. Née Albertine van Nijvenheim (1743–1805). She married Gerard Pater in 1760, and was
divorced in 1764. She moved to Paris and joined the circle of the duc de Choiseul; among her
many admirers was Louis XV.

about it subtly, for as I have already said, it has not prevented me from admiring many charming things in your verses, and I do not perceive that it makes me unjust. What makes your prose preferable to your poetry, I think, is that these vivid, striking thoughts—slightly strange and sometimes even bizarre—, which work so well in your essays and letters, do not accomodate themselves well to the constraints of verse; they are ill at ease there. A brilliant expression often loses half its sparkle when one is obliged to make one line rhyme with another. The next time you want to celebrate Mme Pater, let it be by a Pindaric ode, full of emotion and tumult. People say you're in love with her; it's partly your fault that I cannot yet picture her as very agreeable. In the past you've described her as ridiculous, and I haven't seen her since. My prejudice would cease, no doubt, if I knew her well, and found her

A noble soul—kindness, genius, and pure virtue.

What finer eulogy could there be! That is how prejudices are formed and dispelled; that is how, in the end, one changes. A mere nothing made you think ill of Mme Hasselaer, whom you admired so much, while Mme Pater has assumed such an elevated place; I flatter myself that not everything is equally subject to such vicissitudes, and that I will always have the place in your judgment and in your heart that I have desired to have.

At the moment of my writing this, I regard my sister's marriage as settled. My father is at the Hague for the affairs of my cousins, for whom he is the guardian; at the same time he is making arrangements with the Perponchers. They are in agreement on everything essential, and I think that they are about to choose a house and establish a household. I do not yet know when I will entrust my future brother-in-law with getting this packet to you—which is becoming enormous—, but when you have received it, write me. You can do as I do, take your time, make up a volume; I am in no hurry, but I would be very pleased to have a response to what I have told you and what I have yet to say. And then you will tell me also about yourself, your pleasures, your plans.

We wanted to perform *Le Glorieux;*[2] Obdam was supposed to take part, but I think that the death of my uncle will prevent a gathering that is already rather difficult when we are so dispersed. Bentinck would have played Lisimon, I Lisette. It would be rather amusing if we could do a play together some day, you and I. People say that I have some talent, especially for tragedy. I remember that we talked about that the first time in my life I ever spoke to you. And that the first of your merits that fame reported to me was that you were an excellent actor.

I was about to finish the subject of Perponcher and of our writing by telling you that you need simply address your packet to him, since he will come to Utrecht frequently from now until the month of May.

2. A comedy, *The Vainglorious Man* (1732) by Philippe Néricault Destouches (1680–1754).

When you write me, tell me what has become of the unfortunate Calas family; your report of them has moved me too much for me ever to be indifferent to their destiny; perhaps your long stay in Paris has put you in a position to help the Calas mother, who was there.[3]

Tell me also if you have received the letter that Perponcher sent you in Lausanne some time after the one that you wrote me from the Hague. A pleasant habit quickly takes hold; I must say to my shame that I preferred to argue with you over whether or not we could write to each other, than not receive your letters at all. Although I have been receiving them for no very long period, it's as though I were astonished not to have more of them. It vexes me that they are charming, well-written, interesting; such, in a word, that I might miss them.

I told you that I intended to write to you only when my situation changed; it is not yet changing, and yet I am writing. I find this so ridiculous on my part that I'm afraid you're laughing at me. Well, can't I hold on to this until I've received news of the departure of the man who is coming from so far away to ask me to marry him?[4] That will be news interesting enough that my friendship might be allowed to inform you of it. Meanwhile, I entertain myself for a few moments in conversation with you.

78. *To Constant d'Hermenches, June 29–30, 1763*

I am worried about you, d'Hermenches; Miss Aston said in her last letter that you were sick, and distressed over the condition of your sister-in-law; you were no doubt very fond of her, and her death must have grieved you.

I haven't received your music; those of your friends whom I asked for news of you at the Hague had not had any word of you for a long time. I would like you to write to me, but that is more difficult, and secrecy is more important to me than ever. My brother-in-law is going to Spa ... you will be able to address a letter to him there, and I will tell him how to send it to me; or if there is no very sure channel, he will give it to me himself upon his return. Do not send the music if it is not already on its way before the month of August; it would be a nuisance if it came during the absence of the Councillor.

I hope that Miss Aston has assured you that I was not satirizing a man who is a friend of mine and a woman whom I do not know. It's quite true that in spite of your verses I don't yet have any great opinion of her, but I have as little desire to tear her apart as I do to sing her praises. I would

3. By late fall of 1762 the committee that Voltaire had called together had arranged for Mme Calas to be in Paris and had secured the release of her daughters, who joined her there. They were being introduced among influential people whom the committee had contacted. The case got onto the agenda of the King's council for March 1, 1763.
4. Probably Baron Christian von Brömbse. See Letter 120, n. 4.

say—if I had to speak of her—I would say, as Rousseau said to the Archbishop, "What is there between you and me?"[1]

At this very moment, someone has come to tell me that Perponcher is spending this evening in Utrecht and leaves tomorrow for Spa. I'll send him this letter; he will write the address—I'm afraid of having my handwriting appear on the envelopes—and I'll tell him that he will receive one from you for me.

I have not a moment to lose; farewell, then, Monsieur, believe me your friend forever.

79. *To Constant d'Hermenches, June 30, 1763*

Perponcher came yesterday to spend the night here and does not leave Utrecht until tomorrow. I have just found in my letter case a great deal of writing that I intended for you this winter, although without any clearly determined plan; I am finally sending it to you. It amused me to write it; perhaps it will amuse you to read it; in any case, here it is. I don't really know why I didn't send it sooner. Everything around me has been awkward and uncertain.

Hurry and send the letter I'm asking for to Spa, *To Monsieur de Perponcher in care of Monsieur Mark*. We mustn't risk his no longer being there; later you will be able to write me at leisure, if you don't have the time to respond to everything in that first letter. I know that Monsieur Bondeli is content, that his wife is happy.[1] The one absolutely had to have a bailiwick, the other a husband; if they have few scruples, so much the better.

Hide or burn everything; whether this packet gives you pleasure or bores you, it is still the fruit of friendship and trust; it would be very culpable of you to betray them.

80. *To Constant d'Hermenches, June 30, 1763*

I had written many useless things in the interval of these two dates, but I have had the courage or the stupidity to throw them in the fire, so as to make myself a little less guilty of the *crime of correspondence*, as you called it the other day. What the flames have left you is poor enough not to make you regret the rest, and you deserve much prettier things. It is a pity that this correspondence is a sort of crime, and that it cannot be carried on openly.

1. Christophe de Beaumont, the archbishop of Paris, condemned Rousseau's *Emile*. Rousseau wrote a response (*Lettre à Christophe de Beaumont*) containing this sentence in the first paragraph.
1. In Letter 73 Belle had disapproved of d'Hermenches' role in arranging this marriage.

CR *Letter 80 may have been used as a wrapper around the packet of letters that Belle had been accumulating for over half a year, since October 23, 1762 (Letter 72).*

Belle writes Letter 81 to her prospective brother-in-law to apprise him of events that may have implications for the prospects of his suit. We include it here because the events are part of the story of Belle's and d'Hermenches' correspondence and its status in the Tuyll household. It recounts events that are the subject of later letters.

81. *To Cornelius de Perponcher-Sedlnitzky, October 25–26, 1763*

Dear Perponcher, I'm a thousand times sorrier for the predicament I've got you into than for the vexation I've caused myself; thus I've taken more trouble to remedy the one than the other. Your letter, by some inconceivable blunders, fell into the hands of my dear father; my dear mother, suspecting that it was for me, took it from him. Neither of them had read it; she brought it to me; the letter enclosed had been seen. You can imagine my distress. At first I pretended to know nothing about it, and not to care at all, and I went and threw both letters in the fire to avoid explaining details that would be too embarrassing if they were asked for, and at least to keep them from ever coming to light. Then, seeing that my dear mother was hardly gullible as to my ignorance, and was fairly calm, I thought only of saving you from blame, and taking it on myself. I admitted everything except the name of the author of the letters. I assured my dear mother that you were ignorant of it, that you were doing this for me for the first time, that I had given your address and arranged everything unbeknownst to you. Nonetheless she is angry; I have done what I could to persuade her that your conduct was perfectly natural, and exactly what it should have been, given the relationship between you and me. I will tell her whatever else is necessary.

If she writes to you about it anyway, answer her simply—without piling up assurances or falsehoods—that having received a letter for me with the request to send it to me in a specified way, you did not think you needed to undertake an inquiry that did not concern you, nor suspect me of anything criminal; and that therefore you had followed the instructions that it seemed I had given, and without any sense of wrongdoing; and that you are nonetheless very sorry to have displeased my dear mother, and that you will conduct yourself henceforth so as never to risk losing her good graces or her good opinion. By this simple and specious answer, which accords so well with my explanations, you will, I hope, be made white as snow.

Up to now, my dear father has not looked closely at the absurdity of these envelopes and that address at Maarsen;[1] if he should ask any questions, my

---

1. A commune bordering on Zuylen.

mother has promised to tell him that since you didn't know whether we were in Westerhout[2] or Utrecht, you had sent a blank envelope, so that our neighbor could fill it in if we were still in North Holland. She spoke of news from a letter from Mitie as if it came out of my packet; so she will do what she can to make me appear innocent in his eyes; you will seem innocent to both of them. Whatever happens, I will take everything upon myself, which is only just; I will not vary that by so much as a word. I love you with all my soul, and would like to provide for you a thousand pleasures, unmingled with a single grief.

Write to me about the furnaces ... no, don't write me anything just yet, your letter spoke about them no doubt, and I haven't read it. When my dear mother writes I will ask you again for the answers that I burned; if you were to write to me now what you are supposed to have written to me already, I would be suspected of having informed you of this whole episode.

I am very sorry to have been unable to save those poor letters, but I was so frightened to see my mother enter my room, holding your opened letter in one hand, d'Hermenches' in the other, that as soon as I had them in my possession I made a single leap from the top of the staircase to the bottom, and in less than an instant the big kitchen flames devoured a thousand delights. My dear mother wanted to stop me, but I said "No, I suspect some mystery there, just as you do; I care neither to have it explained to me nor to have to explain it to you, and just to show that this means nothing to me, they're going straight into the fire." When I went back upstairs, I was exhausted with agitation, and with the thundering of my heartbeat. But I have been such a good daughter for so long that by no means could my mother be severe. I recounted to her all sorts of things, I cajoled her, I touched her heart; far from promising that such a thing would never happen again, I said that this could not have been otherwise; I begged her not to treat your innocent indulgence of me as a crime; I told her that as for myself, if they pestered me too much I could always console myself with the idea of an immediate marriage. I added, half laughing, that I had been pressed once again yesterday on the subject of the German baron, and that I would have only to say yes tomorrow. Although she might, deep down, prefer that marriage to another more distant one, I think I frightened her. I laughed, I wept, I finally told her that if I hadn't burned my letter I might have read it to her; certainly it was charming ... Finally, my skill and my frankness won everything I wanted from her affection for me. As for you, just do as I say, and forgive me for having made you guilty.

Copy what you need for an answer if one is required, and then send this letter, all smudged as it is, to Lausanne with the letter that I'm about to write; I want to spare myself the repetition of this ridiculous episode.

I must sleep if I can; almost everyone else is asleep. It's late, and tomor-

2. The Hasselaer country house in the north of Holland.

row at seven we must leave for Woerden.[3] My faithful Doortie[4] is weeping at the harm she has done me for want of using her eyes and her memory; I am weeping too, and I say to myself, whom can you trust? Good honest folk are thoughtless, the wicked deceive us—and our arrangements were so well prepared! Farewell; you will promise to be Mercury no longer; stick to that: I do not want to be the Demon, I don't demand wrongdoing.

The night of the 25th to the 26th

Put the address: *Lausanne, Switzerland;* carry the packet to the post yourself. You mustn't believe, seriously, that I would get married just because of a scolding; I would be very surprised if I made such a strange resolution tomorrow, whatever my dear father and my dear mother might say. Among the follies I uttered tonight, I said that my husband should take care not to be jealous, for in all likelihood he would be deceived—I wanted to make my mother admit that such as I was, I was still better than most.

82. *To Constant d'Hermenches, October 26, 1763*

Zuylen

For pity's sake, D'Hermenches, try to recall everything you wrote me; don't forget anything; your answers to what I said, the Calas family—in a word, try to remember it all, and then write it to me once again. By the letter I'm writing Perponcher, you will see how it has come about that I haven't read a word of yours. Don't tell me I'm mad, and that since I was willing to lie I could have hidden your letter and said that it was burned; I know all that, but it was one falsehood the less, and I was in such a fright, especially for my brother-in-law ... Anyway, the letter is in ashes. Address the one I'm expecting from you to Mlle Phlügerin, chambermaid, care of Monsieur de Zuylen in Utrecht; I will see to it that it gets to me, and then we will drop our sorry correspondence until further notice. You can see that these chambermaids' secrets don't work, and you will certainly agree that there is no pleasure in dealing with an extravagant creature as unlucky as I am. For some time now my mother has been saying to me: "I know more than you think; you are imprudent, and your friends are indiscreet." She said to me tonight: "I knew you had a correspondence, I've been told that you had written to someone about three months ago; it's true that I don't know the name of the man who is writing to you, but I will find out." These may be fabrications with no relationship to the truth; we will see. My dear mother is not ordinarily taken in by fabrications. Yet how would she know they were? All I know is that this is all very unpleasant. Goodbye; I expect

3. A city about fifteen kilometers west of Utrecht, where Belle's cousin Anthony Bentinck was governer.
4. Dorothea Phlügerin, Belle's devoted chambermaid.

to receive your letter in a month. I'm going to bed; for the last several hours I have had no peace of mind, and I need a little rest.

I cannot console myself for the loss of your letter, no doubt so full of charming things, cast into the flames; fortunately you can write more than one good letter.

83. *To Constant d'Hermenches, October 26, 1763*

My mother has written a terrible letter to Perponcher; he has come to believe in all conscience that he must no longer be involved in any of this, and has brought me back my letters. Here they are; I am sorry for this delay. The one that I wrote to my brother-in-law is not really good enough to send you; never mind, I neither want to nor can write another. My only regret for this unfortunate episode is your letter that was burned. My mother has not brought any of it up again, nor has she shown me any resentment; she has also been perfectly pleasant to Perponcher during his stay here. Write to me; everything will be mended. Goodbye for a very long time.

84. *From Constant d'Hermenches, November 17, 1763*

Hermenches

I am in despair! You never have anything but trouble and grief on my account, beautiful, incomparable Agnes! And what pleasure do you get in return? Absolutely none! That letter I had written with a warmth that was worth more than the time that you invited me to put into it—that letter perished in the flames, unread! It's true, it would be easy for me to tell you it was a marvel! But judge for yourself: I had been seized by an admiration and a gratitude that went almost to the point of tears upon receiving your thick packet of letters; it contained a treasure of wit and feeling; it was a well-spring of wise reflections and original thoughts. I opened it while I was ill; I replied to it as soon as I was well enough, with all the effervescence of a fever that had passed into my head and heart. How will I be able—now chilled by this mishap of yours, and still apprehensive of some new incident—to recapture thoughts that had been animated by such freshness and feeling? They would be an insipid warmed-over serving, unworthy of you.

I know what I said to you (because I think it every day): that for your style and the justness of your mind I hold you the peer of Voltaire and Madame de Sévigné; but that you touch me much more than they do, because your mind has more vivacity, your soul more nobility and simplicity, together with that feeling, that instinctive affection, that would make me love you passionately even if you were stupid. If these things had been said in their place, scattered through many pages, you would have read them without having any other impression than that of my sincerity and my good taste; today, perhaps, they would displease you, blurted out point-blank ... No, Mademoiselle; there is no way I can redo my letter ... I regret it all the more because I was waiting for yet more interesting answers, if such a thing is possible.

I regret it almost to the point of thinking we might as well have consented to having my letter read by your mother; so many reflections on duties and prejudices—treated in your style—on friendship, on passions, illnesses, death, would have made the good lady forget her austerities, and her proto-col of decorous etiquette. She would have said: "My daughter, that man thinks well, his reflections are true, they are founded on study and experi-ence; he admires you prodigiously, he praises you to excess. He is too in-tensely attached to you, but even considering that, I see nothing that might corrupt your heart; it's all in your very own tone, it's the language of feel-ing; but he is far from turning your head. Possibly you will never see him again; so go ahead, put an end to so many dangerous precautions; let him write to you directly; I promise that your packets will not be opened ..."

What a bargain for you, clerks of Lausanne and Utrecht—what a lot of postage you would have earned by it! What tranquillity for the innocent and intelligent Agnes! What happiness for me, who hardly know happiness any more! What profit, perhaps, for those who come after us! For if—as I say without any false modesty—if what *I* write deserves only the fate that it has met with in your kitchen, at least it is the steel that draws these brilliant sparks from your mind, and gives the occasion for *your* letters—which certainly do deserve to pass to posterity.

I would, however, like to remember what I answered you about your fine injunction against judging my verses. I assured you, I think, that I have no vanity on this subject, and that I would consider myself fairly condemned if you were to condemn me; after all, who should judge attempts at genius if not genius itself? Besides, I have no pretentions; I became a poet out of a mere joke—it was a question of amusing oneself at the expense of a few countryfolk who were trying to be wits. They were talking about a new play of Voltaire; in six days I wrote a thousand lines of tragic verse, and pre-sented them as coming from him. They were fooled, and others have been fooled since—as I said, even La Sarraz. Note that all my life I have been so much on guard against the mania for writing verses that, in order to resist that itch, I had studied no rule, and I was ignorant of the first rudiments— even to the point that I did not regard the alternation of masculine and femi-nine rhymes as a thing of primary necessity, and I made hiatuses in every line.

Of the Calas family, I said what I can still say today: the case is before the Grand Council. I was able to render them a few services when I was in Paris; I have seen acts of the greatest humanity: the most famous lawyers have written on their behalf; indignation was raised to the highest pitch against the fanatical murderers. But in that country, even more than else-where, attention does not stay long on the same objects. The Calas widow can now only wait to hear her fate from judges who have grown cool and bored, and who are struggling with their fear of stigmatizing a *parlement;* along with that, there is all the disadvantage that her cause must naturally suffer amid all the unrest that troubles the sovereign courts of the realm.[1] But she still has right on her side, and Voltaire continues obstinately to press her case. He has just written *A Treatise on Tolerance*[2] that will please you; we have urged him not to publish it until after the Calas decision, because it concerns and attacks too many people and too many things. Besides, I am in open warfare with him on deism: he wants to establish it, and I maintain that it is a disastrous gift to mankind, who need an object of worship, and that it is not up to him to deny revelation just because it presents absur-dities . . . .[3]

I said to you concerning the sufferings that precede and accompany death that—far from thinking as you do—I find them necessary to prepare us for it, to make us regret life the less; they make of that moment, so often regarded as terrible, a moment of consummation, and one that is often desired.

I replied also, concerning Mme Pater . . . that you should never judge my feeling for her by a few poetic expressions; besides, after all the hard truths with which I began my remarks, didn't simple gallantry require that I say something kinder? And I assure you that, on balance, I think I have de-scribed her rather well; she has all the vices that I reproach her for, and the germ of all the good qualities that I attribute to her; but what an upbringing, and what a fate that unfortunate woman has had! Still, isn't she to be ad-mired for extricating herself from Paris without the slightest damage to her reputation? Surrounded by men who are foolish, indiscreet, wicked; by women who sought her out only to find fault with her; dazzled, carried away by coquetry and unbridled ambition, her virtue is spotless, her virtue is pure, in the opinion of all the best society in Paris. I didn't dare hope it

1. On March 17, 1763 the Grand Council had decided to suspend the verdict of the Toulouse Parlement and had ordered them to turn over the records of the proceedings. They said they would allow a copy to be made if Mme Calas supplied the materials and paid fifteen hundred livres for the job of copying. (Voltaire exclaimed, "I'd copy the *Summa* of St. Thomas for two hundred!") The Grand Council received the records in August. The situation was indeed as d'Hermenches describes it: there was an intense conflict for power between the crown and the *parlements* in the 1760s, and the question of whether it was politic for the Grand Council to overthrow an action by a *parlement* and embarrass a minister of the interior weighed heavily.
2. Voltaire's *Traité sur la tolérance* (1763) contains discussions of the Calas case in particular, and a scathing discourse on the commemorations of the Délivrance in Toulouse.
3. Voltaire had just published a dialogue, *Catéchisme d'un honnête homme*. D'Hermenches wrote a little brochure, *A Monsieur de Voltaire / Réponse d'un Suisse au catéchisme d'un honnête homme*, to which Voltaire responded. These texts can be found in *D'Hermenches: Pamphlets* 14–24.

for her, but it has been confirmed for me everywhere, and by respectable people to whom I had recommended her, and on whose account I trembled when the first rumors of her disaster reached me.[4]

I must also tell you that it was simply circumstances that induced me to write verses for her: I was at Middachten,[5] where each day on which the post arrived, it would rain verses from all the fops and dandies of the French Army; many of them were insipid, and the best were only pretty common-places; vanity seized me, and suddenly there I was, putting a few thoughts to rhyme—and it is you who are deciding their fate by judging them as favorably as you do. To finish my discussion of this woman—about whom you are waging a war with me that I must admit I began—you must know that when I spoke so lightly to you about her I was judging her only by her entourage, and her frivolous and affected surface. Since then, she has quite literally compelled me to be one of her friends. Who is so unsociable that he cannot be won over by being given preference, by flattering considerations that are then cemented by trust and attention? While all the others wore themselves out with flattery, she lent an ear with more pleasure to my lecturings. She still writes to me now and then; in a letter she wrote after the reconciliation with her husband, she said: "If having wealth and being twenty are what make one happy in life, what do I lack for being happy? That's what I was saying to myself three years ago; today it's no longer the same ..." And in another: "How wide of the mark you are, thinking that my misfortunes have brought me to that degree of reason that leads gradually to a solid and durable happiness! I must admit, to my shame, that no one is farther from it than I am; if only I could find some consistency in my reflections! ..." You must agree, Agnes, that this deserves some interest.

I told you that I have not read the letters of Lassay, and I still haven't found them; I think I haven't even looked for them. You gave me a distaste for them, rather than otherwise; those extremely tender expressions can only please very young people, who recognize themselves in them, and who authorize themselves to make use of them. In our riper years, we can still love intensely, but passion is painted less in words than in things; one hides a part of it from oneself, and I think that if I were now obliged to say "I am dying of love, I adore you," I would be as desperate as I was pleased with myself when, young scamp that I was, I had wrested some confession of love by means of an impassioned letter. I remember that a woman gave me back my letters, for fear of being caught, but with the promise that I would keep them. A few years ago she asked to have them back. I loved her very much, but I could not prevent myself from asking her permission to remove a few, and to edit the rest. And yet no one in the universe knows how to

4. Madame Pater's impending divorce.
5. A château in Holland belonging to Count Athlone's family, into which Belle's favorite cousin will marry.

love with more passion and abandon than I do . . .

But Agnes, let's talk about you. Who are all these suitors you have in reserve? Do you live only for the moment, and have you made no fixed system for happiness and for establishing yourself? It seems to me that, in your situation, you can choose your own future; you have reflected enough to know by now what can satisfy you. Why, then, are you willing to be at the disposal of circumstances and events? Only a man of intellect who is wealthy and whom you love should ever make you come to a decision—without which, I fear that you will not be happy, as, for so many reasons, you deserve to be. Your imagination is too lively, your tastes too various and refined, for you ever to marry like another.

What are these ill-starred journeys, which undoubtedly, by your absence, have caused all the tribulations of these letters? I wrote to Monsieur Perponcher about his marriage; please be kind enough to tell me the fate of my felicitations. I still tremble at putting the address on this present rhapsody to you; if I do it no better, you may blame my fear of fire, water, and all the elements—but that's how you wanted it. At least let the idea of all that I think on your behalf, all that I am for you, all that I will be for you all my life, not be separated from the memory of me that you deign to preserve; my respect, loyalty, and unfailing discretion will always be my gage to you for all that you are willing to do for me.

Will I conclude without telling you one of the important points of my last letter? No, I still owe you that sign of obedience. I was consulting you about my plan to quit the service. After many arguments of a perhaps somewhat Cynical philosophy, I said to you that Holland is becoming unbearable to me by the paucity of relationships, charm, advantages and hopes that I find there—after having consumed my youth under more flattering expectations. I asked your advice, as someone who might judge better than I of the effect that such a resolution might produce, and who could weigh the validity of my distaste—which is based principally on the spirit of prejudice and jealousy against me that is so widespread there, even in the midst of a conduct on my part which, I dare to say, is altogether sociable and civil. I think that I could live happily here as philosopher and farmer. The idea of being far from you is the only thing that disturbs my plans—but do I see you in Holland? A certain intuition tells me that some day we will draw closer together; it is one of those delightful images with which I soothe my vexation at all the obstacles I encounter with respect to you: I will finish out my days at Agnes' feet; perhaps she will come to dwell in a land which draws to it all those who love pleasant society and liberty; the land that Voltaire, Haller, Rousseau have chosen for their retreat;[6] or if you become a great lady, you will call me to you, and I will fly wherever you are. Holland is not made for you: I see it only too well from all those barons, all those people

6. Switzerland—where, in fact, Belle will spend the last three decades of her life.

who are lined up to come from so far to court you; and you will simply drop me, in the midst of these people who tear me to pieces, and I will hang myself, you can count on it, as soon as there is no more Agnes. Advise me then, and receive the homage of the truest respect and the most inviolable attachment.

85. *To Constant d'Hermenches, January 10, 1764*

Utrecht

At last, at last, I hope I can answer you; I began a month ago, and again three weeks ago, and I have never been able to finish. The letter that was unfortunately burned deserves, no doubt, a thousand regrets, but since we cannot revive its ashes, let us try to forget it, and think only, Monsieur, of the one that so amply makes up its loss. Favored by all the elements, protected by all the stars, it has arrived in safe harbor. However, this address must be used only rarely. Not only might it become suspect, but there is the nuisance of having to depend on one's servants in that way. They don't know enough about the case to judge that it is innocent, and our secrecy makes them think it may be guilty—for all secrecy seems degrading; and for myself, if I ever wanted to seem a heroine, I think it would be for my chambermaid—though they say that no man is a hero to his valet.

You ascribe to my mother the finest speech in the world, but unfortunately it's very different from the one she would have given. It's not your turning my head that she fears, and even had your letter come from a veritable Cato,[1] she would have had plenty of other reasons not to authorize such a correspondence. She has said nothing to me, she has shown me neither resentment nor suspicion; but to acquiesce explicitly in something that might in any way be wrong—that is what her scrupulous sense of duty will never allow her to do.

Are you really hesitating, Monsieur, between remaining in the service and leaving it? And are you seriously asking my advice? That would be both to show great trust in me and to believe that I have very little judgment. What! without really knowing you, or the Hague, or Lausanne, should I decide whether it is the Hague or Lausanne that suits you—whether you should be a warrior and man of the world or a philosopher and farmer? When it is a question of the fortune and happiness of my friends, I do not give out advice so lightly. All I can say is that, for a soul made for feeling it, the life that is the most independent of other men is also the sweetest. A man who does not seek pleasure so much as he seeks the avoidance of exertion does well to flee the world. We do well to distance ourselves from those who do not love us when we can do without them; but he has need of the pleasures and the

---

1. Cato was the paragon of stoic virtue.

exertions and the stimulation that is found in commerce with other men does better to make his peace with them. The Hague must be a dreadful place for you if you have no friends there; but—allow me to say it—if that's the case, then you are wrong to accept no blame whatsoever for that misfortune. To have no enemies is evidence against one's merit, but to have no friends is evidence against one's character—or at least against one's temperament. Confess it now—confess frankly that you are a little to blame. Either I know nothing at all about reading faces, or else you have a certain haughtiness, and an insistence on your rights, that offends the claims of others. I know only too well that if one has wit it is difficult to avoid displeasing; but at the same time, if one has wit one ought to know how to overcome that difficulty. What would be the use of wit, if it were an insuperable obstacle to our own happiness and to that of others? It would be the worst of all gifts from Heaven, and one would have to pray God to make people of wit yet rarer than they are.

I am just back from the Hague; I have just spent two weeks there, but I heard no talk of your plans; once again, I am too ignorant to give you a wise, well-founded opinion, and too scrupulous to give you a reckless one. Your advice to *me*, to follow a fixed system for establishing myself and my happiness, to choose a future for myself—in short, to marry—seems to me prudent indeed—and all the more so for its being practically cancelled out by what you say next: only a man of wit, rich and beloved, you say, ought ever to persuade me. Do you think that it's easy to find that man? Is it certain—is it even likely—that I will find him? Perhaps I will be less particular; perhaps a rich and worthy gentleman whom I could respect will persuade me. Perhaps not—I simply do not know. I have no system—all that systems do, I think, is lead one methodically astray. I let my inclinations guide me according to circumstances; they are constant enough, uniform enough for me to trust them. It is quite true, I live almost entirely for the moment—but is that so unreasonable? Only the moment is ours, only the moment is certain, we do not know what the future will be, we do not know whether there will be even a little time ahead for us—I mean to say, a future for our projects. God keep me from ever fearing that there may be none for my very being.

But to return to the starting point for all this ratiocination: I haven't even hesitated over the parties who have presented themselves up to now; they didn't suit me. At present I have two suitors in reserve in the depths of Germany; perhaps one of the two will be acceptable to me—we'll have to see; perhaps another one will come forth who will suit me better.

I will wait with equanimity as long as the present moment is pleasant. I am content enough with my situation: my days pass quickly, and they do not pass uselessly. If I were married, I would not give as many hours to the harpsichord or to mathematics, and that would distress me, for I want absolutely to understand Newton, and to become almost as good an accompan-

ist as you. I write, I do handwork; my parents love me, and they are used to
seeing me sometimes slip the shackles of custom; I have permission not to
waste my time with people to whom I have nothing to say, and who say
nothing that I don't already know by heart. You can see, the advantages are
considerable. La Sarraz said to me the other day: "When I shall come to
hear that you are getting married, I will be most surprised; and if you marry
solely according to your own taste, your own ideas, without being swayed
by the circumstance and the advantages of an establishment, your husband
will be such a singular being that I will gladly go fifty leagues to see him." I
told him that he was right, and that such a man would be worth the trouble.

Speaking of La Sarraz, let's say a word about your poems; if you were to
talk from now until tomorrow, with all your eloquence, I wouldn't believe a
word about your giving it all up. One wouldn't write poems if one had no
hope of writing them well; one would burn them if one found them badly
done. Their aim, their sole aim, is to inspire admiration. Monsieur d'Alembert[2] says quite rightly that a man living alone on a desert island might pursue mathematical truths, but he would not write poems. If you leave hiatuses in yours, if you neglect the alternation of rhymes,[3] it's because you
think them good enough to please in spite of these irregularities. No, no—
you have not persuaded me that one might judge them bad without causing
you pain. I don't know that there is a man in the world whose verses I
would dare condemn if his friendship were precious to me; I advise my
friends always to mistrust sincerity on that point.

When you judged ill of Mme Pater on the basis of mere appearances, that
was certainly wrong of you; one cannot hasten too quickly to abandon such
injustices nor show too openly that one *has* abandoned them. If I remember
correctly, it was when we were talking about Mme Hasselaer that I did battle with you over the volatility of your feelings. I share your view of Mme
Pater's imprudences; in the case of a person who is young, ill brought up,
carried away by such a violent torrent, I would pardon even more faults; it's
only the premeditated breaches of probity that she committed out of self-
interest that irrevocably distance me from her. For those, there is no excuse,
because one should have been incapable of committing them; it's not so
much the action I condemn, but rather the heart from which they spring that
I despise. As long as I can say, "Perhaps in that woman's place I would do
no better," then I excuse with humility and indulgence; but when I can no
longer imagine that, I give up the intention of justifying the conduct that is
drawing blame. However, Mme Pater is unhappy, and that alone is enough

2. Jean Le Rond d'Alembert (1717–83), mathematician and philosopher. He was a major
figure of the French Enlightenment: he was author of the *Discours préliminaire* in the *En-
cyclopédie* and a seminal contributor in the development of theoretical physics.
3. The alternation of masculine and feminine rhymes was a rule of French prosody of the
time. A feminine rhyme is one composed of words ending in a mute *e*. In a previous letter
d'Hermenches had spoken of his casual attitude toward such rules.

for me not to unleash myself on her with the ferocity displayed by so many virtuous people.

What you tell me about the Calas family makes me very angry; one of the great imperfections of humanity is the short duration of the best-founded and strongest emotions. But if the members of this Parlement clearly see what they have done, are they not punished enough? If they were to do all the good for that unhappy family that is in their power to do, I might wish that they be left in peace.[4]

I told you that I had just been to the Hague; I must tell you that I thoroughly enjoyed myself. Mlle de Rechteren provoked a quarrel with me that makes her look ridiculous and which I merely found entertaining. But Mme de Degenfeld and the other most agreeable women received me very cordially.[5] As for the men, you know that I get along with them not at all badly. I was often asked whether I had written *The Nobleman;*[6] I said "no" to some, and "yes" to others, but in confidence: I want it to be suspected by the public but not known with certainty. You have read it, no doubt; if not, you must read it. La Sarraz said to me: "I wish I had written it." That may well be, but for its actual author, it has rather too free an air.

Farewell, I have said everything, it seems to me. To give you the advice you requested on a thing of that nature—that simply cannot be done. To tell you what will become of me—whether I will go to Germany or stay in Holland, what kind of a lady I will be—that I cannot tell you because I know not a word about it myself. Please maintain the interest that your friendship has made you take in all this, and believe that the same sentiment makes me ardently wish for your happiness.

4. On June 4, 1764, the Grand Council found that the irregularities in the Toulouse trial warranted their annulling the original conviction, and they took the Calas case to try themselves. On March 9, 1765, they acquitted all five of the accused. The Calas family's possessions had been utterly consumed by their business creditors and by the court costs in the Toulouse proceedings. Voltaire and others had been supporting them in Paris and had paid some fifty thousand livres in lawyers' fees. The king awarded them a grant of thirty-six thousand livres to be shared among them. The Parlement of Toulouse never admitted any fault or made any restitution. See Nixon, *The Calas Case.*
5. Ladies of the Hague, probably among those who "tear her to shreds." Mme de Degenfeld is Louise Suzanne de Nassau, Countess of Degenfeld, wife of the minister plenipotentiary of the United Provinces to the court of Vienna.
6. *Le Noble* was a rather Voltairean story by Belle. It was published in 1763, first in a periodical, *Le Journal étranger*, and then in a separate edition. Belle's parents had it withdrawn from circulation, not without reason. Its heroine, of a noble family, escapes from the ancestral chateau to join her non-noble lover by leaping out onto a platform composed of the portraits of her ancestors, which she has thrown out the window.

86. *From Constant d'Hermenches, February 2, 1764*

Lausanne

Am I not an unlucky man? I don't know *The Nobleman*! I have written everywhere, I have ransacked the bookcases of everyone I know—all in vain: the sublime, the ingenious Agnes has written a book, and I don't know it! Allow me to tell you that in spite of the inestimable value I attach to your letters, this last one humiliates me and mortifies me through and through. If I had the happiness of being what you flattered me I was—to some degree singled out as a friend—, would you have written something, would you have given it to the press without telling me? Friendship is not so reserved! But it all fits together—you deride me because I ask you for advice; you take it literally when I say that I have no friends at the Hague, and then make a formal case against me for it.

I see, fair Agnes, that you were just returning from that place; you had talked about me with La Sarraz, who, while protesting that he holds me in the highest esteem, cannot resist gossiping about me on every occasion; this comes from a certain ricochet of feeling in him that is hard to describe, but which I have perceived. I caught him at it this last year. A friend of mine warned me that he was making loose talk about me, and was generous enough to give me permission to use his name if that became necessary; he authorized me to lay these injuries before La Sarraz as a response to his reproaching me for my silence. He sent me an enormous defense of himself—easily refuted by the facts. That made him uncomfortable and he never wrote again—his embarrassment possibly having turned sour. What a relief it must have been to him to be able to hold forth to a credulous auditor who was predisposed in my favor, but unwilling to admit knowing me well enough to dare defending me. I love La Sarraz tenderly—as one loves a vicious and unfaithful mistress. He has the prettiest wit in the world, a talent for clowning, no bitterness in his heart, a knowledge of many things, and a quite affable character; but he is of all creatures in the world the least reliable in his judgments, his affections, and his demonstrations of friendship; he is loose and indiscreet beyond what a man is allowed to be. I wager that the next time I see him I can make him tear your *Nobleman* to pieces! When the Prince and Princess of Orange were still alive,[1] there were a thousand times when he dealt me mortal blows, all the while believing that he was showing me off to advantage, using as pretext some extraordinary thing that I was supposed to have said on such-and-such an occasion.

You will see that I am dwelling at length on what may well be only a product of my imagination; I beg you to forgive me—but how can I not become heated whenever I see even the slightest danger of losing credit in your mind? You, whose judgments become more interesting to me every day; you in whom I find a precision, a depth, that are astounding—what kind of

1. The parents of the stadholder, Willem V.

being are you? Deshoulières, Scudéry, Sévigné, Lambert, du Châtelet—they do not even come close![2] You are the epitome of all their genius, all their learning, their graces; and beyond all that, you have a mind and a manner that is unique to you. But here I am, praising you—and that was not my plan!

Back to the subject of friends; when I said that I don't have any at the Hague, frankly, I did not think I was saying anything ill of myself, or that you would believe ill of me. I meant to say that in that land, no one knows what it is to love; no one even knows what should be loved. That's the sort of people who inhabit it! Look and see whether there are any connections there that one might want to make or that one might respect. That is the source of my aversion. Everywhere else, I find delightful moments, conversations, the use of talents, instruction; but Agnes, can one find any of this in the Hague? You say that you get along with the men not at all badly; but do you dare say that their manners or their remarks please you? If you don't get along badly with the men, allow me to say that I as well, when I have wanted to, have been in rather good favor with the women; and yet neither my self-esteem nor my taste have been flattered by it for a single moment. If, by some miracle you find a few agreeable people, there is always some infamy that nullifies your respect for them: look at Obdam, Twickel,[3] Bentinck. In that deplorable situation, far from having to be ashamed of myself, I can take pride in having formed and sustained liaisons with people who merit distinction. La Sarraz, Bigot, Maasdam have been my friends for fifteen years; they have continually sought me out and given me their trust.[4] I am in as much favor with Mme de Degenfeld as one can be with a woman when neither love nor intrigue is involved. And since you force me to make a tally of my merits, fair Agnes, I will say that I think few people can say as I can: I have never quarreled with any friend—albeit, I have them in every corner of the world. I am open, trusting, merry, which generally doubles at least one's share of friends. Then, you will say to me, why are you complaining? I complain that this small number of people one might want to

2. Famous women of letters of the seventeenth and eighteenth centuries. Antoinette Deshoulières (1637-94) wrote pastoral poetry; Madeleine de Scudéry (1607-67) was a novelist who had one of the famous *précieux* salons; Marie de Rabutin-Chantal, marquise de Sévigné (1626-96) had an immense correspondence that was regarded as a model of the art of letter-writing; Anne Thérèse de Marguenat de Courcelles, marquise de Lambert (1647-1733), was a fine essayist and had a salon frequented by such people as Montesquieu and Marivaux; Emilie le Tonnelier de Breteuil, marquise du Châtelet (1706-49), a close friend and beloved of Voltaire, was extremely learned in the sciences and translated Newton. One notes the range of talents that d'Hermenches is attributing to Belle when he cites these names.
3. Carel George, count van Wassenaer van Obdam, Heer van Twickel. He is the brother of Obdam, one of Belle's suitors.
4. Jacob Adriaan Bigot was colonel in the Swiss Guards and the chamberlain of Willem V; Baron Aarnoud Joost van der Duyn van Maasdam was lieutenant general of the cavalry and governor of Breda.

know are eclipsed—they are coerced—they are broken to conformity by their needs—which I can never be; it follows that they are shot through with a thousand evil things to which they are in pawn for those needs. That refined sensibility that a delicate, trustworthy intercourse can maintain in Paris, London, Brussels, Geneva, Lausanne, Hermenches—good God, in any place where Agnes might live, if only one could be near there—that sensibility atrophies.

As I said before—you treat me severely throughout your letter. To excuse yourself for not giving me advice, you say to me: "I don't know you." You tell me ironically that either I show great trust in you or else I think you have very little judgment—which is your way of telling me that *I* have none at all. Eh, Mademoiselle! Cannot anyone with sense profit from even the poorest advice? If I know what you would advise me, given that you think I am in such-and-such a disposition, in such-and-such a circumstance, I can draw accurate and useful conclusions regarding an opposite state! Besides, is *opinion* itself nothing? It is not enough for one to know how to make the choice that is intrinsically the best; one must also know whether it would be approved by people whose approval one prizes; one must know what can weaken or strengthen their respect for us.

But in any case, I have postponed my plans for retirement, and for a journey to the Hague. I reflect a great deal; I have had a great deal of experience; whenever I haven't succeeded, I am inclined to believe that I have gone about things badly. Every day I tell myself: when everyone is wrong, everyone must be right—we'll have to see what happens. I have only thought to maintain some moral stature; but since you suspect me of haughtiness, I am wrong. I thought that on a thousand occasions I had sacrificed to the fear of mortifying others—or to simple laziness—anything that might make me stand out from the crowd. You think that I insist too much on my rights; then I must reduce them by half. Besides, what are one's rights other than those that the quality of our sentiments confer on us? I must admit that when I do not find my own very edifying, that is usually taken care of by comparing them to others'. There are two sentiments that are absolutely unknown to me: envy and self-interest. You can see what an Iroquois I must be in Holland!

But is it really true that you are studying mathematics? Where do you find the time? I forget more of it each day, I barely practice my music, and I have never written even a *Commoner*, let alone a *Nobleman*!... That's a rather bad pun, but I don't have the leisure to erase it.

Do me the favor, Mademoiselle, of teaching me your method for enjoying the present moment; I confess that I have not yet learned how. I have always found the moment too slight, and I constantly catch myself worrying about the next day. Without a doubt your philosophy is the best by far—or so people say. Teach me how to do it! I enjoy the present moment only when I am alone, sunk into a chair, in a complete apathy—that is a sort of lethargy that you are surely unacquainted with. Then the slightest contemplation satisfies me, and I dread the moment to come, which will draw me out of it.

Speaking of music; I have just received *Medea*, a tragedy by Glover,[5] that has been much praised; when I opened the book, I fell on this passage, which I have just imitated from the English; I will send you the text another time, if you tell me to:

> O Musique, dont l'art, favorable aux plaisirs,
> Nous les rend plus touchants, fait naître des désirs,
> Pourquoi n'employons-nous ta brillante harmonie
> Que dans les jours heureux, si rares dans la vie?
> Les Noces, les festins, prestiges du bonheur,
> Peuvent sans tes secours satisfaire le coeur!
> Mais c'est dans les ennuis, la douleur, la tristesse,
> Dans les chagrins cuisants, dans l'état de faiblesse,
> Qu'on devrait invoquer ton magique pouvoir
> Et par tes doux accords bannir le désespoir![6]

I was standing there among three harpsichords of different construction and tone that I have in my room, and this passage struck me. I was thinking about a dear friend of mine whom I lost last week; I have been in mourning with her husband continually. He is quite desolate, and I noticed that the idea of those three harpsichords seemed to be distressing him—and behold! Here come Glover and Medea to my rescue.

Mademoiselle, I protest that I am not touchy about criticism of my verses; on the contrary, I swear to you that often, while rereading them after a time, I become indignant toward those who have applauded them or who haven't noticed what I myself find bad in them. If you wish, I will send you some that I wrote to console a deaf-mute: according to what his family tells me all the time, they are even now making his existence noticeably more bearable; he knows them by heart.

But I must finish; my eyes are troubling me, and I have been forbidden to write. So much the better for yours.

Here is something else I am vexed about: you say, *Oh, as far as that goes, no—my mother wouldn't be afraid of your being able to turn my*

5. The English writer Richard Glover (1712–85); his *Medea* was published in 1761.
6. The English original is as follows:
> O Music, sweet artificer of pleasure,
> Why is thy science exercis'd alone
> In festivals, on hymeneal days,
> And in the full assemblies of the happy?
> Ah! how much rather should we court thy skill
> In sorrow's gloomy season, to diffuse
> Thy smooth allurements through the languid ear
> Of self-devour'd affliction, and delude
> The wretched from their sadness. (I.i)

head.[7] And why not, may I ask? Whom might that depend on? The head? or the turner?...

Good night, most adorable of created beings. I consecrate to you my respect and my veneration forever.

I beg you, don't study mathematics. It shrinks the imagination, it desiccates the mind; these proofs are at the expense of feeling; one must believe, and validate, and taste without proofs. Oh, but I see clearly that you have not yet made any great progress in mathematics! Your letters would not be so charming.

Have you read the *Catalogue of the Royal and Noble Authors of England* by Milord Walpole?[8] It gave me a great deal of pleasure. No doubt you know the *Letters* of Lady Montagu.[9] You know all the Tudors and the Stuarts by heart! These are my pastimes; I compose a little music too.

If Mme Pater was lacking in feeling, I renounce her; but I will always excuse her.

Tell me, I beg you, about the quarrel that Mlle de Rechteren picked with you; she is very narrow-minded, poor thing!

CҤ *The "young Scot" Belle mentions in the following letter is James Boswell, whose father had sent him to Utrecht to study law.[10] He had recently made the acquaintance of Samuel Johnson, whom he had already placed in the role of mentor and model. Johnson had accompanied him from London to the North Sea port of Harwich when he set out from England.*

Boswell was in Holland from August 1763 through July 1764. He soon became a friend and frequent visitor of the Tuyll family, and his notes and letters from this period tell us a great deal about the cast of characters in Belle's circle.[11] "Odd and endearing" was Belle's characterization of him: he had about him an amiable absurdity that could charm Dutch high society as it was to charm, after a fashion, Rousseau and Voltaire. Boswell was susceptible to women of all classes; he was entranced by such women of rank and wealth as Mme Geelvinck and the countess of Nassau.

Belle de Zuylen—almost exactly his contemporary—disconcerted him as no woman had ever done. His view of educated women of independent mind was much more conservative than that of his hero Samuel Johnson. "She is a charming creature," he wrote a friend, "But she is a savante *and a* bel esprit, *and has published some things. She is much my superior. One does*

7. Belle will pick it up that he has introduced the notion of *being able* to turn her head.
8. The *Catalogue* (1763) is by Horace Walpole.
9. *Letters Written during Her Travels in Europe, Asia and Africa* (1763), by Lady Mary Wortley Montagu (1689–1762).
10. See Frederick Pottle, *James Boswell: The Earlier Years (1740–1769).*
11. These are to be found in *Boswell in Holland.* For the early stages of Belle's relations with Boswell, see Courtney, *Biography* 93–118.

*not like that."[12] It is fortunate, he thought, that she lacks good sense; other-
wise "she would have unlimited dominion over men, and would overthrow
the dignity of the male sex."[13] He vacillated between the roles of mentor—
which he took up in emulation of Johnson—and of suitor. She put up with
his moralizing with a mixture of teasing and good grace, and was rather
touched by his naïveté and warmheartedness. She enjoyed provoking him by
her views on relations between men and women; "She seemed a frantic
libertine," he noted.[14]*

*Boswell tried to present himself to Belle as the perfect sage. What he did
not tell Belle until much later was that he spent that year in Utrecht doing
battle with an agonizing melancholia that plagued him all his life. Each day
required long lectures to himself ("Be Johnson") and a severe scheduling
(he wrote a long "Inviolable Plan") that was supposed to keep him from
collapsing into indolence and self-hatred. While he led a relatively sober existence in Utrecht, before and after his stay there he habitually consorted
with prostitutes. Sexual abstinence (which he would occasionally aspire to,
usually in vain) was a torment to him, and he was often under treatment for
venereal disease.*

*Boswell was a compulsive advice-seeker, and he consulted everyone he
encountered, all over Europe, great men and small, about how to conduct
his life: how to cure his melancholy, conquer his indolence, think about religion, and find the appropriate wife. He asked all his male friends what he
should do about Belle de Zuylen. As a result, we have an assortment of
views of her expressed in the inimitable diction of the young blades of
eighteenth-century England. It was Boswell far more than d'Hermenches
who was getting Belle talked about.*

*His correspondence with Belle began in mid-June 1764, when he left for
Germany to begin his grand tour.*

87. To Constant d'Hermenches, February 25–March 5, 1764

I'm ready to make you all kinds of apologies, but first, you must
apologize to La Sarraz in your heart. He spoke no ill of you to me—not a
word; and what you say of your friend, on a baseless supposition, is all the
more cruel in that he hopes very much to become my friend. But he will
never know anything about it, I give you my word. If you ever have grave
suspicions against me, I beg you to wait until the crime is proved before you
punish it. But you will say again that I'm deriding you.

Let's talk seriously. Everything that I might know to your disadvantage, I
have known for a long time; from the first moment of our acquaintance, I

12. *Boswell in Holland* 227.
13. *Boswell in Holland* 230.
14. *Boswell in Holland* 287.

was told that you had few friends, although you were very charming. That didn't matter to me—I could easily be the friend of a man who had few friends. If I said what I thought on that occasion, it's because you spoke to me about it, and I believed that sincerity and friendship required such a response. Here's something else that may have made me take a censorious tone: I have recently been reproached for being indolent regarding the faults of my friends, for not reproving them zealously enough for their vagaries of mind and temperament; and indeed, I find that it's of no use. To recognize one's faults one must have a certain modesty, and to combat them, a certain courage that are almost never to be found. I greatly prefer to bend my humor to the whims of others—which is sheer profit for me—than to weary myself in exhortations and remonstrances that are almost always useless. While writing to you I said to myself: this time let us be zealous and sincere. I said to myself also: he praises Mme Pater for liking asperity in his speeches; let's see whether he will like asperity in mine. But, believing I was being only candid, I have been severe; my reflections stumbled on false suppositions. D'Hermenches, I beg your pardon on my knees; from now on, say nothing to me that I cannot take literally. You are right, even bad advice could help you see the best choice; but even so I don't like to give out advice at random, and even while refusing you, haven't I said some things that look a great deal like advice? You shouldn't make me out to be guiltier than I am—for example, you shouldn't change my sentences even as you repeat them. Do you think that I didn't notice that bit of fudging?

As to your other reproach, about *The Nobleman*, I assure you that it was that I simply forgot to mention it rather than that I wanted to keep it a secret from you. It's a trifle whose author was not supposed to be known; as you will see, this little book cost me no more effort than a dozen letters. To repair this wrong, I'm going to tell you that in the *Mercure* or in the *Année littéraire* you will soon see a little work by the same pen.[1] I can't quite make up my mind to tell you the title—it is too strange that I should write such a thing and have it printed. But take a guess, and try to figure out which piece was written by me.

If you guess right, I think you will no longer be so afraid that mathematics is shrinking my imagination—or at least you will find that no harm has been done as yet. I am, however, much more advanced in it than you might think; I study all the properties of conic sections with the greatest diligence. My tutor, who is not polished and is no flatterer, has told me that he has never seen a better aptitude, nor such rapid progress. He was formerly a schoolmaster in North Holland; through his merit he has become examiner of the naval officers in Rotterdam.[2] At present he teaches mathe-

1. This work has not been found.
2. Laurens Praalder (1711-93), mathematician and director of the Utrecht Orphanage. He will reappear in fictionalized guise as Praal, a teacher of mathematics and an atheist, in Isabelle de Charrière's *Trois Femmes* (1795).

matics in a house founded by a rich lady; it is intended to provide instruction for young people from the orphanage who seem to be talented. This my tutor, with the manner of a peasant, is in fact a very clever man, and with all that, so cheerful, so even-tempered, so modest, that he gives science a good name. The more he forgets himself, the more I respect him, and we spend a couple of hours together every day ... But it's too bad for you that I like my tutor, and I'm surprised that I have told you a story so long and so uninteresting; what can it matter to you, this modesty, this school, and our orphans?

What I wanted to tell you is that I don't see yet that my mind is shrinking at all, or my imagination becoming sterile. What I do know is that an hour or two of mathematics frees up my spirit and cheers my heart; it seems to me that I sleep and eat all the better when I have seen some evident and indisputable truths; it consoles me for the obscurities of religion and metaphysics—or rather it makes me forget them; I am very glad that there is something certain in this world. But it is not simply for pleasure that I concern myself with these truths; I find that as soon as one begins to apply oneself to anything at all, it becomes shameful to neglect the knowledge of nature. The order that God has put into the universe is too beautiful for me willingly to stay ignorant of it; like Zadig,[3] I would like to know of physics what is known in my time, and for that, one must have mathematics. I don't like half-knowledge. —There is my justification; however, I thank you for the advice, and I will profit from it; I won't do too many calculations, and I will do many other things. I would be very annoyed if my letters ceased to amuse you.

February 26, before daybreak

I have sat up all night watching over my mother. So near her bed, do I dare continue a letter that would offend her? Yes, I dare; she is sleeping, she is better. I have been tenderly attentive, and she was very touched by it; perhaps, at the bottom of her heart, she would pardon me for this if she knew about it ... By the way, my head is still unturned, and my mother knows it.

I have just finished *Amelia,* which I began at one o'clock.[4] My mind is full of all of this novel's heroes, and you will receive a letter with no common sense in it at all: it will be further than even you could wish from mathematical precision. God preserve me from wanting to be profound, as you say I know how to be; my profundity could only be utter gibberish.

It was silly of me to tell you to look in the *Année littéraire* or the *Mercure* for a little work by me that is about to appear. It's hardly worth looking for,

---

3. The title character in a story by Voltaire. Belle is paraphrasing a sentence from Voltaire's own text. Much later in life, she will write an opera libretto based on *Zadig*. Voltaire, by the way, wrote a layman's introduction to Newton.
4. The novel by Henry Fielding, translated in 1762 by Madame Riccoboni.

and that indication is so vague as to be useless. When I can tell you something less vague, I may write you; up to this point I know nothing myself, except that I've sent the manuscript to my brother in Paris,[5] and I asked him to put it in the *Année littéraire* or in the *Mercure*; I haven't received an answer from him yet. I beg you, Monsieur, not to say a single word about it, either vaguely or any other way.

I have not yet seen the English *Medea;* your imitation gives me a very good impression of it. Certainly I would like you to send me the verses that did so much good for the deaf-mute; these are more than verses, and their success is of another order than vain applause; the satisfaction of the poet is sweet and truly glorious ... As you see, I am dreaming a little: that last sentence limps, I think. I'm having the greatest difficulty keeping my eyes open, and yet I want to take advantage of these moments of liberty. I am already reproaching myself for not having answered soon enough your complaints and your displeasure, which are at least partly justified. Since my intentions are good, you must pardon the expression "glorious satisfaction" and you must pretend to understand what I meant; as for myself, I can't possibly remember or guess what I meant. Never has so sleepy a person as I am held a pen, much less used one to write to a man like you. What's the use of holding forth? I'm dropping with sleepiness; so goodbye.

Eleven o'clock

With the help of tea and coffee, I'm now fairly awake. It would be reasonable to throw this morning's reverie in the fire, but it is easier to let it be. Why be vain with one's friends? Why should one never want to seem a little mad? It would hardly be surprising if my mother's delirium were communicated to my brain. —But from this word "delirium" you are going to think that she is very ill, and you will be scandalized that I amuse myself by writing a letter; you would be quite right to be, if that were so. Thank Heaven, it is not a crime for me to amuse myself; my mother is often delirious when she has a fever, and her fever is merely from a bad cold, we think. Resting my head on her bed, for a long time I watched her peaceful sleep. —Don't you admire my wanting to interest you in what concerns my mother?

Why do you say, "My eyes are troubling me, so much the better for yours?" No, I assure you it is not "so much the better"; my eyes would not be wearied by longer reading—I would have done it with pleasure. Even though you scold, your letter is charming. As much out of self-interest, then, as out of friendship, I would have wanted you not to have trouble with your eyes. Heal them and take care of them: of all the senses, the most precious, to my mind, is sight.

You say that the judgment passed on our actions by people we respect counts for something in the balance of motives that must determine us, and

5. Her oldest brother, Willem René (1743–1839).

that it's partly to learn what people would think of your retirement that you talked to me about it. I understand that so well that I have sharply reproached myself for having neglected the chances I had at the Hague to inform myself about it so I could advise you. Almost six months ago someone told me that you were thinking of leaving the service; I could have mentioned that to La Sarraz, for example, and asked him what he had learned of it, what he thought about it, and what other people would think about it. That was the way to respond to your intentions. If you were to reproach me for having neglected it, I would acknowledge my omission; even so, although you're not reproaching me, I am telling you about it, and I seriously apologize; but I have no other reason for repentance: I am not at all guilty of the excess of prudence that you suspect me of. If La Sarraz had spoken ill of you, and if I had known that he was doing you wrong, I would certainly have dared to contradict and defend you; I know nothing of that single and exclusive attachment to self-interest which makes one always keep it in view, and makes one cravenly sacrifice all other interests to it. Please believe that I will be capable of forgetting it when it's a question of my friends, and even more when it's a question of justice.

Good Lord, all these interruptions! How hard it is to finish a letter that should already be in your hands! You praise my letters with enthusiasm, perhaps with exaggeration; but tell me frankly, Monsieur, this disorder in my ideas, and style, and writing—does it still leave them any grace?

My mother is not entirely recovered; my brother has also been ill; I have hardly left their side, I have a thousand concerns; I can't write a single sentence that is not interrupted; people come in, or call me, I throw down the paper, and my last words are forgotten. Tell me frankly if I bore you; I won't get angry. I will choose my time better, I will no longer write when I'm half-asleep—but if you like what I think in different moments of life, tell me to continue. You think that it is pleasant to live near me; well then, nothing comes closer to it than receiving such letters; but they are not worth keeping, much less rereading, and the fire will do well to burn them, just as the wind does well to carry off my words.

You ask me what I do to enjoy the present moment. Here it is: when it is midnight and I am enjoying myself, I rejoice that it is not one o'clock; then I continue to amuse myself, and I take care not to reflect on the passing of time; I do not say, "One o'clock will strike." In the morning, when I know that I will be bored in the evening, I say to myself, "Let's not think about the evening, let's enjoy the morning," and then the evening is for me as if it were never to come. But when the present bores me or distresses me, my imagination anticipates the future, and then I love it; then I feel that hope is a precious gift from Heaven.

I am rereading Voltaire's *Histoire universelle* with my youngest brother;[6]

6. Vincent.

that's about all I am reading. I am hard to please in that respect—perhaps too hard. I don't know how to look for the good things among the bad and the mediocre; I only want to read what is very well thought and well written. Besides, I have no leisure at present, and however much I want to read Hume,[7] I haven't yet been able to. As for Lady Montagu, I have known her for a long time. I have too many correspondences; they occupy me more than they should by half, and since they find no place during my day, they often encroach on my hours of sleep. The rest is rather well ordered. From ten to eleven I listen to Voltaire, and I do handwork—for you must know that after having never been able to endure any sort of handwork that I knew about, finally this winter I found a kind that amuses me very much and at which I am quite skillful. A new taste that is innocent and easy to satisfy— that's an important acquisition; a thousand moments that I used to abandon to boredom have become, simply by the taste for work, moments of pleasure, moments that count for something in my life.

In my whole day, there is no time better employed than the time I spend reading or chatting with my brother. He is sixteen; he is likeable, perceptive, modest, cheerful, a thousand times more reflective and more prudent than I am; we love each other very much—and none of my advice is a burden to him. Taste, intelligence, feeling—he has everything that makes a likeable man. Since he wants to amount to something, he has asked to be in the service; in a month he is going to join his regiment at Bois-le-Duc. I think I will learn to play the lute when my brother is no longer with me. Isn't that an odd compensation? After our reading I go to my harpsichord teacher; then comes mathematics, which I sometimes also resume in the evening. The rest of my time is given to my father, my mother, my uncle, my clothes, and my concerts.

As for friends, I have many fewer here than you have at the Hague—that is to say, I have none, and I do without them with an ease which sometimes makes me think that I am not worthy to have any. I am aware that I must seem to be condemned by the judgment pronounced by my own lips against people who have no friends; but it does not exactly apply to me. I get along well with everyone, and if I have no friends, it's because I don't live on terms of friendship with anybody. I am much loved by my own family, much loved by my uncle and aunt.[8] There is a very worthy man, enlightened and very civil, who accompanies me on the bass as often as I wish; he comes to visit my brother, and we often talk with pleasure.[9] When I go out to some gathering, I chat and play with a young Scot who is sensible, intelligent, and ingenuous. The others don't suit me at all; I am annoyed when it

7. David Hume (1711–76), whose *History of England* had been published in French in 1763. Belle met Hume in London three years later. Her account of their meeting in April 1767 is in her Letter 271.
8. General Hendrik Willem van Tuyll van Serooskerken and his wife.
9. Perhaps Castillon, a mathematics professor, whom she mentions by name in a later letter.

is rainy or when my spirit is somber, but ordinarily I console myself very well with the kind of solitude in which I live; I have more leisure and more liberty.

You say that the sensibility for pleasant and trustworthy associations is something that gets lost at the Hague—what a bizarre idea! I am persuaded that you would not lose it in Algiers. My brother the sailor[10] had seen nothing for a long time except the ocean and the shores of America; when he returned home he was surprised, it is true, to hear a conversation that resembled nothing he had heard, but he felt its pleasantness all the more. Although he was barely seventeen when he began his métier, what he had loved then he loved even better now. For the month that he spent with us he couldn't bear to have me leave him; I couldn't get him out of my room at night, and sometimes he stayed seated on my bed until two or three in the morning. Believe me, when you know what is worthy of love, you know it forever.

It would be a pity if I spared you a description of a single one of my relatives in this letter; so I will tell you that my sister is the mother of a pretty little girl, and she and her husband are inexpressibly joyful.

You asked me once, a long time ago, whether Perponcher had received your congratulations; yes, he did, and he passed on to me your charming compliment. But the wrath of a mother-in-law is like the wrath of the king whom (I think) Solomon speaks of; so he no longer dares to take the least part in our correspondence.[11]

I did not say that I was flattered very much by getting along well with the men at the Hague, but undoubtedly I enjoyed myself more than I would have if I had displeased everyone there. You yourself admit that there are some there whose approbation is flattering, and whose conversation might please me. I have never had a bad conversation with any of them who know how to have good ones. I thought that there were only a small number of amiable people anywhere, and when I compare the men of the Hague with the women of the Hague, with the men here and in other cities I know, I found that there was a fair amount of wit and merit among them. Yet another reason for believing that I am not especially worthy of having friends is that I get along perfectly well in the company of people who are not well thought of. The moment their minds amuse me, I don't look too closely to see what their hearts are like. On that basis, one could imagine that my own doesn't amount to much.

But speaking of the heart, I remember what you said about your sentiments; others, you said, make yours seem better by comparison with theirs. Permit me to tell you that I find this method of comparison a bad choice when one aspires to perfection in anything. We find on our path so many

10. Diederik (Ditie), her favorite brother.
11. Proverbs 16:14, "The wrath of a king is as messengers of death: but a wise man will pacify it" (King James Version).

dishonest people and so many stupid people for every clever or virtuous man, that if we were to judge ourselves by comparison with others we could achieve satisfaction at a bargain. It is too easy to have the advantage; this arbitrary evaluation is ever subject to miscalculation. In my view it is not a question of what others are, but of what I am, what I can do, what I should be. There might be a kernel of pride and disdain in this system, but it would forestall petty forms of arrogance or vanity.

Have you heard of the verses that are making the rounds of the Hague about your friend Maasdam? I hope you haven't, and that this will be a novelty for you. The first ones were written long ago, after a Jewish wedding where I had played cards with the General before knowing him.[12]

> A son teint noir et basané
> Comme à ses traits et son air sombre
> Je crus Maasdam être du nombre
> Du peuple élu jadis, aujourd'hui dispersé.
> On nomma Général le minois judaïque
> Mais un titre plus magnifique
> A mon opinion n'aurait pu changer rien
> Et j'aurais cru plutôt toute la République
> Conduite par des Juifs, que ce Maasdam, chrétien.[13]

Here are the new ones:

> Après dix-huit mois de mystère
> Quelque ami lassé de se taire
> A publié certain écrit
> Qui ne parlant du coeur ni de l'esprit
> Attaque un peu de Maasdam le visage.
> On le dit courroucé, mais moi je n'en crois rien,
> Je le tiens de moitié trop sage.
> Qu'importe un minois juif quand on est bon chrétien?
> Et quand on n'a pas l'esprit sombre,
> Quand le coeur est exempt de ténébreux soucis,
> Qu'importe si d'épais sourcis
> Sur les yeux jettent un peu d'ombre?
> Contre Apollon, ce beau blondin,

---

12. There were a number of important Portuguese Jewish families at the Hague at this time. They were patrons of music and the theater. Thanks to them, Mozart was invited to the Hague on a number of occasions. The wedding in question was probably that of the Pinto family, which took place in 1763.

13. By his dark and swarthy color, / By his features and his somber air, / I thought that Maasdam was of that people / Once elect, today dispersed. / This Judaic cherub was named General; / But a more magnificent title, in my opinion / Could have changed nothing, / And I would sooner have believed that the whole Republic / Was led by Jews, than that this Maasdam was Christian.

Mars, quoique brun et hâlé, j'en suis sûre,
N'aurait changé d'air ni de chevelure,
Et qu'eût-il fait d'un plus beau teint?
Une histoire bien avérée
Dit qu'il ne plut guère à Vulcain,
Mais beaucoup trop à Cythérée.[14]

I have received a very polite letter from Monsieur de Maasdam. Write me a good long one, if your doctor allows it. I am sorry for you if it's bad for you to read. I can say with good reason: my eyes do not give me trouble, and that's so much the worse for yours. I won't write you for a long time now; life is too short for me very often to write sixteen-page dispatches in the guise of letters. Write and tell me that you are no longer discontented. And stop being annoyed that neither my mother nor I fear for my head. Really, what a childish reproach! Which would you prefer, being written to or being feared?

89. *To Constant d'Hermenches, May 11 and 15, 1764*

Utrecht

Your little letter, Monsieur, has given me great pleasure.[1] It seems to me that you were very slow to answer me; I was afraid that you were ill, that your eyes hurt you too much for you to write. I am very glad that's not the case.

You are not expecting what I am about to say next. To speak of the pleasure that a letter gives is almost to ask for others; but, on the contrary, I am obliged to tell you not to write to me any more. It is rather bizarre that one has to be two hundred leagues away to have any association with me, and that it's all finished as soon as one comes near. You will understand my reasons. First, they open everything that goes between here and the Hague; but that's not the main problem. My chambermaid is German; the letters that you sent by way of her from a long distance were not suspect, but letters coming to her from the Hague, where everyone knows she has no correspondents, would be. We are going to the country—in four days, I think.

---

14. After eighteen months of secrecy / Some friend, weary of keeping silent, / Published a certain writing / Which, speaking neither of the heart nor the mind, / Attacks the face of Maasdam. / They say that he is angry, but I don't believe it at all; / I think he is much too wise. / What does a Jewish face matter, if one is a good Christian? / And when one's mind is not somber, / When the heart is free from dark cares, / What does it matter if thick eyebrows / Cast a little shadow over the eyes? / Against Apollo, that handsome blond, / Mars, although dark and sunburned, / Would not—I'm quite sure— / Have changed his manner or his hair, / And what would he have done with a fairer skin? / A well-confirmed story / Says that he pleased Vulcan hardly at all, / But pleased Cytherea only too well.
1. This letter has not been found.

My father comes into town every day, and the first thing he does is pick up the mail. Your letters might by some inadvertence fall into his hands, and perhaps, as I have said, their address would give rise to suspicions. It was a blunder on the part of the best-intentioned of people that put me in such a predicament last autumn.[2] The occasion was just about like what I've described. We were at Zuylen, and the letters that arrived in Utrecht were all brought to my father. At the moment I cannot imagine anything reliable—any good arrangement for our correspondence. I have thought hard, I have racked my brains, but I see risks on all sides, and while we are at Zuylen, everything is chancy. However, I think that if there were something that you absolutely had to tell me, you could address your letter to Mme Geelvinck *care of Monsieur d'Amerongen d'oud Amelisweerd;*[3] she has been in Amsterdam for two days, but she is coming back Sunday, and will stay here a few weeks more. She is a faithful and discreet friend.

Now let us speak of my misdeeds; I have undoubtedly committed some, and I ask your pardon, since my justification may not be very good. But I assure you that I had no specific intention of keeping my works a secret from you, and that I did not distrust your discretion. Laziness, and the tedium of copying—but even more, certain ideas in which vanity and modesty have their share—these are the causes of my crime. I prefer letting what I do be spread abroad without my spreading it, rather than making it public myself. I dread seeming ridiculous, like those authors who are so enthusiastic about their own works that they bore everyone to death with them and pity those who are unaware of their accomplishments. —I know what you would say, d'Hermenches, but you are not everybody; you are my friend, and for that very reason you would not have been bored to death; I could count on the interest you would have taken in anything I wrote. I know that—and it's for that reason that I admitted I was guilty.

Moreover, I have never confided anything to Mme Blatière, whom I have never seen; whatever was confided had surely passed through many hands before arriving to her from me!

Ask Bentinck for the Garcin epistle and my answer, for the "Portraits of Zélide", and for the epistle to Mme Hasselaer.[4] Say that people in Switzerland have spoken to you about all this. Ask Perponcher for the verses that I addressed to my mother—they are new. Goodbye; midnight is sounding, I

2. Her letter to Perponcher, Letter 81, recounts how d'Hermenches' letter wound up in the kitchen fire.
3. Husband of Mme Geelvinck's sister.
4. The epistle from Garcin (a Swiss pastor) and her answer have not been found, nor has the epistle to Mme Hasselaer. Belle had written a literary self-portrait that is generally referred to as "Portrait of Zélide," but whose title line was *Portrait de Mlle de Z... sous le nom de Zélide, fait par elle-même.* There were then two additions: *Addition au portrait de Zélide,* and *Seconde Addition.* She had also written a portrait of Mme Geelvinck. They have come down to us through copies that Boswell made early in 1764. See *O.C.* 10: 35-44.

dare stay up no longer; I was very ill for some time—a violent cough, fever, vapors. I take cow's milk and quinine; I am told that sleep and idleness are even more necessary for me.

Saturday, May 11

The remark about my tutor greatly amused me. If I spoke of him as of a Saint-Preux, I must have spoken very oddly.[5] Can you imagine anybody who less resembles Saint-Preux than a little man of more than fifty, who wears an old reddish wig all askew, and coarse woolen stockings in all seasons; who's as grubby as a Capuchin, and who, whenever he opens his mouth, drops a shower on me and on my paper? The enthusiasm with which I spoke of him is, then, very different from what you have imagined. I would be very unhappy if my attention were not divided among a number of things; a single object could never suffice for all the activity of my soul; but why does that make you think that I value you the less? How are these things connected?

I am very annoyed at the interruption of our correspondence ... Send at least one long letter for me care of Mme Geelvinck, and above all, tell me about yourself; tell me how you are getting on with everybody, and whether, now that you are back at the Hague, your plans for retirement are taking shaping or being shelved. With a few friends, a taste for study, beautiful walks, and a good theater, it seems to me that you shouldn't be bored. You ask me whether I am ever going to the Hague. No, I think not. People may tell you these days that I am going to be married, but don't believe it until you hear it from me.

I wrote unclearly an address that you must read clearly. My friend's brother-in-law is MONSIEUR D'AMERONGEN D'OUD AMELISWEERD.

Tuesday morning

I have waited for Mme Geelvinck's return to send you this letter; I couldn't bring myself to send your name written in my hand by the post; besides, I wanted to ask her whether she would allow one of your letters to be addressed to her. She is willing, so do write to me.

91. *To Constant d'Hermenches, May 21, 1764*

Zuylen

Good Heavens, what misanthropy! What a black mood![1] There are a thousand things that weary me as they do you, a thousand things distress me; sometimes I weep, sometimes I'm sick, but that doesn't prevent my recognizing what is good or beautiful, or from laughing any time I can.

---

5. Saint-Preux was the hero of Rousseau's *Julie, ou La Nouvelle Héloïse* (1760). He was both the tutor and the lover of Julie.

1. This seems to be in response to a letter from d'Hermenches that has been lost, but no such missing letter is mentioned in the *O.C.*

I am sorry for you, d'Hermenches, from the bottom of my heart. I know my compatriots; but can't you let just a glimmer of philosophy pierce through your gloom, and somehow change the way things affect you? It's only a small part of the day that has to be spent with people one doesn't like: afterwards, one returns to one's books, writing desk, and harpsichord. Nevertheless I understand your disgust; it requires almost a light-hearted-ness—an imagination that can furnish cheerful ideas for itself—to endure the life that I see you leading at present. For I do see you. Your letter paints a striking picture, and it has spread a cloud of sadness over my own mood.

But what on earth are you thinking of when you say: "Come to the Hague"? Do I take a step alone? Do I take a single step freely? I wish that Mme de Boufflers were in Utrecht.[2] I am certainly not as worthy as the eleven hundred virgins, but I am as well worth seeing as their skulls, which people so curiously go to view in the Cologne Cathedral.[3] Perhaps if Mme de Boufflers were in Utrecht, she might be willing to take steps to see me; for, however willing I might be to make all the advances, I think she would have to take the first ones. But it's foolish to linger over that: she will not come to Utrecht, I will not go to the Hague, and we won't see each other; I'm quite annoyed about it.

I passed on to the Widow all your sweet words; she would deserve them even if she were less useful to you. She is charming, and I am fond of her both out of habit and on account of an affinity that grows every day. If your amiable lady goes to Amsterdam or Haarlem, try to have her get to know Mme Hasselaer. I have just spent three weeks with her, I saw her from morning to night, and a part of the night; after a thousand conversations on every subject imaginable, I concluded that if I had to change places with any woman I know, from head to toe, in mind and in heart, it's with Mme Hasselaer that I would do it.

Goodbye, let me not write to you any more for a long time; let me sleep, let me avoid any cause of mishaps and anxiety. I'm in great need of repose and tranquillity.

92. *To Constant d'Hermenches, May 27–30, 1764*

Sunday

Honestly now, is it only the Widow you want to see in Utrecht? Don't you have some plan to engage us to be there together—that is, to expose us to all sorts of embarrassment, and have one of us accused of imprudent

---

2. A well-known figure in society. She had left her husband and become the mistress of the prince de Conti. She was a friend of David Hume and became one of Rousseau's pro-tectresses. Several comments in this letter and the next suggest that Mme de Boufflers was tak-ing a tour of remarkable architectural sights in northern France and the Low Countries.

3. According to legend, St. Ursula and her companions, the eleven hundred virgins, were massacred in Cologne by the order of the king of the Huns.

conduct, the other of a blind and cowardly accommodation? But supposing that I am wrong, and that you are willing to come within two steps of me, in a place where I go two or three times a week without even thinking of seeing me. In that case, I say, your plan would be very reasonable; Mme Geelvinck is much more worthy of such a pilgrimage than some "Notre Dame."[1] If this one were in no way a disadvantage for her, I would tell you to set forth at once, and were you to come on foot through thorns and brambles, an hour's conversation would not be too dearly bought. All through the town, and then in all the Provinces, people would say: "There came a man with a black headband and eyes full of wit, and he spoke tête-à-tête with a young and pretty widow." And society would be scandalized, and the Widow would be very annoyed, and the man with the headband would reproach himself for having caused vexation as the reward for a cordiality that he says is very precious to him.

You think that you do a wonderful thing by saying "I am ashamed at having distressed you by my misanthropy, I only wanted to pay you homage," and so forth; but I prefer a thousand times to have someone speak to me of his troubles because his heart is full of them—thus can I share them and ease them—rather than pay homage to the excellence of my being—it being only very moderately excellent and deserving very little homage.

I am delighted to see you a little more disposed to happiness. Bentinck has told me that you spoke of your woes in such a way as to make everyone die laughing. Boswell saw you for an instant at Monsieur de Maasdam's, and in that instant you were full of wit. I think I spoke to you about him one day; he's a very good friend of mine, and much respected by my father and mother, so that he is always well received when he comes to see me. He came often while I was sick, and he was so surprised to find me always in a very good humor that he almost reproached me for it; it seemed to him almost bizarre and out of place.

Mme Hasselaer tolerates fools, and for that I envy her; but she does not confuse them with people of wit. She knows how to ask the question and give the answer, but she greatly prefers to find people who hear and who respond. She is not at all false, she does not dissimulate; with the public she is polite and prudent, with her friends she is trusting and sincere. If one has only moderate respect for her, then one does not know her at all.

It was of absolutely no use to me to know that Mme de Boufflers was in Utrecht; I couldn't very well say "Monsieur d'Hermenches wrote and told me; she's his friend; we must go see her." It's too bad that I am not a celebrated curiosity; she would have come the day before yesterday, and would have found very good company. I thank you for having wanted to give me the keenest pleasure I know—that of seeing an amiable person—,

1. There seems to be a pun here on the French "une autre dame" ("another lady") and "une Notre Dame," a common name for a church or cathedral.

but this could not be.

You are very clever; one must always answer you, whether one meant to or not. I imagine, however, that this is beginning to interest you somewhat less. In my letters I am a great reasoner—you know that by now, it's no longer news—and at a distance of two hundred leagues one must be satisfied with that; but since we have been less far away from each other you would prefer to hear me speak foolishness. I too would be charmed to see you, but you must keep it in mind that that is impossible.

Send me your verses whenever you please, but I promise nothing yet; I don't know whether I will have the courage to criticize them. All authors say what you say, just as all lovers say that they will be faithful; and in all good faith, they make dupes believe it.

Farewell, Monsieur. Do not set Mme Geelvinck against me any more; she said to me the day before yesterday, "Write, write!" It gives her pleasure, and that argument seemed to me unanswerable. You can well imagine that I care very much about the return of your health, and everything that conduces to your well-being. It would be a great improvement for me to play the harpsichord as you do; I would give everything in the world for your skill. Compared with yours, my fingers only profane an instrument.

I'm sending my letters by way of the Widow, and since I've gone several days without seeing her, this one has aged a little in my writing case.

93. *From Constant d'Hermenches, June 4, 1764*

Your censure is quite just, if you read my writing as literary work, or if you supposed that I laid some claim to writing well.[1] But Mademoiselle, if you had deigned to consider the circumstances, and to see me seizing the opportunity to tell some home truths to a young person for whom anything sublime would be Greek, and on whom nothing not personally directed would make any impression, then you would pardon the mundane images I used in my efforts to correct her and interest her. The person in question needed all those warnings, and if she had found them in a book a thousand times, she would have paid absolutely no attention; it was necessary—quite necessary—to interweave them in her hair.[2] She was grateful to me for it;

1. He is referring to a poem that he had presented to a young woman—possibly Mme Pater, who is first mentioned in Letter 76 of January 1763.
2. There is a poem, "Toilette: A l'Etre singulier qui veut que je le coiffe" [To the singular being who would have me arrange her hair], in *D'Hermenches: Pamphlets* (39–43), in which d'Hermenches uses the details of hairdressing as figures of speech in his advice on manners and morals. It seems likely that this poem—or one like it—contains the "interweaving" in question here. The problem of the accumulation of grease in one's hair was one that people did discuss in Belle's time: see Georges Vigarello, *Concepts of Cleanliness: Changing Attitudes in France since the Middle Ages* 83–84.

she has been more careful on several points, and her sense of emulation has even inspired her to write me a response full of reflections; have I then wasted my time? I am not Addison;[3] I was not rhyme-making for Agnes, and I was undoubtedly more at a level with my audience than that writer is with you! I don't know what I could write that would truly be up to your level, even supposing that you had the imperfection of being unable to think about greasy hair! I don't want to elaborate all this any further; I am persuaded that you understand me perfectly. If my letter is better than my verses, it is certainly because it was intended for you, and the verses were intended for someone else.

How pleased I am, Mademoiselle, to hear you say that you don't like allegories, even in the epic, which is their native habitat; in Virgil, in Homer, they have wearied me and made me impatient a hundred times over. Comparisons are the subalterns of language, and allegories those of genius.

I have just left Mme de Boufflers. She has returned from a very cold journey, but her absence did not chill her feelings for me; perhaps we'll play cards, perhaps we'll dance tonight at the English ball. But good God, how different this ball will be for me! Two years ago I saw Agnes there! She found my minuets quite bad, but I found her conversation excellent, and her grace incomparable.

Your Scot looks on me quite favorably; he said to me this morning, "Je daisir Monsiu de fair votre conessance;"[4] but I fear, my too generous friend, that you have deceived him; he seems to expect each word of mine to be an epigram, and you can't imagine how that holds me back. We will talk about you; that will be worth all the witticisms in the world, and off that will I feast—at this feast. Write me, I beg of you; I put myself humbly at your feet.

94. *To Constant d'Hermenches, June 8, 1764*

We are in complete agreement on allegory. If it is to please me, it must be very short, very clear, and perfectly appropriate. If I had been persuaded that all the characters in the *Iliad* are allegorical, as some Jesuit Father claims, I would never have read it. It is tiresome always to be running back and forth between the visible meaning and the hidden one; the image distracts one from the moral, and the effort of seeking out the moral disturbs the pleasure that the image can give.

When you write, Monsieur, tell me about your son; tell me what he is doing, what he is learning, what you desire to have him know. The educa-

---

3. Joseph Addison (1672–1719), a much-admired playwright, poet, and author of moral essays; with Richard Steele, he founded of the immensely popular journal *The Spectator*.
4. Boswell's mispronounced French for "I desire, sir, to make your acquaintance."

tion of an only son is a very interesting subject, and one which must occupy your thoughts many moments of the day. Besides, I want to think about something that concerns you.

Don't look for my work in the *Année littéraire* or in the *Mercure français*. It was poetry in prose; the reputation of the daughter of a king of France was severely attacked, and for that reason it could not be accepted by the *Mercure* unless I changed the title. Since the public can very well do without it, and since changing the names, places and circumstances would be tedious for me, I think no more will be heard about it.[1]

I am amusing myself just now by writing a comedy.[1] If I finish it and have it performed I will tell you its name immediately, but don't ask to see it beforehand. To show a work to a friend is asking for criticism, asking for advice—and I don't like to ask for it because I don't like to follow it. My work must be my work; like Rousseau, I say that its first success is to please *me*. I know that seems arrogant, and I'm sorry; but isn't there also a bit of vanity—a vanity not altogether noble—in presenting as one's own a work whose faults have been corrected and whose beauties have been enhanced by someone else? I don't even think that desiring my own approval above all is arrogance; it is simply a feeling. What displeases me *always* displeases me, even if it were to please everybody else; and I'm vexed at having done something that displeases me. An action whose motive is known to be criminal only by him who committed it will never appear to him virtuous—he will never applaud himself for it, were the entire universe to applaud him. I think that this is almost the same thing: the author feels that he could have done better; he's vexed at not having done better. The approval we give ourselves is a consolation when we have failed to receive it from others, but the approval of others never replaces our own—it is never so keenly felt.

That is all very poorly expressed; my head is very bad today. If you were not a trifle prejudiced in my favor and very indulgent, I think I would throw my letter in the fire.

How shall I go about telling you that soon, in another two weeks perhaps, we will no longer be writing to each other? In showing me—in such a truthful manner—that my letters were a pleasure to you, you have hit upon my weak point. Yesterday, a footman gave me a rose he had gathered for me; I found that it redeemed twenty acts of negligence, and I realized that we are happy and good in proportion as we provide more pleasant feelings for any being capable of feeling, whether it be in big things or in small ones. Giving pleasure or not can never be a matter of indifference. If a degree more or less of happiness is not indifferent for a dog, what will it be for a man? If it concerns us for a stranger, how can it not for a friend? My letters cannot give you any very great pleasure; it is only a slight degree of happiness—it's merely the rose that I was given. But I was touched by the rose,

1. *Justine.* The text has been lost, but it was read in Belle's circle.

for there are few roses—and there are few pleasures in life. Such as it is, it pains me to take this one away from you. But by continuing it I would be causing myself grave uneasiness, I would be exposing myself to great anxieties; you wouldn't want me to continue.

Please believe that I will resume the correspondence as soon as I can; even if it were not for your satisfaction, I would do it for my own. I am careful not to neglect my own pleasures, and the pleasure of receiving charming letters written with the intelligence of a man of intellect and the heart of a friend is no small thing.

They say that Mme de Boufflers writes so very well—write to her. Unless she keeps her habitual reserve in her letters to Holland, that will take the place of writing to me. I will write you once again when Mme Geelvinck is on the point of leaving.

I am impatiently waiting for Boswell, to learn what the two of you said to each other. He told me the other day that although I was *a charming creature,*[2] he would not be my husband, though my dowry were all the Seven Provinces; and I found that quite right.

Friday, June 8, 1764

Your heart, then, is much better than mine; I don't think I would finish any verses that didn't please my own taste, even if I could hope that they would reform all my contemporaries. D'Hermenches, I beg you to pardon my severity. When someone has wanted to do me a service and has failed, I consider the intention; but when he shows me verses, never. I do not look to see whether they are good as moralizing, but whether they are good as poetry.

You are going dancing; I'm going for walks, and getting wet in the rain. Mme Geelvinck and I were obliged to seek shelter this afternoon, after having followed the river's edge for a long time without noticing that the sky was darkening. These strolls are delightful; but since no pleasures are perfect, I tremble when I hear barking, or when I see a big dog. My aversion to these animals has come on since we have come to have a considerable number of rabid dogs in our province; it is more real and more inconvenient than a horror of greasy hair.[3]

You are playing with Mme de Boufflers, with the beautiful ladies; *I* am playing with my mother, who has the toothache. We enjoyed ourselves so much this evening after supper that it is now very late, so farewell.

2. English in the original.
3. See Letter 93, n. 2.

95. *From Constant d'Hermenches, June 12, 1764*

In this we differ absolutely, or rather, beautiful Agnes, you are deluding yourself. It is always *others* whom we seek to please; we want to captivate either their taste or their esteem. I make exception for the points pertaining directly to what is popularly called "conscience," and which for us are essentially associated with character: honor, probity, humanity ... And even on those very points, public opinion has such a hold on us that we abstain from things that, by our own lights, we find permissible or neutral, if custom, or concern for the judgment of our fellows, prohibits them. In all things, it is superiority that fascinates us; and *you*, who would prefer to do evil rather than good, if this same evil *is* good according to your principles—that is only because either you believe that the others will eventually open their eyes, or your pride is flattered by this kind of firmness that will make you stand out. You believe that in works of taste or wit, it is your approbation alone that guides you. No—you approve of yourself only because you are persuaded that you will be admired. A certain usage mutely dictates to us what is closest to the general taste. Sometimes singularity is one of the surest paths, and we are singular not for our personal satisfaction, but the better to astonish others. I have not been taken in by this charlatanism[1] of Rousseau: his learning, his genius, his experience had taught him what was intrinsically good and pleasing; his stoicism concerning public judgment was merely an additional seasoning. How many good and honest minds has this man not seduced by his Cynic-like tone?[2]

To the shame of humanity, insolence claims rights to our respect. Look at the advantages that the swashbucklers, the haughty lords, the elegant coquettes have in our society. If someone lets it be known that his happiness or his success depends on us, we make him pay for it, and often very dearly. If Voltaire had been better able to hide his immoderate competitiveness, and this ambition of his always to please and to know everything; if one did not know that a satire against him, or a preference for someone else, can absolutely mortify him—then he would be a prodigy, he would be the oracle of most of those same people who so enjoy denigrating him.

If you were on an island where no one knew how to read, and it were certain that what you wrote would vanish along with you, would you write verses, Agnes? or tales, or comedies? You would paint or embroider if the inhabitants of that island could only judge by the sense of sight; you would sing or play the lute if they had only ears; you would learn to swim if they knew no other perfection but that of living in the water.

1. For the significance of *charlatanism,* see Letter 63, n. 1.
2. D'Hermenches writes "son ton Cinique," which is more closely related to its classical origins than the modern English "cynical tone" would suggest. The Cynics followed the principles of Diogenes, who rejected all conventions and disdained all wealth as a hindrance to liberty.

I have often done, thought, and said things contrary to usage and accepted taste; I have ventured these innovations even in fashion, dress, adornment—but always being persuaded that after the first protests I would be imitated and applauded. And what glory! Not only to have had the courage to distinguish oneself but to have known what would please, what would suit others better than they themselves could know! And *you*, Agnes, you have done what is a hundred times worse: you have adopted turns of phrase, usages which not only were not yours, but which you would have criticized if you were not already used to them as conventions. I pick as an example the first thing of yours that I have right here at hand: for all the treasures in the world, you would not have said, "Divinities of Helicon, daughters of Apollo," etc. if you had not found it in the best poets, and if it were not a protocol accepted from Catullus down to our time.[3] When you look closely, you will find a thousand concessions of this nature rendered to what is conventionally pleasing, and which are as exotic to you as it would be to tell your shoemaker that you are his very humble servant, if that weren't the form of address that you came upon already established.

Forgive me for this tirade; I have no wish to reread it, for if I did I'm sure I wouldn't send it to you.

It is certain that there are few things that could distress me as much as giving up your letters. It is much more than a flower that you give me; it is the fruit of my profound admiration for you, it is reward for my esteem, my respect, my attachment; it is the wages of the preference I give you over all my other connections; it is the remedy for the mortal chagrin I feel at not being able to live with you. How you offend me by suggesting ways I might receive other well-written letters! How little you know me! No one in the world could have more aversion for pretty letters than I do; I can show that almost every day I kill off one correspondence or another. This persiflage that so many people consider such a charming thing is unworthy of me if my heart is not fully engaged; and my heart could not belong sometimes to Agnes, and sometimes to Mme de Boufflers! People here think that Milord Holdernesse[4] is madly in love with her—and that Milady is much vexed; they have returned together to Paris, and Milady is staying here with us.

When you tell me of the river at your feet, it makes my mouth water. Why can't I come and protect you against all those mastiffs that frighten you! (Here, they are only a nuisance, but nonetheless they disturb my walks.) I spend whole days at home, and am so idle that I do nothing here. I find the theater here is unbelievably dreary, and that includes the audience.

A very good night to you, Mademoiselle; I deserve your indulgence and your friendship because of all the thoughts of you that I so cherish.

Mr. Boswell has asked me for a letter introducing him to Voltaire, which

---

3. The poem in which she uses these expressions is in *O.C.* 10: 339–41.
4. Robert Darcy, earl of Holdernesse, minister plenipotentiary from England to the Hague.

I have sent to him.[5] He told me that he was going to see you that same day; I was very envious. Since then I have had no sign of life from him.

101. *To Constant d'Hermenches, July 9–10, 1764*

I must seem to have forgotten you; nothing of the sort however, I assure you. I began to write you twice: the first time was in the middle of a bad night; the second was in the intervals of a horrible nose-bleed that made me light-headed, so I could never finish.

I would have liked to go the the Hague today with my father, but he didn't think he should take me; what consoles me is that I would have spent only three days there, I would have seen you very little, and I would have become so tired that I would have needed a long rest upon my return. Today it suddenly occurred to me that you might be anxious about the fate of your last letter, and fear that some unfortunate event might once again have disturbed my peace of mind and our correspondence. It is to forestall your fears or put an end to them that I am writing tonight, even though it will soon be one o'clock.

I have just had supper with ninety peasant men and women. The peasants had been working all day threshing a certain grain whose name I don't know. You can imagine how hot they were, but our peasant, the master of the house, was so pleased to see me, he placed his sweating hands on mine with such good faith, his wife did the honors to my brother and me with such pleasure, our servants also found it so pleasant to be at table with us, that this feast was very enjoyable all the same. For a moment I compared myself with pride to Julie.[1] However, there was no way to dance with them. They embraced each other with a deliberateness, a composure, and an innocence worthy of the Golden Age—worthy too of our phlegmatic country. You would say that the gallant and the girl are speaking to each other in private; she is altogether unguarded. Neither one budges any more than a pillar. Everyone at the dance was equipped with a little pipe; the smoke was ... But farewell, I do better to go to bed than to put you to sleep.

Tuesday morning

If Boswell has not written to you, it is not because he isn't very pleased with you and your letter: he showed it to me. Allow my vanity to remember, word for word, a compliment that—exaggerated as it is—is still very agreeable: *It is said that Mademoiselle de Zuylen writes as well as Voltaire.*

---

5. The letter from d'Hermenches to Boswell accompanying the letter of introduction to Voltaire is extant. See *Boswell in Holland* 262–63.
1. Heroine of Rousseau's *Julie, ou La Nouvelle Héloïse*. Rousseau makes a point that the aristocratic Julie participates in the peasant festivities of her estate as a way of reinforcing affections and loyalties.

That *It is said* seemed to me charming, delicate—not, however, discreet. For if there had not been any secrecy, one would not have thought of saying it; one would have supposed your judgment to be based on the *The Nobleman* and the "Portraits".[2] But no matter—*It is said* pleases me very much.

Boswell left three weeks ago. To the very end, he spoke to me of morality, religion, friendship. He is such a good and honest man that he seems singular in this perverse century.

Goodbye—my mother is waiting for me; we are going to Utrecht for my lessons and to see the fair. Would you like to lend me a little beautiful music, and send it care of Mme Geelvinck? I especially like fine trios or quartets in the style of Campioni and Pugnani. Goodbye—another time I will write less badly and at more length. I am your friend from the bottom of my heart.

102. *From Constant d'Hermenches, July 14, 1764*

The Hague, Saturday

If your heart is not tender, at least it is not altogether barbarous, which is still something! You rescue me, Mademoiselle, from a cruel anxiety. I had two misfortunes to fear, and I am too sincere to tell you that one was not as cruel for me as the other: either your forgetting or tiring of me, or else some incident similar to those that have already befallen us. My fear of your forgetting me was based on the immensity of your distractions and the liveliness of your mind, which makes you continually pass to new objects; and your tiring of me I could attribute to my last letter, for a pedantic refutation can well produce that effect. Finally, without altogether reassuring me on that point, you show me pity, and I throw myself at your feet in gratitude.

I lead a life so insipid that I can hardly talk to you about myself. I still have an ardent desire to go to Utrecht; I imagine that without being too conspicuous I can show up there during the kermess.[1] It's part of the customs of this country; I'll pass for a curious onlooker for the sake of the only real pleasure to which I am susceptible—seeing Agnes! And to make my journey seem yet more natural, I'm asking the Marquis de Bellegarde to come with me.[2] He is staying with me now; he's my closest friend; I will accompany him. Thursday morning we will be within the same city walls as you. Please instruct me in all the conduct I should keep to, and tell the Widow that my friend and I want to ask her to lunch. This Bellegarde is a very rare being, by the sincerity of his character and the nobility of his feelings; he is philo-

---

2. The "Portrait de Zélide" and the additions to it; perhaps also the portrait of Mme Geelvinck. See Letter 89, n. 4.

1. An annual fair or festival celebrated in the Low Countries.

2. François-Eugène-Robert Noyel, Marquis de Bellegarde, seigneur des Marches (1720–90) belonged to a distinguished family from Chambéry in Savoie. He was commanding officer of a regiment in the service of the United Provinces.

sophical, he's cheerful, he's witty, he knows music well, his valet is a very good violinist. We spend our days and our nights laughing, arguing, and playing trios. I'll go look for some trios that are worthy of you; I am happy, divine Agnes, every time I can do something for you.

You are waging a war with me in which I am quite innocent: my *It is said* could be indiscreet if I were speaking of a person less well known than you; I spoke exactly as I would have done if I had never seen your letters, and that is the comportment that I find the most correct in conductiong this sort of thing. There is no one who has ever heard of you who hasn't heard it said that you write like an angel. I didn't want to say to a man who is going to visit Voltaire, and to whom I wouldn't want to appear to be showering you with praise, that you write as well as Voltaire; but charming letters, full of substance and delicacy, are a flower that one can attribute to your age and sex, without seeming banal, because several persons *have said to me* that they have received some letters from you. On the basis of *The Nobleman* and the *Portraits*, I would have been able to judge you myself; but what is said about your letters, neither he nor I are supposed to know by ourselves. On that point, it's entirely natural that I seek to learn what your friend knows, or thinks; it's vexation … desire … curiosity … in short, after the Marquis de Mascarille's *whatever one says,*[3] what could be more ingenious than this *It is said?*

I know you will pity me when you learn that this Micheli,[4] who was killed hunting, was one of my oldest friends, my neighbor in the Swiss countryside; that I had seen him full of life and friendliness only a few hours before, then saw him stretched out on his floor, bathed in his blood, and left to the care of the ignoble hands of strangers.

If I dared, I would ask you to send me a little note for Tuesday or Wednesday; I leave that to the dictates of your generosity. My respect and my admiration for you, which I hereby express, will always be my most cherished guide.

103. *To Constant d'Hermenches, July 16–17, 1764*

Zuylen

Why aren't you a charlatan or a professional actor? You certainly don't lack the talent for it, and you might be here now.[1] I'm sometimes very weary of never living with my friends.

---

3. Mascarille is a character in Molière's *Les Précieuses ridicules*; however, d'Hermenches is confusing him with Trissotin in *Les Femmes savantes*. The phrase he quotes shows up quite meaninglessly merely to fill in the meter of a vapid poem over which much is being made by the ladies.

4. A colonel in the Swiss Guards.

1. That is, as a performer at the fair in Utrecht. Zuylen is close enough for one to go back and forth for an evening's visit. For her use of "charlatan," see Letter 63, n. 1.

Monday evening, [the 16th]

That's a beginning that has been awaiting its continuation for four days; now that it's so old I would have torn it up if it were not proof that, far from forgetting you, I want you here. I look for you in the crowd, I complain at not finding you there. I swear to you that I thought of asking you to come; if I haven't done so, it is purely out of delicacy for my parents' sake. Now you come without my asking you; it's not my fault, and I'm very glad you're coming; but follow my instructions carefully. I have told the Widow that she must receive you—I have entreated her, and she will receive you. That will be Thursday morning. You may hear from her whether I'm in town or not. You will take a turn about the fair, and if you find me there with my mother, so much the better; if we go to the opera that evening, better yet. We will chat quite openly, and people will get used to seeing you. If we are not in town that day, send a card to my father at our house; he will surely be there. Say that you and Monsieur de Bellegarde will come to see us at Zuylen after dinner, and then indeed come; see for yourself a little what the tone of the household is like and try to fall in with it. I will be doing some handwork; I'll talk with you about it, very simply, and then you will discuss the news a little with my dear mother, and you will reason a little with my dear father, and after that whatever you wish. You will say that you have come to keep your friend company, and to see the fair, and to see us; and then ask what we are doing the next day, as if it went without saying that you would see us every day.

Goodbye, the dinner bell is ringing, I will return quickly. You must know that it's only today that the Widow was able to give me your letter.

Do you know that my uncle's country house is in this village? You need only act as if you were an old friend of his—ask him to dinner for Friday, for instance. What I can't do is promise that you and I will be able to do just as we please, that we will be able to walk alone together a little, that we will be able to talk quietly together; on the contrary, I insist that you not try it. If you have something to tell me, write, and give your letter to Mme Geelvinck; I will reply by the same channel. That way I will let you know whether you can prolong your stay without any awkwardness for me, or whether it would be a favor to me for you to leave after a few days.

We are expecting any time now Mme de Schoonenberg, a cousin of my father's—a woman of great merit, of extraordinary courage and strength— with her daughter-in-law, who is the wife of that unfortunate Schoonenberg who is condemned to death.[2] We are upset about her coming; she is young and beautiful, and we're afraid that there may be a sort of incongruity between her conduct and her situation. It is to be hoped that she will not see many people at our house; it isn't suitable for her to be much in evidence. If

---

2. Schoonenberg had killed his father-in-law, and wounded his mother-in-law; he had then fled to Germany.

I see that your visits wouldn't be welcome while she is here, I will warn you before she comes. It's not that she is in the least coquettish or extravagant; she conducts herself very well. She still loves her husband; she hardly knew her father, but it takes a great deal of sense and delicacy for a woman whose husband has killed her father to conduct herself in a way that is appropriate to the magnitude of her misfortune.

These instructions are becoming as long as a plenipotentiary's, but never mind, there is still another important point: you must be prudent and discreet regarding the Widow. She isn't in her own house, but at her sister's; her mother is there as well, and I think that her father will be there. If you go there often, if you seem too attentive, they will be very displeased and she will be very embarrassed. That's enough of that.

It's six o'clock, I haven't slept; I have just got up to write you. Tell me no more that I am a cool, capricious friend; say no more, when you praise my heart, that it is "not altogether barbarous;" speak no more of my forgetting you or tiring of you. The refutation that you call pedantic seemed to me solidly thought out, forcefully and agreeably expressed. I find that you are at least three-quarters right; the rest deserves our discussing it some day at leisure. There is no man who does not wish to be esteemed by his fellows, no author who does not write to please the public; but are we satisfied to see ourselves esteemed when we have little esteem for ourselves, to please others when we displease ourselves? I think not. If a century from now, and in all the centuries to come, *Le Devin du village* were to seem a bad opera and *Le Maréchal-Ferrant* a beautiful one, I wouldn't write *Le Devin du Village*—but neither would I write *Le Maréchal-Ferrant*.[3] If in all centuries, to all men, the style of Rousseau were to appear insipid and that of Formey pleasing, I don't think that Rousseau would try to write like Formey.[4] During my childhood I was passionate about all kinds of glory; there was nothing I didn't envy in whatever people applauded. And yet Cicero's consulate did not seem to me glorious; the thanks of the Senate, the acclamations of the people made not the least impression on me; I in no way envied the man who had saved his country. A man who is superior to all other men would put his own approbation above all others'; and I don't know whether it's not absurd to say that God created worlds and men for his glory. These are very curious and very interesting subjects of speculation. Read the *Theory of Moral Sentiments* of Dr. Smith.[5] If you don't find it at the Hague, mention it so that I can offer it to you and lend it to you, or else I will give it to Mme Geelvinck.

3. *Le Devin de village* [The village soothsayer] is an opera by Rousseau; *Le Maréchal-Ferrant* [The blacksmith] is by François-André Danican-Philidor.
4. Jean-Henri-Samuel Formey (1711–97), a French pastor who became a protégé of Frederick the Great and perpetual secretary of the Academy of Berlin. He adapted and popularized certain works of Rousseau (such as *Emile*), making them less controversial.
5. This work by Adam Smith, published in 1759, was especially admired in France.

Moreover, it is quite true, Monsieur, that my comedy is written with the intention of pleasing others, and that's just as well for it, if it is indeed better that it has not been burned before now.[6] If it had been written only to please me, it would no longer exist, for it often displeases me. Sometimes I would like it to be in verse, and it's in prose; sometimes I'd like to have it sung, and it must be recited; to have it make people laugh, and it may make them weep. The characters are better than I am, and that seems to me sometimes humiliating, sometimes hypocritical.

If I had known that Monsieur Micheli was your friend, I would have pitied you indeed, and I would have written you. Although I didn't know him, so strange and cruel a fate has greatly touched me.

I think that Monsieur de Bellegarde is not a marrying man, which is too bad; since he is so likeable, he would have only to take me for his wife while passing through. I am often weary of the state of dependency. If I were free, I would be worth a great deal more.

If we are not in town on Thursday, don't announce yourself by letter, but come straight to my uncle's after dinner and then to our house.

104. *To Constant d'Hermenches, July 21–22, 1764*

How unlucky I am! I was in desperate need of sleep, and I thought I was sleepy; I complain, I hurry through the end of supper, but then I find in my room seventeen English pages from Boswell; I read them and go to bed.[1] The seventeen thousand thoughts of my friend Boswell, a faint memory of Monsieur d'Hermenches, the conversation of the Marquis and of the Englishmen—it's all spinning around in my head so giddily that I haven't been able to stay in bed more than a quarter of an hour. Here I am, pen in hand; that pen will move to the bidding of a crazed head. Don't expect me to be rational; don't imagine for a minute that I'm writing to please you; I'm writing because I can do nothing else. No, truly, I'm hardly thinking about pleasing you; you do not deserve such attention—I am annoyed.

Didn't you understand my letter, or did you neglect to read it? I asked you to come to my uncle's after dinner on Thursday, and then to our house. I thought you could not fail to do so, and that your only business was to see me; so I was preoccupied and anxious about your visit from eleven in the morning. What welcome will he receive? Will I be suspected of having known about this journey, of having arranged it with him? Etc., etc., etc. Already I was not feeling too well, and with these anxieties coming on top

6. Her comedy *Justine*, now lost.
1. Boswell's long letter of July 9—of a truly breathtaking fatuity—is Letter 99 in *O.C.* 1: 196, or see *Boswell in Holland* 307–17. He lists her faults: her "ungoverned vivacity," her religious scepticism, her "libertine sentiments." While he assures her that she is not a proper wife for him, he insists that she confess her passion for him.

of it, I became really ill. When I am troubled about something, it's not evident in my face; but in my heart, my body, everything is upset. I said to myself: he will have to be really charming to repay me for what I'm going through.

We were alone; we would have spent the whole evening together. You do not come. I cannot imagine why. Attractive as the Widow is, I know that you prefer to be with her friend, so it is not for her that you have left me ... Next time, no more such journeys, I beg you—don't have me write any more long and useless instructions, nor have me fear and languish. A half-hour's visit, a few words spoken in a crowded theater—really, it isn't worth it. If we had seen each other Thursday, we would have seen each other yesterday; but you hardly care about it at all. It turns out that *you*, who write such beautiful letters, such lovely things, who put so high a value on the happiness of seeing me—you are, when all's said and done, rather indifferent; whereas *I*, with a more or less barbarous heart—I am truly a friend, who feels intensely the pleasure of being with you, and is vexed at knowing that you are two steps away from me without my profiting from it at all.

You are much shrewder than I am; however, I am not so stupid that I fail to understand all this. You are not as bored at the Hague as you say; boredom for boredom, you'd have done as well to stay another couple of days in Utrecht, and in the evenings you would have come to Zuylen. Beauties of style count for something in your complaints and your wishes; I will no longer so readily be taken in by them; and when my occupations or my pleasures prevent me from writing for five or six weeks, I will not think you dead on my account. So much the better; it is fortunate indeed that Utrecht—where you also can stay only a few days—has fewer charms and the Hague fewer horrors than you say, but in the future be sincere: speak to me no more of that insipid, sad life that you lead far from me, and which is in such need of the relief that my letters provide. Come now, confess frankly: all that is only half-true.

I thank you for having me make the acquaintance of Monsieur de Bellegarde; that is really a great pleasure. I am charmed with him; tell me what he says about me. It is not very apparent that he has any desire to marry me, and I don't know what my parents would say about it; but for myself, I think that to be the wife of a respectable man—a man of wit, a man of the world, one who travels, who likes good company, who has birth and fortune—would be a very agreeable thing. My design is to be a respectable wife; but there are a hundred thousand husbands with whom that would be so difficult for me that I couldn't guarantee it. God protect me from a fool! God protect me from a jealous husband—unless I were to love him madly! It is a thing to notice, that when jealousy is completely unjust, it neither disturbs nor offends. At this moment I would quite willingly marry the Marquis. I would please him, I would amuse him; I would be quite as good as a mistress, and I wouldn't be any more of a hindrance. He is many years older than I am, but we'll stay up late and play trios.

You see that I'm being crazy; don't answer me about my craziness; tomorrow I will become serious again. Besides, all this is very chaste—as I write it my heart is guilty of nothing; but between chaste and decorous there is a great deal of difference.

Farewell, Monsieur, I hope that in two or three years we will see each other for a quarter of an hour. Farewell.

I have slept from two o'clock until about five; now it's six; I have to write to you a little more. My poor head! Three hours of rest out of forty-five hours of activity! How glad I would be to see you today. When I sleep well, I am sensible; when I don't sleep, I am over-sensitive; my swift and agile spirits bring my soul twenty times more ideas and sensations than usual. I don't know whether I've said that quite right metaphysically, but I can't express any better what I am feeling, and you will understand me. I hope that today and tomorrow you encounter, instead of me and my spirits, only leaden bodies, frozen imaginations, hearts of stone! I hope that you are bored to death, that you regret not having spent the fine early morning in the Utrecht mall with *The Theory of Moral Sentiments*, which I would have sent you, and the evening in the lovely woods of Zuylen with me. I hope that you write me of *real* troubles this time, which I will now completely disregard! I hope ... but that's enough of imprecations. The abandoned Calypso railed no worse against Telemachus. *His* departure, however, was much more cruel.[2]

I dare not send you this letter through the Widow as usual: if I were to write you so many pages after having seen you only yesterday, it would suggest to her a passion. Neither her heart nor her intellect know that when one has just spoken to one's friends is precisely the time when one has the most to say to them. That's when the well-springs of discourse are open; that's never when they dry up. Or at least that's what always happens to me. In a few days I count on being able to do without you, just like anyone else, but today it is hard for me. There are a thousand interesting subjects that were not even broached between us, and not one was discussed in its necessary and natural scope. I am truly vexed at your departure.

I have reread what I wrote to you last night; the joke about staying up late and playing music instead of going to bed is in even worse taste because the Marquis is young—quite as young as he needs to be. I ask pardon both of him and of decorum.

Really, it is a very difficult thing for me to marry well, and it would be a terrible thing if I were to marry badly. What a life I would lead with a man I didn't love, with a crude or ignorant man! I have been repelled by the

---

2. Calypso was the nymph in the *Odyssey* who for seven years kept Ulysses from returning home. However, Belle is referring to the immensely popular novel *Télémaque* (1699) by Fénelon, in which it is Ulysses' son Telemachus who visits Calypso while seeking his father. When he leaves, Calypso is beside herself with grief and rage.

marriages that have been proposed to me thus far. Last year, I said to a young man who might have wanted to marry me: "Do you know *Cinna?*" "Yes, I have read it in Latin."[3] One of them is traveling just now; I was told, "Wait a little before you absolutely say no. See him when he returns, if you are not yet married; perhaps he will improve." I learned three days ago that he was a thoroughly bad lot, and that the person who had presented him to us and praised him had acted like a scoundrel, and I was wicked enough to be very glad—I was so happy to be able to say *no*, irrevocably, with everyone's approval. The Count of Anhalt[4] is very slow to arrive; some say that it isn't his fault; others think that he cannot make up his mind to marry me. He is right, I think; for a man who is sensible and merely ordinary, this isn't a thing to be desired. Besides, I doubt that I myself have the courage to marry him. The subjects of his master[5] are slaves, and what I want above all is to be free.

Write me a good long letter as soon as possible. Tell me what you made of all of us, and whether this château pleased you. It seems to me that they were not too vexed at seeing you; perhaps all that was needed was a few days, for you to be liked, esteemed, loved ... Really, it's ridiculous to leave; returning is not the same thing as staying. Farewell, then, for a very long time.

105. *To Constant d'Hermenches, July 22, 1764*

I have just read your strange letter![1] There is no need of long reflections to know what the heart feels, what the mind thinks, when one knows oneself well; one needs no preparation to tell the truth, without artifice, as I intend to do all my life; thus my response is ready. If it were at all likely that with my character and turn of mind, in the situation into which I was born, I might marry a man whom my heart's passion would place above all other men—then I would not listen to your proposition. If within my own country, within my own religion, I knew a man who exactly resembled your friend, and if that man wanted to marry me, I would prefer him. Since these things are not the case, I will accept the Marquis' suit, assuming that my fortune is appropriate, that my parents permit it, and that his ideas and mine are the same on a certain few items that I will tell you with a candor befitting you and me. My sister is being given three thousand florins a year, which is the revenue of one hundred thousand; I will be given the same

---

3. Corneille's *Cinna* (1640) is in French.
4. Friedrich, count of Anhalt-Dessau (1732–94). He was aide-de-camp of King Frederick II of Prussia (Frederick the Great). He later entered the service of Empress Catherine of Russia (Catherine the Great).
5. Frederick the Great.
1. This letter has never been found.

amount. My mother is almost as young as I am;[2] I don't know what her fortune amounts to, but I imagine that upon her death my children would have eighty to one hundred thousand florins to add to the hundred thousand of my dowry.

I don't think I can tell you any more about it today; I have already been interrupted; I've been having my lovely cousin[3] sing some old songs and play some old airs, and I'm about to go back to it. You and the Marquis are in my thoughts; I respect you, and I thank you. I am sending you the foolish things I wrote last night as if there had never been a question of anything serious since then, and to amuse you after taking up your time, I am sending along part of Boswell's letter as well.[4] Send it back to me tomorrow, and tomorrow also I will write to you. I am your friend forever.

Sunday night

If you can imagine how tired and overwhelmed I am, how many poor shabby things I have said today, you will easily excuse the bad style and the scrawl.

106. *From Constant d'Hermenches, July 24, 1764*

It is because one is a martyr and a hero that one incurs your indignation, adorable Agnes! Where, then, is probity to be found? I have not taken a single step that was not dictated by the most zealous and sincere attentiveness; you reproach me for the pains you took to send me directions, and those directions in my hands were what the compass is in a pilot's hand on a stormy sea.

My response to your injustice is precisely what you said concerning ill-

2. Belle's mother was in fact only sixteen when Belle was born.
3. Anna Elisabeth van Tuyll van Serooskerken (Annebetje) was the daughter of Belle's paternal uncle Jan Maximiliaan (the uncle whose death Belle described). She was and would continue to be Belle's favorite cousin and best friend.
4. It is not known exactly what part of Boswell's letter she sent, but from their comments later, it seems that it included the following passage:

You may say perhaps that you cannot prevent your mind from soaring into the regions of perplexity. Allow me to deny this. Suppose you should be seized with a strange inclination to touch the ceiling of your bedchamber while you stood upon the floor. You would in that case stretch your arm till it was very sore without coming much nearer your aim. You would tell me that you had got such a habit of doing this that you really could not help it, although you owned it to be very ridiculous. I would answer, "My dear Zélide, while your arms are unemployed, no doubt they will take their usual curious direction, but if you will sit quietly down and embroider a waistcoat for your brother, I defy your hands to mount, and I assure you that by degrees they will forget their bad habit and rest as peaceable as the charming Comtesse d'Aumale's. Just so is your mind to be managed. Study history, plain and certain parts of knowledge, and above all endeavour to relish the common affairs of life." (*Boswell in Holland* 311–12)

founded jealousy: it does not offend. I pity you for being so unacquainted with attentiveness! We arrived on the designated day; no one was there at your house in town. The next day, despairing at not having met you at the fair, I wrote a card asking permission to pay our respects at your house. We received a response *by word of mouth* that you could not receive us, and that the family was leaving for the country. My companion, who was unaware of your instructions, laughed at me and wanted to abandon the plan of being introduced to you; you may gather this by the joke he wrote out while I paced back and forth across the room in meditation. The cards sent by your father and uncle were a pretext to try our luck the next day at Zuylen; no one proposed that we return, nor that we remain in Utrecht, and he wanted to continue his journey. Could I, without compromising you, stay in that inn alone and make another attempt? My heart knows what it cost me! In thorny situations where my interests are at stake, I am much more tremulous than I am shrewd; such is my regard for you that the least remark, the least reproach that you might have endured because of me would not have been redeemed by a whole week's enjoyment of the delightful sight of you. That is the truth, and those are the wrongs I have committed.

On Sunday, since I couldn't find a carriage to leave in the morning, I tried to cover my sojourn in your neighborhood by a visit to Mme Pater, who had been casting reproachful glances at me for my neglect of her ever since my arrival in Holland. You may, if you wish, give that visit the most unjust interpretation: that I have done more for that woman, whom people say I am in love with, than I have done for you, and that therefore I put you on a par with her. That logic will devastate me, and I will not complain about it any more than about the rest of your letter; its "beauties of style that are sweeping me along." Agnes, can you really utter such words?

You have made the impression on my friend that you will always make on any creature of feeling; he said to me (because, like his sister,[1] I often urge him to get married): "My word, now there is a woman I could love to distraction, but I would not be to her liking, and our religions are different, and besides she is expecting a suitor ..." And thence comes the idea that I have communicated to you. I am certain that I would only have to indicate a mere word of possibility for him to be at your feet; but he is incapable of knowing how to do any of the things that would be necessary to win the consent of your parents. You, then, who have so much influence and ascendancy over them, you would have to ascertain whether the thing would please them; it would even be necessary that they should, to a certain point, desire it in order that my friend might not be exposed to a refusal, or to certain details of contractual matters that are always odious.

A hundred thousand florins is a fine dowry for the daughter of a family of quality; but for you to be happy and comfortable they would have to give

---

1. Charlotte de Bellegarde, who managed her brother's affairs.

them to you in capital, because we[2] have fine lands and a good estate which demands just such a rounding-out; your fortune would be backed up by our lands, and you would double your revenue.[3] Our sister is a prodigy of merit and wit; she is devoted to her brother's household, and you would be in paradise with those people. There is the seigneurie of Thonon on the shores of Lake Geneva, and the Marquisate of les Marches between Lyon and Geneva, just two leagues from Chambéry where we have a house; in Holland he has his own regiment, and the rank of general at the next promotion; there are the Prince of Rohan-Rochefort and Mme de Brionne who are first cousins in Paris; the governors of Dresden, Alexandria, and Nice for uncles; General Oglethorpe is an uncle in England, from whom we hope to inherit; the Marquise of Mérode-Westerloo as niece in the Low Countries—that is our estate and our circumstances. But we would not have a big enough fortune to figure in Paris, London, or the Hague; one would have to be content with the comfort of a provincial lord in Savoie, and with the status of travelers everywhere else.

See what you want to do and what suits you. I can answer for my friend, but if there are steps to be taken with respect to your parents, I know in advance that he will never know how to do it, and that it will be up to you and me. That's why he is still a vagabond; to love, to please, is his lot; to do what it takes to accomplish the thing he most desires, that's just what he's incapable of.

I am charmed by the English letter. I find things in it that move me and make me quite discount its pedantic form. It remains to be seen how one can reduce these estimable principles to everyday practice; that's the reef on which all these moralizers generally split. Except for a veritable Diogenes,[4] they are severe only with respect to the things that have nothing to do with their own dominant appetites. And then the passage on the sacrifice of Jesus Christ is weak beside the rest; how can someone who reasons logically comprehend that the crucified Son of God could—and should—expiate the sins of so many millions of creatures by an act that has no connection (I say, still reasoning logically) with the justice of the Almighty? This is a dilemma that

2. D'Hermenches is imitating the usage of attorneys in using "we" for Bellegarde, as though his were the voice of his principal.

3. D'Hermenches has begun to develop a position with respect to the dowry from which disagreements with Belle's father will arise. The capital that generates Mitie's income is not alienated from the Tuyll estates: at her death it will not devolve to the estate of her husband but will remain with the van Tuyll family. Mitie's dowry is not fl 100,000 but is a 3000-a-year lifetime annuity. Annuity contracts based on actuarial life expectancies were known in the eighteenth century—and certainly to van Tuyll's Amsterdam in-laws. The cash value of Mitie's annuity contract, basing the evaluation on the 3 percent return rate that both Belle and d'Hermenches have been assuming and on a lifespan expectancy even as long as 65 years, would have been a little less than fl 70,000.

4. D'Hermenches says "à moins d'être ciniques." See Letter 95, n. 2, for the particular resonances of this term as he uses it.

will strike any reflective being, whether he is seated in front of his work, or reaching on tiptoe for the ceiling ...[5]

We found your countryside charming, the house very noble, and the welcome of Madame your mother much more favorable than we had dared hope. The Widow had put my friend off them, even while telling us that we must go there. The customs of this country are so strange to the eyes of people accustomed to living in high society elsewhere that it is impossible not to be either chilled, or else greatly flattered by whatever consideration that one may receive—which is always the case with me and with my companion.

The thickness of our packets should not worry you as far as the Widow is concerned; she thinks that we are passing literary works back and forth, and that's what I've confirmed.

It is not enough to have failed in the purpose of my journey, to have seen you so little, and to be so inhumanely addressed by you. During this short time I have lost my case in the most unjust of lawsuits with a wretch who filed claims against my late brother, the most upright and most generous of men. I have suffered, as happens to me almost everyday, the effects of the aversion of fools and clods.

Good night, my unjust friend, but friend whom even so I regard as a gift from Heaven. Let us understand each other better in the future; let us see things in in a rosier light, and above all, take care that your mind does not wear out its envelope. Your existence will always be precious to those who know you, and as for me, it is absolutely essential to mine. I assure you of my respectful and passionate devotion.

The Hague, Tuesday the 24th

I have been to pay my respects to Madame your sister. The sound of her voice gave me pleasure because it reminds me of yours.

107. To Constant d'Hermenches, July 25, 1764

The other day I thought only of answering you without delay; without deliberating an instant, I showed you an entire trust; I did not speak to you, Monsieur, of my gratitude, but I hope that you have guessed how keen it is. Today, however, let me speak of it; let me tell you that I admire both your heart and your conduct. If what you are doing costs you some effort, you

5. Along with his general moralistic discourse and the advice about reaching for ceilings quoted in Letter 105, n. 4, Boswell had also written, "I think I see a very great probability that Jesus Christ had a divine commission to reveal to mankind a certainty of immortality and an amiable collection of precepts for their conduct in this life; and that by His death He atoned for the offences of the world, which God's justice required satisfaction for" (*Boswell in Holland* 311).

are right to call it the most sublime effort. So it is true, then, that I am dear to you, that it is my happiness you desire, without any thought for yourself! Whatever the outcome, I will be eternally grateful. I have never been more flattered in my life. The Marquis sees me for a moment and I please him; you who know me and who are his friend, you hope that I will become his wife.

I say you know me—but is that really true, really certain? For, while I have never adorned myself with false virtues in my letters, I have expressed to you only the best of my thought; you have been able to see, perhaps, that I knew how to reason soundly, but you do not know whether I act reasonably. Even if you knew everything about my conduct, you could still not know *me*, for I am not free to act as I please. In order to assess people, to know what they are, and what they will always be, one would have to see into their souls' depths, independently of circumstances—which can change. You would see into my soul that way if I had intended you to, for I know it well; but aside from the fact that such a spectacle had nothing to interest you, I had reasons for hiding a part of it.

For as long as I have known you, I have been told a thousand times that you were the most libertine and the most adroit of men, and that a woman was guilty of the greatest imprudence in having any connection with you. These accusations of libertinage were supported by stories both old and new; I saw well enough for myself that you were ingratiating, that you always managed to get me to write to you; that from the first moment of our acquaintance you had attached me to yourself to whatever degree you chose. Those were not sufficient reasons to make me give up a connection that pleased me, and for which I had no reason to reproach myself; but it was enough to prevent indiscreet outpourings, which in any case were not called for by the circumstances. I have put between you and me a reserve that is more scrupulous than is habitual with me.

Prudence aside, I had a stronger motive: I believed that we would become better friends if we spoke the language of virtue, and no other; and I was pleased to think that our correspondence—which prejudice would call a crime—would perhaps, instead of familiarizing me with licentiousness, reconcile you with duty. Do you find me proud and extravagant? No, you find me candid and full of the best intentions. But self-praise is not the point here; let me go on. You have seen, then, how much I respect virtue and reason; and you have not been able to see to what degree I could forget them. Perhaps you suspect it: my countenance speaks, and experience gives you insight; but that is not enough. Today I wish to be sure that you know me; indeed I owe you and your friend that abandon, that unreserved sincerity. Perhaps my language will not be decorous, but what is decorum at the cost of probity?

Well then: If I were to love, if I were free, it would be very difficult for me to be chaste. My senses are like my heart and my mind, avid to be pleased, sensitive to the most vivid and to the most delicate impressions. Not one of the objects that present themselves to my view—not a sound— passes by without bringing me a sensation of pleasure or pain; the most imperceptible odor delights or disturbs me; the very air that I breathe—now a little softer, now a little finer—works on me with all the variations that it undergoes itself. So you may judge of the rest; you may judge of my desires and distastes. If I had neither a father nor a mother I would be a Ninon,[1] perhaps—but being more fastidious and more constant than she, I would not have so *many* lovers. If the first one had been lovable, I think I would not have changed, and in that case I do not know that I would have been very culpable; at least I could have redeemed by my virtues the offense I had given to society in shaking off the yoke of a wisely established rule. I *have* a father and a mother: I do not want to cause their death or poison their life. So I will not be a Ninon; I would like to be the wife of a man of character— a faithful and virtuous wife—, but for that, I must love and be loved.

When I ask myself whether—supposing I didn't much love my husband—I would love no other; whether the sole idea of duty, the remembrance of my vows, would defend me against love, against opportunity, one summer night ... I blush at my response. But if we do love each other, and if my husband deigns to concern himself with pleasing me, if he values my affection, if he says to me "If you are unfaithful, I will not kill you, but I will be all the more unhappy at losing my esteem for you because it may be that I would love you still"—in that case, I say—I think, I hope, I firmly believe— that I will flee from everything that could seduce me, and that I would never fail in the laws of virtue. Is that enough, Monsieur, for you to be able to give me to your best friend without a qualm? Is it more, is it less than he could promise himself from another woman? Surely I will be warmly attached to him; if he wishes, I will be his friend, his mistress; I will never neglect to please him and amuse him; surely too he will love me. But will he do something on his part to keep this happiness from flickering out? Suppose I were to seem to him capable of a misstep: would he treat me from then on only with distrust and scorn, or would he attach me to himself, would he hold me by tokens of tenderness and trust? Suppose that my heart, my heart alone had been guilty for a moment: would an avowal, a sincere repentance, obtain forgiveness?

"Open up your heart to me, in all its recesses," you say. Ah! I hope you are satisfied. What do you think of this heart, now that it is opened up? Tell me frankly whether you despise it—whether after this letter you find me much less than what you had thought me to be. Beyond that, I am not demanding that you answer for the Marquis concerning what I have just

---

1. Anne (Ninon) de Lenclos (1620–1705) was celebrated for her wit and beauty. She was also famous for the number of her love affairs, the longevity of her charm, and her capacity to keep her lovers as friends. Her salon was much frequented by the free-thinkers of her time.

said. What you have told me, what I have seen, persuades me that I would be happier with him than with another. It is not for myself that I have fears, it is you and he that I do not wish to deceive.

The issue of temperament is almost as important as that of virtue—no, it is more important; a woman who has love-affairs is more tolerable than a shrew, and I would much prefer an unfaithful husband to a sullen or brutal one. I am certainly not spiteful, or scolding, or fussy, or capricious; however, I am not even-tempered; these sensitive organs, this boiling blood of mine, these keen sensations make my health and spirits subject to changes that I have never seen as extreme, as rapid, as strange, in anybody else. If I were not recognizable by my heart and my face, I could be taken from one moment to the next for two different people—for six people, sometimes, in the course of a day. Everything has the power to affect me; there is not a moment in life that is indifferent to me—all my moments are happy or unhappy—they are all *something*. Provided that I am never unjust, never sour, never carried away by anger, will he pardon me if sometimes I drown him with a flood of words, and then sometimes fall silent for hours? If I sometimes abandon myself on a whim to an immoderate gaiety; if I weep sometimes, hardly knowing the reason? Those vapors of mine caused by inactivity, those vapors of exhaustion when I have been too busy—will they make me ridiculous and unbearable? I can certainly repress all that—silence my joys and laugh while I grieve; but it is with strangers that one constrains oneself to that point rather than with a husband that one loves. Besides, if I were to drive him to distraction, he would have only to tell me to be quiet; if I were to pester him with a tune, a book, a tone of voice—some little thing—he would have only to laugh at me and leave me alone to amuse myself with my folly. Sometimes a musician, sometimes a geometer, sometimes a self-styled poet, now a frivolous woman, now a passionate woman, then a cool and tranquil philosopher—this diversity might even please him; I am sure at least that I would not bore him, that he would not weary of me; and as for the depth of my heart, he would find it the same every day. My fits of impatience are rare and short; anger I know hardly at all; I am gentle and patient when I am unwell; when I weep I do not scold.

There, that is finished; I have said everything, I think; you can judge of me as of my fortune. If I am not worthy enough, or if I am not rich enough, say so frankly—but don't try to be tactful, say it directly. Do with my confession what you will, show it entire or in part; I abandon myself to your good judgment and to your friendship.

It remains for me to explain to you those points on which I would like to know whether the Marquis's ideas and mine would match. That will be for this evening after dinner, unless I send you this today and take up my pen again tomorrow.

108. *To Constant d'Hermenches, July 25, 1764*

You tell me that the Marquis will make his way, but what is this way? Isn't there a law that obliges our Catholic officers to quit the service when they take Protestant wives?[1] But you must know how things stand better than I do, so that's not my business. The question of the fortune, which I don't understand very well, I leave entirely up to your decisions. It is enough for me to see that it is not forgotten in your counsel; I am not so romantic as to disdain it.

If the Marquis were older and less attractive, I would be afraid that for him marriage meant retirement. I hate those aging suitors who take a wife to help them through the winter, who invite her to warm herself next to a wretched little fire after they have already spent their springtime and summer, and have gathered flowers and fruits without her. No sooner have they set up a household than they subject everything to an austere rule that they had not observed before. —I say all that simply to amuse myself, for it is clear that this is not at all the case here; your friend is younger than I thought, and he seems no more in retirement than I am. I would be charmed to be his wife.

Wednesday evening, the 25th, at midnight

I received your letter tonight. You must pardon my injustices, for they were a proof of friendship. Why should you care whether I'm fair with you? One is fair with anybody; but for me to get angry unreasonably, out of pure friendship—that's a favor I reserved for you. You certainly could go to Mme Pater's, but since you stayed there either to see her or for lack of horses, you should not have said to me "I'm staying today so that I can write you this."

Your letter gave me real pleasure. I'm very glad that the knights entered the castle in spite of the enchanter—but for a brave chevalier, you really are too timorous; since I said to you "Come," you could indeed have come, even at the risk of throwing everything into discord and disorder. I admire you, however, since you demand it. Yesterday someone said to me: "Monsieur had more to do here than you thought, he was coming to see Mme Rouel ..." Those are stupidities that I should blush at having remembered.

My mother is pleasant when she wants to be; she has intellect and sense, and can even be delightfully witty. I am, however, vexed with her just now: during supper she interrupted my outbursts of laughter, which annoyed her—the first such laughter that has escaped from me in several days. I assured her that it didn't do her as much harm as it did me good, but mean

---

1. Belle is mistaken here and corrects her error in Letter 112. Laws were passed by the States-General in 1738 and 1739 that prohibited Protestant men in military or political service from marrying Catholic women, under penalty of losing their positions. In 1750 marriages between Catholics and Protestants were forbidden for men under twenty-five and women under twenty (*O.C.* 1: 570).

while I had lost the thread of my gaiety; still, it seems to me that I am finding it again with you.

Let's speak seriously a moment about this marriage. First, you must clear up the matter of this law I mentioned to you, which is on my mind; you must tactfully find out whether, supposing it exists, one cannot evade it or get a dispensation. You name many fine names to me; but I am more interested in the Marquis and his sister, whom I have heard described a thousand times in terms like yours. There would be no difficulty about my receiving the hundred thousand florins.[2] One must not spend the whole year on one's property—that could be boring—but a visit now and then to Chambéry, or a bit of traveling, are enough. Since I am being sought through gates of bronze, amid giants and monsters, I will lack for good company nowhere; I have no need of great cities.

I am a trifle vexed that my spelling is more correct than that of the Marquis, but that is because he is such a great lord.[3]

By the way, does he know that I don't have sixteen quarters?[4]

I saw Chambéry once; I was barely ten years old, but I remember everything: the warm welcome we received, a thousand kind attentions I encountered—first in a lovely promenade filled with fine society and then from people of quality where I was taken to visit. I remember a verdant grotto with a natural waterfall, which gave me infinite pleasure. I have been twice to the baths at Aix;[5] the poverty of the Savoyards distressed me, I groaned when I heard about the *taille*,[6] and I cursed the sovereign; but I liked the subjects, who seemed to me the best people, the most polite, the most obliging in the world. The locations of all these lands are charming. Lausanne is not far off, so we could see each other without hindrance or blame. I think, as you do, that I would be in paradise. One should, however, obtain clear assurances that my children would not be taken from me to be given to inept and superstitious priests. I say *my children*, without circumlocution or indirection; perhaps that isn't proper.

2. Clearly she has not discussed the structure of Mitie's dowry with her father. This ratification of d'Hermenches' misconstruing of the value of Mitie's dowry will come back to disturb things later on. See Letter 106, n. 3.

3. Correct spelling was regarded as bourgeois. Bellegarde's spelling was atrocious.

4. "Quarters" here is a term of heraldry—the divisions on the heraldic shield, the number of them indicating the extent of the noble lineage. For one to belong to the highest nobility, all sixteen of one's great-great-grandparents needed to have been noble. Since her mother comes from the bourgeoisie, Belle does not meet this requirement—the whole idea of which she satirizes in her novella *The Nobleman*.

5. Aix-les-Bains and Chambéry are in what was the duchy of Savoie in Belle's time.

6. A tax from which nobles and churchmen were exempt.

109. *To Constant d'Hermenches, July 26, 1764*

I am very sorry, d'Hermenches, about your lawsuit, and about the iniquities that caused you to lose it. You should no longer consider your journey a failure. That moment when we saw each other was pleasant, in spite of the constraint that surrounds me. Then too, I beg you to count for a great deal the rights you have acquired to my eternal gratitude, the proofs of attachment that you have given me, the respect that you have inspired in me, the boundless trust that flows from it and that I take such pleasure in showing you. Even if our projects were to fail utterly, I will never regret the strange letter I sent you yesterday. On the contrary: I will always be glad to have shown myself as I am to a man who is so sincerely devoted to me; you have the right to know me. Respond to my trust by reporting to me exactly the impression that this letter made on you. It is presently in your hands; have you read it more than once? Are you surprised? Are you contemptuous of me? Do you love me more than before? Do you still find me worthy of being the wife of your friend, the sister of his sister? —I'm going to suppose for the moment that you still find me worthy, and that you can give me completely satisfying assurances on the points that are quite rightly close to my heart. Let us talk of ways to make this succeed.

To engage my father to giving me away without knowing the Marquis— that is impossible. He would only see the obstacle of religion, and he would see no way to overcome that obstacle. Here is the best plan I can think of. I will write a letter from you to my father, in which you will ask him whether a man of the highest distinction—a man whose intellect and probity are admired, who has a noble and generous soul, who is of a suitable age, is rich enough, and is in all respects such as he would choose for the husband of a beloved daughter—except that he is Roman Catholic—could win me as a wife. You will present to him all the motives likely to win him—motives that I know perfectly. You will entreat him to show me your letter, to know what I think; you will not name the Marquis, but we will be shrewd—we will be able to guess. If I am consulted, I will say what is necessary. Supposing that my father doesn't reject the thing out of hand, the Marquis will do what he can to see us now and then. We will keep all this an inviolable secret, both out of consideration for him and to avoid the gossip of a family in which there are few heads fit to decide my fate. Questions of financial interests won't stand in the way; my father is the most upright, the most disinterested of men; and surely the marriage will take place.

This first consent once given, I would dare answer for the rest; but it is this consent that is very much in doubt. My mother will surely not find the thing to her liking; the best we can hope for is that she will refuse to decide, as she often does, and I would not push my scruples so far as to be constrained by aversions that she would not express. From now on, there is nothing, I think, that I cannot demand of you. Once it is really decided between us that this matter is advantageous to us both, I might ask you to say in this letter to my father that on such and such a day, at some particular hour, you will be in Utrecht to receive the reply directly from him; then your eloquence could show off reason to its best advantage. —Tell me what you think of all that.

But aren't you rather rash to answer for the Marquis's heart? Is it quite certain that this sister, who so deserves to be listened to, whose generosity earns her so many rights in the matter, finds me a good enough match for her brother? —that the difference of religion will not repel her? Who knows whether the Marquis has not already all but forgotten me?

I expect *enormous* responses from you. Do not, however, neglect your own affairs. Don't stay up all night, as I do; write at your leisure.

I have started taking quinine again; I will pay people to remind me, since I'm always forgetting.

I am very touched by your recommendation; I am very glad to be so prized by you. We deserve a great deal from each other: I by my sentiments, you by both your sentiments and your conduct. Farewell; if some new idea comes to me, I will write to you in a few days.

110. *To Constant d'Hermenches, July 27–28, 1764*

This morning I gave the Widow the letter I wrote yesterday; she gave me yours, which I am very satisfied with.[1] If we were together, I would point out to you a few apparent contradictions, but I don't know whether I will have the leisure to spell them out. The main thing is that you are pleased with me, and that if you are surprised, it is by finding me truer and better than you had thought. If you truly think that knowing me is a benefit for you, you should be grateful to me for having made the first advances. Do you remember, at the Duke's? —four years ago? You took no notice of me, but I saw you. I spoke to you first—"Monsieur, you're not dancing?"—to begin the conversation. I have never bothered about etiquette; and whenever I have encountered what might be called a physiognomy, I have always had a passion for getting it to speak. —But what a digression!

The manner in which you propose to broach all this to my parents is entirely impracticable.[2] They are too subtle themselves for subtlety to succeed on them. My father has all the penetration that sagacity of mind can give, accompanied by the most invariable sang-froid; he would perceive the truth at once, if I spoke of this idea as of a thing even slightly probable and substantial; otherwise, he would think I was mad. That, however, would be the last thing to occur to him; the first would be a correspondence with you. No, I cannot begin with that, I would spoil everything; they would be

---

1. The letter she is referring to has not been found.
2. Apparently "the manner" described in the missing letter.

prejudiced against our plans at the outset. If I speak at all, I must say more; I must speak forcefully rather than cleverly; I must speak boldly, and then—in the thick of the fray—pull from my pocket a letter which I would have received from you directly by the post, openly addressed to me.

There are occasions when one must astonish, stupefy—forestall all objections, force all minds to surrender. So many things are unimportant and neutral to me, and there are so many things that would seem to be important (my suitors, for instance) but that I have discussed only jokingly—saying silly things—that when for once I show a serious, firm, decisive will, it cannot fail to make a telling impression.

The only risk in this method is that if they are *not* impressed, the whole affair will be completely broken off—or at any rate, it will be difficult to find a thread with which to take it up again. Perhaps I will be expressly forbidden to have any commerce with you; but never mind, I know how to take risks when I must. I never lose my head, and out of the very disorder of these heated discussions there sometimes arise unanswerable arguments which suddenly decide the matter, or at least leave strong impressions.

Another method—gentler, less bold—would be for me to attach to your letter to me one from me to my father, and give them to him one evening as I leave him; I would entreat him to read and reflect. My letter would be written with good sense and energy, and with a persuasive gentleness. Consider whether you want to write to me or to my father; whether it's the method that I described to you yesterday, or today's, that seems the most effective. When that is decided, send me a draft of your letter; but you must allow me to change or add or cut it, as I wish. Quite honestly, I am the best person in the world for managing minds that I know well, when I want to—though I rarely want to, because I have no ambition to govern.

I still have it in mind that if you speak to my father after he is already informed, responding to his objections and emphasizing all the advantages, you will get farther than you will by letters alone. But that he should commit himself without knowing the Marquis—you must not even think of it. It would even be absurd, and I myself would not wish it. Provided that the Marquis doesn't have to play the ridiculous role of declared lover-cum-suitor—that it isn't a question of tiresome zealousness, or entreaties, or discussions of financial interests—and that he may be sure of being treated with all the discretion and consideration that he deserves, then I don't see what would prevent him from making our acquaintance. My father and my mother have only seen him in passing at Spa twelve years ago; he was there with Mme de la Rive, and he seemed so ill and so worn out that it was difficult the other day to persuade them that he was not forty at that time.[3] He now seems to everyone much healthier, and he even looks younger. For myself, I can rely on your judgment in all the good things that you say

3. He was actually thirty-two when they saw him at Spa.

about your friend, but my parents cannot—for they do not know you at all. And to be infatuated with the name, the titles, the connections, to the point of paying attention to nothing else, would be utterly unworthy of the sensible people that they are.

Consider, then, just when it would suit the Marquis to come see us, and a little before that time—in these matters there must not be long intervals, for everything cools off—a little before that time you will write to my father or to me. If possible, you will speak to him two or three days after having written, and if my parents then wish to meet the Marquis, I consider the thing accomplished. He need make no special effort to please; his naturally polite demeanor, and his good and generous heart—which shows without his thinking about it—are all that's necessary. He will certainly neither do nor say anything that will offend, or that will persuade them that I would be unhappy with him; they will see all the evidence to the contrary, and will leave the choice to me. No one seeing him with me during these first few days will guess his intentions. You could accompany him; people will think that neither of you have anything particular to do and that, since you find me rather good company, you come to enjoy yourselves. If, against all likelihood, by some unheard-of events, the affair having come to this point were still to fail, I can guarantee that no one would know about it.

I find it quite appropriate that the Marquis had not been able to endure me in the character of "marvel." Nothing in the world is more detestable. His hatred for pretentions of wit and for metaphysics do not put me off in the slightest. For a long time now, I haven't concerned myself with things I cannot understand, except perhaps for ten minutes a month at the most. At fourteen I wanted to understand everything—but since then I have given it up. Boswell is wrong to think that I wear myself out in speculations.[4] A sort of scepticism that is very humble and rather tranquil—that's as far as I go. When I have more insight and better health I will perhaps see certainties; at present I see at best only probabilities, and I experience only doubts. But even if I did have a passion for metaphysics, that would inconvenience no one; there is only Monsieur Castillon, a professor in Berlin, with whom I like to discuss it.[5] As for my intellectual pretentions, they too were a form of childishness that I think I have outgrown. It no longer occurs to me to demonstrate some point that, when it exists, demonstrates itself perfectly well—that loses half its grace by being elaborately displayed and eagerly thrust upon the audience. Sometimes I am seen speaking with an absorbed, animated air to an interesting man; people think I am filled with a desire to seem to him sublime, when in fact I am only concerned with enjoying my-

4. She refers here to Boswell's letter of July 9, 1764: "Pray make a firm resolution never to think of metaphysics. Speculations of that kind are absurd in a man, but in a woman are more absurd than I choose to express." Letter 99 in *O.C.* 1: 200; or *Boswell in Holland* 311.
5. Giovanni Francesco Salvemini di Castiglione, professor of mathematics in Utrecht and then in Berlin. He was one of the many intellectuals that Frederick the Great attracted to his court.

self; it's only the interest of our conversation—its gaiety or its arguments—that animates my gestures and my face.

What makes me and my mind such great friends is its excellence for everyday use. It makes me the soul of this house; it can be amused by a little thing, and can amuse others with it; it is cherished by my brothers, my sister, my brother-in-law—by all those whom it lives among; that is certainly evidence in its favor. I ask you to recall if ever, in any of my letters, I have said pretty things that had nothing to do with the subject—thoughts paraded out expressly to show you how witty I am. When I was a little girl, I did it all the time; I would slip in my fine idea quickly, wherever I could, dying of fear that the occasion to say it would never return. At this point my vanity is more refined and more tranquil. The Marquis will hardly have reason to complain on that score; and then, after all, people make fun of me all the time without my getting miffed or hurt by it.

Provided I am allowed to go my way with my lessons, my readings, my writing, as I do here—perhaps even a little more freely—I will be content. Surely the Marquis will not think of hindering me in this; neither my mind nor my erudition will inconvenience him, and what can the rest matter to him? Not for a throne would I give up the things that occupy me in my room. If I were to cease to learn, I would die of boredom in the midst of all the pleasures and grandeurs the world could offer. Consider that my tastes have held up—against prejudice, against endless ridicule, against the example of laziness and stupidity offered by three-quarters of my compatriots, against the leaden air of this country—and you will agree that these tastes are part of my being. If the Marquis likes to read aloud, I will learn history while I embroider his vests. I do not know how to talk all day, or spend a whole day in company; my head gets exhausted, and in the evening I'm yawning, I'm miserable, I'm half dead.

How fortunate you are, Monsieur, not to get bored with me! Every day a packet, with eight or ten pages of writing! —By the way, there is a passage in this letter that seems horribly dissonant: "Perhaps I will be expressly forbidden to have any commerce with you, but never mind ..." That will wound your eyes on a first reading; it wounds mine, although I understand what it really means. Ah! certainly it matters to me a great deal that all commerce between us not be broken off; but that will never happen—it would be futile to forbid it. They may be able to make our commerce difficult, perhaps even sink it for a time, but it will always resurface; I hope that there will not be even an interruption, ever, in the feelings of friendship and gratitude that my heart has sworn to you.

Saturday morning, the 28th

I'm going to send my letter, and then continue to write to you a little. It is to give you pleasure that I announce this, for I will not be outdone by you in the expression of friendship.

111. *From Constant d'Hermenches, July 29, 1764*

The Hague, Sunday

It's a delight for me to follow all that your vivid and subtle imagination prompts in you about our conversations, and I am more amazed each day to see that even in trifles, as well as in the most serious things, you are always guided by an exquisite good sense and a rectitude that I idolize. Why can I not, incomparable Agnes, offer in return for so many precious things, phrases that are worthy of you? But if we were in each other's presence, a nod of the head and, from time to time, a genuflection would be my portion of the dialogue; and in my letters, alas, you will find only repeated praises which would become insipid if fresh subjects did not continually renew them. I will therefore reply as clerk to master to the items in your two letters for which you require explanations.

I have informed myself about the law: it was made for Mme d'Usson,[6] and is enforced only in the case where the parents want to apply it. A Catholic officer can marry a Protestant without any difficulty, if the parents of the girl consent; and to be assured of this consent, it is only a question of a longer interval in the announcements and the bans. Thus, the Marquis can be the happiest of mortals, without giving up the possibility of one day commanding the armies of the Republic. He and his sister are not at all bigoted—not even slightly; and I even think that when you are all under the same roof, there would be no difference of religion but what would be indispensable for the exterior observance; unless I am sorely mistaken, the feelings among you about dogmas would be as similar as they are about morality. That answers the item of education, etc. Never would priests be an obstacle to your desires and your duties. Your tastes for reading, for activity, the ardors of your genius—those will all be treasures for people who can repay you in kind, and will only strengthen the bonds among you. You will be free, you will be your own mistress, if ever any woman in the world was such—and all the more because I see you as the most reasonable and the most useful of women. Thus I can only reply to all your doubts on these points: "Yes, Mademoiselle ... have no doubts, dear Agnes ... one would be very sorry if you were other than what you are ... this is what makes us desire you ...."

Let us get down to the means for bringing this all about. I am waiting for

---

6. Margaretha Cornelia van de Poll, a Dutch Protestant, was the widow of Cornelis Munter. In 1755 in the Hague she married a Catholic, the comte d'Usson, brother of the French ambassador to the Hague. Her father, burgomaster of Amsterdam, had vehemently opposed the marriage and had tried to get a law passed to make it even more difficult for Protestants and Catholics to marry. There were long debates over this proposed law; the only provision that was passed was one that protected wives' property by prohibiting communal estates between husband and wife. The case of Mme d'Usson will be a continual reference point in the discussions of a marriage between Belle and Bellegarde, and d'Hermenches will have a good deal of contact with them socially (*O.C.* 1: 571).

a letter from my friend, in which I will learn of his reflections since we left each other, and obtain precise instructions concerning what he wishes of me. At that point I will write to you, or to Monsieur your father—it is up to you to decide. But since (as I expect and hope) you will be sending me the model of that letter, I will only copy it; it is the most legitimate homage due to your genius to make use of none other but it in this matter that must concern you most in the world. Do you doubt that I will meet with your father, if you find it necessary?

Remember however, fair Agnes, that in your very first letter you dazzled me by the ease with which you spoke of arranging this marriage. I thought that you were assured of your parents' consent as soon as your choice fell on a gentleman of birth and wealth; and here now, instead of our marrying like great lords, you put us through the drill of suitors. The Marquis will certainly do everything that you prescribe; but once you have made up your mind, would it not be far more pleasant for you—assuming you trust my word on the facts and on his reputation—to dispense completely and generously with these troublesome preambles? That was how *I* got married; I loved my wife madly, but I said to her: "Your willingness is enough for me; speak to your parents, assure yourself of their consent; I have my parents' consent in my pocket." If she hadn't done it, I would have returned to the army as I had come from it; and since then never a word of financial interests has been pronounced between her family and me. I fear, dear Agnes, that this man will never come forward unless I tell him: "You are accepted, it is up to you to confirm the idea and the esteem that people have of you." If Monsieur your father does not want to have such a son-in-law, then I fear—I fear for our plans; and if he does not want him, it is either because he does not love you, or because *you* do not want him.

Good night, my honored friend. Bear in mind that I am in a rage because of this lawsuit that I have lost. I am making my judges tremble for fear that their stupidity and their partiality will be revealed. They have judged me to be unjust; I have in hand what it would take to show them up as corrupt, but it is only a question of one hundred twenty-seven florins for the heirs of my late brother—is it worth giving it an instant of one's tranquillity for that? Philosophy says no; public safety, self-esteem say yes.

Ah, my God, Agnes, how happy I will be when I can think that in fleeing this country I will not be separating myself from you! I spend many bitter days, because quite precisely one perceives that one lives in society only at the level of the dregs of society everywhere else. To be alone in my garden writing you would be a delight; to have a horrible headache would be only a passing ill; but to find instead of men only oxen and bears, and to be obliged to see them—that is an ever-bleeding wound. Good night.

It was not *in order to write to you* that I didn't leave by the morning boat on Sunday; I went to Wijk because I had to wait for the evening boat in Utrecht. So where is the contradiction?

⚮ *The project of arranging a marriage between Belle and Bellegarde went on for four years. During that time they exchanged a few letters by way of d'Hermenches. Two letters of Bellegarde to Belle and a fragment of one from her to him are extant, but there is reason to believe there were others. There were also several letters that Bellegarde wrote to d'Hermenches that he forwarded to Belle, but most of these have also been lost.*

112. *To Constant d'Hermenches, July 29 and August 3-4, 1764*

I think I was wrong concerning the law I mentioned to you: I think it's a Protestant officer who can't marry a Catholic woman without losing his rank. So much the better that there's no difficulty on that point.

Don't you think you need the approval of Mademoiselle de Bellegarde before trying anything? If she refuses me, I'll not be at all mortified or offended; she doesn't know me. If one should have even a moment of regret after having taken me—it's that alone that I could not bear.

It seems to me that if I were a libertine, it would be in the style of the Marquis rather than in yours; you seek conquests, I would only seek pleasures. However, I would not get carried away as the Marquis does—I don't know how to get carried away; I would love my mistress very much, but I would not have the happiness of believing her to be more perfect than she was. Perhaps in winning over a woman's mind, I would sometimes, like you, have no other design than that of keeping seducers at a distance; but I would forget my design, and sooner or later I would take their place. It would certainly be the surest and pleasantest way of being her guardian. It is your ambition, you say, that a woman should pass from your hands a little better than she was before. Yes, sometimes that is so, I think. You will impart delicacy, decorum, a certain dignity to a woman who is imprudent, impulsive, and indiscreet. But, says Dr. Smith, after the glory of reforming one's age, there is none greater than that of corrupting it.[1] When there comes along no woman to improve, but rather there appears one to seduce, what do you do? Suppose that much ado was made about the virtue of this woman—that the most subtle, the most successful, had failed with her? You are much given to disdaining what people generally find most admirable; but I would be surprised if you made no effort to please someone who had disdained the whole world before she saw you. Perhaps generosity would hold you back when you saw victory within your grasp. Satisfied with being able to say: "It would only depend on me," you would now say: "It is my wish, I permit it, let her be virtuous"; and there would be a double glory in bringing her back to virtue after having made her long for vice.

---

1. She has been reading Adam Smith's *The Theory of Moral Sentiments*.

Friday evening

I return to this old letter, which I have not had time to finish; I can continue to write on the same sheet. What do dates matter? What does the order of subjects matter? Only in my heart would I like to see less disorder and confusion. I am not at peace; I am anxious and at war with myself—not about the matter itself, which still seems to me good, and attractive; I still desire its success.

As to the means, however, my thinking continually varies. Sometimes I hate our roundabout methods—this atmosphere of conspiracy. It seems to me that I am becoming guilty toward my father, whom I am deceiving; and that you yourself will find that my conduct is undermining that probity—that rectitude—that is the virtue I value most and the one by which I would hope to redeem my failings and my faults. In your heart of hearts, are you not saying: "What aptitude for intrigue! Such eagerness for a man she has seen for only a few moments!" Aren't you accusing me of an indecent impatience to see myself married, or an excessive inclination for independence, or some other sentiment which would do me even less honor? It may well be that if the affair succeeds, and, having done with it, you are less busy than you are at present and are thinking calmly about what I am doing—so many letters written, so many measures taken in less than two weeks—you and the Marquis may be surprised that you no longer find in your heart of hearts the same sentiment of esteem that you thought you owed me earlier.

I beg you, d'Hermenches, be my casuist: you who know women, and who know so well how the world judges them, prevent me from doing anything that might debase me. I must not engender contempt in the man whose wife I would like to become; but above all I do not want him to believe me false, for I am not. If you answer me: "We will never let him know the history of the letter," that in itself will prove that I should not have written it. In that very ineptness for which you reproach the Marquis, in that very clumsiness, there is something likeable; in the talent for succeeding in everything one wants, there is something to be feared. One is rarely sure enough of the intentions of men not to fear that they may do harm when when they are free to do so. A man who always has a subtle poison in his pocket, whatever his reputation as a good and honest man, would seem a little dangerous. It is easy for you to apply these maxims. I leave you the absolute master of my letter, the judge of my conduct; but be scrupulous in my place.

Tell your friend (if it's not overdoing things) that he should not desire to be other than what he is; I would hardly have wished, I think, to be the wife of a god or a king, whereas I would be very happy to become *his* wife. Yes—tell him that whatever happens, I want him to know that I am flattered by his choice, and grateful for his sentiments; that I have been charmed by his wit, and that I believe what you say about his heart.

His letter gave me great pleasure; I reread it three or four times, always looking for the expressions of tenderness, and seeing them again with even more joy than his expressions of admiration. I think it's a sign that if I become his wife I will love him very much, for I have always found it unbearable to think of a husband who would love me passionately and whom I would hardly love at all.

No doubt there is pleasure in being very rich, but it is one of the pleasures that I can most easily do without. What cures one of that fancy is to see just which people are rich: to see most often avarice coupled with treasures, bad taste covered with gilt, the ugliest Jewesses decked out in the finest diamonds. Soon, whatever we might have in common with these Croesuses no longer appears worthy of our vanity; we create for ourselves a vanity of a completely different sort. The Marquis and I would be, I think, agreeable enough company not to need to be very opulent. Fools do well to have footmen, six spirited horses, and a golden coach; people enjoy seeing them on the avenue, and forget how tedious they will be in the house; if they were to come alone on foot, the house would not be open to them.

Consider the difference when your friend and his wife would go pay a visit. Since we know how to talk in company, we have no need to gamble for high stakes. Since we know what elegance is, we have no need of profusion. To give me out as "the most reasonable and the most useful of women"—that is what my conscience does not permit. Sometimes I would prevent extravagances, as you say one should do; but sometimes too I would propose them. For example, a trip to Paris, reasonable or not, I wouldn't refuse—I have long desired it. What might somewhat cool that desire if I were the Marquis' wife is that he is too great a lord, and the names of his relatives are too fine. I might need to conform to their fine airs—and I don't like those in high places, nor fine airs, nor conforming. My passion would be to see Paris on foot and by hackney, to see the arts, the artists and the artisans; to hear the people speak, and La Clairon act;[2] I would make—purely at random—some acquaintances I would like, others who would make me laugh; I would pay a great deal for lessons from Rameau;[3] and a week before my departure, just to sample a bit of everything, I would make the acquaintance of the hairdresser and of high society. If I ever make such a journey, would you like to come along? —No, the great ladies would recognize you.

Let's return to our marriage and my household management. I have always been told that I wouldn't have any at all, that my husband would be greatly to be pitied, that I would be the worst housewife in the world. It's only my mother's old chambermaid, a woman of great good sense, who has

<hr />

2. Claire de La Tude, known as La Clairon (1723–1803); one of the most famous and admired actresses of her time, particularly in classical roles.
3. Jean-Philippe Rameau (1683–1764), great French composer and music theorist.

sometimes reassured me. She says to me: "It's true that you will run up wild expenses for two or three weeks; but then for three months you won't buy anything, you won't dress up, you will think neither of drinking nor of eating; and your friends will be so witty that they too will forget these gross things, and at the end of the year it will be exactly as if you had been orderly and economical all along." This maid is right, I think: if I am in charge, there will be highs and lows, as in everything that I do. During the time that I don't know how to run the household, other people will; I will follow with docility and pleasure the order that I find already established. I think, really, that it would all work itself out with the greatest of ease, and that we would find ourselves quite as rich as necessary to be very happy. If the Marquis were very wealthy, it is quite certain that I would not do everything I'm doing at present to marry him; my motives would appear ambiguous, and perhaps people would be contemptuous of my zealousness.

I will write the letter that is to be from you to my father. I hope that I won't have to play a long role of dissimulation. You could not believe how much these subterfuges cost me; and the more attractive the end, the more scrupulous I am about the means. To procure for myself a pleasure—one of your letters—I would tell a falsehood that I would certainly not tell if it would win me a fortune. It must be, then, that I regard this marriage as a pleasure and not as a fortune, lest I find myself contemptible. I am often stricken with remorse: what! write a letter that two days from now I will pretend to read with surprise!

The most innocent art partakes of perfidy.[4]

Ah, that is very true! If you come to have the slightest, most passing feeling of scorn, if you think for an instant that my art degrades me, throw everything into the fire and let it never be thought of again, for I refuse to be degraded.

It's written—that letter; can you not tell by the disorder of this page I've written since? My wits have flown; I drank some coffee at midnight, the day has returned and I haven't yet let go my pen. At the end, while I was writing that long model-letter, I no longer knew what it was for. It all seems to me only a dream, with no verisimilitude.

If you don't burn anything, write me a word on Saturday, and on Sunday send the letter to my father. I choose Sunday because Monday is the last day that my cousin de Tuyll is here.[5] I'm very fond of her; talking with her will distract me from my mortal anxieties. I must not die; that would break off all our plans even more surely than Calvin's schism and the infallibility of the Pope.

4. "L'art le plus innocent tient de la perfidie," Voltaire, *Zaïre* IV.ii. The line would be familiar to d'Hermenches, who had played the leading role of Orosmane.
5. Annebetje.

Farewell, Monsieur, at this moment you have only a madwoman for a friend. I still have a hundred things to say to you; I am saving them for when I have my wits back.

> Friday night ... early morning
> ... later, Saturday

An hour of rest has restored me; now I can see, and think, and judge. I am confirming what I did this last night; I will not retract the letter; you may send it. Tomorrow I will write you once again, and then no more until the decision is made. Your letters will be put in a packet, sealed, and left with the Widow. I will abandon the care of my keys; everything will be open in my room, and my conduct will leave no occasion for suspicion.

You speak of a first letter of mine, which dazzled you. Such was not my intention; I may have expressed myself badly; but I have never had to answer except for myself. I myself rely on you, but I do not control the trust of my mother and father. Besides, you are perfectly free to say to them if they offer many hopes: "That is not enough to make my friend approach you; he must have complete certainty, a signed promise." If you fear the least unpleasantness for him, you are free to abandon this whole project; you are also free to write him and ask what he wishes. In that case I give up the choice of Monday, and I will arm myself with courage for another day. I have no wish to ask anyone to go to more trouble to have me than I'm worth; and I don't think I'm worth a great deal of trouble. Your praises of me, precious and touching as they are, cannot blind me. I do not know what my parents will do; I know that I'm doing everything I can, and I abandon to you the care of the rest.

That manner of dialogue in which you would say nothing is quite ill-conceived.[6] Don't you see that it is your mind that makes mine say the things that you find good or charming? Do not take what I have said for ill humor. I feel for you only gratitude and sincere friendship.

113. *To Constant d'Hermenches, August 3, 1764*

[This is Belle's draft for the letter that d'Hermenches will send to her father.]

The idea that I am about to present to you, Monsieur, could seem absurd to those who judge superficially: that is, those who know just how attached you are to our religion and how conscientiously you fulfill its duties, but who are unaware of how averse you are to restricting the goodness of God within narrow confines, or to thinking that the devotees of any other religion—His creatures like us, our brothers—would be excluded from His favors. For myself, Monsieur, I am not unaware of it; I have not been able to

---

6. See the beginning of his Letter 111.

forget that long and serious conversation that I had with you one night at the ball. The noise and the dancing in no way distracted me from what you were saying, which deserved full attention. From that conversation, I learned that you had as much humanity and true philosophy as religion; that you were still more a Christian than a Calvinist. Thus, without further preamble, and without fear of too greatly astonishing you, I dare to propose to you a Roman Catholic as a son-in-law.

It is for my best friend that I am speaking. I know him as I know myself, and although I have rarely seen your daughter, I think I know her well enough by her own conversation, by that of her friends, of mere ac-quaintances, of jealous women, of the entire public—to come to this conclusion: if there exists a man who would suit her, it is my friend; and if there exists a woman who would suit my friend, it is Mademoiselle de Zuylen.

They have the same humanity, the same generosity; they are capable of the same virtues; they both love the arts and those who are distinguished in them; their tastes would meet and join; and, mutually, the talents of each would be a source of pleasures for the other. You know as well as I do, Monsieur, those talents that Heaven lavished on your daughter, and which a distinguished education has cultivated in her along with her virtues. These are precious gifts, which ought to earn good marriages, but which often stand in the way of them. There are few men who would not be intimidated by such gifts; there are still fewer who could please the possessor of them, who would appreciate them and recognize them. My friend has enough in-tellect to desire that his wife have a great deal; enough knowledge to permit that his wife be learned—in short, it is your daughter, such as she is, who charms him, whom he loves, whom he desires, whom he needs in order to be happy. He, in turn, pleases her—or will please her, I dare answer for it. If she becomes his wife, her heart and her inclination will accord with her duty to prefer him above all others. She will enjoy herself with him; at home or in company, she will be happy being with him. The presence of an amiable husband who will respect her too much to experience jealousy, far from hindering her, will increase her pleasures; and her reputation, like her happiness, will be far safer than it would be with a husband who would be, for such a woman, always in the way, and who, even if he were not incon-venient, would at any rate simply be forgotten.

I would enumerate for you, Monsieur, the titles, the fine connections of the person who desires to enter into your family, if I believed that these things had much power over a man like you. It will suffice to say that he is of distinguished birth, that his house is one of the most respected in his country—in short, the proudest and most scrupulous would find nothing to object to on that head. He wishes he were yet richer than he is, so as to make your daughter yet more happy; for myself, I find that he is rich enough. Their favorite pleasures are not the most costly. They would have no need of elaborate display. There is a kind of vanity that seeks magnificence; there is another kind, more meritorious, that disdains it, that wants to shine without its help, without anything imposing, anything that dazzles and deceives the gaze—that is the kind of vanity appropriate to your daughter and my friend. A noble and respectable ease suitable to their rank is what they would enjoy in the country of their chief abode; and the journeys they would make to Holland to see their relatives and to pay their respects would not unduly tax their means.

If love, gentleness, a perfect evenness of temper, and the most generous sentiments can bring a woman happiness, Mademoiselle de Zuylen would become the happiest of women in marrying my friend. All those who know him well offer the same praises; no one has ever been able to reproach him except for those faults that are all too ordinary during the age of passions. But they have not spoiled his heart; they have not inured him to dissoluteness; they have not made him insensible to the gentle pleasures of a legitimate union. He was hoping for those pleasures; he was hoping for children, for a life's companion; but that companion had to be amiable, sensitive; he had to love her. He saw your daughter; if he wins her, he will never love anyone else.

Please believe me, Monsieur, you would choose him for your son-in-law if you had the choice of any man on earth. The difference in religion is the only obstacle that might make you hesitate; but that obstacle is more formidable to prejudice than it is to reason. Never, Monsieur, will anyone think of "converting"—as the zealots say—converting your daughter. Those whom she will live with, while they respect their own religion, are far from being bigots. Her children will be Catholic, but they will be none the less *hers*, entrusted to her care. She will render them reasonable; she will inspire in them the duties of all religions; there will be no difference between her children and those of her sister except the name, the ceremonies, and perhaps a few difficult dogmas on which God seems to permit doubt, and will pardon error. The essential dogmas, all the precepts, will be the same. Ah, Monsieur! what can be accomplished by books, philosophers, exhortations of true Christians, in comparison with such examples to inspire in all those who claim to be Christian the spirit of tolerance and peace! If Catholic fathers and Protestant mothers in Toulouse were to raise their children together, those children would no longer celebrate those hideous festivals,[1] and never again would an innocent old man perish on the wheel.

These considerations, feeble as they may be for ordinary hearts, are worthy of touching yours, Monsieur, especially when they are joined with fatherly tenderness. If they determine your consent and that of Madame de Zuylen, then perhaps ignorant and prejudiced people will protest; you will not listen to them, and soon they will fall silent. But the wise will admire you; and, what is sweeter yet, you will approve of yourself.

---

1. The Délivrance celebrations. See the translator's comments that follow Letter 68.

Before anything else, I would have asked for the consent of your daughter if I had had less hope of obtaining it. But as I have depicted the man who desires her—that is to say, such as he is—, she undoubtedly sees that he is the man who is to make her happy. That free, entire, heartfelt consent, without which my friend would not be happy at all—if she does not give that, then everything I have said falls of itself and becomes bootless. May I hope, Monsieur, that you will show this letter only to her and to Madame de Zuylen? I would be chagrined if people other than you were to guess the name that I have not pronounced. And what advice could you need? Other people would see no better than you do what might doom this project, but others would not see as well as you do what justifies it: that an ordinary marriage will hardly suit—and will even fail—a girl who is not ordinary; that in certain cases, instead of timidly weighing the disadvantages, one must boldly seize the advantages. Other people will love your daughter less than you and her mother do, Monsieur; they will have the leisure to be guided by what is conventional, and will not be so touched by the pleasure of seeing her placed according to her inclination, according to her mind, absolute mistress of her actions; passionately loved by her husband, and governed by duty alone, which becomes much more powerful when it is accompanied by no arbitrary and superfluous constraint.

I will go to your house to ask for your response, Thursday or Friday. Be good enough, Monsieur, to write me which of these days best suits you. If you fear that this journey to Utrecht may seem extraordinary, I will be at Woerden so that I may have the honor of speaking to you, or else at Alphen—wherever you please. Then I will give you all the necessary explanations concerning my friend's fortune, and you will be good enough to tell me what Mademoiselle would bring him. For while we are thinking about what is agreeable and beautiful, we must not forget what is necessary. I have taken this concern on myself for two reasons: first, that the great failing of my friend is that he does not understand the details of these things; second, that since he cannot yet form any conjecture as to the success of a plan that seems so extraordinary, he prefers not to make it public, nor to expose himself to a refusal.

I flatter myself, Monsieur, that you do not fear that my predilection and the warmth of my friendship can make me change or exaggerate the slightest thing. This temptation—perhaps the most dangerous of all because its motive would seem to excuse me—would, however, not seduce me. In an occasion of this importance, I would dishonor myself in my own eyes if I said a single word that was not dictated by truth.

I have the honor of being ... etc.

If you want to add a word about the attentiveness and the passion that the Marquis shows in his letters, that's your business; I have already suffered enough showering myself with such ridiculous praise. Say, if you like, that you will show him passages of these letters. I pity you for having to copy such a long scribble. If something displeases you, change it; if something is missing, add it.

114. *To Constant d'Hermenches, August 4, 1764*

Saturday morning

The end of yesterday's letter was written in the morning in town; upon my return here I reread your last letters, and I saw that since I had not grasped your thought very well at first, I had not given a proper answer at the end; my tone was not quite right.

What I said remains true, however. You offer me the example of yourself and Madame d'Hermenches, but the situation was very different: she had probably seen you more than for just one evening, she loved you, and her parents knew you. When she spoke to them about you, when she praised you, when she said that you were just the man to make her happy, she had other proofs to give than the letters of a man with whom she was not allowed to have any correspondence. She could say a thousand more things than I could—and you were not Catholic.

If my father, after showing me this letter that I know so well, asks me who this person is, I will name the Marquis without hesitating; and if he wants to know how I know it, I will recount to him faithfully the little bit of conversation that we had, you and I, as we left the Opera. He will immediately see how I am disposed; I will then say everything necessary. But you have no idea how difficult it is to behave with those whom we are dependent upon when we and they are made completely differently, and yet we love and respect them—when they oppose a never-changing prudence to our vivacity.

My mother has come to read in my room; there is only my writing-table between us; I am tempted to tell her everything. Perhaps, perhaps I will take her into my confidence before your letter arrives; perhaps afterwards. She is more impulsive—I know better how to stir her up, and I speak to her more candidly than to my father. But she is so firmly decided against the merit of works![1] We shall see. She has asked me in such good faith to keep on writing!... Subterfuges are hateful.

Let us talk about your lawsuit. I am no longer surprised enough at seeing inept men led to the most glaring iniquities by puerile motives to get as angry with them as you do; I can say to you more or less what Philinte says to the Misanthrope:

---

1. A wry reference to a point in Catholic-Protestant theological controversies: namely, whether salvation is obtained through faith or through the performance of "works"—by which, a contentious Protestant would say, Catholics mean merely formal, ritualistic penance and a priest's absolution.

> And it's no more a matter for disgust
> That men are knavish, selfish and unjust,
> Than that the vulture dines upon the dead,
> And wolves are furious, and apes ill-bred.[2]

We are both wrong, or rather we are both unhappy. You demand too much from men; I expect almost nothing. You get angry with them; I am disposed rather to scorn them. Bears, oxen, scoundrels, and fools outrage your heart or make it bleed; as for me, I look at them a moment, and laugh; then I turn away my eyes, and forget them. Your reflections against my compatriots are too harsh. In any country, one loses lawsuits that one should win. There is good in this country that you are unaware of. Here it isn't amorous intrigue that is the dominant vice; that's not the one that the most decent people tolerate. At least they insist that it be hidden—no flagrant love affairs; only with the greatest difficulty are such things pardoned or forgotten. Moreover, foreigners find there is a sort of prejudice against them; and if the slightest thing can be found to say against them, then nothing is verified, and they are left out in the cold, since no one has any interest in befriending them. Here people are heavy; they seem at first tiresome, off-putting, unbearable; they neglect all charms of society; that is true in all the cities, all the houses. But not everywhere does one have the unfeeling, base, mean-spirited heart that you find in the high society of the Hague. Nowhere have I seen people more ridiculous nor more contemptible; but you would be unjust to judge the whole nation by them.

As for your lawsuit, think no more about it; or think about it only to pity justice for being in such corrupt hands, and the judges for being devoid of all conscience. If the thing can have a laughable aspect, seize upon it quickly; that is of more consolation than any reasoning—and next time bring your lawsuits only to the court of Holland. I would not disapprove of your exposing the corruption of your judges if it could make them more just, if it didn't embitter anyone against you, or roil up your blood. But if the utility were dubious and the drawbacks certain, I wouldn't take the trouble. I dare not preach to you my profound indifference to the evils that surround me only from afar. I disapprove of this indifference of mine; I find it criminal; I would like it if I got indignant more often. It is a bad thing not to respect society, and to pardon one's fellows everything out of pure disdain.

Supposing that you were to send the letter, remove that phrase: ... *absolute mistress of my actions;* that would not be the case, nor should it be. If what I have you say about libertinage is not exactly true, or if it might seem hypocritical coming from you, don't say it. Tomorrow I will send for your letter at the Widow's house; I'm waiting for it impatiently. Unless it's to amuse myself for a moment by telling you things that aren't urgent, like

---

2. Molière, *Le Misanthrope*, I.i. Translation is that of Richard Wilbur, *The Misanthrope* (New York: Harcourt Brace, 1965).

those I wrote a week ago, I intend not to write you for some time; I must avoid any appearance of secrecy in my conduct. Farewell; I am so weary of thinking, of condemning myself, of excusing myself! If I keep on with this I will soon no longer be able to think—but I will always love you. I wish I were at peace in the depths of Savoie.

115. *From Constant d'Hermenches, August 5, 1764*

Can you know me so little—or so little know the true power of enchantment, and of esteem and affection—that you can imagine that the confidence with which you honor me, and what you unveil to me of what goes on in your mind mind and heart, could do other than increase my veneration for you? No, Mademoiselle, you analyze too well the properties of a true and honest heart for your fears on that subject to be sincere! Even if I had known you only on this occasion, you would have bound me by the most sacred veneration and admiration! And to punish you, I ought not even to answer you concerning these doubts!

Tomorrow I intend to write that letter that is so important to your fate and that of my friend. I find him enviable, if only in the preferences that you already give him over me: his kind of libertinage pleases you better than mine—and yet the one is of the senses, the other is of the intellect; his clumsiness pleases you better than my skill! Go on like this, and it will be I who will repent having revealed myself before you as I have done ...

It is kind of you to involve yourself in the petty annoyances of my lawsuit. It isn't the Dutch that I have to blame for the lack of equity and enlightenment; it isn't the fogs of this country, but rather the degenerate Swiss, and the spirit of flattery that poisons everything and gains ground every day in a country where liberty exists neither in actions nor in feelings.

Your version of a journey to Paris is admirable; what pleasures are in store when one bases them on principles as true and solid as yours! You will be a great lady wherever you are; you will reign over hearts and minds as well. I have only a moment to tell you that every day I am more deeply struck by the sublimity of your character.

116. *To Constant d'Hermenches, August 6, 1764*

Monday morning

I received your letter yesterday just as I was going to bed; I could hardly sleep because of it.[1] I admire you sincerely; I admire you immensely. What you are doing seems to me beautiful, great, difficult. A person who does not

---

1. Here Belle is answering not Letter 115 but an earlier letter that has been lost. She seems to be referring to feelings, fears, and losses not explicitly treated in other letters that we have.

know what it is to love would say: she cannot be yours, so giving her to your friend is not a sacrifice. Myself, I judge it very differently. I feel only too keenly that to add, by one's own hand, new separations to the old ones and to put an eternal and invincible obstacle to one's desire demands a courageous and sublime generosity. Giving one's beloved in marriage to one's best friend is quite another thing from giving her to any other man; one imposes forever the most rigorous law—not on one's actions, but on one's gaze, one's desires, the most secret movements of one's soul. You entreat me to reassure you; it would be easy for me to recite to you all the commonplaces of modesty: to tell you that seeing me oftener you would cease to love me. But that would not be true; on the contrary, I think that if you love me even a little at present you would love me much more hereafter. The liberty of our commerce and the marks of friendship and confidence that no consideration could oblige me to refuse you would have that effect.

Permit me, d'Hermenches, the pride of believing that no woman will ever hold precisely the same place in your heart that I could. But as for love—all that you would need for being quite tranquil near me you will find, perhaps, by falling in love at the first opportunity with a more beautiful woman; you will see a thousand more beautiful women whose charms, combined with a bit of intelligence, will help you be, with respect to me, all that you will want to be. Ever since we have known each other, I have always had your esteem and your liking; but haven't you been in love many times? My image may have given you a moment of emotion now and then; but hasn't it also, in a thousand other moments, left your heart perfectly tranquil? And then, couldn't it be that one gets used to regarding the wife of one's friend as something altogether beyond one's reach, whom it would be absurd to desire, impossible to possess, so that we don't even think about it?

If there were any foundation for your fears, I would be tempted to say to you: "Break it off, I don't want you to be unhappy; I don't want you to avoid a friend like Bellegarde, and I don't want him to lose a friend like you. It is very unlikely that I could compensate for it; on the contrary, I truly think that he would lose by the exchange, and that instead of the good service that you would like to render him at the expense of your own happiness, you would do him an ill one; find another wife for him, and remain friends."

"But," you say, "Heaven will reward virtue." It is already a reward for your intentions that you can say those words: I think that they are accompanied by a very pleasurable feeling; I would like to experience it myself. Up to now, I admit, I have had few claims on rewards from Heaven; they have had no part either in my consolations or my hopes.

Who could ever guess the subjects and the style of our letters? I myself am surprised by them, and I find that I'm happy that I decided to become your friend in spite of all the opinions, all the talk.

When you write to my father, send a letter for me to Mme Geelvinck at the same time, so that I will be warned. If my father delays speaking to me, I will ask him several days later whether he hasn't received a letter; I will tell him about our conversation at the opera, and I will add that since this affair seems agreeable to me, I wish that someone would write to him about it, and that then it would be worth our consideration. There are moments when success seems to me almost impossible, others where I find it very likely. Goodbye; I will continue to write to you, and to love you.

117. *To Constant d'Hermenches, August 6, 1764*

Monday evening

I am at the Widow's; she has given me your letter. Ah! why do you utter these reproaches against me, when I think only of admiring you and thanking you! It's at myself and not at you that I have aimed these insults; reread my letter, you will see that there is no other possible meaning. You will see in this one that I do not deserve a harsh rejoinder, and that in revealing yourself before me you have only secured a firmer hold on my heart. Farewell.

118. *From Constant d'Hermenches, August 7, 1764*

The Hague

Yesterday, Monday, I launched the letter; as I told you, it is the best reply that I could make to your letter. I have perhaps blasphemed in speaking of Heaven; if it has given me a virtuous heart, can I ask for rewards for what this heart makes me do? Besides, I see a good, a present charm, which makes me forget all the rest: I will at least be able to see you freely; I will enjoy your friendship, your intellect, your consolations. If I have ever imagined happiness on this earth, it is in thinking that we will live in each others' company, and that we are going to make a trio of perfect intimacy such as no poet, I think, has ever yet dared imagine. If I were to become your husband, I would be more troubled; between the moments of sensual ecstasy, all the intervals would be spent in the fear of not making you happy enough, of making you put up with my bouts of ill humor, with all the contradictions that have always been part of my life—who can tell? becoming unfeeling, perhaps unfaithful; reproaching myself for it without being able to correct myself! I do not want to hide from you that in this pitiless regimen you lay out for me, equity will enter for nothing—for on that article our man would not himself hold anything sacred; my wife, my sister, my daughter, my mother, all would be fair game for him; only the fear of distressing me could restrain him—and this is the libertinage that you prefer to mine?

I would like to go to Utrecht; Mme de Degenfeld is leaving because her husband must leave his regiment in the command of one of his subordinates during the Duke's absence; they are going to Mme de Nassau's and to Cleves.

What does the Widow say? What does she think of our correspondence? When it turns out that I shall have been nothing but your intendant, to compensate her ... Yes, yes, it will have to be you who does up the envelopes. It is good of me to joke about it, isn't it?

119. *To Constant d'Hermenches, August 7-8, 1764*

Tuesday evening

You should fall to your knees and implore my pardon. What! so unjustly to scold someone who is anxious and disturbed, and who has no constant feeling except her gratitude and affection for you! What! To change your style on purpose! But even if your wrongs were only those of having so thoroughly misunderstood me, I would demand that a blush of embarrassment and repentance cover your whole face. Did I ever tell you that the Marquis' libertinage pleased me better than yours? Will you dare maintain that I said it? I had written you a letter such as perhaps no woman in such situation has ever written, nor will ever write. You have answered me as perhaps no libertine has ever responded. Since I have a moment of leisure, I am resuming this conversation with the same confidence, the perfect freedom that had begun it.

It was quite unnecessary, I admit, to tell you just *how* I would be a libertine, if I were to be one; but, after all, I enjoy saying it. Were it not for the puppy who follows my dear father around—and whom I think I heard a little too close to me—I would have continued. I would have questioned whether what you said was true—that women do much more for vanity than for pleasure. I would have affirmed with full conviction that, in my case, pride would be weak against love; but that the horror of the crime of betrayal, the fear of being odious to myself forever if I were to offend a husband who loved me and did not suspect me—these would be much stronger weapons of defense. If I were to love with passion, and believed I was loved as much in return, then the possibility of scorn, of disgust would not come to my mind; but I might never forget for a single moment the horror of being despicable. In general, the fear of being despicable concerns me much more than the fear of being despised.

I would have said all these things a little better and more pertinently if I had not been interrupted; a week later, that very sheet comes out of my drawer,[1] and I see in it only a very humble confession of my sensitivity to pleasure; a confession which must please you in that it was a new proof of unlimited trust; a confession which by my lights placed me beneath you. I send it to you so that you can see the whole succession of my ideas, and because I find that to burn what one has written to a friend is a sign of reserve or culpable pride—I send it, and you scold me. I could not say that the libertinage of the Marquis pleases me more than yours without being both mad and ungrateful. It's all the better for me—valuing you as I do, your heart, the services you render me—that you can love a woman quite otherwise than the way he does. A few innocent letters written from two hundred leagues away would not have won or kept his affection; he would not concern himself with me as you do. Really, d'Hermenches, if you had *wanted* to understand me, you would have found nothing to make you angry.

Your letter has passed through my hands into those of my father as we were arriving in town. Instead of the turmoil that I was feeling before, a sudden calm came over me. He looked at the address attentively; the people who were waiting for him prevented him from reading it; he had opened it, however, and I distinctly saw your writing. He was occupied the whole morning; we came back in company with others, and there were people here when we arrived. My father shut himself in his room before dinner. The rest of the day he was cheerful, or pretended to be. Toward the end of dinner, this evening, we talked about religion: the Jews, the prophecies, morality, the union of Christian churches; I said what I thought as the occasion arose. My dear mother has surely been informed by a rather long conversation that they had together, but they have said nothing to me. Tomorrow I'll see what's to be done, I'll have one of your letters, I'll do some thinking ...

For now, I'm going to bed; for a long time now I've had only a little sleep. My cousin de Tuyll was finding that my hours of sleep were lost hours for her; she left this morning.[2] Last evening, she wanted to spend the night on a chair in my room so that, she said, "if you wake up I can hear you talking right away." At half past twelve, she was still sitting on my bed; at five-thirty she was already there again. Farewell; since it is now after midnight, I find that I have been awake for a long time.

Wednesday morning

This uninteresting detail about my sleep, which may well make you nod off, you owe to my pride at seeing myself loved by a young girl perhaps as much as by you.

1. Her Letter 112.
2. Annebetje.

120. *To Constant d'Hermenches, August 9–10, 1764*

Thursday morning

You are a little less saintly in this letter than in the last one, but on the other hand you are more fortunate, and thus, I think, you haven't lost much on the exchange. I'm about to report what's going on here.

Tuesday, the day before yesterday, when our company had left, after supper I abandoned myself somewhat to my distractions; I wanted my parents to suspect something; I wanted them to speak to me soon. Yesterday morning, I made some outburst about "the things of this world," which my mother noticed; I went with her and my father to Utrecht, where I had no particular business, simply to be alone with them. In the coach they began by making small talk; then they mentioned Boswell, who has written them a letter full of admiration for me (he doesn't want them to tell me a single word of it). I told them all his reasons for not marrying me; I made fun of it all; I told them tales (true tales). I told them that at the very most, if I became much more reasonable, more prudent, more reserved, Boswell might in time try to have me marry his best friend in Scotland.[1] We were all in high spirits. In Utrecht, as soon as I was alone I wrote a letter to my father in order to open the conversation, and to beg him not to be secretive with me about something that concerned me, etc. The letter's style was flaccid and negligent, so it would not resemble the one from you.[2]

After a brief mechanics lesson, which was the pretext of my journey, I found myself alone with my mother. "You are pale," she said to me, "what's wrong? Is something troubling you?" "No," I said, "but there's something on my mind." "Is it a secret?" "No—if you like, it won't be one for you. You won't repeat any of this except as I wish?" —"I give you my word," she said.

I asked her first if she had learned anything new; she said yes. I next told her about your proposal at the Opera, and I begged her to question me, promising that I would answer, but she refused.

"There would be no point," I said, "in concealing from you that I have learned a number of things since then. I wouldn't for the world mention it to my father, but, I can tell *you* that I have obtained as much assurance as possible on the question of raising children: although my children would be Catholic, they would not be taken from me; I would see them, I would raise them myself . . ."

"Why don't you want to tell your father that?" she interrupted, looking rather pleased. "Because," I said, "that way he would learn of my correspondence with Monsieur d'Hermenches." "He knows about it already,"

---

1. William Johnson Temple.

2. That is, so that it would not resemble the elegant style of the letter that Belle had written for d'Hermenches to send to her father, which he had rewritten slightly and then sent under his own name.

she said; "at least I think he does; he has had the chance to know about it, just as I do." I asked her if she could subtly find that out and let me know (that would have simplified matters). She told me no, that she was afraid of exposing me, and that it had never come up between them.

I showed her the letter; she was pleased with it. "But," she said, "we wouldn't think of replying without talking to you." And then she declared that she had already said everything she wanted to say to my father; that the affair was no longer up to her. "Excuse me," I said to her, "if what you have said is that you are definitely opposed to it, then the matter is already decided." In her tone and her gesture, I thought I perceived that she claimed to disapprove more than she really did; but she did not explain herself, either for or against. I tore up the letter, which now seemed to me useless; we returned to Zuylen.

After dinner my mother had me take a long stroll alone with her. It was raining, but that didn't bother her; she took pleasure in talking to me about all sorts of things, cheerfully and trustingly. I talked to her a little about our enterprise; she said that surely it had been premeditated on the part of the Marquis. "Not so," I assured her. "At the very most *you* might have thought of it before the visit, but not Monsieur de Bellegarde." "Come now! If you believe *that*," she said, "you've been thoroughly taken in. After he's had fifty mistresses, he's fallen in love with you at first sight! But after all what does that matter—you would be more flattered, but to me it makes no difference." And then she asked me to change the subject.

After the walk, my father talked to her at length; she called me to her when she had left him and said that I could go talk to him. "You can also put it off until tomorrow," she said. "Why put it off?" I said to her. "Surely my dear father is not in a bad humor?" "No, not at all, but you may not be pleased; the two of you may not agree." That kindly attentiveness seemed to me a good sign.

I went up, and found my father in the corridor. I gave him my arm, and we began the conversation in a quiet, gentle tone, walking in step together. He spoke to me about your letter, which he did not think he needed to show me. It contained a great deal that was flattering for him and for me, which we owed to your politeness and to your desire to succeed; he gave me a very precise summary of it.

"Would you rather begin," he said, "by telling us your opinion, or by hearing ours?" "Ah!" I replied, "since it isn't yet an irrevocable decision, but simply a conversation, it makes no difference." And we began to chat, both of us trying to avoid seeming closed-minded. The difference of religion is an obstacle; I expressed my ideas on this; I agreed that it would be better if things were otherwise, but I said I thought that an amiable Catholic husband was better than a disagreeable Protestant one.

"Perhaps the Marquis has more debts than it would be fitting for us to pay."—"That is something that we can learn quite precisely."

"The Marquis is not rich, and he likes to spend, he likes to travel."—"Age and family cares change those tastes."

"We do not know anything about his character."—"We can make inquiries."

"But you ask us not to consult anyone."—"It's precisely by *not* consulting—if we go about it right—that we can find out the truth."

"His morals ... "—"An amiable wife who seeks to please can always hope to make her husband faithful."

We returned to the question of religion, and of children. You had spoken of the resources that existed for them in Catholic countries. I said that you were mistaken if you thought that I wanted to make use of that kind of wealth; that my sons would not be made priests, and that no one would talk to my daughters about becoming nuns. After they turned twenty-five they would do as they pleased; but beforehand, whether they were poor or rich, there would be no question of it, that I would not allow it, and that all conditions would be based on that. Indeed, without that clause I would break off all negotiations in an instant, irrevocably. At a time when all sensible people among the Catholics protest against absurd vows that lead to licentiousness and that depopulate the world, I, a Protestant, will have no part in that abuse. No—if they wanted to make my son coadjutor of Rome while still a child, I would never consent to it.

I know that for many people there is little conformity between their reasonings and their actions; that those who declaim against convents would nonetheless put their daughters there if it favored the fortune of an elder son. But I am not made that way. I rarely go to great lengths in reasonings; I have few fixed principles; I have no systems. But when a line of reasoning seems to me just, evident, indisputable, it immediately becomes an invariable rule of my conduct. Although my voice is gentle, my resolutions are firm. Thus—no abbés, no monks, no nuns. That my children might be Catholic—that does not distress me at all; that is not in conflict with my ideas. But that is enough; one must not demand anything more. And could the Marquis demand that I be deprived of a mother's rights? If I were capable of giving them up, I would have no heart, I would be unworthy of being his wife!... No, he must be glad to recognize that for me there are sacred, inviolable duties, which nothing would make me renounce.

We talked about education, my father and I; I said that it would not be forgotten in our marriage contracts, and that a convent education should be out of the question. My father said that such a clause would make me suspect; that the Marquis would perhaps not be free to change what is customary; that there would be protests against him that would cause unpleasantness, disputes—but I cannot believe it. I trust the assurances that you have given me; I will rely on the promises that no one will refuse to give me. One would have to be devoid of all soul, all compassion, not to feel how hard it would be for me to see my children tormented by people who would only speak to them of me when they are talking about the hellfire to which every heretic is eternally condemned.

My father said, "You cannot prevent the servants, the aunts—everyone— saying to them: "It's too bad your mother is damned." "Ah!" I replied, "they may believe it for a moment; but when I hold them tenderly, they will no longer believe it. At least I will not be obliged to see a little daughter coming out of a cloister, ill-brought-up, badly dressed, her imagination sullied by all the foul talk of those convent schools—to see her misjudge me, tremble at my errors and, with pious moans, implore the Holy Virgin to convert me. Besides, if it turns out that in spite of my tenderness and care, my daughters are bigoted and foolish, and want to cloister themselves at the age of twenty-five, that will be their business."

After all these speeches and many others—always gentle, polite, moderate, reasonable—I begged my dear father to let me present a favorable picture of this marriage. "If I were happy, good, beloved, if my home in Savoie pleased me, if I came from time to time to see you, tenderly and joyfully, if my children were lovable, if Monsieur de Bellegarde found himself to be the most fortunate of husbands—wouldn't you be glad?" "Yes, but how long would it be before we could be certain of such a happy future! We could also paint a very different picture ..."

I said to him: "It would vex me to stay unmarried forever, and even to stay unmarried a long while; do you know a man who might suit me? Those who most ardently hope to see me settle down in this country can name only two parties that I could accept; and there are many things to be said against each.[3] One of the two has no wish to get married; the other, whom I have never seen, has vital reasons for seeking certain advantages that he would not have if he were to marry me; thus he does not care about seeing me, although his friends urge it. Two from two leaves zero.

"So much for this country. Let's consider the foreigners. The German baron—I want absolutely nothing to do with him.[4] Even supposing that what we have been told is false, my distaste will always be an invincible obstacle; the hatred and the boredom he would inspire in me would make me miserable, and even if I could make him live in Paris, it would still be a horrible marriage.

"The Count of Anhalt is the slave of his king, or else is put off by my reputation.

"Boswell will never marry me. If he were to do so, he would have a thousand regrets, for he is convinced that I do not suit him, and I don't know whether I would like to live in Scotland. The idea of marrying his friend— that is a hare-brained scheme. And as for that litany of reforms—I will not

3. Belle is referring to Count Jacob van Obdam and Baron Adolf van Pallandt.
4. Baron Christian von Brömbse (1742–1808). Belle's initial impression of him had been fairly favorable (see Letter 76, n. 4). Later she received a report about him, the content of which is unknown but which apparently disqualified him utterly.

undertake them for a man I've never seen.[5]

"But to live with an amiable, witty man, who wants me as I am, who knows the world, who would not be jealous without reason, who loves music, who would love me . . ."

When we got to that point, my dear father went downstairs to send off a letter; we then had a friendly game of comet together. Today we haven't discussed any of this, but my dear mother has seemed a little more ill-disposed than I had hoped. However, I know her; she will not make matters worse. She has said what she thought she should say, and she won't go back on it. But there will be no insinuations, no malign interpretations; she will let my father decide, and she will not, by so much as a word to him, do any more injury to my hopes.

The supper bell has rung. I have finished my long narration; I wanted to let you know where things stand. I may have given you a number of tedious, useless details; once my pen starts to recount, it is not sparing of words, at least with its friends. Tell me whether I bore you, or whether you enjoy seeing us and hearing us hold forth at length.

My father has not spoken to me of the proposed interview; I have not dared be the first to mention it. I don't know how much he wants to reflect before he answers you. I don't know whether you could come before receiving his answer; if it is too late in arriving, perhaps that would spoil things; I simply don't know. Think about it, please, and write me. When the time is right, I will put more warmth into my arguments, I will press ardently and forcefully. Unfortunately I cannot be pressing and ardent about the Marquis himself—his person, his heart—without appearing mad. "You have only seen him once," they tell me, and that is true. However, they speak of you and of him only with great respect. My mother admits that he is very polite, very amiable. My father does not appear to have the least mistrust of you. —By the way, it is certain that he is unaware of our correspondence. Goodnight, I'm exhausted, I'm going to sleep.

Let us be sure we understand each other: I would not make my children envisage the cloister as something really odious. Simply, I do not want it to be presented to them as very holy, or very attractive; I do not want them to be told that one goes straight from there to Heaven, just as from heresy one goes straight to Hell. I would not forbid them to pray for my conversion . . . But it's too much to explain; you understand me perfectly well—by now you read into my soul as well as I do. My mother says that it's not the question of children—who perhaps will never come—that bothers her. I will try to persuade them that I will be neither more nor less Protestant and Christian in Savoie than in Holland.

---

5. The long letter from Boswell mentioned in her Letter 104 contains the litany in question: "Could you live quietly in the country six months in the year? Could you make yourself agreeable to plain honest neighbours? Could you talk like any other woman and have your fancy as much at command as your harpsichord?" And so on (*Boswell in Holland* 315–16).

Friday morning

If this business is not absolutely impossible, d'Hermenches, we *must* make it succeed; I wish it more than ever; you wish it as the happiest thing that could happen for you, for me, for your friend. Unless my father is utterly resolved, it has to succeed. I will, however, be a docile and respectful daughter; so far, my parents' conduct is both kind and reasonable.

Have you thought of the figure we would cut, you and I, if this business were to fail? It would not be worth much. What would become of this blaze of correspondence? Would it be extinguished? —And everything I have confided to you—what would you do with that? Perhaps we would weary of not seeing each other—and yet we would not see each other. If ever another husband presented me to you, you would be obliged to forget everything, to suppose I had said nothing, to see nothing . . .

By the way, that's a fine piece of reasoning you offer! In the line of conduct you describe, you say, equity would count for nothing, for our man himself would consider everything his for the taking—my wife, my sister. etc. When I know that a man would seize my fortune if it suited him, I can then take his without breach of equity. That's a nice kind of equity.

There is no sort of libertinage that I prefer, but would you like to know what libertinage I hate? It's the doctrinaire kind. I met with it again yesterday, reading some of the poetry of Chaulieu,[6] who is otherwise such a likeable poet. I read the teachings of theologians with boredom, those of freethinkers with horror, those of libertines with distaste. That one should want to extend the realm of vice, make licentiousness into a system—that I cannot bear. That one might love, that one might forget oneself—that I can forgive . . . Ah! how dangerous, that inclination to forget oneself! I will be good, however—yes, I hope, I will be good.

You find yourself quite fortunate not to be marrying me. Your reasons for not envying the Marquis are all very fine, but, I beg you, don't go so far as to feel sorry for him.

121. *To Constant d'Hermenches, August 11, 1764*

Saturday morning

Don't expect anything favorable; however, things are not completely hopeless.

Yesterday morning there was nothing new concerning our business.

Yesterday after dinner, my father followed me into the garden where I was walking alone; we began our conversation, not with the dispassion of Wednesday, but rather with a great deal of intensity. There were several

---

6. Guillaume Amfrye, abbé de Chaulieu (1639-1720). He was part of the libertine society of the Regency that Voltaire frequented in his youth.

small incidents that worked us up to the necessary pitch. In particular, when I heard him condemn the welcome I had given the Marquis—singling him out with approval and pleasure—as being contrary to decorum, as if I were throwing myself at people, in a way that is bound to displease the men themselves—I got angry in earnest, and I declared that no motive could ever make me go to the trouble of hiding a feeling that I had no reason to blush for; that it had never been a question of love-making in my heart, but that any amiable man must seem amiable to me; that if there were twenty such all together they would all please me, and I would let that be seen by all of them, and that they would hardly be likely to think that I was in love with them. I said that a man who would be displeased by that would displease me likewise, and would never become my husband, were he the greatest match in the world. Such a blunt contradiction did not satisfy my father, as you can imagine. I would not back down; however, on this point we tempered our responses, and got down to the matter itself.

The great objection, the great fear, is that I will be living with people— whether my close relations or others—who, sooner or later, would find themselves obliged to use all possible means to make me change religion, as a consequence of that dogma accepted by any good Catholic: *No salvation outside the Church;* as a result, either I will change, or I will find myself unhappy. I told him that there was no Inquisition in Savoie; that the most ardent zeal grew weary; that the Marquis himself was surely not a bigot and would not bother me about this; that he would be most unlikely to allow others to come torment me in his house; that if he was too easy-going to be the master there, then I would be the mistress, and I would prevent pious busybodies from coming continually to preach.

I said a hundred thousand other things during twenty turns around the garden; believe me, I said everything there was to say. All the issues were discussed; I put forth all the motives; my tastes, my situation furnished me with a thousand pressing arguments. I was heard; I was right, but the objection was not destroyed. From my point of view it seemed to me exaggerated, and did not touch me at all. One thing, however, *did* touch me. "Have you thought about the shock, the distress you would cause all the people who love you?" "That hardly matters to me," I replied, "so long as I have your consent and my mother's. Besides, I have hardly any friends, and as for the remarks of mean-spirited, prejudiced people—I wouldn't hear them." "We would hear them in your place," said my father sadly. —"No, no," I said to him; "you will not hear them either; no one will dare to make them in your presence ..." "That silence," my father interrupted, "that tactful silence that people affect would hurt me very much." I made no rejoinder. I will not seek my own happiness at the expense of his.

Finally, my father's conclusion was that this sole obstacle of religion was such that it did not seem to him necessary to ask for explanations on any other point, and that the suit could not be accepted.

After a few moments of silence, I told him that his word was final, that it always would be, that my arguments were not meant to be a revolt, and that thus I believed I could express them and show my surprise. Then I reminded him of everything he had always said about tolerance, and of his plans for reunion[1]—impossible to carry out by discussions, definitions, and treaties; possible if one gave free scope to the natural influences of the mind, of feeling, of habit, to work among the adherents of different religious sects, united by ties of love and blood.

At the moment when I was speaking to him forcefully about his own ideas, he interrupted me to ask me if I had told you about them. "Monsieur d'Hermenches," he said, "has written me the same things." I replied, simply, "No," with an affirmative air of truthfulness that cost me some effort to adopt. I had hit on my father's weak point—no, it's not a weak point, I'm expressing myself badly—I had touched his most sensitive heartstring. The conversation became more tender, and, on the surface, more tranquil. I told him what I had expected on his part; I said yet again everything that came into my mind. Finally, after two hours of conversation and rapid pacing around the garden—which my father had tried several times to escape from—he said to me: "We know at present quite as much as is necessary, and perhaps more. If you wish, I will not reply tomorrow, but will wait until the day after; if you have something more to say, you will have the chance to say it."

We rejoined my mother, who was having tea in front of the house. I was hot, my heart was beating; I ran in to change my clothes, I returned. But a young girl from my uncle's household had come to interrupt our emotion-laden silence with her small talk; I could stand it no longer, and went up into my room. My father, tenderly anxious, came to look for me immediately; he found me half-reclining on my bed, with a volume of Voltaire in my hand. He spoke to me with great kindness about the turmoil that this conversation might have caused me, about the upset ...

"Perhaps you would rather talk about this some more, and more calmly?" ... I said that it didn't matter, that the upset didn't amount to anything, that I was not so frail; that I was vexed, and necessarily so, at seeing the failure of an opportunity so exactly suited to me—one that was unique, that would not come again, that promised me the pleasantest life, the happiest future. The fortune will be enough for me, all my tastes will be satisfied; I know the country and I love it, its inhabitants are cheerful and good-natured; it will be so easy for me to be loved by them; the Marquis's sister is spoken of only with admiration; what can one hope or even imagine that might be better? What society could be more amiable? In what situation in the world would I be better placed for my happiness and my duties?

1. The reconciliation of the Catholic and Protestant churches.

My father listened with a sort of approval and sensitivity. "I too can imagine this picture," he said. "My imagination does not run wild, it's not given to romantic fancy," I added. "Here is what it has shown me about all the marriages suggested to me so far: see whether these pictures are not accurate." And thereupon I drew for him five or six, all of them striking, in which no trait, good or bad, was forgotten. "A motive for you that is almost an objection for me in this business," I said, "is the obligation that I will impose on myself to justify the Marquis's choice, my own choice, and your indulgence in such an extraordinary thing, by the most irreproachable and the most generous conduct that my heart makes me capable of. My obligations will be greater than they would be in any other marriage; I will want you to applaud yourself for having to such an extent acceded to your tenderness for me. I will do everything I can so that the Catholics will not blame the Marquis and the Protestants will approve of you. My task will be difficult, but I do not despair of fulfilling it. And what will people dare to say when they see me return to your house to visit with my husband—him content, myself happy, and still your daughter, loved by you, respected by all those who come near me ... Believe me, my dear father, the speechifiers would find nobody to listen to them. People would approve of you for having known me so well, for having loved me, for having let my own liking decide the most important thing in my life ..."

I took advantage of the mood I had put him in to undermine his principal objection; I acknowledged the possibilities, but I showed him that all the probabilities were in my favor, and that in things of this nature one could only act on probabilities. "It would be possible," I said, "for Monsieur and Mme de Perponcher and their two daughters and younger son to have all the power in my brother-in-law's house, and for my sister always to be contradicted and very unhappy. Were you afraid of that? Did you think about it?"

My father would have liked to yield; he said: "That's enough for today," in a gentle, uncertain, affectionate tone. I remained lying down. My mother came in shortly after. She thought I was ill, and came intending to help me; but when she found me well, calm, hopeful-looking, she hardened, and after a long silence—which unfortunately I undertook to break—she spoke to me harshly. When she saw me weep, she was sorry; but I see that I had been wrong about her that first day.

That's where we are now. I will still do everything I can; if nothing succeeds for me, it's because my father and mother cannot consent except by failing in their own principles and impairing their own happiness; in that case I must no longer desire success. From this point on, for me to try to contrive with you any new tactics would be unworthy in a way that you would not like to think me capable of. That is finished. If you or the Marquis want to try something now or at some point in the future, you are free to do so; but I can no longer be involved.

If they refuse my request, at least I will have more freedom, and I promise you that whatever it costs, I will go to spend some time with my sister at the beginning of winter.

To show some of your letters, to admit our correspondence, would be a bold attack; the danger of it frightens me, but the hope of its success may perhaps tempt me. To demand the freedom of a married woman—the freedom to go when I wish to the Hague, to Amsterdam, to England and to Paris when the occasion arises—for that, I have already laid the groundwork, and from that I can expect something. Goodbye.

122. *From Constant d'Hermenches, August 11, 1764*

If these were details from a novel only half as well-written, I would still read them avidly; judge the effect on me of things that concern the person in the universe closest to my heart! Put aside the most engaging style that I know, and reflections whose truth strikes me on every page ... Far from imagining that anything that comes from you could have the slightest relation to boredom, if you really understand you must see me in a continual state of enthusiasm—speechless with amazement. You must never go to the unnecessary trouble of explaining, justifying your expressions, your avowals, your thoughts. Your letters are my sole recreation, they charm away all my griefs and woes—and I assure you that I have a great many of them. Why, then, waste a single stroke of your pen to speak of boredom? That is a word that must be banished from the lexicon of all those who have the good fortune of having some connection with you.

If I did not completely trust your judgment I would criticize your having mentioning our correspondence to your mother. I would also have wished you to wait for your father's decision—I think it would have been more advantageous for you. I cannot imagine that, fundamentally, this marriage would not be to his liking—especially at a moment when the Count of Anhalt is conducting himself so strangely, and seeing that your parents were already accustomed to the idea of your living far from them. As for Scotland, I tremble at the very idea. It is a wilderness; a land of ferocious customs, where I would never allow the most wretched of beings that I cared anything about to go. But, after all, given the key in which the overture has been pitched, I gladly leave it up to you to sustain the modulation to the end: it is touching and majestic, and everything that you have been good enough to report to me of your private conversations instills in me the greatest veneration for the tone and character of your household.

It seems to me that you could easily propose that I be invited to come see you to discuss in person a matter so important to the rest of your life; and you can count on my presenting myself in a way that will not be at all discordant. As for the controversy concerning child-rearing and sectarian prejudices, you are pushing yourself to anticipate much more than you need to do; you will be able to raise your family as you wish without any opposition, and you have nothing to fear from the disapproval of others. Bellegarde and his sister spend their lives among Genevans; they don't believe that those who pray to God in French are heretics; and they would send away at once any priest, servant, or relative who would attach the slightest distinction to the difference of religion in a household whose soul and sovereign you would be. I will inform your family of this at the first opportunity.

I adore what you say about doctrinaire libertines; I am their exact antipodes, and it is always my wish to draw some good for society even from licentiousness and frailty. If one is not chaste, one should at least be decorous; if not virtuous, one should be humble; if one has no honor, one should at least have civility. You put me in the dock for what I said about equity, and I think you do it quite unjustly. There is a difference between robbing a man because he is a thief and having no scruples about winning a hundred louis from our friend at the gaming table when we know that he is resolved to win the same from us. When I see that someone whom I'm duelling with is afraid of killing me, I only aim at his arm; but if he approaches with elbow bent and aims at my body, the sort of equity that I am talking about does not prevent me from piercing him if I can.

Twickel was at my place this morning; he had a great deal to say to me about marriages and households; he told me that he didn't want a woman more intelligent than he. He would like to marry your cousin,[1] but he says that she drinks eleven glasses of beer a day. This conversation followed strangely upon the reading of your letter. I am at your feet, adorable Agnes.

123. *To Constant d'Hermenches, August 13-14, 1764*

Tuesday morning

Truly, I am as touched by your tender and flattering remarks as if they were all new to me—as if you were feeling them for the first time.

I cannot continue recounting the details today; I only want to tell you that I am alive, that I am well, that things have changed a little, that I will not get to the point of showing your letters—that is, not even the least word of your letters, for to show them entire has never entered my mind—, and, finally, that it is not yet impossible that I may belong to Monsieur de Bellegarde.

You are right to admire my father. There is no man in the world whose probity, equity, and moderation I respect more. I have never seen in anyone such a perfect equanimity of soul. Vexation, pleasure, anger, tenderness

---

1. Anna Elisabeth van Tuyll van Serooskerken (Annebetje).

never change anything in his conduct, never influence his decisions. And this heroic impartiality is not accompanied by the stiff-necked pride that so often goes along with it; no display, not a word that might announce what he is. Sully[1] took pleasure in using rigorous condemnations, and loud and haughty pronouncements, to show off his stubborn and magnanimous virtue. My father, on the contrary, seems so modest and gentle that one is always surprised to find him so firm.

As for my mother, equally generous and more impetuous, she sometimes forgets how much she loves her daughter; but she does not forget it for long, and she never forgets that she must keep my secret, and that one must be just and true. The Roman matrons of Rome's finest days were not more virtuous, nor, for the essential things, had they more grandeur.

She had spoken to me a long time ago about our correspondence; therefore I was risking nothing in what I did—I no longer had her indignation to fear, and I could win her to my side by my honesty. My dear father, who is very attentive to things in themselves, pays little attention to the manner of them; I assure you that so far I have made no blunder.

The eleven glasses of beer made me laugh, because my cousin doesn't care whether Twickel is counting two or twenty; but nothing is more untrue. It is true that she eats and drinks more than is fitting for a beautiful demoiselle; I have begged her to change her diet for the sake of her health and her complexion. She is doing it; she writes me that she is also sleeping less than usual, in order to preserve the habit of mental activity she had acquired when she was with me; at my entreaty, she reads aloud and recites verses to learn to articulate. This deference to my advice touches me all the more because my aunt—who for other reasons cannot bear either me or my sister—makes fun of it continually and ridicules her docility. Monsieur van Twickel does as the fox does:

They are too green, said he.[2]

He would have wanted her, in spite of the beer, if my uncle had not declared that he would never tolerate this marriage. But if he must have a wife who is his inferior, then she is not for him. She has, I think, quite as much intellect, and a hundred times more character—a noble and firm heart. Her mind is not much cultivated; however, she makes distinctions between the good and the better with as much discernment as the connoisseurs, but with more eagerness. Her impressions, her thoughts, her utterances—they are all original, all her own. She writes and speaks not well, but sometimes with an astonishing energy, and always in a way that reveals integrity and a beautiful soul. One would think that I am forgetting everything in the pleasure of depicting—no, no, I am forgetting nothing.

1. The duc de Sully (1560–1641), fellow soldier and minister of Henri IV of France.
2. In La Fontaine's fable "The Fox and the Grapes."

124. *To Constant d'Hermenches, August 15–16, 1764*

Wednesday

After attentively reading the letter I received from you yesterday, I tore it up; it's the first, I think, to have met with that fate. You mustn't think that it was out of ill-humor; but it seemed to me that I should not put it in my pocket. My main reason was that I could die today, and I wouldn't have wanted for anything in the world to have it found after my death in my writing case. I would rather be suspected of all the frailties of love than of causing your unjust harshness toward my parents. Yes, it is unjust; and if it is my fault that you have misjudged them, I am guilty. I might be discontent with my lot, but I had nothing to reproach them with; they follow their ideas as I do my own; they follow their principles as I follow my likings.

You cannot, Monsieur, be astonished at their reluctance; although this century is enlightened, these marriages are nonetheless no more common than they were. In our whole country, among the people of some position, you would not find a single father more disposed than mine is to accept such a proposition. Mme Geelvinck is her own mistress; if she spoke of marrying a Roman Catholic she would only be answered by insults, and if she were to marry him, I am sure that she would never appear again before her relatives ... Ah! do not think that I have been won over, changed, contented; no— but even in distress, one must be just; I must let neither my father nor my mother be accused of wrongs they have not committed. My mother has not tried to outwit me; I misunderstood her at first, and that was my fault. She is brusque, but sincere; the distress she caused me on Friday came merely from a mood. When she speaks while she is angry, it comes out in short sentences at intervals, which become stronger and harsher until they offend or wound. Then the ill-humor ceases; her heart is moved, and, in repentance, she tries to soften, to efface the damage done by the harsh tones and the scornful words.

If grief and discontent are, as you believe, capable of producing some effect, then I have reason to hope. I am in an inconceivable state of exhaustion, languor, sadness; I have no need to dissemble anything in this respect. An hour ago I could neither hear nor think at all, and could find not a single word to reply to my mother; but I think I've somewhat recovered now, and by means of the coffee I'm about to drink, I will be able to tell you everything you don't know. Whether I recount them well or badly, you will like my details because they come from me. —But I am beginning too sadly; one would think that everything is finished for good, impossible; and that is not the case.

My accounts have gotten up to Friday evening. On the Saturday morning I wrote to you, I hardly left my room. At table, not a word was spoken; I took a walk with my mother without speaking; I was annoyed and displeased, and I didn't hide it. My father came into my room that evening; he said to me; "I wish to reply to Monsieur d'Hermenches. I can say nothing either for myself or for your mother except that the obstacle of religion cannot be compensated for by any advantage, and thus we have no need of further information. But you are not of the same opinion; I can say that, and I can request on your behalf the information that is being offered. Thus you can see whether the match suits you, whether the advantages outweigh the difficulties; in a year and a few months, you will have reached your majority, and will no longer need our consent."

I answered that I was quite willing to have it known what I thought of this affair; and that he could say whatever he wished about it; that I had not yet thought about the use that I could make of the liberty to determine my own future; that I would perhaps take advantage of it (just how, I did not know); but that surely it would be a hundred times pleasanter for me to marry with his consent, and, when I married, to be regarded as his daughter, rather than as a stranger.

"Who knows," I said "whether the Marquis would even want me under those circumstances? Everything would change. I would have no right to expect to be treated like your other children as to my fortune; equity would no longer impose any obligations upon you; it would be pure grace ..." My father said that in that respect there was never any obligation for parents, and he gave me to understand that if I took advantage of my rights to marry without consent, my fortune would not suffer for it. We spoke a while longer, very calmly; I said that the idea of seeing myself solely responsible for my choice, my future, did not frighten me at all, but rather that I preferred that, starting now, he let me decide it: that would make my position more graceful, and would amount to the same thing for him.

"If you were to let me marry at present," I said to him, "you could reply to those who criticized you: 'My daughter wished it.' If I had reached my majority, people would still condemn you, and if you say: 'My daughter wished it, she was free to do as she pleased,' the zealots would say to you: 'you should have given her nothing, and disinherited her forever.' So it is simply a question of knowing whether the first of these choices is contrary to your principles, contrary to what you believe your duty to be. It seems to me that it cannot be contrary, but you alone, my dear father, can judge that. God keep me from engaging you to a thing that you could some day reproach yourself for; but be so good as to examine that question again." He said that he was willing to do so.

Supper was fairly cheerful, our minds fairly free. I reproached myself for my own discontent, I said to myself: they are doing what they can. On Sunday we spoke of none of this. I went piously to church; the minister got himself so thoroughly entangled in a definition of faith that mine was not at all enlightened by it, nor my heart more attached to our sermons.

Monday, not a word about our marriage; I set my hopes on my father's reflections; I wrote to you without recounting our last conversation, hoping to be able soon to tell you something pleasanter. Yesterday morning, I finished this letter, which I wanted to carry into town. While we were having lunch, my father renewed the request that he had made Saturday that I put in writing what I was thinking, so that he could the better write it in his own letter. He had always supposed that the difference of religion was a difficulty for me as well as for him, and that it was only a question of degree. I believed that my good faith required that he know the truth. I told him that at a time when I was sad, overwhelmed by the vapors, my mind full of the most disturbing doubts about religion, I had sometimes said that I found Roman Catholics very fortunate to be obliged to be ignorant, to have an unquestioning faith in the Church and their curé; that this feeling of their security—their peace of mind on thorny, unresolvable questions—would put me at my ease with them; that I would share their peace of mind ... I reminded him of those things that I had said in the past, and I told him that I still had something of that feeling. He thought that, simply, I didn't like to hear obscure points of religion argued about or even discussed. I explained to him that it wasn't that; that in our church, where each person is required to instruct himself, it pleased me no more than it did him to see indifferent, negligent people who would one day reproach themselves for their ignorance. At that point, someone came in and the conversation ended.

We went to Utrecht; my father was more pensive in the carriage than I had ever seen him. I was given your letter;[1] I did not find it strange, but unjust; I found that it was permissible for you to judge my parents more or less as you did, but that it was not permissible for me to tolerate patiently these condemnation, and I meditated with some impatience the response that would justify them. We returned to Zuylen (I seem like an old crone of a story-teller with all my exact circumstances, but I no longer dare excuse myself to you, nor suspect that I might weary you—you have so strongly forbidden it!).

We returned, then, and scarcely were we in the house when my father said to me: "What you said this morning has increased my anxiety; not by much it is true ..." I must admit that this caused me to despair. I tried to prove to him that he had not understood me, since his conclusion was so opposite to the one he should naturally have drawn; I showed him that all those ideas of mine came from an almost insurmountable disposition to doubt everything that was not absolutely evident; that I surely would not be persuaded by the least rational religion where I had not been persuaded by the most rational; that I would not sooner adopt contradictory opinions than obscure ones. That I could not even imagine a persuasion so entire, so complete, that it could make me leave the religion of my fathers, in which I had been raised; and that if unfortunately my doubts were to increase to the point of making the two religions equal and indistinguishable to me, still I would never change; that no self-interest, no notion of expedience, would commit me to

---

1. The one she tore up: see the beginning of this letter.

an action which seems so cowardly when self-interest is its motive. I begged
my father to conclude nothing based on a conversation that had been interrupted before I had more than half-way explained my position.

We dined in silence. Your letter appeared to me less unjust; I believed
that indeed, with my good faith and my ideas—just, fine (in my opinion)
and true, exactly true—however bizarre that they might appear—I was
wrecking everything; that neither my mind nor my heart were of any use in
furthering the success of an enterprise—in short, I was impatient, outraged,
despondent. I went up to my room immediately after dinner, and began to
write to my father. He came up a moment later to show me the draft of his
response; I read it, I put it down without saying a single word, and I continued to write. My father finally said to me: "I wanted to talk about your own
ideas, but I thought that it would weaken what I said about ours; tell me
what you think about this, because it is time to respond." "I no longer dare
speak," I said to him, "because I am afraid of harming my own case; but I
beg you not to send your letter until tomorrow." He consented, and left me.

At that moment I was hardly more just than you are. I continued to write,
and to be perfectly candid, come what may.[2] I declared point-blank that the
difference of religion was an obstacle for me only because it was one for my
father and mother; that far from my conscience being alarmed by this, it was
more at peace than it would be in a marriage with a man of my own religion; that, doubting practically everything, and yet finding myself obliged
to use what insight I had for the instructions of my children, I had always
been afraid to make of them very bad Protestants; that if, on the contrary, I
found that I did not have to instruct children who were to be Catholic, I
would be responsible only for the duties about which I had no doubt; that by
speaking reason to them and trying to inspire in them the love of virtue by
my example, I hoped to make of them Catholics who would be happier,
more tolerant, more enlightened, better Christians than they would have
been without me. I beseeched him not to retract the offer to leave me free
when I reached my majority, and to frame his answer in such a way that the
Marquis could still think of me without injury to an appropriate pride. I
made him the solemn promise he had seemed to desire on Saturday: not to
commit my word before either he permitted it or I reached the age of
twenty-five.

I promised him, if he were to give his consent at present, much more reg-
ularity in the observance of religion than I had shown heretofore and a conduct on my part that would not give rise to criticism. I protested against so
prompt a decision contrary to all my desires; I let it be understood that there
were also unpleasant consequences to fear from this refusal; I proposed to
decide nothing until he had the opportunity to speak to you at the Hague;
and I finished by saying that I presently believed that my future was being

2. The letter she wrote—the summary of which follows here—has not been found.

judged on the basis of possibilities that had no likelihood. My letter was eight pages long; it was as forceful and energetic as such a letter can be. I had refused to go for a walk; I had not wanted to budge from my room, and I was in such turmoil that my mother was frightened when she came to see me; but I maintained that I was very well, I gave her my letter for my father, and we remained silent for a long time.

Finally, at the first opportunity to speak, I uttered a thousand wild things that would have amused you in spite of our distress. It happens without fail, any time that I am chagrined; always, from the turmoil of my mind, from the fire in my head, a thousand bizarre ideas are born whose pell-mell course I cannot control, and which make me laugh in the midst of despair. I haven't seen that madness in anyone else; it is not, however, unique, for Richardson gives precisely the same character to the griefs of Lovelace.[3] Whether it is a kind of delirium that proves the greatest sensibility, or whether, on the contrary, it proves a flightiness that prevents my soul from ever being completely concentrated on a single object—that I will not undertake to determine at the moment. My dear mother, after listening to me for a long time, went on her way. I remained alone in the dark, stretched out on my bed; I would have wished that you, rather than my letters, lived in my writing case, and that I had only to open it to have a conversation with you—but on the condition that your faculties and your talents would confine themselves to hearing me and responding to me. Such as you are, and with your piratical ideas of equity, you would be a very dangerous guest.

I had got to that point when flashes of lightning illuminated my room; my sister, frightened by the thunder, came looking for company. I found it hard to persuade her that there was no more danger in the dark than there was in the midst of twenty candles. She sat beside my bed, and to distract her I had her tell me a story about Mademoiselle Bonne,[4] which she had just finished. But after all that, I was afraid of becoming really ill; my blood had mounted to my head, and I was so cold that I couldn't get warm; that didn't seem natural to me.

Fortunately, everything is back in order. This morning, my father looked so distressed that I was very touched. He complained of a few expressions in my letter that were too strong, in which I didn't seem to do justice to his good intentions. Later, he came to show me what he wanted to add to his letter. I did what I could to obtain yet more, but when I saw that he really could not grant more without thinking that he was failing in his duty, far from pressing him I assured him that I would not want to be happy at the

3. Lovelace is the arch-seducer in Samuel Richardson's *Clarissa, or The History of a Young Lady* (1747–48). It is interesting that Belle compares herself to him rather than to the novel's heroine.
4. A character who is a governess in the didactic novels of Jeanne-Marie Le Prince de Beaumont (1711–80), highly popular at the time.

expense of his happiness and peace of mind, and that he should not have a moment of remorse or repentance on my account; that I thanked him; that I would not commit myself.

Goodbye, d'Hermenches, I am out of paper.

Thursday morning

Thank God, my father and mother are in town, and I am free to write. After I went to bed I could no more sleep than I did when I was writing to you; however, my face did not betray me, I was not suspected of having stayed awake, or of having spent the night writing. That, at least, is a piece of luck.

I'm sure you find my confession of scepticism quite useless, quite out of place; you would like me to keep to myself the sort of tranquillity that I will be able to find in the midst of a Catholic people, and my sublimities concerning my children. You are right if you consider only what is politic; but was I to dictate to my father ideas that were not mine? Was I to have him write: *My daughter finds, as we do, that the difference of religion is an obstacle; it is not without difficulty that it could be resolved ... however ...*—when his daughter, at the bottom of her heart, finds no obstacle, and feels no difficulty? You would love me much the less if I considered only the outcome, and if I were so unscrupulous about the means of procuring it.

You wanted me to prevent my father from answering you himself; besides the fact that there was no time, and that he would not consent to my writing you for anything in the world, I don't know how I could have resolved to speak to you less honestly than I ordinarily do—to speak two different languages. At least, I would like my conduct to be such that if it came to be known, a completely impartial judge would not condemn me.

Have no fear that I might reveal our correspondence to them. The pain I suffer in assuming the bold language of frankness when it is not truly mine; the hope that they might find motives for consent in what you say, and find in my very faults reasons for my marrying—so they may be rid of the arduous care of my conduct—that's what made it occur to me; but I think that it is not a good idea after all, and since it troubles you, that is enough to make me give it up. You have rights as worthy of respect, perhaps, as those of my parents; your friendship and your services have earned them for you, and never, unless forced to it, will I risk making our commerce impossible, or breaking this bond that unites us and that you so love.

My God, I was in distress yesterday! We were talking, my father and I, about the answer he was to give. I proposed that he make it quite vague, and wait for the opportunity to talk with you. He said to me: "What would be the use of that? His letter contains all the strongest arguments; there is nothing to add; I would not be persuaded, but my ideas could be disarranged so that my response would be less clear." I proposed that in his expressions he leave some doubt concerning the immutability of his ideas and resolution, if only out of politeness and out of kindness for me, so that we might not appear too separate in our views, and so that one might see that I could one day marry the Marquis without quarreling with my parents and without being banished from the paternal house. He said that it was enough to refrain from saying that his reluctance was unchangeable and eternal; that for him to ask for information for me was enough proof of his moderation, and that it was all that he could do; that perhaps one day he would find that it is still too much ... "Then don't ask for it," I interrupted; "I'll obtain it when it's necessary, that is no more pressing than my marriage."

But he explained his motives to me: he wanted, if possible, to prevent your addressing yourself to me; he was still only too afraid of a correspondence between us, through which you would commit me to giving my word as of now, and which, besides seeming dangerous to him, would be improper according to his views. "You understand that perfectly well," he said. "Yes," I said, lowering my head, "but believe me, since I have promised you to remain free, nothing in the world would oblige me to give my word until I am free to give my heart and my hand." It seemed to me that he was going to speak again of you and of a correspondence. What should I have done? Should I have promised not to write to you? No; I would have wanted neither to break my promise nor to keep it. Could I refuse to do it if I had been asked? I would have refused, but God! what suspicions! what indignation! What would have become of me? —I thoroughly concealed my turmoil, and to bring the conversation to an end I left my room, a hundred times more wrought up than I can express.

My father hesitated about explaining the motive of his request for information. You could say: "What's the use, since he cannot overlook the obstacle of religion?" But he thinks that you will guess, or that at least you will think that it is not for nothing that he makes the request. Explaining himself further would perhaps also entail explaining himself on the question of my dowry, and that would be premature. His intention, he has said to me, was to make no distinction between my sister and me. If you ask him about it, he will not be surprised; he expects it, and will answer you.

You must admit that if this conduct is not bold and brilliant—if it is not such as, even while making small minds indignant, would arouse the admiration of genuinely reasonable people—at least it is honest, gentle and equitable. Here is, precisely, what determines it: my father finds that it is possible that I might change religion, or that, if I do not change it, I might be unhappy; and not wanting to be responsible for such an outcome, he refuses to give his consent. I told him that I did not want to remain unmarried. It is possible that no match will present itself that would please me as much and would be more suitable, and fearing all the other possibilities, he does not want to prevent this marriage forever; he does not want to go on being master by the control of my fortune when he will no longer be master by law. I told him yesterday that if he could be reproached for one thing, it was that, conducting himself by excellent rules, he neglected the just exceptions.

Well then, he doesn't intend to give an absolute refusal, and he has just told me as he was leaving that he would make his letter as polite as possible.

At present I think I have done everything I could do; to take further measures with you to alter a decision that I appeared to be content with would be contrary to probity, or at least to that precious scrupulousness which allows one to look into one's own heart with esteem and pleasure. If you want to try something more, you are free to do so, but it will be without me; I will merely support you by saying in good faith what I hope for. In the name of God, whatever you say, do not let them suspect that it was through me that you have learned of the objections in their full force. If you speak too well and with too much zeal, you will seem too well informed; press for nothing, leave something to time, to circumstances, and to my discontent, if it lasts.

Yesterday it had reached a pitch you cannot imagine; I walked all day, sometimes outdoors, sometimes in the house; in the evening I begged my mother, who was reading, to read aloud, but I didn't understand a syllable. I walked back and forth, and were it not for this movement, I would have doubted my own existence. My mother was greatly disturbed by this; she ran to find me in the house; she gently pointed out to me that she could not see the reason for this excessive sadness. I said to her, in my distress, that I was complaining of nothing; that, simply, I was exhausted and overwhelmed, and that I no longer had a single distinct thought. She wanted to have someone stay up to watch over me, but I refused; I wanted only coffee and a writing desk. My role was very difficult; and even if it had not taken its toll for me to appear always in need of explanations about things that had been explained long ago ... to seem in doubt when I was convinced ... to put into my discourse a warmth always calculated according to the effect it was supposed to produce, concerning insights that I was supposed to have and not those that in fact I had ... to put precise limits to the expression of my inclination ... to tell the truth without betraying my secret—even if there were not, in addition to all that, the turmoil of fear and hope, my role would still have been extremely trying. I still need to explain the promise that I made to my father, to remain free until I am allowed to marry, either by him or by my age. I will keep that promise inviolably, and I want the Marquis to be as free as I am.

If he has it in mind to marry a girl of twenty-three and not one of twenty-five; if he wants to see in his wife's parents, as in his wife herself, an unqualified joy; if he takes a liking to a more attractive woman; or if, consulting less his heart than the conventions, he wants one who is richer than I am; if he forgets me; if he learns something to my disadvantage; if his sister urges him to take a Catholic wife; if he loses the desire to get married—he has only to write to you on the instant, and you will tell me, and everything will be finished. He will not need a single reason to disengage himself—the slightest whim will suffice, and, far from being indignant, I will never speak of him except with respect; I will be interested all my life in his happiness, and I will always be flattered to have pleased him for a little while. If he marries me, I want him to be happy, to regret nothing, to prefer me to everything; I have no other ambition. On my part, it will be the same: I will be able to give him up, and to tell you so without appearing guilty and without incurring your reproaches. Thus the word given to my father will be kept. In fifteen months, if my father has in no way backed down from his resolution, and if I have not changed, I will write to you that I belong to the Marquis, if he still wants me; and at that point, let there be no delays, no dragging out of things, no preparations; wedding clothes, adornments will not slow down a thing. I will be his wife by my will alone, and I will make him, I hope, the happiest of husbands.

I would be happy to see him in the interval—at the Hague, for example, if I were to go there; but that should not disturb the least of his plans, nor give him the slightest trouble.

Have I said everything at last? What a letter! Don't expect another for several days; I must have some rest at night, and my mornings are not free when my father is here. He often stays all day in the country; I can then neither write freely nor send my messengers to carry my letters into town. Farewell; it is time to send off this one. The story is complete and finished. You have seen my heart in all its moments; see in it above all my friendship and my gratitude.

The Response from Monsieur de Tuyll to Constant d'Hermenches[5]

Zuylen, Thursday, August 16, 1764

Dear Sir,

The manner in which you have done me the honor of proposing your idea to me could only contribute to making it desirable, and it would have in itself some very favorable aspects if the matter of religion did not appear to us—to Madame de Zuylen and to me—an absolute obstacle.

We are far from harboring any bitterness against those who are of another religion than ours; nor do we think that one can put limits on God's goodness. But it is one thing to love tolerance and wish all people well, and quite another thing to consent to an alliance such as the one in question.

The judgment of absolute condemnation that Roman Catholics pass on any person who is not of their Church; the ensuing obligation to convert by various means; the fear that my daughter might be drawn sooner or later into error or hypocrisy; the remorse that could follow; the apprehension of domestic dissensions and vexations that she might have to endure if she does not yield—not necessarily on the part of her husband, but on the part of the ecclesiastics and other zealots who would be all around her; the chagrin of

5. This letter appears in *O.C.* as a note to Letter 124 (*O.C.* 1: 576, n. 4).

seeing her children raised in a convent or, in any case, in a religion so different in so many respects, and particularly in that intolerance which would make them believe their mother was damned; the effect that would produce; finally, the distrust that she would cause by wanting to give her own care to their upbringing, whatever good intentions she might have not to contravene any agreement—all that is too strong for us to consent that a daughter whom we cherish should run those risks.

To that must be added the fact that we would distress our whole family, and that we would be condemned by all those whom we esteem and respect.

I beg you, Sir, at least to excuse our reasons and our scruples to your friend, even if you cannot justify them; their basis is in the nature of circumstances that we do not control.

But in a little over a year, my daughter will be free to give her hand where she pleases. If toward that time, in the event that things remain as they are, you are able to send me information concerning the birth, the possessions, and the financial situation of your friend, I do not refuse to communicate them to my daughter (nor to provide whatever such information as would be necessary); after which, being sufficiently informed, she will be able to state her wishes.

Moreover, Sir, the marks of approbation throughout your letter can only be precious to me coming from a person as enlightened as yourself. It is with these sentiments and those of the greatest respect that I am, Sir, your very humble and obedient servant.

D. J. van Tuyll van Serooskerken

Zuylen, August 16, 1764

125. *From Constant d'Hermenches, August 17, 1764*

Friday, August 17

This coffee you always speak of drives me to despair; you will burn your blood—it makes me shudder. Take opium, sleep—don't even write at all; and bear in mind that it is better to be a live martyr than a dead marquise.[1]

I must begin by saying, my adorable friend, that I received no letter from you from Tuesday; the last is the one that I answered—see whether there is one missing.[2] I was terribly uneasy at seeing nothing from you all these mornings, and today I am in a state of turmoil.

I have just replied to your father; my sentences are a little long, which is always the case when I do not want to say the half of what I think. I believe, however, that I took the only suitable tack: to break nothing off, to embar-

1. D'Hermenches had first written "virgin" and then crossed it out and replaced it with "martyr." Belle will remark on this in Letter 127.
2. In Letter 127 of August 20, Belle reports the letter found. It is Letter 123 of August 14.

rass him a little, and not to compromise our little triumvirate. I have found nothing very civil or very flattering for me in this response; and yet I deserved some consideration—for what motive can be ascribed to me? You are not a millionairess, so I can hardly be suspected of seeking what is called a good bargain for my friend; and one ought always to be pleased when a highly acceptable man thinks about one's daughter. At any rate, insist on seeing my letter, and advise me as to what can be done. I shall not write anything yet to the Marquis; he is waiting for my response quite peaceably while I am turning myself inside out to plead his cause, and that irritates me; but such is his character. If I tell him that he can come forward in fifteen months, he will doubtless think that that period of time has to do with the Count d'Anhalt; it is better to let him thrash about, and then steer him according to circumstances.

As for you, follow my maxim; I take all measures to succeed in what I think is to my advantage; but I believe in destiny, and I do not torment myself at all if I fail. Your tone of distress was good as a strategy, but as a feeling, get rid of it immediately, and do not waste a minute of your beautiful life in vain regrets. You are so young, and you use your time so well, that the future cannot fail to offer you a variety of pleasing prospects. But it does seem to me that you should be able to ease the chains of the paternal household, and I do not think that at your age, and having your letters patent as a genius, you can be forbidden to write to such-and-such a person, nor that you should be obliged by your scruples to reply to any questions on that head.

I have no other resentment against your parents except what is aroused by opposition to one's desire. If they really think that you will be converted, I cannot blame them; but then I blame you for having put too much metaphysics into this business—and believe me, metaphysics is a great poison in this material world! You ought simply to have said: "I will let myself be burned rather than change religion; if I marry a Catholic, it will be absolutely necessary that he think as I do on such-and-such points; he will have to give me such-and-such an assurance, I will take such-and-such a precaution. If he likes me, he will consent; if he doesn't like me enough, I don't want any of this." I am sure that your family would have been much less anxious; and if there is some casuist in your family, he would have decided that this marriage could redound to the greater glory of God, and that it must take place. It is quite certain that Bellegarde is absolutely not at all Catholic, nor is his sister; so as I have told you since my first letter, everyone—and you above all—are getting hung up on imaginary snags.

I am still of the opinion that you should ask permission to write to me, or say that you have written me: this matter concerns you too closely for that not to be permitted. And if they are unjust enough to regard me as a man suspect, with whom you are exposing yourself to risk, then—on account of that injustice—they do not deserve to be treated with consideration.

Don't you also think, Agnes, that they are playing for time, to see what the Count of Anhalt will do? In all this there are things in which I find so many disparities that it affects my whole way of thinking about them; they would let you go to Brandenburg ... to Scotland ... and they do not want a man who serves in this country; one would say that they do not love you! At other times there is such a sensitivity in the liberty that they promise you ... If I have used terms that have displeased you in one of my letters, pardon me for them; my trust, my abandon with you is such that even without my carefully grooming my expressions, I always expect that you will give them their true sense; and the surest key is the truth, the desire to please you, and the passion for being useful to you. Write to me still—that's essential to me ...

... but no coffee, I beg you on my knees!

126. *To Constant d'Hermenches, August 17–19, 1764*

Friday evening

Good evening. I am sad and tranquil—in a mood for talking with friends. I would give anything to dare write to you, but my mother's chambermaid told me yesterday that all my friends together were not worth the health that I would ruin for them; that I must sleep, that I was getting too thin; finally, she made me promise that for two weeks I would be in bed at eleven-thirty. I have just sent my German girl[1] to see what is the precise minute by the clock; she says that I have not a moment to lose to get undressed. I do not want to break my promises; I respect the feeling that makes them so dear to a woman of that kind. I take pleasure in banishing the signs of a chilly deference, and in replacing it all around me by love and love's care. Except for the girl who serves me, I command no one in this house; I have never wished to take on the least authority, but for my sake, they would betray my father and mother. Goodnight; I am not boasting—I am sharing with you a feeling that occupies me just now, and that pleases me. I impatiently await a letter from you. —In fact, the clock has just struck eleven-thirty.

Saturday morning

We were speaking yesterday of deference; I was saying that I banished it—that its chilly submissiveness was a burden to me compared with the lively, animated attentions of affection. In my heart, that is always true; I have no interest in being deferred to. I want people to grant me much without thinking that they owe me anything; I do not want to impose, I want to please. Boswell thought that was very bad. He preferred to see me wearing a big hoop, with a long dress, lace dangling from my headdress, looking very serious, and holding my smile in check until people drew near—rather than

---

1. Belle's chambermaid Dorothea Phlügerin (Dortie).

in short skirts, looking free and merry. "How can you possibly," he said "neglect making yourself respected when it would be so easy! Instead of always trying to be friendly, why don't you make people wait a little while before you consent to be amiable, to please, to entertain, to give yourself over to the company; and then, after some period of freedom, resume a tone of reserve. Save all those wild things that you say to anyone who will listen, and that are not understood, or are misinterpreted—save them for me, your friend—say them in English. You should have more consideration for the jealousies of friendship; you should feel that it desires some privileges, and that it is offended at seeing everyone treated the same way ... Everyone is at ease with you! That is terrible! People so unworthy of being at ease with you!"

I find, however, that he is partly right; and if I were not afraid of seeming ridiculously affected, and still more afraid of being tormented by constraint, I would perhaps try. You must see how his idea fits with his character. He respects humanity; he wants those who honor it to be distinguished, and receive homage; he likes to have virtue announce itself by an imposing exterior, and to have whatever accompanies it take on an air of grandeur which would subdue the vulgar in advance. The austerity of his morals does not make him condemn the pleasures of a lively imagination, or free conversation; but he wants them to be taken as recreation; he wants me to relax with *him*, to amuse myself, as a prince among his favorites forgets the purple and the power. Obdam, on the other hand, said to me the other day, "Oh, drop that air of gravity that you always assume whenever you walk into a room; don't go to so much trouble to spoil your expression even for an instant; trust that if people love you a great deal, they will always respect you enough."

Something beyond just the difference in character makes what is an agreeable sentiment for one a burden for the other; what makes their judgments so opposite comes down to their amour propre. Boswell can take pleasure in advance in a respect that he counts on attaining some day; Obdam can have no pretentions but to be amiable.

Sunday evening

What I wrote yesterday and the day before just to give myself the pleasure of speaking to you does not have the grace of aptness; however, I don't want to tear it up; these are ideas that have amused me, that will perhaps amuse you; and I have no other sheet of paper in this room.

You accuse me—and me above all—of *getting hung up on imaginary snags*. Either you have a bad memory, or you are in a very bad mood. I asked you only one thing: Will my children, if I have any, be left with me? Will I be able to raise them without a convent, without priests? You answered me: "Yes, you will be able to." I was satisfied. Then you suggested the need for yet more precautions, by speaking of the resources that there were for children in Catholic countries: I said that I didn't want my daughters to be nuns, nor my sons priests—the former unhappy, the latter perjuring themselves with absurd vows. Did I say anything else? Perhaps my imagination has given itself over to useless picturings, but only on these two subjects, and only because of an active mind rather than a feeling of fear. Where are those *imaginary snags*? Except for the the children I've spoken of, I see nothing that might seem to be imaginary in all this. When I received your answers on these two points, I made no objections, had no fears; I see no obstacle; I foresee only pleasures. I said to my father, exactly as you wished: "Let us obtain assurances on that point; let us require some promises. A request is being made of us; we are allowed to set some conditions, and to grant only according to these conditions. If they don't suit the marquis, he has only to say so, but then I will not be his wife."

127. *To Constant d'Hermenches, August 18–20, 1764*

Saturday evening

And you, you vex me too! I would like to see you for just a half an hour, not to say a word of friendship to you—I wouldn't even give you my hand, I think, if we were alone together; I would scold you. I would tell you that some of your orders are utterly impractical and contradictory— that there are things that burn my blood quite as much as the strongest coffee. *You* can say whatever you wish, you are master of your own actions; you cannot even imagine what dependence is like. *No more coffee*, you say, *I shudder; get some sleep;* and then, *Write: that is essential to me* —as if I could freely choose among all the hours of the day. One thing, however, did amuse me: you say *It is better to live as a virgin* ... —and then you strike out "virgin" to put "martyr" in its place, as if the two things were just about synonymous. You may not be so wrong at that; your blunder broke up the course of my ill humor by making me laugh.

Well, then—it is better to live a virgin *or* a martyr, as tranquilly as one can, than to restart a useless hubbub ... restart it? Redouble it! Inflame people's minds! Embitter them! Alienate them—by admitting our correspondence, or by insisting that I be allowed to continue it. Once more, I repeat, they would never permit it. If, in the heat of discussion, I had been willing to take the greatest risks, I could have said: "I know more than you think I do; Monsieur d'Hermenches, with whom I have been corresponding for two years, has given me all the information I asked for ... Listen, I will read you a portion of his letters; but above all, do not take them from me ... Bear in mind that since I write to him in spite of your forbidding it, since I have confided in a man I did not know, since I have in all things a firm and decided will that is mine alone, that has yielded neither to upbringing nor to convention, it is better to let me marry according to my fancy, lest fancies take me that would please you even less ..."

Perhaps that wouldn't have done a great deal of harm, but at present it can no longer do the slightest good; I would quite uselessly disturb the peace that is beginning to be restored; I would render you suspect, and make myself almost odious. The prejudices that accompany virtues are strong in virtuous people.

After supper

This evening, two hours ago, if someone had spoken—you, the Marquis, someone other than myself—who knows what we might have accomplished? My father came into my room and said to me: "I already have Monsieur d'Hermenches' response; it seems to me that he took my thought very well." "May I read the letter?" I said. "But it's so flattering." "Oh, what does it matter, I've been praised before." He gave it to me. "Read it aloud," he said. I read it well, in a merry, laughing voice.[1] "*For the present*," my father repeated, seeming pleased also, as if he were glad that the refusal was only for the moment. "Now admit," I said to him, in a free and cajoling manner, "admit that if you could manage a truce in your arguments with yourself, you wouldn't really be sorry?" "Ah!" he answered, "I don't know enough about all this, and truly, I would fear the consequences . . ." "That I might change religion? —Surely you see that it's simply not possible; it would never happen." He said little in reply, and still seemed cheerful. A word from the Marquis, if he had been there, who knows . . . But has a girl ever before been required to perform miracles all by herself to get a husband? Goodbye, I'm going to bed.

Sunday

I'm really very pleased that the Marquis is a great lord—for *his* sake, and for his wife's, whoever she may be; but just now, for the matter at hand, it would be much more convenient for me if he were a younger son, without châteaux or title, and if he commanded only a company instead of a regiment. Then he would be heard to say, "I love her. Give her to me quickly or I may just take her. Don't reflect too long about the upbringing of our children . . ." Everybody would see that he was in love, and that I was only *somewhat* severe. If he tried to see me alone, no one would suspect that it would be to talk about either the Pope or Calvin.

It's lucky that the fine decorum in which the so-called damsels of high birth wrap themselves touches me not at all. But *you*—not satisfied with what I do that causes me no scruples or reluctance, you want to commit me to doing more than I think I should, and you use an ill-chosen stratagem: according to you, if you tell the Marquis that he can present himself in fifteen months, he will think that this period of time has some connection with the Count of Anhalt. Ah, no! He certainly will not. When I say that I was born

1. This is not the letter of which Belle was the ghostwriter but d'Hermenches' response to Belle's father's response to it.

October 20, 1740, he will see that the period of fifteen months pertains only to me.

No one in this house has ever been concerned in the least with the Count of Anhalt except me; at a time when I was dreadfully bored, that proposition was put to me in the most flattering, the most dazzling way imaginable. The King, who was in a better humor then than now, and who was struck by the reports of Catt,[2] hoped to see me at his court; I have even learned that before the Count's designs were known, there was another suitor whom the King thought of sending to me. I saw letters from the mother, the sisters, the friends of Monsieur d'Anhalt: I was a divinity whom men wanted to see descend from heaven (that is to say, Utrecht) to dwell among them. His Majesty has had some misfortune, and apparently no longer cares to be entertained; the Count believes, perhaps, that a divinity who's a *bel esprit* would not suit him. For myself, I got a look at his letters; I got a look at some Germans; I was less bored at home—and so the Count's behavior grieved me not at all. Since the matter was indifferent to me, and I am not at all proud, I was not even vexed; many people spoke to me about it, and I only laughed. My mother wanted to break everything off; I begged her to let the affair go along at its own pace. I am convinced that if the Count were to come, he would go back alone; but if we wish it, he will not come at all, and I think that he would be obliged to me for having extricated him; it would cost me merely a word to my father. Rest assured that that matter will in no way harm this one. The tyranny of the master, the corruption of the court, have always appalled a man who has a heart both virtuous and republican.[3]

My mother has always shuddered and wept at the thought of my going so far away. Too often—and again today—we quarrel, she is angry, she won't look at me; but she loves me; I am the cause of her griefs sometimes, but also of her consolations, her joys, her amusement; she cannot live without her daughter except at the price of boredom and languor. For her, I am like those favorites of great lords, who can take liberties that are pleasing twenty times, and are displeasing on the twenty-first. They fall into disgrace, but they are called back, because one cannot do without them. If I marry the Marquis, once the first upset has died down, I think that it will simply be up to us to come as often and to stay as long as we would like. I would prefer to marry now rather than a year from now; but if that cannot be, what consoles me is the thought that before leaving them, before causing them a kind of grief, I will be able to have my parents spend another pleasant year, and to have for another year their happiness as my first concern.

Really, I wonder at your touchiness! To scan my father's letter for compliments or expressions of thanks! To waste your time proving to me that

2. Henri-Alexandre de Catt (1725–95) had been a tutor to Belle's brothers. He later became lector at the court of Frederick the Great.
3. "The master" is Frederick. By "a man" Belle specifically means her father.

you deserve them! You deserve a great deal from *me*, for it is *I* whom you are trying to oblige. But if it was your design to win the gratitude of my father and mother, you should have told me. I would have warned you that not loving me, not writing to me, not giving me a Roman Catholic for a husband, but rather leaving me alone in my ancestral castle was the best thing you could do. My father, who is the coolest, the most circumspect, the most sincere of men, will never be other than coolly polite with those whom he hardly knows, and will never show himself grateful for something that does not yet please him.

Your letter of yesterday pleased him as much as any letter on this subject could. It's very good; I reread twice the passage about a Countess de Belle-garde who was Protestant; that is factual proof.[4] The passage in which you said that if there were any risk of a change of religion, it would be on the part of the Marquis—that flattered and amused him. He is pleased when someone makes him perceive that I am worth a little more than another; otherwise, he is hardly aware of it. My letters patent as a genius have never been produced before his eyes; genius, supposing that it exists, nearly always goes about incognito in the paternal household, and indeed they often find me much too proud. They require of me all the humility of a very ordinary person, and they are right: who asked me to be a genius? It carries no obligations, and gives me no sort of privilege; it only increases the number of causes for anxiety. They see that I do not care at all about public esteem, that I may perhaps aspire to fame, and that I love pleasure ... They tremble. But, precisely, they value me enough not to be surprised or dazzled by any suitor; besides, they do not overrate grandeur. The idea of my becoming Countess of Anhalt did not give them the slightest gratification; there was talk of restoring to the counts of Anhalt the title of prince, and that would have displeased them greatly. A rank in my own country, upheld with intelligence and with the éclat that a fortune gives—that would have flattered them. They would have taken pride in seeing me the greatest lady in my own country and the most amiable, doing the honors and giving the rank distinction; patriotism entered into it as much as vanity. Yet I was only allowed a glimpse of that feeling, and they would not have taken a single step for that marriage, which would have pleased people, and which was somewhat desired by Monsieur and Madame de ... guess, for I do not trust the post.[5] Besides, it is impossible, this marriage, and it is not an obstacle.

---

4. Marie-Aurore, Comtesse Rutowska, was the legitimized daughter of August II, king of Poland, elector of Saxony, and of the comtesse Aurore de Koenigsmark. But d'Hermenches is wrong: she was not Protestant.

5. The prince of Orange, Willem V, was in search of a wife; various foreign princesses were considered as brides for him, but there was also talk of his marrying a girl of the Dutch nobility. It seems likely that the count and countess of Degenfeld-Nassau put forth Belle's name. The prince married a Prussian princess, the niece of Frederick the Great, in 1767. Years later, in 1781, he is reported to have remarked: "Could one ever have thought that the daughter of Monsieur van Zuylen would marry Monsieur de Charrière?" (*O.C.* 1: 578, n. 1).

To tell the Marquis that he may ask for my hand again in fifteen months—that's not at all the thing to do. Without needing to come forward himself, he will know from me whether I still want to be his wife; and supposing that he still wants to be my husband, he will be. Everything will be seen to and arranged; all that will be left will be the ceremony. For myself, thank God, I have no need to maintain the reserve due to a title; I am, by birth, far beneath a certain ugly creature, a German canoness, who came here yesterday: she has sixteen quarters, she is a countess, people call her Madame; she is fortunate indeed if the name keeps her from being a martyr, for a virgin she will be eternally, I think. As to fortune, there are a hundred thousand girls who have more than I do; thus, when I give myself, it should be unpretentiously. Are you afraid, perhaps, that the Marquis no longer cares about me? Well, then, he will take another; he will find much better matches. If you want to try to persuade my father right now, it's up to you; but truly, I don't know whether I can meddle in it further without crime or shame.

Soon, you can write to say that you have letters from your friend; that he offers all possible assurances for my conscience; that he says that to raise these objections is not to know him; that priests are powerless in his household, although he respects their ministry, etc. Send one of his letters; in it, have him speak of his aunt—of how she was treated, and that I would be treated just the same way; that I would be happy and tranquil; that he would see to it that no one dared torment the woman he loved. If he can do it without compromising himself, have him write me; have him say: "I am not requesting any response from you just yet, but I beg you to tell your father that the friend of Monsieur d'Hermenches does not think that you are damned; that no one and nothing would disturb your peace of mind, nor attack your beliefs ..." If that cannot be done, come to see us in a while, but if a somewhat chilly reception would put you off, do not come; leave me a virgin. That's all I know about the matter.

My father leaves tomorrow for Arnhem; I will have more freedom during the week he's away. I may write you tomorrow; it is one o'clock, we are expecting a large company for dinner, and I must get dressed. Farewell, farewell—I would give you my hand; how do you tell a man that you love him, when he is neither a lover nor merely an old friend?

Monday morning

Myself, I do not believe in destiny; so in something of great importance to me, I would be extremely vexed not to have employed the best of means to arrive at my goal. If indeed "metaphysics" had harmed my case, I would have been very angry at it and at myself; but really, I have no reason to reproach myself. *I would let myself be burned rather than change* ... Since neither is that true nor is it in my style, it would not have made the slightest impression. I have asked myself a thousand times about Henry IV—whether he didn't in fact do quite the right thing in going to Mass.[6] And then, everybody knows that the mood to be a martyr no more lasts forever than the mood to be a virgin—supposing that one *is* sometimes in such a mood.

If I were dealing with people devoid of good sense, infatuated with titles and grandeur, I would have said: "What a pleasure it will be for you to address letters to me! To say as often as you please: 'My daughter the Marquise!'" If my parents were fanatic bigots, I could have said: "It is evident that God calls me to convert all the Savoyards, from the high nobility down to a little boy carrying a marmot or cleaning shoes.[7] How many souls won for Heaven and for Calvin!" But since my parents are people who reason, one must reason with them; since they raised objections, I had to reply. Were it not for my arguments and all the efforts of my eloquence, they would not have left room to reconsider the matter when I reach my majority; they would not themselves have reminded me that I would then be free to do as I wish.

I assure you that no one is thinking of the Count of Anhalt. I wish that it were indeed to play for time that they are putting things off. A firm declaration on my part never to marry him would wrap things up, but that affair is regarded as finished and quite unimportant.

You are free to tell the Marquis only what you think appropriate; but here is one of my metaphysical scruples:[8] if he is unaware of the true state of things, he will neglect to think about any other woman; one may cross his path who would suit him, and he will not look at her, thinking that he is already halfway my husband, and bound by honor not to make any other plans. He will also think that I am bound to him; and so I was, by the consent I had given, until my father's answer. But at present I am free—I have promised to be. Laugh at my subtle distinctions if you must, but don't correct me for them. My letters are so free that they are hardly decent; I must preserve the delicacy of the most scrupulous probity. If the inclinations of my heart are not pure, at least the maxims of my reason should be.

Mme d'Havrincourt,[9] scandalized by the freedom of my manner, by my unlowered eyes, exclaimed when she learned who I was: "A demoiselle! That one, a demoiselle!" What would the good woman say if she saw my letters? —By the way, Tuesday's letter has been found;[10] the Widow wrote me; I don't know whether she added it to yesterday's packet. I was not

---

6. When France was torn by its Wars of Religion in the sixteenth century, Henri de Navarre, a Protestant, was able to reconcile the country and rule it as Henri IV only by converting to Catholicism. He is reported to have said, "Paris is worth a mass."

7. Young Savoyard boys were to be seen on country roads and streets carrying tame marmots for display or doing odd jobs. See Vissière, *Correspondance* 167, n. 73.

8. "Metaphysical" in the sense of "elaborately abstruse."

9. Wife of the French ambassador to the Hague.

10. Her Letter 123 of August 14, 1764, in which she gave descriptions of the character of her parents. D'Hermenches had expected to receive it and had asked about it in Letter 125.

greatly concerned—it contained only some fine character portraits—but I am sorry for your anxiety.

You must, however, get used to somewhat fewer letters; and if our marriage falls through for the present, we will have to talk about something else—to forget that one gets married, that one loves sometimes, that one can become a mother. Let us rather give ourselves over to the chimeras of metaphysics: you can guess my reasons.

If, as people claim, a woman's reputation is the most precious of all possessions, happy the women who have no heart! Happier yet those who have no senses! They acquire the greatest of possessions at a very low price; they acquire, without virtue, the reputation of being virtuous. As for the others—no matter what they do, a single glance reveals their desire; no one ever believes that they have the strength to resist. Farewell, my friend; although I am not guilty, I will blush when I see you again. Do not scorn me; is it more virtuous to be born in Greenland than in Italy?

I am curious to see my father's letter; send it to me. Send me some trios; while playing the harpsichord, one thinks of nothing else. I read all the novels I can get my hands on.

Urge the Marquis to be prudent, whatever happens. A week of diet, he said, gives him ten years of life ... For my part, whatever happens, I will try to be better in a year than I am today, steadier, gentler, more even-tempered, etc.

128. *To Constant d'Hermenches, August 21, 1764*

Utrecht

I have seen the Widow; she has nothing for me; I am annoyed. I beg you to write to me generously, disinterestedly; I must write to Boswell, to my governesses, to my cousins, to my friends—to everybody whom you cause me to neglect.

My trust in you tells you how much I love and respect you; you may count on an affection that can withstand anything—that henceforth not even you could destroy. Take care not to groom your words too much; let me scold sometimes without much reason for it, and be sure that, even if you were to hurt me, I will love you all my life.

129. *From Constant d'Hermenches, August 21, 1764*

You defend metaphysics—so be it: you have much more intellect than I, your thoughts are precise and strong; you have all the fire of youth to support a seductive logic; and in all these respects you leave me far behind, divine Agnes! My experience and my reflections, in a head cluttered with a thousand different cares and anxieties, must naturally weaken my discourse and scatter contradictions throughout. I submit, then to all your censures, and you see me at your knees, in the best faith in the world, to admire and to be instructed. Were I to draw together the quintessence of everything I know, of the best of my thought in my whole life, still I could not produce the equivalent of one of those pages that you steal from your sleep, yet written by you with so much ease and rapidity that it seems that your pen should set the paper afire; from the very beginning it has carried that flame into my heart. I will never in my life expose you to risk; but some day I want to extract everything from your letters that is striking, and true, and fresh; it will be a precious collection, and the truest likeness of you that one could have.

It's just as well that I had enough of a headache yesterday not to be able to write to you. I was furious with Bellegarde, and if I hadn't known him so throroughly, I was going to accuse him; he hadn't written to me since the letter that you saw. Here are two of his letters at once; since they repeat each other, I'm only sending you one, with the trust that I owe you on the particular matter that he speaks of on the third page.[1] Everything is in agreement; you need only prescribe what we must do. But above all, calm your mind, and think about your health; you have too many good things to do with it, and too many years ahead of you to abuse it.

I have just had my son here; it's a pleasure, but, like all pleasures, mingled with concern: his health did not flourish in England, and if I bring him back, I waste part of the studies he was doing there. A brother of mine in Namur, a true philosopher, learned and full of virtues, asks me to send him there;[2] I think that I will do it, for he would be lost here. I will have to take him there immediately. Let's have at it, then; let us abandon our English frock-coats and loose hair for a sword and a bun,[3] since English pudding doesn't do for the body what I hoped Horace and Tacitus would do for the mind. But first, I would like to take twenty-four hours to go to Utrecht. Instruct me; I would like to live, think, and write only for you, and yet I must tear myself away. Here are three letters and as many messages from Monsieur de Larrey and from the Count of Voronzov,[4] who insist on dining with me two days in a row; what do you say about Monsieur de Larrey, who takes this into his head after suspending any kind of exchange or politeness for fourteen years?

1. The letter was lost. The matter in question is unknown.
2. Louis-Arnold-Juste Constant de Rebecque (1726–1812). In 1767 he was to become the father of Benjamin Constant, with whom, many years later, Belle had one of the most important friendships of her life.
3. A men's style of hair knotted at the back of the neck.
4. The comte de Larrey occupied important official posts, involving at least one diplomatic mission to arrange a royal marriage. Alexandre Romanovitch Voronzov was minister plenipotentiary from Russia to the Hague.

My son is very sensible and adaptable, and full of ambition; I am joyful at the thought of making him your page in the ancient castle of Les Marches.[5] The letter that was delayed finally reached me;[6] I would have mourned it forever if it had been lost; even the scraps of your envelopes mean something to me. I will read you this evening, and if something occurs to me worthy of having the same fate in *your* hands, I will do myself the honor of writing to you (as the Germans say). Here I am, still in ecstasy, loving you with all the faculties of my soul, my heart, and my mind. That earns me the hand to kiss, I think, with permission to aspire as far as the cheek ... Blush at refusing it to me, and I will blush to think of taking advantage of it; and that is how heroes and martyrs are made!

130. *To Constant d'Hermenches, August 23, 1764*

There is no one, man or woman, to whom I write as I do to you, with whom my letters so naturally follow my mood; I know that you always understand me, and you love me too much ever to scorn me, whatever I may say. Not only do I take pleasure in yielding unreservedly to your scrutiny the workings of my mind and the impulses of my heart, I also find it the honest thing to do. The Marquis knows me only through you; you scarcely know me except through my letters. I want to appear in them such as I am, and if you were to say to me one day: "You are too capricious, you are too impetuous, you are too sensual, etc. .... I cannot give you as a wife to my friend ..." I would perhaps be humiliated, but I would not repent of my frankness; but still, you owe it less to the motive of integrity than to the pleasure of trust, and even if that fine motive were to cease, the frankness would not.

Love my letters then, praise them; I am always flattered by it, but never unfairly, never at the expense of a man I love; you are inconsiderate of *me* when you speak ill of your letters, your thoughts, your reflections.

Tomorrow, I will answer you telling you how to proceed. I haven't the time today. I have been to town, but only to dine a moment with Mme Hassclacr, who has arrived from Spa. She brought me here on her way. I was not able to see the Widow, nor to ask her for the letter that she may have had for me; I will send again this evening. I want this letter of mine to be on its way, and I do not want your letter to waste its time in hands other than my own. I hope that you have dined well at Monsieur de Larrey's; after fourteen years of indifference, his being polite and friendly is not at all flattering; in my view, it was by now only a question of a good dinner.

I admire as I must heroes and martyrs; but I find it dangerous to put oneself in the situation of needing to be one for very long. I am afraid that we

5. Bellegarde's chateau in Savoie.
6. Letter 123 of August 14.

grow weary of living hoisted to so high a level; we tire of those difficult and sublime virtues, and after having applauded ourselves a while, we relax our effort by abandoning them. There's a story about a carter—an apprentice-philosopher—who wanted to become master of his passions. He finally triumphed over himself enough to pass in front of a cabaret without having any liquor; but hardly had he taken ten steps when he turned back, saying, "That effort deserves a drink." That's a Dutch tale. It loses something in translation.

Farewell, d'Hermenches, farewell. Let us never have reason to blush. I hope that either you have no need to be a martyr and a hero, or that you are always capable of being one; I leave the pains and the honor of it to you. Ask me permission only for what I may grant: if it were a kiss you desired, I would let you take it.

Thursday evening, August 23, 1764

I blushed. I hope you're satisfied.

I am very pleased about your son, and I promise to love him very much, at Les Marches or elsewhere. What a pleasure if I could complete his upbringing! —if I could lead him to appreciate what is good, honest, lovable, sooner than he would have without me!

For the first time, I feel the hope of rendering you some service, of repaying yours with something besides friendship; you can imagine how this hope flatters my imagination, how sweet it is to my heart! But still, the idea of owing you much and never being at all useful to you was not burdensome to me; I am willing to be obliged to you, I love you enough for that. Do not let the pleasure of seeing your son be clouded by useless worries that may be unfounded. He is not ill, or you would have told me; he is only delicate. Time may make him more robust—there are a thousand examples that should give you that hope; and besides, one rarely sees a strong soul, a sensitive heart, a subtle mind accompanied by sinews of steel and invulnerable health. Perhaps the former advantages are not worth as much as the latter ones, but at least they offer consolation. I had dinner the day before yesterday with the most robust young man in the province; if you had seen how he was surprised, then utterly dismayed by an attack of migraine—if you had seen his countenance and his despondency, you would not have wished either his appetite or his stoutness for your son.

He will understand Horace and Tacitus a little later—but he will understand them, and it will be at an age when he will best appreciate their beauties. We may even read them together—who can say? I don't know a word of their language; perhaps your son will teach me the rudiments, and then I will study the poets to be able to explain them to him. —Now those are castles in the air!... My dear father! I promise nothing, I will promise nothing.

Be at peace, then, regarding your son. *Sensible, adaptable, full of ambition:* have you not every reason to be satisfied? It seems to me that you do very well to send him to your brother; meanwhile, give yourself over to the pleasure of being happy with your son and showing him affection. What a harsh and false maxim it is that orders parents to conceal from their children how much they love them! What! to conceal the most natural, the most legitimate, the sweetest of all feelings for him in whom it arises, the sweetest for him who is the object of it! A father's tenderness is the most powerful of his rights; an affectionate, grateful son can neither avoid it nor fail to recognize it. Let us try to do our best, but if we fail to achieve absolute perfection, let it be rather out of gentleness, out of mildness, than out of an excess of severity ... I could talk for an hour on this, but you know better than I do what is fitting, and you know how to love.

131. *To Constant d'Hermenches, August 26, 1764*

[Sunday]

I think that the Marquis would like me to go in search of him, like Ruth went to find Boaz or Booz—I no longer know his name; he didn't even wake up, that fine fellow. If I were near Les Marches, who knows whether I wouldn't go to glean the fields after the harvesters? But here that style of courtship is not practicable. I trust that you have read the Bible and that you understand me.[1]

You ask me for instructions; here is what seems to me the most straightforward and honest conduct. Simply tell the Marquis that you have written to me; that, your letters having confirmed the idea that his conversation gives of his mind and the favorable impression that his countenance gives of his heart, I have been flattered and charmed by his intentions; that, relying on your word, I have believed that he loved me, that he would love me, that I would be perfectly happy; that, as a consequence of that persuasion, I have consented and accepted, with the single condition that my children, if I had any, would be raised with me, although in the religion of their fathers, and not in a convent; that my sons would not be priests, nor my daughters nuns, at least before the age of twenty-five. Say that you have written to my father about this without naming the Marquis; tell him or send his response. Add that I have promised my father not to engage my word without his permission, or before becoming my own mistress; thus I am free, and the Marquis is as free as I am. You can also say that my making use of my independence will do no harm to my fortune. That, I think, is the whole story. If it is all the same to the Marquis whether I am his in fourteen months or sooner, and with or without the consent of my parents, and if the risk of not having me

---

1. Ruth, a young widow, left her own country of Moab to follow her widowed mother-in-law, Naomi, to Bethlehem. Naomi's rich kinsman Boaz allowed Ruth to glean the corn fields. Ruth went in to Boaz while he was sleeping and lay at his feet, claiming his protection. He eventually married her.

at all does not disturb him, why should he go to any trouble? Let him measure out his efforts according to the interests of his heart. If it turns out that I never become his wife, I do not want him to reproach you for having involved him unnecessarily in tedious concerns.

But whatever happens, if he wants to take some measures to see me, here is what seems to me the most natural and the least likely to reveal our secret. I know that Bentinck is to come to Woerden fairly soon.[2] Ask him whether he will be there alone or with his wife; if he is coming alone, suggest to him that you spend a few days there together, sharing expenses; tell him that you like to shoot ducks, that you want to go hunting, and that you would rather like to do it in the neighborhood of Utrecht. If that works, let the Marquis know the time and circumstances; let him arrive at the Hague by chance when you are about to go to Woerden, and let him—without any fixed plan, quite casually—join the party.

From Woerden, one can easily come to have dinner at Zuylen, and if Bentinck spends a few days here, you could spend them with Bellegarde in Utrecht, and from there your visits would be more frequent and easier. You would come after dinner, and we could play music until evening, and play comet with my mother and me, and with Mme Geelvinck, if I can get her to leave her sister. Depending on the circumstances, we can talk, and try to overcome the obstacles—or simply take pleasure in each other's company. The Marquis is wrong in thinking that *form*[3] is so important in our house; all the court he need pay is to enjoy himself with us. When we are in Utrecht this winter, you have only to introduce the fashion of coming to see me as something very agreeable; you will find some gentlemen who have nothing better to do, such as Golofkine or Reinst, to accompany you once or twice; the Marquis, if he is around, will come without surprising anybody. People will make fun of you at first, but you will say that the fashion of *fontanges* and of farthingales was still more ridiculous.[4]

If you come to Utrecht, let it be passing by on your way to Namur; say that you want your son to know us and for us to love him. My brother will give him the warmest of welcomes. I am going to Mme Hasselaer's at the beginning of next week. Friday, you would find me in town. Mme Geelvinck would take you to my mathematics tutor's; I would invite you to dinner with us, or to come to Zuylen after dinner. You would tell my father that I would have more power than the Church in that household, and that people would not believe that I was destined to keep company eternally with Satan and his henchmen. You would speak of the Marquis's aunt[5]—in short, you would be the holy apostle of tolerance and marriage, without indicating

2. Anthony Bentinck, her cousin by marriage, was governor of Woerden—a town some fifteen kilometers west of Utrecht, between Utrecht and the Hague.
3. English in the original.
4. The *fontange* was a beribboned hair adornment of the late seventeenth century.
5. The aunt that d'Hermenches mistakenly thought was Protestant. See Belle's Letter 127.

any deliberate plan to change their minds. Say nothing about Purgatory, for you, good Protestant though you are, you must think in your soul that mine has great need of it.

It's with a pleasurable emotion that I read certain sentences from the Marquis. He is right in thinking that I would value the slightest things that were done for me. Habit does not weaken my sensations; every day the same things touch me and please me. The most distant past has claims upon my feelings; my gratitude is eternal, and it's a regrettable effect of the same cause that my memory is vindictive, even while my heart wants to pardon. To be both chaste and sensual; to give lavishly of the flowers of pleasure and receive them in return, and all within the bond of duty—that would indeed be a heavenly happiness. When we love and want to please, nothing is indifferent; every instant counts for something; in nature, everything lives, everything moves us ...

That's enough of that. Write and tell me how many times you have hated me and how many times you have loved me in the course of this letter; heap insults of all kinds upon me; tell me that a young girl must not imagine having children, or at least not talk about it so freely—but these conventionalities are not my way of doing things, especially with you; surely you do not find it wrong that I hope to be a mother, and that I suppose that I will be. Well then, my children will be Catholic. It must be so, and I am willing—provided that people trust my promise to speak to them of their religion only with respect: I would be in despair if they were removed from my care, and if people distrusted me. One of my most cherished hopes is one day to raise my sons; I will study night and day to learn everything one could wish, everything that they will have to know, so that I can teach it to them afterwards. I hate tutors; will I be allowed to teach my sons in their place? Will I be allowed to try to make of them happy men and useful citizens? Far from preventing others from making good Catholics of them when it is time, I myself, if that's what's desired, will instruct them in the dogmas of their religion, and I will teach them its morals; they can be unaware for a long time that there is more than one way of worshiping God in their house. It would be useless for me to hide how much this means to me—you see it only too clearly.

Answer me about what I have just said; tell me also that I will be free to write tales, verses, letters—anything I please; that I will no longer be lectured incessantly about prudence, propriety, etc; that I will only be reproached for what is really wrong; that people will be content to see me apply myself to correcting my real faults, and will otherwise leave me my character such as nature gave it to me; on these conditions, I swear to do all the good I am capable of. It is up to you, Monsieur, to judge how far that will go.

132. *From Constant d'Hermenches, August 27, 1764*

I bless Heaven, perhaps for the first time in my life, with an entire and complete sincerity. It has made me a gift that I had always hoped for, that seemed my due, and that for the last several years I had despaired of obtaining. I used to bless Heaven only out of resignation, and sometimes by comparison; but today my heart is so full, so wrung by emotion, my joy is so pure, that I do not know what adversities, what injustices I could complain of, after the treasure that has fallen to my lot! What radiance your friendship and your penetrating mind have brought to my existence! Ah! if only this fortune had befallen me earlier, what might I not be today! I, who only know and desire good in its perfection, who would never stop with anything short of its extremes! Yes—from things animal to things sublime, I always push ahead, and when there is anything left to do, it seems to me that nothing has yet been done—a tendency as harmful to the organism as it might be sublime for mental existence! If I am at table, I keep on eating—unless experience makes me stop and reflect—as much as my stomach will hold. If I am hunting, I return home half-dead, and insist on bringing back the last piece of game. If I am playing music, I must play on until the end of the work, and perform in a single concert all the beautiful pieces known. If I am reading—even a bad book, or a journal, a gazette, etc.—I can skip over nothing. In the past, I would plumb the most insipid conversation to its very bottom—I have stopped doing that; but the fierceness that makes me want to embrace everything—that is still with me.

With direction, or encouragement, or criticism, one could make something excellent out of such a bizarre nature; but who has taken the trouble to attend to me or make me more moderate? What disinterested and enlightened friend have I ever had? I have been feared; I have been blamed; if I have committed faults, the jealous have rejoiced and my friends have believed that they were doing a great deal for me if they defended or excused me; but never has anyone corrected me. It took a being as sublime as you, divine Agnes! whose affection seemed to be reserved for me in the Book of Destinies, who was to present the Truth, and in doing so please me. Once again, I bless Heaven; but, alas, if so much interest should fade, if you grow weary of me, lose your liking of me—as can hardly fail to happen—how wretched I will be! Come what may, we must enjoy the present.

I spoke to you of a woman friend, who used to be my lover.[1] Why do you seize upon a circumstance which according to my principles, I admit, is indifferent, and which as to sentiment is a hundred times more odious than it is amiable? You admire her scruples, and you say nothing about her harsh and bilious character—she only ever scolds, she never flatters! That vice, I admit to you, is more offensive in my eyes, even on the part of a mistress, than libertinage!

1. Neither the friend nor the exchanges d'Hermenches refers to here are identified.

There is one other person in the world who is intimately attached to me, and from whom I expected the happiness that your generosity grants me; you must get to know her too. She is a relative of mine, rare by virtue of her talents, by the nobility and quixotism of her sentiments, generous to excess, the victim and even the martyr of all her relations; exquisite taste, discreet as Hippocrates, gentle, caressing—generous in the largest sense of the term, with a chaste and delicate mind, even passing for a prodigy in this respect. She is younger than I am, and with a pleasing face; from childhood we have loved each other to the point of almost forgetting that we were close relatives. She has so tender a heart and so humble an expression—one that you cannot fail to understand—that I can believe that she felt passion for me—a passion of homage, because she found me a marvelous being; the passion of instinct, the tribute that the one sex pays to the other.

Well now, could I have hidden anything from her? . . . For a long time she was the recipient of my most secret thoughts; she shared my plans, my aversions, my choices; but how far she is from you! Nothing clear-cut in her decisions; although her taste was of the surest, she was the slave of the conventions of proper upbringing and prescribed conduct; whatever wore the livery of evil was always evil. She did not know how to decide candidly what is beautiful or good if it did not present itself in a form already known; she would confess to me her lapses, her missteps, but without discussing them, without bringing to them those nuances which denote conviction and a frank heart. She's like a bishop who admits to his confessor, in the humble setting of the confessional, that he has a concubine; as he leaves, he sees some poor devil on his knees waiting for his blessing, and excommunicates or anathematizes him. She has never spoken to me of the misdeeds that she thinks I have committed, but she has sometimes favored or flattered them, and always excused them. I had cured her of a blind prejudice for me; that has turned into a distrust so extreme that she now quakes as she praises me, and I no longer know when she is really pleased. Her criticisms are never authentic, explicit; she looks for some circumlocution, some amelioration of them, and her praises are so full of superlatives that they are no longer anything but empty phrases. So, Agnes, I admit it to you, I am often bored with her, although I still seek her out; we never write to each other, although she writes very well—albeit without gaiety, without digressions; she writes like Deshoulières, Fontenelle, and the Hôtel de Rambouillet in their grave mode.[2] Either her imagination is bottled up, or it lacks resilience. At the same time she has the most violent passions; she loves to the point of sacrificing everything, she is ready to die—however, she is not yet dead, and is always indignant at the suspicion that she will not die.

---

2. Mme Deshoulières (1697–94) was a dramatist and poet; Bernard Le Bovier de Fontenelle (1657–1757) was a poet and philosopher who wrote of serious subjects in a light style (he was a popularizer of science). The Hôtel de Rambouillet was the first of the great seventeenth-century salons, held by the marquise de Rambouillet (1588–1655).

She knows you well through the little Aston woman; she loves you madly, she puts you in the first rank among charming women and gifted geniuses; she would very easily pardon you for a passion, a misstep—she would even be glad of it; but she does not pardon your "Portrait", nor the verses on Maasdam,[3] nor the letters you send everywhere on earth—but does she know you? Myself, I did not know you! All that is known of you is only a coarse outer rind, compared to the beauties that I discover in your soul!... Now here is a letter in a tone that must be to your liking; I have begun by a digression that has put me a thousand leagues from my subject, and I cannot possibly take it up again today, so I send you this.

Let me make a confession, however, for I do not want you to give me crowns that I don't deserve. I attach neither obligation nor very great esteem to virtue—or what is called the supreme virtue in women; I do not believe that there is such a thing as crime on this point. That has made me spend twenty years of my life in the horrors of combat and remorse. And finally, whether by philosophy or reasoning (for I don't believe that it is by corruption), I have come to believe that the thing is quite indifferent in itself, and that the Creator does not greatly worry about whether it is a man of this name or that who has gotten an heir with a woman named something else, or whether it is he who has the same name as she. *He* has not decided that the child of Mr. Such-and-Such must have his hundred thousand florins of income rather than share them with other children. Fundamentally, with the permission and the capacity to be born there come to all of us the same rights to these riches, which are distributed at random, and of which the Creator is always the sovereign proprietor. Thus all his creatures have a right to them; it is only circumstances that determine into whose hands they fall.

I take this issue as far as I can, to give you an idea of what I think about everything that is related to it. True virtue, I think, is to fulfill one's vocation, not to disturb the order of society (that's the real barrier), and true honor is to avoid making oneself contemptible. Thus, as a man, I will not let myself be cudgeled, nor verbally insulted; as a woman, I will not be vanquished, and no one will make indecent remarks to me ... But for all that, have I sworn that if the being who is dearest to me comes to my room and persuades me that he cannot be happy unless I let myself be struck by him (assuming I can be sure that this will not degrade me afterward)—have I sworn that I will not offer him my cheek? Yes, I will do it; and since you have so nicely untangled my thoughts on a number of points, I must confess to you that everything that you conjecture about the motives that have often made me triumph over myself—aside from the respect that you have rightly guessed—has to do with this instinct that I have discovered in myself: with regard to women, my heart and my mind are what a hound is with regard to

3. The "Portrait de Zélide" and its additions, and the verses at the end of Letter 87.

his game in the field; he pursues it and devours it. And if this same animal stops, and, by its action, performs (in the terms of my comparison) the equivalent of reasoning, the hound licks it and takes it under his protection. Nevertheless it is true that the hare is sometimes so appetizing, and the hound so hungry, that death may ensue.

—You will suit Bellegarde marvelously, and I will be crushed; he would have told me word for word what you tell me about the story of the young girl, and you are right in many ways: first, I am wrong to exercise any kind of seduction whatsoever if I want to be strict in my principles, and there is always an element of seduction when one takes advantage of occasions for pleasing. A deliberate seduction is more culpable—however innocent its means may appear—than a seduction dictated by instinct or passion, which is only a tribute payment to human fragility, whatever ravages it brings in its wake. But if in my seduction I let all its dangers be known, and all the ways of avoiding them—if I see that what induced the yielding has been fulfilled, and that anything more I might demand would be extortion—do I do any harm?

There is nothing in society so awkward, so sullen, as what one might call an official virgin. Thus, it is not necessarily respect for innocence that would stop me, for in that case it is only a word; a trollop often has more real innocence than a nun, and, I wager, will better fulfill many duties . . .

But Good Lord, I must finish. I am going to write what I must to Bellegarde; you tell me to come to Woerden, and you are going to Arnhem; how does that fit together? I had agreed with Anthony to go spend the night there a week from tomorrow, but where will you be? I cannot send my son off on Friday, but may I come pay you a visit? If Mme Hasselaer were clever, she would have invited me, if you have let her know that I am one of your friends. You have not grasped my idea on equity concerning Bellegarde's wife; it is only a passing remark, but one of better logic than you give it credit for.

133. *To Constant d'Hermenches, August 28, 1764*

Utrecht, Tuesday

I am afraid that you are ill. It is most unusual that you haven't sent a single word of response either to my letter of Thursday or the enormous packet of Sunday.

If you can do it without doing yourself any harm, write me just a couple of lines tomorrow; tomorrow too, I think I will write you a couple of lines.

I forgot to tell you that the letter from my father was not in its final form when he showed it to me. It was his intention not to speak of the approaching time of my independence nor, for the present, to ask for information. I said some things to you that you cannot have understood, and that must have seemed to you utterly garbled.

My brother and I are in town to enjoy ourselves and do some business; we refused a grand dinner at the house of Mme Geelvinck, and ordered a little dinner from the inn. If only you had been there to share it! We were free and alone, we could have said anything we pleased. All that was missing was a pitcher of water, so my head is a little dizzy. Farewell; I impatiently await news of you and your arteries. I love you today in a rather stupefied way, but as always, a great deal.

134. *From Constant d'Hermenches, August 30, 1764*

There is no artery, except the big one in the heart, that could put me in such a state that I would leave you anxious about the fate of your generous packets; still, I believe that with the last surges of my heart will say: "Divine Agnes, I am dead, I can no longer write to you." So you will have received my letter, or letters, because normally what departs arrives. It is nonetheless true that these delays displease me; I am not the sort of person who likes being waited for, and you are the sort who should be paid in advance. Here is a word from your suitor. Although I could not go any further with my letter, I can prove to you my existence in an undisagreeable way by sending you his today.

I was tied up this morning by a party going to the kermess; I didn't get back until evening. I received both your greetings together, and now I have to take my son to dine at Mme de la Perrière's. I find myself engulfed by strangers and social commitments without taking any pleasure in it; duty and propriety utterly fail to compensate me for the fact that I cannot send you yet another of my scribblings ...

You need not send me back the letters from the Marquis that I pass on to you; I do not want to stand in the way of my friend's having all the happinesses possible, and it *is* one to put the expression of his feelings into your hands. The Widow doesn't know that she is only the envelope of an envelope! Do me the favor of telling me, you who are an academician, what is the word for the part she plays? I have taken it from her![1]

Agnes, if you were to tell Mme Hasselaer that I am much better company than all the people she makes so much of, that I appreciate her and value her better than any of them; that she received me very ill two years ago; that I am less offended than piqued at her joking about me at (among other places) Breda, where she said that I *write tragedies;* that, finally, you think highly of me—don't you think that she would invite me to come and see her? And would that not be more seemly for all three of us? I will never present myself at her house without her wishing it. You may remember that two years ago it was by following your advice that I made a fool of myself; it could

1. The female go-between in a clandestine affair is a stock figure in early fiction and comedy.

happen that I fare no better this year, and since your mother is present, there must be a very explicit agreement so that you don't risk being frowned upon, or being accused—and in good faith, Agnes, I do not find my self worthy of causing you a single bad moment. I prefer to return to Utrecht as soon as I have the Marquis' response; I will announce myself to your father and ask permission to see him at home and present my son to him.

—Why don't you like me to tell you stories of amorous adventures? It seems to me that the best touchstone of the human heart is to see it in its weaknesses. I wish that you would write me a little account of everything that you have been told to my disadvantage. I would take the truth as a corrective; you would know me better, and it is no small thing for me to gain something in your opinion!

You have defined something that I have often wondered about myself: *a kind of charlatan!*[2] I believe it, and I think that it is a fault, in spite of the way your favorable prejudice makes you judge of it. It indicates a distrust of oneself, and yet the effect clashes with the self-esteem of others; one is envied and often even scorned to the same degree that one shows oneself to good advantage. No, Agnes, that charlatanism should not please you! If I am guilty of it, help me to correct myself! It is a consequence of that injustice innate to all men, which, when one has been in the world a while, forces one to show off. The most honest, prudent people, offended and hurt by the pretentions of the fatuous and the arrogant, cannot refrain themselves from compensating by a mechanical reflex, at the expense of humble and modest people—at the expense of the inner sense of equity itself. Every day, I, charlatan that I am, I listen in silence to people who shamelessly command the attention and admiration of others on matters that I know better than they do; that I possess and they do not. Connections and relatives, a clever remark, a talent much inflated by people who know nothing about it—they exploit these things year after year, and throughout a whole country! A sort of rage—not at their advantages, but at being their dupe—can then throw me into a different kind of exaggerated overstatement—not *their* kind, for I despise that too much, and I think there is a substrate of truth in my character that is unchanging—, so that often I see that people take what I say at a discount; I suffer the humiliation of needing to prove mathematically what I say, or to have a third party as witness; in short, I am less likely to be believed than many dolts, whom I hear telling lies in the blandest of tones!

Cat some light on these contrasts, dear Agnes, I beg you! Never could reflections and reasonings fall on ground better disposed to receive them; you could certainly make me, if not better, at least cleverer and happier!

There is a sort of charlatanism indispensable in this century; it is the prestige that titles shed on birth, and the precedence that is accorded them.

2. See Letter 63, n. 1.

In the past, out of a republican sentiment I inherited from my father, I found it very grand to be a better gentleman than a count or a baron. To have borne the same name for several centuries and to let it pass unknown that my name had been illustrious in earlier times seemed to me the finest of titles; to add a *de* to it was a degradation and a diploma or proof of common birth. Today, with the eyes of experience, I see that the public does not judge of things in this way; a title, even usurped, gives a mechanical but a real consideration, even among the very best people. Do you remember the Comte de Saint-Germain?[3] Would you have been as eager to see him if you had heard that a mere Monsieur Germain was in the room? One does not go digging around in the archives, even of one's best friend; but one likes him to have a resounding name: that is a *useful* charlatanism—one that I regarded with scorn, and whose corruption has made great progress among the Dutch! That black ribbon of mine that makes people laugh and provokes witticisms and inanities on the part of the rabble of Utrecht—you yourself do not know that it is there on account of a war-wound! A cannonball sent my hat flying, bruised my left shoulder, and dilated the blood vessels of that part of my head to such an extent that ten years later they had to be tied off, cut, and excised! To spread that around might win me a promotion—might be more useful charlatanism!

Adorable Agnes, look at how many ideas spring from one well-chosen and luminous word on your part!

Before I finish, I must recount to you an amorous adventure, even though you might not want me to. Your uncle the general plays a role in it, as well as my quixotism; it always makes me laugh when I recall it. A few years ago someone wrote me that a stranger had arrived who would be very glad to make my acquaintance. I went to meet her, and found her in a house of ill repute, and in the hands of a woman who was doing the honors of the house. The young person seemed melancholy and unfortunate, with beautiful features and a modest bearing, and yet she presented herself as someone who was dedicating herself to libertinage. I was repelled by all this; she replied awkwardly to questions of mine prompted by her situation and my feeling about it; her countenance contradicted the resolution that she appeared to have taken. Piqued that my very humane speeches had made no impression on her, I heaped humiliating remarks on her; I made her blush with a few epithets, and finally reduced her to tears by throwing money at her, that being the object of a profession that I detested. She began to weep; I was immediately touched, and calmed her by a gentler tone. I explained to her that I had exaggerated nothing; that she was authorizing the most ignominious treatment, and that in a few days she would be exposed to enduring the caprices of men far more brutal than I. This picture threw her into an

---

3. A famous adventurer who claimed to have the secret of immortality—another kind of *charlatan*. In 1760 the French sought to have him extradited from Holland, where he was living.

indescribable state, and finally wrenched from her some words that were both reasonable and moving.

She described her situation in the most heartrending terms, and gave me a sort of respect for her: having run away from her honest parents, she was seduced, abducted, abandoned, dragged into a distant land, stripped of her money and all aid, and reduced to putting herself at the mercy of that woman, who had seemed compassionate and hospitable. She was under obligation to her; she was under her continual surveillance; the woman had shown her only one way to escape from her misfortune. She saw the precipice down which she was about to fall, and chose silence, out of a singular kind of pride. I asked her whether she was sincere, whether she wanted to give herself over to some respectable way of life; her responses delighted me. I told her that I would pay her debts and find a boarding house for her until she received news of her family, or found a way to make a living; and as a first condition, no man would be admitted to that boarding house, not even me. She accepted with joy, and with doubts about my sincerity that persuaded me of her own.

I went to make arrangements, and I sent a carriage with her new host to transport her; she replied, with distress, that the monster had suspected something, that she had taken her clothes, guarded her continually, and made terrible threats against me if she left the house. I had no wish to make a scene, and found myself perplexed; I congratulated myself, however, that she was not yet known by any young men. I ran into your uncle, and recounted this adventure to him; after a good deal of talk, I entreated him to go into this house under the pretext of being the girl's lover; to speak to her for me, encourage her, help her pack up her clothes, pay for her, and take her away on his own authority; I would wait for him in the street, and we would take her to her refuge. We strode forth like Crusaders; he enters the house; I remain outside as planned, blowing on my fingers (it was very cold). Finally, after two hours of impatient waiting, I knock on the door, and in a low voice I ask to speak to that gentleman. At the third-story window there appears an immense nightcap: it is he, who says to me in a whisper: "My dear friend, don't take it ill, but I'm staying here." I had a moment of indignation, and went off cursing hypocrisy, my generosity, and his lust; then I burst out laughing like a fool. The next day he told me that he had been seduced by the opportunity and by the fresh beauty of the fair penitent; that he had found it inconvenient to remove her from that place at that hour, that she had offered little resistance, and that he had spent a very good night, "but that he would take care never to expose himself again to such a test." I wanted him at least to redress his wrongs and complete *my* good designs; he found a thousand reasons not to, and I learned since that he had made several visits more to the young lady. An absent friend to whom by chance I was writing at the time learned through me about the existence of this person; he left in secret to go see her, without telling me about it, and gave her help. She has become virtuous; she is fairly happy; she hid from me for a long time, and showed only a great deal of embarrassment when I met her ...

Goodnight, niece of the man in the big nightcap! Perhaps the mail is already on the road.

The big nightcap is the reason why the postmaster had already donned his own; my letter has been brought back to me. If I have some time, I will write you another; this one was only good if it was delivered at full gallop.

135. *To Constant d'Hermenches, August 30, 1764*

Now I am reassured as to your arteries, and well-informed as to your heart. As soon as I have some time, I will write you a long and worthy response. For today, though, just a word about these hounds who run after the hare, and then do nothing about it. I understand very well their pleasure, but I dislike their instinct. At the moment when the hare wants to be eaten, why don't they eat it? It's very cruel, always to want the opposite of what it wants, and to make it look ridiculous, after having tormented it, and exhausted it, and made it suffer agonies of fear—and all that just to be able to say: "I am a clever hound who is behaving like a great man; born master of your whole species, I want you to recognize your weakness and my power. You would like something from me; what I delight in receiving, you would delight in granting—but no, the adventure would be banal. I want to distinguish myself from my fellows; it costs me something, as it does you, but no matter. Go your way and remember that you are only a feeble little creature, with whom I could have done anything I pleased; but you seem rather likeable to me, you have talents, I will bring you along ..."

Don't you see the figure they cut? I pity the hare. And the hound? ... He is my friend.

August 30, 1764

I leave tomorrow for Wijk and return the 17th or 18th. Mme Hasselaer could not invite you, for twenty reasons.

I thought that Bentinck would come to Woerden later. Write me tomorrow about everything you intend to do.

136. *From Constant d'Hermenches, August 30, 1764*

The Hague

Here, Mademoiselle, is a piece of scribbling from your suitor.[1] You will see that we are a little scatterbrained, but that's what utterly kind-hearted people are like, those who are to make a woman of your caliber happy; a pedant, a methodical type, would make you die of boredom. If he must take measures regarding your parents, that is how he will do it; you may judge whether he should be allowed to! I no longer have any steps to take except according to your instructions. It is not a good idea to talk to the General;[2] he must serve us only to support what's really going on without realizing it. This is an enterprise worthy of your sublime genius; if, on mature consideration, this marriage suits you, you must not let it fall through; you will never find one like it—it is utterly poetic. But what pleases me about it is that you will certainly be completely happy; you will not live in opulence, but you will live much more nobly and pleasantly than the Bentincks, the Perponchers, etc. You will be a lady on her estate to whom people will go pay their respects, who will do good around her, who will, without any fuss, come with the Colonel or the General from Les Marches to see her parents from time to time.

As for his expenses, you will increase them only by very little; it will be up to you to keep him from extravagances of purchases, runnings-about, etc. With your hundred thousand florins—which will be secured by our lands—we will round them out, we will clear them of debts, and we will have the most distinguished estate in our province. If to those hundred thousand florins one wants to add a few thousand more, so much the better; we will use them to buy some new clothes, and to make a journey to Paris immediately. Although I speak of money, don't think for a minute that that's what we are seeking; you know that there are dowagers in these lands who might not be at all displeased at becoming marquises. Here is the Marquis' fortune: He draws in leases from his lands ten thousand Piedmont livres of income; along with that, he has châteaux and a house in Chambéry, well-maintained carriages and horses, and all the advantages that can be drawn from his land: woods, kitchen gardens, etc. He has four to five thousand florins of income from the State, and from your dowry he will draw, in his own country, eight or nine thousand livres in income—that in a country where for most expenses a livre purchases as much as a florin. His sister is no less than a genius at household management, to whom one would readily give six thousand livres a year if her presence could be paid for in money.

You know what I am to you, dear Agnes!

---

1. This letter from Bellegarde has not been found.
2. Anthony Bentinck, Belle's cousin by marriage.

137. *From Constant d'Hermenches, August 31, 1764*

Friday the 31st

But we completely misunderstand each other! I do not give myself out to be someone who refuses a tasty morsel on principle; there has to be a reason, or a pleasure stronger than appetite, to make me let slip a prey. If it's in order to be eaten that the hare stops in its tracks, it would be harsh and stupid not to profit by it, and that is indeed the object of the hunt. But I say that just as flight and ruse arouse the desire to triumph, so too a reasoned resistance or a cry for mercy would elicit generosity and reflection. From everything that I have said on this subject, you should see in me a person who would regret anything that he might obtain at the price of sincere remorse, or at the cost of the happiness of the person he loves or prefers. My God, I don't like to cheat; but I am dizzy with delight and am the happiest of men with what I win by mutual agreement, and with the pleasures that I can repay by attentions and services—refusing to exploit my influence or circumstances to make someone do what will make her unhappy the moment after, that is all my heroism consists of! I am a conqueror by instinct; but the evils that conquests carry in their wake moderate or inhibit that instinct; I want to be a king and not a usurper. If you respond to that by saying that passion can easily confuse those fine distinctions, you will be absolutely right; so I can only respond by my principles and a few experiences.

I had some rights over La Martin; she had come here on account of an attachment to me; she was waiting for me. A man of her station in life became attached to her; he can make her everyday life happy—he can marry her.[1] I stayed away a long time—I'm always here and there; I put no obstacle in the way of their liaison. When I showed up, he beat his head against the walls; she was embarrassed; she would have refused me nothing. But didn't I do better not to disturb this household, nor to exploit the desire she still has for me? However, Bellegarde said: "You must be out of your mind to be so cool toward this woman! These are very strange scruples!" But I, who could neither compensate her, nor accept the sharing of her—I let him talk, and was glad of what I had done.

I see by what I have received this morning that everything I said about Mme Hasselaer makes no sense. All I can do is entreat you to return to Utrecht sooner than you said, and to write to me instead of playing whist with Colonel van der Dussen. I must absolutely go to Namur, and who knows what will become of me after that! Spending the winter at the Hague is a terrible enterprise; it means risking boredom—and my purse.

Allow me, my good Agnes, to send you a little scrap of my tragedy. Here is a monologue that more or less presents the exposition of the subject, and

1. Marie Martin, an actress who, through d'Hermenches' recommendation, worked in the French theater at the Hague. The man in question was a fellow actor named Dugué.

by which you can measure what I might have done if I had continued: Statira has been madly in love with Hephestion, from the moment she saw him; she believed that he was Alexander.[2] Ever since she has known Alexander, she has been refusing to carry out the commitments she had made; people are urging her, threatening her; she wants to conceal her secret from the whole world. This is what she says to her confidante:

[*The rest of this letter is missing.*]

138. *To Constant d'Hermenches, September 1–2, 1764*

Saturday at midnight

I will not return from Westerhout a moment sooner than I said; my inclination, my admiration are all with Mme Hasselaer. I will play whist with Colonel van der Dussen, and I will not write to you except at night or early in the morning before dawn; yes, I will write to you because I intended to yesterday and the day before. Today I am displeased with you; what was the point of telling me that tale? To punish you, I won't tell you whether I found it funny; whether the big nightcap provided by the witch expressly for these encounters made me laugh; whether I admired you—no, I will tell you nothing; I will show you, when I have the leisure, how one can manage not to be a charlatan; I will tell you stories in which I myself do not come off particularly well.

Meanwhile, I'll tell you about a little mortification I have just experienced. Last evening, from five until nine, I had given all my attention to my sister; I had entertained her, instructed her, lectured her about all sorts of things. "Ah! sister!" she exclaimed. "Nobody talks the way you do! What you say is so true, your imagination is so vivid! You think and speak so well! When you take an interest in what's happening to somebody, when you want to make people better and happier, they are so flattered! The way you present things is so cheerful, so entertaining! . . ."

Today we hardly saw each other at all; her tone seemed a bit severe, but I was busy, and since I do not love her utterly to the point of adoration, I had not been particularly distressed by it, and I hadn't paid too much attention.

This evening, I was reading your letters quietly in my room; she comes in, grumbling, to bring me something that she had made for me and that she said she could not finish. "But," I say, "you've done enough, you've done the hardest part, I'll have my maid work on it." I thank her warmly; she throws it on my bed with a contemptuous air, continues to speak to me disdainfully, and goes off without looking at me. I follow her: "What's the matter, Mitie? Sister! What's wrong? Tell me! Have I hurt you? Could I

2. Statira was the second wife of Alexander the Great; Hephestion was a Macedonian general and a favorite of Alexander. The first act of a tragedy entitled *Statira par mr d'Herm.* has been preserved in the Bibliothèque Publique et Universitaire in Geneva.

have upset you in some way?" "No, you haven't hurt me." "Have I hurt someone else, then?" "No." I was going back to my room, somewhat relieved, having satisfied myself that she was merely in a bad mood; but she said to me as she was going downstairs, "Maybe it's stupid of me, maybe it's nothing ... but last night I could not stay in your room when I saw that you had the indecency to undress in front of Perponcher: to take off your corset! to show yourself in your chemise! That seemed so dreadful to me!...." "Ah!" I said to her cheerfully, as I gently closed the door, "I'm glad it's only that." But in spite of my patience, I was still stung by her treatment of me. You could hardly have been harsher or more insulting with the girl in your night-cap story. I shouldn't omit to say that right after my little disrobing maneuver I had said to Mitie and her husband: "You must admit that I get undressed quite decently—I learned how to do it when my brothers were around; last winter my brother the sailor would never leave my room until I had gotten into bed, too sleepy to talk ..." So I didn't think that I had particularly disgraced myself. My sister is leaving tomorrow with her heart full of contempt for me. I am humble enough to ask myself whether she is right; perhaps there is some advantage to her grumpy reserve, and my free and easy ways may come from laxness. I overcame my pride enough to ask her to do an errand for me, but she showed no desire to do it; she did not honor me with so much as a glance all through supper. One could hardly have shown more horror or disdain if instead of my sister and her husband, it had been *you* in my room, or if Bellegarde had lifted the scarf from my breast. It is so arbitrary—the meaning of the words "decency" and "modesty"! How varied are ideas about virtue!

Her ill humor and injustice are surely excessive; I don't think I am obliged to say that Mitie did well to treat me like some degraded creature. Nevertheless, if someone took it into his head to change the basis of her ideas on this point, and to rob her of the dignity that springs from that excessive delicacy, I would rip his heart out. I would let myself be trampled on rather than tell her to be less scrupulous. Never again, lest the example alter her, will I do in her presence what I did yesterday. I will not remove so much as a pin.

My story has nothing interesting about it, perhaps, but since it's on my mind I mention it; it just happened recently, and I am still surprised and humiliated by it. Goodbye; I'm going to sleep.

Sunday morning

The subject of *Statira* seems fine to me; there are some beautiful lines, some prosaic ones, and some that are weakened by overblown epithets. *Héros* is aspirated; there is one syllable too many in that line, if I'm not wrong about the *h*.[1] Statira does not take advantage of the situation in

---

1. That is, *héros* begins with an aspirated *h*, and the vowel in the preceding article is not elided: one writes *le héros*, not *l'héros*.

describing her lover; what she says is cold compared to what she could say. But don't take my word for this; I am in such a bad mood that I'm in no state to admire anything—I take the greatest pleasure in criticizing.

My sister, however, has come to say goodbye to me; she embraced me and asked what errands I wanted done, in spite of my indecency. Goodbye; I'm about to leave for Wijk. My father may be going to the Hague next week. Do as you please—I understand nothing about the arrangements. I could not return earlier than the 17th or the 18th even if I wanted to; but I neither can nor want to. Do not stay another moment in Holland when your business is finished. The way things are going, I would gain almost nothing by it, and even if I were to gain a great deal, I don't want you to stay here a minute longer on my account.

CR *Belle has gone off to her friend Susanna Hasselaer's home at Westerhout, north of Amsterdam near Wijk aan Zee, where she will spend most of September. While Belle is at Westerhout she is also having late-night conversations with another suitor, one whom her parents rather favor: Adolf Werner Carel Willem, Baron van Pallandt. She does not mention this to d'Hermenches immediately, but there will be repercussions later on.*

139. To Constant d'Hermenches, September 4, 1764

Westerhout

What was I saying the last time? Nothing very tender or even obliging, I think. I was in a bad mood; I found your tale nasty;[1] the hour, the carriage, indeed, everything about our journey seemed badly arranged, and I didn't dare say what I thought about it with the frankness—with the complaining and the scoffing—that makes one forget the reason for one's bad mood. I was also very displeased with myself. All of that must have influenced my letter. I will be more gentle now, I hope. One single torment has taken the place of several: I can't sleep.

The pleasure of seeing Mme Hasselaer again made me spend the first night without closing my eyes: neither my books nor my writing case had been put in my room, so you can imagine how long that night was. This one is hardly better; I have been reflecting a long time; everyone is sleeping; I don't know what time it is. These virgin insomnias are the most boring, painful things in the world.

Mme Hasselaer protests that she never made any kind of joke about you; she remembers everything she saw, everything that was said at Breda, and she cannot remember anybody's talking about you or even mentioning your

---

1. The story that d'Hermenches told about her uncle and a young prostitute in his Letter 134.

name. She is neither deceitful nor thoughtless; you can be sure that there is not a word of truth in that accusation. We spoke of the pleasure there would be in having you here; she doesn't dare invite you for fear of displeasing my mother—that's all that holds her back. She would be delighted to see you; she knows no more charming man in the world, she says, and begs me to be on my guard lest I fall in love with you. I don't know where you got your notion about Colonel van Dussen; he's not around, and is not expected.

Sunday, when we arrived, we found a great deal of company: Monsieur Rendorp,[2] whom I like very much, Mme Hogguer,[3] who is very pleasant; the young Boulanger girls, who are very affectionate and who are much taken with me because they had been told that I was such a wit (!), and expected on that account to find me very rude; it is always pleasant to make people happy by a flattering greeting. The rest of the company was good enough to play whist with, so that I wasn't bored. Three of those who were staying here left yesterday; we no longer have anyone except Monsieur Bost,[4] who seems to me a good fellow; he has read a lot and remembers what he has read. He lets us take walks by ourselves, Mme Hasselaer and me, when we want to. He has as much wit as he needs, with a few more pretensions—but gentle undemanding pretensions; he already tolerates my laughing interruptions when he's saying things that make good sense—for he does have good sense and the gift of registering the pretty things that are said, and even of saying some himself. I am sure that he will get used to my impatient outbursts, and that we will get along splendidly. We spent yesterday in a way that just suits my laziness: no visitors, no wit; in the evening, everyone sitting around the table, each reading quietly or doing handwork or making houses of cards ... Don't you see that I'm all but asleep? What calm, just now, in my mind! But since you may have no need of an opiate, farewell.

Tuesday, after dinner

I was not so calm after receiving the packet of yours that was the one before the last one: the letter all about you, your women friends, your principles. I was so preoccupied with it for two days that I was incapable of doing anything with the slightest attention. One morning I was so weary from having tried a half-dozen books, having started I know not how many letters; so weary from all the emotions and reflections that your letter had aroused, and from the effort it took not to respond to it, that finally I nearly fell asleep, and it took the dinner bell to restore my wits to their normal motion. You may ask me, "Why try so hard not to answer?" It's because I had other things to do, and if I had begun a response it would have absorbed me utterly; sometimes one must master one's impulses.

2. Alderman and then burgomaster of Amsterdam.
3. A banker's wife.
4. Jan Bost, a lawyer, who was to marry Mme Hasselaer many years later.

But what a bizarre contradiction! All my reflections veritably exuded a severe virtue: a thousand arguments arrayed themselves against your principles; and a thousand emotions, the fire of imagination—and some other fire (I know not what)—and the languor that follows it, inspired me to forget my own.

I will answer you, d'Hermenches, I insist. If you have already forgotten your letter, I will return it to you. But truly, these discussions are dangerous: reason argues, but the heart goes soft and the senses go up in flames. One never believes more firmly, Mr. Brown[5] said the other day, than when one does not know why; I think that women are never more virtuous than when they do not know why. My sister surely does not know why there was any harm in my getting undressed, and yet she sets greater store by propriety than I do by virtue.

I was quite convinced that a great many hares were eaten, and, for a moment, I took advantage of the broad sense in which one could take what you said simply to enjoy the joke. But I am not ready to undertake the interrogation you ask me to make. Perhaps you would be perfectly sincere, but it would cost you something; if one of those adventures had no creditable side, you would have to dose your style with too much of that charlatanism[6] that you want to be rid of.

Since I have not yet seen you use it to belittle humble and modest people, you will allow me not to be as severe with it as you are. I look at it as a game that does not ill-become you, and that amuses me. I have never had the desire to correct the superficial flaws of people I love when they have neither offended me nor prevented me from loving them at the first glance; it seems to me that they come with them. When I think of you, your air and your tone come to my mind at once, and I cannot hate the strokes with which you are drawn in my imagination. If a benevolent gentleness and a philosophical indifference retain their place in your soul, then the modest will no longer be belittled; the fatuous will be free to enjoy their frivolous advantages; your arteries will be the healthier; and without your having deliberately tried to change tone, it will come about that you will no longer be a charlatan—except with me, who rather like charlatanism, and with others who at least are not distressed by it. Then it will only amount to the art of suffusing your descriptions of things with a brilliant coloration that will enhance them, and produce an illusion that pleases even though one recognizes it for what it is.

Although I don't want to *ask* you for such-and-such a story, I am willing to have you tell me stories. I consent to the humiliation of sometimes finding myself inferior to all the characters in them: the pleasure of feeling

---

5. Robert Brown (1728–77), minister of the English Presbyterian Church in Utrecht and a good friend of the Tuyll family. He was friend of Boswell's and is frequently mentioned in his Holland journals.
6. See Letter 63, n. 1.

my esteem for you increase is worth what it costs me in pride. But beyond this pleasure, I promise myself an advantage that is yet more substantial: I feel that no argument has such power over me to combat a bent for the licentious as does a close look at most of the women who abandon themselves to it. Pride and contempt can accomplish what virtue cannot—nor can reason, nor fear of remorse, of abasement, of unhappiness. I shudder at the thought of finding myself confounded in the category with those whom I scorn. My God! If ever, with you counting on your fingers the women who have loved you too much, I were to find myself between La Martin and some other of her kind! The count might go rather high—but you would stop there out of discretion. I can almost hear you saying: "That one now (I mustn't name her) she was a little different; that one was not an actress." And as for me, who knows where I would wind up? Who knows whether I might arrive at one of those cold arrangements so different from love that I can't even imagine the pleasure in them? And in your place, who knows whether I wouldn't debate with what I would call my *probity* and my *delicacy* whether or not I ought to disturb a household like La Martin's? All these humiliating images overclouded my spirit Saturday night to a point you cannot imagine; my sister's contempt finished me off,[7] and I think I took out my anger on you.

But why are these emotions only momentary? Why is it that what *sometimes* seems so odious doesn't *always* seem so? I do not know how others feel after a deep look into themselves, but as for me, as long as I am an impartial spectator of my own heart I do not risk becoming vain. (I should say *spectatress*.) Besides, I share the Marquis's view: if you love La Martin, you might have her. After all, this marriage will not be any great settlement for her; it would only have been delayed perhaps; and then it will hardly matter to society, or even to the theatre, whether the little thespians-to-be are named Dugué,[8] or are born without any name; the only element that justifies your scruples is that lover, bashing his head against the wall. Poor man! He loves her, then! But she loves *you*, you say. If only she had torn out three of her hairs and made one little scratch across her breast, I would have drawn straws to see which side was that of generosity—whether leaving her or taking her should be called noble behavior, delicacy, etc.

I will keep the Marquis's letters with pleasure; I love them, I will love him, you may be sure of it, and he will not be unhappy. Here is the address to put on my letters. I have a hundred thousand things to say to you.

7. The episode of the corset, recounted in her Letter 138.
8. The actor and Marie Martin's lover, referred to in d'Hermenches' Letter 137.

140. *To Constant d'Hermenches, September 6, 1764*

Westerhout

My letter was taken to the post too late the day before yesterday, and I am very annoyed; I would have liked to receive one from you today. Yesterday I was too overcome with the vapors to add any more words to the packet. I read Mandeville[1] in the morning, and spent the afternoon in Mme Hasselaer's room, lying at her feet. Having loosened the tight lacings in our clothing, we chatted for several hours with the tranquil, luxurious delight of friendship and reason. She is never more charming than when she is not the hostess, when it is not a question of form, nor of scrupulously dividing her attention among friends and mere acquaintances, nor of smiling for the sake of smiling—but when she simply gives herself over to herself, to me, to whatever she likes.

At the hour when she was to receive company, I readjusted my clothes and hurried over to Mlle de Mauclerc's; we spent the evening alone together, without any light, both of us sick, but enjoying ourselves as much as we could. She has a clever mind, an excellent heart, a sure sense of what is right, a scrupulous sincerity. Were it not for an undefinable something that is not at all affectation, yet nonetheless robs her phrases, her tones, her gestures of their simplicity and naturalness, I would find her one of the most amiable women I know. —You see that so far neither of us has lost anything for not being together at Westerhout; I have only spoken, only lived tête-à-tête, and I would not have been tête-à-tête with you.

If you have other bits of *Statira*,[2] send them to me—not to afford me the pride of judging them, but rather the pleasure of reading them.

I am rather impatient to know the Marquis's responses. Eight or ten days ago my father gave me a letter from Monsieur Catt,[3] in which he spoke strongly about the Count of Anhalt. There had been rumors in Berlin that I was marrying another German,[4] which caused some surprise and a little consternation; Catt had told the Count that he should secure his possession of me; that no matter how hard he looked, he would never find anyone who would make him as happy as Mlle de Z. I was greatly amused by that style of recommending me. The Count had understood very well, but his situation is awkward. Catt sent along a letter from the Count to him, in which he

1. Bernard Mandeville was a British philosopher and satirist born in Holland. Adam Smith devotes some space to his work in *The Theory of Moral Sentiments*, which Belle had been reading. Here she is probably reading Mandeville's *The Fable of the Bees, or Private Vices, Public Benefits* (1705).
2. D'Hermenches' tragedy about Alexander the Great, which he and Belle discussed in Letters 137 and 138.
3. Formerly tutor to the Tuyll children, now reader at the court of Frederick the Great. See Belle's Letter 127. It was he whose enthusiastic description of Belle had aroused the interest of the count of Anhalt.
4. Von Brömbse of Holstein.

spoke of arrangements that had already been made since their conversation, of letters that were going out, etc.—all of which was utterly obscure to me. A moment later I gave the letters back to my father, saying: "There is an item missing in the collection; it's the response of Monsieur Catt to the Count, and I have supplied it." And indeed, I had written that the Count could be reassured, that he need neither journey nor write; that I would marry neither him nor the Baron from Holstein. Bantering all the while, I had signed the letter, and my father—who saw that I was not joking, and who did not want a serious and official action taken—bantering all the while, tore it up. I, laughing, threw it into the pond—for we are both admirable, my father and I, at being quite aware of what we are doing even when we seem only to be joking. But whether the letter wound up in the pond or in a writing case, my hand had still signed my resolution.

The next day, I told my mother that I had made up my mind, and that it seemed to me more reasonable and more generous to warn the Count, and to prevent a long and useless journey. "This refusal," I said, "does not entail any promise to someone else; I have promised to be free, and I will be." The next day, my father asked me to dictate myself his response to Catt; he softened a little, he wanted it to be from me: "My daughter requests me to tell you ..." The form hardly matters; but if I know myself, if the nature of my resolutions is presently what it has always been, then this thing is certain, and unalterable, and this marriage is no longer in the category of the possible. Do not say a word about this to the Marquis; he would believe that it is for him that I have broken this off, and that the measures I have taken obligate him; that would be a mistake that would distress me greatly. The Count of Anhalt is not the last suitor in the world; and were I never to marry, what does it matter to the honor of the Marquis? You cannot imagine how important this term "liberty" is to me. Each morning the Marquis must wake up with the liberty to want no longer what he wanted the night before.

Farewell, I'm going to Mme Hasselaer, who is getting dressed.

141. *To Constant d'Hermenches, September 7, 1764*

Friday

What! not a word from Monsieur d'Hermenches. Mad creature that I am! I thought that you could not have let so many days go by without writing me, without at least scolding me, without reproaching me for the harshness and the injustice of some of the words that my hateful pen traced as I was leaving Zuylen. I thought that your letter was only awaiting my directions to come, to fly to me. But not at all; you are in no hurry either to insult me or to flatter me; you leave me ... Well, I will not seek revenge. Whenever I can, I will give you news of me; if you do not get my letters, at least my thoughts will be with you; sometimes, when I am at the feet of Mme Hasselaer, as I listen to her, and talk to her, and make her smile, I will think of you and I will wish you were here.

Yesterday I spent away from armchairs and tête-à-têtes. I would have liked you to be here; you would have found me a little crazy, however—in fact, it often occurs to me that it must be hard for you to get used to me. "How can it be," you would say, "how can that possibly amuse you? How can that man make you laugh? How can you be so affectionate toward a woman, kiss her hands and arms, follow her, seek her out, tell her a thousand times that she is charming?"

Yesterday Monsieur Bost and I tried to see which of us could run the faster. In all modesty, I can say that there is no woman who runs like I do. Afterwards I quarreled with him and Mme Hasselaer until the middle of the night.

Farewell. If I can't write any more before the post leaves, I will still continue for tomorrow's.

142. *From Constant d'Hermenches, September 7–8, 1764*

The Hague

Your bad humor would have given me more pleasure than pain; it would be the token of the sincerity of all your impulses; and it is a precious mark of friendship not to give a studied response—but rather to criticize, to yawn with boredom, without contriving to be tactful. Then whether people laugh at us or praise us, we can be assured that it is not merely out of complaisance or affectation.

But I am devastated—what I feared has happened to me. I had foreseen it, I warned you about it, and none the less I have fallen into the trap: you are already disgusted with me! Will there not be, then, one being on this earth to whom one can show oneself naked, without losing the prestige that is accorded only to reserve and to studied circumspection? Since people are used to assuming that all mortals are worth less than meets the eye, if we show ourselves as we are, we lose all the value we have left. If someone blames himself for some weakness: "Oh," people say, "That's a vice of his!" If you admit to one misstep, that authorizes attributing to you a thousand. "You said that once, and I have the right to believe that you still think it!" That is how people judge; "The force of habit has drawn you in and will always carry you along." Why do most honest gamblers never, after a certain time, say what their losses really are, but always exaggerate them? Because it is established that a man who says that he has won a hundred *louis* has really won two hundred, and on the basis of that conventional inflation, the evaluation is made. The novice who says frankly what he has lost and what he has won is a swindler who ruins everybody, for people make their calculations based on half of the indicated loss and on the double of the gain; they envy him, curse him, and avoid him.

I have expressed myself miserably, and you have misunderstood me about all the stories I've told you. I will take care not to tell you more; your little apologue about La Martin makes me shudder, and makes me indignant with myself. I thought that you would simply judge that I was more generous and sensible than libertine and tyrannical; that the senses did not make as much impression on me as did reflection and thoughts about the consequences of an intrigue in which appetite is but little engaged, and the heart not at all; that—more than is the case with other men—the temptation of an ordinary intrigue had less power over me than the fear any torment. The first frenzy of the senses having passed, age and experience have left me enough sensuality to hold my own in the world, but have made me more scrupulous, more refined, more prudent ... Forgive me if I say again these few words on my own behalf.

There is no reason to be distressed by your sister's opinion; it is good and useful, but it proves your innocence and the purity of your impulses. You knew in your conscience that there was no coquetry or affectation in your free and easy behavior; you should thank and bless the person who warns you that people can judge otherwise. Where is the humiliation in all this, I ask you? Are you still unaware that one must serve weak minds according to the weakness of their faculties? If your sister should ever go so far as to unlace herself in front of someone, she will go to bed with him—that's all the conclusion you can logically draw from her being so scandalized.

I didn't receive your letter until two days after it was written, and the reason for it appeared on the envelope; thus, don't be concerned; I am delighted to be able to send you two from my friend. You will see that he too makes rhymes;[1] you will see the impression made on him by your father's reply, and by what I sent him on your behalf. If you are living happily and tranquilly at Beverwijk, half of my wishes are fulfilled; the other half would be to be able to witness it, to see you, to admire you in the calm of the casual acquaintances who surround you. But you are sending me away: "I don't want you to stay a minute longer in Holland on my account," you say.

I would count myself very fortunate if you found my poetry worthy of your corrections, but it would be asking too much to request that you point out to me the prosaic lines. Those are easy to change; I have already corrected one or two inflated epithets. I don't know why she should say anything more about Hephestion at that moment, which is one of constraint, in which she must not mention anything that has not also struck everyone else. In a following scene, she abandons herself more to her feelings, and manifests all the strength and unhappiness of her passion.

I am counting the days, and I am trying to reach the 17th or the 18th, when I will certainly bring my son through Utrecht, if you wish.

---

1. Bellegarde's poetry, alas, has not been found.

What you tell me about Mme Hasselaer flatters me. Believe me, there is no one in the universe who aspires more to seeing people pleased with him, than I do; the *coloration* I apply to things is intended to make them more agreeable and more interesting; I let myself get carried away by the desire to give the greatest satisfaction possible. Every day I am bored, and I put up with it rather than leave a circle where I think I am giving pleasure, or which my departure will disturb; but—cruel fault!—I become embittered toward the absurdities and the vices of people I love the most—and often at the expense of the opinion people will have of my character.

You can be very sure that Monsieur d'Hermenches will never neglect you; you can be sure that if he exists, he exists for you; that he can die of grief through your indifference or your disgust, but that while he lives you will be in his heart and in his mind far above all other beings.

I have just had your cousin Tuyll to dinner;[2] his features have some slight resemblance to yours—a thrill went through me. I went to get Monsieur Arkel;[3] it is as though I can draw nearer to you when I see people who are fond of you.

Your letter of today did me good—but why is it you who are at the feet of someone, kissing her arms? I always imagine that people should be at *your* feet!

I believe you as I would an oracle about everything you tell me. Here is proof of it: I thought that Mlle Mauclerc gave herself intolerable airs— La Sarraz and others had talked to me enough about her, and I myself found her style quite bad—and now I want to get to know her. But you mustn't think that I require marvelous things to amuse or interest me! No one knows better how to loll about. When I'm in the country I can converse for whole evenings with my farmer and his wife and children; I am never bored by scarcity of company, but I am unhappy when I am constrained.

What you tell me about the dispatches from Berlin is very interesting and important to know. You don't say whether your parents would desire this match; neither do you say whether the gentleman is amiable. Even if I had no other interest in the matter, I think I would say, as I do at present, that I have no very high opinion of a marriage arranged by a tutor. Even if Berlin were as close to Lausanne as Chambéry is, I think I would expect you to dislike it there. This is a business in which everything seems to me very precarious.

When I recall that I had a sister-in-law[4] who was very prudish and genuinely chaste; and that as we got more and more familiar and trustful, little by little she would get dressed and undressed in front of me; and that, without noticing, I just happened to be present at the time she went to bed; and

2. Frederik Christiaan Hendrik van Tuyll van Serooskerken (1742–1805), who had once been interested in marrying Belle.
3. A cavalry colonel, later adjutant general to Prince Willem V.
4. Charlotte Pictet, wife of his brother Samuel.

that under pretexts that I myself was blind to, I was still there when she was in bed; that I got her into the habit of chatting on that bed, and enjoying it; that on this account I was neglecting parties and invitations; and that finally, in a moment of delirium, I passionately desired to slip into that bed; that she joked and had too much wit to let me see that she believed my intention to be real; that I went so far as to make all the usual arguments to prove to her that it was all simple and innocent; that I acted like the languishing lover, and was about to unsettle her heart and her senses—then I say: you ought not to have been distressed at your sister; the prejudice is a good one, it is an indispensable barrier within families. Haven't I caught myself finding pleasure in lacing up my own sister,[5] who came all innocently to ask me this favor? I am only familiar with two feelings regarding women, distaste or desire; I never feel indifference; but I am familiar with a certain decency, a self-respect, which is difficult to define. I will trust myself in a tête-à-tête; Venus herself, at the mercy of my good faith, will remain untouched; whether out of modesty, an amour-propre that fears failure or an amour-propre that fears to reveal itself as weaker than the weaker sex, I will be pedantically reserved. But amidst obstacles, in the urgency of the moment, deep in shadow, at the moment when one can escape into the crowd, and escape reproaches and mutual embarrassment, I need a double portion of reason ... So! Do I, indeed, recount only things to my advantage, adorable Agnes?

You want some more of my thrown-together writings? Willingly: here's the end of the scene of which you already have a scrap. I don't know whether I'm being blind, but it seems to me that this sort of dialogue (if it is elevated enough) would be preferable to the dramatic writing of today; I except Corneille, Racine, and Voltaire in their good plays. You must tell me your thoughts about it; I am not obstinate, and I have no pretensions—and even if I were stuffed with them, everything falls before you, everything is at your feet, I swear it, divine and delicious person!

143. *To Constant d'Hermenches, September 8–11, 1764*

Saturday

Heavens! how crazy and wretched men are! Without any likelihood—what am I saying?—against all likelihood, against the very evidence, you persuade yourself of something that devastates you! That I could become disgusted with you! Is it because I write to you continually that you think so? or because I make you the confidant—indeed, the witness—of all the impulses of my soul? Is it, in short, because every characteristic of your soul interests me, moves me, fills me with indignation or delight? If the time

5. Angélique Constant, who became the marquise de Langallerie.

ever comes when, instead of being impolitic, tender, and trusting, I am cold
and polite; when I write short letters and long apologias—then I will allow
you to think that I am growing tired of you. Until then, do not let a ridiculous and bothersome fear trouble a heart that I would like to make happy.
Tell me your stories, show me yourself as you are, be yourself without
reservation, and let me—sometimes sinner, sometimes penitent, sometimes
saint—make my confessions, apologues and homilies. If the Marquis did not
exist, I would think you were very artful. I will say more: if the Marquis
did not exist, then after our correspondence—which has of late burst into a
blaze—after all the confessions, I would believe myself to be in your hands;
and if I did not put whole seas between you and me, it would be entirely up
to you whether or not to see me the weakest of women. But, without the
Marquis, there would never have been these letters, these confessions—
which proves that I am not so extravagant after all; for to rely on my virtue,
when your letters are more captivating than all other letters, your discourse
more captivating than any other; when you play on my feelings at will;
when I have taught you to read in my eyes every sensation of mine, each of
my ideas—then for me to rely on principles, on duty, would be already to
have lost my head. But again I say, I had not lost it; and even without the
Marquis, my prudent reserve would have saved me from you almost as well
as my feelings for him will save me—as well as yours for him, for me, and
for virtue.

I am not sending you away, d'Hermenches—how can you say such a
thing? I made a thousand plans to see you this autumn and winter, here, at
Zuylen, in Utrecht. Not one of them suited you; what do you expect me to
do? Do you want me to make you stay six months longer at the Hague for
the sake of seeing me there for perhaps six days? I am not begging you to
come here; but if you come, if you would like to spend a few days at Wijk
with your son— that is, sleep there and spend the day with us—I promise to
receive you with all possible friendship and pleasure and freedom.

Will you go to Woerden?

I am very sleepy; my style shows it a little, I think; I will love you until I
fall asleep, that is for a few more moments; truly, I love you very much. If
you have been so base as to use your suspicious complaints to win sweet
words from me, you haven't succeeded badly at all.

Sunday

Sweet words aren't enough; I owe you an apology. My bad humor prevented me from telling you how much your conduct with the beautiful penitent girl seemed to me admirable—but could you have failed to understand?
Could you have doubted that I admired it? You insult my judgment and my
heart to think that I underrate you. I will not let one mistaken perception rob
me of the pleasure of believing you. I am not constrained by habit, and, if I
know myself, each new object will make a new impression on me without
old impressions changing and distorting it. You thought that I would see

you more as generous and sensible than as libertine and tyrannical, etc.; indeed, I do see you that way—you are not mistaken! *Forgive me*, you say, *if again I say a few words on my own behalf.* Oh, my God! Please, no humility! I am not fit to have this humble language addressed to me. There was nothing offensive to you in what my imagination painted for me regarding La Martin; rather it was I whom I refused to forgive, I whom I wanted to picture in that humiliating position, loved, and then abandoned—just like the women who are scorned. Let me be afraid sometimes—of you, of myself, of love, of its sensual pleasures; too often my soul becomes complacent and tame, and would like to let itself be seduced. Farewell.

Tuesday morning

By a fine scruple of mine, the letter that I wrote you Saturday has waited for the one that I have just written,[1] which you will do with as you please. My heart insisted that I write it, and I never oppose its wishes without strong reasons. If you find it inappropriate—more likely to displease than to give great pleasure—burn it quickly, for it is intended to give pleasure. I have in my writing case another letter for you that I began I don't know how many days ago. I will finish it when I can; neither your letters nor mine grow old as others do.

I'm not ill-placed at the feet of Mme Hasselaer; even you would not not want to see our roles switched. She has quite another kind of dignity from mine, in both her character and her conduct. She doesn't hesitate between bad and good; she consistently follows what is good. Moreover, she doesn't claim so much homage; she is sensitive to it out of friendship and not out of pride; she repays me by gestures of affection, by a continuous interest in me, and by an indulgence that I would not have expected in a person as cold as she has always been represented to me. There is no predicament that she would not want to extricate me from; no faults, no weaknesses that she would not pardon in me, in spite of her austere prudence. When I reproach her for putting up with a style of badinage which, for all that it comes from France, is nonetheless revolting—a tone that supposes that all men are lovers and perpetually desiring something from a woman—and when I say that this bores and displeases me, that it is impossible for me to laugh at it, that I am scandalized and astonished that *she* can—she listens to me, and doesn't get angry. Indeed, to my mind nothing is so cold, and in such bad taste as these witticisms that are too polite, too decorous to give rise to the image of pleasure, or to arouse desire in our senses, and yet are too free to be virtuous, since they suppose inclinations that duty condemns. I'm expressing myself rather badly, but I think you understand me. A lively, amusing double-entendre can entertain me; I can forgive the playfulness of an imagination afire; if a man who loves me asks me ardently for what he desires, I may not be offended—for that is passion or nature. But when a

---

1. A letter for Bellegarde.

man who does not love me thinks to make himself agreeable by making speeches which I will have to find meaningless if I want not to be offended—that I find intolerable.

Goodbye; I could amuse myself about that and other things for another hour or two, but I cannot—I must leave you.

I hardly dare send you or receive from you any more letters; my father has arrived. I don't dare wish you to come; I don't want to forbid it. Write me once more while I am here, and tell me when and for how long you will be in Utrecht—but no, wait—the time depends upon our return, so I will let you know.

You will like my cousin even more when you learn that he loves me passionately; that's a secret between him and me, so don't joke about it. He has the heart of a king. Farewell; mine is yours, at least as much as it can be.

The last part of *Statira* you sent me has more fire than the first; it gave me great pleasure. I am not pleased with what she says about Hephestion, because a woman who speaks of the first moment when she saw her lover cannot speak of it as she would of an ordinary moment. It's the most fascinating moment—she thinks it's the first moment of her life; a lightning bolt has distinguished it from all the rest. A blind man whose sight is restored will not speak with indifference of the first ray of light that struck his eyes. Whether she wants to confide her secret or keep it, something must indicate that Statira loved Hephestion as soon as she saw him; this occasion above all, this single moment of error which was the first moment of love must have something striking about it. See what fire and grace Racine put in these two confessions:

> Je le vis, je rougis, je palis à sa vue,
> Un trouble s'empara de mon âme éperdue;
> Mes yeux ne voyaient plus, je ne pouvais parler . . .[2]

All the impetuosity of Phèdre's passion can be felt from this first instant; how head-long it is, what force in its expression!

This is milder:

> Je le vis, son regard n'avait rien de farouche;
> Je sentis le reproche expirer dans ma bouche;
> Je sentis contre moi mon coeur se déclarer . . .[3]

To find that Hephestion has the air of a sovereign isn't enough. That might be a part of the impression that he has made, but Statira's heart found much more than that.

---

2. *Phèdre,* I.iii: "I saw him, I blushed, I paled at his sight, / A turmoil overcame my bewildered soul; / My eyes no longer saw, I could no longer speak."
The second line quoted is actually "Un trouble s'eleva dans mon âme éperdue."—"A turmoil welled up in . . . ."
3. From Racine's *Iphigénie* II.i: "I saw him; there was nothing savage in his gaze; / I felt my reproaches die away in my very mouth; / I felt my heart declare itself against me."

The Marquis' verses are sometimes charming in their ideas, and the rhyme lends itself to it with good grace; but the meter doesn't want to join the party. Let him abandon the Phrynés and the Laïs;[4] if ever ... I will repay him abundantly for these privations. His letter gave me real pleasure; I am moved to esteem and gratitude. It's up to the the Fates whether I will be moved to a more tender love.

I have written two long pages on my knees in three minutes; that's enough. Goodbye.

144. *From Constant d'Hermenches, September 12, 1764*

Without a doubt, your mind is beyond everything I ever hoped to find in any living creature! It's precisely that offensive tone (which does not come from France, but from some border garrison at the closest) which I cannot bear, and which Mme Hasselaer likes and encourages, that keeps her from treating me as well as she treats others, and that keeps me from admiring her, or rather that nourishes in my heart a certain resentment against her. I had said this to you once before in other terms, and you were tremendously angry with me; but you authorize me to say it once more: if I had used this wretched jargon with her, I would have been much better received, and even now—in spite of all the relatives—I would be staying on the same floor of the house as you.

Today's packet from you is balm for friendship, but it does nothing for the amour-propre. Why deny it—I will be only the more biddable for it— you have quite made your pronouncement on the matter of me! Throughout what your generous heart and frank soul make you say, there is not a single construction that does not tell me how I have sunk in your opinion. It isn't your fault, it isn't mine; it's the nature of things, it's the ordinary effect of a prestige dimmed by familiarity. As I once said, I have taken off my wig! ...

Your letter[1] is something too wise and too precious for me not to let it go its way; why would I refuse to make my friend the happiest and the vainest of men, if he wishes? But after that, my divine friend, think about yourself; do not let yourself get carried away by your intensity. Bellegarde will not die of grief if he does not win you—honesty obliges me to point this out to you; do not let your own fate be altered by it either.

I am sending you a letter that I have just received;[2] it is all for me, and I beg you to send it back to me. It will make you laugh, and will show you

4. Courtesans of Greek antiquity whose names were often used conventionally in love poetry like that written by Bellegarde, but Belle is using their names also as code words for the real courtesans that Bellegarde probably consorts with.
1. The letter she is sending to Bellegarde through d'Hermenches.
2. A letter from Bellegarde. This paragraph, including the remark about being an oracle, apparently relate to its contents.

just whom we are dealing with. I have crossed out a platitude that might have made you judge him unjustly, and that displeased me; don't, I implore of you, let that make you want to know what it is! Since I am an oracle, you must believe me about this. That scolding you give me is very prettily expressed; you show me off well in the eyes of my friend. But there is a tinge of ridicule that will not escape him. The masters of Eton never dare appear before their pupils without their long robes; I must not appear between the two of you except in the form of a man who invariably wants your reciprocal good, and whose precautions and foresight must not be weakened by anything in the world.

I can make no better reply to your astute reflections on Statira's passion than by sending you the monologue that follows what you already have. I do not believe that the same passion always manifests itself by the same expressions; moreover, it's precisely because Racine had spoken thus before me that I was unable to imitate him. I feel just how much a couple of felicitous lines would give of that grace that my monologue is lacking. Your criticism is just, and perhaps some turn of expression will still come to me that corresponds to your idea, if I go so far as to take up this trifle again. As for my heroine, I am giving her a character particular to her; I am trying to make her captivating even to the least tender hearts, and I am seeking as much of pity and compassion in her favor as can be justified. It's up to you to determine what point I can reach. You must enter a little more into detail, I beg you.

I notice a curious agitation in your whole being since you have been in the country; even a man who had never seen agreeable women—however combustible he might be—could not be as wild about Mme Hasselaer as you seem to be. I leave you for Monsieur Verelst,[3] who has just arrived, and whom I like as much as you like your hostess; and now here is Twickel, who always comes to play my harpsichord just when I would like to write to you. Do not reproach me for all the letters that you write me; if you knew how precious they are to me and how I savor them, you would reproach yourself for not writing more.

145. *To Constant d'Hermenches, September 13–18, 1764*

I am sending you back the letter from the Marquis, and I'm tempted to send back yours along with it. Really, how thoughtless can you be, to reproach me for being agitated! *I notice,* you say, *a curious agitation in your whole being since you have been in the country.* You go on to say that I am too attached to Mme Hasselaer. Good Lord! Do you intend to be jealous of everything that amuses me, of everything I love!

3. Minister plenipotentiary from the United Provinces to Berlin.

Take care; you risk making of me a source of distress rather than of enjoyment. If I marry your friend, you will be less content than you think; if I live far from you, you will not be content at all ... But—no, you don't need to take care at all, if you don't want to; I will see to it myself. For my own peace of mind and yours, so that everything can proceed on its natural and reasonable course, we absolutely must not write to each other so often; we must be less preoccupied with each other. Think how many letters we've exchanged in the last two months! If that were to continue, we would soon be utterly useless to the rest of society. It is obviously not your intention to have only one concern in life; it is certainly not mine. I have as many concerns as the Marquis does, and although I do not gad about as much. I am no less active than he is, and no more disposed, when some enterprise fails, to stand mulling over the wreckage while everything else slides. Virgin or no virgin, Marquise or the most insignificant little matron in the world, I hope I will always be *something*. But for that, one must not waste one's time, nor render oneself incapable—by an occupation that overheats the imagination and the heart—of attending to less fascinating things; one must not abandon oneself over to anyone, be it friend or lover.

You speak endlessly of distaste, of disillusionment; but who can say whether in three days it will not be you who will have had enough of me? Why would I be silly enough to think that impossible? I am not as proud as people think; I find that I am made exactly like those women whom one forgets—there are merely arbitrary differences that determine nothing.

The Marquis, you say, will not die of grief. Ah! Truly, I believe it! On how many quarter-hour occasions has he seen me? But if I myself were to die tomorrow, I can promise you that you would live, and everyone else would live, and the universe would go its way perfectly well. If anyone at all were to be distressed, it would be those who have known me all my life, those I laugh and cry with. They would grieve for a while; they would find a certain empty place in their existence; they would seek me still. And then, eventually, they would cease to look for me; you and they would find a thousand other concerns, and soon it would no longer seem that I had been—neither I myself, nor my death. You would be surprised at how easy it is to come to terms with anything. Not marrying me would cost a reasonable man at most a dinner and a night's sleep. *At most*—I repeat. I have never believed that it would cause any serious unhappiness.

Goodbye; I'm going to bed, it's late. If I'm agitated, it's the madness of writing to you that causes it—forever secrecy, concealment, worry. You, I think, are ungrateful. Goodbye.

Tomorrow we will see whether I know any better what I am saying and whether I am less bitter. —No, I am as I must be, and I'm speaking only the truth.

Thursday, the 13th, at midnight

For three days it has been impossible for me to write; forgive me if I have held onto a letter which perhaps required a response, but I could resolve neither to send it back by itself nor to send it in the company only of the expressions of an irritated mind—a heart that seemed ungrateful. I used against you an opinion that you offered me in good faith and friendship: you say to me: *the Marquis will not die*, and instead of thanking you, I get angry. My pride rebels at the idea that you could think me so vain as to need this advice; I seize upon your words, I take advantage of your thought to tell you harsh and disagreeable things.

But then too—why make my blood boil, telling me that my whole being is agitated since I have been here? Heavens! Who do you think is agitating it? Do you honestly think that my admiration for Mme Hasselaer might have had that effect? The first day, in the joy of seeing her again, that was possible—but ten or twelve days of agitation at being near a woman!... I thought I saw in your reproach a fund of ill-humor that made me tremble for the consequences. My dear d'Hermenches, if I am unjust, if indeed my letters are of a style that shows agitation, then I owe you the humblest apologies; I would wish that a few endearments, a penitent glance might quickly efface an odious impression. Truly, I am not agitated. I sleep, I eat just as I do at Zuylen. Everywhere I am, there are highs and lows in my health; wherever I am, a whole morning of conversation and promenading around without any time to myself, without reading, gives me the the cruellest malaise; that has nothing to do with Westerhout. If in one of those bad moments, or in the middle of the night after I have been in conversations till an hour past midnight, I have written you an incoherent, disjointed letter, don't attribute that to Mme Hasselaer. But let's return to what I was saying to you the other day.

It's true that our correspondence often agitates me, but it is also true that its pleasure and usefulness are not too dearly bought at the price of a little repose. It's true that I want to write to you less, but it's for reasons that may flatter you: our letters are too interesting. For two months now I have had no taste for proofs in mechanics, nor for those algebraic derivations that are such a beautiful thing. I've neglected the harp, I've neglected my women friends. As long as the issue was a marriage that was to determine my destiny, I found that I could neglect everything else. At this point, everything has been said on that matter, and yet our correspondence is as intense as ever; that's not good for us. I simply must return to my algebra, to my tranquil friendships; and you also, to your attachments and your own affairs. If you are not distracted from anything important on my account, so much the better—it does you credit—, but that isn't the case with me. I fear that you have too great a share in my thoughts; that I am getting used to being preoccupied—too intensely preoccupied—with you. I absolutely do not want that to happen: how could it all turn out? A passion perhaps; perhaps a breaking-off. I love you too much to take subtle measures without explaining my motives to you. I will never be reproached for being secretively prudent with a man to whom I have promised and given my trust; listen to me and approve my resolutions.

I think it is very doubtful that the Marquis will still be interested in me a year from now; in the month of March he may be at the other end of the world. A taste acquired in two hours soon fades away with so many distractions; moreover, I am persuaded that neither my father nor my mother will ever give a formal consent. They will say (and perhaps without chagrin): "You are free, do what you wish." They may behave in a friendly manner to the Marquis; if they like him, they will be very pleased, but that formal approval that would make them responsible for the outcome, and that would excite public indignation—that they will not give. And why would they give it, since it would be superfluous? And why would I ask for it? That would not be a loving gesture from me; it would be very ungenerous.

If I see in this marriage the happiness of my life, I am firm enough to choose it, and it matters little to me that people denounce me; but I must not wish for my parents to bear the blame for a thing that concerns only my own happiness. I can sacrifice what belongs to me, but I must not wish for others to sacrifice unnecessarily a reputation that is theirs and that is an essential part of their happiness. And what is the difference between what people would say about me and what they would say about my father? They would say that I am mad; but they would say that he is giving a dangerous example, that he is attacking the security of religion and of the country. If my father had been able to scorn these stupid speeches, I would have thanked Heaven, and I would have married. But he fears them; he thinks he can avoid them by making me wait for the time of my independence. I must be content, especially since the Marquis does not wish to make any effort to marry me sooner; and when the time comes, I can sound out their hearts. But I must not ask them to give a formal consent; I will not press them—that is decided.

If the Marquis insists that they give a formal consent, then we will not spend our lives together—you will live in his castles without me. What will we do then about this habit that attaches us to each other? Will you be content to write to me all your life without ever seeing me? —Yes, that will be possible, *if* from now on you write to me with a tranquil heart—if sometimes you forget me in order to devote yourself to other things—if you think about me only now and then. But after a fiery correspondence, intense and tender, we will want to see each other, d'Hermenches. We will seek each other out if we do not quarrel; and then beware of passion, jealousy, impulse, delirium, and dissoluteness. If I do not marry your friend, if I am always thinking about you, then one day I will become your mistress—unless either we live at opposite ends of the earth or you stop loving me altogether.

Those are my essential reasons; there are others as well: I cannot bear to neglect the things I do—to be learning nothing, to do only a single thing for a single person. A certain pride and an ardent desire for growth, for knowledge, for perfection, make me revolt against that state. If our correspondence is going to continue to please me and not make me blush, it must leave my mind available for attention to things where fancy and sensibility have no part. The most responsive springs of my soul must not be kept in ceaseless motion. I must guard against a dangerous languor that weakens the mind, corrupts the heart and allows the passions to triumph.

My father left this morning for Utrecht; my mother and I will stay here perhaps a few days longer than we had planned. I neither asked for that nor refused it; I am very pleased about it because of Mme Hasselaer, but sorry when I think of you; you must not reproach me about this. Don't put off your trip to Namur any longer, and if you pass by Utrecht, try to see my father. When you return follow the same route; you will certainly find me there. I would give anything in the world for people to become accustomed to seeing you without anxiety, and to have you stay for a while. We would have a better visit than we have had thus far; we would talk. After that, more friendship than ever, but fewer letters.

You will send me the Marquis's letters when you think it appropriate, but we will let that business rest until he raises it again himself. I ask you on my knees, I beg you, I demand that you not press him—stop reproaching him for his gadding about, and let him follow his own impulses. I can conceive no humiliation comparable to that of becoming the wife of a man who would desire me only *somewhat;* you yourself do not think I am made for that, I'm quite sure. Let us wait until March, and let's arm ourselves for any event by proceeding prudently.

I'm very glad that you sent my letter; it seems to me that joking about the oracle can do no harm.

I've just learned that we are leaving Westerhout next Saturday; be in Utrecht before us, or come there only two or three days later; let's not have our meeting look like a contrived rendez-vous.

I don't know how the term "quarrel" slipped into this letter; I promise that I will never have a serious quarrel with you. That you might stop loving me, that you might tire of me—I place that among the improbable possibilities.

Although I'm about to be writing to you much less, still, I will write you tomorrow or this evening. Please send me a letter, long or short, by Thursday. Tell me whether you are angry, or whether you still love me; to tell you how much I care about that would be to tell you that I love you tenderly.

146. *From Constant d'Hermenches, September 20, 1764*

The Hague

Trop de prudence entraîne trop de soin.
Je ne sais point prévoir les malheurs de si loin.[1]

If we take pleasure in writing to each other, why not satisfy ourselves? Even if I catch a fever from it, it is still better than the one that I've had for three days from a damned indigestion. By coarse appetites, or even by boredom, we do ourselves more harm every day than we do by these orgies of the heart and mind for which you would reproach yourself.

Now tell me, for the love of God, what is there left for you to learn? What better have you to do than to enjoy yourself? You already know only too much; you are preparing for yourself infinite torments in the world; it will be peopled only by—in your eyes—the ignorant and stupid. While you are young and pretty, the pleasure of being a marvel sustains you; but you will weary of it. And if you get into the habit of this sublimity of duties and occupations, they will only dig for you a terrible emptiness for the future. Already, what is merely middling is horrible in your view, and you are wearing yourself out; by turning so much inwards toward yourself you are pushing yourself to your very limit. Yes—I want to combat and weaken, if possible, that agitation that torments you at any least event, and, yes, I would prefer that you waste your time in what you call mulling over the wreckage, rather than continually meditate on novel ways of arming yourself.

I have never been in the Marquis's châteaux; he has always stayed with us, because we are a better class of people than those he would have had us meet, and I will go there only when there will be someone better than us: that is certainly you, and you exclusively. Without romanticizing his feelings, I am convinced that if you do not change your mind, you will be his wife, for he will meet no one who is worth what you are. He ought to be getting married; that's why I have applied myself to this project. He is logical and philosophical in his way, and I have no need to tell him anything in this respect. You must also believe that, out of respect for you, I would not do it; Heaven does not provide twice in a lifetime circumstances as favorable to a mortal's aims; thus, I firmly consider the matter in your hands.

Agnes, for three weeks now you have owed me masses of letters in response to mine; you haven't written me for a long time except to talk about passion—anger, reproaches, affairs, justifications ... Be a good fellow, won't you, and write me one of your good long letters that are a whole course of instruction for me. Your remark on jealousy is well taken; I will be on my guard: it's the dregs of sentiments that are too intense.

---

1. "Too much prudence entails too much care. / I cannot foresee misfortunes from so far away." From Racine's *Andromaque* I.ii.

Do you know what's happening to me? I'm beginning to enjoy myself with these scoundrels here, and I may be sorry to leave. There are more people here who like me than I believed, and all in all, my role isn't bad, in spite of things so shocking that at a first glance it would seem that I shouldn't stay here a moment. Were it not for that agitation of yours that I complain about, I would like very much to discuss these things with you, for there is no one who sees things more clearly, nor who judges of things more sanely. I would also be enchanted to go into more detail, even about common everyday things; but that would be to profane the tribunal of your fiery imagination—your thoughts, your actions, your discourse, are always on an epic scale.

This Twickel has just given me a very sad picture of his household. His father and mother are dying of vexation over the conduct of Obdam; they would like to marry off Charles, and they never find what they want. The demoiselle of the nineteen glasses of beer (for he insists on that point) is destined for Lord Athlone;[2] they think that there are commitments, and a bill for damages he owes Rosette. She is having supper at my place tomorrow; he would like me to find out the truth about it, and I don't want to get involved. For three days now, I have scarcely left my bed; I'm giving this supper at the urging of Verelst and Count Voronzow,[3] who are dying to have supper with La Martin.

I'm waiting for your letter about your departure from Wijk, so that mine will reach you in Utrecht. I have a prodigious need to talk to you; perhaps when we see each other you will not be so anxious about the consequences of our correspondence. I do not flatter you all that much; I contradict you often, and often I don't get your point; my conversation is sometimes heavy; and besides all that, I'm already getting some gray hairs. Oh no, Agnes, never, never will you find me worthy of being your lover; I know you better than you know yourself. That very rapidity with which—as you yourself admit—you need to pass from thing to thing will always exclude me from the happiness of being able to make you love me alone. Have me as an admirer—as an adorer—for that I am; there will be no risk in it for you. We will always be friends, always writing to each other. You will confide to me all your joys and sorrows; leave it to me to make sure that their cause will not be your humble servant.

2. The demoiselle in question (see Letter 122) is Belle's cousin Annebetje, who did indeed marry Lord Athlone. Twickel and Obdam are the sons of Wilhelm van Wassenaer Obdam, ambassador to France. Their full names are Carel [Charles] George, Count van Wassenaer van Obdam, Heer van Twickel; and Jacob Jan, Count van Wassenaer van Obdam. Jacob van Obdam, the elder, has been a suitor of Belle. He seems to have some sort of arrangement with an actress of the French theater of the Hague, named Rosette Baptiste.
3. Verelst is minister plenipotentiary from the United Provinces to Berlin. Voronzow is minister plenipotentiary from Russia to the Hague.

147. *To Constant d'Hermenches, September 25, 1764*

Westerhout, Tuesday

I am leaving in an hour, but I will stop for two days in Amsterdam; I'm traveling with my aunt and uncle. My mother has been at Zuylen since Saturday. I say two days in Amsterdam, but who knows whether we will stay there longer. I'll write you as soon as I am back in my ancestral castle, and then, at my leisure, I will give you the long answers I owe you.

Goodbye, d'Hermenches. Reading your last letter, I admired the fact that an extreme levity and gray hair have come to you at the same time and all of a sudden.

149. *To Constant d'Hermenches, September 30, 1764*

Zuylen

After enduring a great deal of tedium in Amsterdam, and sleeping night and day—resting up from the all-night conversations of Westerhout—I arrived here the evening before last.

I hope to see you, and yet I fear the remarks, the conjectures, the public— but especially my father and mother. Come without warning me in advance; it doesn't matter which day. Tell everybody at the Hague that you are taking your son to Namur, that you will pass by Utrecht, and that you propose to see me; say, quite naturally, that it's because of me that you are choosing that route. Someone said to me three or four months ago that you didn't speak my name, that you didn't simply ask for news of me as you would of anybody else. I think that must have been a mistake—the air of secrecy is a sort of indiscretion you wouldn't be capable of; but just now it makes me think to make this request of you. When you are here, let us be as open and direct, as unhypocritical as possible; let's talk about everything except our correspondence. If you are badly received, leave quickly; if not, stay, but not too long. I am eager to make my long responses to your long letters.

My imagination is not so epic that I do not enter willingly into all the details that might be useful to you. But do I know your world well enough—the people you're dealing with—for my judgments to be of any value? One of the men among my friends said to me the other day, "You don't know men, you will be duped a hundred times over by the most mediocre minds." Another exclaimed the following day about my perceptiveness, and said "You have only to open your eyes, and you see immediately all virtues, all foibles, all absurdities; after ten years, I still don't know that woman any better than you do though you have seen her for only two hours." Which one should I believe? Yet both are right; I don't know exactly how, but it is certain that I am both very perceptive and very easy to dupe. My mind sees, but my heart and my conduct do not always take its insights into account; each, I think, goes its separate way.

Good night, I'm falling asleep. Good night, dear d'Hermenches.

151. *To Constant d'Hermenches, October 3, 1764*

Zuylen

It seems to me that you can forward what I wrote last evening.[1]

Your letter touches me. See what habit is, and how dangerous it can be! A thousand little things keep me from writing, and it makes you almost unhappy! It's not my embarrassment about saying what I think of your verses that has caused this silence. Since you can bear the truth about the most delicate points of amour-propre, I'm no longer afraid to judge a tragedy you appear to have abandoned. I will say to you quite directly that I am not at all content with the monologue: it lacks warmth, and the verses are weak. Across the gaps in the sentences one ought to see ideas that are more sequential. The vivacity of sentiment makes the speaker neglect the links, but the listener must be able to perceive them; otherwise, a monologue is merely a delirium, and the character merely by thrashing about on his chair without speaking would tell us just as much.

To undertake a tragedy or an epic poem is to have a courage I can scarcely imagine. Those who succeed to the degree that is needed seem to me demigods. Always to say beautiful things, put them in rhyme and meter, please the ear, satisfy the reason, touch the heart; to say things as well as Racine and Voltaire without saying them in the same way; to observe so many rules, avoid so many shoals—truly, it's magic.

I have a hundred things to say to you; rather than trying to put them in order, I'll take them at random, as they come to mind.

You are still wrong about Mme Hasselaer; if you haven't succeeded with her, it's not at all because you don't have a certain style of making chat. She puts up with it, she adopts it; but even though I detest it, she doesn't find me the worse company. It isn't necessary, it's merely what's done. I have already told you, you seem to her very amiable—a man of wit, amusing, even charming. If she lived in the same city as you, and could see you without shocking anyone and without your demanding to be singled out in any way, you would be one of the men whose company she would enjoy the most in her whole circle. She can get something out of any conversation; she understands the most subtle, she finds charm in the most substantial. You would have the vexation of seeing her chat with the Villates[2] as well, but she makes no mistake about the differences, and she has quite another way of listening to them.

Mlle de Mauclerc complained to me the other day that Mme Hasselaer tolerated the most vapid conversation, got along with the most inferior company, listened to everybody; "Yes," I said, "but her good taste asserts itself—she lets her mind wander to other things."

I yield to your opinion of Mlle de Mauclerc's style—some of her phrases,

---

1. A clandestine letter to Bellegarde, sent by way of d'Hermenches.
2. The baron des Villates was a lieutenant general in the service of the United Provinces.

the expression of her eyes—it's the German tortuousness; it's Mme de Boet-selaer[3] with less experience of the world. But that she has a just and subtle mind, the most sprightly wit, and an excellent heart—for that you can take my word. You could see her twenty times without seeing any of that; she does not concern herself with appearing amiable in company; she day-dreams, or contents herself with listening. There is, I think a certain distortion to which very sensitive women are subject when they are virtuous: it's a certain languor; an interest *so* delicate, *so* detailed, in everything that concerns their friends and relatives—emotions, anxieties; one must have a double dose of good taste for all that to be agreeable and not appear as affectation and simpering. In Geneva, I remember, so many women talk about *sensibility!* I mentioned it the other day to a Genevan lady who understood me very well, and spoke to me of several societies where people were *so very sensitive!* Mlle de Mauclerc has too good a mind for these stupidities, and yet she is also of the class of sensitive and virtuous women.

You don't admit that the kind of talk we complain about has come from France; and I maintain that it has indeed come from there, and I imagine its origin to be in the ancient chivalry where gallantry had so important a place. The tone of that gallantry has changed along with customs, but it hasn't ceased to be the stupidest thing in the world; look at Saint-Evremond, the letters of Chaulieu, those of Fontenelle.[4] Certainly French platitudes become a hundred times flatter in the mouths of the Dutch, but believe me, were it not for the French, we would never have thought of quipping for a half an hour on an equivocal word to which the speaker attached no meaning, and to which the recipient wanted no meaning to be attached. We would not speak so much of conquests, jealousies, etc; a woman who does not care about being loved would not say a thousand things about the passion of a man who doesn't love her. These vapid remarks that have no beginning or end, no reason or verisimilitude—were it not for the French they would never have entered our thick heads.

Mme de Tuyll said to me that when she was in Spa she was tired to death of hearing General de Chabot, a fairly inhumane warrior who had lived beyond the age of being a pretty fellow, speak eternally of the power of women, and seeing him still play the lover. I am convinced that this is not the best French style, but, without prejudice, I assure you that it comes from there, and that France sends us many other quirks that, grafted onto ours, do us as much harm as her fine manners and her coiffures do us good.

I had believed that truth, to be accepted, had no need of assurances piled one on another, of protestations, of vows; I told you that far from being dis-

---

3. Undoubtedly the wife of Baron Nicholas van Boetselaer, the tax collector of the province of Holland.
4. French literati of the late seventeenth and early eighteenth centuries, whose writings are here cited as examples of preciosity.

gusted with you, I love you much more since I had come to know you better; and since that is true, believable, just, natural, I thought I would be
believed at once, and that I had persuaded you once and for all. I was
wrong; you revert to your opinion; you speak of a diminished prestige, and
it seems that you miss the time when we didn't know each other—you miss
the distance that in part hid us from each other's eyes. Then you were for
me like a statue or a picture, placed in the distance. Fine coloring, correct
proportions, an elegant contour can please me at that distance; my eye is
drawn to those beauties; but do you think that, having seen other pictures,
other statues, I am unaware that the bad is mingled with the good? Do you
think that from the beauty of the whole I conclude that all the details are
beautiful? That would be very naïve. If I can, I draw near, I look and I see;
I distinguish the most beautiful traits from those that are less beautiful; I admire and I criticize. If the beauties outweigh the defects, I admire more and
I love more than before. That, d'Hermenches, is my history with respect to
you. If you saw into my heart, there might be a moment when you would be
displeased; but there are a thousand moments when you would be quite
satisfied.

While emptying my writing case, I saw this tumble out of it; I am sending
it to you.[5]

I have reread the monologue, and I have found that my criticism was
somewhat unjust. Except for the ending, it's not that the ideas lack connections, but rather that they lack body, force. It is still true that I don't like
the monologue, and that I love you no less for not writing fine monologues.
It doesn't much matter to me how you speak when you are alone, provided
that you speak well to me when we are together.

Tell me whether the transaction concerning your company has already
been made, and whether you are free or committed to it, so that I may know
whether my reflections will come too late—supposing that I have any to
make.

152. *From Constant d'Hermenches, October 8, 1764*

The Hague

Everything that you reply to my last packet is of the most sublime delicacy—charming Agnes! —and will most delightfully nourish the eagerness
of those who reign at Les Marches; I will send it off tomorrow. You will do
very well not to consult the so-called oracle;[1] you are much more
knowledgeable than he is, and he will always count himself fortunate to
have you for *his* oracle.

---

5. The preceding paragraph.
1. The "oracle" is d'Hermenches himself. It seems Belle referred to him that way in a letter to
Bellegarde. See d'Hermenches' Letter 144.

If you find my monologue bad, it must be that it is; if I had continued that folly, I would however have left it not as a showpiece, but simply as necessary to the exposition. I have always wished, as you do, that its poetry were more sinewy.

However, your verdict on the philosophical shortcomings of my opinion of tutors will not find me so docile. It's my experience of the scope of different positions in life that guides me—an experience that you cannot have, and on which you will permit me to rely, rather than on the superiority that I accord you in metaphysics. Those people have a sort of theoretical enthusiasm that can be regulated neither by knowledge of the world nor by familiarity with certain sentiments, and which is rarely proportioned to the practices of everyday life—just like a young girl who wants to rule her heart and govern her lover according to the novels she has read; or like Monsieur de Soubise,[2] who talks of war to absolute perfection, who knows tactics very well, and who knows neither how to capture a camp, nor organize a march. Monsieur Catt may have told the King and the counts that you were a marvel, that you would be a treasure in marriage—and yet not, for all that, give a faithful account of what would suit you, and what would suit your husband. It's like your chambermaid, who will say that sunlight is more brilliant than moonlight, and could not give the reason for it. How could this man appreciate you? He hasn't known how to obtain for the King anyone who could raise young gentlemen; I know for a fact that he has just put in place there a scoundrel and a fool. It's not that I'm attacking him, Agnes; it's rather that I'm defending myself, whom you are scolding. I'm convinced that the King will not have listened to him more that a few minutes concerning you, and that he was simply boasting about the rest. You should know the fatuity of that kind of Swiss.

I have done nothing about my retirement; I even confess to you that I am becoming reconciled with my position, or at least with living at the Hague. I know that it's because I am dragged along by a detestable laziness, and a sort of independence that a man should blush at. Would you believe that I am weighing the advantages of my own home, where I bring together interests, gaiety, sociability, and a certain authority, against my idle crowds, the languor that reigns here, and my perfect uselessness? But I am here without duties, without constraints; all the hours of the day are mine, and I am not obliged to make any effort of any kind. One becomes stupefied in such a métier, but it is seductive, when one has tasted of everything as I have. It can happen from one moment to another that I will be awakened, and then your arguments will be precious to me; thus, don't refuse to give them to me if they come to the tip of your pen; I am waiting for them, and I am at your feet.

2. Charles de Rohan, prince de Soubise, marshall of France (1715–87). He suffered a notable defeat at the Battle of Rossbach (1757). He was in command during part of the Seven Years' War and was generally blamed for much of France's embarrassment in it.

To judge of my lethargy, you should know that for six months I have not written a single note of music, nor opened my harpsichord four times. I wanted to go over a scene of a tragedy: it was impossible for me. I still have not taken a turn about the woods; I have not been to Scheveningen;[3] but I read all day with delight, and the rest of the time I listen to platitudes, risqué remarks, even dirty jokes, without being bored. So that you don't imitate me, I will close now, and put myself at your feet.

153. *To Constant d'Hermenches, October 17, 1764*

Zuylen, [Wednesday]

Good Lord! How long it's been since I've written you! Your last letter was a little cool; it didn't give me all the usual pleasure. You had grown dull, you said, in your idle crowds and your laziness. As for me, every day I have been too wide awake; walking, talking, listening—it all went too slowly for me; running and thinking were the only things that I could do. I have gone a long time without eating and sleeping; the opium that I'm obliged to take is a sorry remedy. But now that I'm writing you, let's not talk any more of our ills; this is a pleasure that should banish the very idea of them.

My father is going to the Hague next Monday or Tuesday for a conference about rivers. You must see him if you are there; you must speak to him a little about the Marquis, about my conscience, about everything that is appropriate and right about our project. Perhaps I will write to him when he is at the Hague; I will beg him to see you and listen to you, and I will make one last effort to obtain a permission that would make me your friend's wife in six months. I don't dare flatter myself that I will have any success, but at least the reasons I will use to support my request will serve to justify my conduct if, one day, profiting from my independence, I consult only myself, my own taste, my own ideas of happiness. I have spent three months without any rest; I would like some repose, but I don't know where to find it. Too many activities here, too many pleasures there. I think that I would like to spend two weeks at my aunt's at the Hague—the aunt who can't stand me, but that doesn't matter, I love her daughter;[1] I would sleep, and I would see you at the theater. At my sister's I would be freer but less tranquil. We will see whether I can make one of my plans succeed. But you— what is becoming of your plan to come here to see me, to take your son to Namur?

Since nothing has been settled in your transaction, I'm willing to tell you

3. A fishing port near the Hague.
1. The aunt, Jeanne van Tuyll van Serooskerken-de Geer, was the second wife of Belle's paternal uncle Jan Maximiliaan and stepmother of Belle's favorite cousin Annebetje.

my objections to your retirement. In the world, said Mme de Maintenon, one's thoughts turn toward God; in a convent, one's thoughts turn back toward the world.[2] At the Hague, you turn back toward your country, your house, your family; if you suffer from boredom and annoyance there, you foresee with joy the day, the very hour, of your departure. "When I suffer too much," you can say to yourself, "I will leave for good, and I will not return." Any pain that we can end seems to us a temporary pain, and that simple possibility makes of it a bearable pain. After being bored at the Hague, you love your home more than before. It gains by comparison, which adorns it with a new charm—and as sound policy, it should be so adorned. One must try to find agreeable—and continually agreeable—what one cannot change. With a head and a heart such as you have described yours to be, one is never perfectly happy; one is always cursing one thing or another. Well then, it is much better to curse a foreign country than your own—curse the Dutch rather than the Swiss. Besides, in ten years our slug-gishness will displease you less than it does today; and then too, it seems to me that complete independence is not agreeable. When, like you, one is in the prime of life, one is ashamed to see the world go its way without us. It is better to have some bond with society: by the services one renders it, by the prominence one receives from it, by reciprocal duties and aid.

You seem to be reconciling yourself with your stay in the Hague; believe me, that comes in great part from your seeing yourself ready to leave it. That feeling of indulgence will increase if you do indeed leave it—I mean for good. Things will look quite different to you from the way they have seemed up to now. Such is the bad luck of the human mind, that distance weakens annoying impressions, and exaggerates to us the impressions of pleasure. Often a friend who leaves or dies becomes, instead of the quite or-dinary man that he had always seemed, a perfect friend, an inestimable treasure. You have too much wit to be susceptible to such illusions; you will not go as far as that, but still, you will say to yourself: "Did I have so much to complain about? Wouldn't a little indulgence and patience, and a more philosophical attitude, have made the annoyances quite bearable? Have I ap-preciated enough the pleasant side of things? Have I profited as much as I could from the country and its inhabitants?" Especially if you leave behind you enemies, and people who are displeased with you, you will be sorry not to have won them to you before leaving them; you will think that you could have done so; you will be sorry not to be missed by everyone, every-where...

That, I think, is all I know that might make you hesitate about your retire-ment. There is little order in my writing this evening and even less elo-

2. Françoise d'Aubigné, marquise de Maintenon (1635-1719), was the morganatic wife of Louis XIV after the death of his queen Marie-Thérèse in 1683. She was also a considerable in-tellectual figure and leader in pedagogy.

quence, but it seems to me that my head—light and tired as it is—has nevertheless some reason in it.

If I can, tomorrow I will join another letter to this one; if not, I will write to you the first day, without even waiting for your answer. Good night, dear d'Hermenches, good night. If I believed in destiny, I would ask for its book instantly, I would quickly search for my page. Will I belong to Bellegarde? Will he love me very much, with all his heart? And will you always be my friend?

154. *To Constant d'Hermenches, October 18, 1764*

Zuylen

I was by no means forgetting you while I wasn't writing to you. Your indigestion reminded me of what you said once about the stubborn ardor that makes you play, hunt, eat to excess. You say you want to kill the last partridge, finish the last page of a book, leave nothing undone, go as far as possible in everything you undertake. That causes indigestion, but the opposite extreme is at least as troublesome—no, I think it's much worse. Why can't you give me something of your fierceness! I would be happy to rid myself of an excessive delicacy that has all the disadvantages of inconstancy along with many others. The third rubber of whist is unbearable to me, and the obligation to play three of them makes me already hate the first. I am always afraid of having too much of everything. A big portion of the best dish puts me off; I almost never empty a glass; I eat half of ten peaches, ten pears, rather than an entire peach or pear, always trying them all, and holding out for nothing less than perfection, which one so rarely finds! When a book is less than excellent, for fear of finding a single page ... but I am foolish to go on and on about such a ridiculous trait that I shouldn't even admit to myself; I should never think about it except to make myself ashamed of it, to blush for it.

I assure you, d'Hermenches, that I read and reread your letters; not a syllable escapes me; everything in them gives me a keen and constant pleasure. Write me, then, tomorrow if you can; it has been a long time since I have received real letters from you; the last one, as I said, was cool. I think that you were apologizing for contradicting me, saying that it was I who scolded you first—my God, what does it matter! I can't bear such civilities in my friends; if you were often that civil, I too would have to become polite.

You answer me seriously about what I said—that I would no longer consult you—and you say that I am much more knowledgeable than you; you're making fun of your friend. The Marquis complains in his letter that I had submitted my letter to your decision; what I said is only a joke in response to that reproach. I don't imagine myself at all knowledgeable, and I would consult you in a thousand situations with all the docility and trust imaginable. We may have argued about the talents that a tutor may or may not have, or something like that; but we have no dispute over Monsieur Catt— by no means do I take him for an intelligent man. If the King of Prussia had known him as I do, he wouldn't have gone to so much trouble to get him. At the beginning he spent a great deal of time with the King, who even wrote some bad verses against Mme van Berchem, the unfaithful mistress of Catt. He wrote us: "The King has made fun of Mme de Limiers,[1] and permits me to send you this piece." Indeed, it was a piece of mockery. He reads with His Majesty for an hour or two every day, and when he stops to make reflections, "Read, Monsieur Catt, go on reading," the King always says. Poor fellow! He was wished for, and sought out in the most flattering way; he was dazzled; and then he was left to be ruined. Misfortunes and no compensation; the fatigues of attachment and no reward; employment and almost no salary. That King and that court should only be seen at a distance. The only happiness Catt has received is becoming a member of the Academy.

I am boring you, perhaps, recalling old tales that you have already forgotten; but never mind—as you say, you know how to endure boredom. I would have liked to have supper with you that particular evening with La Martin and La Rosette, and be known only by you.[2] I think I would have greatly enjoyed myself. However, I have a few prejudices against Monsieur Verelst: his big blond face is the first, and his light blue eyes the second. I was only a child when I saw him, but my memory is faithful, and the upbringing of his son, whom I have seen from close up, has, I think, forever spoiled things for my esteem. Is it true that La Martin has a great deal of wit, in every way, and a superior discernment in everything? If I were to go to the Hague without my father or my mother, and stay with my sister, you could have me meet her.

You are quite right not to mix in the affairs of the Twickel household. Charles's trustfulness is only his incapacity to keep his mouth shut. I am rather fond of him, however, and I can't bear to see people being rude to him. He's unhappy; let him play on your harpsichord.

Please tell me what you think of my arguments against retirement. They are hardly brilliant, for they are very badly written; you can judge them quite impartially.

Do not believe that I think you would be useless to society outside of the Hague and outside of the service; far from it. I believe and I know that you do a thousand kinds of good at home. It's at the Hague, rather, that you are almost useless; it is independence and idleness that keep you there today. However, it seems to me that professional connections have a certain advantage. It's difficult for me to express my idea; but, for example, I find it

1. The widow Mme de Limiers remarried and became Mme van Berchem.
2. The evening is referred to in d'Hermenches' Letter 146. He had arranged a supper for two diplomats and two actresses—a gathering that a woman of Belle's class could never join.

unfortunate for my uncle[3] that he's no longer obliged to spend a few months of the year at Court. He doesn't like it; but, being always free, he is too free. No obligation to go to the country or return at a certain fixed time; nothing determined in his life; thus, he always has the trouble of deliberating, the embarrassment of choices, the risk of choosing badly. I am nearly always annoyed when dinner and supper interrupt me, but would I be happy for long if I were never interrupted? Will Switzerland please you long, when you will no longer be mingling a bit of Holland with it? I don't really know; but think about it, and be happy.

There's another prejudice in what you say about the business of the Count of Anhalt. Monsieur Catt had apparently found me attractive. I learned a few months after his departure that he had found a way to obtain the pretty portrait of me that is a good likeness. Perhaps he had shown it to the Count; at least he spoke often to him of me. He would put His Majesty to sleep with the description of my charms. The King liked that tale as much as another; he had it repeated to him, and one day he advised me to avoid Fénelon,[4] whom I was reading at the time. The imagination of the Count heats up; he writes, he has others write and speak—not through Monsieur Catt, who has not even named him in his letters as long as the negotiation has been going on. At present he will be the envoy of my refusals—that's all. My father has written him twice under my dictation. But even if he had negotiated this business, what does it matter, if it had succeeded? "I will never have a high opinion," you say, "of a marriage made by a tutor." So any man who educates young people must not find any merit in me, nor speak of me, nor be interested in what concerns me. D'Hermenches, should a philosopher have such prejudices? I would as soon believe in spirits and consult the gypsies.

Farewell for today; I am a little sick. This humid weather affects my nerves.

155. *From Constant d'Hermenches, October 20, 1764*

The Hague

It is in the irrevocable order of things, dear Agnes, that I will be your impassioned friend until my last breath. Your genius will always have my admiration, your virtues my esteem; your graces and your ingenuity my astonishment, and your indulgence, along with your trust, my sincere and unchanging gratitude. All the books of the Sibyls could tell you nothing so certain; why, then would you want to consult the Destinies about me? I

---

3. Hendrik van Tuyll van Serooskerken, lieutenant general in the cavalry and adjutant general to Willem V.

4. François de Salignac de La Mothe-Fénelon, French prelate and writer. His immensely popular work *Télémaque* was a criticism, in fictional guise, of tyrannical kings.

quite believe that you will be my friend's wife; he is going to busy himself seriously with his sister regarding everything that can procure him the means to achieve that, and in the state of things in your household I foresee nothing that can overturn an arrangement that circumstances and your choice have miraculously brought about. The Marquis will not love you as much as I do; he will not feel to that supreme degree all that you are worth; but you will be happier than if you belonged to a man who would prize you as I do; more ceremony, a bit of mockery and mutual influence will lead to more liberty, and I think that you need flattery more than you do tenderness; that's the case with all people as sensitive as you.

I'm not of the opinion that you should make any more efforts with your father. It's enough, I think, that you tell him that you want to get married; on our side, we will do the rest. No match will present itself between now and then whose advantages we cannot counterbalance. As soon as your father is here I will take steps to see him alone and discuss this affair as a calm and detached negotiator—I think that's the best.

I haven't a word to reply to your reasoning about my thoughts on retiring; all your arguments occurred to me when I was deliberating. I can tell you that it was never my intention to remain entirely idle. I have been offered a decoration at the Court of Vienna, which would give me a footing for anything that might present itself thereafter. It is now entirely up to me whether I shall enter into the service of France; I have some very positive letters on this subject from Choiseul's people.[1] Not wanting, however, to start up one transaction before having finished another, if I had left I would, as a matter of principle, have completed that.

Besides, you do not know me well if you think that I would miss my position and this country, whatever the future might hold in store for me. My experience persuades me that I am so constituted as to enjoy myself everywhere, and to find that the place where I am is the most agreeable of all places. It's a great deal of indolence and laziness, and a small amount of skill in knowing how to create for myself interests and occupations in all situations. In Paris I can't conceive that one might exist elsewhere; I savor everything, I fill every moment, and disdain everything that isn't there. In my city,[2] I am the busiest of citizens. I laugh at country-dwellers and their proud idleness, and I am no sooner on my own land than I have to be kidnapped to be brought back among the living. When I came to the Hague, I can say that it was with a horror and a distaste that I didn't believe could be overcome; only the idea of drawing nearer to you sustained me. That lasted

1. The options open to d'Hermenches in France have been brought about at least partly through the agency of Voltaire. The duc de Choiseul (1719–85) was, at various times, minister of foreign affairs and—what's important here—of war and of the navy. He was a long-time friend of Voltaire, who had written both to him and to his sister on d'Hermenches' behalf (*Voltaire's Correspondence* 54: 267–68; 55: 51–52).
2. Lausanne.

a long time; today I no longer find I am bound there by chains, but by many little catches. I'm getting used to this pointlessness, this sort of abjection; I see in it independence, conveniences; without playing any role, I have a rather good position here that allows me to ignore the rest. If here one is judged crudely, unjustly, one can also judge others, and that at least balances things out. I will say more: from here I don't care a fig about my little Lausanne folk, and I miss neither my beautiful house, nor my gardens, nor my hunting, nor my good meals, nor my theater because I see the absurdity and the foibles of all the people I have need of there; that center escapes my view in the distance.

There, again, is a frank portrayal of this character that shamelessly shows itself to you, as it is, and that finds pleasure in it. You portray yours too, such as I feared you were, but such as I know so many people of wit and charm to be: always seeking pleasure and perfection in what they do not have. Experience and a long acquaintance with the world will be the only remedies.

Imagination moves more quickly than the actions of life, and seizes on only the interpretable outlines; the imagination is a picture that presents all objects at once, as a little volume often encompasses a complete course in a very large field of knowledge, or an entire eventful life. Thence come the discontent of those who know pleasure only by speculation; thence come the faults of those who know everything about an art, but who have never practiced it. Just now I listen and I enjoy myself; I occupy myself with things that formerly I regarded with the utmost disdain. Who knows whether one day you will not be delighted to play four rubbers of whist with your sister-in-law, your curé, your children's tutor in your château of Les Marches?

I still think of going to Utrecht, but I haven't yet found the occasion. I'm keeping my son with me because until now he hasn't wasted a moment here. He is getting accustomed to me; he is quickly shedding that exterior shell of prejudices and false enthusiasms that makes young people so gauche; he is receiving good instruction from the English chaplain who takes an interest in him and spends his days with him. My brother will be very much surprised to have nothing left to do except to sustain sensible conversation with him, and give him trainers for physical exercise.

Agnes, I had a singular pleasure the other day at that same Duke's, and at a party like the one where I met you: I danced, I chatted, I looked at your cousin, your sister—I attended only to the Tuylls! They were a bit scared, almost impolite; but I noticed the effect of your influence on your cousin.[3] Since I am your friend, she was willing to listen to me, and dance, and respond. The next day I had my work cut out for me. That sweet girl was mercilessly criticized; Mme Degenfeld, who has the intolerable fault of denigrating all the women who attract attention, fell upon her and upon your

3. Annebetje.

sister, seconded by her entire cohort. I was able to rout them by a comparison with all the other women of the Hague; at least no one could dispute with me her decent and modest air; no one could cite any ignoble gesture, any base word, any stupid airs, and I carried it off by laughing at what they were saying about her good appetite and her big hands, and by concluding that it was better to eat one's fill than to starve oneself to look slim, or not dare do anything for fear of having red hands. This Mme Degenfeld, who is exalted to the heavens here at the Hague, does well to stay here; anywhere else she would be hissed and booed, or else she would have to change her behavior. But here, even I myself coddle her, and lavish praise upon her, because she is without comparison better than the rest.

La Martin has natural good sense, and a decorum in conversation that she has acquired by experience; she also has the qualities of an honorable man who used to be a libertine, and she has the wit as well. But she is still far from having the elevation of soul and genius that would merit the portrait of her that you have been given. What makes me respect and admire her here is that she is so utterly free of pretentions of any kind, and so far from the pettinesses of women of her condition, and of the world.

I must leave you, my dear Agnes, with the greatest regret.

CR *D'Hermenches' situation at this stage in his life is greatly influenced by events in military history that are associated with the name of the duc de Choiseul. D'Hermenches held the rank of colonel in the army of the Allies in Holland. He owned a company, but aspired to owning a regiment and commanding it—to becoming a line officer rather than a staff officer. The meaning of the ownership and command of companies and regiments, and the structure of opportunities for a professional military officer were changing. In the years following France's embarrassment in the Seven Years' War, Choiseul introduced sweeping reforms in the structure, priorities, and personnel of the French army.[4]*

Before Choiseul's reforms, there was no real military organization above the level of the regiment except in time of war. A regiment usually comprised a couple of battalions, each comprising a couple of companies. Captains recruited and owned companies and colonels held commissions from the king and owned regiments. Officers may or may not have had military training or experience—often colonels had none whatsover and left military command to their lieutenant colonels. They held their offices by privilege of birth coupled with a monetary investment—some captains owned companies when they were only fifteen or sixteen years old. Common soldiers were recruited by the owners of companies according to a wide range of criteria and inducements, and training was haphazard. In time of war, brigades,

4. See Kennett, *The French Armies.*

divisions, and armies were pieced together from regiments and commanded by the états majors—*the staff headquarters—whose field marshals, commanding generals, and staff officers became active for the occasion.*

Early in the 1760s Choiseul, as minister of war, began radically to change things. A permanent staff headquarters was established; common soldiers were recruited to become soldiers of the king rather than soldiers of their captains. Commissions were granted only after military training in newly established academies; grand maneuvers, in which divisions and corps executed movements and exercises, were held yearly.

Choiseul's reforms were epochal: French military history is divided into pre- and post-Choiseul eras. It was into this newly conceived military profession that d'Hermenches was invited.

157. *To Constant d'Hermenches, October 28, 1764*

I have just had a quarrel with my dear mother, such a sharp one that I refused to accompany her to church. I'll make up with her in an hour or two, and I won't waste my time just now reproaching or distressing myself. We needed a few frank little disputes to get us past the formal reserve that the business with the Marquis had put between us in the last three months. To be sometimes in the wrong, and to have a mutual experience of it does more good than one might think for friendship and trust. People say that my tone is sharp, imperious—offensive, in short—in a dispute; I am persuaded that there is some truth in this, and I will watch out for it. Meanwhile, in lieu of penitence, I am deliciously dividing my solitude between you and a cup of coffee.

Tell me no more, I beg you, that I am such as you have feared to find me, always seeking pleasure and perfection in what I do not have. In truth, I very often have what I seek; the perfection of things of which I make my pleasures consist are to be found twenty times in a day. A book that pleases me, some needlework that becomes pretty under my hand, the liberty of thinking without saying anything—that is usually enough. Whenever I feel that I can leave off what I am doing, toss aside my book, change my handwork, run or sit as I please—I'm perfectly happy. But to have in front of me a whole day of company, to have to dance all night or play cards for three hours—that causes unbearable surfeit. I've had too much of it before I begin.

I'm extremely pleased with your whole letter. So you are happier than I had thought. If I can, I will go to the Hague toward the end of next month. I will have supper at Mme de Degenfeld's; she has shown me that she would like to get to know me. Her gravity is pleased to amuse itself with me, as the rich and powerful play with their monkeys; but that doesn't bother me, I will still enjoy myself—monkeys, in their turn, are amused by the rich and powerful. Indeed I thought that this elegant deliberateness, this decorous manner, this so-prudent tone and air of a great lady were the ornaments of a mind tainted by a thousand little meannesses. One hardly has the time to elaborate one's words so much when one has a wealth of ideas. It's like the princess in Madame de Sévigné: writing only quite mediocre letters at long intervals, she would spend an hour sharpening her pens, and made flourishes on all the B's and L's.

With Mlle de Tuyll[1] it's just the opposite: no affectation; everything exterior is neglected—but her soul and mind are capable of the best and most beautiful things. She had written me before your conversations with her. Talk with her again the next time you see her.

My sister has another kind of wit that is not easy to come to know. She has more discernment and taste than intellect, which makes her very hard to please; along with that, a proud timidity. But the noblest frankness and the most decided aversion for everything that is degrading elicit the respect of all who know her. That is something that I want to dwell on a moment with pride: of all the Tuylls of my acquaintance there is not one miser, not one deceiver, not one coward, not one woman of easy virtue, not a one who would commit a base act for any self-interest whatsoever—no one, in fact, who is not beneficent and capable of generous acts.

Sunday evening

Instead of reproaches and excuses, we burst out laughing, my mother and I, when we saw each other again; she told me that I had missed nothing by not hearing the sermon. We are here—that is, at Zuylen—alone together, she and I; I am not bored a moment; the days are too short. Today I find that one has to be very stupid to be bored when one is free and alone. But in company I am not like you; the feeling of boredom is compounded by reflection on the uselessness of my existence in a tedious circle. My empty chair, I say to myself on such occasions, would do as well as I; thus in that moment I live for nothing, I do not even live . . . and those are times of horrible impatience. This winter in Utrecht, I will see as few people as possible, but when I see them I will try to overcome my distaste; I will try to amuse, to be liked—to soften just a little the rebukes that will be launched from all sides on my conduct if I marry your friend. People will still say that it's unpardonable; but I don't want my feelings to be poisoned, nor have a thousand voices cry out in unison that I have neither religion nor principles nor affection for my parents. I will also try to remember this as a motive for assiduous politeness at the Hague. I will court Mme de Degenfeld a little. They say that she is a good friend, and what she says is credited by a great number of people.

The Countess of Nassau has given birth; people laugh and talk.[2] To me, all that seems certain is the pleasure that having a child will bring to a

---

1. Her cousin Annebetje.
2. Johanna Gevaerts (1733–79), wife of count Hendrik Karel de Nassau La Lecq de Beverweerd, thirty-four years her senior. Her reputation continued to slide. See Belle's Letter 255.

woman who has only an old fool for a husband; and rather than spoiling by vague conjectures the feeling that makes me share her joy, I will go and congratulate her wholeheartedly. I rather like this woman, and I don't know why. Her lectures bore me; her curiosities are tedious; people assure me that she is not at all my friend, although she seems to be—and yet, she interests me. What is curious about her—supposing indeed that she is given to love affairs—is that she has none of the faults and none of the charms ordinarily ascribed to women who are. No outbursts of jealousy; no pestering; none of that nonchalant self-forgetfulness that is so dangerous but so appealing. Her mind is rigid: she lectures, subdivides, talks politics in a tone that suggests that she doesn't know how to talk of love.

But that's too much talk about a woman who apparently does not interest you at all. Let's talk about your affairs. They say that Vienna is a delightful place to live. I'm too uninformed about everything one would have to know to have a clear wish that you choose this or that, but I'm not sorry to see that you have some disposition to stay as you are. You have no chains binding you to the Hague, you say, but rather little catches. If one can be satisfied with little catches, it's a great happiness not to have chains; life is the sweeter for it, the soul calmer and freer. We do better to enjoy ourselves than to bind ourselves—at least for anyone who does not think himself dead when he is free of passion. In any case, it is very good of you to read what I write about something of which I see only certain aspects. If there enter into your decision none of those passions that obscure for a time even the best vision, you are surely deciding well. —I'm writing badly; my pen, and ink, and head are balking; there is only my heart that tends quite naturally to love you, and that wants me to tell you so. Farewell, d'Hermenches, farewell.

I am delighted by what you tell me about your son. Indeed, he is by no means wasting his time, and you are right to postpone his departure.

We speak of uselessness and indolence in the tone of casuists who are too exacting in the matter of the employment of our time. When one is happy, one must not examine it so closely. Life is not useless, when it is sweet; and then, an indolence that would rest the blood and calm the passions by keeping away everything that excites them, that would dispose us to be easily content with other men and with fortune—such an indolence would be more useful than the best directed activity. Be then usefully idle.

158. *To Constant d'Hermenches, October 29, 1764*

Zuylen

It would not be proper to go into town tomorrow and to bring nothing for you, Monsieur. Let's chat a moment, then, but above all let's not talk about me. What are you doing? What do you say when you are not thinking about our enterprise? Whom do you love, aside from the people you want to marry off, and whom you love so well?

On the eve of that Saturday,[1] when for a moment we breathed the same air, someone said to me (someone who doesn't know you at all) that people didn't think that you were made to be a friend. I said that people were wrong; that you had a heart for loving, for hating, for being a friend, or a lover—indeed for all kinds of feeling; that, although I had seen you only rarely, I had quickly been able to distinguish you in just that way from those whom people put in the same category as you; from people who have intrigues and habits and even attachments without being capable of love or friendship, and who are incapable of the least sacrifice for the object of what they call their passion; that surely you did not resemble them at all; that you loved; that you know how to be generous. I am very glad to have seen all that before I received any incontestable proof, and to have given you my trust in spite of all the gossip, by a sort of prejudice that is a thousand times sweeter and more flattering than an esteem based precisely on solid reasons. The one is a gift given by the heart; the other is a justice that one cannot refuse. In the first instance, even though everybody exclaims that it's an act of rashness, something tells you that it is not, and that you will not be deceived. At present, I am truly in your hands; my whole reputation is entrusted to you. You have found my confessions honorable and my conduct irreproachable in all this, but there would be few people who would judge as you do! Are my letters in your keeping safe from thieves, and safe from all perfidy? I am so careless myself that I can fear the carelessness of my friends without insulting them.

But once again, what are you doing? It looks so likely that we will not be getting married any time soon that I would like to see your mind somewhat detached from that business and busy with other things. If it were less boring in Utrecht, I would propose to you to come spend a little time here this winter; it would be easy now, I think, to have my father and mother see you with me without anxiety—and what do we care about the others? But people find it too boring here; it would be only too obvious that you come only on my account, and we would not see each other enough; but I will try to go to the Hague.

This isn't a question I'm asking you—that would be ridiculous—but I would be rather curious to know whether just now you have a mistress of any sort, or a lady that you're courting, or a girl, or, after all, nobody; whether friendship, the happiness of others, the hope for the sweet, secure companionship of the people you love the most—whether these are enough in themselves to occupy you. —I'm sure you see that there is not the least need to respond; I am amusing myself aimlessly, telling you whatever comes into my mind.

1. At the time of the kermess in Utrecht. See her Letter 104.

There occurred to me yesterday an entirely new method of putting an end to all discussions of libertinage based on a physiognomy that people misjudge. Instead of calling such talk malicious, I said that it was indecent; that women should not concern themselves with a man's morals; that they shouldn't even think about it; that they should not become experts in physiognomies; that instead of admiring the delicacy of these women of such rigid virtue, I found it vulgar of them to allow themselves such a subject of conversation. It seems to me that if that caught on, it would be an excellent thing; it would put me in an odor of sanctity and rare innocence, and it would justify perfectly my connection with you. "So simple at her age! How beautiful!" people would say. But seriously, it would at least cut down on gossip, and on the repetition of old stories. I remember that none of those that people regaled me with on the subject of your love affairs made much impression on me. "Yes, very well," I would say, "I believe you, but what does it matter to me?"

One very slight thing bothered me more: my eldest aunt, whom you no longer remember—a remarkable little person if there ever was one—, recalled four years ago, at the beginning of our acquaintance, that ten or twelve years earlier you mistreated a little dog that Madame d'Hermenches loved very much. I have not forgotten it, because I was angry about it. To love a woman other than one's own wife is less a crime than a misfortune; to sacrifice passion to duty is a difficult thing to do. But not to beat one's wife's dog is so easy that beating it is cruel. In general, there is more cruelty in inflicting little griefs than big ones.

159. *From Constant d'Hermenches, November 1, 1764*

The Hague

I haven't been able to see your father; I tried to visit him, but he did not receive me. All he did was send a lackey to my place with a calling card (for I was at home, and would have received him); he has not shown himself at any play, or concert, or parade, or gathering. Yes indeed, the Tuyll are worthy people; but they are very cold, cheerless, unsociable, and, I think, rather full of their own virtues and nobility; with all that, they fall somewhat short where noble bearing and manners are concerned. I must admit to you (and I say it apropos of Mme de Degenfeld) that as much as I admire and respect all virtues, I detest that stiffness and gravity that professionally virtuous people affect; they push others toward vice. What good did Cato do in his time? He made people mock him, and he perished miserably, as did all his followers.

I had supper yesterday at your sister's house, her husband insisted on it; La Sarraz and Obdam were there. I said, jokingly, that it was a convocation of roués; this supper was going to become tedious, so I employed all my means to enliven things—with some success. La Sarraz, who (all things considered) is the most agreeable man in the Hague, fell into stories about chamber pots—it is the usual basis of his jokes, a habit he acquired with the Princess Royal.[1] After they had laughed for a bit, I pushed the conversation toward more elevated subjects; we talked about literature, customs, illnesses, death; we came back to comical things, and La Sarraz was still there with his chamber pot. Your sister laughed at his scatological jokes, but reddened with anger at any double-entendre. This was all very interesting to me because she's your sister; often I imagined you in our midst. We drank to your health; I asked your sister permission to do so, and she blushed; finally I ended the gathering. I am curious to know what she thought, and whether she is pleased. Colonel Prevost,[2] a great boaster about his profession but a very good man, had not a word to say. I had supper on Sunday and Tuesday with your cousin;[3] I played cards with her the first day, along with Ambassador Wassenaer and Monster.[4] One could hardly be more awkward—almost sullen; but I find some charm in her because of what you have told me about her; her awkwardness is only naïveté and absent-mindedness, but the others do not judge it so. I exalted her as much as I could, but I have ceased to be her cavalier—to avoid stupid raillery, and also for lack of things to say to her, for she supplies nothing at all. At the Duke's ball, she was badly dressed; she lacks bearing; but she's beautiful, and she has a very noble and honest gaze. Today I dined with her sister, who says nothing either. How is it with all these Dutch women? If they have not drunk seven or eight glasses of *vinn roudge*, they can hardly pronounce a word; and the Tuyll are sober people. And you, Agnes, on what milk have you suckled? You are the vampire of all the souls of this country's inhabitants; it's a divine fire that inspires you. Your brother too lacks vivacity; but I love them all, for the nobility of their sentiments, and for the love of you, who are my idol.

Those transitions from ambition to indolence that you depict so well are the continual struggle that goes on in my thoughts. Often I say to myself: Why do I not become an extraordinary man? In literature, war, or business, one only has to work, and to seek one's place. The moment after: —What madness not to follow the impulses of our desires and needs! Augustus was no happier after having conquered the universe; the King of Prussia is melancholy; Voltaire is criticized, torn to pieces, despised. All the famous people are judged by fools. Cornabé died dejected and worn out by work; Kniphausen, my friend, a man rare in his wit and his skill in negotiation—of the most charming character, the most agreeable countenance—after having

1. Anne of Hanover (1709-59), daughter of George II of England, wife of the stadholder Willem IV, and mother of the present stadholder, Willem V. She had been the regent of the young Willem V after her husband's death.
2. The brother of a former governess of Belle's, Jeanne-Louise Prevost.
3. Annebetje.
4. Unico Wilhelm van Wassenaer Obdam, ambassador to France, was the father of d'Hermenches' friends Obdam and Twickel. Frederik Unico van Monster was a captain.

consumed his goods and the prime of his life in the service of a grand king, languishes in obscurity.[5] Let us remain obscure, I then say, without going to so much trouble, and let Fortune, if it please her, come to seek me out by my fireside with the person who gives me the most pleasure; or in my bed, with a book in my hand; —and then comes remorse over wasted time, so many cares and words expended on small things, so many hours sacrificed to idleness or the daily routine of the world, leaving not the slightest trace. Then I blush, and I loathe myself; I wonder what is the reason for my existence, and I see that I do not deserve to exist; I can't comprehend it . . .

Agnes, you are far superior to me! Be aware of your good fortune, and of the excellence of the organization of your temperament. But who knows whether at a certain age you may not have more anxieties? Even now I could already wish for you less celebrity; more than once I could have wished that people not say: "Is that the author of *The Nobleman*?" However, it is impossible to be distinguished by more wit, nor by a more sublime character.

Other times, I push my reflections further: if men after their death preserve some awareness of what goes on in the world, isn't that perhaps the true reward and punishment that religion and philosophy tell us of? It seems, when one follows them in the labors and trials that they brave in this life, that all great souls are impelled toward that goal—a renown that one enjoys very rarely. The heroes—whether heroes in war or heroes in their studies—who have enjoyed none of the luxuries that the sensual man feeds on will be magnificently recompensed if they see that after their lifetimes they are venerated, imitated; that they are the ornaments of their families and their countries, and that their existence is truly still useful and precious to the human race. These rewards would certainly be fixed and irrevocable, for the most exact justice is dealt to those who are no more: each great man has his place, each work is appreciated and consecrated for posterity. Those who have dazzled us by great talents or grand actions dazzle us no longer; we weigh their merit; we expose their weaknesses to the light of day. According to this principle, imagine the torment of a man who has seen himself honored, who has believed himself loved and respected in his circle, if he sees that after his death he is forgotten—that precisely nothing remains of him. His goods, his titles have passed to another; his merit, his wit—all unknown, and his portrait goes to decorate some antechamber; he is dead for posterity as he is for his contemporaries. So far as this passive existence goes, he suffers the fate of mere matter, and that is indeed a punishment. Construing in this way, all other beings will be sunk to nothing; the ill or the good that they have done is lost in the cycle of exigencies, and I do not see that in all fairness it would be possible to establish a Hell or a Paradise

5. François Cornabé was colonel of a Swiss regiment, then later a general, responsible for the external correspondence of the United Provinces. Baron Ferdinand van Kniphausen became deputy from Groningen to the Council of State in 1766.

in any other way; everything will depend on the degree of sentiment and of purposive calculation in each person.

See then, Agnes, how one cannot keep oneself from tackling all sorts of subjects when one is fortunate enough to hold converse with you!

I do not think as you do that there will be any great outcry when you marry the Marquis; his position is very suitable for you, and if he follows my idea, which is to bring into it all possible formality and ceremony, I think that people will judge that you are doing well. The issue of religion will not cause a sensation among society people; fundamentally, it is they who join together and judge; the others will be edified. I beg you to send me back the letter from his sister.

I wouldn't be going to Vienna, but to Brussels, where I can live with my oldest and most faithful friends;[6] I can get some money from my employment, receive a decoration, and live independently. If I am willing to go to France, I am offered employment there; what do you advise me? I'm quite old, I'm lazy; I would have to act like a competent man, even a pedant; I would have to pay court; I think that I would make a name for myself, but at some cost to my convenience. I would have to abandon my son to his fate, until some favorable circumstance arose. But at least I wouldn't see a coarse peasant from Neuchâtel, without any sort of merit, become my superior;[7] I would live with men, and not with the little Hops, Horsts, Reynsts, Vernands, Fagels, Anthonys, Cruinings, Obdams—all of them false, fools or scoundrels. What do you think of all this, Agnes?

So come to the Hague; I will enjoy seeing you doing battle with Mme Degenfeld; she will be impressed by you, and it will be delightful; I will point out to you little things that will keep you from losing an inch of terrain to her. But first, come! For once in your life, be free to do something for my benefit!

160. *From Constant d'Hermenches, November 1, 1764*

The Hague

[The beginning of this letter is missing.]

... true in the sense that you have been told; it is certain that I often wage war on her dogs, because she has the foible of loving them to the point of being ridiculous, and yet she has enough sense to recognize this ridiculousness. Often she is impolite to the people she likes the most, and all because of her dogs; often she carelessly lets strangers be inconvenienced by these animals; they divert all her attention and her care. I have done her the

6. Probably the duke and duchess of Arenberg, good friends of d'Hermenches who are mentioned a number of times in later letters. He was a field marshal and owner of a regiment in the service of the Holy Roman Empire.
7. Claude-François Sandoz, a Swiss officer in the service of Holland.

service of making her feel, by all kinds of means, this intolerable rudeness, and I have had the generosity to take on myself the blame for that sort of maliciousness that is attributed to me, in order to excuse or conceal all the better her foolishness and her weakness. I have constantly played this role with Mme d'Hermenches: I enjoy letting her pass for a model, a marvel; and I take on myself all the blame for the sharp remarks, the neglectfulness, the harshness. How happy I would be if someone of a just and penetrating insight like yours had witnessed me in my conduct and my principles! I dare to believe that you would have decided that I was, of all those who have ever existed, the being who knows how to love the most nobly and the most truly; I am so sure on this point that often I have let appearances wrong me, and thereby laid myself open to the gossip of little minds. No woman will ever have a husband of my caliber, I dare say, when these relationships are understood in their whole extent, and in their largest purpose.

I have no mistress; I have a thousand little adventures in which—by I know not what twist of fate—there is always something singular and romantic; to which I bring not intrigue, but rather generosity and morality— not that I make it my study, but it happens that circumstances make me find more satisfaction in that turn of things than in another. When my arteries permit, I will tell you all about it; I even offer, if you will tell me about all the scandalous stories you've heard about me, to give you the true versions. If you can believe me, you will be astonished. The other day, one of the prettiest girls in the Hague, whom I had been eying (as all the men do) sent word to me that she wanted to see me. After many negotiations as to the place and time, after various incidents and uncertainties, we finally met. As soon as we were alone, she dissolved into tears and wanted to run away. I showed my astonishment, and perhaps a little indignation; she threw her arms around my neck, kissed me, told me that she had loved me for a long time, that she had ventured to see me; that she was handing herself over to me, but that for the love of God I was to leave her in peace. While she multiplied her tears and kisses, I was frozen; I begged her to compose herself. We talked more calmly; she revealed to me that she was still in a state of innocence; that her plan had been to destroy it, and that she was repenting . . . I urged her to keep her chastity, I made her accept a small present, and I let her go. She is as pretty as an angel!

I have no affair with a woman except with one whom I loved thirteen years ago. For three years we lived on terms of a limitless familiarity, and yet without my ever having won from her all I desired; her scruples kept increasing. For five years we have been writing to each other, and hardly ever speaking. She was very young; she has become a very amiable woman; it was I who formed her mind and heart. Everyone loves her, and seeks her out; she is noted for her wit, delicacy, taste, character; and would you believe that all I have from all that are some letters—rather tender ones, it is true, but ones in which she never ceases to scold me, reproach me, blame me? You can well imagine that this commerce would have ended a long time ago if my silence did not provoke yet stronger reproaches ...

My God! what a lot of foolishness I am writing! Is it really to the being who has the most genius, taste and superiority in the whole universe that I dare address such a rhapsody!

Thursday evening

You wanted me to talk about myself: I could hardly do it more diligently; this will cure you, I hope.

161. *To Constant d'Hermenches, November 3–6, 1764*

Good evening, d'Hermenches. Quickly, before I go to bed, I must thank you for the pleasure your letter has given me. I received it only today; Mme Geelvinck sometimes lets a good two days go by without coming to see me, even though we live within the same city walls. I had to laugh at the account of the supper, and all the Tuylls, and the Dutch ladies, and the red wine to loosen their heavy tongues. However, I am sorry about my cousin; she has all the merit that I have described to you, but such a horrible education for high society! I sent her some pretty dress material; my aunt said that at best it was only good for a man's dressing gown. Monsieur van Rhoon[1] came in: "Who chose that?" "My cousin." "It's ugly, it's horrible!" And then no one dares use it. Things balance each other out. Believe me, I would be wrong to be proud. If it were only a *divine* fire that burned in me ... I am not of ice, but then, I am not so very chaste. You will not say that my gaze is chaste. (My heart—let it not be taken in—is not either.) Now that I have taught you to read it so well, I will not often dare to raise my eyes before you.

Goodbye, I'm going to bed. My cousins are much better than I am. Farewell, Father Confessor. I do not believe in your Hell, but I do believe in Purgatory.

Sunday

It is six-thirty by the sound of the bell, and already I am holding a pen. Three hours ago I was already thinking of getting up. You speak of my father; he would sleep less than I do if he could see my heart in broad daylight. But he could never know it; no matter what I said, he would see laxness of principle, but he would not imagine the fire of passions. Passions alone can conceive of passions; every time reason enters into discourse with passion, reason shows that it cannot conceive of passion; they speak two different languages; they cannot understand each other.

By the way, my father is not all abristle with that gravity of virtue that you speak of regarding Mme Degenfeld. He does not declaim against the

---

1. The father of Anthony Bentinck.

vicious person, or even against vice; he seems rather to be unaware of them, and not to want to know them. He is a man accustomed to paintings of a cheerful landscape where nature is to be seen in its happiness and beauty; he turns his eyes away from the horrors of a tempest, or the martyrdom of St. Laurence burned on a grill, or of a Last Judgment. The painter may surpass himself in these horrible subjects; my father sees only an imitation all the more horrible as it is more perfect; he admires, but he returns to the landscape.

It is a curious thing, the effects of this moderate, wise, mild character. My father has that influence on his whole family that a superiority of mind and knowledge should give when one uses them continually in the service of others. The lexicon of the whole family is formed on his thoughts That is to say, he limits himself to expressions of decorum, rectitude, virtue, a sincere but cool politeness. No exclamations, no vivid expressions, no chamber pots. It's only my mother who knows how to exaggerate. You should see how little I am understood when I give way to my indignations or my enthusiasms. It is truly an astonishing thing that I am called Dutch and Tuyll. Providence must have insisted absolutely that I be what I am. The physical and the moral seem to have opposed it with all their might. My family have been not wrong, perhaps; all things considered, I have nothing to reproach them with; what has all this fire to do with happiness? You say that my brother lacks vivacity; well, so much the better! What would he do with vivacity in his country? Here one is vivacious all alone. Good sense, a generous heart, the kinds of knowledge that are useful in one's profession and agreeable in society; a taste for occupying oneself, an easy humor, varied and moderate pleasures—for someone I love, that is what I wish.

Vincent is scandalized by the malicious tone that prevails at the Hague; he says that people mock whatever is decent and gossip about whatever is not. The duping of Starrenburg,[2] who was advised to get a new suit of clothes to please his mistress—that he finds pitiful. The less wit the other has, the more he finds the game stupid and wretched. We have been reading Plutarch's *Lives* since yesterday. We will read some novels. I want to try all means to separate in his mind the idea of a book from the idea of hard labor. Young men are so slow to acquire the idea of reading for pleasure!

My father has been slightly ill, and still busy at the Hague; that's why you haven't seen him. This whole business of dikes and rivers in this province depends on him and M. Brouwer. Well, this M. Brouwer, who is unique for his sagacity and knowledge, is thought by many people not to have any religion. My father sees him every day, admires him, enjoys being with him, and is careful not to clear up this accusation; he simply avoids the idea of it. One could be his best friend and have mistresses, provided that

2. Willem Lodevijk, count van Wassenaer, seigneur de Starrenburg, captain of the dikes of the Rhine Basin, and ambassador to Russia and Austria.

one didn't talk to him about it. What is also curious is that among us, errors are banished from conversation as well as vices. My father thinks that silence is better than refutation. My sister was much surprised to hear talk of ghosts at school—she didn't even know the word.

The conclusion of all this is that I want you to think well of my father. Enlightened, modest, laborious, lenient, full of respect for the Creator and benevolence for the creature, useful to his friends, even more useful to his country—whatever Paradise you might imagine, my father will enter it.

My letter has been waiting for a sequel for several days; it was not interesting enough to go off by itself. Besides, I was hoping from one day to the next to be able to tell you something positive about my visit to the Hague, but no day brought any more certainty than the one before. I promise to do what I can. They will have to prevent me quite directly from making this journey; I will not give it up just to please. I am very impatient to see you; but do you not feel that our meeting will be strange—at least the first moment? One hardly blushes while writing; but one blushes when gazed at to the depths of the heart.

Let's talk about something else; let's talk about Paradise. Yours is not so badly imagined, provided that it is only *one* Paradise, while we wait for another. When the world comes to an end, there will no longer be anything to see for those who busied themselves by watching it; they will have to find another occupation, other pleasures, other pains. Another supposition that will be necessary for your hypothesis: the souls of the dead would be happy or unhappy not precisely by the good or ill report of them that remains on earth, but by the good or bad consequences of what they had done there. Without that, there would be no punishment for the secret crime, no recompense for the modest virtue of a ploughman. I want him to be aware of the abundant harvests from the lands he has improved; of the happiness of a family that he has raised for work and virtue; he must be able to see his grandson, a brave soldier, and his granddaughter, a rich farmwoman. It is not a question for him of immortality—his name is not made for glory. Oblivion would be a hell only for the vain and the ambitious, especially for bad authors. They would see their books successively relegated to the corner of a library, rejected in a sale, turned into tobacco cones, and finally used as curlpapers. Those who had done neither good nor ill in this world, having left no trace of their life, finding no consequence of their actions, would be bored in the other world, and this punishment would be all the more just in that usually they bored everybody in this world. When I have the time, I will tell you about the Paradise and the Hell that I imagine.

I don't know Brussels at all; I can't advise you; I'm sorry. For your sake I would be happy to give up that kind of amour-propre that makes one so afraid of being responsible for events. If I thought I saw what would most favor your happiness, I would tell you, at the risk of having to recognize later that I was wrong.

Meanwhile, would it be impossible for you to see people in a different light, and to reverse the conclusion you made after enumerating your acquaintances at the Hague—to see in Obdam an man of wit, in Monsieur Reynst a good fellow, in Monsieur Horst a gentleman? I speak of the last only by hearsay, so what I say means nothing.

My sister had been very apprehensive about this congregation of wits at supper, but she admitted the next day that she had enjoyed it more than she would have thought.

Goodbye; I have answered all these points quickly because I have to get dressed and receive some young ladies and Mme Geelvinck—a very innocent little party at which I do not deserve to enjoy myself. Goodbye; I would as soon see you as these virgins; they are, however, very amiable, and they are better than I am.

Tuesday night

At this moment I can't look for the letter from Monsieur de Bellegarde any more than you can look for the trios.

162. *To Constant d'Hermenches, November 8-9, 1764*

I think, finally, that I will be free to go to the Hague; we have had a rather long conversation, my mother and I; we spoke calmly and reasonably about everything—you, your friend, the impression of myself that it was in my own interests to give in public. After the conversation she said that she loved me a little less than before, but she said it jokingly, and while accepting my caresses. So I will go to the Hague; we will see each other, d'Hermenches, with a good deal of liberty—not, however, with complete liberty, and so much the better.

Do you know what I am afraid of? Of approaching you provocatively, caressingly. One of the brakes that stops sensual women is the fear of indiscretion, and with you it seems to me that I would have nothing to fear. If I were to give you a kiss, would you betray me? Perhaps you would think yourself obliged to tell your friend to give up a woman more given to the wild passions of love than to delicate tenderness ... I don't know what you would say; but be careful not to try to set my senses ablaze. You know me so well that there would be little glory in exciting a guilty emotion; there would be a great deal more in remaining my good and prudent friend. Be austere, even, if necessary. I hope it won't be; I hope that I will not give you the glory of such a triumph; but when all's said and done, I wouldn't dare to answer for myself on such a unique occasion, when a man who is sensual, a libertine until now, thought to be dangerous, finds himself in possession of all the secrets of my heart, of my most intimate trust, and is so attached to me that I cannot fear from him either treachery or scorn. No—since, after everything that I have said to you, you do not despise me, my caresses would not make me despicable ... You would receive them, however, with a tincture of remorse that would spoil all the pleasure. I won't offer any at all, I hope, I believe; but I wanted to tell you my fears and my scruples.

You are grateful for my sincerity, and I myself find pleasure in it; I regard it almost as a duty; and it is satisfying to me to prove to you how much I trust you by saying things that people simply do not say. The least scrupulous women give their weaknesses out to be an excess of sensibility, of complaisance; I think they are false; if they are sincere, I congratulate them. You are too discreet to answer me. Draw back your hand, if it were to happen that I tried to give you mine. Goodbye. I'm going to bed. Goodbye.

Thursday night

Friday

As soon as the time is set for my journey to the Hague I will let you know. Tomorrow I'm going to Amsterdam for two days.

163. *From Constant d'Hermenches, November 13, 1764*

I give you my word of honor, dear Agnes, that I respect and esteem your father in a way that should satisfy you, and that everything I know of him requires of me. I also like your cousin very much, and if I have complained of her it is because of this very sentiment: I would like people to do her more justice; I would prefer that the only beautiful soul who may be here should be seen in its true light—not that it is cruelly obscured by its material shell, for she is not at all sullen; she has a noble gaze and expression, and she doesn't talk nonsense. But let's leave your relatives, and let it be me that occupies you the most today, for I am unhappy—all the more in that my fate is in my own hands, and I am going to be responsible for that of my whole life.

Just an hour ago I receive from Vienna a letter telling me that I am going to be made the Emperor's chamberlain; and one from Paris, in which I am told that the King is offering me ten thousand livres of salary, a staff position in a Swiss regiment, my rank as a colonel and expectations of all the favors that such a beginning promises: many friends, and a good reputation.

I have been completely disenchanted with things here; the late Princess[1] had ruined me by obligations on my company that threw me into debts—I have not been dupe enough to pay for them directly out of my own pocket.[2]

1. Princess of Orange, regent of the young stadholder. See Letter 159, n. 1.
2. The owner of a military company was paid by the state for its services, but he was financially responsible for its maintenance and operations. As with a business franchise, one might make or lose money.

I saw no means of advancement; a coarse peasant from Neuchâtel[3] was the man who should make a place for me, and under whom it oppresses me to serve; the Duke[4] treated me rather coldly; people said that I had enemies; the regiment is ill-furnished with officers—not a man who isn't petty-minded and vain. It pains me to see all your young people thinking themselves quite superior to us as soon as they take office, and having that opinion fortified by the regard of the Stadholder.

But the Hague is a place where one lives freely; there are some good people here; little is demanded of one; I can take as many leaves as I please; I will soon be a major general; I can eventually own the regiment. The chamberlain's key will give me some distinction if I stay here, and at least parity vis-a-vis the people of the Court, who are greatly impressed by it; and in all the other courts it gives prerogatives. In the Netherlands, I am free of everything, and I am treated with distinction at the Court of Brussels; do I want to attach myself to it? The door is open for me; what shall I do?

If I am given forty thousand florins for my company, as Golofkine[5] has offered me, and if I make my fortune in France in a few years—or if I should die—I will certainly have made a wise decision to accept what is presenting itself; I am nearer my home; my position calls upon me often to live in Paris; but I must also get accustomed to a laborious life, a garrison life, full of endless petty details. The salaries are about the same in compensating for the cost of living in these countries, but here it is more permissible, it is even authorized, to live stingily, and without any amenities—your General Cannenburg makes a good day of it at everybody's parties, and eats like the very devil at suppers, without gambling, in uniform, wearing black stockings, cadenettes,[6] and his wife's old lace cuffs. I will be a general here in two years; in France, I may not become one in ten years, but I have only to live, and I will have a regiment that will bear my name; here, never. I will live among charming people, I will be dependent on my best friends; I will have a military cross and sash. On the other hand, that key will mean nothing to me; perhaps I will have to give it back at the first war.[7]

Put all this together, genius, and dictate your oracles; it is a fine thing to possess all the charms of youth while ordering the conduct of a gray-haired soldier. I have only a very few days to make up my mind, and I have no one here in whom it would be wise to confide. Better yet: come to the Hague, force circumstances a little; this is the season of fêtes and balls; say that you

---

3. Claude-François Sandoz, mentioned in his Letter 159, n. 7.
4. The duke of Brunswick, commander of the Allied troops in the Netherlands.
5. Gabriel-Marie-Ernst, comte de Golofkine, colonel in the Swiss Guards; an adjutant of the Stadholder Willem V.
6. A military hair-style, in which a braid was worn on each side of the face.
7. That is, the honorary key of the emperor's chamberlain will mean nothing in France.

want to take advantage of it—it would take only one bereavement or one least untoward event to spoil the rest of the winter season. Come, and you will make my Paradise.

The Paradise of mine that you want to change is much simpler than you understood. The good ploughman will be neither happy nor unhappy; he will not know whether his children have turned out well or badly; if people speak well of him he will know about it, and I am not at all opposed to beings undergoing another modification after this life. If you find them too idle merely savoring their fame, let them have employment; hidden crimes will be punished by remorse or by annihilation; but I would regard pain or pleasure as a second creation for all those millions of beings who have only followed instinct or stupidity.

I haven't written you these last few days because you were in Amsterdam; today I am writing you nothing that's worth anything because my head is spinning—and is there not good reason, Agnes? Bear in mind that if I refuse, I offend—indeed, I alienate forever—some powerful friends who think they have performed miracles for me. And indeed it is a miracle to have this opportunity in a time of peace and reform.[8] My son is no obstacle; he is really a good boy; people will be glad to keep him here, they will be glad to have him there, and he is of such a good temperament that my care is not indispensable to him, as you see in the letter that Mr. Yorke's chaplain[9] has written me; please send it back to me so that I can copy it for Madame d'Hermenches.

But, Agnes, I'm forty years old; I may be an invalid in a few years, and will not be able to claim the same indulgences except by serving in a land where I and mine were born. On the other hand, with forty thousand florins more, I have eight thousand livres of income for life; and then I can do without all the services; I can round out my lands, increase my daughter's dowry without acquiring one sou of debts, and, safe at home, can tranquilly defy events and ambition. The Duchess of Arenberg, who does not suspect the pressure I am under, writes me that she has arrived in Brussels; she is asking me to act in their theater and direct their plays, and is delighted about this key.

You must admit that this is a very singular postal delivery! Forgive the writer, who only brings you cumbersome, badly-posed questions.

By the way, I cannot fail to wonder at the range of your mind's play in the reflections you make on our meeting. Your imagination is everything; that is what carries the fire; your senses count for nothing, as you will see when we meet. If I make bold to kiss your hand in a corridor, or to press it while we are dancing, I will merely seem pitiful to you. The finest letters most often produce the coolest meetings, just as the most tender rendezvous

---

8. The sweeping reforms of the French military structure executed by Choiseul.
9. Archibald Maclaine, chaplain of Sir Joseph Yorke, the British ambassador.

are followed by the most laconic love-notes. I am not at all worried about our meeting. It is still a person worthy of all my respect, all my admiration, in whom I have put all my confidence, and whom I love with all the faculties of my soul, to whom I will pay homage; I would be unable to fear, or premeditate, or seek to know anything about impulses guided by such sentiments. Good night, Agnes; I am going to the ball, where I will undoubtedly see things very differently from the way I did yesterday.

164. *To Constant d'Hermenches, November 18, 1764*

I am still in Amsterdam. I am thinking of you. I will write to you tonight. At this moment, after a few hours of reflection I like the forty thousand florins and France. When you become yet more philosophical, if you find you are getting old, you need only leave everything and live on your own lands; but why so early? There would be a sort of pleasure in saying to the Hague: "It would be to my advantage to leave you, but a certain inclination based on long association of friendship and habit attach me to you. I love you, cold Hollanders, even though you grumble against me and I against you; I will continue to serve you. I am becoming wiser than I was; I will leave your wives and daughters alone; I will do good without mixing it with evil; I will no longer have a single enemy ..." If that is too much to promise them, if you have but little feeling for them, then leave them light-heartedly. "Goodbye, good night. Fine company awaits me over there!"

You are very cool, or else very modest. My senses are obliged to you. Farewell.

165. *To Constant d'Hermenches, November 19, 1764*

Amsterdam

I think today as I did yesterday, dear d'Hermenches. An impulse of the heart must make you choose Holland, or else you must choose France. As I see it, serving foreigners is never very reasonable. It is to your own country that you owe your blood. I mean by *country* the society whose laws protect you, the land whose production nourishes you, the dwelling-place of your parents and friends. It is *that* country that you must defend, out of both self-interest and gratitude; to serve foreigners who have done you no good against foreigners who have done you no harm—custom authorizes it, but wisdom does not approve it. If you could regard Holland as your country, I would say to you: refuse all offers. But you live here only as a foreigner; your wife, your goods, are in Switzerland; you are there yourself as much as you can be, you only make journeys here; yet does your heart feel nothing for us? Ask yourself what you would feel if, as a warrior for the King of France, you were compelled to attack Holland or the allies that defend it. If your heart makes no answer, and is not moved at this, then accept France. Here, the chamberlain's key would be ridiculed as much as respected. In Brussels people are bored; I have no desire to see you busied with politics after having been for so long a brave officer. Once we have established our reputation on one basis, let's not subject ourselves to public injustices on another. According to my reasoning, you should serve neither France nor our country. —I said that that was the counsel of wisdom, but custom can on many occasions replace wisdom. Long before our time, so many things have been subjected to it; we would have to go so far back to separate the laws of reason from traditions of prejudice that one can easily, I think, relax a little on that point.

You would be bored, I fear, if you left the service entirely. Once again— if sentiment does not speak strongly for us, become French. You will live with your friends, you will be more happy; being a general among us is not enough, it seems to me, to balance the advantages that you would find in France. In ten or twelve years, if you are weary of the constraints and the garrison life, you will go to live in your lands; perhaps you will still be young and vigorous ten years from now; perhaps you will enjoy for a long time the pleasure of having a fine regiment bear your name.

As you see, I favor selling quickly to Golofkine and accepting the ten thousand francs of salary. You do not love us enough and you are not enough loved to find happiness in any idealistic attachment to Holland. I will stop there; unless your heart decides for you by one of those sudden impulses that makes any contrary choice bitter, accept, accept. Each moment of displeasure in this country would make you repent.

I deserve your trust in my heart; I do not deserve deference to my insight; but all things considered I am a hundred times more proud, more vain, more charmed, more grateful than you can imagine at the value you put on my advice. If friendship illuminated the mind as much as it warms the soul, then you could establish me as arbiter of your actions.

Farewell, dear d'Hermenches; I will see you if I can. Give our Marquis a thousand assurances of esteem, affection, the tenderest remembrance. In spite of your dilemmas, you must write to him quickly. Write to me tomorrow or the day after. Address your letter simply to Mlle de Zuylen, care of Monsieur Hasselaer, Alderman. Farewell. You are so busy that I could embrace you without your noticing.

168. *To Constant d'Hermenches, November 25, 1764*

I have only a moment, I will only say a word to you, but this word will give you pleasure. I am going to the Hague Friday the 30th at the earliest, the following Tuesday at the latest. If the river threatens to freeze, I may go

Wednesday or Thursday. Finally we will see each other; that is as certain as the future can be. I am very impatient to talk to you about your affairs. I have imagined nothing new, and it still seems to me that what I said to you is right; but whatever the wishes of our hearts may be, or the efforts of our mind, we so often see mistakenly! If only she were more reliable, the oracle that you so honor by your trust! Then the responses of friendship would secure your happiness.

CR *During Belle's visit to Mme Hasselaer's house at Westerhout back in September, she had spent a good deal of time with a possible Dutch suitor, Baron Adolf Werner Carel Willem van Pallandt. She now has reason to fear that Pallandt has been damaging her reputation by relaying her imprudent remarks, by talking about the prospects of her marrying Bellegarde, and by advertising the fact that he was in her room chatting until two in the morning. Belle is particularly worried that Pallandt's indiscretion might diminish her in the eyes of d'Hermenches and Bellegarde.*

There exist a dozen letters from Belle to Pallandt (none from him to her) written between October and late March 1765, expressing considerable anxiety, self-justification, and anger. She doesn't trust him, but she seems to be attracted to him.

170. *To Constant d'Hermenches, November 28, 1764*

I am in despair. You suspect me. People have told you horrors about me, and you have believed them. Otherwise, where would this long silence come from? Why not a word of reply to my three letters? I thought that there was one soul in the world for whom I was above suspicion, and that that soul was yours. I thought that my own confessions would scarcely persuade you that I am guilty ... But I was wrong; the public—that is to say, envy, error, malevolence—triumph over me in your mind. You do not even deign to question me to clarify things for yourself; you leave me without a word for twelve days—me, who take such a keen interest in whatever affects you. After you have asked me for advice about a choice on which your fortune, your happiness depends, you leave me ignorant of what your choice will be.

Don't write to me any more. I am going to the Hague Monday or Tuesday; come to see me the day after. Whatever people may say, I will be able to find a moment as soon as possible to speak to you alone. Supposing that I have been blackened in your mind, I will subject myself to the most rigorous interrogation, and if after having heard the truth you find that I am culpable, I will throw myself at your feet, in the most humble attitude; I will expiate my fault by my regrets and by my tears. Farewell; never have I been so sad.

CR *During the month of December Belle and d'Hermenches see each other at various society gatherings at the Hague.*

171. *To Constant d'Hermenches, December 4 or 5, 1764*

The Hague

As I said, I don't know how to talk to you the way I know how to write to you. It's a man I see before me—a man I haven't spoken to ten times in my life; it is natural to be disconcerted and to dare not pronounce certain words that decorum seems to forbid, or that are usually accompanied by blushes. Well then, let us write. Everything I have said has been sincere; I do not know whether Pallandt loves me and wants to marry me; and supposing that he did, I don't know what I would want. Comparing what I have seen of him with what you tell me of the Marquis, my happiness with your friend would be more assured, my days more peaceful, my liberty greater. If I made the other choice I would feel my parents' joy; public approbation, although much less precious, would nonetheless make its impression on my heart—a light impression however, too weak a compensation for a lesser degree of happiness. But enough of that comparison, which perhaps will never be necessary, and whose result I do not know; at present it is only a question of an abstract reflection on Pallandt and all the suitors that I might have.

I have found that when people mentioned those forty-seven years, the difference of age was too great ...[1] Say what you will, d'Hermenches, I do have senses; my desires cannot be deceived on that score; in ten years my senses may still be alive. I would like then, as I would like today, to caress my disciple even while I'm preaching the immortality of the soul, and receive caresses as the reward for my sermons; and after announcing the pure joys of Heaven, experience the sensual joys of earth. You say that your friend is younger than people have told me; I believe you, and you could easily clarify this uncertainty.

But can you reassure me as to the horrible consequences that libertinage can have for a wife and children?[2] I believe that your friend is too decent a man to expose me to them if he thought that there was reason to fear; but for some time now, various occurrences have taught me things that make me tremble. Forgotten illnesses that were believed to be cured ... To bring children into the world ... In Utrecht, a beautiful woman, still young, has died in a state that they have not dared describe to me; it was from her father, they say, that she received the poison. Another woman—diseased at

---

1. Bellegarde was forty-four in 1764, though apparently Belle had the impression that he was forty-seven.
2. She is referring to the possibility that Bellegarde may have syphilis.

birth, believed to be cured during her childhood, too chaste to be suspected by her husband—has given him this horrible disease: he is dead or is dying; they have children, and one trembles for them. It would be dreadful for me to have to fear for my own; perhaps my pain would not be only that of fear; perhaps I would see them unhealthy, feeble ...

You can feel how cruel a thought this is for me. If, when you see the Marquis, you could demand that he recall all the adventures of his life, that he consider rigorously whether he, I, my children, would have anything to fear ... We will see, we must think about this. You would be inconsolable at seeing me unhappy. Goodbye; I want to sleep tonight and see you tomorrow.

CR *D'Hermenches leaves abruptly on December 25, 1764, to take up his new position in the service of France, where he will be posted as adjutant of a Swiss regiment, the Eptingen Regiment. Instead of saying goodbye to Belle, he leaves her the following letter. They will not meet again until 1772, in her new home after her marriage.*

173. *From Constant d'Hermenches, December 25, 1764*

My heart is too torn for me to dare present you with such a hideous object, incomparable Agnes! who are fashioned to accept only the flower and the exquisite aspect of things. When I go back over these days spent in the same city as you, and consumed with boredom and invincible nuisances, it seems to me a monstrous lacuna in my life. But what can reason and experience teach us, other than that frail creatures must conform to their fate! Mine was to die of regret at going away from you; to feel all the cruelty of that departure in the charms of your presence, and to surmount so much grief by the supreme effort of my philosophy. I am leaving; I am almost glad not to have found you this morning; your gaiety, your anxieties, your volubility on Sunday killed me ...

Write to *Paris, care of the Baron de Besenval, Lieutenant General and Inspector General of the Swiss Guards, Rue de Grenelle.*

In the whole universe I know no man who will be able to live happily with you nor who will make you content, except the Marquis.

175. *To Constant d'Hermenches, December 25–27, 1764*

The Hague, Tuesday

Though I am used to living away from you, I would not have thought the news of your departure would have taken me as it did. I had sent you a card asking you to come again if you were leaving tomorrow; I had just sent it off when your messenger arrived. I don't know who he is; I didn't see what he looked like. When he told me "Monsieur d'Hermenches left half an hour ago," it froze me; for a moment, a painful amazement held me motionless. To utter my complaint would have been equally ridiculous and imprudent; I had to contain myself and be still.

Even so, being displeased with you as well as distressed, I couldn't keep from asking myself what you had been doing all day yesterday. You dined in town, so you had time to go out; why didn't you come see me? You would have found me sad and full of tenderness. You are carrying away with you an image that is too light-hearted; your memory rehearses my last bantering, which was quite out of place.

You should have told me you were leaving. Would I not have been discreet? Wouldn't I have found a way to see you alone for a moment? —But perhaps you didn't want to say goodbye to me in private. Why do you say that my lightheartedness and my agitation killed you? I have only your letter; how I wish it could speak! I ask it for explanations, but it has no answers. Did you think that my misgivings were likely to demolish our plans? My gaiety, set beside the possibility of our never being together—did that displease you; did it irritate you? Did you see indifference in it towards yourself and your affection? In that case, you are very mistaken. If what you say means something else, explain it to me; that reading of it distresses me. Far from being indifferent, that evening I felt—even through all my joking—that to see you love another woman in my presence would make us have a falling out; that if there were one whom you praised to me with enthusiasm, I would do just as you would—I would challenge every one of her merits. In a word, I would be jealous.

I thought of this again as I got into bed; I felt I would do a great deal to preserve that supreme preference—that sovereignty—that I think your heart accords me. My imagination sought you, my desires caressed you until I fell asleep. Goodbye, d'Hermenches, I'm going to bed. Even in my dreams, I will miss you.

Wednesday morning

I have just received a terrible piece of news. The sweetest, the most virtuous of women, my first cousin, still young, beautiful, whom I have always loved, has just died.[1] She leaves a child born two weeks ago; her husband, her mother, her sisters, who idolized her, are utterly desolate. All the circumstances are painful, and make things bad ... many things broke off my writing. I had been calm and sad all morning; then suddenly, after rereading the letter telling me of the death of my cousin, and after speaking of her to Charles van Twickel, I had a violent attack of the vapors, which lasted more than an hour; this evening I am well again. I will put on mourning, though I

---

1. Isabella Agneta van Lockhorst, the daughter of Belle's father's sister.

am not obliged to, and I will refuse the parties for tomorrow and the day after. I will not greatly enjoy parties without you. For me, your departure makes the Hague more deserted than if half its inhabitants had left.

You do me wrong to think that a broken heart is not something to present to me. If I wanted to see only cheerful things, if I knew how to share only the pleasures and not the pains of life, I would not deserve to have a single friend, and I would make any man unhappy who would link his fate to mine; for the Marquis himself I would be a hateful wife. No—to see the effort, the regrets it cost you to leave me would have been sweet; but what I would have wanted would have increased your pain. I would have embraced you; perhaps I would have felt the beating of your heart under my hand.

D'Hermenches, believe me, let a man and a woman of feeling never trust friendship. It is very different from love: it does not with the same rapture pursue a shadow, the traces of footsteps pressed in the sand. They will not sleep with me—those gloves that you left here—; and I will not kiss your letters. There are not the same suspicions, the same anxieties, but the effects are alike, the manifestations are more or less the same. In the end, friendship and love could well be confused in caresses that would delight all that quickens our feelings. The self-confident air of virtue that I adopt in talking about our liaison and our correspondence—it is a hypocritical air. It is not really always so innocent ... Apropos of that, what do you do with my letters? Do you burn them? Aren't they exposed to risks in your travels? This one and the last ought to perish in the flames. Outbursts hardly creditable to me and merely transient in my soul should not be immortalized in your writing case. Goodbye.

Thursday

Don't say a word about all the things that are licentious in this letter; I am ashamed of them. Even so, I cannot bring myself to tear it up. I even want to go on for one more moment—and then I hope I will never come back to it. This is the last time, I hope, that I abuse the liberty of showing myself just as I am. I repeat, loving and loving resemble each other; unless friends are disagreeable—or are a hundred years old—they are dangerous. With you, I always find the proof of it. Believe me, I was not thinking of my portfolio when I followed you into the darkness Saturday night; you had already answered my question; I pretended not to hear you, I asked again and kept running toward you ... I was asking for a kiss.

Now for something that is not so tender: I intend to write to you almost not at all. I will have a great many things to do in Utrecht, and nothing needs so much attending to as a secret correspondence; so for a while my letters will take their leave of you. Truth to tell, I don't like writing half so much when my letters have far to go. During their long journey, I'm uncomfortable with the inanities I write; it seems to me that they give themselves airs by having themselves carried a hundred—two hundred—leagues, and arriving only to appear outlandish. All this, for example; does it deserve to go to Paris, where the ladies are so admirable? Perhaps if you run out of gazettes, you can use these pages for curling papers when you go to see them.

I permit you to forget me a little; and indeed, you would do it without permission. You have no need of my letters while you are occupied with business and pleasure. Still, try to find a few moments for me; instruct me, so that I can share what concerns you and amuses you.

You can write me here until I tell you of my return to Utrecht. I may stay here for a while. I have a brother who is to arrive any day from London. Last year he thought of being in love with my cousin—he thought of it himself without anyone giving him the idea; but an idea that amounted to the same thing had been in my aunt's head for a long time.[2] She spoke about it; my father, who is my cousin's guardian, is too scrupulous to show the slightest partiality in favor of his son; he scarcely replies, shows not a bit of eagerness; not a word that might alert my cousin—and besides, my brother can do as he likes; it's up to him to love and to speak up. My brother is the prettiest fellow and the most indolent man in the country. He is coming, and I'm waiting for him. If they love each other, I will beg them to say so, since that will please everybody, and my beloved cousin could well become my sister. So you see I have things to do as well as you, and secret business— for not a soul is informed about all this. Neither brother nor sister. Nobody.

Rereading my letter, I find a tone of arrogance in one of my sentences; however, my thought was not arrogant: I did not for a minute imagine that it was because of me alone that your heart was torn, or that nothing about leaving here was costly to you except leaving me. You had other friends here, old friends; you may love them a little less than me, but you have loved them longer. It is really from them that your departure separates you—you and I are destined to be separated. A little later, it is I who would have been leaving.

I hope that I will belong to the Marquis; I think that you're right. But what outcries! At the moment you came looking for me Tuesday I was attending vespers with Mme Torck, her son, and Twickel. We had gone to hear Father Urbain,[3] who is said to be a wizard of a preacher. We heard him. I have had many thoughts about these things; I followed carefully all the discussion I've heard about them. I will be torn to pieces, anathematized—but it doesn't matter so long as I am happy and my parents are not unhappy. Write to the Marquis, tell him that I would have very much liked to see him here.

If there is some new development with Pallandt, I will write you in all possible sincerity.

Goodbye; love me well. You are going to be admired and cherished, but for all that, do not scorn my affection: rely on it that—sometimes foolish,

2. The brother is Ditie; the cousin is Annebetje.
3. A popular Carmelite preacher.

sometimes wise—Belle de Zuylen will always be your friend. —I was forgetting my fine name. Farewell.

I reread your letter to Voltaire; I read it aloud, and found nothing to fault in it, but only what is fine and good.[4]

177. *To Constant d'Hermenches, January 28, 1765*[1]

Utrecht

You want me to write you often; can that be so precious to you, so necessary, in these first moments of business, of glory and pleasures? I have to believe you, however; I have never had reason to reproach you for falsity or even exaggeration; your actions have always borne witness to the truth of your words; in you, everything is consistent, everything pleases me and elicits my gratitude. I am willing, then, to believe that it cost you something too, to be so perfectly prudent, and that you would have wept as you said goodbye. I would have wept too; you did very well to spare both of us all that emotion.

After your departure, I saw a great deal of the Torck ladies, Mme de Twickel, sometimes Mme Spaen. I often had supper with Mme de Degenfeld; I read the comedy[2] to her; I paid her long visits before the hour that she usually receives guests. She liked me; my attentions flattered her, and they were sincere, for I find her very agreeable. The last evening, I ran to her house on foot, at eight o'clock. It was raining, and it seemed to her mad but charming. The novelty of receiving such simple signs of affection amused her; great ladies ordinarily receive so many gestures of deference and so few of affection! For myself, all those curtsies soon bore me. I had a little outburst of honest anger in her presence, which put me at ease; no more formality between us since. I embraced her as she was fastening my cloak; she scolded me and teased me, and we were the best friends in the world. She has told my cousin that she was fond of me and missed me very much.

I will write to Mademoiselle de Marquette about her marriage; she is marrying Gabriel Golofkine, and I will try to maintain friendly relations with that whole household, which is undoubtedly the best in the Hague. —You asked me for details, but you will surely not ask for any more; the length of these will put you off them for life.

Even so, I'm not through yet. I still want to tell you that at the ball and at various gatherings, it was your friends that I chatted with: Maasdam, La

---

4. The letter to Voltaire was d'Hermenches' response to Voltaire's position on deism. It was d'Hermenches' position that human beings need an object of worship. See Letter 84, n. 3.

1. This letter is in answer to one from d'Hermenches that is missing.

2. Probably Belle's lost comedy *Justine*.

Sarraz; the Golofkines stood out by the friendship that they showed for you. I struck up a friendship with Count Pierre;[3] we continually played cards, dined, and talked together. I like his straightforward tone, his frankness, his wit, and his good heart.

But can I delay any longer talking to you about your letter and its astonishing success? I mean your letter to Voltaire. I read it one evening at Mme de Twickel's, in the presence of Mme Torck and Mme de Noordwijk. After having long thought of you—with no reason at all—as a free-thinker, they now declared you a saint—with a sudden rush of charity and a pious enthusiasm that made me almost burst out laughing. Each of the ladies reproached herself for the injustice that she had done you in her heart, and if they have gone to confession since, you will have figured in the sins they confessed. A few days later, Monsieur Chais, the pastor, told me that he had copied it as well; he praised it as an intelligent man does, and very highly. He told me that he would be curious to see Voltaire's response; I told him that if Voltaire sent a reply it would not be difficult for me to have it, and that I would get it for him.[4] That's the good side of this business; but if you only knew how many times I had to swear that you were the author! If you knew how stubbornly certain people maintained that even if you had been able to write that beautiful letter, you couldn't have sent it. I firmly maintained that you had not only written it but sent it; I discredited all the injustices as well as I could, sometimes resorting to jokes, sometimes to serious reasoning. Mme de Degenfeld registers your worth; she and her supper guests miss you. Maasdam is really fond of you; his frown cleared and his tongue came untied more than once to speak to me about you; he hoped that you had written to me. Write to them—it would make them happy—and to La Sarraz; don't give your enemies the pleasure of thinking that you are forgetting your friends.

There are many dolts and fools at the Hague. I stayed there more than three weeks after you left. When my brother arrived,[5] I said farewell; although I was pleased with many people and many things, I did not shed a tear or heave a sigh. I was eager to come home and entertain my mother a little; besides, I was somewhat tired of my sister and her household; and then a certain detachment, a certain distaste for my country, a certain joy at being independent of its inhabitants and being able to leave them if I wish without losing a thing—those feelings left me no more than did my shadow. While I was paying my visits, going around alone in a carriage and looking at streets and houses, I said to myself: This is the prettiest and most brilliant city in my country. Well now, if I were never to return except for a few

---

3. Pierre Golofkine. It was his brother, Gabriel Golofkine, who had bought d'Hermenches' company.
4. The reply is in *D'Hermenches: Pamphlets* 24.
5. Vincent.

days at a time, and as a foreigner—would that be so bad? And I answered: No. For indeed, unless something altogether unexpected happens, I intend to return only as a married woman. I behaved well; I didn't make anybody angry; I have made a number of sensible people cast aside their prejudices. That's enough. If I leave my country, people will perhaps feel that they might have taken some pleasure in keeping me here; if I stay here, fewer nasty remarks, fewer false and unjust judgments will make my stay less disagreeable.

Farewell, dear d'Hermenches; I will write to you next Thursday or Monday. I love you very much. You wouldn't want me to embrace you.

178. *From Constant d'Hermenches, February 5, 1765*

Paris, care of M. de Besenval, Rue de Grenelle

O gift from Heaven, divine friend, why would I delay answering you even a moment? Why would I not want more of your details? On the contrary; I protest that since I have stopped seeing you I have had no more true pleasures except those I find in reading your letters. I am fortunate; I bless Heaven for the decision I made; but I am not enjoying myself. Illusions have no more power over me; unfortunately, I see the truth of things, and the only glimmers of light are to be found in those intimate relationships of the heart, that rapport of minds, that truth of character that attach me to you.

So you have now experienced what I have felt over many months, seeing the houses, the streets, the inhabitants of the Hague; I have long savored the hope of separating myself from it. I must say that my happiness is more passive than otherwise, and that anyone who resigns himself to live in Holland must be either stupid or abandoned by Fortune. What better proof than your enthusiasm for that Countess,[1] who (between you and me) would be regarded anywhere else as a rather insipid creature; her rigidity of character and her laxness of heart and mind can win her homage only in a country where a thousand vices turn her faults into virtues of a sort. Here, I must say, one's character is forced to become agreeable; one can find many that are excellent; and one practices a virtue unique to estimable French people, which consists in a sustained politeness and a zeal for rendering service, for showing interest in the persons with whom one has any connection—virtues which, if I have any at all, form the basis of my character. I perceive that I please people here more than I am pleased myself; the haughtiness of the women, the self-importance of the men, this continual theatricality in clothes, in manners, in expressions, are so many fetters to my gaiety. I dare

1. Mme de Degenfeld.

to say it, and people do not take offense; but one must at least behave as everyone else does, and my independence suffers from it.

As ever, I am still madly fond of your brother;[2] I have offered him all my service, and I would gladly present him to *le beau monde*, but he is rather like his country—chill and formal; and besides, we live far from each other. He cherishes you with passion and enthusiasm, and seeing how well we get along together, I have yielded to his insistence and have told him what he may know of the matter of the Marquis; that is to say, my letter to your father, the answer, your frame of mind, and the wishes of the Marquis. He entered warmly into the project, and reproached himself for having responded to you vaguely; he must have written to you by now. I see that you will be able to do with him everything that you need to. The unhappy fellow shudders at the idea of returning to Holland; I have, however, reconciled him with his situation, and made him feel that a man of quality is better placed as a participant in the government of his own country than anywhere else, and that it entirely his choice to play a role and marry somebody rich.

I am charmed by what you tell me about the success of my letter,[3] but have you corrected its faults of style? You would be doing me a bad turn to let copies circulate with barbarous sentences. But tell me, did people claim that I had stolen it from someone else, since they disputed my authorship? You think you go too minutely into details, but I swear to you Agnes that you don't tell me half the things I would like to know; for instance, you must tell your friend what his friends think of him—how they judge him.

I am staying in Paris for the whole month, so I count on more than one letter from you; ask me questions if something piques your curiosity. I dare not use the Utrecht address, since I don't know whether the Widow is there. For God's sake, go see the Widow, and let's take care of her; we must pull her out the mire she's in; we must marry her off in this country—she will be the happiest creature in the world; she will enjoy herself, she will become known, and her character will be formed. Mme d'Usson[4] is so striking an example on all these points that there is nothing to add. I beg you, Agnes, bring her around to this point of view; we will need it for our friend; you will come to see her with the Marquis. Here is a letter from him.[5]

Voltaire has not answered me, as I knew in advance; here is his last letter, and here is what he wrote to Monsieur de Richelieu about me;[6] it may even

2. Willem René, Belle's eldest brother, who is in Paris at that time.
3. His letter to Voltaire on deism.
4. See d'Hermenches' Letter 111. Mme d'Usson was a Dutch Protestant who had been widowed. She married the Catholic comte d'Usson, brother of the French ambassador. Her case is often cited in the letters in discussions of mixed marriages, but here the issue is how well she has taken to life in France.
5. The letter is not extant.
6. Louis-François Armand de Vignerot du Plessis, duc de Richelieu (1696–1788) was the

be that his niece[7] has stolen my writing, and I would not be sorry. I adore you and respect you.

180. *To Constant d'Hermenches, February 14–18, 1765*

Utrecht

I have been wanting to write you for many days, dear d'Hermenches; I have even begun; but your distance, my ignorance about your present concerns, the uncertainty of my fate and the variety of my thoughts—all this keeps me from writing. To say everything that I think I would have to write too much; to say only a part of it could give you a false impression and would not satisfy me. I impatiently await one of your letters; address them as before to Mlle Phlügerin,[1] care of Monsieur de Zuylen.

Mme Geelvinck is soon going to the Hague, and then I don't know where. Don't write me often; let's be more careful than ever to avoid accidents. All is well at present, so let's not upset the calm that is being restored.

My mother warns me that her ideas have not changed—although she no longer shows anxiety or distance from me—and that she still fears and condemns what she has always feared and condemned. She says so but since she is cheerful, tranquil and tender, isn't it clear that her mind is getting accustomed in spite of her to what repelled her so at first? I have no fear of a lasting indignation; they will never forbid me to return to the paternal home. They love me, I amuse and console them, and in spite of the opposing sentiments, they do not despise the depths of my heart. But what joy it would be for them if they could see me take by choice a distinguished husband among my compatriots!

Pallandt hasn't written me for more than a month. His conduct is bizarre. You know that I had demanded that he send me back my letters, and he has

---

grandnephew of Cardinal Richelieu. He became a distinguished soldier and diplomat and was eventually made marshall of France. He was in the battle of Fontenoy of 1745, in which d'Hermenches was wounded. The duc de Richelieu was also notorious as a Don Juan and there are references to this aspect of his reputation in subsequent letters.

The letter in question contains this passage: "My hero, permit me the liberty of boasting to you of the honor I have of being the friend of M. d'Hermenches, son of the very devil of a general in the service of Holland, who for forty years fought against the French. The son has preferred to fight for you. He is presently in your service, and has desired, quite rightly, to be presented to the general who has best sustained the glory of France. . . . I can certify that he is the man who knows the most in all the world about the art of declamation. I had the honor of playing old Lusignan with him [in *Zaïre*]. He played Orosmane to my great satisfaction" (original French in *Voltaire's Correspondence* 57: 73–74).

7. Mme Denis was Voltaire's mistress as well as his niece.

1. Belle's chambermaid.

never been willing to do it; he could have come to see me on his way to the Hague, and he took another route, or did not stop here. If things remain where they are between us, then far from hurting the Marquis' cause, he is serving it. My conduct toward Pallandt is irreproachable in all respects, and will satisfy my father and my mother if I tell them about it. They will see that their satisfaction has not been forgotten; that I have not dismissed something that could please them, and that I will have at least hesitated, compared, reflected. I have said and I repeat it: in my entire country, Obdam and Pallandt are the only ones who could make me hesitate. Never fear on my part, dear d'Hermenches, a culpable reserve. If something were to happen that would affect your friend, my letters telling you about it would seek you out at the ends of the earth. I am more attached to you than ever; you are lovable, and you know how to love; doesn't that redeem a multitude of sins?

Do you have any news of the Marquis? You will see him in Paris, perhaps. When he is in Maastricht and you in Lille, you will be able to see him. Besides what I charge you to tell him, say to him anything you please; I have an equal trust in your prudence and your zeal. I will be happy—I believe it. Tranquil, beloved, treated with tenderness—if my parents consent, I will be happy. The other day there was a question of another suitor, also a foreigner; I told my mother distinctly that I would not change; she didn't tell me I was wrong. Let us patiently let two or three months go by; we will see more clearly into my destiny.

I am wonderfully well; I'm gaining weight, I'm sleeping, I often speak of you to my mother and father, and I am getting them used to being interested in what affects you. I am playing my harpsichord; I am bored with mechanics, and yet I am learning it. Must not one know why a lever is a lever, and how a scale is made, and where Archimedes would have put his fulcrum to lift the earth? I too am bored at social gatherings, but I pretend to enjoy them; I go to the trouble of dressing well even though there is no one I want to please; I am very polite, I make a great many curtsies, and in my heart I say, "Goodbye, goodbye, this is the last winter." [2]

My brother loves my cousin[3] and tells her so, but very softly; no one but you knows it, or even suspects it. Only once have I accused you of indiscretion; it was about Mme Geelvinck. You should have told me everything in a transport of trust, persuaded that thinking and talking to me were the same thing; or else you should have told me nothing at all, and resisted the pleasure of letting me know that you had paid for her obligingness by an important service. See how delicate and discreet I am! In my conversations with my friend I have not tried to get her to tell me a secret that I am still rather curious about. I would not be surprised, in the end, if she were to marry our

2. Belle will reach her majority at the age of twenty-five on October 25, 1765.
3. Ditie is in love with Belle's favorite cousin Anna Elisabeth (Annebetje).

Colonel van Hardenbroek.[4] I hope so; he is a decent man, and what is she doing with her freedom? —Poor mouse, I wish I could give you yours! (I am talking to a mouse trapped behind my tapestry, whose anguish I share.) If we were perfectly free, you and I, we would not be constantly separated.

Goodbye; I embrace you; at a hundred leagues' distance, I think that is allowed. Did you notice the peignoir that I kept on during our long conversation? It was a good precaution. If I had come close to you, your black suit, whitened by my powder, would have been a tattletale—perhaps a slanderer.

Tell me whether you now breathe easily and are no longer coughing. Tell me what you are doing with my letters. I'm a little uneasy about them. Couldn't they get lost in your travels? If you are unwilling to burn them, send them on ahead to Switzerland. I do not reproach myself for them. They are not guilty, but they are unguarded; neither a husband nor the public would pardon me for them. Sometimes it seems to me that sooner or later everything gets told, everything is known; and I tremble, in spite of the perfect trust that my heart has in yours. Ah! d'Hermenches, may it never repent of it! Goodbye; I hope that my memory may never for a moment damage your happiness, but I also hope that you never love anyone more than you love me.

As I reread this I admire that sequence *I'm sleeping, I often speak of you*... Sleeping is a pleasure, but speaking often of you is one also.

Thursday, at midnight, February 14, 1765

All that I have in my writing case is a single half-sheet of white paper that is part of a letter from my mother. Never mind, let's fill it; I promised, and I am thinking too much of you at this moment not to write to you. Perhaps too, even now, you are thinking of me; you are having supper with some ladies, and you are thinking that you love me better than any of them; or else you return home, and seated at a corner of your fireside, it is me you would like to see seated at the other corner. My feelings are the same, dear d'Hermenches; my stove is as good as your fire, my room is warm; I would like for just an hour to give you my chambermaid's place and chat with you at my ease. But who knows whether even today you haven't fallen in love? I must not let myself be too much taken in by the sweet things you say; you may very well be dining with a lady you love more than me. Your sweet words, d'Hermenches, please both my heart and my vanity; it would be forgivable to be dazzled by them. Never exaggerate by so much as a word; it would be a deception, for I take everything literally, and I take it as Gospel that your greatest pleasure in Paris is a bit of writing from Utrecht.

You tell me to ask you questions; nothing in that country piques my curiosity except what concerns you. Tell me what you are doing, what you love, what you admire; let your own imagination choose the subject of your descriptions. I am very glad that you are made uneasy by all that theatri-

---

4. Governor of Berg-op-Zoom.

cality, all those grave rules that savoir-faire dictates about trifles. I detest a slave who is happy. Never, never will I be subjected to that insane constraint. People complain about duty when it is a question of virtues that maintain order and peace of mind in society, and they are mad enough to load themselves down voluntarily with a heavy, useless yoke! *Manners, expressions, clothes*—all of these will forever be according to my taste and my convenience. You do very well to submit—you are French just now; but, once again, you do well to be ill at ease. I said to you a long time ago that you are a bit of a charlatan;[5] but what I love in you is that you do not need to be. You have mannerisms and fragrances; what I like, and what makes me forgive them and not find you the more foppish, is that if your fragrances and colors are taken away, you have lost nothing. I see many people who would not be so likeable if their hair were not curled; the whole pretty exterior that decorates them seems to have become essential to their composition. Go ahead, let your hair go uncurled—I will still love you.

Goodnight. I will finish this another day. A thousand compliments to the Marquis. He should not wish for a crown; let him be as he is, which is all he needs to please me. If some day the news of our plan were to become public, then whether it fails or succeeds, I will make no secret of the consent I had given. I hope that if it fails it will not be known; but if people find out that the Marquis wanted me, it will be known at the same time that I wanted to belong to him, and that only the difference of religion made an obstacle for my parents. Goodbye.

I have it in mind tonight—as I did this morning—that sooner or later everything is known; but if this were known, it seems to me that the Marquis would hardly be embarrassed; everything would be equal between us, as I just said, and neither of us would blush.

The two pages that I wrote you yesterday have cost me several hours of sleep; to be thinking after midnight about one's friend and one's suitor is worse than coffee.

Sooner or later everything gets told: that was my text yesterday. A proof that everything gets told is that the lover of Mme Huffel[6] is boasting—and who should boast less? What favors are less precious? What is less flattering, less seductive for one's vanity? You would not, you said, dining at Mme Spaen's, have challenged her to give the French names of all the dishes. I believe it; but I would not have repeated to La Sarraz, as you did, that Mme Huffel was sending letters and jewels. At bottom, it was a matter of indifference that Mme de Spaen was making herself ridiculous in a way that she has done a million times in her life; but the reputation of Mme Huffel is not a matter of indifference. Because she is ugly and stupid, people do not spare her; it's for that very reason that she is the more to be spared; the

5. See Letter 63, n. 1.
6. The widow of a bailiff.

poor woman has nothing to lose. Perhaps you find my sermon a very poor one; but notice and approve at least this: that none of your words escapes me; I pay attention to everything; I retain everything; not one of your gestures is lost for me. If I judge you rigorously, it's because I love you tenderly. What pleasure I take in praising you! —especially to those whom error or prejudice distance from you.

You speak of Mme de Degenfeld: I am no enthusiast for her merits; she seemed to me cold and haughty, and haughtiness is always accompanied by many little pettinesses. I think as you do that she needs the bland background of the other women of the Hague to be greatly admired; I also think that without that little air of royalty that she gives her house and her suppers, and her titles and her fortune, she would not receive all the distinctions she is accorded. But don't exaggerate; don't be unjust; recognize that she has discernment, good manners, and quite as much wit as is necessary in conversation. People say that she has integrity, that she is a sincere and constant friend: in any country that would be respected. I was not someone much to her taste, I think; and yet, in addition to the friendship that she showed me at the Hague, she has written a thousand kindly things about me to Mme de Nassau, in a letter full of praise. Not only am I grateful for it, but it does her honor in my mind; it proves that she can accept a little less deference and a little more liberty. Really, I find her very amiable; even the haughtiness I mentioned I only knew by hearsay—I have only seen her very polite. One day, thinking that she had hurt my feelings, she wrote me a letter and made apologies with the best grace in the world.

One tells one's friend, you say, what his friends think about him. This is what General van Maasdam said, in a brusque tone: "Have you received news of Constant?" I answered that I hadn't, and added: "Don't you miss him?" "Of course I do." "He has always told me that you were a good friend of his." "He was right." "And people say that when you are a friend, it is for life." "How could it be otherwise?"

La Sarraz said that you did very well to leave us and go to France; that you would enjoy yourself there; that your talents would be respected and cherished; that here no one took any account of them, that here they like mediocre people, and forgive nothing in really amiable people, etc. Pierrot Golofkine thought that you were wrong not to write to me; he called you *our friend*, carried in his pocket the letter that you had written to Gabriel, read a few items from it, and spoke of you with his easy and kindly air. Mme de Degenfeld found your departure a loss for society here, and said your company was most agreeable.

That's what I have retained of the remarks of your friends. I would not have been done so soon if I were to tell you all the remarks of your enemies. I won't bother with the ones concerning disputes and formalities I understand nothing about, but I can't prevent myself from saying a word about those that I do understand, and that distress me. First, your enemies claim that you had already entered the service of France—that you had the act in your pocket—before concluding and before asking for your discharge. I claimed the contrary, giving my opinion as a very well-founded conjecture—even letting it be thought that I was certain of this. And indeed, if I compare the date of that letter I received from you in Amsterdam, in which you consulted me—you spoke of your hesitations and weighed the arguments for and against—with the time that your agreement was concluded, I am persuaded that you had deliberated before the conclusion, but that you had not yet accepted. There is more: you wrote me that you had just received the offer from Paris, and that you had been offered forty thousand florins; so the price was set before you were able to decide in favor of France. That your resolution had preceded your resignation is quite natural and certainly quite innocent; that you had already committed yourself to France before resigning here I don't believe—and what use would it have been to you? They say that if it had been known that you were leaving for France, you would not have received forty thousand florins for a company that you would have had to leave for nothing; and I reply that you needed the forty thousand florins, and that if you had not received them, you would not have gone to France. They say that the sum is exorbitant, and that you have duped your friend. But since the value of the merchandise is arbitrary, and since Golofkine is not a child, and had all the time he needed to reflect and consult, that could never be called dupery. And yet the imputation is troubling; one does not like being accused of having duped his friend, or even to have demanded too high a price. I hope that this imputation will fall away; what will contribute to destroying it is that the Golofkines seem content; they speak of you in a friendly way. Quite sincerely, I assure you, Pierrot rejoiced at learning that you were enjoying yourself in Paris; I was not as close to the other, but, by everything I have seen and heard, I think I was able to conclude that his remarks concerning you were very courteous.

Now this, d'Hermenches, is what I can neither understand nor forgive. What! Do you who are rich and who understand generosity, demand two hundred ducats for your journey?[7] Haven't you made a hundred unnecessary journeys that no one paid you for? For a thousand florins more, did you need to give your transaction that unseemly air? Many people had talked to me about it at the Hague, even before your departure; I didn't dare tell you what I thought about it, and I tried to believe that they were mistaken; but they were not, the thing has been confirmed, it is indeed true, and I can no longer be silent after what I have been told. And it's not only the two hundred ducats; there is also an allowance for your son. In the name of God, do not accept it. Make do with a fine suit of clothes the less, and one party the less, and no allowance. Think of some way out—say that you found you had more funds than you thought, or pretend to forget that clause—but no al-

---

7. A ducat was five florins of the period, or about twenty dollars in 1999.

lowance. I would be in despair if the son of my friend—my wealthy friend—received a private pension. That tail end of your bargain is too much: the journey, the pension distress me.

Monday morning, February 18

Is my zeal perhaps too intense? The tone I dare take—is it not ridiculous? I don't know; but if you love my friendship can you blame my intensity? Would you want me to listen patiently, like a cool and passive friend, to remarks that harm you in even my mind? Should I be silent when I condemn you, and only speak when I admire you? I conceal nothing from you; my heart has shown itself without reserve; my essential and constant faults, my momentary follies and weaknesses—I have hidden nothing; you count, then, on the most perfect frankness, and if I were to hide a single one of my feelings, a feeling which concerns you, I would be guilty of a hateful treachery that would make me forever unworthy of your affection. I would pardon you for rivalling Monsieur de Richelieu in the most glorious conquests in Paris—loving, charming everyone, being Love's favorite;[8] but I demand a generosity above all suspicion; an idealistic disinterestedness—perfect, irreproachable. I also want you not to forget me. I dare challenge any and all friends and mistresses ever to love you more or better than I love you.

If you say a single word concerning what I say when you write to the Hague—if you show the least suspicion, the least ill-humor—if you complain of mean and unjust remarks, I will never forgive you; I will call that a use of my frankness that is directly contrary to my intention, and you will get no more frankness from me.

What you said to my brother is excellent. I thank you for it, I love you, I reproach you; I would like to have everyone in the whole world—even the envious, even your enemies—be compelled to admire you.

182. *From Constant d'Hermenches, February 24, 1765*

Paris

That sublimity that characterizes you in everything was bound to apply itself also to that touchstone of humanity, self-interest—that common center where the hero finds himself almost always as petty as the coward. If it were possible, divine Agnes, for my enthusiasm for you to increase, it would be because of the sentiments that you show me in that letter, and in the motive of courageous friendship that impels you to speak to me thus. Far from finding you too bold, I find you only too perfect. I am persuaded that you would do just as you prescribe for me; but as for me—who am sublime only in my way of loving—before dispelling your indignation, I must admit to you that I could have been guilty of everything that shocks you, without

---

8. That is, rivaling the duc de Richelieu's considerable reputation as a libertine.

being any the less at ease with myself. Yes—I would have had my post-horses, my dinner, my supper, paid for by the person with whom I had made a transaction; yet worse, I would have reserved for myself what you call an allowance, and which is basically only interest income, not only for my child, but for me, for my mother, for you, without thinking that I was injuring what I owe to nobility of feelings; I would sell for a hundred thousand crowns what is only worth a hundred sous to whoever took the fancy to pay, and so forth . . .

But that is not at all what happened to me, because at bottom I am more of a Don Quixote about money than I wish to appear, and also because I like to see people content with me, and to have the superiority of having been accommodating. The two hundred ducats were part of the arrangement, like the rest. Golofkine offered me forty-five thousand florins; there were delays in the payments; to expedite matters, I said, "Guarantee forty thousand to my account, and give me a thousand in cash because I need them so that I can leave immediately." And thus it was done. Do you find that very ignoble? . . . You, who if you were a duchess or a princess, would in that state easily go over to receiving favors and bribes, for that is the way business is done!

I have not bargained for any allowance for my son; on the contrary, one had been assigned to him earlier, and I stipulated that it would not be in force until he reaches his majority, at which time he will do what suits him; but for the present, he draws nothing but what comes to him, and if he did have an allowance—as is common practice—where do you get the idea that it would go into the pocket of a private individual? It would be an increase of pay for a company that belongs to the Prince, that I raised myself, for which I have ruined myself, that was in my possession for seventeen years, and in which all my descendants and kinsmen had more rights than a Russian who arrived in the regiment the day before yesterday.

As for dupery, they are fools and dolts who accuse me of it. Golofkine is only too happy with the good bargain he has made. Born in the service of the State, having been in combat—of which I bear the scars—at the end of twenty-eight years, I had eaten up twice forty thousand florins in the service, and consumed the best years of my life. Besides, it's they who have provoked me, it's they who—by vile ruses, by unworthy means—have wanted to get the best of me, and have tried more than a year ago to disgust me and intimidate me. Bellegarde will tell you that before I thought of coming to France, he was charged with proposing to me a more advantageous retirement than the one I have received; that I had the honesty not to want to enter into negotiation with Golofkine because it would have discomfited an officer whom I respect, and who is his senior; and that I sacrificed everything to tell this officer about it and let him know about what was being hatched. It is true than since then I have been adroit enough to assure my future elsewhere; does that harm anyone? I responded to the Duke's indifference and to Golofkine's eagerness without granting those others the pleasure of having shut me out for money. Agnes, if I had been able to get them to pay a hundred thousand crowns and come here as Marshall of France, I would glory in it all the more ...

Besides, where do you get the idea that Gabriel is my friend? You pride yourself on being my friend, and you admit to that title a personnage who is so utterly null and insipid! I can compare that only with the humbleness that comes through in your phrases when you speak of Mme Degenfeld: *that air of royalty in her house ... She wrote you a letter when she thought she had hurt your feelings ... Her titles ... She can accept a little less deference ... She has written a thousand kindly things about you to Mme de Nassau ...* But Agnes, do you really mean it? Should the eagle speak that way of the other birds? What then is this deference, or rather this impressionability? I must confess to you that I don't recognize you, and that I would a hundred times rather have duped ten Russians than be for one moment the dupe of my own vanity by the attentions, or rather the civilities, of a silly goose with a title. For, after all, I must speak out: if she welcomed you, it was under compulsion and as a ruse. I demanded it of her; she saw that people of taste and intelligence admired you, that La Sarraz and I had suppressed all the mockery of you, and because, finally, she believed that it was the fashionable thing to have you as a friend, under obligation to her, and in correspondence with her. I was transported with admiration at the skill, the suppleness and the wit with which you managed at the first supper you had there; we called her "respectable," but I had no doubt that you found her an affected prude in the depths of her heart, and she was just that. I was indignant at the superficial welcome she gave you. I knew her—she is fond of no one and she detests all women. But she is vain, and I was sure I could keep her in hand; if that had not been so, I would have kept you from coming. And you, poor, honest dupe! You are wearing yourself out trying to find virtues in her, and you take pride in her indulgence; but do you know that in this country—called a country of slaves, but in fact the only one that is free—no one would speak or even think about anyone so fulsomely? I repeat: she shines at the Hague because she is surrounded by abominations; she is a decent person, but since you want me to explain myself: Yes, I refuse to grant that she has any discernment, sincerity, or constancy; as for friendship, she doesn't even know what it is, and her *savoir-vivre* is in the worst taste, and of the most banal conventionality. She is not mean-hearted, it is true, but a thousand pettinesses, a thousand prejudices in her mind ...

I'm getting heated about this subject like a fool, I who haven't the time to say two words to you, and who still wanted to argue with you about the injustice that curiosity is making you commit (which, perhaps you didn't recognize in yourself): you reproach me for having been indiscreet about the Widow—what am I saying? for having been indelicate, because I told you that I had done her a service, and didn't give you the details. But it seems to me that that is all one should say about it to one's friend, who is interested in the matter. Either I fail to understand refinements and sublimities, or nothing seems to me more appropriate than to say what is likely to be agreeable to the person to whom one is speaking without harming the person about whom one is speaking; and that is the case.

As as for the Huffel widow, I intended to praise her by what I said (which I don't remember having said to La Sarraz): that she had the intelligence to give jewels and write letters—to be capable of a tender sentiment and a generous action. I don't understand through what lens you are seeing this as the destruction of her reputation; to begin with, does one have a reputation in Holland? Tell me, in all good conscience, whether a hundred love letters would deprive her of one quarter of a suitor for her widow's dower! And besides, why must one be considerate of a stupid, sullen, boring woman, who behaves badly, who has six times the gold that you do, while you who conduct yourself well, who have wit and the grace of all the archangels— you get torn to shreds? I still say that it is ill-done to get Mme Spaen to make herself ridiculous; it would be as bad as if it were I to whom she sent jewels, it were I who had engaged her to write to me, and that then I had spread the word about it. On that score, I must observe what people have told me a hundred times, and that I have experienced to my grief: La Sarraz is very dangerous through his indiscretion, and indecently gossipy; I never told him what her fortune is.

Another grievance: are you seriously saying that it's only Obdam that you could marry, etc.? Seriously, Agnes, would you marry him? What, you, a man so disparaged? As for Pallandt, you are getting only what you deserve; he wanted to have letters from you; you blindly sent them to him, and he is keeping them, and surely he is having people read them. I repeat: get out of the habit of looking for decency and nobility of sentiment in the wretched climate you're living in: those are exotic virtues there that persist only as particular gifts from Heaven, and that cannot be propagated.

But I am scribbling just as I am arriving frozen from Versailles where I had gone on leave (they are keeping me here this week for some business I know nothing about). There I find an adorable woman, the idol of my host (the man with the finest face, the most agreeable mind, the gayest humor, the most solid character, warmest heart, the best style), Mme de Ségur, plunged into the horrors of a hideous smallpox. A week ago today we were in the midst of the delights of a masked ball of which she was the chief ornament and charm; perhaps we will only see henceforth a cadaver or a monster. The Court and the City are devastated by it; she is thirty years old, she has two children, and she has this lover who will go mad from it. I am going to be with him; good night, dear Agnes.

Burn this letter, I beg you; it means nothing, but the mail was leaving, and I could not be silent a moment.

185. *To Constant d'Hermenches, February 25–28, 1765*

The hour for the mail is past, and this letter will not leave for three days. Where will it find you? You are to leave Paris at the end of this month. Will I receive a letter Thursday giving me your address in Lille? Let us keep on writing. I want to busy my pen with two interesting subjects: I want to talk to you about Mme Geelvinck.

I shuddered when I read the plan that you were forming for her. My God! let's let her be happy! Let's leave her in the position for which she was born. Let us be satisfied with departing from order ourselves, but let us not destroy it. Who are we to disturb, transplant, change the ordinary course of things, to direct a destiny that does not belong to us, to make ourselves responsible for someone else's happiness? I am bored in my country, but I do not hate my nation. Would I tear away from it one of its ornaments? Would I want to make an amiable and rich woman who can spread happiness around her dislike my fatherland? Would I plant quarrels between my friend and the kinsmen she loves? If I made the slightest attempt at it, if I dared thus arrange her future, I would deserve the anger, the coldness that she has been made to feel towards me. People are putting me at odds with her. They have repeated to her remarks that I let slip when I was in a joking mood. They have added slander to their reports. I know this as of yesterday: I learned it from her. I am in despair. I've just returned from being with her, overwhelmed with chagrin. This morning I met her at my music master's; I turned so pale that she exclaimed at it. If only I were completely innocent! I would console myself, and I would scorn—without being upset myself—the vile and barbarous souls that take pleasure in distressing me. Mme Geelvinck will not come around; if she were angry, I would have some hope, but she smiles, and bows politely. She says to me: "How pale you are! I'm sorry you're not well." Mme Geelvinck has a benevolent soul, but not a loving one. She is always obliging, but she has no real preferences. Cosmopolites don't love their country; people who please all of society do not satisfy their friends. Her heart is noble and generous; she is discreet and helpful; but—and this I have seen in no one but her—her virtues cost her so little that they lose some of their value; her services cost her so little that one's gratitude is diminished. She doesn't feel them, she hardly knows they exist.

Monday, February 25

I continue; this is the 27th, I think, and I am as sad as ever. Do you know, d'Hermenches, the unhappiness of a person who assesses the goods and ills attached to her destiny not according to the judgments of her reason, but at the whim of an imagination that exaggerates everything? She perceives this exaggeration, and cannot effect a remedy for it. Reason labors, reflects, condemns error, establishes truth—all in vain; it does not persuade; the impression remains. A thousand ridiculous hypochondrias, a thousand

·extravagant fantasies drive away all repose. The harm people have done me in the eyes of Mme Geelvinck, her displeasure with me, have caused me infinite pain; if that alone continued to distress me, I would understand myself; if this chagrin produced analogous ones, I would still understand; but no, at the moment when I am distressed about Mme Geelvinck, anxieties and cares that have not the remotest connection with the ones at hand present themselves to my mind, seize hold of it, plant themselves there, and will not budge. They are trifles—and these trifles make me wretched. They are follies that I would not dare describe to the person who loved me the most, for fear he'd think I belonged in a madhouse; and these follies my entire reason cannot destroy.

Let us be humble, d'Hermenches; we are very frail. Those who have a great deal of wit are not very different from those who have none. Each faculty of the mind has disadvantages that balance the advantages. What a help, for example, is memory! but also what a torment! As long as I have known myself, there is nothing I have read or seen, there is not a single pleasure that I do not remember; but also I have not had a moment of grief that is not present to me. Horrible recapitulations, before which we are defenseless, serve to eternalize what we have suffered and to make us seek in the past, with the saddest solicitude, the origin of our suffering. Imagination, then, coming to the aid of memory to torment us, makes present for us all the painful possibilities of the future. D'Hermenches, a lively and strong imagination is a terrible gift of nature; another such gift—all too fertile in suffering—is a sensitive heart ... Your friend is mad this morning, overwhelmed by the blackest vapors, hoping for nothing, wishing for nothing, detesting everything. I run to my tutor. I play on the harpsichord a trio written for the cello; a bad violinist accompanies me. I find in this trio a few measures, or rather a few sounds, a few notes that transport me; my senses and my heart are moved, sweeter tears moisten my eyes. I rediscover the idea of pleasure and happiness.

February 28

It annoys me not to be getting any of your letters. I who know nothing, see nothing new, I write you these immense packets; and you who have changed position, occupations, friends, way of life—who have new perspectives that are interesting because they *are* new—you choose the smallest piece of paper, and since the last time we saw each other you have only filled two or three nice little pages. That isn't good. Remember that each item of your destiny, of your pleasures and your pains, is important to me. I'm not asking you for witty descriptions, portraits ready to be printed—but just some details about you. Egoism is not displeasing among friends. I hate political news; I don't care to hear about literary events; but what you are doing, what you would like to do, which people you like, which others annoy you—you couldn't give me too much of that.

The other day, I had an attack of distrust so sweeping that you yourself were not exempt. I was afraid of everything—fate, and my friend, and my shadow. I feared for my letters, and I decided to ask you to reread them when you had nothing to do in your garrison, and to burn those that we wouldn't want to have read by anyone at all. I thought that if there was something in those letters that you wanted to keep, it would be easy to dictate it to some ignorant person, who would know how to write but would not understand what he was writing, let alone guess the author of the letters. It would then no longer be in my handwriting; nothing would betray me, and thieves could carry off your writing case without any ill consequences for me. In that moment of distrust, I thought I saw the thieves, the stolen writing case, the lock pried open, the letters read; I heard Ill-Fame publish them everywhere, piling on, adding things, interpreting; and all around me there sprang up jealousy, suspicions, bitterness. This black dream dissipated; I am not giving you any orders, dear d'Hermenches, but I put into your safekeeping my reputation and my peace of mind.

You asked me if those who did not think you were the author of the letter to Voltaire were accusing you of having stolen it from someone else. No, they were not saying that; they spelled out nothing, and proved nothing. Ill-willed remarks are usually vague. They found the letter too Christian to be from a libertine who is a favorite of Voltaire, that's all. It would have been ridiculously pedantic to look in that letter for a few lapses to correct that no one would have noticed. No, I didn't do it; I would not have found them, or if I had tried to change them I would have only have made them worse. All I said was that you had written hastily, and that you had mentioned to me a great many errors.

The Marquis says that he does not fear false allegations that I might hear about him. He is right, he is not to fear them; any ill that is said about him will not easily be believed. Write to him that I request the same incredulity, and that if I did not hope for it on his part as he expects it on mine, I would be afraid that every day that he spends in my country might make me lose something in his good opinion.

You know how I am on the issue of good faith. I think you should tell him when you see him (writing would not be as good) that all things considered, you don't think that any foreigner could be a successful rival to him, but that if a perfectly suitable match presented itself in these provinces, it could be serious competition. Say that in passing, or say nothing at all: I leave it up to you.

Pallandt seems to me thoroughly confused. He would like, I think, to forget me or to hate me, and he can't manage to do the one or the other; to love me without reserve, that he cannot or will not do either. "Reflection will always be to your disadvantage," you said one day; perhaps you are right, but Pallandt may be thinking: "If I don't have her, someone else will take her; one can be not altogether crazy, and still want to marry her."

Farewell; never have I seen a more bizarre rhapsody than this letter.

186. *To Constant d'Hermenches, March 2, 1765*

I devoured your letter, I reread it, and I'm taking up my pen. Thank God I spoke out so sharply and so persistently! The impression that so distressed me has been dispelled. When we love only a little, suspicion is bearable; we might as well let it remain, rather than risk no longer loving at all! But when we love a great deal, we must hide nothing; we must probe all the depths, condemn, get angry, question. Tact, constraint, and suspicions extinguish affection, just as a damp fog would first obscure, then entirely extinguish the flame of a lamp. Let us not quarrel about our theories of generosity; mine may well be the generosity of fable, yours that of history, without our loving each other a bit the less. It's enough for me that the two hundred ducats are something quite simple, quite right, and amicably exchanged; that Golofkine didn't pay too high a price, and that the allowance was a false report.

As for the ridiculous widow,[1] who hardly deserved the honor of being named in our letters, I don't want to talk about her any more; but I must justify La Sarraz. He repeated nothing to me. We were together at the ball; *you* tell us that the lady was lying, when she claimed "she couldn't fall in love with a man;"—that she *was* in love—that she wrote, and gave presents. You said it to both of us; he hasn't mentioned it to me since. Don't be annoyed that she is six times richer than I am; doesn't she need wealth six times more than I do? If she were poor, who would look at her? If I became a shopgirl, a dressmaker, a servant, wouldn't you love me just as much as today, and much more than all the queens and financiers' wives in the world? You would give me money, and you wouldn't even want me to thank you; a kiss would pay my debt. But if Mme Huffel gave herself entirely for a ducat, would you pay a ducat?[2] Let's leave her her riches without vexation or envy, and let's not think any more about her love, which can only be a homely beast of a love.

I had to laugh at the passage about Mme de Degenfeld. So you absolutely insist that I be as disapproving as you? I am already only too disposed to it. The people I know from close up so rarely give me the pleasure of approving, I am usually so annoyed, so disgusted, that I like to believe there is merit in those I hardly know, and who seem to deserve it; it's an illusion that pleases me until further notice. Notice has been given: you who know Mme de Degenfeld, you refuse to grant her discernment, sincerity, constancy, the friendship for which others praise her; I believe you, I submit. I wanted to write to Mlle de Marquette; I would have included some friendly words about Mme de Degenfeld; but she doesn't deserve them. I thought that Gabriel was your friend; I was mistaken; people had told me that he was a fine chap; you assure me that he is null and insipid. Very well! I

1. Not Mme Geelvinck but Mme Huffel, referred to in Belle's Letter 180.
2. About twenty dollars in 1999.

won't write. I quite saw that good form along with the desire to see my *bel esprit* in vassalage at her suppers and to receive its liege homage counted a great deal in the Countess's welcome. But I profited from that vanity and was glad to profit from it; and I still find it better taste to receive me because I pass for having some wit than to send me away because of it—which people do every day. If I have been grateful to Mme de Degenfeld for departing a little from her titles, her rigidity, her superiority, to enjoy my familiarity, it's not that I respect her titles, nor that I believe her to be superior, nor that I find her rigidity bearable, nor that I think people have a right to haughtiness and impertinence under any circumstances. But I have judged, according to the notions that she herself has about all these things, that I had some obligation to her. If an American makes you a present of a necklace of coral or of red, blue, and yellow glass, if it's his most beautiful necklace, wouldn't you be much obliged, even though the gift itself was fit only to be thrown out the window? Besides, I am usually so ill received that it is an intoxicating pleasure to be warmly welcomed.

Apropos of my praises of her and my gratitude, you say, *Should the eagle speak thus of the other birds?* Coming from you, these words flatter me if they are sincere. But if the animal were to say continually: "I am the eagle, I am the bird of Jupiter; I fly higher than any other winged creature;" if he admired nothing, or almost nothing; and if, living in a country where eagles do not abound, he were to fill his head with his superiority over everything that surrounds him—admit that your friend the eagle would be a very unhappy animal, and more ridiculous than all the countesses of the Holy Roman Empire.

Your last complaint is Obdam and Pallandt. I haven't said that I wanted to marry Obdam; I haven't thought it either. I only said that he and Pallandt are the only men in the Republic over whom my parents could insist that I hesitate; the only ones whom they could make me compare in some way with Bellegarde. I know for a fact that Charles van Twickel, with three million florins, would not make me deliberate a minute. I'm not so certain about what his brother's intelligence, together with my parents' desire and the urging of his family, could make me resolve; however, I see it as a thousand to one that he could not make me resolve to marry. As for Pallandt, I assure you that he's not passing my letters around.[3] He's not a dishonorable man; besides, I have hardly written him except to pick a quarrel with him. Our adventure does him little honor in the public's eye and does me not the slightest wrong. He is consoling himself for the public blame and is making peace with himself by earning and regaining my trust; surely he won't want to add a crowning touch to bad behavior that he openly admits regretting.

Rest assured, d'Hermenches, that it's your friend I would like to belong to, and that if he were here, if I had my father's and mother's consent, I

3. For the brothers Obdam and Twickel, see Letter 146, n. 2. For Pallandt see p. 218.

would give myself joyously this very day, this very moment, with all my heart, and without hesitation. But will we obtain this consent? Would we want to do without it? Let's wait and see what the future brings.

Write to me. Tell me the news of Mme de Ségur; her fate interests me. Why didn't she get herself inoculated? Thanks to my parents and my perseverance, you need not fear seeing me die of smallpox. —Did I ever tell you that I had the procedure repeated three times? I would pity Mme de Ségur less for dying, if she is in love, than for losing her beauty and no longer being loved. If we die young, we leave engraved in the hearts of those who love us a beautiful, touching, ineffaceable image. If I were to die today, you would love me all your life. People would no longer tear my reputation to shreds. Mme Geelvinck would be sorry for her harsh behavior, and would pardon me for jokes that were innocent in intention. My parents and the Marquis would join in missing me ... Truly, it would not be so hard to die. However, I hope that Mme de Ségur lives.

Have your servant write the envelopes of your letters; your handwriting is too well known here. Give me an address in Lille. Love me very much.
Those are all the orders I have to give you. Above all, a long letter, with no more quarreling.

March 2, 1775

What we said about Obdam and Pallandt is only pure speculation, for Obdam will never love me, and Pallandt—even supposing that he loves me—has a thousand reasons not to marry me.

I won't destroy your letter; too much do I love the fire with which it is all asparkle.

188. *From Constant d'Hermenches, March 7, 1765*

Paris

Agnes, I love you more than ever, for I see that I am truly your friend. You write me a letter in which there is a great deal of wit (you could not do otherwise) but not a great deal of good sense. You confide in me your vapors, your anxieties, your dreams—all of them tokens of a trust that is precious to me and that I beg you to continue, for it is the task of friendship to sponge up those fogs that obscure the soul. I will not answer you concerning them because when you receive my letter, it is likely that you won't even remember what you have written me. You found yourself unhappy; this can only be by an adverse disposition of your senses; for what would be the use of wit, youth, learning, talents, if they did not make us happier than those who have been less favored with such gifts? What would I myself be, who am past my prime, who have no very intense sensations, whose destiny is set, and who cannot cheer my imagination with castles in Spain? I, who have a son to raise, a daughter to marry off, a wife to care for, debts to pay, lawsuits to pursue? I who am unsure of pleasing, and who must take all the steps myself? Nevertheless, I do not complain; I even allow myself to be envied.

Here is a letter from the Marquis;[1] you see that he persists, and that he is preoccupied only with you. As time goes on, the more am I persuaded that it is with him alone that you will be happy, because it is he alone who will always be at ease with you.

I'm still in Paris; I'm not answering him; I had written to him to pass through Lille, where I will be next week. If you want to write him a word, I see no reason not to.

I'm sorry if you have displeased the Widow to the point of no longer counting her among your devoted friends; it would have been so easy to keep her, but—allow me to say it—I thought you had nothing womanish about you except your skirts, yet it occurred to me that I was mistaken about that when I perceived in you a few traces of that tendency to demean other women—a tendency that costs your sex so many of its advantages and puts you, one after another, at our mercy. I beg you, do something to repair things between you. I am attached to her, and I protest that this sentiment has no other source than that trust that she inspired in you, and which, as you know, so surprised me.

You ask me to report on my pursuits here. I am living in the most agreeable and most distinguished circle in Paris; it's no more trouble than living in a mediocre one. They aren't *beaux esprits*, but they are the wittiest people in France, of the most elegant style, the highest birth, and the greatest wealth; all association with them is sustained by a noble and complete familiarity, because one risks nothing in showing oneself as one is and in saying what one thinks. If one has weaknesses, it is for reasons and with behavior for which one can respect oneself. People gamble only a little; joke a great deal; tell lively stories; recount pranks. Beside all that, I have a great many duties to fulfill. Custom requires that you pay visits almost every day to particular acquaintances. You are received at any hour; you lounge into an armchair; you learn the latest gossip; you go on to someplace else. You involve yourself in the passion of the day—sickness, pleasure, an unusual event; you talk about your own affairs, you find aid and counsel. And then, I've an immense amount of writing to do; for three weeks I haven't been to a single play. I'm making love to no one; it's too serious a commitment in this country, and intrigues with easy women are too expensive; I'm limiting myself to a few passing flirtations that are reciprocated in the same spirit.

I had your brother to dinner last night with people he enjoyed. He sees company, but there is a difference that struck him between men of the highest social circles and those one finds at the houses of women who may be as amiable as any others but are of the second and third order.

Goodnight.

---

1. This letter has not been found.

191. *From Constant d'Hermenches, March 28, 1765*

Lille

Dear Agnes, here I am in Lille; I am waiting for your letters, but perhaps you do not dare address any to me. Let me tell you, then, that I have taken possession of my post; that I find a very well-composed regiment, officers who have welcomed me with incredible courtesies, many Knights of Malta and Saint-Louis who all claim to be delighted at being under my orders; a very well-trained, well-disciplined corps, where the respect I receive is greater than if I had been a colonel in the Guards; so I am content.[1]

But what a life! I'm up at six in the morning; there are infinite amounts of writing, accounts, orders, manoeuvres; it all gets muddled in my head, but I must manage to fit it all in. Lille is one of the most brilliant cities; twenty houses as good as the best in Paris, and thirty others; people who are delighted to receive a colonel who comes from Paris—however, people who are titled and very rich. The commandants and generals give me dinners, suppers, balls, and present me everywhere. There are concerts, a cabaret, and a theater where Dalainville[2] does what he was doing at the Hague; his brother Molé is giving us eight performances that lend luster to this theater.

That is the physical side of my existence; the moral side is very philosophical. You know the things that alone can satisfy me, and you know that I do not have those things. I already see how I might make some arrangements with pretty women; I even see that they will fight over my attentions, but I will give them to no one. I am giving myself over to my profession, and if I can find leisure for reading and making a little music, I will be very pleased. I have met once again the woman who received my first homages twenty years ago; she was not young even then, so you may judge of her decrepitude at present; however, she has a great deal of wit, a good house, and I am charmed to see her again. She finds me taller, and quite brilliant. I do not miss Paris at all, but I miss the moments I have spent with you at certain balls. I have no news of the Marquis; I don't know what route he has taken; I'm about to write to him. I have the very strong impression that before this year is out I will have the chance to welcome both of you at Lille.

Good night, dear and divine Agnes.

1. D'Hermenches is apparently being treated with the deference and respect appropriate to his permanent rank of colonel but, on account of his transfer into the French service, his duty assignment seems to be that of regimental adjutant—normally that of a major.
2. Dalainville's real name was Louis-François Molé. He and his brother François-René were French actors.

194. *To Constant d'Hermenches, April 5, 1765*

Utrecht, Monday

Your letter, which I received this morning, has given me a very great pleasure. You are contented, you say; how sweet, pleasant, and rare is that word. You are respected, loved, flattered and wise; what more can one ask? I myself am far from being contented; for days I was continually dying of anxiety, vexation, vapors. I had a fever and a dreadful loss of appetite; today, I am more or less myself again and am enjoying chatting with my sister. There is no sort of annoyance that I am spared; I won't spell it all out. I must not trouble your heart's peace by the pains of my own; besides, I have only a moment to write.

I have written a long letter to the Marquis; I would like him to come here, but I fear that the reception would not be gracious and that he would too quickly be put off by it. Will he hold firm, confronted with a cold welcome and stern faces? He will always do as he pleases, but if—knowing my situation better than he does, and knowing the turn of mind of my father and mother, what they will one day think, what I myself will be—if I wanted to give myself to him in spite of my family's disapproval, I would prefer that he not refuse me. Tell me as soon as possible whether he would be free to leave Maastricht for a few days before the end of the exercise, supposing I should want him to. In a few days, I will know better than today what I wish, and I will write to him. I would not take it amiss if he should show a little interest in me so that people would not undertake to blacken me in his eyes. I'm dying for fear of that, and of the possibility that such gossip might cost me the perfect respect that I think he feels for me at present. I know how to be silent about other people's secrets, but not my own. Before long I am sure that my intentions will be known because of my own imprudence; tell the Marquis to participate in that indiscretion. I detest mystery in honest things, and this secrecy could harm me. I would like the Marquis to let it be perceived that he loves me, and that he would not welcome any attempts to make him hate me. He can add that it is not utterly impossible that I may become his wife; that at least he will do what he can for that to happen. Tell him all that, I beg you. I will write to you Monday.

I must end this letter. Have you received the one in which I said so many foolish things about the Countess de D. and a great many other things? I had written *eagle* in the masculine for a whole page; I didn't know its gender, as if there had never been a Roman eagle.[1]

Continue this chaste way of life that you have adopted. No *arrangements;* it's an ugly thing and an ugly word. I still have an old letter of yours to refute on the rights and duties of marriage.[2] Thank God, you have not per-

---

1. In this context the gender of *aigle* is feminine; Belle corrects herself by remembering the expression *une aigle romaine.*
2. This letter has been lost.

suaded me. The very discussion of it—even being able to entertain the idea—is too much. The prudes will say ... let them say it. But until I manage to convert you, leave the wives to their husbands.

Farewell, d'Hermenches; in loving me you love your best friend.

196. To Constant d'Hermenches, May 3–6, 1765

I am sorry to hear about your fever, dear d'Hermenches.[1] If only you could convalesce somewhere near me; I would take care of you, entertain you, and forget my own ailments. I would gladly exchange my vapors for your fever or for La Sarraz's apoplexy. Who would have thought, when we heard him joking, that soon everything would have been said, and that we would never see him again? I was thunderstruck and moved by that sudden death. I who maintain the idea of immortality, I find it hard to imagine what his soul is presently doing in the other world, where there are no more princes to amuse, no more chamberpots, no more absurdities, no more barons. There are people who do not seem made for living, and others who do not seem made for dying; unfortunately, death is made for everybody. It would be a quite skillful person who could be gracefully young, gracefully middle-aged, gracefully old, and die with the same good grace. —In spite of all my efforts, you have refused to read my Doctor Smith;[2] if you had read him, you would sense my idea still better, and you would imagine the *becomingness, the propriety*[3] I have in mind. Nothing has made me so sad as the letters of Saint-Evremond when he was old.[4]

There is no longer anything for you to miss at the Hague, now that La Sarraz is dead. Maasdam is quite mute and Bigot hardly talks, and when Obdam has the gout I see no recourse except to yawn in these question-and-answer kinds of conversations.

Your departure had already cost the Countess's supper three quarters of its charms; from now on it will be horribly gloomy. Twickel will shine, and there is nothing so melancholy as his gaiety. Add to that some people who want to get married and who are forced to wait without any reason; they now only have one thing to say to each other, and nobody wants them to say it. It must be the pinnacle of languor and boredom. Moreover, people are saying that some of the guests fear that the Countess may retire to Germany, and—being more prudent than grateful—they sometimes prefer the supper given by Mme Nagell ... That, my dear friend, is a rather banal piece of nasty gossip; you will pardon its bad taste in favor of the subject, which is

1. The letter she is referring to has been lost.
2. Adam Smith's *Theory of Moral Sentiments* (1759).
3. English in the original.
4. Charles de Marguetel de Saint-Denis, seigneur de Saint-Evremond (1614–1703), was a gifted French satirist and letter-writer who lived as an exile in England and Holland.

not disagreeable to you. Is nasty gossip about your friends at the Hague ever unwelcome?

Mme de Degenfeld has found, people say, so much resemblance between *Justine* and *The New Pamela*[5] that she has considered it not impossible that I took my play from it. It's also the conjecture of many other experts. Notice that *The New Pamela* is so banal, so badly written that I couldn't read six pages of it. Never mind—those who imagine this great resemblance may also find *The New Pamela* a pretty novel; thus, I am not insulted. What will seem still more extraordinary to you is that a man whom I hardly know, apparently piqued that I refused to show him *Justine*, said in full company that he had seen the first acts two years ago, and that since then I was burning with desire to make the play public. "I have seen those first acts too," exclaimed another man, and M. Spaen, who had not seen a single act, nonetheless set about to judge the play, to point out all its faults, to the great satisfaction of the assembly that was dining at his place. That scene took place a long time ago. Even now *Justine* damages me in many people's minds; love is too well depicted, it shows too much experience, etc. On the other hand, Maasdam, his children, and their friends are enchanted; the general wept reading it, for the second time since he was in the cradle. People still applaud me in Mme van Twickel's room, and Obdam speaks only with the greatest praise of the style, the dialogue, and the imagination. He had many remarks to make about the construction, and especially the plotting of the play; he sent me a very detailed critique, which was quite accurate in some places and wrong, I think, in others. I gave him a very lively and, I dare say, a very pretty response. If you are curious to see all that, you need only indicate a way to send it to you; I will ask for a copy of my response. The packet will be quite big: forty to fifty pages; it's almost a book. I don't know whether Obdam has said all he has to say; I think not, and I expect that we will discuss it a little more.

The Teutonic Chapter[6] is assembling here at the end of this month. My mother is going to the Hague with my sister in twelve days; I would not be at all put out if the Marquis came during her absence, which will last five or six weeks. He has sent me a letter full of financial discussions.[7] That is quite all right; my own had provided the occasion for it. But it's so serious that it seems almost ill-humored; I'm sending him an answer today that must seem—I know not what. Between you and me, if this project fails, I think it will be entirely his fault. He wants so explicitly an official approval! Never

5. In Letter 177, Belle mentions reading her comedy *Justine* to Mme de Degenfeld. *Fanni, ou L'Heureux repentir* (1764) by Baculard d'Arnaud was called *La Nouvelle Paméla* as an allusion to Samuel Richardson's *Pamela*.

6. The Teutonic Knights, a military order founded in the twelfth century during the Third Crusade.

7. This letter, in Bellegarde's execrable spelling, is the first of two extant letters he sent to Belle. It is Letter 195 in *O.C.*, dated April 7, 1765.

mind, let him do as he pleases; in fact, the advantage for him is not so considerable nor so certain that he should be forced to take me; and then it may very well be true that I am mistaken, and that my father and mother, seeing that he lets everything be determined by them, will be rather taken with him, and won't be able to resolve to break off the project. We can be lavish with signs of distaste and aversion for a thing we have decided about, but pronouncing a decisive refusal is not done so lightly ... We'll have to see; don't urge the Marquis to do anything, and let him do what he will.

I instructed him about everything in my preceding letter, and today I reassured him about any conflicts of material interests; there won't be any. From one side, a hundred thousand florins will be asked for; from the other, they will be granted or refused, without a fight. Besides, if my father only wanted to give the revenue just now and refused the capital, I think that in a year or two he would give the capital. The Marquis would be wrong to break things off because of that; if he knew the terrain, he would say, without greatly insisting, "I am sure, Monsieur, that you will soon see that I am not as bad a manager of money as one might think, and then you will give me the sum without difficulty." But don't say anything about all that; I could still be wrong. Let's not take more responsibility for the outcome than we need to; if our mistake involved some vexing miscalculations, we might be reproached for it.[8]

And then—what kind of woman are we giving the Marquis? The most bizarre creature who has ever existed. We should be wary of giving him a bad present; let us not urge him to accept it. Maclaine, reversing Piron's witticism,[9] said to me the other day, "You who have the wit of forty people ..." —But one could add: "... and the folly of a hundred." The more I see myself, the more I am surprised; the more I look at myself, the less I know myself. What can one say, for example, of a person who has suffered with heroic courage—reading, laughing, singing now and then—the most horrible pains in the mouth, the head, the neck, the brain; and who, after fifteen months spent peacefully, free of pain, is now in despair that her teeth, which look beautiful, are not sound—who thinks that at any moment she is about to lose them, dreams about it at night, examines them a hundred time a day, imagines that one is good for nothing if one does not have perfect teeth, is astonished at finding friends, lovers, a husband ... I no longer set great store by history; I no longer believe historians. Can human beings be known? It would depend on nothing but me whether I pass for something great, and what am I?

8. Possible alternative calculations are discussed in Letter 106, n. 3.
9. Archibald Maclaine was the chaplain of the British Embassy. He is alluding to the French wit Alexis Piron's remark about the forty-member French Academy: "There are forty of them with the wit of four."

Monday, May 6

Mme Geelvinck has pardoned me for everything, as generously as one could imagine. We are on as friendly terms as ever; that is, I seek her by inclination, and out of a need to see someone whom I love; and she lets herself be found sometimes, sees me then with pleasure, loves me, speaks to me tenderly. But she has no need of me; she is happier, more things satisfy her, she doesn't seek me out. Never mind, I must be content; our quarrel was no less a dishonor for me than a torment. I told her of the interest you took in her, and your admiration for her, for her heart, for her generosity, her obligingness; she told me the story of her letters. I remembered all the things you said, and I laughed at how they embellished the episode.[10] "Down to the last line, the last scrap, I have returned everything to her," you said. It would have been difficult to return what had been burned. It's an admirable thing, how precisely I recall everything you say. Speaking to me of these letters, you said ... "One can think anything one pleases about a woman who writes." Ah! you would not have said as much before our correspondence was so well established. It was quite the contrary; nothing, you said, was more innocent and inconsequential; and I simply believed you.

While we're on the subject: although I am no longer in a panic regarding my letters, I beg you to think a little about their safety; for instance, do not fight a duel without burning them first or taking measures to have them pass without fail into reliable hands. You must realize that although they were blamelessly written and dictated by an innocent heart, they would destroy my reputation forever. I am still amazed at my trust in a man who is always described to me as devoid of all principle, as one for whom nothing is sacred. Let them say what they will; I will respect you and I will not fear you. Say a word to me to persuade me that I need not fear Fortune either, and that you are sheltering my letters from her treacheries. You had believed, you say somewhere, that I had nothing of my sex except the skirts, but that you are beginning to believe that I have that weakness common to women that makes them attack each other and puts them at the mercy of men. You are wrong; my jokes have no sex, and make no such distinction; I make fun of men and women alike, without ever being malicious or jealous. A few imprudent jokes, innocently intended, were my whole crime against my friend; they had been envenomed by the abominable race of tattle-tales.

Another word about our great project. Nothing is more singular than my situation; nothing is less conceivable for someone who doesn't know all the souls of this house. My mother especially is astonishing: she is indignant, she says she doesn't love me; and each word of gaiety, each glance of sadness or anxiety on my part will cheer her or distress her—each is an event

---

10. The episode in question is apparently recounted in the missing letter.

for her. She claims that she has little esteem for me, that she is becoming indifferent to everything that concerns me; and yet, what she complains of is not seeing me enough, not talking often enough with me. The other day, after long conversations, we arrived at the subject of Mme d'Usson;[11] she found the parents ridiculous in their opposition—even culpable in some of the means they had employed to prevent the marriage. "She was a widow and free, why didn't they let her do as she pleased?" But my mother thought they were crazy: after the disdainful behavior and the tokens of scorn that they had endured from her, she found them quite crazy, I say, for seeing her when she made a journey to this country. "I would have sent her packing." "What!" I exclaimed, "their daughter! Wasn't she still their child?" "Daughter or not," said my mother as she left the room, "she had gone off to Paris and she had only to stay there." Five minutes later, she comes back on purpose to say: "After a hasty speech one doesn't know what one is saying; don't pay any attention to my last words." And then everything resumes its accustomed tone, without any sharpness, without bitterness; a little reserve on my part, a little anxiety on the part of my parents—that's all that can be seen between us. It will, I think, be as difficult for the Marquis to make my parents say "No" as "Yes"; he can't imagine any middle ground; he thinks that it will be in spite of them or else with their consent; that they will be pleased or else at odds; and myself, I regard these two things as equally impossible. I said as much to my dear mother; I said: "The Marquis will imagine nothing between approval and opposition, and he will never advise me to do anything against your wishes." "He may be wrong," she answers, "you are free." In a word, it's a mixture of tenderness and delicacy that seems odd to anyone who is not initiated into the metaphysics of this household. They will not approve, but they will not forbid; I don't believe they will even advise me against it. The Marquis, I think, will only need to understand us to be able to marry me.

197. *From Constant d'Hermenches, May 18, 1765*

Lille

I was yielding to all my enthusiasm and my gratitude for your letters; I was happy and flattered, when I came to two or three passages of your last letter, which overturned all that felicity. You were in your reproachful mode, Agnes, which is not so serious; but there are some things that one must never say, because they cannot be based on any of the privileges of the familiar style: *Is nasty gossip about your friends at the Hague ever unwelcome?* That is funny, and it made me laugh, even though it touched on my character. When a remark is witty, I can't quarrel with you about it. But

11. The Dutch Protestant widow who married a French Catholic.

there is nothing funny about the satiric remark on the story of the Widow's letters. *I laughed at the how the things you said embellished the episode—* that makes me weep; weep if simply putting someone more at ease by saying that you have read nothing—that you know nothing, that everything was burned—and then reporting the matter differently to a friend (you love the friend enough to prefer the crime of a breach of discretion to a breach of trust!) makes one a charlatan.[1] Besides, I would like you to tell me in all good faith whether you didn't contrive to wrest this confession from the Widow: you sometimes say more than you know, and the Widow will have been much on her guard not to be concealing from you what you were able to let her think you already knew.[2]

But how can you say to me, Agnes! —for there is no joking or gaiety in this—: *I am still amazed at my trust in a man who is always described to me as devoid of all principle, as one for whom nothing is sacred.* If you are constantly told such a thing, you must either believe it, or else flee those who say it as if they were monsters. But no one has said anything like this to you; my greatest adversaries have never denied that I have an honest, generous, grateful heart, especially warm in friendship, and very obliging toward everyone. *Those* are *principles;* that is what is *sacred,* I think.

That comparison, or rather the application that you make of that maxim: *One can think anything at all about a woman who writes* is again humiliating for me, and cruel and unjust on your part; yes, I said that a woman does wrong to write too frivolously; but I also said that she does well to write when she has found a friend such as I am—or at least she does not do wrong; that's what I say to you at present, as I said it before having seen any of your writing. It's the same with your letters as it is with your playwriting; I urged you to let me see it, to read it to Mme de Degenfeld; I advised you not to make it public. You see what happens: Mme Degenfeld and I have done it justice; others use it against you, still others tear it to shreds, etc. On that basis, would you have the right to say to me: *I simply believed you when I showed my play to everybody?*

Don't be concerned about your letters; several no longer exist[3] and the others are enclosed in two sealed envelopes labeled as manuscripts. One of them is addressed to you; I am presently going to put on it the address of the Widow.

Have no anxiety about the woman we are giving to the Marquis; she's just what he needs; a monotonous, flat character would not satisfy him nearly as much. Do not be vexed if your teeth are less than perfect; a few perfections the less is an advantage for your husband; it's so many the fewer pretensions. Besides, they will have to fall out sooner or later.

1. See Letter 63, n. 1.
2. There are some obscurities here concerning Mme Geelvinck that would probably be cleared up if we had the lost letter from d'Hermenches that Belle referred to in Letter 196.
3. It seems that almost all of Belle's letters to him are extant but a number of his are missing.

—I have a bad headache; goodbye.

C. d'H.

I am waiting for answers from the Marquis on all the advice I have given him. I am sure that the marriage will go forward, and even without alembicating himself, the Marquis will please your parents.[4]

198. *To Constant d'Hermenches, May 22, 1765*

Never have I had so much pleasure in seeing your writing as I did this morning, nor so little in reading your letter. The evening before last, someone who came from the Hague, someone who knows that I am greatly attached to you, said to me brusquely: "Monsieur d'Hermenches has fought with an officer of his regiment; he has received a mortal wound, and may no longer be alive." At first I did not believe a word of it. You have said so many good things about your regiment, you were so pleased with the officers! And then, since you were just recovering from an illness that left you very weak at the same time the duel was supposed to be taking place, one might well have been able to kill you, but one could hardly have proposed fighting with you. In short, I believed not a word of this news, but the truth of it was so strongly affirmed that I could not keep myself from being anxious. I wrote to the Marquis, without knowing whether I wanted to send my letter. Yesterday, I questioned the unwelcome messenger, and since he was to be at the Hague this morning, I begged him to find out more and to write to me. Then the tone and the phrases changed; he assured me that I had no reason for anxiety; the injury had been common knowledge for a week; if you had died of it, it would have been known for some time, and he had no doubt that you had recovered. I kept my letter, and although I didn't think I had great reason for fear, I ardently wished to receive one from you today.

It has come; you can judge how it was received; but you scold me, you are displeased, you are ungrateful. Yes—it is ungrateful to look for things to blame in my expressions when I love you with my whole heart. Allow me, my dear d'Hermenches, to fill my mind with the joy of knowing that you are full of life, and not with the gloomy care of justifying a few bad sentences that you should not even notice. I am not, however, entirely innocent, since I have caused you pain. Accept the humble excuses that I make to you on my knees, with real regret, and count on my word of honor to avoid in the future everything that might displease you, offend you, or distress you for a single instant.

It was several days after the reconciliation, as I was talking with the

---

4. A reference to her description of "the metaphysics of this household," at the end of her previous letter.

Widow about everything that concerned her—suitors, marriages—when she told me of her acquaintance, her liaison, her correspondence with M.,[1] treating it very lightly, and not believing that she was making a confession, but simply telling the story of an imprudence into which her heart, she said, did not enter at all, and I think that she told the truth. I saw her every day at the time of her suitor's death; we spoke about it together; I know for certain that she did not weep for him as one does for a man one really loves. She said to me: "I'm sorry to hear it; that news came as a blow; I knew him well enough to have played comet with him often; he was an honest and amiable man."

As for the people who speak ill of you, let them talk; I forgive them, as I forgive the man I spoke with the other evening for having caused me the pain of thinking that you had been killed. But they will gain nothing by it. If the whole universe were to tell me not to love you—even if you yourself were to tell me not to write to you any more—I would not stop writing you or loving you.

It was La Sarraz more than anyone else who made my comedy public. I don't really care; derision I simply ignore; the criticisms are useful, and give me pleasure.

Goodbye. You are ungrateful.

200. *To Constant d'Hermenches, May 29–30, 1765*

I hope that by now you are writing me some tender words to make up for your reproaches. Someone has written to me from the Hague that your wound did not put you in mortal danger; tell me what really is the case— whether this wound is fable or truth. Write to me: since your departure, you have only written me short letters; you used to like to write me long ones, and I loved receiving them. I don't know whether it's the state of my nerves, or simply sadness—but I would only have to add another word here to dissolve in tears. Even now my eyes are filling; the least emotion would make the tears overflow.

My mother is away; my sister, who has just had a son, is doing well. I am alone in the house with my father, who fell quite ill with a colic the day before yesterday. We were dining in the country with the Widow; yesterday he had some pains and fever, but today he is much better. I am taking good care of him; he likes that; he is cheerful, I entertain him—with not a word about the Marquis or our disagreement on that score. Deliberately to distress parents to whom I am attached, and who merit that attachment—would I have the heart? I am grateful to the Marquis for disliking that hateful idea even more than I do. In a moment, I will ask your advice about him.

1. "M." has not been identified.

My hypochondria that focused on my teeth is going away. My dentist made fun of me, and told me that with the care I took of them they would perfectly well last my whole life, if I lived as long as Methuselah. To agonize over something that neither offends the eyes nor affects the health—really, that's being altogether too adept at tormenting oneself; I am beginning to get over that obsession.

You're entirely wrong in what you say on that subject. Before my teeth bothered me I only thought about them as a necessity, and not as any pretension. It is only recently that people have pointed out to me that I have the whitest teeth in the world; if I wanted to, I could form and maintain pretensions about them. It is untrue that pretensions may hurt my husband, and the sense of my imperfections serve him—far from it; my pretensions and the desire to approach perfection in all things will create his happiness. If I did not love him, he would be the most unhappy of all creatures. You said to me one day that you understood very well how I would make a husband die of grief—but if I love him, if I love him! I can do nothing halfway; I have no lukewarm desires, no limited ambitions. I will have the desire and the ambition to make him the happiest of men, to see him incessantly bless the fate that gave me to him; I will want him not for a single moment in the twenty-four hours to be nostalgic for another time, prefer another woman, prefer other pleasures. All my pretensions will turn to his advantage; the most inventive coquetry will be less ingenious than my heart. To be loved always if I live, long wept for if I die, like that lady I resemble: that is a rare and touching glory, to which I will aspire and for which I will do everything—that is, I will if my husband deserves it, if he knows how to love and to weep.

I want to ask your advice, you who know the Marquis—and men in general—better than I do. As you know, I showed from the very beginning a desire to accept the proposal. I am neither prudish nor proud, and I said what I thought. As soon as it seemed to me reasonable to write to him, the Marquis had no trouble in getting me to do it; my letters, while perfectly decent and respectable, evince trust and friendship. I am already so inaccessible by circumstances—I cannot also barricade myself by affectation and reserve; so I have not done ill, nor am I doing so now. However, it is certain that his conquest of me will not have the merit of difficulty. It is to be hoped that this merit is not essential in his eyes, and that he does not resemble those who value something only by what it has cost—who value a woman by the resistance she offered; evaluated thus, I would be worth very little to the Marquis. He is going to come here: tell me how to conduct myself. Obviously I will not behave foolishly; but can I continue as I have begun without the risk of losing his respect? Suppose he were to ask me to find a way for him to speak to me alone, freely, for a few moments; would he in his heart take it amiss if I consented? Would he think me imprudent and ill-behaved if I am free, frank, without distrust towards a man whom it is not at all certain that I will marry? In a word: can I simply let myself go, or are there rules to observe, measures to take to protect myself from scorn, or suspicion, or jealousy?

Goodbye. I will ask you the rest another time; for the present I haven't the leisure to write more. Goodbye, my dear d'Hermenches. —People speak ill of your friend's health.[1] In the name of God, don't repeat this to him, give him no more advice; let him do what he will. I will be your friend as long as I am a being with feeling and life.

201. *To Constant d'Hermenches, May 30, 1765*

Utrecht

My letter left only two hours ago; it's simply for my own enjoyment that I continue. At eight o'clock I ran over to my friend Mr. Brown[1] to take a stroll with his wife and his sister-in-law, two pleasant Swiss women, very kind, very simple—the only women I see in Utrecht. I came back at nine-thirty to take care of my father's supper; mine took only a quarter of an hour. I arranged his room for the night; he went to bed; and here I am. If by chance you think I don't know how to look after things, you do me an injustice; my father is very pleased with the way I've been taking care of him since he's been sick. Before that I arranged dinners and suppers perfectly nicely, and was a passable hostess; but always with men and Swiss women as guests. The other women of my acquaintance are too difficult; they require too much fuss; they want one to have only the precise amount of wit necessary to amuse them and to make them shine; they want one to divide one's attentions and affectionate gestures among them in exactly equal portions; otherwise those who feel neglected spread gossip and slander. My mother says that in the last nine or ten months she has begun to believe that one day I will be competent in domestic economy, and be able to manage a household well; I thanked her for the compliment, which gave me great pleasure. The desire to fulfill my duty, then, influences my mind and attention, and gives me talents. It seems to me that this bodes well.

That brings us to the subject of the household which perhaps will be established, but is not yet. Before I go any further, I beg of you to communicate to the Marquis only what I wish of the things that I say on this subject, since the whole affair is so uncertain. Promise me this, so that I can tell you about remarks I hear whenever I please, without being indiscreet about the people who make them. If something disturbs me and bothers me, you must help me clarify it as if Bellegarde were not someone who mattered to you—

---

1. Bellegarde may have syphilis.
1. Robert Brown, a Scot, was pastor of the Presbyterian Church in Utrecht. He and his family are often mentioned in *Boswell in Holland*.

without prejudice or partiality. I am asking you to take care of your own happiness when I ask you to act prudently in respect to mine. What regrets you would have if I had any regrets! What would you not suffer if I were suffering![2]

Supposing that I have no regrets to fear, that everything works out, and your two friends are destined to spend their days and nights together: tell me your opinion on an interesting point, before and after marriage. As I have said, since you know men and the Marquis much better than I do, you can help me conduct myself properly. The question is whether, with a lover and a husband, it is better to conceal carefully one's shortcomings, one's foibles, one's odd little habits—in which case one is more respected, and one's peace of mind is less disturbed—, or to reveal them, confide everything, admit everything, ask for consolations and indulgence—in which case one is more loved, and one loves a hundred times more. The one choice is more heroic; the other more tender; the first choice offers fewer inconveniences, the second more sweetness. Which of the two is the better; which of the two will the Marquis prefer? Perhaps the choice will depend very little on your advice and my will. If the Marquis had a character very different from mine, I could not, I think, tell him everything I feel and think; if he were very trusting, very affectionate and tender, I could hide nothing from him. However, I would be very glad to know your thought, and I will try to fit my conduct to it.

Goodbye. I wish you a good night. It's still a long time until the mail leaves, more's the pity.

202. *From Constant d'Hermenches, June 5, 1765*

Lille

It is only the fever that is killing me, dear Agnes, and I am not writing you at as much length as I would like, because just now a line is more difficult for me than a whole epistle used to be. I have fallen sick again, I've suffered a great deal once again, and I am steeped in drugs, fasting, and my various pursuits. I haven't had the slightest quarrel with anyone; I am showered more and more with attentions and acts of kindness. That is the physical side of my situation; the moral side is still immensely concerned with you, and I am more upset than you can be at your situation and at the least of your annoyances.

The Marquis will come see you at the end of this month. He deserves all your trust, and deserves to possess you, I assure you. He will not think the less of you for your correspondence. But no secret meetings! A very prudent, very reasonable letter has often resulted in quite a mad conversation.

2. This seems to refer again to Bellegarde's health, and the question of venereal disease.

Besides, think of what you might risk with regard to the public and your confidants. A foreigner, a man whom you have hardly seen two or three times! ... He himself would only admire you more if you refuse him everything of this kind; but for God's sake don't give any romantic reasons for refusing! Simply say that you don't want to; and treat him all the better for it in his visits, at the risk of displeasing your parents. Your marriage must be the fruit of a deliberate resolution, and not of an intrigue.

And that, my friend, is my answer to what you ask. If your parents love you, they will consent to what you wish; if they are at all sensitive, the Marquis will please them; if they are of good faith, they will give you the means to take advantage of their consent to your choice; it will be in the arrangements of financial interests that this good faith will be seen. You can only become a marquise by guaranteeing the title with your hundred thousand florins; one must entrust the dowry to whomever one is willing to entrust one's daughter to: that is the principle of the whole business. Don't let your imagination catch fire, nor your mind get carried away; forget during this time that you are Sappho,[1] so that you may become a wife, a mother, a citizen ...

My letters can no longer treat of any other subject; all other subjects seem insignificant to me; but you, who know how to pay attention to everything, supplement them by the image of everything that friendship and the most lively and respectful esteem could tell you and present to you on my part. Make up the dialogue, in your moments of leisure or of the vapors; deign to answer me; I will correct, as I always permit myself to do, any errors I may find.

Give me news of the Widow: what is she doing? What are her plans, her desires?

I must leave you to go take care of things that are not worth the most worn-out of your slippers, but for which I must go to more trouble than for the most delightful being in the world, which is you! My humble respects.

203. *To Constant d'Hermenches, June 9, 1765*

Zuylen

I dared not send you my letter, which was written more than a week ago, because people were still talking about a duel and its aftermath; the Marquis himself wrote me that there were rumors about it in Maastricht. Since I knew that you were very much alive, I was fairly calm, but I kept my letter. I will send it to you, ancient though it is; your letters and mine do not grow old as others do.

---

1. Greek lyric poet (610–580 B.C.). Her name was often used in the period as the symbol of the woman intellectual and artist.

It's just this morning that I received the bad news that you give me of your health, and your excellent advice; I promise to follow it. Although I see no reason to fear a *mad conversation*, I promise you that there will be no private conversation at all; I will be not only well-behaved, but prudent, as much as will be in my power. My situation is more critical, more difficult, more disagreeable than one can imagine ... but you know that, and since that causes you pain, I should not be bothering you with it yet more. You are sick, and I should be cheering you up and alleviating your cares instead of loading you down with my own.

I am very sorry that you have been sick for so long. To be a little ill now and then is so intrinsically a part of the human condition that it is unreasonable to complain, either for oneself or for one's friends; but you have been sick for too long! Do you neglect your health, or do you have a bad doctor? Watch out for drugs, and do not allow other ills to be added artificially to those that you want to be cured of. In most illnesses, doctors do more for the imagination of the weak than they do for their health. I avoid them, and when they are consulted I rarely take what they prescribe. With calm, patience, and the proper diet, one gets well without them.

The Widow is well, and is going to spend her summer traveling through our Provinces; she is going to Gelderland, she will go to Cleves, and I have asked her to come to Zuylen. Her desires do not go much further than her enjoyments, for she is happy; her plans, I think, are non-existent or undetermined. Happy creature! She does not spend her life committing imprudences and having to repair them; her character doesn't close off all the well-trodden and easy paths to happiness; she doesn't distress and worry her father, her mother, and her best friends. Let's leave that subject; in any case, there's nothing more to say about it; we must wait as calmly as possible for what reason, circumstances, and my parents will ordain. However my parents may conduct themselves, I will not put it into doubt *that they love me, that they are sensitive, and that they are of good faith.* I have proofs of it that would be difficult to gainsay; you do not have them, and I couldn't blame you much for thinking differently from me, but you will be giving me no pleasure by telling me so.

On the other hand, you give me great pleasure in warning me of my errors and making me fear my faults. In telling me how a *mad conversation* would be inexcusable, *a stranger, a man I would only have seen two or three times* ... you seem to think you should believe it impossible. Not at all; those circumstances do not prevent you from fearing it, and you say it simply, without indirection. I find you are right, and I love you ten times more for this bold sincerity, which considers only my interests and makes no compromises with my vanity. A single impulse of devotion is more precious to me than a hundred flattering speeches.

As reward, dear d'Hermenches, I embrace you tenderly, and so good night; no more fever, I hope, but if you do have any, dream of me in your delirium, and love me ...

As long as I am in the country, send your letters care of M. Spruyt, bookseller, in the *Koorstraat* in Utrecht.

204. *From Constant d'Hermenches, June 15, 1765*

Lille

You ask me for a piece of advice, dear Agnes, that I give you with the greatest pleasure in the world. Must one show oneself such as one is to one's lover or husband? Yes, without a doubt; if one wishes to keep them forever, it's a risk one must take; and especially with the Marquis, you run no risk, as I have told you many times. This is the most honest soul I know, and what's more, he has a passion for everything that is attached to him. I would not want to take him as my confidant if you were to fall madly in love at first sight with someone else; but, except for that, you can tell him anything; he will help you, he will console you, and he will always be gentle and obliging—I have told you that from the beginning. But I have also told you that he is a little scatterbrained; that is, he will not enter into these infinite details that you and I are capable of; he loves to hold forth, but always according to his own imagination, never according to the reality of facts. You will correct in him that little infirmity that makes him a bit ridiculous in society; he, in turn will correct in you that somewhat romantic, rather metaphysical turn of mind; he will make fun of you, and will preach simplicity to you. In my eyes, dissimulation is the most execrable of vices in an intimate relationship; it offends and degrades both parties, and like Zaïre[1] you have no need of it; you are delightful to sound out and to follow in all your impulses—which will not be lost on the Marquis, and will bind him ever closer to you. So be at rest on that point. What torment, what madness to have to watch oneself continually with someone with whom one is spending one's life! Out of twenty women who take lovers, nineteen of them do it to have someone to talk to about their little miseries, and receive some sympathy; put yourself on these terms with our friend, and all these aims will be met.

I detest and scorn many women for this one fault, for dissimulation. My wife, who is always cited to me as perfection itself, has deprived me of the very happiness of having a wife, because she was born secretive and makes a scrupulous habit of it; and on my part I no longer find any comfort in telling her what is troubling me, because she always presents to me a calm and composed surface. There is a kinswoman of mine who has almost as much wit as you and infinite talents and social charm; I took a mortal dislike to her because she is sly; because I finally noticed that she was hiding many

1. The heroine of Voltaire's play of that name. D'Hermenches played the leading man in Voltaire's own private productions of it.

things from me, and that, unbeknownst to me, she was playing up to people I hated, and whom, to please me, she pretended to hate as well.

Dear Agnes, you need take no other precaution against the Marquis except not letting yourself be indoctrinated by him, for, as I have said, to him it's all only imaginative play. He knows much better how to hold forth than how to act; it will be up to you to have him make good decisions, and give consistency and decorum to his ways of doing things. I can answer for it that he will be only too happy to hand this kind of care over to you; that is how his sister manages things.

What you say to me about doctors, for example, is stolen from the Marquis; it's a declamation in exactly his taste: *One must not listen to them, nor make oneself sick by what they say!* And how the devil do you expect someone to cure himself of the tertian fever?[2] I have three doctors, and I take quinine in a triple ratio to the general ignorance about how it produces its effect. God wants there to be doctors, as he wants there to be bakers; let us study the properties of herbs, and let's learn how to knead bread, and then we will require neither the one nor the other.

I am cured, but I am weak and on a diet. I love you and respect you beyond all expression. I am indignant at the Marquis, who doesn't write to me. I am at your feet.

205. *To Constant d'Hermenches, June 17, 1765*

I am going to spend a few days at Rosendaal with Mme de Voorschoten;[1] I have told the Marquis about it, and when I will return.

On the subject of my fortune: my mother said something the other day that did not seem to bode well, nor promise that things would be easy. I am not mentioning it at all to the Marquis in my letter; if they like him, everything may change. That may not be an issue in any detail until after October[2] when I will have made up my mind (supposing that I do). Whatever my parents do in that regard, I will not think that I have a right to complain. My conscience is mine; it is up to me to assess the difference of religion; but their fortune is theirs, and if they say, "We will not depart from the arrangement we prescribed for ourselves in order to favor a marriage that is repugnant to our principles," you must not think that I will find fault with that, nor that anyone will please me by blaming them. I hope, however, that they will say otherwise.

Although my father has said nothing to me, I know for a certainty that he has been told that Bellegarde had been very sick, and that his health had

---

2. A fever whose symptoms are acute on alternate days.
1. Mme de Voorschoten's château, Rosendaal, was in Gelderland.
2. Belle will reach her majority on October 20, 1765.

greatly suffered. I have been told yet worse: that he had been ill more than once, that the disease had been palliated but not cured ... Ah! if that is true! If it is false, I would like to know it, be convinced by it, be able to convince those who are interested in my future. All the probabilities are in favor of the Marquis. His letters seem to come from a the most honorable man; am I rich enough, am I a great enough catch for anyone to be willing, in deceiving me, to run the most terrible risks for himself? However ... I would like the two of you to see each other, and to have you interrogate his conscience. But still, don't think that I am more alarmed than I am; I have had this unpleasant information for a long time, and have given it little credence—nor do I do anything about it one way or the other. People say so many things that are simply false! From the slightest conjectures they so often create a certainty. Take care that the Marquis knows of this only what he must know. I could arouse in him unjust suspicions against his friends. No—he must know nothing, and suspect nobody. I myself do not know who the indiscreet and the slanderers are. The accusation appears to me rather public; those who spoke to me were only trying to be obliging. I will see Bellegarde; I am impatient to see him. Ah! how he will have to love me! How sweet marriage will have to be to make up for what it is costing me!

206. *To Constant d'Hermenches, August 1, 1765*

Zuylen

I have begun more than one letter to you, my dear d'Hermenches, but they were never worth continuing: I would have wanted to give you the details of all the little events, but the little events led to nothing, and so the details would not have been interesting. I would have wanted to say to you: such-and-such a thing is sure, or at least likely, but up to now I see neither certainty nor likelihood regarding anything at all—neither for nor against. Bellegarde has just spent a week in Utrecht; we saw each other fairly freely, a little while each day. We were very much strangers to each other, and yet we spoke to each other trustingly; there prevailed between us a certain formality, and yet we pleased each other and liked each other. You know us well enough to imagine how that all went together. Another time, I hope the Marquis will be a little less polite; then I will be less reserved and more at ease. I think that I am not naturally polite; except with people like Mme Spaen, whom I make fun of even as I am complimenting her, politeness hampers me; it's a balancing act in which I can barely stay upright. With the Marquis it was a bit like dancing on the high wire—my body erect, all movements deliberate, no impulsive capers, no lapses of attention, nor brusqueness, nor outbursts of gaiety, nor tender tones. We were too polite.

By the last evening I had just barely began to find my natural manner; it is true that we didn't see each other continuously long enough for us to be-

come really well acquainted; our least awkward meetings were at the kermess, where my brother, who accompanied us, discreetly let us talk alone.
But one must be on more familiar terms than we were to take any great advantage from these tête-à-têtes in the midst of the crowd. There were a hundred things that I didn't dare say to him or ask him; a hundred others for
which I meditated the exordium. Once again, we were too polite.

Do you remember when you and I met? You reproached me for something
or other from our second word; at our third, we were friends for life. You
knew me at once; you saw into me. I was young and vain; I loved the sway
you wanted to have over me. The Marquis does not see into me at all; he
respects me more than I am worth, and makes more fuss about it than I
deserve. The advantage in all this is that finding each other very agreeable
even now, we sense that we will do so even more when we have complete
freedom; we will like each other much more after marriage (if there is any
marriage) than we do beforehand, which is a very rare thing.

So far I encounter no disappointment; everything is as you had told me.
The kind of refinement, and prudence, and cautious behavior that accompanies stupidity as often as wit—Bellegarde has none of that. He has
rather the kind of simplicity that often goes along with wit, and that is never
separate from frankness, and good faith, and an honest and generous heart.
It causes him to make blunders, but it is likeable and endearing; it dispels
all mistrust, and disposes one to friendliness.

And that's what I think is going on in my mother's heart. Between her
and me, the situation is always peculiar; she does not forgive me for being
willing to have my children attend Mass, and yet she rather likes to have me
talk to her about the Marquis. I said to her the other day: "If you continue
to love me and wish me well, you will see me as often as you like. I detest
my country, but I love my family home; the Marquis is obliging, and he
will bring me back here whenever I wish, or will let me return." She was
noticeably pleased by all that.

My sister is here; her children will be Protestants—and yet what a
difference! It is with me that my mother likes to read, and chat, and take
walks, in spite of my heresies. She cannot do without me; each sign of tenderness from me is precious, in spite of my manifest impatience to lavish
more ardent ones on someone other than my mother. For all that my sister is
much more orthodox and much more decorous, she is not amusing to be
with, and they do not love her heart as much as they do mine. I tell you all
this, my dear d'Hermenches, not with pride, but with joy, and as something
that astonishes me.

In a week or two I will tell you if this is all going in the right direction; I
would give anything for it to succeed. You wrote me a charming letter; you
advised me to be sincere—advice that I would so like to follow! If ever I had
something to say that I didn't want to say to Bellegarde, I would say it to
you; if ever I had need of intercession with his kindness, it's to you that I

would address myself. His humor is obliging, his heart seems to me tender and kind; but his ideas seem difficult to alter, and when by some misfortune he adopts a false one, he bases it on the underpinnings of his imagination in such a way that it is not, I think, a short-lived error. So much the better, perhaps; I will be able to charm his imagination more easily than I can satisfy a rigorous reason; I will love his illusions and their stubbornness, if they are favorable to me.

Goodbye; write to me. I love you very much; I would find great pleasure in talking to you, and often I am weary of a destiny that continually separates us, who would be so happy together. I beg you to make this separation more bearable by writing me long letters. —What letters we were writing a year ago! You will never have a friend more tender nor more devoted than I am.

The Marquis' playfulness is pleasant, and his gaiety is charming.

207. *From Constant d'Hermenches, August 4, 1765*

Lille

I was waiting for today's mail with the most intense impatience, thinking that it would bring me news of you, sublime Agnes! or news of the Marquis. I am dying to know what is going on with you, and you leave me in the dark! That's not fair. Not an hour goes by when I am not calculating what your situation is, and what your state of mind must be. The Marquis has written me that a rampart of ice makes you unapproachable. He has nothing but the highest praise for you. I didn't write while you were running about, because I had nothing to say that was worth the distraction, for you are one of those people who always have more things going on than others; more is demanded of you; you take in more things than anybody, and my ancient devotion is only at all welcome when you are peacefully alone at home and have some time to yourself. I only have a few moments today; besides, I do not know whether I am writing to a married lady, or a maiden; one who has been promised, or refused; who is vexed, or who's well-pleased. We will resume our conversations when this romance has been sorted out. I know that I cannot do without your trust and your remembering me. I haven't answered your letter from Rosendaal because it was on a subject that I had responded to several times; you must believe me—me and my friend—and not bother yourself with what a third or a fourth person might suppose.[1] I would also like to know whether your brother has returned from Paris.

I am living the life of a recluse here; in the midst of a great deal of good company, I am giving myself entirely to my work. I have not the energy to

---

1. This, again, is the issue of syphilis.

know how to divide myself between pleasure and business; however, I have just spent a few delightful days with the Duchess of Arenberg at Enghien.

I have a favor to ask you, dear Agnes: there lives at Heeze en Leende—land belonging to your family—a pensioned Swiss officer named Egenberge. He has a wife who is as deserving as can be: she is sensible, hard-working, honest, clever. Do me the pleasure of recommending her strongly to your family, so that they might render her service when necessary, and offer her that kind of protection that is so pleasing to people who are neither rich, nor noble, nor of high society. Don't name me in this recommendation; I will tell you another time who this woman is. I am at your feet, adorable and unique friend!

209. *To Constant d'Hermenches, August 12, 1765*

You didn't know, you say, whether you were writing to a married lady or a maiden; how on earth do you think I would have managed to become a married lady in so little time? You may be assured that I am a still a maiden, as much as one can be; almost too much to suit me. I am not yet either *promised* or *refused;* sometimes I am *vexed,* sometimes I am *well-pleased.* Your letter is charming, and gave me great pleasure. Your letters are always good, whether I am running all over the countryside or whether I'm yawning on my chair, and you should write to me whenever you have the desire to, without considering anything other than that desire, which flatters and pleases me and which, like any feeling from the heart, gives infinite value to what it produces.

You have made such a point of the example of a sister of the Comte de Saxe, who, according to you, professed Protestantism in the middle of Savoie; a single little circumstance overturns all the proofs that one might draw from that: she is Catholic.[1] It has turned out that Bellegarde absolutely did not know at all whether he could have me as a legitimate wife in his country, or whether my children could inherit. My father wrote him a polite letter the day before yesterday telling him that before going any further it would be necessary to clarify that point; a week earlier I had written him the same thing, clearly specifying each of the items on which he should consult people who were well-informed. Your friend is less a man of method than a man of good faith. I would like there to be no need of dispensations; if there is a need, we must spare no efforts to obtain them.

I'm not surprised that he speaks of a rampart of ice; and yet believe me, the rampart was less icy than it seemed to be; it was of snow, which melts rather easily.

1. Marie-Aurore, comtesse Rutowska, legitimized daughter of Comtesse Aurore de Koenigsmark and King August II of Poland, elector of Saxony. Belle had mentioned her in Letter 127.

The Marquis sent my father his mother's marriage contract, almost a hundred pages long, I think; I suspect him of never having read it. It carries eight hundred thousand francs in dowry, to which he says he is sole heir. I suppose he is the heir by right, and not in fact, and that the dowry no longer exists; for in the inventory of his fortune, not a word is said of it. My father thought the same, and did not understand at all how this document could be of any use; he never mentions it without laughing. This contract has done some good by its very uselessness, for when we laugh we are in a mood to be pleased; and when we see that people understand nothing about the business that they have to negotiate with us, it happens—I don't know how—that we take a liking to them, and want to make the business take the turn that they desire; their very incompetence seems to charge us with the care of their interests.

My father seems to me quite persuaded of the perfect good faith of the Marquis, and is very pleased with his conduct. However, do not expect too much; nothing is certain yet; I don't even know whether one can say that success is probable. As for the question of capital or revenue, it is clear where the advantage is for Bellegarde and for me. However, for my parents to do otherwise for me than for my sister is to favor a marriage that at heart one disapproves of; that is unpleasant. Suppose that I were to die without children, and that my fortune, either whole or in part, were to come back to my relatives in this country—would it not be difficult to get the capital back?[2] I think, however, that when the matter hinges only on that, my parents will grant what is asked; but if they do not grant the whole thing at first, they will, I imagine, do enough and give sufficient hope so that the Marquis would be in the wrong to break the thing off. I will never cease to view my parents as absolutely free to do what they wish on this point. I hope however, as I have said, that they will grant without restriction what is asked; to bring that about I will do everything that one can do decently and without falling short of that scrupulous disinterestedness which is so dear to me. If, against all expectation, this business were to be ended because of financial interests, I would not want anyone in the world to know it.

There, you will say, she is being quixotic again. Very well; but that way of being quixotic is part of me; the moment it were destroyed, I would no longer exist, or would no longer respect myself. I know of no one who has taken more literally than I do everything that the philosophers and the novels say about detachment from riches; they have made me swallow the whole line.

A recommendation on my part to Mme de Heeze and Leende would be a patent of eternal disgrace for M. and Mme d'Egenberge. I would have recommended them to my cousin under the seal of secrecy, and she would

---

2. See Letter 106, n. 3, for the difference between Mitie's dowry and the arrangement that Bellegarde wants.

have tried to make them agreeable to my aunt, but unfortunately neither the one nor the other are at Heeze, and they may not go there for a long time.[3] I told M. Singendonck,[4] who's going to spend the hunting season there, to see them, inform himself of their affairs, and render them service if he could. If the lady should be young or pretty, I have demanded that he not fall in love with her, nor any man that he might bring with him, and he has promised me that my prohibition would be observed.

You could perfectly well have repeated your answers as often as I repeated my alarms; the subject is too serious for me not to be allowed to go on a little and ramble a bit about it.[5] People do not get tired of frightening me, or at least they are doing their best; they have told me that the cold humors[6] were passed from father to son in almost all the families in Chambéry; but besides my thinking it's an old wives' tale, or at least a great exaggeration, the Marquis has no look of the cold humor about him, and what do I care about the other fathers-to-sons! However, answer me.

Whenever the occasion presents itself, tell Bellegarde or write to him that he will have to bring me back to visit my parents often; that I must be allowed to be here often. Everything I see here tells me that my parents' pleasure in seeing me will compensate, and will make them pardon and forget all the drawbacks; not to see me would be the most poignant grief, if not for the reason, at least for the heart.

Goodbye, my dear d'Hermenches. —I have written this hastily.

210. *To Constant d'Hermenches, August 22, 1765*

I am in a bad mood. Aren't there already enough big obstacles in life without the little complications? My father wrote on the ninth of this month to Bellegarde; I receive a letter from him yesterday that showed that on the eighteenth he had not yet received the letter from my father. As for information regarding the validity of a marriage such as ours in his country, he has not yet taken the first step to obtain it; this is going to drag on an intolerable length of time. And what will happen, when all's said and done? Between you and me, I think that such a matter could not be in worse hands. Bellegarde will not know how to choose his informants or his agents; he will see neither the ways nor the means; he will believe that what is merely difficult

---

3. Heeze and Leende are villages in Brabant where Belle's aunt, Johanna Elisabeth de Geer, the widow of Jan Maximiliaan van Tuyll, owns property. Belle thinks she cannot do much for the Egenberges because her aunt dislikes her. The cousin is Anna Elisabeth (Annebetje), the aunt's step-daughter, of whom Belle is so fond.

4. One of the brothers of Maria-Anna Singendonck, the wife of Belle's uncle Hendrik Willem van Tuyll.

5. The issue is, again, the possibility that the marquis may have syphilis.

6. Scrofula.

is impossible, and as for me—after having moved heaven and earth for more than a year to remove the obstacles that we had foreseen, I will have the vexation of seeing my efforts and my successes overturned by some blunder.

I would like to be in the Marquis's place just now, and be acquainted with his friends and the court and Turin, and know what he knows. I would see our business through, even if the laws are against us—or at least, so I imagine. What would be very useful to us and make those who give out the permits more lenient, is that the Marquis would only have to want to live in this country and he would be able to do without the permissions altogether. In a poor country like Savoie, they don't like to have the great families move away, and they like to have foreigners whom they suppose to have considerable fortunes come to live there. If the Court approves, I think that it would easily obtain the papal dispensation; besides, in Rome, you can get anything with influence and money.

Why didn't we think of all this sooner! You would have helped us gather this information; at present you are up to your neck in your new military duties, and all you can do for us is to wish us well.

I beg you to have a little remorse at having lulled us with the supposed Protestantism of the sister of the Comte de Saxe. Really, you did badly to affirm to my father with so much assurance something that you didn't know at all. It took Bellegarde a long time to recall that aunt, and he didn't know what I was talking about. He is amiable, charming, full of wit; but he is not at all deft, and I am afraid he'll spoil everything. (Are you aware that people with much wit and no deftness are worth much more than others? I am sometimes vexed with myself because of a certain adroitness of mine that makes me succeed in anything I please. The talent for intrigue is always a little damaging to good faith. It is so difficult not to exercise one's talents—to put them aside until there is a pressing need!) I like the Marquis very much just as he is, but at this juncture I wish he could put matters in the hands of a friend who is a trifle less estimable and slightly more adroit, and that the business at this end could be decided; I would do on my side everything that I could to bring my father and mother around, and finally everything would be in place, and then a few words of liturgy and then ... I would be so happy to have arrived at the denouement that I would spare myself all those mincing little displays of prudery; I would not waste any time weeping, as is the convention, after having wasted so much time arranging, and persuading, etc. One rather good thing—that stupid law which condemns one to play the tedious roles of fiancés for three months has not passed into our province; we will be married like other people.

I am bored beyond all expression; for according to the explicit order you gave me, I have only this matter in my head—not the least bit of wit, neither in verse nor prose. I write nothing but long letters to Bellegarde from time to time—I don't produce dissertations, I merely write trifles and rhapsodies; one has to cheer oneself up somehow. I don't know what to do with my energy; I don't play a single note of music. I keep my mother company, I do a little embroidery—that's how my day is spent. My sister is a prudish, ill-humored child; although she has quite as much wit and attractiveness as she needs to be likeable, she is bad company. The days are long, the weeks infinite. It was a year ago that I said: today is the first of June; surely it was a year ago; that's a strange thing, a year of three months, but no matter, that's the way it is—so that it's been a year and a half since I saw you last. That's a long time; I am very impatient to see you. My dear mother wanted to go to Cleves for a pleasure trip at the beginning of September, and in spite of my unworthiness I was to be the soul of that party. But now my poor aunt is dying of convulsions.[1] She's an old maid who never had a great deal of sense; for some time now she has had so little that it hardly counts. Thus the loss is not great, but that would upset our plans for now. If, against all likelihood, she recovers a bit, I hope that we will make our journey.

I beg you to send me a dispensation for a few bad jokes about your protégée Mme Spaen. What else is there to do in this tedious time? There is a great dearth of amusement here, and while I'm waiting for marriage I have to live somehow. Tell me, what do you predict regarding permissions, dispensations and so forth? They have to be water-tight, in absolutely correct form; I must be a legitimate spouse, and my children legitimate as well, without my ever having to change church for any consideration whatsoever: for I will not change. Mme de Nassau is leaving her husband and is coming to live in a house that my father has just finished building next to us in Utrecht.

I am still in a bad mood; I thought that it would pass if I talked to you, but not at all. Goodbye then; I am in too bad a mood to love very much, but I love you as much as I can.

211. *From Constant d'Hermenches, August 28, 1765*

Lille

I was going to write to you, dear, beautiful Agnes, to demonstrate to you, by solid arguments, what you say to me with such infinite charm: that a husband who is a man of wit and a little clumsy is not at all a bad bargain for a woman who has more wit than he does—and just at that point I receive your letter. That's just what I was saying already last year: a husband who understands business too well often drives his wife mad; if you were to doubt it, I would tell you to ask my wife what she thinks. So be impatient if you must; but no chagrin or ill humor. The Marquis, as I have told you, is unbearable in everything that is a matter of detail or organization. His good faith makes him negligent and often even culpable; it will be up to you to correct all

1. A sister of Belle's father, Anna Elisabeth, who died in May 1766 at the age of fifty-two.

that. That's what I was saying a year ago, and it is why I regard you as a treasure for him, all the other merits aside. If he knew how to get married, don't you think he would have been married a long time ago? As an only son, titled, charming, he could have chosen anyone he pleased; do you think that if he were at all methodical about his own affairs, he would be obliged to beg for your hundred thousand florins, and to be dependent on so many circumstances? I have omitted nothing in my exposition of the subject; please reread my letters if you still have them. He cannot settle in Holland, but he can have you live in comfort in his country. As for that aunt, I knew her as the sister of the Comte de Saxe, who died a Protestant; could I have guessed that the wretched woman would not be of the same religion as a hero?[1]

The Marquis has left for his country; he has put all the ardor he is capable of in the arrangement of his happiness; he writes me about it in those terms, and I have no doubt that it will all work out. The King is rather devout, but he will permit one of his subjects to make a good marriage; on your side, it seems to me that you have made great progress with your parents. I count absolutely on the Marquis' sister, who is more clever than all of us!

Go to Cleves; you will do well to do so; one must distract and amuse oneself. As for me, I am killing myself with labor, without distraction or pleasure, and yet I do not complain. Mention M. d'Hodicq to Mme de Spaen; he's a Frenchman who has let it be known (or so I am told) that he had enjoyed the favors of that lady. He has just obtained a fine post, and is going to marry a rich widow here, who seemed to be about to marry someone else. I put myself at your feet, my charming friend.

212. *To Constant d'Hermenches, September 4, 1765*

Good evening. It is late already, midnight or thereabouts. Tomorrow I am getting up at five o'clock; however, I must still say good night to you. I have saved you as a treat after all the other tasks and farewells. I have just finished a panel of my dress. The most colorful border! the prettiest thing! I talk to you about trivia because I love you, because it's a pleasure for me to talk to you; your letters, on the other hand, are so terse and laconic that I think you no longer love me. The last one is charming, it is true, but too short by half. What has become of the time when you preferred the pleasure of writing to me over all other things! In those days, a word gave birth to a page; the subject was you and me. Just now you have related a piece of news: Monsieur d'Hodicq is getting married! God bless him! I have never

---

1. Maurice, comte de Saxe (1696–1750), was a French general and one of the great military heroes of his time, especially in the War of the Austrian Succession. He was credited with the French victory at Fontenoy, in which d'Hermenches was wounded.

seen him. Do you find I have become too crazy, or is our liaison getting too old?[1]

I would like to learn very soon that Mlle des Marches[2] sees a way to obtain a permission from the King and a dispensation from the Pope. The Holy Father, they say, does not get involved in anything; it is only a question of presenting things to him in the way one would like him to see them. In Rome, everything is to be had with influence and money. Will we get what we want? I hope so. Write a line or two to Mlle de Marches. My father quite rightly insists on this legitimacy; he must be told very positively the possibilities and probabilities and means that we see for obtaining what would make this marriage legitimate; then it will be necessary actually to receive the dispensations and show them to us, and then the Marquis will be embarked on the sea of marriage. May it not be for him a stormy sea! Too much calm would bore him; a gentle wind must stir up a pleasant undulation, and he will be lulled by the ebb and flow of the waves.

I am enjoying myself this evening; this morning, it was the contrary; I woke up with the most lugubrious ideas on the very subject that I am enjoying just now. This morning I was saying:

> Tout au monde est mêlé d'amertume et de charmes
> La guerre a ses douceurs, l'hymen a ses alarmes.[3]

My God! if there should happen to me what they say sometimes happens—if the warmth of my love were soon to inspire only distaste, and if Bellegarde were to pass from indifference to scorn or jealousy! ... I am ardent, my friend, and I feel strongly that between repugnance for my husband and rapture, there would be no middle ground. I would find myself pitiable if the first advances I had ever made were not received with gratitude and pleasure.

Here I am again, being much too free-spoken with you. I think that you would like me to get rid of that tone; you may be beginning to find it no longer decorous, and you would be right. But at any rate it will not be said that you have been unaware of a single one of my ideas on marriage.

Reread my last letters; write me long answers, and I hope I will find packets from you, care of *Spruyt, Bookseller, in Utrecht* (that's my summer address) upon my return from Cleves. I have not accused you of having deceived me about the character of the Marquis; on the contrary, I have admired the truth of what you have told me regarding the things I can judge of today. I have no intention of playing the mistress of the household, com-

---

1. Belle has missed the point, or else deliberately ignored it. D'Hermenches was responding to her requesting "a dispensation for a few bad jokes about ... Mme de Spaen."
2. Bellegarde's sister.
3. From La Fontaine's *Fables*: "Le Meunier, son fils, et l'âne" [The miller, his son, and the ass]. "Everything is mingled with bitterness and charms; / War has its sweetness, a wedding its alarms."

petent in everything; I mean to leave to the Marquis' sister an authority that surely she will make better use of than I would know how to make; it seems to me that they will be pleased with me for that deference, which will cost me nothing, and will win me flattering kindnesses for which I will be very grateful.

I like your referring me to your wife to learn what an inconvenience a clever husband can be. Another charming sentence: *Could I have guessed that the wretched woman would not be of the same religion as the hero?* But if it is true that you wrote charming sentences, it is no less true that you have been unpardonably irresponsible and reckless.

I am dying of fear that we may learn that Mme de La Perrière[4] has changed church to legitimize her marriage; in that case, it will take very strong evidence to persuade us that she would have been free not to change—that it was her fault, her free choice to change.

What makes a strange effect, annoys my friends, and, I think, amuses my enemies, is that the Marquis publicly denies what I freely admit.[5] I cannot change my character, nor accustom myself to sustain a falsehood that does no one any good; if I found it bad or shameful to marry, I would not get married; if it is good, then let it be known. The Marquis, for his part, follows his own humor and method; that does not bother me, but it is rather odd. Goodbye; without being a wizard, you have gathered that we are leaving tomorrow for Cleves.

One o'clock in the morning

How foolish to be writing so late.

Whether I get married or not, love me still; bear in mind that I am still free, and that it would take only a whim of mine ... Farewell.

213. *From Constant d'Hermenches, September 15, 1765*

Lille

You are absolutely right, charming Agnes! I have indeed changed, and you have in me a very dull correspondent! The fact is that right up to this very day I have not been able to dispose of my time as I pleased. There have been similar modifications to my costume, my actions, and my thoughts: I wear clothes that are short, close-fitting and simple; all my steps are counted as by a watch; my tone is grave and imperative, and my thoughts tend only to the renunciation of anything pleasant, anything unrelated to my present situation. But my heart is the same, nonetheless, my dear Agnes; if I were to open the smallest window into the feelings locked up in there, you would see them inundate whole notebooks of paper as it used to do—but I must

4. The wife of a certain diplomat.
5. That the marriage negotiations are going on.

not. I am putting myself to a test worthy of a great man. I dare to say it to you: I no longer count myself for anything; I no longer have any other pretensions than that of seeing whether one can exist without having any, and without satisfying one's tastes. I am succeeding; I am gaining a strength and a method in my character that had been lacking. If I am becoming more laconic, I will be no less whole-hearted to my friends; perhaps less agreeable, but more interesting, more easy-going.

Can you really believe that your letters, which gave my life its savor at a time when I was being frittered away and distracted by trivialities, would now have lost their value in my eyes? No, you cannot believe it. A day will come when we will be together again, when you will find the same warmth in my attention, when, I think, you will be charmed with me. But right now the situation of my mind and that of your fate do not lend themselves to such close commerce as before. I pay you sincere homage, I humbly raise my hat to you as we pass, but I cannot sit down; things are up in the air for both of us.

I am waiting for news of the Marquis's return home. You are right, we must let his sister do what she can, and I strongly urge you not to put more of your own effort into it than you have done so far; it is up to them to show the greatest efforts to possess you. I must confess that I would have preferred that you had not admitted this marriage prospect to simply anyone who was curious about it; the Marquis and I have kept it quite secret, but with all your metaphysics and your superior genius, it is not possible for you to stay in the beaten paths; otherwise you would have liked that sort of dishonesty which makes young girls show a horror of marriage until the moment when the priest has blessed them.

So you are in Cleves now; I regret all the pearls you are throwing away there, but so long as you get some pleasure out of it I will be happy. You can imagine whether I have any, at this moment. I had arranged to spend my winter here; the expenses have been laid out; this is the best city in the kingdom; I have agreeable and useful connections here. I receive the order to march with my regiment to Landrecies and Avesne, two holes where there are only barracks and provisioners. Farewell Lille, fruit of all my labor; I will be worse off than I would be in the countryside, and my regiment will lose much of its beauty and order. I am not in despair, however, because I am like Horace's sage;[1] if I can live without you, without my friends, I can more easily go from Lille to Landrecies. My resource will be to begin to read again, to hunt, and to travel more easily to Brussels, Paris, the Hague. All these troubles fall on my body like a thunderbolt; I was about to set forth tranquilly to play music in a delightful country setting with the Bishop of Tournai. Farewell, my dear Agnes; write me at *Landrecies in Hainaut,* by way of Valenciennes. I am at your feet.

1. The sage described in Horace's *Odes,* whose equanimity makes him invulnerable to the caprices of Fortune.

CR *D'Hermenches is now established at his post in Landrecies in north-eastern France. Belle reached her majority on October 20, 1765, and as he had promised, her father began a formal exchange of information with Bellegarde.*

216. *To Constant d'Hermenches, November 25, 1765*

I didn't want to write to you; but I am beginning a letter; I don't know whether I will finish it. My father has answered the Marquis: he is requesting more extended and better established clarifications as to the legitimacy of the marriage; to that end he is requesting answers from the highest court of justice on several questions that he is proposing, item by item. I find it only fair that since he is being asked for his consent, he should want to know on what basis to grant it, and to take all the precautions that his prudence suggests to him. If I find that prudence a little inconvenient, it isn't his fault; it's mine, or that of circumstances. Provided that the law is not opposed to us, or that the sovereign can and will dispense with the law in such a way that wife and children have nothing to fear, my parents will make no obstacle; Bellegarde will have me if he wants me. The question is: will he want me?

My father is offering fifty thousand florins of capital, and a thousand florins a year;[1] he is content with the dower[2] that the Marquis is willing to give, and proposes to offer him an equivalent. If you knew our affairs as I do, you would find this very good—that I would be foolish to ask for more, and ungrateful not to be content with this. I have written to Bellegarde that he should refuse without further ado if these offers do not suit him; I have said everything I should say, my soul being as you know it to be. I have promised always to be his friend if I cannot be his wife; I will keep my word, without any difficulty. I will not blame him, I will not be vexed; I will even be obliged to him for not exposing himself to regrets.

I have asked him to send you my letter, supposing that the affair be broken off by the question of fortune; but I want you to be the only man in the universe who knows about the cause of this breaking-off; I have promised in my heart to the Marquis, to my parents, to myself, never to open my mouth about it to anyone at all. If the truth were clearly known, it would justify both Bellegarde and my parents; but when is it that truth is not obscured by hateful suspicions? No one of those whom I love must be suspected because of me, much less by my own doing. So be discreet; if the affair breaks off, do not suspect, or accuse, or blame. I dare tell you—I who

1. If Bellegarde were to use the fl 50,000 to purchase a life annuity for Belle, it would yield about fl 2,165 a year, so that, with van Tuyll adding fl 1,000, Belle would be receiving about fl 165 more than Mitie. See Letter 106, n. 3.
2. Capital reserved for the wife in case she is widowed.

know all the details—that you would be unjust; I must add that you would distress me. But how I wish that this business would succeed, and that I might belong to your friend!

I am on very good terms with my parents. Everything persuades me that if I marry Bellegarde, my father will conduct himself as if this marriage pleased him, as if this son-in-law were of his choice. And really, he finds him a great lord, and he believes he is honest and amiable as well—kind, gentle ...

217. *From Constant d'Hermenches, November 27, 1765*

Raismes[1]

In me you can see, charming Agnes, one of those survivors of a ship-wreck who, after long wandering on a savage isle, have lost the use of speech, yet still find some possibility of existence without what attached them the most intimately to the world; these survivors have often been found to be very amiable people, and the quality of their heart has not been altered by the suspension of all its functions. I was already unworthy of your correspondence when I was in Lille; what can I be worth here? I arrived here very sick; for six weeks I have lain ill in bed or at my fireside; I have been weighed down with various cares and business. I have not known how to seize a moment that seemed appropriate for writing you. You are one of those beings to whom it is a profanation to present oneself when one is stupid and morose; you do not believe in these sorts of infirmities, and I have often seen you attribute to the will something that is only a physical obstacle. Why is that? It's because you are never at a loss, you are always sparkling; and because—rare being that you are—you are not acquainted with any of the ups and downs that characterize humanity.

I certainly owed you a whole volume of letters; my heart was full of things to say to you; and that is precisely why I have never found the oppor-tune moment to set myself down to it. Today, to punish myself and to show you how ashamed I am, I am scribbling this on the corner of the mantel-piece, with the post horses waiting at the door and twenty people here in the apartment of the Marquis de Cernay,[2] whose house I have come to for a change of air and whom I am leaving to return to my Landrecies—which is a hole like Woerden or Naardan,[3] but is at least inhabited by species of Frenchmen.

I am lodged in a barracks that I have covered with wrapping-paper and maps, and I live here like a hermit after discharging the daily duties of my post. I have received my beautiful harpsichord from the Hague, and many

1. A city in northern France.
2. Seigneur de Raismes; lieutenant general of the king's armies.
3. Small Dutch cities.

books; I am drinking only water and am constrained to a diet. And that, my dear Agnes, is the sum of my existence these days.

But let's talk about Raismes. Heaven has led me to a woman there who bears an astonishing resemblance to you. She is very beautiful, with the kind of beauty that you have; she is gentle as an angel; she is madly fond of pleasure; she is full of talents, and is prodigiously witty, with a wit like true coin—an everyday wit and a metaphysical turn of mind when it's called for—however, not as strong as yours. I am looking at her just now as I am writing to you, to see whether I am not mistaken; her name is Mme d'Orchival (it's only fair that you know the name of the person I'm comparing you to). She will spend the winter three leagues from here, where she has a fine house; and who knows whether I, who am clumsy enough to let myself starve for your news and give you the worst possible opinion of me simply for lack of writing a letter, will not be just as negligent with your mirror image! It is quite possible that I will go several months without visiting her. My dear Agnes, you have quite a monstrous friend here; however, you must not exchange him, believe me, any more than I would exchange the most lukewarm of your letters for all the bounties of this new acquaintance. The same concern for you consumes me still; the same admiration, the same enthusiasm inspires me. It's because I think that it cannot be otherwise, nor could you suspect me of the least change, that I so disgracefully neglect ex pressions of it.

But it is also a bit your fault, and that of the Marquis. He writes me that he is waiting for an answer from your father to begin taking measures at the court in Turin;[4] you write me that you will tell me everything; and both of you leave me waiting for the mail every day to learn the news that will determine your fate. Has your father replied? Has he consulted you? Are you persisting in your intentions? Without trying to excuse myself, I am obliged to tell you that you owed me all these details; and the Marquis, in each mail, tells me: *I have no answer.* It is time for you to know your destiny, and I cannot suspect your vigilant and ardent mind of stopping halfway; but it is important to my happiness and to my existence to be informed about it, for I belong more to you than to myself.

218. *From Constant d'Hermenches, December 4, 1765*

Landrecies

A few days ago you will have received one of my letters, adorable Agnes, in which you see a friend who is anxious, ashamed, but still concerned for you as for the being who is in all the world the closest to his heart. The let-

---

4. The court of Savoie, which is part of the kingdom of Sardinia. Its capital was Turin.

ter of yours that I received today distresses me;[1] I see that our affairs are going down that trivial path of debate over finances. You have given your verdict, and thus my reflections are no longer pertinent; but since you must know what your best and most tender servant and friend thinks in all circumstances, allow me to say that the offer made to the Marquis resembles a maneuver to get rid of him, rather than conditions that he might have expected.

For more than a year we had been assuming that you would have a dowry, either in income or otherwise, of a hundred thousand florins; that was the arrangement made for your younger sister, who was marrying a man whom your family had not chosen, and whom she herself had not absolutely decided on. The Marquis frankly presented himself on this assumption, disdaining the wealth that he could have found in other marriages that would not have satisfied his other sentiments, but able to support you only on condition of certain arrangements. You should have said at the outset: "You will have only half the capital, and the revenue of two fifths of the rest."[2]

I have no news of the Marquis since my last letter; thus I'm only speaking to you according to my own common sense; as for him, I do not know what his decision will be. I can see him from here, in despair, torn between desiring a thing that will make his happiness and trying to adjust his calculations accordingly, and being too honest a man to be willing to be romantic at the risk of having you ill provided for. You must admit that a thousand florins are only half the revenue of the missing payment in the dowry that you had declared. —It is dreadful to be in the situation of discussing such wretched details, but these matters are to the sweet conversations of marriage what childbirth and its sequels are to its embraces.

You misjudge me if you think that I could ever make disclosures that might destroy our plans; but you misjudge the world even more if you think that this can be kept a secret. Everything is known eventually, once matters have to pass through different hands. The d'Havrincourts,[3] who were passing through here, have received letters from Holland mentioning your marriage as a virtual certainty. I replied that I would be charmed, that it would be a very good thing, but that I knew nothing about it. My advice, if you asked me, would be to put it to your parents that the Marquis will have enough to do to get permission from his court, without being tormented over financial matters; and that you should ask them to deal with you more

1. Letter 216 of November 25.
2. Here again is the misunderstanding about Mitie's dowry. See Letter 106, n. 3, and Letter 216, n. 1. In any case, d'Hermenches must have meant two thirds.
3. The marquis d'Havrincourt was the ambassador of France to the Hague. It was his wife who looked over Belle at a society gathering and said, "That one, a demoiselle!" (See Belle's Letter 127 of August 1764.)

generously, telling them that if they make distinctions between you and your younger sister it is only fair that they be in your favor, given your position as the eldest daughter and a marquise. If these remonstrances were to be at all fruitful, I would like you to send word to the Marquis immediately without waiting for his reply. It seems to me that things have gone so far that this cannot be broken off without its being very disagreeable to you, and I put myself in the place of the poor Marquis and his sister: they will be in despair. As for the dower[4] that your father is offering, I am certain that the Marquis will not accept it, so suppress that item altogether. It is a question of establishing oneself properly, solidly; all the rest will go of itself and, I am sure, to the pleasure and the greatest satisfaction of your family.

I tell you nothing of myself, my dear Agnes; today, I am too full of these great concerns; you and the Marquis are the the creatures that I count on the most in the whole universe, with whom I share my thoughts most freely. I have returned to my hole, and to the pleasure of being the complete philosopher-hermit. The Duc de Choiseul has made a gesture on my behalf that would make you love this country.[5] An officer wrote a letter against me; he sends me the letter, and the writer is in prison for three months.

I am at your feet.

219. *To Constant d'Hermenches, December 5, 1765*

Have no fear of reproaches, nor of those cold, proud expressions of forgiveness: *Monsieur, do as you please, do not trouble yourself; if you find no more pleasure in writing to me, write me no more.*[1] That's what is usually said, but that's what I will never say to you. Sometimes I am tempted to love you more than one loves a friend, but never to love you less than one loves the best and the most lovable of friends. I have been chagrined by your silence without being offended by it; my last letter was laconic; that was enough punishment. I meant to write you a long letter to put in this mail; I would certainly have written it even if I had not received yours. I have received it with great pleasure, and I have reread it more than once.

I am very sorry that you are ill and on a diet. I would like to be still closer to Landrecies than Mme d'Orchival. It seems to me that two months spent calmly with me, with rest and a quiet mind, without doctors or medicines, would put you right; but you would have to avoid all frenzy, and not stir up your blood nor fatigue your mind. I would put my words on a diet, and thus do you no harm. No, of this I am very sure: you will not forget me

4. Capital reserved in case of widowhood.
5. For Choiseul, see the translators' comments that follow Letter 155.
1. This is in answer to his Letter 217 of November 27.

for any new acquaintance, even though in her resemblance to me she were more beautiful than I; nor will I exchange my friend, silent as he is, for anything in the world. Of all the men in the world you are the one in whom I have the most entire and the most natural trust; I have no prudence, or reserve, or prudery with you, and—what is more extraordinary—I no longer have any vanity before you, so that all my follies, all the failings that diminish me in my own eyes—I always feel disposed to tell you of them. If we lived together, I would conceal nothing; perhaps I think that you have a better opinion of me than I have of myself, and I expect to see myself reassured, raised up, more highly valued by the judgment that you would bring to bear on my confidences.

Good Lord, how tender and sweet I'm being! The style of Mme d'Orchival, sweet *as an angel*, is not more benign than that; I am not ordinarily very sweet, but I love you, and today I am a little sad; I could even say *very*. I! *Unacquainted with all the ups and downs that characterize humanity!* My dear d'Hermenches, can you think it? Then you no longer know me. The difference between us is that your spirit is sometimes downcast when you are ill, and mine is extravagant when I am in full health. I assure you that I am half mad more than half the time.

I will weary you a little this evening with my fantasies, and manias, and hypochondrias, if I have the leisure; at present I must tell you quickly a word about the Marquis and our enterprise. But what can I tell you? I think I reported to you in my last letter everything that is important and new. I think that the decision is almost in his power. If he goes to a little trouble, it seems to me that he will be able to obtain the clarifications asked for in the form that my father prescribes; then a permission from the Court—would he not get that as well? But before anything else he must know whether the conditions suit him; on that point I do not want him to have any illusions or make any sacrifice for me. I told you how I had written him; since then I have received another of his letters, and I replied in a friendly manner, hardly speaking of our matter. He very much hopes, he says, that it will succeed; I hope for it even more, which is as it should be: I am younger, and very intense about what I desire, and I have more interest invested in this. If the affair falls through, he can find something better, or continue a way of life that pleases him and that he was resolved to continue before all this started. As for me, I will never find such a good marriage, and I can no longer endure celibacy—that is, celibacy in the strictest sense; for to live without a husband and without any hindrance is not at all a horrible state. If I do not marry Bellegarde, I will begin by not wanting to marry anyone else; then I will renounce marriage altogether. Then whose business will it be, this so-called virtue of chastity? Will I not be free? To whom will I have promised a privation that is tiresome for me and does no good for anybody? Then he who cannot become my husband would be, if he wished, my lover.

Goodbye; I would say a great deal more, but General Eliott[2] and his wife want to take me to our Dutch theater. Long live the English, for their freedom of commerce, for an ease that is not a particular tone, or air, or convention—which is not a kind of constraint, as with the French—but true ease, true liberty. These people are fond of me, make much of me, and want me to visit them in England. I speak English like an Englishwoman. I will write you Monday, for here they are.

220. *To Constant d'Hermenches, December 7, 1765*

See how I love you, see how I keep my word to you! I have a hundred things to say to you. Did you manage to read and understand the end of my last letter? I didn't have the time to reread it, but I am so used to making horrible mistakes of absent-mindedness that I am always afraid of being unintelligible. I was telling you about Mr. and Mrs. Eliott; the husband has a distinguished war record on the French coast, in Germany, in America—wherever there has been combat; he speaks all languages; he is a very humane soldier and an enlightened, polite, amiable man, no longer young. He has just brought his son to Brunswick; he makes much of his daughter, who is here; his children are the same age as yours, but he is ten years older than you are. I have never seen a husband whose attentions to his wife are more mannerly, more agreeable, more courteous; she listens to him, admires him, feels honored by his reputation, by the people he knows, by the approval that he wins everywhere. They make a couple that it's a pleasure to see: no vapidity or affectation or indifference. They don't like either gambling or the ceremonials of great gatherings any more than I do, so we get along very well together. Mrs. Eliott speaks only English; she gets along splendidly with me, who understand her language and her English gaiety. In my own eccentricities I have quite a bit of that *humour*[1] that they find only in their island; that amuses her, and in a few awkward gestures of affection she shows me a hundred times more friendship than a Frenchwoman would in a thousand superlative protestations.

If you could see with what delight she imagines my stay at her home in England, the beer I will drink, the oratorios of Handel she'll take me to! This will surprise you—for all that they are only here by chance, in the worst of lodgings, without any motive for staying here, and with very few connections, they cannot bring themselves to leave Utrecht and they find it hard to return to London, where they are building, and where they should be. I like to see people good-natured and content—who, having reached the

2. George Augustus Eliott (1717–90). He will distinguish himself in 1782 by his defense of Gibraltar, for which he will receive the title of Lord Heathfield.
1. In the early eighteenth century the French borrowed the English spelling of *humour*—which Belle uses—to express just what she is referring to here.

age when most people only have plans and cares and worries, enjoy themselves instead, and forget themselves. Since one ought not to be *too* happy, the General has the misfortune of not greatly enjoying all the talk of dogs and horses that is the main topic in the society of most of his compatriots. In the past he has been a close friend of La Sarraz. I go on and on about this—but can you be bored by what amuses me?

221. *To Constant d'Hermenches, December 11–12, 1765*

Wednesday

I have just received your letter;[1] I have only skimmed it—the beginning, the end—I have skipped the rest; that detail is simply too painful; I am allowed to spare myself. What does it matter whether my parents are right or wrong? I don't want to know. It is impossible for me to change anything about this; they may yet change of their own accord; I know nothing about it; I hardly even wish it. I would not like to be so far indebted to anyone in the world, not even my father and mother. It would distress me if they acted in my favor in a way that would seem onerous to them. There is no happiness that I would want to purchase at that price. I confess, this is not so much generosity as hauteur and inflexibility of character. But, whether it is vice or virtue, this sentiment is ineffaceably imprinted in my heart.

Write to the Marquis; tell him on my behalf and on your own to refuse—that is, advise him to refuse, and assure him that this will not put him on bad terms with me; that I am, nonetheless, in despair at losing him; that I am greatly attached to him, that nothing will compensate me for the loss of him; that it is not my fault ... say everything that should be said. His letter to my father can be very polite, and not offensive to anybody; if he prefers, he can write to me, so that I can show the letter; then we can continue the correspondence, if it pleases him ...

There is only one page of your letter that I am not reading at all; I can respond to the whole content of the three others. It is my fault, I have said a hundred times, that the thing has been known to the public. I don't dare tell you how that came about, you would make fun of me. That ridiculous failing of mine—not being able to be silent about my own concerns when they greatly preoccupy me—has often given me cause to blush; on that point

En un mot, je suis femme.[2]

I will mend my ways. When all's said and done, this does me no particular harm; I will never disown my honorable intentions. On the contrary, if henceforth I live only to divert myself and do nothing at all—that is, if I only write poetry, if I pay attention only to the stars, if my sovereign glory

1. His Letter 218, with his financial calculations.
2. "In a word, I am a woman." From Racine's *Athalie*, III.iii.

is to understand Horace and Juvenal, and if then some sensible person reproaches me for the uselessness of my life, I will reply: "Once in my life I did everything in my power to be of more value, to be more useful, to fulfill better the aim of my existence." If anyone has some other reproach for me, I will reply: "At one time I was resolved to follow the established order in society; at one time I wanted absolutely to be a respectable woman." If the bonds of marriage are denied me the only time that I might have entered into them with pleasure, I regard myself as forever free. No, it is not likely that I will marry; I see the chances as a thousand to one against it. That state suited me only in certain circumstances, with all the attractions and all the charms that were attached to it, and which I will never find again. Something that seems to me very certain—that has been planted irrevocably in my head—is that I will never get married in the future except *sans dot;*[3] at the very most I will accept a yearly allowance for clothes, but nothing beyond. I have never made vows; and if it were not for that I would make this one. You must not think, however, that this is a bad joke, dictated by bitterness toward my parents; I do not know whether you would forgive me for it—I would certainly not forgive myself.

I find you unjust with respect to them. They wanted to treat my sister and me with complete equality, offering three thousand florins a year; the Marquis had and still has the right to accept them or not. That offer doesn't suit him; he is quite right, but it's not my father's fault. You would like them to do more for me than for my sister;[4] by what right would I claim such a preference? My right as the eldest is nothing at all, as you know perfectly well, and your predilections are blinding you. Perponcher pleased my mother very much;[5] there was no objection to him; it is true that since his ancestors were noblemen in Guyenne and not here, he cannot enter our corps of nobles, and therefore was not regarded as one of our best matches. But everything else was as it should be—fortune, connections, character—, and he was not Catholic. My sister hesitated, but it would have been vexing to see her send away the best match in the world simply because he was not as grand as she is and not as amusing as I am.

In passing, I will relate a rather curious observation: my sister is prodigiously jealous of her husband—jealous only of his preferences, but to such a degree that a woman passionately in love with a libertine husband would not torment herself more. She cannot endure to see him in conversation with even the women to whom he is the most necessarily attached: his cousin

3. "Without a dowry": an allusion to Molière's *L'Avare* (*The Miser*) I.vii, in which the miserly father Harpagon keeps repeating that term—*sans dot*—as a condition of his daughter's marriage. D'Hermenches will pick up the term later, in his Letter 248 of August 1766.

4. Apparently Belle has come to realize that a hundred thousand in cash is a bigger dowry than three thousand a year for life—a point she confounded in her early communications to d'Hermenches. See Letter 106, n. 3.

5. Her sister's husband.

Mme de Voorschoten, his wife's cousins, or me, her own sister. You see how ridiculous it all is! He still adores her, and avoids everything that it pleases his wife to forbid him.

My father and mother have just left to attend the betrothal of my cousin de Tuyll and Milord d'Athlone.[6] Imagine it! My sister didn't ask me to accompany them and to stay with her. I don't know, however, whether it's out of jealousy or some other bad humor. She has done well; I would not have gone. I am all alone in the house—what freedom! But it is of no value, since nothing invites me to abuse it. Saturday I will go for a few days to the Widow, in Amsterdam; only for two or three days. I write with great disorder; my head is in a muddle.

You say that since this affair has gone so far it cannot be broken off without much unpleasantness for me. Yes, I would be very sorry, because I would lose my best-founded hope of happiness; but that it should have gone so far and become public will add nothing to my chagrin—that circumstance is a matter of indifference to me. Let us be careful lest no one in the world know the cause or rather the circumstances of this breaking-off; I answer for myself, and I count absolutely on your secrecy on this point.

Do not feel too sorry for the Marquis or his sister; you have no idea of the extent of my vapors, my weakness of spirits, my dispositions to the most somber melancholy; I have entirely lost the faculty of judging things in my imagination according to the measure and weight of reason. Farewell. In truth, your *sublime* friend is only a madwoman.

Do not fail to write to Bellegarde right away; cheer him up, put his mind at its ordinary ease; do not let him regret me for more than a week. How great a loss is a woman, after all? There are so many! They are so often merely in the way! Perhaps he should bless Heaven. Tell him all that, and to think no more about it.

I like very much the last words of your letter: surely you immediately wrote to the Duc de Choiseul to have your enemy set free.[7] Goodbye, dear d'Hermenches, I love you very much; and if I were allowed, I would embrace you in gratitude for your friendship, which is so faithful and tender and sustained. Keep to yourself what I have said about my sister; if you were here, I have a few stories that would make you laugh; if you were here—I on one side of the fireplace, you on the other—what pleasure! We would be alone . . . we would talk.

December 12

I see that my long scribbling of yesterday morning is not worth a great deal. Not only had I not read your entire letter, but I had misunderstood

---

6. Her favorite cousin Anna Elisabeth (Annebetje) married Frederik Christiaan Reinhard, count van Reede, fifth count of Athlone. His family were Dutch, but were made Irish peers by William III in 1692. From here on Belle refers to Annebetje as Madame or Milady Athlone.
7. A reference to the end of d'Hermenches' Letter 218.

part of what I had read. For instance, I had thought that you were reproaching me for the d'Havrincourts' knowing of our business, but that was not the case; I recommended that you keep secret the circumstances of the breaking-off, but you had already promised it. Never mind, I won't throw all that in the fire; it is up to you to burn it after reading it with some slight impatience. I'm about to fatten this packet of combustible material, fit only for the fire, so that you may have yet a brighter flame. I have now read and understood everything. You insist on counting three percent, as if money could only be invested in this country; but don't we have capital in France and England at a much higher interest rate? I have just made some calculations, and I find that at three and a half percent, the three thousand florins that have been given to my sister, and that would also be offered to the Marquis ... well, see what the capital must then be:

3.5 is to 100 as 3000 is to	*85,714 $^2/_7$*
Subtract from that:	*50,000*
There remains:	*35,714 $^2/_7$*

It is true that at 3½ percent they would yield 1,250, and only 1,000 are being offered. That's where I'm caught; I was counting on a different result when I began the calculation. Apparently one must figure an even higher rate of interest, because my father, who is no scatterbrain, would rather give three thousand florins a year than what he is offering, and he is consenting to give fifty thousand only to accommodate the Marquis.[8] —Let's talk no more about it, my dear d'Hermenches, I don't understand any of it; I can't absolutely say that I find my parents easy-going in this affair, but neither could I accuse them of being ungenerous. If they were to marry off my three brothers it would be impossible for them to give them the same annual sum that my sister and I receive without cutting back considerably from their own present expenditures.

Again, let's talk no more about it. If I had it to do all over again, I would set my cap for some moneybags who would not be lovable and to whom I would not be faithful. Where is it leading me, all my fine fastidiousness in marriage matters? To nothing but a thousand headaches.

It is impossible for me to speak to my parents in the way that you urge me to; besides, it would be useless.

8. Belle's calculation would have given her the answers she expected if she had used 4 percent: fl2,000 are needed to bring van Tuyll's 1,000 up to Mitie's 3,000, so the question is, "At what interest rate will fl50,000 yield fl2,000?"

223. *From Constant d'Hermenches, January 20, 1766*

Brussels

You must think me altogether dead, my divine friend, or absolutely incapable of writing to you. I am not at all dead—I live to love you and admire you—, but I have just been engaged in travels that, without my intending it, have taken me away from you and from my letters for more than six weeks. Finally I stop at Brussels, to throw myself at your feet. God, how tempted I am to slip over to Utrecht while I'm so nearby! But could I see you there without creating a scandal?

I have received news from the Marquis; he is desolate. He was confronted with insurmountable objections; he wrote you about it, for he adores your letters as I do. He is going to return to your Provinces, and I hope that he will see me on the way. That's all I can say about it at this moment. I am very sad at the turn that this affair has taken; I hope, however, and I implore you, that it not affect your happiness or your good humor.

Mine is restored a little by my travels. My illnesses, the dreadful garrison, the stupidity of my surroundings, the multiplicity of dealings, and, finally, a barbarous element I am condemned to live among, had formed a crust over my whole being. I have seen some of my friends; I have tasted a little of the delights of society, and here I am again, a new person.

I spent some time with my friend General Sarsfield in Lille;[1] he's an Englishman established and born in France, and who has won honors here. He has the best of both nations in virtue and in mind; he has given me his friendship and his trust. We were so seldom separated (only for a few hours of sleep) that I never found a moment to write to you as I wished; we worked a little on military matters, and did errands. From there I met the Duc d'Arenberg in Mons, where he was attending to his properties. This is a friend of twenty-one years standing, and I am perhaps the only intimate friend he has in this world. He gave parties upon parties, and without forgetting you, dear Agnes, I was swept up in a whirlwind of canonesses, which took up all my time; finally, I've come here to see the Duchesse d'Arenberg. Learn for yourself what kind of woman she is, and you will decide whether I owe her my attentions. I am staying in her townhouse, and these two amiable and faithful creatures fill all the moments of my day with everything that can occupy the taste and the heart.

In the midst of all that, I see you before me—you accompany me everywhere. I curse the fate—and the canals—that separate us, and I've made up my mind to tell you so quickly, on the run, however disjointedly, and without waiting any longer to be sitting down to write the letter I owe you with the responses to the thousand interesting things you told me.

1. The vicomte de Sarsfield, inspector-general of cavalry. His family, originally from Ireland, had moved to Brittany in the time of Cromwell to escape religious persecution.

I learn that there is a General Eliott here, with his wife; I immediately inquire whether he comes from Utrecht. Yes, and he is going to Flanders. I send word offering him help in any way I can, but he left this morning. How vexed I am—he had just seen Agnes! When you wrote to me about an Eliott I believed that it was the one who had been in our service, and who had been married in Lorraine, and whose children are rather unhappy in France; what you said about his happiness with this second wife hardly interested me.[2]

I have no pretensions, my dear Agnes, but believe me, if you knew the resourcefulness, the devotion, the charms of friendship among the French, your enthusiasm would be only for them. The heart must be the same among persons made of the same stuff, whatever the country; but in France there is applied to friendship a structure of rites—of sanctions and assent—which, while making it just as solid, strip it of that somberness, that too-gaping openness, those gross liberties of friendships in other countries.

I am going to see my son in Namur, and then I return to Landrecies; I beg you to write to me there that you are not angry at my incongruous silence, and that you are sure of all my adoration and my impassioned respect. Tell me what you have done about the Widow. My dear friends, do not remain in Holland, I beg you! I have a fine letter from the Comtesse de Degenfeld. People are showing around a letter from Rousseau to the Swiss, and one from the King of Prussia to Rousseau;[3] do you want to see them?

CR *Since Belle does not readily regard objections as insurmountable, she presents herself incognito to the Jansenist archbishop of Utrecht. This particular archbishop is in the midst of a doctrinal controversy, and his authority, which he regards as legitimate, is not recognized by Rome. He tells her that he is in no position to help her but that she might be able to obtain a dispensation by applying directly to the Vatican.*[4]

2. There were two General Eliotts. See Letter 225.
3. Rousseau had been in flight from both French and Swiss authorities, who were incensed by his *Emile* and his *Contrat social*. He wrote a number of letters justifying himself, and we cannot be sure which one is being referred to here. David Hume offered him refuge in England, which he accepted in January 1766. At that point Horace Walpole and some friends played a practical joke on him and circulated a fake letter in the Parisian salons, ostensibly from Frederick the Great inviting him to live in Prussia. Both the practical joke and the rather insulting terms of the letter could only have added fuel to Rousseau's already well-developed paranoia (Vissière, *Correspondance* 324).
4. The account we have of this venture is found in the fragment of a letter Belle wrote to Bellegarde in January 1766 (Letter 224, *O.C.* 1: 453).

225. *To Constant d'Hermenches, January 26-27, 1766*

Good evening. Now as for me, nothing prevents me from writing you except a pile of books—Tacitus, Sallust, dictionaries; I throw them under the table, by which means it is disencumbered, and I am writing. I was extremely sorry to hear that you were sick; your letter gave me great pleasure by telling me that you are in better health, more cheerful, and reconciled with nature, life, and society. The rest made no great impression; if I had been angry because of your silence, I would be still. I know that excuses on that subject are worthless, and that when one wants to write, one writes. I see nothing in all that enumeration of obstacles except that you had little desire to write; fortunately that is not a crime, and I am not so unreasonably proud as to claim continual attentions.

Let us not quarrel any more about the French and the English; we only half understand each other. You have adopted a little of what I call jargon: You say, *The heart must be the same in persons made of the same stuff.* I do not know two hearts that are the same, and I do not know what the same "stuff" in people means. My friendship knows no etiquette; it has its highs and lows like my moods, and I have not composed my feelings into a code of conduct. So far I think that my judgments are better than yours because they are more natural, truer, less subordinate to prejudices and to fashion. But on the other hand one should not go by what I say as to the social conventions because I am not sociable—I am bizarre, difficult, unobliging, and any kind of constraint seems to me a torture. If the praise that you sometimes lavish on certain people and customs is not altogether deserved, I, on the other hand, feel acutely that my distastes are often unjust—that is, they prove nothing about anyone else, and have their source only in my own disposition. All is well, then; you live with the French; it is fortunate that you like them. I hardly know them, and I will apparently never live among them; it doesn't matter that I don't much like them. I would certainly like the superior people in France, perhaps more than people of equal merit in any other country, because they are more communicative. But this communicative tendency itself makes me impatient with people of mediocre merit, who make up the greatest number everywhere, and I find it terrible to see myself pursued by commonplaces, insipidities, trivia, attentions, when I would a thousand times rather read, write, think, or sleep in peace.

Goodbye, my friend, I am falling asleep; I do better to go to bed than to put you to sleep.

January 26

Do you remember that one day in Westerhout, on your way back from England,[1] you defended against Madame Hasselaer the very thing that you

---

1. At Mme Hasselaer's house in Westerhout in September, 1762 (when d'Hermenches' arrival had embarrassed Belle), there seems to have been an argument about French versus English manners: at that time d'Hermenches was defending English manners.

combat today? You really lost a great deal in not seeing General Eliott. The one you are talking about, who was in our service, died a few years ago.

Madame Geelvinck is very well, and lives very happily; or at least so I gathered during the week I spent with her in Amsterdam. She seems to me as happy among the Dutch as you are among the French, and I beg that neither of you change your lot.

The business of the Marquis is less hopeless than you think. My father wrote to him last Tuesday; it was too late, I think, for Bellegarde to receive the letter. I pointed out to my father that the letter would no longer reach him in Chambéry, and to support my conjectures about the time of his departure I naturally cited a letter that I have received from him. My father said only a word of reproof about our corresponding, did not scold at all, and hesitated about writing. However, he was rather eager to send the letter that was already dictated in his head; having noticed that, I did not want to delay what could be a good impulse, so I changed my mind and altered my advice. My father wrote, and consulted me with very good grace about the address of Monsieur de Bellegarde, quite aware that I had written him much more often than he had. I have not read the letter, but I know that he backed off from the declarations he had demanded at first; he is perfectly content with the accounting that the Marquis sent, and if we can obtain a dispensation from the Pope and a permission from the King,[2] my parents will believe me well and duly married.

As for the finances, I think my father showed in that same letter that he would not be obstinate and limit himself to his first offers. I do not know how far his indulgence may go, or whether he will do enough for what the Marquis's affairs require. But I imagine that if the Marquis generally accepts the offers my father has made with the augmentations that he seems disposed to make; if, continuing to let my father see his financial needs, he relies a little on him for arrangements; if, finally, he is willing to hope and wait for something from time and circumstances, then I imagine, I say, that our marriage can take place. If, on the contrary he thinks that he should not yield, not wait, nor run any of the risks of uncertainty, the marriage will not take place. I repeat: I will blame neither the Marquis nor my father, whatever they decide. I am now only a spectator. To try to make them decide against their interests in favor of my own, I would have to cease to be myself.

It's always at midnight that I write to you, and I never put down the pen without telling you that I'm about to go to bed; this formula for a farewell is becoming very tedious; however, I cannot resolve to omit it tonight. I need the excuse of the hour for you to forgive the insipidity and the excessive disorder that prevails in this letter. Besides writing it with the greatest lethargy, I have incessantly put one word in the place of another; interruptions and bad pens have made this whole letter disgraceful, abominable, and

2. The king of Sardinia, of which the Duchy of Savoie was a part.

disagreeable for both eyes and mind. If I had the time, I would rewrite it; I would do a clean copy. We write each other so rarely that we ought to put a little ceremony into it. Forgive me; another time I will have more energy, I will love you more, and I will write better.

January 27, Monday evening

I'm afraid that I'm being ungrateful, and I'm returning to the house to add a few words to my letter. Since you have for so long taken such a keen interest in my concerns, and since you implore me so affectionately not to let my happiness and good humor be altered by the shipwreck of my desires, I must inform you and reassure you; I must not affect a hateful terseness with as good a friend as you. I will confess to you, then, that the constant opposition that Fate presents to my plans sometimes distresses me—it irritates and sours me. But I am too proud, I claim to be too superior to Fortune to show my distress, and I have too many resources in the things I do and in my imagination not to be—twenty times in the course of a day—distracted, amused, cheered, and of as good a humor as if I could hope for everything I desire. It would only be up to me to marry advantageously, but I do not want to; I will not give up Bellegarde except at the last extremity, and if I am obliged to give him up, I'm going to England to visit Mrs. Eliott. My fate or my fancy then will lead me where they please. I'm quite profitably engaged in explicating Tacitus, Sallust and Cicero with M. de Guiffardière[3] (whom you know, I think); I'm still rather bad at it, but I'm on the point of doing well. I write in Dutch, I translate from English; I am resuming a little algebra and geometry; I'm trying to find the time to do a little music, and aside from my sick aunts I see no one, except our English minister and his family.[4] It seems to me that by now you have a fairly precise idea of what I am like, and that you can well imagine the philosophical attitude, mingled with a great deal of hauteur, that makes me adopt an air of indifference to everything that concerns me.

I am not so indifferent to my friends (for I still have some, although the public pitilessly tears me to shreds), and I have had a great deal of pleasure in seeing my cousin de Tuyll again—now Milady Athlone. She spent a week here with Milord, who is a pleasant enough fellow, but as fussy as an old

3. Pastor Charles de Guiffardière. He will later become reader for Queen Charlotte of England (consort of George III) and teach history to the royal princesses. Belle is probably unaware that in 1763 Guiffardière wrote to Boswell about her in the following terms: "Ah, Sir, if I am not very much mistaken, you are going shortly to triumph over the charms of the fascinating De Zuylen and find yourself often in a situation to prove the sweet transports that a fond heart feels at the feet of the adorable object of its wishes.

"However, when you are sure of your conquest, do not fight with useless scruples, thinking that your mistress's honour consists in her chastity! Above, all, no timidity. And if she ever takes it into her head to faint during a tête-à-tête, do not call for help. She would not be at all grateful to you for such officiousness." (Boswell in Holland 75)

4. Robert Brown.

man; he's a fool, in my opinion. She is as beautiful and charming as ever; she is pleased with her situation; having a character like hers, one finds value in everything, one is satisfied everywhere. Her husband took her straight from the Hague to the countryside. She found no company there other than icicles, mud, and fog; she is enjoying herself, however, arranging her household and regretting nothing. After a week spent here very agreeably, her husband wants her to to go take communion in Amerongen; she left with as good grace as a pious old woman. Fortunately we have got Milord to agree to their returning. We had a rather nice subscription ball, where she greatly enjoyed herself: she will return to take part in the one that we are giving in a week.

Does the Comtesse de Degenfeld talk to you about Madame de Nassau?[5] This woman's reputation is ruined in the eyes of three quarters of the public; pity and a sense of justice involve me in daily quarrels on her behalf. Farewell; the post is about to leave; I don't even have time to reread this scribbling.

226. *To Constant d'Hermenches, February 24, 1766*

Are you in a bad humor, my dear D'Hermenches, because I was, and because I showed it? Perhaps I have sulked in a disagreeable manner; if that's so, I ask your pardon. Don't *you* sulk any longer; I prefer to have you scold: write to me. I am in despair over Bellegarde. The affair does not, however, seem irretrievably broken off; my parents do not seem to have taken any decisive resolution. They don't talk about it at all; when they say a word it is in kindness. Bellegarde will see them in the Hague, and perhaps they will come to an understanding.

Pallandt has asked Madame Geelvinck to marry him; she has refused. It seems to me that she has been raised far above me; I look up at her from down below.

Do me a favor, my dear friend. I know that if the thing is possible you will do it since I ask it, so without any other motive of persuasion I will tell you what it is. A young man named Blin, from a large family of good people of modest means was discharged after the war; he has come to this country, where he had relatives, to ask to do military service. You know that we have enough discharged officers to provide for: the poor boy has been able to obtain nothing but respect and good wishes for his happiness. My uncle became very much interested in his case, and even wrote to an old friend, an officer in France, who has the power do something for him. So far he has done nothing. During his stay in Utrecht this young man gave evidence of an excellent character and good judgment rare for his age; he

5. See Letter 157, n. 2.

rendered services to his family in a delicate affair that is too long to recount. I am sure that he deserves to have you take him under your wing and try to place him in the militia that is being levied just now. I told my uncle that you were in favor with the minister, and that I would write to you. Here is his address.

Goodbye. I will write to you from The Hague.

227. *From Constant d'Hermenches, February 26, 1766*

Le Quesnoy[1]

I am quite tempted, charming Agnes, to write to you against the Marquis. I have been waiting for him for a month with the greatest eagerness, anticipating the delight of seeing him, of talking about you with him and then giving you our news. And then he doesn't come—and yet he had to pass just a few leagues from here to go to Holland. You must agree that when one treats one's best friend in this way, one deserves to lose credit with the most charming of women; but he is undoubtedly visiting you, and he will give you reasons that will only make me seem malicious. Therefore I will merely beg you to pity me for being thus separated from you and from him; pity me too for not writing to you more often. I cannot define what it is that prevents me—perhaps my reflection on myself. You have a thousand times more wit and more ideas than I, you are more learned; there is not one of your letters that isn't an admirable picture of the rarest of all beings. Myself, I am always the same; my existence rolls along on a small number of principles and tastes that you know; all the rest is filled by a routine of daily occupations which don't contain enough substance to furnish a single line for our correspondence. I love you passionately; I regard you as my most intimate, my most generous, my surest friend; because this sentiment is so deeply rooted in my soul that it is like a second nature there, I no longer speak to you of it—I am no longer even aware of it as I used to be except by fits and starts.

I have concentrated everything I feel for you on the desire to see you married and happy; everything unrelated to it seems to me trivial, and that is precisely why my pen is no longer inspired to talk to you of other details, or to communicate my thoughts to you. Without even noticing it, I postpone all of that to a time when we will be able to talk at our ease, and dispute our different opinions other than by arguments and definitions—on which you are much stronger than I am, while I have more experience and a calmer imagination. I am sure that we will always agree when we start from the same point, and for that we must see each other, hear each other, pick our examples near at hand; but imbecile that I am, I deprive myself of a precious

---

1. A city in northern France, near Landrecies.

treasure in not profiting from the permission that you give me to write to you! I have no news of you! You must recognize that your dictum on this is not infallible; one does not *write whenever one wants to!* A card, a note, yes—but to write coherently several sheets of paper—addressed to a single person—a multitude of things that present themselves to the mind—for that I need the right circumstances; I want to take my time, and I never find it quite to my liking. It's with this as it is with salvation—you put it off until the next day, and you wind up being damned ... That's what I greatly fear, my dear Agnes, because it would be Hell for me if you were to condemn me to the smallest degree less of warmth in your friendship and your trust.

I am so tormented by paperwork and insipid correspondences that my work-table has become like a torture chamber; I undergo my punishment as rapidly as I can, and then I leave it with rapture. I have nothing to distract me but an armchair in the corner by my fireside, a book, sometimes my harpsichord. There, your image comes to revive my spirits; I speak to you ardently; I report to you everything I read that is interesting and that pleases me; I teach you all my tunes. Ah, if only one didn't have to bend one's back, clutch a pen between the fingers, and fix one's gaze on blank paper, you would know that there are very few days when I do not devote several hours to you! Sometimes while taking a stroll, sometimes in my bed, or in that armchair; the wretched writing-table is the place where you are the most incongruous. If the place I take at your writing-table is that of Tacitus and Sallust, perforce I find it unworthy of your dignity to make you take the place of the king's directives or the regimental accounts;[2] indeed, do not believe that this present paper comes from that same place!

I am at the home of the woman who resembles you; she is witty and sweet, and she showers me with friendliness. She loves her duties, her husband, her daughter; she has invited me to play music, and I have come here for a concert. After supper, we talked of you, and that came naturally; the subject was the prejudices of different nations, and what makes up the distinctive amusement of each one. The resemblance of your features, and what you wrote me in your last letter on the English and the French—in which, parenthetically, you tell me rather severely and with great injustice that I have taken up the *jargon* of the latter—have inspired me to tell you my story, and I write this to you before I go to bed. If only you had spent the evening with us! There were three or four titled men, former military officers; they had polished manners, lively conversation, and charming naughtiness in the games that we played after supper; seven women, all of some talent, all of agreeable countenance enhanced by good taste in their informal dress; a decorous tone, open but decorous manners; a bit reserved, but with fire in their eyes, and a singular vivacity in all the movements of our little games. I said to myself: if only Agnes were here! She would find

2. He is referring to her Letter 225.

this style more agreeble than the awkward and gloomy air of the English, or the coarse, brazen air of Dutch women. If, fundamentally, wit belongs to all countries, admit that the country where education is the best and the most cultivated is also where the society must be the most pleasant, and the most interesting ... Do you find, Agnes, that this is yet more *jargon*? When French company is bad, it is more detestable than that of any other country because it combines the vices and foolishness of all conditions; that, perhaps, is what I was denigrating at Mme Hasselaer's, since she could hardly know anything else!

I do not speak to you at all of your affairs, my divine friend; it is from you that I should hear about them. The Marquis is probably in Holland, but whatever happens, I beg of you, don't make plans to go be the Sappho[3] of England, much less go there to shun the world that you hardly know. You have studied everything, delved into everything; there is only one thing that you have no idea of as yet, and that is the society of people who are cultivated, gay, and amiable, and who have lived in the great world; you must have that totality to be able to make reliable judgments about men.

This letter will find you amidst the tumult of the Hague; it resembles the amorphous crowd that you will see there and that would prevent you from reading it if I made it any longer. Make curling-papers of it, I beg you, Agnes: it will then seem to me that it is I who have made those beautiful ringlets around your head.

If you are at the Hague, see my son; he's homely, but he has wit; he is stubborn, and rather unfeeling about what people do for him, so treat him quite cavalierly.

Tomorrow I will be at Landrecies.

228. *From Constant d'Hermenches, March 2, 1766*

Landrecies

Really, the Marquis de Bellegarde is a fellow of the highest merit— amiable, civilized; if I were a woman, I would like to have him for my husband, at the very least! What do you say, charming Agnes, to this change of tone? It's because he has come to see me! He went out of his way to seek me, and we have just parted. He is cheerful, sensible, refreshing; he speaks wonderfully well; how can one not like such people! Ah! how we talked about Agnes! As good luck would have it, the woman who resembles you had come to dinner at my place; they met—all of which means that for several days now you have been the principal object of my activities.

The Marquis will be at the Hague on the 7th. He fears your parents' resolutions; he spoke to them clearly, like an honest man; he must have the

---

3. That is, don't go in the character of the woman poet and intellectual.

hundred thousand florins.[1] If you are to be a well-established marquise, there must be enough money; it's dreadful, but he proves it, and it's just what I have said from our first discussions: this sum is absolutely necessary for him.

My dear Agnes, I am so devoted to your happiness that perhaps I am more tormented over this uncertainty than you and the Marquis are. I do not share that quixotism of yours that makes you hesitate to ask your father for the means to be happy, and I find some fault in your repugnance for incurring great obligations to those by whom one was given life; these are grand sentiments that I do not admit at all in my code, even supposing that I found them in my heart.

The mail is leaving; farewell, my good friend, I would like this letter to be in Holland before the Marquis, so that I may appear unjust in your eyes for as short a time as possible. He left this very moment; goodbye.

ᘒ *Bellegarde was at the Hague early in March, where Belle and her circle saw him. Her friends' reactions were not encouraging, as she says in a letter to her brother Vincent. Annebetje thought that he looked very old next to Belle in her festive mood and attire; her brother Willem René said to her in his blunt and jocular Dutch, "Yes, when you are far away, you will sometimes be sorry that you didn't stay here in Holland with the biggest fool."[2] But Belle refused to be discouraged.*

230. *To Constant d'Hermenches, March 23, 1766*

My dear friend, I am about to tell you some important news: my father and my mother are granting the dowry. Don't talk about it; they absolutely do not want people to know about it.[1] You say that the hatred of great obligations, the repugnance to ask something even of a father and a mother, would not be in your code, even if it were in your heart. Perhaps you are right, but I have no other code than that of my heart. As a consequence of this disposition, good or bad, not only did I not ask, but I recapitulated the reasons to refuse. I asked that they not decide except after very thoughtful examination; and no sooner had my dear mother insinuated to me her consent than I pressed her to think about it again, and to consider whether she

1. The history of these problematic florins goes back to d'Hermenches' understanding of Mitie's dowry in Letter 106 (see note 3 there) and Belle's confirmation of it in Letter 108, and can be traced through Letters 136, 202, 216, and 218.
2. Letter 232, *O.C.* 1: 466.
1. Mme van Tuyll's merchant family as well as the family of Belle's sister's husband would have recognized that fl 100,000 would be about fl 30,000 more than the value of Mitie's 3,000-a-year annuity for life. See Letter 106, n. 3.

would ever regret it. I promised not to show the slightest displeasure, not to have a single moment of ill-humor ...

The dowry, then will be given; the debts will be paid. My father is no longer asking for anything but clarifications, arrangements, guarantees; and for that it will be easy, I think, to satisfy him. But one simply must have the dispensations. Bellegarde imagines that it is impossible to obtain one from Rome, and he got the idea because a fool of a nuncio from Brussels, who they say is authorized to grant it, wrote to him that such marriages are quite illicit. This letter, which is only the most inane verbiage, has alarmed the Marquis as if it were decisive. It seems that he didn't even read it, but I did, thank God, and I saw that it meant nothing. He would like to do without the Pope's permission and content himself with the King's;[2] I do not know whether my father would be content with that. I think that in a few days I will be able to show him how to obtain the dispensation from Rome, tell him whom to address, and how much it costs. I am very pleased, and it seems to me that Bellegarde is also.

You speak to me in your last letter about the people living in Heeze and Leende that you brought to my attention last year.[3] You told me then to introduce them to my aunt and her family, but neither my aunt nor my cousin has returned to Heeze. I charged M. Singendonck to see them, to find out what they desired and what sort of service they might need. He tried to visit them; they did not receive him, and he has been unable to learn anything about them except that Monsieur d'Egenberge hunts a great deal and apparently very much wants permission to hunt on my aunt's land. I spoke about it to my cousin; he told me that he absolutely did not dare give that permission without his mother's consent. To ask such a thing of Madame de Tuyll would be to court a refusal. What do you want me to say or do? Munificence is precisely the virtue of my country, or at least of my province. You are unjust; one can say enough bad things about us without slandering us. Goodbye; the post is leaving.[4]

231. *To Constant d'Hermenches, March 24, 1766*

Utrecht, [Monday]

Do I not have three charming, wonderful letters from you—one of six pages, one of four, one of two pages that are worth ten?[1] And yet, I don't write. Sometimes it's the tumult at the Hague, sometimes the weariness of my spirits, sometimes the tedium of always speaking to you of my lot with

---

2. The king of Sardinia.
3. The previous August there had been an exchange between Belle and d'Hermenches about this. He apparently brought up the issue again in a letter that has been lost.
4. This letter may not have been sent.
1. Only two of the three letters have been found.

uncertainty that keeps me from writing. God knows how long I would still delay, if it were not a question of my protégé; because today I am again sick with a cold, and unsure of things. Thursday, I will still be unsure and Monday, and so on ...

But I must talk to you about your son and about my protégé. It was impossible for me to see your son—I don't call a mere visit really seeing him; I would have had to invite him, make much of him, and entertain him, so that I might then question him and preach to him a little. If I had been at home, or if I had even had some leisure, I would have done all that. All I have been able to do has been to talk about him at length with Bellegarde, to support your recommendations with all my eloquence so that they would not be treated lightly, and to warn him off the habit of salt. He writes me[2] that he has done his duty; apparently he will report to you. Don't be too anxious about him; your son is young, there are people who grow up late and who turn out better than the precocious ones; there are several ways of having merit. You say that he is intelligent; Richardson[3] wrote last year that he had a good heart; with these two things there is always reason to hope. But couldn't you give him someone to keep an eye on him, or at least have him stay with some officer among your friends? It seems to me that he is very young to be left entirely to himself, and since he hates making any effort, he will do nothing at all. If I had had any sense when I was at the Hague, or had had my wits about me, I would have tried to talk about him to Vernand,[4] and, according to what he replied, I would either have stopped or else have continued to speak.

As for my protégé,[5] he has, I think, a very good reputation, but cuts a rather poor figure—neither tall, nor handsome, nor very well put together; and I think that he has little money, for he has a great many sisters and brothers. I told the Marquis of my request; he told me that the militia was the most dreary and dismal thing in the world, and that I was doing my protégé no favor at all; but that to help him get back into a regiment would be a fine thing if that could be done for someone who is neither a handsome fellow nor a rich one. Otherwise, dear d'Hermenches, forget that I said anything; however, I would be very obliged to you.

You see that I write in great haste. The post is about to leave—which is too bad, because I would have a great many things to say to you. You probably know the military news; you know that the Comtesse de Degenfeld is mad about the Comte de Denhausen; but you have no idea how bored I was at her house, and how much I missed you. What an emptiness and languor

2. The letter has not been found.
3. Probably Robert Richardson, chaplain to Sir Joseph Yorke, British Ambassador to the Hague.
4. *Général-major*, proprietor of a Swiss company in Holland.
5. Blin: see Belle's Letter 226.

your absence has left! However, I like Gabriel and his wife.[6] They wanted to invite me to a supper party with Bellegarde; after a little deliberation, we had accepted; no one would have known anything about it. Madame de Degenfeld was ill; it would have been just our two couples, but she became yet more ill, and all plans were upset.

Van Monster is fond of you and misses you very much; he looks so bored that he is boring. I do not speak of Bellegarde; there would be too much to say, and the post would leave without us.

233. From Constant d'Hermenches, April 20, 1766

A thousand and a thousand pardons, dear and adorable Agnes, for not writing you sooner, for not thanking you for the news that you give me of these hundred thousand florins, and for not jumping with joy in your very presence. I have been submerged in mourning—my father-in-law, and my charming sister-in-law,[1] dead in the same week; and here, under my eyes, practically at my side, a captain in the regiment, whom I was very fond of, and who was very close to me. I didn't have the time to see to his burial myself; I was ordered to Lille to receive the Crown Prince of Brunswick.[2] I made the tour of the principal garrisons of this country with him. He was given an admirable reception, and he has won the admiration and affection of all our French. He was astonished to see the changes in the state of our military, and I admit that I was more pleased to be a major in this country than a general where I was destined to be ... He left yesterday for Paris, where he will surely be well received; prepare yourself to wear hairstyles, etc. *à la prince héréditaire*. As for me personally, he has treated me wonderfully well, and told me that he would write me from Paris. I found occasion to speak to him about you, as I went down the list of the women of Holland, which he knows very well; I gave him no small desire to have the chance to admire you.

But let's talk about this marriage. Bellegarde has written to me that his courage and hope have been renewed. I think, as he does, that you do not need a dispensation from Rome; I am even sure of it. So get that out of your parents' head; it would be money very badly spent, and would involve long delays; the consent of the King is enough, according to everyone I have consulted:

Trop de prudence entraîne trop de soin[3]

6. Golofkine. It was he who had bought d'Hermenches' company.
1. Charlotte Pictet, wife of his brother Samuel.
2. Karl Wilhelm Ferdinand (1735–1806), from 1780 duke of Brunswick. Benjamin Constant will spend six years in his court, from 1789 to 1795.
3. "Too much prudence entails too much care." From Racine's *Andromaque*. See Letter 146.

and whatever you may say, the nuncio at Brussels is right: it is not this sort of dispensation that one requests in Rome, and Rome does not break marriages unless asked to; and who would take it into his head to unmarry you?

I leave you, adorable friend, and you see how I count on your indulgence; I am obliged to leave for Landrecies this very minute. I am at your feet.

234. *From Constant d'Hermenches, May 4, 1766*

Landrecies

My dear Agnes, there is nothing bizarre in my conduct toward you; I am, as always, your passionate friend; I am more anxious than you are, perhaps, about the uncertainty of your situation, and that discomfits all the faculties of my affection for you. With each post I expect to receive some assurance. You must not blame the Marquis; he is convinced that this dispensation of the Pope is something that must not be requested. As I wrote you, I agree with him; it would be a very difficult undertaking, which would cost a great deal of money, and is not customary. Madame d'Usson had none, and is she not securely married?

And be careful, my dear friend, not to do me an injustice concerning the Marquis. I told you from the beginning that he is a scatterbrain; I have continually emphasized that side of his character, which is perhaps not the least of his contributions to your happiness. It is not in his power to follow any matter through consistently, although he loves to hold forth. Thus, do not expect him to know how to court you in a conventionally romantic way. Observe his manner, and sound out for yourself how much or how little satisfaction you will find in a union with him. In no way does he disguise himself; that is an enormous advantage you have, and your perceptiveness protects you from all danger. I have always said that he is pleasant to live with, easy-going, cheerful; that he never has a moment of ill-humor, and is undemanding of the people that he loves. But don't expect the little attentions, the courtesy, the thoughtfulness of ordinary people. Look at my letters of the last two years; I have always been saying the same thing. I write him in a very different style: I scold him, I get angry at his epicurean way of life; I tell him that if I were in your place I would interpret the behavior that he thinks of as philosophical as a lack of delicacy. He turns my arguments back on me, and tells me that he will always love his wife more than I love mine. I tell him that mine possessed a man of twenty, ardent to procure for her all pleasures and spare her all cares; that she was neither so amiable, nor so resourceful as a companion, friend, etc. That is where we are.

I hope that you will have received my letter from Valenciennes, where I had just left the Prince of Brunswick. Since then I live a completely mechanical life: drill twice a day, fatiguing details, and a continual performance that is unsustainable in the long run; add to that two deaths in my family, and affairs that would require my presence, and judge whether I can be an agreeable correspondent. Judge me as you have known me, and believe that you will find me always the same. This is only a passing moment; thus, do not remove from me the slightest particle of your trust and your friendship; it would be a criminal injustice. I am at your feet, my dear Agnes.

235. *To Constant d'Hermenches, May 8, 1766*

I was not in too good a mood the last time I wrote to you. People were continually making remarks to me, telling me on all sides so very eagerly that the Marquis talked about our marriage as if he hardly cared about it. There were all sorts of conjectures, predictions that he himself would make the difficulties insurmountable; people assured me with pathos that I was the dupe of my credulity. Finally, such a thing seemed to me not obvious, but at least possible; I thought that people might have spoken ill of me to him, and that thereupon he might have changed his mind without knowing how to break things off properly. I grew alarmed, and wrote to him. He was somewhat vexed; however, he consented to enter into all the details necessary to put my mind at rest, make me approve of his conduct, and persuade me of his sentiments. I hastened to apologize to him, and I promised that in the future I would listen to no telltale and harbor no suspicion; and thus ended our little squabble, which left us very good friends.

It's for the love of chronology, apparently, that I began with an old story, while I have something much more interesting to say. The Marquis has been here; I saw him the day before yesterday all evening; yesterday, we were together morning, afternoon and evening. He left this morning to go to Brussels; from there, to Maastricht; from there, to Germany, and then to Chambéry, Turin, and then, I hope, to my bedroom. My mother is still not feeling well; she took this pretext not to see him. However, she is pleasant to me, and doesn't say sour or disobliging things about the Marquis.

My father received him with very good grace; they talked politely and cheerfully, just as I had hoped. Yesterday morning, at seven, he came into my room before leaving for an inspection of the dikes, charged me to pay his compliments to Bellegarde, and told me that if my mother did not want to receive him during his visit with me I must try to have someone else there. Still half-asleep, I promised; but I invited no one. When he came back in the evening, my father found the two of us chatting alone together, but we looked so proper and even so serious, seated at each end of a big table, that he did not appear at all shocked; after a little conversation, he even went out and left us alone. We said a great many things; for all that he was well-spoken, when Bellegarde held forth with his oratory as though I were a stranger it was not the best part of our visit. There still prevails something of a formality between us, and a perceptive third party would see that our respective tones were formed at a great remove. That doesn't matter; they will grow closer to each other, and when they are not completely in unison I can guarantee that their dissonance will not be disagreeable. We went over many necessary things; he tells me his plans; he wishes that I were already his, and that I could accompany him to Germany; we would spend the winter, he says, in Savoie, and would return to Paris in the spring. Now *that* speech was very good, and the look of pleasure and tenderness that accompanied it was worth a great deal. Toward the evening, when the light was low, when we were no longer talking continually, but softly, a few words at a time, of things that concerned us—it was then that I was the most at ease: I am sure you sense that.

The Pope and the nuncio have not been forgotten; my father still insists on the dispensation. *Rome,* you say, *does not break marriages unless asked to; and who would take it into his head to unmarry you?* A motive to declare my marriage null could very well occur to someone two or three generations from now who could thereby relieve the Marquis's heirs of their wealth and lands. If omitting the formality of a dispensation exposes the heirs to such a risk, then a dispensation we must certainly obtain. We will see whether one can do without it—whether my father can be persuaded to do without it. If not, we must then think only of the means of obtaining it.

I told the Marquis about the tour you did with the Crown Prince; we spoke of you a great deal; I mentioned his admiration for your military status, and for the changes in it that have taken place. I said that you were pleased to be where you are; however, it seems to me that Bellegarde would like to see you a major general here.

Goodbye, my dear d'Hermenches, I hope that henceforth your friends and relatives will stop dying, for I would like you not to have cause for grief, and I would like not to go for centuries without receiving news of you.

236. *To Constant d'Hermenches, May 15, 1766*

You are very much afraid that I am unjust and that, forgetting your letters, I am accusing you of not having depicted Bellegarde as he is. Be reassured, my dear d'Hermenches, I am just; I have forgotten nothing, and I do not accuse you at all. Thus far, I have found no reason to complain of Bellegarde's not loving me enough; having no passion myself, I don't demand a violent love. He has always written to me assiduously; he has seemed very pleased to see me; that's all very good, that's enough ... or at any rate, so I say. Perhaps I think it, but do I feel it? Is my heart satisfied? Does *it* find that that's enough—that I love enough, that I am loved enough? That's a complicated question; what would be the use of untangling it? It's better to say simply *Nihil est ab omni* ...[1] It is a curious thing, to be moving heaven and earth, doing battle with monsters, filling up abysses, for a marriage without passion.

When I am far from the Marquis, my imagination does what it wants with him, with his heart, with mine, with our days, with our nights; I bring it all close together; then we speak, we understand each other, we love each other, I embrace him, and I await the reward for my chastity, for this painful deprivation.

When I see him, we are strangers; I am polite and ill at ease; the rapport that I had imagined gives way to all the real disparities that the differences in age, country, way of life, and character inevitably set between us. He speaks and I listen to him; I am not tempted to interrupt him, and when he has finished, I don't know how to rejoin; rather like those actors who can't pick up their lines on cue from each other—when the one has finished, the other doesn't know how to rejoin. I also speak, but it isn't my natural voice; it's some kind of falsetto, which annoys even me, and which I adopt in spite of myself for fear of annoying him, or displeasing him, or not being understood if I were to say what comes into my mind in my ordinary tone, unaffectedly and unreservedly. I'm always on the watch for things that will please me in what he says—to hear simple, true words, that come from the heart, that are feelings rather than nice phrases, or sound thoughts rather than some ghost of a dissertation. I listen, I notice them and I retain them, and I hope that those things will multiply and that when we are living together he will not fatigue himself in discourses with me or in making long speeches; that he will say a simple single word, and that he will hear a simple single word. I see quite well, however, that very often he will not hear me; that will be a little hard. Here I am often bored to death; people do not think as I do, but when I speak, they understand me: everything I feel is felt, everything I think is understood. This change will cause me pain; I will be a stranger to everybody, but *Nihil est ab omni parte*, etc.

In the morning, when he left me, he had given me two kisses that I had received very warmly, with emotion and pleasure. In the afternoon we were alone: *He hoped that I would do him the favor of writing him. It was an honor for his sister that I asked for news of her.* You cannot imagine how this ceremoniousness disorients me; how I—who am seldom awkward, rarely embarrassed—how clumsy and stupid I become. I no longer see any way but one for us to become better acquainted; I hope that it will succeed for us better than our conversations.

However, we have sometimes talked very well together—about how we would enjoy traveling to Dresden together; about how persuaded we are that we can be very happy with each other, and that we can avoid all the ridiculousness, all the failings, all the unpleasantnesses that have given us a dis-

1. Horace, *Odes* II.xvi. *Nihil est ab omni parte beatum*: "Nothing is happy in all its aspects."

taste for marriage up to now, and prevented us from ever envying the lot of any husband or any wife of our acquaintance. Bellegarde is certainly very likeable; I am not so foolish as to think that the only good style is my own. I still ardently desire this marriage; any other would be odious and impossible for me. If some other might offer more lavish delights, none would be so free from vexations. I will be free; nobody will come pedantically preaching my duties to me, and that in itself will pique my vanity to fulfill them. I will be content, I hope; if sometimes I should feel some emptiness, some languor in the soul, I shall say: *Nihil est* ...

Goodbye. Answer me quickly, and tell me whether this rhapsody does not seem to you quite absurd and quite boring: absurd, no, I think it is not.

237. *To Constant d'Hermenches, May 24, 1766*

I replied in advance to your letter, and explained the one of mine that you are answering. I wish that a man like you would affirm positively only what he knows for a certainty, and not put forth as proof of his notions an example that proves the contrary. I have heard it said a hundred times that Madame d'Usson was not properly married, and that if she had children their legitimacy and their father's name, title, and wealth would all be disputed in France. On the basis of what Bellegarde has told me, the letters he has shown me, and the memorandum that has been prepared by one of his jurisconsult friends, I do think that in Savoie it would not be the same thing and that we could do without the dispensation. But still, I don't know enough about it to convince my father; and he, who has not the same interest that I do in facilitating the affair, also does not have the same tendency to take the path of least resistance.

The last time that Madame d'Usson came into this country, her father said to her: "If you want me to receive Monsieur d'Usson as my son-in-law, prove to me that you are his wife, that your marriage is valid, that your rights could not be disputed." She could not satisfy him; I will not expose myself to the same doubts and the same unpleasantnesses. If my father consents to it, I will marry without a dispensation; otherwise, the decision is his to make. I don't believe that it is so difficult a thing to obtain; people are imagining it to be so, it seems to me, on very slight evidence. I will shortly know more about it, and I will tell you what I have learned.

238. *From Constant d'Hermenches, May 26, 1766*

Paris

A thousand pardons, my divine Agnes, if I leave you uncertain as to my existence; I was obliged to come to Paris; it is a sweet constraint, but I am so busy that I have not yet had a moment to go even to a single play. There are reviews, drill, journeys to Versailles that have turned me away from my regular duties; the most pleasant and most permanent duty of my heart is unquestionably thinking of you and loving you. I do it in very good faith, you may be sure of it. I questioned Madame d'Usson about her marriage: she asked for a dispensation from the Pope; the Holy Father advised her to get married in any case, and then he granted the dispensation, which I have seen. It was the Duc de Choiseul, then ambassador to Rome, who managed the affair without its costing them a penny.

I don't understand a thing about these eternal travels of the Marquis; he hasn't written me at all; I hope that marriage will cure him of these mad-dog ways, for one gets giddy merely trying to follow him on the map. I am here until the 7th of June; I am staying at the house of Monsieur de Besenval, rue Grenelle; by the 10th I will be in Landrecies. I prostrate myself before you, my sublime friend; in great haste, as you see.

239. *From Constant d'Hermenches, June 9, 1766*

Paris

I do not despair of seeing you one day at the head of armies, accomplishing marvels like Mademoiselle d'Arc; you will not be divinely inspired, but you will be educated and enlightened, and they won't burn you. Indeed, what do you have left to learn, amazing Agnes, except military science? Here you are, intimate with the Latin poets, simply because it occurred to you that one must know Latin; you are truly an astonishing creature! Since you love Virgil, you must be mad about Horace. He's my friend; it is in him that one finds the quintessence of taste, morality, and philosophy. All the fine things that people have said since—they all belong to him; I am always amazed that men who have been working, and thinking, and composing for so many centuries have hardly equaled the genius of the Ancients. One of these days you will take up the study of medicine, and you will be astonished to see that our Boerhaves and our Tronchins,[1] in spite of the accumulation of aids and experiments, do not surpass Hippocrates.

I am returning to Landrecies, and I'm taking my Horace with me; I have never learned him by heart, but he is familiar to me, and I will be thinking that I'm occupied the same way that you are. Read his satires as well, especially the one on discontent with one's lot.[2]

Bellegarde has seen Monsieur d'Usson in Aix; I hope that they will have discussed business; d'Usson is an honest and prudent fellow, who can give

1. Hermann Boerhave (1668–1738), renowned Dutch physician, teacher, and medical writer. Théodore Tronchin (1709–81), Genevan physician, studied under Boerhave at the University of Leyden. Tronchin was Voltaire's doctor, and one of the most famous physicians in Europe. He popularized the practice of inoculation against smallpox.
2. Horace's *Satires* I.i.

excellent advice. I am writing to the Marquis, who is in Berlin today. Madame d'Usson indeed says that her father does not want to see his son-in-law, but it is certain that there is more ill-humor than reasoning in this. It is true that the marriage could be contested in France if the Gallican Church refused to accept the papal dispensations;[3] but Madame d'Usson received at Court as the Comtesse d'Usson cancels that pettifoggery as far as the law courts are concerned.

You see very clearly Bellegarde as he is, and I can very well see you with him. *I* would be more attentive, I would treasure more the thousand rare qualities you possess; your heart and your mind would be more at ease with me. But I might not be as good a husband; I would disturb you, I would let nothing go by; whatever is not to my taste would be a subject for despair. He does not appreciate everything, but he will not criticize anything. —That's what I think about your union. You have all [...][4]

Favor me with your letters to Landrecies, where I will be until August; after that time, I will be free. I am at your feet, my adorable friend.

240. *To Constant d'Hermenches, June 18–19, 1766*

A few hours ago I wanted to ask you a favor, which was to stop writing me. I'm being harassed on all sides. It seems that everyone who writes to me, everyone who is involved in my affairs is shooting at me, and nobody misses. With all the best intentions, you are killing me just like the others. You could not imagine any sinister thought that did not occur to me after reading your letter, nor could you imagine how much better it seemed to me to be killed outright rather than be martyred in that fashion. One could then write my epitaph; perhaps it would be said that I was worth something, and that I showed promise of being worth yet more. I would be out of this whole predicament; no more suitor, no more Pope, no more advice ... If I don't want to throw myself in the river, I can get married in Scotland,[1] marry a good Protestant whenever I please—a man who's in love with me and who will inherit twenty-six thousand florins in income.

3. Gallicanism was a tradition within French Catholicism of resistance to papal authority.
4. The sheet on which this letter was written has been cut, and a dozen or so lines are missing. Much of Belle's answer to this letter seems to be addressed to things in those missing lines.
1. To William Johnson Temple, Boswell's friend. On the basis of Boswell's description of her, Temple had declared his adoration in a letter to Boswell of May 22, 1764: "I am already in love with Mademoiselle de Zuylen. Charming creature! young and handsome, *une savante et bel esprit*. Tell her an Englishman adores her and would think it the greatest happiness of his life to have it in his power to prostrate himself at her feet." In a journal entry of May 25, 1764, Boswell recounts how he relayed this to Belle: "I delivered to Zélide the fine compliments which my friend Temple had charged me to deliver: that is to say, the warm sentiments of adoration. She was much pleased" (*Boswell in Holland* 250, 259).

But why am I indulging in this nonsense? I will limit myself to the effects of your letter. It arrived a moment before dinner; we had company. I have never been able to keep myself from weeping like a child; I simply wept outright at table instead of eating, and instead of conversing with people I conversed with you and meditated my response. It's lucky for you that a bone-chilling shudder and an overwhelming despondency kept me from leaving the table as people wanted me to do; you would have received a terrible letter. But I blamed everything on the vapors, and merely hid my face to dry my tears; I remained at table, and between dinner and supper I forgot a part of what I wanted to say to you. But seriously, speak to me only of Horace, and no more of the Marquis. Lightly, without thinking too much about it, you write whatever comes into your head, and as I said, it's a piercing shaft that goes from Landrecies to Zuylen, straight to my heart. Do you remember the Greek who shot an arrow into the midst of the Trojan army during the truce?[2] It's precisely that. I seem to remember that it wounded the handsome Paris, and that Venus, hiding him in a cloud, quickly went to bathe him and cure him. But I have no gods at my service; the dart enters deep, and makes a horrible wound.

You are young, you say (although I have calmed down since dinner, I have a great desire to shoot back the splinters of the arrow, and to sharpen them so that they will at least scratch you), *You are young,* you say. *A year is soon passed.*[3] What does that mean, pray tell? Would you want me to spend yet another year like this one? I would rather die. And what would that year accomplish? At the end of the year, would the wind or Noah's dove carry a papal dispensation to the feet of the Marquis? If I don't bestir myself to procure it for him he will certainly get it in no way other than by a miracle. Well, I don't know that he deserves one, or that I do either. This, you say, should not be taken on as a challenge. What do you mean? That I should not persist in trying to bring about my marriage? If that's what you mean, say so clearly, and tell me to give it up; perhaps you would not be so very wrong, but still it is not yet my idea. You have done everything in the world to give me the opposite idea; you have preached to me of marriage, the Marquis, and persistence. I am not disposed to change plans every day.

The rakish manners you reproach him for don't matter in the least to me; I too have rather strange manners at times, which I would be very glad to have people overlook. You are right, I believe, to think that you would not be as good a husband, and I'm not asking you to marry me. Ah, my God! were it not for my plans, my hopes, and my passion for liberty, I swear to you that I wouldn't still be having you arranging a marriage for me. That is what sustains me—that, and the respect that I have for constancy, and the

2. Book III of the *Iliad*.
3. Much of what she says in this letter seems to be in response to the missing part of d'Hermenches' Letter 239.

contempt I would feel for myself if I were to drop the Marquis, who has given me no reason for complaint; who is today just as he was when I absolutely wanted him; about whom people have no more bad things to say—that is, no new accusation; and who had not promised me to be clever or diligent in seeking a dispensation. Simply to drop him, to marry someone else out of weariness or frivolity—that would be, it seems to me, a despicable way to act. To wait with my arms crossed for—how long? A year? —Assuredly I will not do that.

His journey to Berlin seemed to me, as it did to him, almost indispensable. I haven't dreamed of complaining about it; what would he have done in Utrecht? Unless he went to Rome, he could do nothing to advance our affairs, and in Rome he might well have spoiled them. He didn't even understand the letter from the nuncio in Brussels.[4] As he was leaving I promised him I would gather all the information possible concerning this dispensation, and give it to him and tell him what to do. And indeed, I have obtained information; without naming us, people have written to Rome. Monsieur Piccolomini[5] sent all the necessary explanations; I received them yesterday, and I busied myself with them today. I had already planned how to manage it: there are a thousand things to be discussed with my father; I was to write by the first post to the Marquis and tell him what letter he should write. Then yours arrives. *Make no more advances, take no more measures*, you say, *above all write short letters* ... At that point, I come down with the fever.

If I were reasonable, perhaps, I would see things otherwise; but my patience is worn out—so many people have been after me, worrying me, vexing me! My blood boils at the slightest thing; everything infuriates me, and I wish that your letter had drowned a thousand times in the infinity of water that it crossed before it arrived in my aquatic country. And now has not everything been upended in my mind? Am I not hesitating over the whole affair? I cannot write to the Marquis, for that would be *taking measures, making advances*—and yet I had promised him. I cannot write because letters must be short, and I cannot remove phrases from sentences, nor words from phrases, nor cut a few letters and a few syllables from words— and yet he had asked me to write to him. If it is to please him that I must write short letters to a man who never sees me, I would just as soon marry the great Mogul by proxy; and he could certainly marry an African heiress rather than me to pay off his châteaux's mortgages. If you have good reasons to think that my letters are too long—if he has complained about it—, if he does not yet think me necessary to his happiness, if the measures I take displease him, then have the kindness to tell me so; I will not wait a year, and everything is finished. Otherwise, have the kindness to write me quickly

4. See her Letter 230.
5. Enea Silvio Piccolomini-Ristchini, cardinal and governor of Rome.

that your letter made very little sense, and put things back as they were. Goodbye.

Zuylen, at ten o'clock in the evening, Wednesday, June 18

June 19

Yesterday I wrote you, all in a penstroke, everything my imagination dictated; I hope I said nothing that might make you angry. I am very sure of your intention, and that it is still the quintessence of good friendship; I think I said so, and that is enough for you not to be angry, just as it is certainly enough for me to be content. But really, perhaps one should not, at the moment one is about to leave Paris, write hastily on an important subject to an impetuous, sensitive person in a rather isolated countryside, who has all the leisure in the world to create dreadful monsters for herself.

I wanted to go into town this morning; there I would have found, I think, a letter from the Marquis that I could have spoken to you about before sealing this one, but the rain prevented my uncle from going and taking me with him. I will write you another day about what he tells me, supposing that it restores my head to a state of reasonable composure. But answer me first anyway. Do not think that it is the unmarried state that I find intolerable for another year; it's the state of uncertainty with respect to the Marquis. If that uncertainty were necessary and natural, as it has been up to now, perhaps I would endure it; but finding the Marquis too indecisive or not eager enough—that's a fine reason to postpone things! That would rather be a reason to break things off at once.

I am by no means at a loss about what to do with myself—less than ever at present; you must believe it, on my word of honor. I said yesterday that I could perfectly well get married in Scotland; I'm not at all sure, however, that I want that husband, or any other, or that if I break off with the Marquis I would say "*if it's not you, then it's your brother*[6] that I will marry; it's all the same,"—and rush off to marriage. It's not at all the same. I have become attached to him; no château pleases me except the one in Savoie, and certainly I will not get married out of despair. An unmarried state that would be well-defined and established, and no longer a waiting period, would suit my humor much better. My brothers and Horace and Virgil would be much better for me than a marriage that would not be entirely according to my taste. You should have seen how brusquely I interrupted a sort of declaration that Charles van Twickel was beginning to make to me; I quickly spoke of something else, and seemed not even to have heard.

Send me quickly two words of reply, and then let us drop this tedious subject—it were all well and good if it were merely tedious, but it is really distressing. On all sides, as I have said, people are at me, and I cry for mercy right and left. I am cutting back on my dealings with people as much

6. From La Fontaine, "The Wolf and the Lamb," *Fables* I. x.

as I can. You do not know that I had quarreled with Mme Hasselaer; we had been thoroughly reconciled, but the continuation of the distress caused by her—by her weakness, that is, which I regard as the instrument of M. van Pallandt's hatred[7]—has made me give up all connection with her. It isn't at all a quarrel; I simply wanted to protect myself from that source of chagrin. I make a great secret of it because it seems to me that all the wrong is on her side. Keep it a secret for me. Someday I will tell you all about it in detail—that is, if my scruples and my respect for my friend do not make me keep silent. I have never seen anyone do as much harm as she has done me—and than without any bad intention, but only out of weakness, insensitivity, slowness of judgment and a faulty view of things. Her character is a curious thing: the good prevails infinitely over the things that one can complain of. If nothing strange had happened between us, things would still go along perfectly well. But what was enough for things to just go along is not enough to put things back from a total upset. Just as one needs more strength to rise than to keep oneself standing, it would have taken more heart after our quarrel than during our tranquil friendship, and the *more* was not there. I hoped to find it, but it wasn't to be found. You will not be surprised at all that.

I talked a great deal with my uncle and General Crönstrom about your son. I spoke well of him, but said that you were vexed about some bad habits of his—an inflexible tone, a lack of diligence; that you hoped that your friends would take an interest in him, to correct him and give him some advice and models for emulation. They say that the officers of his regiment could render him these services. My uncle, who is full of good intentions, and who may remember your connection with the episode of the big nightcap in the window,[8] wants to find out more about your son and talk to d'Aubonne[9] about him; meanwhile, my cousin Crönstrom, who is going to the Hague, will testify to the interest that we take in him. If something more than words comes out of this, I will let you know. You had given Bellegarde a large commission; what a choice of preceptor! I saw him preparing his speech. It would indeed be a good sign if your son had profited from it; for that, he would have needed an admirable predisposition, for I know of no less persuasive style in all the world. I think that the women that he won over were won over in advance; and assuredly, if I were he, I would not number seduction among my sins. As for me, if my imagination had seduced me for him during his absence, his tone would unseduce me. Besides, although he says he loves me very much, perhaps he loved more in the past.

I have not been doing any Latin for three weeks, since my tutor[10] has

7. See her Letter 170.
8. A reference to d'Hermenches' story about her uncle, hendrik van Tuyll, and a young prostitute. See his Letter 134.
9. A Swiss officer in the Dutch service.
10. Charles de Guiffardière. See Letter 225, n. 3.

been off courting. I am doing nothing; I am becoming extremely stupid. You say that I am young, but I have hours and hours of exhaustion that make me believe that I am at least a hundred years old.

Are you very sure that Madame d'Usson has been received at Court? I was told very positively just the other day that she had not been presented.

243. *From Constant d'Hermenches, June 28, 1766*

It is not a bad way to proceed, when one is full of bile, to unload it onto one's best friend; it brings relief, and isn't dangerous. So, dear Agnes, you did very well to treat me like a dog because you were in a bad mood, and because, tormented by all and sundry, you found it good to confound me in the category with your tormentors. You have done well, I say, to address your wrath to me; I love you none the less for it, and it is a touchstone applied to my attachment to you for which I am grateful, because it proves to me all the more that it is of the most sterling quality. But my dear friend, one must keep to the truth; chagrin and opposition can bring one to extremes, to absurdities, to outrageous things; but never to falsehoods; and if you said to me that I write to you thoughtlessly, that I let fly sharpened arrows at random, that I write from Paris with less reflection than from anywhere else, when it is a question of the fate of someone to whom I am attached—I would tell you, adorable Agnes, that you do more than go astray. You betray the justice that is due me from you; you slander me! The expression is harsh; don't be offended; I'm using a lawyer's style, which is less cruel than the arrow of that Greek . . .

I hasten to justify that rag of a letter,[1] which I am so far from disavowing that I will repeat its main points to you, like so many aphorisms that apply to your situation:

1. The expectation about a year—and I would find a year quite manageable at your age—is based on the supposition that this postponement (which I do not approve of on my friend's part) might by itself put you off this marriage. But I say that it would not be the postponement itself that would induce you to break things off, since for the last two years you have had generosity enough to accommodate to circumstances: I ask this third year of you for my friend supposing that no other reflection might make you change your feelings.

2. But if you were to come to envisage this affair as less agreeable, less suitable; if you were to come to have an aversion for my friend, then I say that you must not make a challenge of this marriage project and do out of stubbornness against those who oppose you what you would not otherwise do by choice.

1. His Letter 239 of June 9.

3. I thought it was necessary to impress on my friend the degree of happiness that he hopes for from your union; I am allowed to frighten him about the unfortunate effect that his tone and his inattentive conduct could produce in this affair—which you must not consummate if he does not keenly desire it. I am allowed then to tell you what I am doing in that respect, because your happiness, your satisfaction, your good name are closer to my heart than his are.

4. It is in that same spirit that I recommend that you make no more advances; that has been my method since the beginning of this affair. Remember it, my dear Agnes, look in my letters, if you still have them (I have all of yours); the Marquis must beseech you not to be put off; he must be afraid of it, otherwise you are not in the position that I want you in. I know my man, he's an admirable fellow at heart, but which of us doesn't slack off when we feel that are others watching out for us? There are few men who don't become negligent when they feel sure of things; and if you yourself think that he cannot be reproached for the crime of seduction,[2] must not you avoid it all the more in your dealings with him?

5. He does not feel the value of your letters; I have said it a thousand times. He doesn't read long letters; he doesn't understand them; as long as I've known him he makes jokes about them—that is, for the last twenty-five years; you say, yourself, that he didn't know how to read the letter from the nuncio. I have never seen him read two pages of a book consecutively; he never opens Voltaire except to criticize him. Is it then thoughtlessness on my part to say to you, Agnes, *Answer his short letters with yet shorter ones*? He will write you long ones; he will go down on his knees to have you write him. If that position doesn't please you, then by all means write him volumes—I tell you I don't believe he will read them. I tell you this not because I am leaving Paris, but because I am in Landrecies, where I think about you as I do in the Hague, at Hermenches, in London, and wherever fate leads me.

To this letter of his that you send me, I would reply to him that it gave me great pleasure, but that you were not worried about him ... As for the dispensation, I would tell him that he knows what you think, that he can act accordingly and let you know everything that can contribute to determining your common future. (N.B. His story of the sojourn in Aix is a result of my reproaches, because for a long time I have forbidden him to go to that region—where he has never done anything but commit stupidities and make bad acquaintances. This desire to excuse himself in your eyes pleases me very much.) I would tell him, in short, in three or four lines, what you are doing, what your father thinks, what you think must be done; and I would

---

2. Belle had said in Letter 240 that she found no one less persuasive than Bellegarde—that he should not count seduction among his crimes.

like—without my asking him—to have Monsieur le Marquis tell me positively when his travels will end.

I'm not working against him; I want to help him. This man—whom I persist in regarding as worthy of you, and whom I make my most intimate friend—has, throughout his life, lost everything by his lack of perseverence, by this scatterbrained manner, by his accursed travels where he never sees what he should be looking for. He has mismanaged his fortune; he has done nothing for his reputation and has perverted many of the gifts that he had received from nature. You are called upon to remedy all that; you will succeed up to a certain point. But rather than compromise yourself further, rather than take one step more, after having proven your good faith and your greatness of soul—yes, yes, I say: Go to Scotland, to Muscovy, or rather take a vow of celibate liberty. I say this against my own interests, for I have no hope of living near you except when you are the wife of the Marquis; but from beginning to end I have been sublime and heroic in this affair, and I will not cease to be so ... And you do me the outrage of confounding me with all those crackpots whom you have become dependent upon through your passion for new acquaintances! You compare my letter with the ones from those frivolous correspondences that you have attracted right and left!

I owe you a thousand thanks for what you tell me about my son; he has been with me since my return from Paris, and it's a happy event. He is acquiring some taste for the military, and some ambition; he is full of good sense, and has not yet been corrupted. If your uncles make known their interest in him, it will be a noble action; may they make that cowardly, feeble automaton d'Aubonne blush—he who, owing me everything that one can owe to friendship and to the thousand services I have done him, has never done me anything but harm and hasn't deigned to see this poor unhappy little fellow a single time during his whole stay in the Hague. That would be incredible in any other country, but in the Hague such contemptible behavior is only too common. My whole misfortune is that this child is very delicate; nature made a mistake—he has acquired the temperament of his mother.

Bear in mind, when you happen to be annoyed with your parents, that I myself have a mother, the most unreasonable of beings, whom I still adored and respected like a divinity just ten years ago; who married me off at the age of nineteen, without giving me anything to live on, to a sickly woman—older than me and without any fortune—simply for the pleasure of arranging a marriage between a child who imagined he was in love and a daughter-in-law who she believed would be easy to manage because she is gentle. And then—just imagine—after that she heaps reproaches on me because that wife is not robust and her children are delicate; and to infuriate us, she is presently marrying off my brother Juste (the one known as "the Philosopher") to a girl young enough to be his granddaughter, and who hasn't a penny to her name—and once again, simply because she thinks that this daughter-in-law will be manipulable, and because she likes to arrange marriages.[3] As for me, I laugh at all that. I am detaching myself from the whole world; I am trying to make my existence independent of circumstances that I can do nothing about. But I want to exist in the hearts of my friends—at Zuylen, in Paris, in Enghien, and a few others scattered over the surface of the earth; to have around me people who respect me, and to whom I do some good; and to have as my superiors people to whom I wish to pay no other court than to prove to them that I am worth something. And that, my dear Agnes, is the existence of the surest friend that you could ever have; receive his homage and his respects—in great haste.

245. *To Constant d'Hermenches, July 11, 1766*

To leave only in three days

My dear friend, I ask your pardon for my letter, since you have found that it was all bile, ill humor, calumny. Let's not argue any more. You are surely more in the right than I, who am crazy—but you are really not as right as you think. You have always talked about his scatterbrained style and character, but it was precisely to tell me that if I didn't do everything, nothing would get done: that, you said, was the character of people who are completely goodhearted ... Bellegarde was incapable of details, too thoughtless to complete any difficult thing ... He adored my letters just as you do ... Would he not have been married a long time ago if he knew how to get married? ...

I asked whether my taking measures would not put him off, and you said no; but you asked me not to see him alone, because after the the most prudent letters often comes the maddest conversation.[1] You must believe me about all that, my friend, as if you were rereading your own letters, for they are written in my head. I often lack good sense, but my memory never deceives me; it is the only one of my faculties that is indisputable and that the awkwardness of my situation has not upset. Except for your last letters, I have not heard of the boredom that mine must cause Monsieur de Bellegarde, nor of the risk I was running in hastening to smooth away obstacles, nor of what there was to be gained in his affection, in his attentions, in his way of appreciating me, by a more reserved conduct. You never said a word about it, and I did not have the wit to guess it; if I had guessed it, I would have yielded to the obstacles a long time ago.

3. Juste Constant married Henriette de Chandieu in 1766. She was sixteen years younger than he. Their son, Benjamin Constant, was born in 1767, and Henriette died two weeks later.
1. See d'Hermenches' Letter 202 of a year earlier.

To obtain on the one side, by my eagerness for this marriage, a sort of approval and a hundred thousand florins from my parents; to obtain on the other side some sign of eagerness from Monsieur de Bellegarde by indicating a *lack* of eagerness; to arrange everything to compensate for his incompetence, and yet appear not to wish for anything, so that his desire to have me might become more keen—that was much too difficult a game.

I thought that Monsieur de Bellegarde suited me; that he did not love me enough—did not value *anything* enough—to combat the obstacles that separate us if I myself didn't try to remove them; but that he loved me enough to wish to see them smoothed away, and that, if we were to live together one day, he would be pleased and happy, and would thank me. If I had thought that he no longer desired me, or that he would despise me for taking these steps, you can imagine whether I would have taken them. If I had believed that he would love me more if I let him do everything, or even that he would know how to succeed without me, I would have made not the slightest move. We will see whether I will have reason to repent the moves I have made.

It is too late, my dear friend, to follow your advice; for, seeing my father and Monsieur Piccolomini and everything else as well disposed as they can be, and a situation that we'll not see again if I let it be lost, and not having strong enough reasons on the other hand to change my conduct suddenly, I wrote on Tuesday in my ordinary style to Bellegarde, and I prescribed precisely what he had to do. If that succeeds, you will be very pleased about it, as will I; if not, we will not indulge in useless recapitulations of our ideas or of our conduct. The temperament that God gave me is my star; it has never been able to deny itself, either for good or for ill. I am sometimes in despair over it; then I console myself, saying that it is an instrument in the hands of Providence and that what it has caused me to lose did not suit me. For instance, if Bellegarde is cooled off by my long letters and if, perceiving that, I break off the marriage, must one greatly blame the long letters? I don't dawdle, I think, when I write; if I write a great number of things, it's because I have a great number of them in my head and in my soul. If there are too many by half for Bellegarde, I hope that he will look for a wife who has only half my head and half my soul; as for me, I will be glad to keep them entire for someone they will suit, or for myself alone.

Goodbye; I love you extremely. Yes, certainly, you are a hero. But still have the heroism not to want always to be right. As for me, twenty times a day I am wrong and admit it; and, provided there is nothing for which my heart can be reproached, that doesn't bother me. I find my wit more stupid than the stupidity of others, and my experience equal to that of my sister's child, for all the use I can get out of it. There is no one but Bellegarde who is clumsier than I am.

◌ʒ *During the summer of 1766 d'Hermenches was not the only man Belle was writing to in secret—she was also writing to the man who would become her husband. Charles-Emmanuel de Charrière, born in 1735, had been tutor to the Tuyll sons since 1763, and he stayed on in the household, probably as secretary, at least until 1765. His home, which he shared with an elderly father and two unmarried sisters, was in Colombier, near Neuchâtel. He was a quiet, self-contained, and highly intelligent man who loved mathematics. Only one of Belle's letters to him is extant. The earliest one we have from him was written in Colombier and dated July 7, 1766. It gives us an idea of some of Belle's late-night conversations with him, her subsequent correspondence, and the troubling effects of both on the modest and scrupulous Charrière:*

... Mademoiselle, you are inconceivable! Why do you recall to me memories you have forbidden me to preserve? How can you say you are my friend, when you disturb my happiness by making me perceive how sweet it would be for me if you were something more?

The passage in which you speak of "prudery" transported me back into your room; it was midnight, the whole house was silent, and we were talking, just the two of us, alone. You, Mademoiselle, like a physicist performing experiments, you were imparting to your heart and to mine now a greater, now a lesser degree of heat. You were observing, you were reflecting; and for you, our feelings were never anything other than phenomena. As for me, I rather resembled—as you remarked—a young pupil who repeats his lesson full of fine phrases, and who forgets at every moment that it is his role to play the sage. Oh, how like a madman I played that role! Mademoiselle, I will return to Utrecht. In the name of God, no longer stay up with me late into the night; do not again have so much kindness for me if you have decided not to have yet more.

Do you want to know the result of all that passed between us? I admire the subtlety of your penetration, the accuracy of your discernment, the honesty which is, so to speak, the instinct of your heart; the inconsistency of your ideas astounds me. I have attached myself to you by all the bonds of respect and friendship, and without a doubt I have done so for life. Well—for one must say everything—those moments that I have spent with you leave me with regrets and desires ... Oh, Mademoiselle! will we ever talk again together late into the night? [...][2]

2. Letter 244 in *O.C.* 1: 486–87.

246. *To Constant d'Hermenches, July 31, 1766*

Utrecht

I am a little uncomfortable, slightly ill at ease, my dear D'Hermenches; I would like to explain the reason, but how should I go about it? I don't like to complain; that is boring for others, mortifying for oneself, and sometimes dishonest. I promised Monsieur de Bellegarde not to listen to any complaint against him; isn't it yet worse to complain myself? Well then, these will not be complaints; I will speak to you of myself, without accusing him. Sometimes, I have found that he was inattentive, but I was not offended by it—he hardly knows me. When he comes to know me well, I will be much more annoyed if he doesn't think that having me is a very good thing. There were many obstacles; I believed that I was more capable than he was of smoothing them away. I did my best; I succeeded. At present, it seems to me that he should take advantage, eagerly and without delay, of the opportunities I am offering him. It seems to me that he must have received long ago a letter from me, which he ought naturally to have hastened to answer; but he does not hasten. I am not fashioned to endure patiently the slightest coldness; even less to scold and weep and complain. I have been careful not to let my father notice that I think I have some reason to suspect the Marquis. They would seize onto that, and would no longer tolerate my even thinking about this marriage; neither he nor my mother nor my brothers would tolerate it. Thus I see only one thing to do, which is to clear up this suspicion. I must not lightly give up a plan on which I made my happiness depend; but if indeed I find coolness and indifference, I will break it off immediately, and no more will be said about it. The other day I jokingly threatened Monsieur de Bellegarde with a German lord; but I'm not joking now. If we break it off, and if I am weak enough to fear the appearance of abandonment that the breaking of a commitment might give me—a commitment that I desired quite openly and visibly to the public view—then I will accept the offer that this German has made to come see me. He bears a fine name; that will be good—not to marry but to refuse—, and *so it will look very well.*[1]

It's not the delays in themselves that displease me—you have seen how for two years they have seemed quite tolerable; and even if they were to last yet longer, I swear that it would not greatly distress me. As a matter of fact, my situation has never been as free nor as pleasant as it is at the moment; I rarely speak of the Marquis with my father and my mother, and when we do speak of him, it is without acrimony. This distant suitor makes my situation seem unremarkable, which suits me very well—as if I were a married woman far from her husband. I go and come as I please, without anyone finding fault. If something displeases me, the hope of a change of state arises in my heart, and comes on cue to put me at ease. Thus, my friend, I would pardon circumstances for many delays, but I would not pardon the

1. English in the original.

Marquis for even the merest shadow of one; the more I have been frank and eager in the measures I have had to take for him, the less I could endure the appearance of coolness. This same conduct, which I thought earned me gratitude, could produce a completely contrary feeling that assuredly I will never expose myself to.

Answer me, reassure me, or clear up my suspicions; you are free to tell them to your friend if that serves some purpose, but I want to be informed, and to know the truth. If tomorrow I receive a fine letter from Dresden,[2] I will be a little ashamed of this one; never mind, one must say what one thinks, even if one has to unsay it later.

Goodbye; I am going to give a French lesson to a pretty and charming Englishwoman, whom I'm mad about, as she is about me. I see her every day, and we never stop talking English; I keep forgetting it and relearning it—all I need is a week for either. I have many more friends this summer than usual; I'm going to Middachten to my cousin's; to Rosendaal; perhaps to Bosbeek, to stay with Mme Geelvinck's mother. Do you know that her father died? She is extremely distressed. I could very well end up making a trip to England; I like travelling as much as your friend does. God knows when I would return! He would not lose much.

247. *From Constant d'Hermenches, August 5, 1766*

Landrecies

I find your wrongs so sublime, my charming Agnes, that I would trade them willingly for all my right reasonings; I am even ashamed, for if I am right and you are wrong it is because I know the perversity of mankind—its distrust, its deviousness—and because you have the soul of an angel. You reason and act according to your principles; they are noble and excellent. I reason on the basis of experience; unfortunately, that is the best guide to success.

I was just beginning this when I received your second letter. It almost makes my answer for me, and you go so far as to defend my friend. Fear nothing on his part—he will never fail you. But, as I have told you, expect from him all possible clumsiness; count more on his indulgence if you have a few faults than on his admiration for all the perfections that you have above others. Don't even mention this German lord, nor a journey to England; he would stoically tell you to do what you want and that he will put up with it. Always bear in mind that with his name, his likeable qualities, and a very honorable existence, he would not still be a bachelor at the age of forty-five if he had known how to get married, or rather if he had not been all his life a marriage-spoiler. I have had no letter from him since he left

2. That is, from Bellegarde.

Holland. I scolded him; perhaps he is annoyed, but I'm not disturbed by it. He will return. I would disturb myself about it if I could be useful to you by writing to him, but I don't think that is the case. Give him your news; do not undo anything of what you have done; but let him come to you, and don't metaphysicalize with a man who, I swear to you, never turns a page. You will see him again, still courteous, cheerful, attentive, and as pleased with himself as if he had cracked his head against walls to win you. Enjoy your resources, and the liberty that this marriage plan has procured for you, and bear in mind that except for painful crises, the present moment of our existence is always the most agreeable.

I am writing this on the run, my dear Agnes; I am returning from an immense circuit through Flanders and Artois. Out of a childish curiosity, I have been to see the castles of my ancestors, in Rebecque;[1] I rediscovered the time when they were *Messires* because they were ruining themselves for the Pope in the Crusades, and the time when they were driven out like beggars because of Calvin. The moment I arrive, I receive a personal order to report to camp; that requires a thousand arrangements, and I must be there by the evening of the 7th. If I find a blank piece of paper in the camp it will be for you, my dear friend. On your part, write me here; I will return to undertake the journey to Switzerland.

Speaking of Switzerland, you must know that the Crown Prince spent two days in Lausanne. He stayed with me; he shut himself up in my study and wrote me a charming letter. Isn't it curious that if I had been at the Hague I would perhaps never have dined with him even once, for all my general's brevet; and that here in this country, where I am merely a French major, he has hardly left my side and has followed me to Switzerland? Go tell that to those who ridicule me for having left the land of tedium.

If I had a moment, I would write to the dear Widow about her bereavement, for I'm still fond of her. Speak to her about me, I beg you, dear Agnes; I still hope to see her again and that we may all meet one day under a happy sky, cheerful, content, and enjoying life. Adieu, divine Agnes.

248. *To Constant d'Hermenches, August 21–25, 1766*

Zuylen, Thursday

Here are a couple of quick words I will send you this evening, if I can; otherwise, I will keep them for Monday. What has become of our lovely correspondence? Who would ever have believed that it would be ruined to the point of no longer being anything but self-justifications and a list of

---

1. The Constant family originally came from Artois, where they owned the domain of Rebecque. They had left Artois for Switzerland to avoid religious persecution during the sixteenth century.

grievances? It will rise again, I am sure, from this sad decline and will become again what it was—gay, reasonable, useful. If I were to die for it, I will still say that there is a little contradiction in your advice; I permit you to say, in turn, that there is always excess in my conduct, and that my soul is like a little ball suspended on a long cord, which makes a huge swing at the least bump and bounces off the ceiling—sometimes from one side, sometimes the other. Let's not touch it any more just now; it is at rest in its natural position; it is at ease.

I received your letter at Middachten,[1] where I spent a week with all the pleasures—and all the pleasure—imaginable. I still love my cousin madly; we had the Count of Hompesch, Henri Saumaise, Reede[2] whom I've always liked so much, a young Bernese whose name is hard to write—something like Charner—, my sailor brother, and my sailor cousin;[3] they all got along very well together. We played cards, we sang, we ran races; the party at Rosendaal[4] was superb—a fairy-land, with truly supernatural fireworks, a marvelous light-show. There was only one little mishap at Middachten: I almost broke my thigh falling from a stool I had climbed on that broke under me; but that interrupted my gaiety only for a moment, and instead of pitying me and being sorry, everyone was pleased, in spite of my aches and pains and the cries I let out from time to time—they were pleased because I couldn't leave. They had lunch, they played cards on my bed; my cousin Reede and my brother didn't budge from there all morning. I would still be there if it were not for Monsieur de La Tour,[5] who had started up my portrait again, and who was impatiently waiting for me.

I made my way back Monday and Tuesday; my bruise obliged me to travel slowly. It isn't yet healed. The swelling is stubborn, and the whole thigh is a horrible color. I am so busy with my portrait that I have only a few moment to write—and I had a thousand letters to write. This one was begun Thursday and it's now Monday. I write in my bed, just as I am waking up; all the moments that I am not obliged to give to my portrait I give to my thigh.

I wrote to the Widow everything you told me to tell her, except the desire to see her again under a cheerful sky, etc.; our sky is perfectly fine and quite cheerful, for she is adored and happy. Good Lord, how relentless you are, and how prejudiced! For you, it was "the land of tedium"; very well, I

1. The chateau of the Athlone family.
2. Count Arent Willem van Reede, brother of Lord Athlone and brother-in-law of Belle's cousin Annebetje.
3. Her brother Ditie and her cousin Reinout Diederik, both of whom were in the navy.
4. A chateau belonging to the family of Torck-van Rosendaal-van Voorschoten.
5. Maurice Quentin de La Tour (1704–88), one of the finest painters of the eighteenth century. He was famous for his pastel portraits of Diderot, Voltaire, d'Alembert, Louis XV, Mme de Pompadour, and Rousseau. The travails of La Tour in his efforts to capture Belle's charm on canvas are described in subsequent letters. The result was the splendid and often-reproduced portrait of her that is now in the Musée d'Art et d'Histoire in Geneva.

believe it, and you did well to leave; but we must be looking at objects through a glass that is singularly favorable to our judgments to persuade ourselves that everything that does not please us is absolutely bad, and that what bores us must necessarily bore everybody. You would almost make me love my country by abusing it so excessively. In order to be just, I look for its good sides; I find in it a thousand advantages. Except for Tscharner, all the inhabitants of Middachten were Dutch; however, it was far from being the dwelling-place of tedium. Allow me to say it, my dear d'Hermenches, you are not making great progress in becoming philosophical. In the presence of Hompesch and Tscharner and everyone at Middachten, I recounted that the Crown Prince had been to your house,[6] and that he had shut himself up in your study to write to you from there. That is charming, and very flattering on the part of a hero.

I have never seen anyone ridicule the decision you made; Bellegarde is the only person I've heard talk about it. He is annoyed that you are not a general, and in spite of everything I could say, he cannot persuade himself that one can prefer Landrecies to the Hague—except for the forty thousand florins, which, like the *"sans dot"* in *The Miser,* justify everything.[7] If you regretted having left us, I don't think a visit from the Crown Prince would console you.

I am writing very badly, and in great haste; I can't wait to see my two brothers again, who, after five years of separation, met yesterday in my room. While the sailor was coming back from Newfoundland, the other had left for Paris.[8] And when the latter was returning from Paris, the former was in the Mediterranean. And he returns from the Mediterranean just as the other had left for Aix. Willem returned from Aix Thursday night; Ditie had gone to Amsterdam Thursday morning. Each was despairing of ever seeing the other again. Finally, yesterday, they met; they wept; they embraced each other. Their joy was touching to see.

Write to me. I still love you very much, although I argue about everything. We would soon no longer love each other if we had to hide what we think. As I reread my letter, I see that I spoke of the party at Rosendaal as if you couldn't fail to know what it was or why it was being given—I don't know whether people write to you about these things, and I don't think you bother to read our gazettes. I must tell you, then, that Monsieur de Rosendaal was giving this party for the Prince,[9] who was at Arnhem for his installation ceremony. I think that I am ever so slightly in favor with the Duke;

6. The future duke of Brunswick. See Letter 233, n. 2.
7. Again an allusion to Molière's *The Miser* I.vii, echoing her application of it to her own situation in Letter 221. The forty thousand florins are the price that d'Hermenches received when he sold his company.
8. Ditie and Willem René, respectively.
9. William of Orange, who officially became stadholder (Willem V) in 1766, when he reached the age of eighteen. The duke of Brunswick was his guardian.

he always talks to me a great deal, and I dance and play cards with the Prince. If this is favor, it's a very small degree of favor; I don't believe I'm cut out to obtain a greater one.

Farewell, my very dear friend.

249. *From Constant d'Hermenches, August 30, 1766*

Compiègne

My dear Agnes, I have found here many delightful little things that, taken together, almost add up to an entire happiness and which I must tell you about, for it is, I think, a duty of friendship. I was invited to the Camps,[1] and all those who had asked to be invited were refused. The Duc de Choiseul told the King that he had counted on making a good acquisition in placing me in his service, but that I was far surpassing his expectations; and then he told me so himself. He assured me that I would be brigadier in the next field exercises, and he is having my regiment brought up with that intention.[2] He then told me that surely I would make a fortune in this country and that he is sorry to see me stationed in so remote a place. He left me the choice of all the garrisons in the kingdom; I asked for Besançon—the best of the cities, and eighteen leagues from my home—and I will have it. Meanwhile, in order not to be too far from the camp, I asked for Mézières,[3] and I march there in two weeks; he gave me permission to have a governorship,[4] something that had never been granted to a foreigner or a Protestant. Provided that the King, who is very much against the old practices, doesn't oppose it, I'm going to have one—about the size of the palm of my hand. As the Duke was leaving us yesterday, he said to me: "I cannot see you without the cross. Why have you not asked for it?" "Because," I said, "They are not being given, and it is even forbidden to ask for one." "Oh, that does not apply to you, I want you to have it this very evening," and immediately there is an order to make me a chevalier; but one must have the King's order, one must have a cross, clerks, a commander; I will have to wait three days, and I am going to Paris for it.

All the officers in the Swiss Guards at the Hague—those louts—protested that my son could not be allowed not to rejoin his unit; Vernand had written me a pathetic letter to that effect. I, in turn, wrote a pretty letter, French-style, to your Duke, and he sends all those pettifoggers packing, and orders

1. For the large-scale summer field exercises called the Grand Maneuvers.
2. A brigadier was the commanding officer of a brigade, comprising two or more regiments. His rank might be anything from lieutenant colonel (or, rarely, major) on up. Before Choiseul's reforms, a brigade had been formed only during war or during the Grand Maneuvers. See the translators' comments that follow Letter 155.
3. A city in northern France.
4. The command of a fortress or garrison.

the egregious Sandoz[5] to inform me of me a six-month leave for the young-ster, whom I'm taking off to Switzerland with me.

And you, dear and divine friend, what are your adventures? You should only have heavenly ones! This Marquis runs all over the world, and hasn't written me a word since his departure; you must, however, marry him—for he will bring you to France, where you will see people who are gay, pol-ished, who speak charmingly, gently, and who are the most refined in all the arts, talents, tastes; who are light as the wind, and yet heroic in conduct; yes, you must marry him. (Although the Comte d'Usson does tell me that he had immediately begun to pay court at Aix-la-Chapelle to some or an-other princess or Milady.) For example, if you only had a true notion of Villers-Cotterêts[6]—which is a country estate of the Duc d'Orleans that I continually run to from here—you would throw all Dutch country manors into the sea. It may not have such beautiful tulips, but it is the Palace of Happiness. There are often seventy of us, each sleeping in a delightful apartment, and each can have, if he likes, his little repast in private and at any hour. People don't use their pencils here as they do at Madame Hasse-laer's; they use them to write little verses and jokes. Ah! how marvelous you would be there, Agnes! Fat Madame d'Usson has her corner there, what do you say to that? Such is the influence of a good example. They act com-edies and do improvisations, and then they have a café-theater. Oh! what a delightful thing these café-theaters are! Thirty little tables in a big, well-lit apartment; abbés, eccentrics, poets, travelers, authors. Madame d'Usson is the hostess; each asks for what he wants; d'Usson and his waiters in white aprons and loose-flowing hair serve you. Each does his reading or his dia-logue and improvises a scene; one recounts the latest news; the other, a story; those who are accomplished singers climb into the orchestra and sing—it's a sort of local Ranelagh[7]—there are theatrical sketches and danc-ing and hunting parties and gambling; this goes on for three weeks.

Agnes, have you spoken very seriously about me to the Widow Geel-vinck, my friend whom I love and whom, I take it, you love also? Have you told her that if it were not more worthy to think keenly about one's friends rather than to write them conventional letters of condolence, she would have one from me? I'll wager that you did not; a slight word, perhaps, muttered between your teeth, that the poor Widow may not have heard—that's not what I want. I order you to take up a pen at once, and to tell her for a half-page about my way of being concerned for her.

I meant only to write you three lines on my knee, to inform you about my

---

5. Vernand and Sandoz are Swiss officers; the duke of Brunswick is commander-in-chief.
6. A small town north of Paris. Its chateau, belonging to the ducs d'Orléans, was the site of lavish fêtes.
7. Lord Ranelagh had installed a ballroom and theater on his property, which were widely im-itated in France. The term "Ranelagh" was used in French to indicate this kind of light enter-tainment.

little existence, and here I've written three pages. I don't know whether you won't find them utterly mad, but let us see how it will all sit, next to your philosophy, your metaphysics, your logic, your English, your Latin, and, by Heaven! your mathematics!

You should also know that I'm going to Paris for a very few days; from there to Landrecies and Avesnes, then to the Duc d'Arenberg's in Enghien for a week; then I return to take the Eptingen Regiment to Mézières, because it's on my route to Switzerland; and then straight to Hermenches, where I have already ordered a café to be set up and where I mean to hunt like a Nimrod for two months. Be so good as to write me in Landrecies until the 15th of September, or in Mézières until the 21st; and after that in Switzerland. I deserve it, for on my honor, even in this Palace of Happiness I have described to you, I am still—as I am everywhere—on my knees in adoration before your heart, your mind; were it not for this wretched Savoyard[8] I would say: before your image. Good night then, you who must be only an ethereal essence for me ...

But the point of all this is that d'Usson is writing to Rome, that it's a pleasure for him to do it, and that he has a friend there who will take care of your business. It is quite certain that Mme d'Usson has been presented to the royal family, and that she is as well received at the Court as if the priest had had his part in it.

Good night, once again, my sublime friend.

My postilion drives more like the Devil even than the one who will carry this packet to you.

When you think of me, imagine whether a bit of blue ribbon would fit nicely in my buttonhole, and in your thoughts.[9]

250. *To Constant d'Hermenches, September 6–7, 1766*

I have just received your letter. I'm very glad to hear about your successes. The cross, the little governorship that can lead to a bigger one, the honors, the praises, the minister's favor, these good and convenient garrisons—it all delights me, and I congratulate you on it, and I hope that the King fulfills all the fine hopes that so agreeably smile upon you.

As for Villers-Cotterêts, that is perhaps more interesting to those who are there than to those one writes to. No matter how hard I torture my imagination, I cannot force it to take pleasure in your description—gay and amiable as it is. You think that I would be marvelous there; no, in truth, I would be very stupid there, and if ever I were to appear there I would pity you for

---

8. Bellegarde.

9. The blue ribbon accompanied the Croix de Mérite, which was instituted by Louis XV in 1759. For Protestant officers in foreign regiments serving France it corresponded to the Croix de Saint-Louis, which was reserved for Catholics.

having announced me other than as a very awkward foreigner. I would enjoy the spectacle for a few moments, that is all. You may find that it is impolite to speak in this tone about what amuses you; really, I feel that's the case, and I would tear all this up if I had a great deal of leisure; but the hour presses, and we would like to go to Leiden tomorrow to see some pictures. The post is about to leave; we will not be back by the following day; thus, I am dashing this off, and I ask of your indulgent friendship a general absolution for the innumerable outbursts of sincerity this letter may contain. Since I am not French, I need a great deal of time and reflection to be polite.

You must marry him, you say of Bellegarde. Do you think that sentence makes much impression on me? *You really must marry him so that he will bring you to France.* Do you think that such an argument, presented in that way, will move me to marry? I am very tired of seeming to be counseled and led about as if I were an utter fool, and I can almost hear you from where I am, holding forth in a manner that—for all that it may be flattering, full of friendship, inspired by affection—is quite unpleasant for me. One must, you are no doubt saying, tear her away from the fatherland of tedium and bring her to the dwelling-place of happiness; she is made to live here, etc. My discourse is flat, but I know that yours is elegant—I haven't the time to arrange my sentences; but however fine it may be, it doesn't suit *me*, and rather than seem to be letting myself be thus married by the arrangements of anyone in the world, I would break off the finest match in the universe. It seems to me that I would make a strange figure, letting my future be arranged for me that way—I, the most independent and willful person, and the most attached even to the very air of independence. And what outcries there would be if I were to disappoint your conjectures, if I recited neither verses nor tales at Villers-Cotterêts, if I were to yawn at M. d'Usson's café, if I found the French disagreeable, and if I wanted to live at Les Marches more or less the way I live at Zuylen! What outcries, what *disappointment*,[1] what insults I would hear against my country, against my prejudices!

Will you allow me to tell you where the Bellegarde story is at this point, and the effect that your letter produces? You will curse; never mind, I am used to telling you the truth. He sent me the letter for Rome; it is addressed to Rendorp, but it is to be sent to Monsieur de Piccolomini. In the postscript he says that he is spending the winter in Chambéry in order to receive letters addressed to him there. I receive with that letter a long epistle for me, full of fine phrases and protestations; he replies to everything I have written, and claims that my long letters are very agreeable. I answer him the next day that everything is very well, but that we are not pressed to ask for the dispensation, since he is spending the winter in Chambéry; that once it is obtained, this dispensation would be a commitment, and that I do not want us to be engaged longer than is necessary; that I will keep his letter until the

---

1. English in the original.

time when I think it is appropriate to send it; that meanwhile, I am going to ask my father for permission to spend two months in England; that, in spite of his polite assurances, I think letters seem very heavy, especially when they are growing old, and that I beg him to burn mine ... The next day, I told my father a part of the truth; I showed him the letter for Rome; I asked permission to write to Mrs. Eliott to know whether she can receive me at the beginning of November. He told me that he would think about it, and I hope that he will consent to my project, which I am looking forward to immensely.

I was afraid of having put a little of my intensity in my letter to Bellegarde; my intensity, I must admit, has quite a tinge of brusqueness. I wrote a little letter to soften it; it was to leave yesterday; happily I forgot it, I received your letter, and mine will not be sent.

You will do well, I think, to beg M. d'Usson *not* to write; we have enough with M. de Piccolomini; at the least, M. d'Usson must not promise any money; it would be disagreeable to pay for a dispensation that no one would use. I am not as docile as one might think, and if the slightest distaste, the slightest bad humor were to seize me, I am quite capable of tearing up the dispensation, curtsying politely to the appellants, and telling them that it is impossible for me to take advantage of their good offices. In the eyes of Monsieur d'Usson, especially considering what he has told you about Aix,[2] I must seem like a financier's daughter whom one takes to pay off the mortgage on one's lands, and who, by the hope of getting out of a tedious household, along with with the bait of a title, is enticed to marry—against wind and tide—a man who neglects her. That doesn't suit me at all; I am not rich enough, and I am too proud. Ask M. d'Usson to pour his coffee at Villers-Cotterêts, and to stop meddling in my marriage.

That's enough about all this; but you may be sure that this is not a whim of mine, and that everything I am writing is what I think, down to the last syllable. Let's say no more about it. From here on, people should let us manage our interests as we can and as we wish—Bellegarde and I.

Sunday morning, the 7th

We didn't go to Leiden, and I am taking up my pen again. I liked the beginning of your letter very much: *I have found here many delightful little things that, taken together, almost add up to an entire happiness.* You see that I still know how to applaud. Really, that is true and is charmingly said. Fortune, circumstances, powerful people, friends, pleasures all yield in their several ways their small satisfactions, no one of which is very considerable; but all together they make us as content as if we were happy.

You ask me what my adventures are; they are very simple, and rather good ones. The swelling in my thigh is beginning to come down, which is

---

2. Aix-la-Chapelle. D'Hermenches had mentioned Bellegarde's flirting (at least) with various women there.

indeed a piece of luck, for people had me worried about an abscess. My cousin d'Athlone arrives in Utrecht at the end of the week; I have just received a letter from her in which she asks me to take the time immediately after her child is born to go off to Rosendaal or to Madame Geelvinck's for ten days or so, for it would be cruel, she says, to be almost within sight without having me continually by her bed, and she thinks that I would not be allowed to be there for fear that we would talk too much. There is nothing so precious in life as one's friends, in my opinion, and nothing so charming as the signs and the speech and the loving gestures of friendship.

For the last two weeks I have been spending every morning with my uncle, and I dine there with La Tour, when he has been working for two or three hours on my portrait. I don't get at all bored, because he knows how to talk, he is witty, and he has seen many things and known curious people; besides, we have company. I give him an incredible amount of trouble, and sometimes he is taken with a feverish anxiety about not succeeding—for he absolutely wants the portrait to be my very self.

All three of my brothers are here, each one very likeable in his own way, and so eager to talk with me that I hardly have the time to go to bed and to get up. I love them very much, and that gives me great pleasure. I'm doing very well.

I end as I began, by finding myself grossly impolite about Villers-Cotterêts, and I ask your pardon. Infatuations annoy me; I say nothing about it when I'm being polite, but with you I have wanted to follow my mood. God knows how many platitudes there are among those little verses, those comedies, etc ... and all for vanity's sake and for showing how witty one is! And that you should be infatuated with that! Let's not start it up again, I meant to apologize and I'm making things worse.

Don't forget to warn M. d'Usson: I am obliged to him for his services, but I don't want any for the present, and tell him that seriously—not prettily; not nicely. There are things I detest joking about. Say that ... it doesn't matter, but he mustn't buy any dispensation yet, and not a word—I beg you—of my caprices, nor of the Marquis, nor of Aix. I don't need remarks from your charming nation—*light as the wind*—and since I am accustomed to seeing and thinking and acting as I please, when I'm given a lot advice I feel tyrannized by it, and ... but will I never end this babbling! You've understood me. I will say no more, and I beg you to believe that I am your best friend, in spite of this outburst that I can't control.

I relayed very clearly to Mme Geelvinck your heartfelt tenderness, your constant affection for her, but I have neither the wit nor the leisure to imagine a full page. Write to both of us from Switzerland: a good letter to me, a charming one to her.

Sunday evening

The farther I get away from the moment I was angry, the closer I get to justice and truth. I have let slip some unjust expressions. Have you advised me too much? Have you sought to extenuate the disadvantages—exaggerate the advantages? Have you claimed to be arranging my marriage? Certainly not; thus, I should not be afraid of being tyrannized; I should not have flared up over a single word; I could have spoken *charmingly* and *nicely*, as in the *Palace of Happiness*, instead of giving way to my boiling impatience; but please, do not reproach me, you see that I am not being easy on myself. Let us live in peace with each other.

Give me some errands to do in England; if my father lets me go, and I don't drown between Helvoet and Harwich, I will do a thousand things for you. I will write to Mme Geelvinck about the pretty blue ribbon,[3] and all the other pleasant things, and how much people in that country are finding that you deserve honors and a fortune. I will be very happy to write those things, and she will be happy to learn them; with the omission of a few of your expressions, such as *that worthy Widow ... whom you say you love*, I'll send her your letter. Say what you will, but I do love her. Villers-Cotterêts would entertain her perhaps more than me, and the pleasure that she would find there would make up for the crime of my aversion. Perhaps, even, if I were made much of there, I would find it all charming, and the pleasantry of white aprons and loose-flowing hair absolutely delightful; I'm hopelessly stupid at improvisations, but I would listen to the music, and that would help me get by.

I think that you must write as if on your own initiative to M. d'Usson, saying that you do not think one need be in haste to solicit Rome, and that all that could be done at present would be to prepare the way for another time, when it would be necessary to ask for his friend's help.

Goodbye, I'm falling asleep, and I'm scribbling and tangling up my sentences. I end by embracing you, in spite of Savoie.

251. *From Constant d'Hermenches, September 18, 1766*

Enghien

I submit my case to you yourself, my dear Agnes, when you will be in a position to compare, whether I slander your country or whether I am merely a scandalmonger. We have agreed between us always to speak and to search for the truth: you think it's a mania of mine to put you off the people you live with! No, Agnes—if you didn't have the opportunity to live elsewhere, if it were not certain that you have enough resources of intellect and character to find good everywhere, I would never have raised the question. There are people whom I spend my life berating because they don't know how to accommodate themselves to what is around them; there are people to whom I maintain that the French are frivolous and worthless, and that they would

3. The Croix de Mérite. See Letter 249, n. 9.

be bored in Paris ... but to you, I must tell the truth. A while ago I found myself in Paris with two women who are very good friends of mine, and to whom I owe a great deal. One of them happened to speak of a man who was much in fashion, who appeared to have all kinds of wit and talent, and whom I had known for a long time to be a very dull, vapid fellow. The women were overjoyed that they were going to act in a play with this man, and thereby admit him into their society. I said nothing; they said to me: "But you know him, why don't you say something?" Finally they pushed me and I was seized with pity; to pull them out of their ridiculous infatuation, I described my man. One of them protested indignantly, and said to one of my friends that she would never have believed that I was malicious, etc. I said nothing in response; but during my last visit, they thanked me a thousand times, telling me that my remarks had put them on their guard, and that indeed the man in question was a complete nonentity; that they were much obliged to me that they hadn't thrown themselves at his head, as so many others have done who don't know how get out situations. I replied: "Whatever the risk, I cannot keep myself from telling my friends the truth."

In your desire to prove me wrong you cite as examples of delightful company a Saumaise, a Hompesch; but Agnes, I protest to you that those people would not be successful even in my little Lausanne. Poor Saumaise has no manners, and is extremely stupid; and Hompesch, if it's Heiden Hompesch, is the most lumpish and disgusting of men; if it's his brother Vincent,[1] I like him better, but he's quite gloomy. Your Swiss Tscharner is a stiff little fellow escaped from some German university, who must have found you quite mad. Tell me in good conscience: do you think that in Middachten you were appreciated for what you were worth? You must have astonished them, perhaps even made them laugh, because you are wonderful with all kinds of people—you would warm a Laplander. But how can the admiration of Laplanders satisfy you? This may be jealousy, coquetry, even fatuity on my part—but the essential is nonetheless true!

I too have been to Middachten, and I had a fine time there. I was the Richelieu of the canton;[2] I eclipsed the rank of Hartemberg, the arguings of the Randwijcks, the languishing sighs of Colonel Schmid; all the young fops from the French camps who had been there before me were forgotten. I answered their letters; I amused myself (not without a bit of mischievousness). Well then, I wasn't in love, but it was better that way; I saw that people were taken with me, and that was all I needed to be happy. You haven't had these piquant little pleasures, Agnes, and yet there you are, being ecstatic.

You also scold me about the Widow, because you describe her as happy; I would wager, however, that that good soul, in the midst of the love of all her fellow citizens that you so exalt, has to endure vexations, harassments,

1. A captain in the Dragoons.
2. The duc de Richelieu, a notorious Don Juan. See d'Hermenches' Letter 178, n. 6.

rudeness. Then too, I can't bear to have people content themselves with something that isn't suitable when one could have something better; and when I compare the lot, the life, the regard, and the delights that Mme d'Usson enjoys, I tear out my hair at leaving the Widow there—that good Widow who would be more stimulating, and whom I would like better. You and she do very well to enjoy the present moment. That's wise; that's what I was doing in Landrecies, where really my days flowed by with more satisfaction than they ever had in the Hague; but for all that, I have not said that Landrecies wasn't a hole, and that the society there wasn't pitiable. Today, I write to you from the bosom of happiness; it's in the most beautiful place in the universe, with my intimate friends, the Duc and Duchesse d'Arenberg. He's an eccentric in all ways, and insupportable for many people, but solid, sensible, and very affectionate to me. She is the model of all perfections— beautiful, gay, without airs or pretentions. Here we don't have the refinements or the fêtes of Villers-Cotterêts, but it's an easy, comfortable daily existence, where people are completely themselves; where one finds the present like the past, and sees that the future will be the same. I'm a mad fellow here, like a mischievous boy, because the hubbub and hurly-burly don't drag me in out of this sphere; I have my own sphere like this at Compiègne—at Villers-Cotterêts, it was different.

I have my son with me here; we are in a charming pavillion in the park. I keep him busy, I make him reflect, reason; and then he goes to amuse himself with the sons of the household. The elder is his age, and the second has just obtained the La Marck regiment in France as heir of that house, whose name he will take.[3]

Myself—in the midst of all these people whose contemporary I am and whom I have known for more than twenty years—I find myself young; I'm the strongest and the gayest. This blue ribbon and little cross give me a certain chivalric air, which is better currency than the patent of a Dutch major general in my pocket. Everybody says so, even the people who were distressed by my moving over to France; indeed, Agnes, would I have been able to do all that I'm doing now? Wouldn't I be hemmed in by all the mediocre superiors, by all the formal leave-granting, and by that confounded conventionality of the Hague that insists that one be oh-so-careful about the places one goes and the people one sees? Would I see you more often? Would I have been admitted to Middachten? Would Turk,[4] who has lived with me, lodged with me, on whom I have always lavished kindness— would he have invited me to Rosendaal? That's what's so horrible about your country—they are not even decent in the courtesies that they should reciprocate. I, a lowly officer, I entertained—had into my house—all of Hol-

3. These are the Arenberg sons. The younger was to fight in the American War of Independence. The comte de La Marck was his grandfather.
4. A deformation, probably deliberate, of the name of Jan Torck.

land's upper crust, both at the Hague and in Switzerland. I have never received the slightest reciprocation, and several have avoided me; all have
torn me to shreds. Draw up a list of all those from your country who have
travelled from home; you will find that I have been of service to them all—
the latest being Pallandt and Rendorp, who has recently been to visit me.
Well now, none of those people, when they returned to Holland, paid me a
single visit, and if it came to inviting someone to their homes or their
country-house parties it was the Colonels Van der Dussen, Saumaise, etc.,
that they asked. M. de Rhoon, Charles Bentinck, who were at my home in
the Hague, who had supper there gaily enough—do you think they have ever
offered me so much as a glass of water? No, Agnes, M. de Rhoon was so
churlish as to give balls where he would invite all the Hague and leave me at
home, because he was using the lists of M. de Boetzelaer—and this while
his fat son Anthony was dining every day at my place and borrowing my
money. The Fagels and the Spaens didn't treat me any better.[5] That nasty
little clerk, for example, whose son was at my place from morning to night
in Lausanne, at Hermenches, while the father bowed down to the ground at
the Hague when he met me—I've had nothing more from him, although he
invited Milady Holderness and Mme de Boufflers, whom he saw me with
every day at their homes and at Mme Degenfeld's, and who were my
friends. He was continually rude enough to have them to supper and to dinner at his country estate one whole summer without my knowing even today
where that estate is.

Well. I could go on with these things till tomorrow, my dear friend—and
you want me not to detest the way of living and the conduct of such a country? By Heaven, I paid dearly enough for the right to rail at them—so dearly
that I take no joy in it. Bellegarde, believe me, thinks as I do—he who is the
only happy warrior; for he has never served them, and he is better paid than
anybody; and he is a general there, merely by dint of his having spent a few
seasons at Spa and a few springtimes at the Hague. It's he who encouraged
me the most to make the decision that I did; and as for the title of general—I
don't know whether I am happily deluding myself, or really seeing it that
way—but it seems to me that it would be a sobriquet, and that I can't imagine speaking of a Dutch general as anything but a joke. And you, Agnes,
what do you think? It's a marquise you want to be, not a general's wife,
isn't it?

I learn with much joy that our Marquis has finished his travels in Germany; he passed by my place, thinking he would find me there; he stopped
by my parents', who are always delighted to see him, and he promised that

5. Count Willem Bentinck van Rhoon, second son of the duke of Portland; he was an important advisor to the prince of Orange, and father of Anthony Bentinck, who is married to one of
Belle's cousins (the sister of Annebetje). Charles Bentinck is the third son of the duke of Portland. Van Boetzelaer was the general tax collector of Holland. Henric Fagel was clerk of the
States-General; his daughter married Belle's brother Willem René in 1771.

when I had returned he would come back. So he is surely occupied as he should be by this lovely romance of which the divine, the adorable Agnes is the prize. If I have a moment to myself, I will go to Les Marches, where she is to live.

You must believe, Agnes, that I am always the same—that is, always worthy of your friendship; if I don't metaphysicalize with you it's because I would like to cure you of that; if there are no epigrams in my letters it's because I am no longer trying to charm you. I am more philosophical than ever because I am not so mad as I was; I talk about the objects that fall under my senses, without going to look for subjects of discussion in the empyrean: *Homo sum, et humani nihil a me alienum puto.*[6]

I could still talk to you about a charming stay that I had between Villers-Cotterêts and Enghien at Raismes, at that estate where I still meet your image, that woman who resembles you; she's an angel in character and friendship. She was at Spa. Ask about her—her name is Mme d'Orchival. But without giving her name, ask: "Have you seen someone who resembles me?" We are very good friends; she is very sad that I'm leaving.

At that same château there was also a pretty little woman, a *bel esprit*, who really does have a great deal of wit; I don't know whether I mentioned her to you. Last year she was full of pretensions, literature, learning of all kinds; she lives in the ancient Château des Coucy in Champagne, and she has had all the time in the world to read and form a high opinion of herself. A few conversations where we teased her a little, a couple of well-reasoned letters, have utterly changed that woman; now she's everything one could wish. Agnes, if I were not so reasonable, there was a charming scenario for me; for she admitted to me that she would like to make a conquest of me, and ever since last year her vanity had been in a ferment. I left, with the promise that one always makes, to pass by Coucy on my way back from Switzerland.

Among all these delightful things the famous Lagarde[7]—the French musician who has written so many delightful songs, and who with his harp suggests the very image of Orpheus—would sing with a young girl whom he comes from Paris to meet every year, to hear, he says, the clearest, steadiest voice, the most supple throat that he has heard anywhere in France. Lagarde has a very fine voice; these two have given me an idea of the perfection of singing and of musicianship that was already clear in my mind, but whose execution I had not yet found; you surely know, Agnes, the *Duos* of Lagarde, *Les Soirées de l'Isle-Adam*, the opera *Aeglé*.

You describe for me very touchingly the reunion of your brothers; they are rare, these fraternal affections, and they last only as long as there are

6. Terence, *Heauton Timorumenos* (*The Self-Tormenter*) I.i.25, "I am a man, and think nothing human foreign to me."
7. Pierre Lagarde (1717–?), French singer and composer.

common interests. But there is something in your blood of the heroic, which I very much like; it lends a touch of the pompous or the overblown, but it carries with it and sustains many virtues. It is certain that a Tuyll thinks about another Tuyll differently from the way he thinks about any other man—isn't this so, Agnes? And other people can feel that; in a family where people respect each other and support each other, there is an atmosphere of gravity and nobility that is imposing. I know two or three such families in the world, from which have issued people of great merit.

Have I nattered on enough, my dear friend? This letter will not be worth much, but at least you will see that the ill you may say of it doesn't discourage me at all, and that my ardor and my abandon with you are stronger than my vanity.

We are all about to be separated; I'm going to pass through Mézières where my regiment is marching, on my way to Switzerland; I'm counting on being at Hermenches on the 28th. It's there or in Lausanne that I will await your letters with rapture. Fill them with reprimands or derision—they will be nonetheless dear to me; everything that comes from you is precious, divine Agnes, including the satire of my being enchanted by the attentions of the Crown Prince! I am at your feet.

CdH

I'm impatient to know how the smallpox will have treated the Comtesse de Degenfeld; if she were to be scarred, that would be a grim embassy-spoiler.[8]

This letter is in answer to yours of the 25th of August, which is the last one I've received; perhaps I'll find one at the regiment. Be good enough to tell me more about that thigh; what color is it just now? Do you remember the green head and the blue thigh of Madame de Sévigné?[9]

252. *To Constant d'Hermenches, September 25, 1766*

Your letter made me laugh, my dear d'Hermenches; I needed it badly, for I was all too serious—even glum. I have my days of self-examination, of general confessions of my faults, my imprudence, my blunders; it never ends, and there is no way for me to obtain my own absolution. I am a truly Jansenist confessor, of the most rigid Port-Royal type, and I refuse to hear of any Jesuitical laxity.[1] Would you believe that during dinner, although the

8. D'Hermenches coins the term *trouble-ambassade,* modeled on *trouble-fête*—"spoilsport." M. de Degenfeld is about to be the ambassador of the United Provinces at Vienna.

9. It is not known whether Belle remembers. Your translators do not.

1. Jansenism was a seventeenth-century reform movement within the Roman Catholic Church. While the Jansenists never made common cause with the Calvinists, they too emphasized predestination and called for an austere and uncompromising way of life. The abbey of Port-

company was large, things got to a point where I couldn't keep myself from weeping? After dinner I got your letter; it brought my imagination back to a more normal condition. You see how fit I am for the beau monde: yesterday, I spoke not at all; today, I weep.

I had known for a long time that Bellegarde, far from being angry with you, was impatiently seeking you out; it was a criminal negligence on my part not to tell you. If you go to Les Marches, describe it to me—make it neither beautiful nor ugly, but paint it as it is. I am curious to know whether it will be my home one day. Many strange things are going on in my heart. For a long time I whipped up my imagination; I thought I desired something—and in order to desire, to be eager, I needed this heat that I was giving to my imagination. Those letters—which you find so long, so ridiculous, and romantic, and metaphysical—maintained that heat; now that all those delays, and your advice, and an interval of absence and silence have cooled my imagination, I look around me and I hardly know any more what I desired. What I wrote I remember only with surprise, and I blush and I think I am mad—and that item in my self-examination is terrible. You will tell me, "So much the better that you have recovered from your illusions and see things as they are." Yes—perhaps. But seeing these things, will I ever marry? If the difficulties smooth out by themselves, I believe I will. But I no longer have, I think, the zeal that makes one overcome obstacles. I tell you this in strictest confidence . . . if I become a marquise, he must not know that for several months I cared a good deal less about being one; but I care even less about being Rhinegravine of Salm. Does a title console one for anything? Does it fill the empty places of the soul? Perhaps I am not capable of loving; however, I would like to love, and especially I would like to be loved. Gratitude would lead to affection; I would be responsive to gestures of tenderness. One can cure oneself of vanity, but sensitivity still remains; a little cat who comes to purr on my knees gives me more pleasure than a wit who praises me. —Don't say a word about the Rhinegravine; people would believe that I am boasting.

You are very fortunate to be hearing excellent music; it's the thing that delights me the most in all the world, and of all your pleasures it's the only one that I envy. Last Sunday we took La Tour to Zyst to have him hear the Hernutes;[2] it is admirable music of its kind. We saw the sunset in the woods, a dappling of fire on those beautiful trees, and between the leaves a dazzling red light; the moment after, the moon took the place of the sun; the light turned white; it was enchanting; then we went into the church. The

---

Royal became the spiritual and pedagogical center of Jansenism; it was suppressed and destroyed by order of the pope and of Louis XIV in the early eighteenth century. The most famous Jansenist was Pascal, who wrote polemics against Jesuit casuistry that were widely read.

2. Zyst is a small town near Utrecht and the home of the Moravian community of the Hernutes, a Christian sect founded in 1722.

cleanliness and contemplativeness made a lovely scene, and the gentle, devout music of the organ, violins, flutes, with the pure line of song banish the passions of the heart for more than an hour and gave us a glimpse of the compelling charm there is in seclusion and worship. In that church, one is a thousand leagues away from the world ... but that will not amuse you, any more than Villers-Cotterêts amuses me.

Let us talk of your description of my dear Middachten. I had a good laugh over it. Indeed, I will not insist to you that Saumaise is a genius, but he's a good fellow—often that's enough; and Vincent Hompesch does let himself have fun, and Reede has a good deal of wit. It is quite true that the Milord his brother is very stupid, but I am a great deal fonder of Madame d'Athlone than you are of Madame Pater, and she is a great deal fonder of me, and there was good fellowship at Middachten. In short, although you spoke your piece about it very well and were very funny about it, I found myself much at ease and contented there. Wait until I have made the acquaintance of all your admirable French friends and your charming lady friends; with any luck at all, I'll make you laugh at them yourself. I have not so entirely given up my former talent that I will not rediscover it with you one of these days.

Let's not argue any more about Mme Geelvinck; we would argue forever. I talked to her about you a great deal in a long letter. I would like her to have the courage to indulge her curiosity and take a tour to Paris with me; but the same traits of character that make a person at ease everywhere and that let one adapt to everything and satisfy everybody exclude impulsive whims like those. One does not desire anything at all with intensity; the slightest thing holds one back ... That's enough; you're well acquainted with that temperament; our friend is indeed unique as to kindness and generosity; she has an admirable heart. Just now she is busy comforting her mother in the country,[3] and she says and does on all occasions things that make people cherish her. I have been thinking for a long while of going to spend a few days there, but I am mired in uncertainties. My journey to England, the one to Rosendaal, my cousin d'Athlone's approaching confinement—all these things leave me hanging for the present. The most attractive plans would give way to the pleasure of keeping my cousin company; but I am so indignant about her husband and he is so jealous of me, that I do not know whether I can honorably continue going there. I would feel that a great loss, but a fool makes people shun his house in spite of themselves. Besides, I believe I would only be anticipating him: some day he will forbid his wife to see me. Just imagine—it is I, whose heart you find so idealistically good, who arouse suspicion; it is believed, I think, that I am a dangerous connection and that I'm capable of giving dubious advice. Well, I don't know what's behind all this, but I could cry out as you do at the horrible

3. Mme Geelvinck had recently lost her father.

injustice and accuse a great many people—for Milord has not imagined this all alone.

At present I have nothing to say for my compatriots; you are right to detest them; everything you report to me tells of their dreadful ingratitude and rudeness. However, remember what I have said a thousand times: you know only the Hague, yet you incessantly say: "The Dutch, your nation ..." In our province, the respectable people either would not have accepted your civilities, or would have reciprocated them. When I reflect on the behavior that you so rightly complain of, I find two causes for it: your merit and your reputation as a libertine. Your libertinage alone would have had no effect; but the fathers and husbands were afraid of you because you were attractive, while the mothers and daughters did not dare defend you because you passed yourself off as a libertine—a trifle conceitedly, in the past, if I am not mistaken? I begin to be persuaded that all men are conceited; I can think of no exceptions except two or three taciturn fellows; the rest are less occupied with enjoying love and pleasure than with talking and writing about them. The cads make a great deal of noise and tell all, while the others speak softly and insinuate; but that's the only difference.

Madame de Degenfeld will not be at all scarred; she has recovered. I have written her a wretched little letter which I found very hard to write; I no longer know how to write except to you and those like you, where I am allowed to use the wrong word and then do great crossings out when the expression is too far from the thought; I no longer know how to spin out finicky little formulas or ladle on expressions like *I have the honor, the pleasure of ... I am filled with admiration* ...; and when I have put myself through infinite torments to do so, I can only laugh at what I've produced.

I will ask everybody returning from Spa for news of my image.[4] Speaking of image, the portrait that La Tour has been doing of me was admirable; we thought we could arrive at a perfect resemblance; every day we thought it would be the last session; there was nothing left except the slightest thing to add to the eyes, but that very slight thing refused to come. He searched, he retouched; my expression changed continually. I didn't get impatient, but the painter despaired, and at the end he had to erase the most beautiful painting in the world—but by then there was no longer any resemblance or any hope of achieving one. However, he starts all over again every morning, and sticks to me like a shadow all day; fortunately, he's very pleasant, and recounts a thousand curious things. Here he is, reading in my room beside me; it was the only way I could get him to let me write. He has done an excellent portrait of my uncle, and has refreshed the one that I had done of my mother some time ago, so that now it is charming, and gives me infinite pleasure.

My thigh is still a little swollen and a bit blue, but by now it's nothing;

---

4. The woman he said resembled her, Mme d'Orchival.

that good blood of mine saved me from an abscess. Write me long letters when you have some real leisure. I will write you another little letter as soon as I can. It is sweet of you to put up with my rudeness; so please accept as well my sincere assurances of friendship.

253. *From Constant d'Hermenches, September 25, 1766*

So it was very wrong of me to come out with that little remark about the Marquis's amusements at the watering-places. For Agnes, philosophical as you think you are—absolute, decisive—you are nonetheless a trifle jealous; your pride is stung. There's nothing wrong with that, but you really mustn't thunder at me as you do, nor go running off to England merely because *he* is running around in Savoie. Besides, if the match suits you, assuming that the man is honest, tender, tactful, delicate—such as you deserve—a hundred leagues more or less shouldn't change the intrinsic state of things. Remember too that this whole affair springs from that sentence you wrote me two years ago: *This Marquis you are so fond of—wouldn't he be a suitable husband for me?* What did I do? I answered: *Yes, certainly, he suits you, for you please him immensely, and he has everything essential to your happiness ...* I say no more, so that I will be scolded only in proportion to these few words.

But, I beg you, don't go off to England just like that; of all countries, it's the one I fear the most for the disposition of your mind. What you need is a little constraint and a great deal of amusement, and that's exactly what you won't find in that country. You are a marvelous person—sublime, gay; do you want to become singular and melancholy? It's bound to happen; you will not have the charm of being original, for there are many English demoiselles, of great wit and propriety, who travel alone, and who, when all's said and done, would admit, if they were honest, that they are not any happier than if they had stayed by their fireside. This friendship, this passion I have for you, which places me above all your friends, your parents—even yourself—will not let me speak otherwise to you, even though I risk seeing you scrutinize each word, each sentence of this letter (written very hastily), to prove to me that I don't know what I am talking about.

I am leaving for Hermenches. I have just escaped being killed: a wretched postilion caused my post chaise to be thrown from the height of a bridge into the river. Luckily I and my son had gotten down and were afoot, but I lost a great deal and it was all a great bother.

This city of Mézières rather pleases me; the Meuse amuses itself by winding its way around it. I watch it in fascination: each of these drops of water will pass into your country; some will carry you, others will serve to wash your feet, etc.; I am always tempted to give them messages for you. If one ever went bathing in Holland, who's to say whether I wouldn't throw myself into the river, in the hope of taking you by surprise?

Farewell, dear Agnes; even though you rail against me and against poor old d'Usson, who can't do anything about it, I am none the less very tenderly and very respectfully devoted to you.

254. *To Constant d'Hermenches, October 5–7, 1766*

Zuylen, Sunday

You will permit me, my dear friend, not to change this time from white to black like a madwoman. Your letter would only stand to profit from the closest scrutiny; a sincere friendship strongly and simply expressed is pure gold—or rather a substance a hundred times more precious.

Here is what I've done, what I've resolved, and what is in my heart. I am not jealous; I was stung for a moment, since I didn't think that the Marquis's soul contains such a great dose of tenderness that he couldn't give me all of it without my having too much; a moment, I say, only a moment—I am neither so vain nor so passionate as not to pardon quite easily such an insignificant offense. I had asked my father's permission a long time before I received your letter; so it's not hurt feelings that made me decide. I didn't urge him any more strongly after receiving the letter; I have spoken of it rarely and lightly. However, I have obtained permission, or just about. I am waiting for a letter from Mrs. Eliott; if she can receive me, I will go. I will not go alone, but with my brother. In six weeks I will become neither bizarre nor melancholy; I make no claim of being "singular." The extra distance from Utrecht to London between the Marquis and me will change nothing in our affairs if I do not want to change them.

After long reflections I wrote a very civil and very cheerful letter to the Marquis, in which I even apologize for what might have been sharp and brusque in my preceding one. However, I insisted that he burn all my old letters written a year ago when I thought that I would marry him shortly— letters that, in the light of all these delays, now seem ridiculous; I confirm my plan to make a little journey to England, and I tell him of the likelihood of his succeeding; I then tell him that you have told me of M. d'Usson's solicitations, and that I have asked you to suspend them, adding that if he had some reason to prefer that way of proceeding to the one involving M. Piccolomini he should please let me know. Just in case, I keep in a drawer, along with my hair ornaments and necklaces, the letter that was written for Rome; the only harm that has come to it is having spent some days next to my thigh, where it absorbed so much *eau d'arquebusade*[1] and drugs of all kinds that it could serve as a plaster for the Holy Father if he were so unfortunate as to tumble down from the Holy Seat, as I did from my stool.

---

1. A concoction for healing wounds.

I have spelled out quite precisely, I think, my management of my journey and of the Marquis; as for you, I hope that I will commit no more injustices, and neither thunder nor rail against you.

By now you must have received from me a letter that shows you that my mind is restored to its good sense, and my heart to its friendship—which, however, in all seriousness, it had never departed from; and I have never misjudged your friendship—it was merely its manners that displeased me a little.

To prove to you how much I respect it, I'm going confide to you something I have never told anyone: it isn't jealousy that torments me, it's the hundred thousand florins. When I asked for them, I was already uncomfortable about them at times, and at other times I thought they were almost owed to me; at present, they weigh upon me. I look at my brothers; I find that they have more need of such a sum than I do, and that they have more right to it. It would be impossible for my parents to give that much to all of us. It was surely not to Monsieur de Bellegarde that my mother intended her fortune to go; she is not buying with it a son-in-law who pleases her. Every day the household becomes more expensive to maintain—horses, journeys, etc. I would like to see my brothers get established without having to marry the daughters of East Indian traders; the more unselfish I see them with respect to me, the more I would like to be generous.[2] My parents do not speak of this at all; they seem content, and, I believe, no longer think about this dowry. But it's my turn now, and I think about it on their behalf. I was pleased, and I still am, at the idea of restoring the financial affairs of Monsieur de Bellegarde and his household, but this pleasure is troubled: the least display of luxury would distress me if it were to cost my father and mother any comfort. Am I not made to constitute a fortune rather than to pay my husband's debts? It seems to me that a very rich man, provided that he loved me a great deal, would suit me very well; I would insist that my parents give me each year no more than what was necessary to pay for my books, my cards, my letters ...

Goodnight; I am writing in bed, and my candle is going out. You would like to blame me, but you will at any rate hear me, and that's all I wish. Besides, if I become Madame de Bellegarde, I will put all these considerations aside and will, I hope, no longer see anything but the good sides; or, at least, I will be silent about the others.

One of the most important considerations, and one which continues to worry me sometimes, concerns the children. To have none at all would distress me; to have sickly ones would distress me yet more. Since I seem to be sensible and good-natured, people often confide rather strange things to

2. At issue is not merely Belle's income during her life. Her father's estate produced income enough for two daughters' dowries, and under terms like those of Mitie's dowry, it would continue to do so in the next generation; if van Tuyll gives a hundred thousand florins to Bellegarde it might not. See Letter 106, n. 3.

me; they know that they risk nothing by telling me everything, and they think that they might gain something by it. Sometimes it's a piece of advice, sometimes it's praise, other times pity. Anyway, people speak to me, and one remark leads to another; men speak to me as naturally—though without indecency—as they would to another man (my attraction to libertines is not increased by it). What ailments! What remedies! What dreadful consequences!

Fat Anthony's children[3] are as beautiful as his tales are nasty, and in proportion, he makes as many children as tales. I saw them today; they have been married for six years and my cousin is pregnant for the sixth time. I told them about your honors and your prosperity—that is, Compiègne, the cross, the choice of garrisons, and the hopes in general offered by the Minister's favor; as for advancement to come and the possibility of a little governorship, I don't say a word for fear of being indiscreet; one must boast of *what is now yours* and not of *what you will have*. That's a rule that I respect with regard to my friends, and that I always violate for myself.

You see how I speak of you to our friend by the little letter that you received because of me.

I'm going to call *yesterday* the day that in the other page I called *today*; this is the third evening that I take up this letter again on my way to bed. You think I need some constraint. Why? Do I make ill use of my liberty? When I am "singular," it is only to return from custom to reason.

Yesterday morning, I wanted to go see my cousins in town; there was some difficulty obtaining the carriage, and my brothers didn't think of offering to take me in the chaise; the weather was very fine; heat never bothers me. I start off on foot with my mother's chambermaid and the groom, and with the greatest of ease, without any fatigue, I arrive in Utrecht in an hour. Isn't that all very fine, very healthy, and was my visit any less pleasant than if I had arrived by carriage? Madame d'Athlone asked me to help her dress; my dress was hitched up as it had been during my journey; Mme Bentinck exclaimed about how short my skirts were. I look down and I see that having forgotten my underskirt, I had on only my petticoats; people found my absent-mindedness very funny. We sit down at table; during dessert somebody tells me some story or other; at an interesting point, I throw myself against the back of my chair to rock as I usually do. It was not constructed to sustain such a sudden movement; my feet, which were too close to the chair, slip forward, the heavy back tips and takes me with it and I fall completely over and pick myself up, and am back in my place, seated—all in the blink of an eye and without my thigh having even noticed the adventure that put it within a hairsbreadth of a relapse. My elbow remembers something of it, but it's nothing; we were in fits of laughter. Madame Bentinck is still laughing. For some time now I do nothing but fall.

3. Anthony Bentinck, whom d'Hermenches had called "fat Anthony" in Letter 251.

Let's talk about the more serious fall that you barely avoided. That postilion was destined to make you remember that *one cannot be happy in all things*. One would feel the loss of the belongings in your chaise, and the nuisance of it all, were it not for the relief at your having prudently got out of the chaise; that makes up for all the rest. I'm so happy to be able to picture you and your son safe and dry on the bank watching the chaise pitch over, and perhaps swearing a little at the poor postilion—whom the river was punishing enough—I'm so happy, I tell you, that I can't pay attention to the other things. —That sentence is very badly written. Your whole letter is simply one felicitous stroke of the pen.

I'm saving a few trifles for Friday; this letter bores me too much for me to make it longer. I'm beginning to write like a pig. At least for a while, in the name of God, let's drop all talk of marriage. In spite of everything I have said in this letter, and in the one that I sent you a week ago, it is very likely that I will marry Bellegarde, and with joy; so let me do as I please, and be at peace yourself.

Write me, you who write so well, and who love me so wholeheartedly.

255. *To Constant d'Hermenches, October 7, 1766*

If you notice the date, you will see that the same day has seen the end of my long letter and the beginning of this one. Let's hope that today's second one doesn't resemble the first! I admire you for not yet having broken off such a leaden correspondence. If we were to write for long in this tone, I would ask for a position with the Lieutenant of Police, because I would soon be capable only of writing court reports.

Tell me what our abductors and abductresses are doing in Lausanne. It is not often that one is both as stupid and as as mad as those five people. Madame de Nassau disgraces herself to such a point that it is no longer possible to see her. There has never been more indecent libertinage nor such scorn for public opinion,[1] and yet she always talked with me as if she were a veritable Lucretia;[2] I would answer nothing—nothing at all—, and it was up to her to interpret my silence. I haven't seen her at all for three months.

Mme de Hammerstein has just left; she was wearing a little hat that made us die laughing. I said that her husband is very fortunate that she has the virtue of her fifty years with the hat of fifteen; unfortunately the face goes with the virtue, and leaves the hat so far behind that one is astonished at seeing them together. I asked her for news of my look-alike, because she

1. The countess of Nassau Beverweerd. See Belle's Letter 157, where she mentions the gossip surrounding the birth of the countess's child.
2. A Roman noblewoman who committed suicide (c. 509 B.C.) after being raped. Her name became the symbol of outraged virtue.

comes from Spa.³ She told me that indeed there was a lady from Hainaut who always reminded her of Mademoiselle de Zuylen; moreover, she claims that I am prettier. One must be careful in talking to me about resemblance; I have become insupportably vain on that point since La Tour has often been seeing Mme d'Etioles⁴ in my face, and the beautiful Princesse de Rohan in my portrait. For two months, now, he has been working on the second one, and he paints me every morning, all morning long, so that I do nothing at all except inform myself about the court at Versailles and all sorts of things about Paris. We also conducted more reasoned conversations; he's an intelligent man, and very courteous. —I said the second portrait; I mean the second one finished; I told you, I think, that the first was destroyed; I hope that he will let this one live, because it really is alive; to efface it would be a murder. His obsession is wanting to put into it everything I say and think and feel, and he's killing himself. To compensate him, I converse with him almost the entire day, and this morning I very nearly let myself be kissed.

By the way, why do you tell me your thoughts about the Meuse? I immerse myself every day in cold water. Some time ago I took this folly too far and came down with a bad fever—it could still happen that I might forget myself in the water, and that's dangerous. One day when I had received a letter from you I failed to notice that the water was freezing my feet and sending all the heat to my heart and head; I kept reading peacefully on, and when I was done, I was most uncomfortable. I'm afraid the same thing might happen again when I think of you. I will ask each drop: Have you seen him? Were you his mirror?

Tell me whether you lost any papers. I would hope that you had lost only my letters. For some time now they have become so leaden that it seems to me they would sink straight to the the bottom, and truly there is nothing I would less like to fish out.

Tell me about your son. I wish you would take care not to be too much in disfavor with this country, at least with those who can help or hinder. Any ill humor of yours, too freely displayed, could have a disagreeable influence for your son. But if, being in favor with Monsieur de Choiseul, you could transplant him advantageously, perhaps you would be rendering him a service. I understand nothing of all this—it's something that passed though my head and that I wanted to tell you just in case. I have also been thinking about the little governorship; if it's not a very good thing in itself, it would perhaps be prudent not to worry about it, lest that new arrangement disturb and damage your prospects of a more considerable advancement.

We are being visited by the beautiful Mme de Schoonenberg, whom you saw here one day without noticing her.⁵ However, her face is charming, and

3. The Mme d'Orchival of Letter 251.
4. Madame de Pompadour, favorite of Louis XV. La Tour had painted her portrait in 1754.
5. See Belle's Letter 103 of July 1764. Mme de Schoonenberg's husband had killed her father, wounded her mother, and fled to Germany.

the dignity of her mother-in-law is amazing. I have never seen anything so close to perfection; you would be astonished and charmed by her reason, her wit, her pleasant gaiety, the many amusing and unstudied remarks she makes, which, in spite of so many misfortunes and a background of darkest sadness, animate the conversation and entertain everyone.

If I were the Prince of Orange, and married a young princess, I would ask Mme de Schoonenberg to take an apartment near the Court, without a title, or any restrictions on her freedom; I would make this position so attractive that her family's interest would force her to accept, and my wife would go talk with her every day for an hour or two. That would be a good bit better than the court prudes—the ladies-in-waiting and maids of honor—with their protocol, their stupidity, and their adulation. The princess would be a little more sensible for it, and the little princes a little better brought up. You saw her when she had just arrived from her journey, but you didn't really see her; she was tired and very troubled.

Goodbye, my dear d'Hermenches. I am very pleased; the spell is broken; my pen was able to trace other words than our eternal refrain.

257. *From Constant d'Hermenches, October 28, 1766*

Hermenches

Here I am, perched in my woods, excellent Agnes. I admire the way the imagination always knows how to bend toward the principal object of our interest. When I was on the banks of the Meuse, it seemed to me that I had only to throw myself into it to be near you, to touch you; my thoughts followed its course, and it was as hard for them to leave you as it is for a river to flow back up toward its source. Today, a hundred leagues farther away, in the steepest of terrain, here I am—nonetheless at your feet. In this lofty atmosphere I approach regions created for you, and (to speak altogether oracularly) it seems to me that you speak to me from the height of Olympus, from Parnassus, from all those dwelling-places consecrated to beings superior to humanity.

That is the advantage that I have over that mortal[1] who says, quite materially, that he is distressed by the delays that keep him from holding in his arms one whom I will always hold close in my heart. I rejoice in the portion that destiny has given me: your friendship, your letters, your trust; I have only to sit under the first pine tree and open my portfolio. The Pope, a priest, a marriage bed, have no right to come trouble me and make me find the present moment unbearable by the expectation of more rapturous moments. Your presence would strain the reach of my fine metaphysics, and the beautiful portrait by La Tour could not offer you more charmingly to my

---

1. Bellegarde.

eyes than you are painted in my mind; I see you, I hear you as perfect; I want to feel myself perfectly happy ... You must at least admit, Agnes, that I deserve to be, with such a lofty virtue.

You have no idea of what is to be called "countryside." In Holland, your well-groomed landscape always presents you with a framed picture that constricts the imagination: straight paths, symmetrical vistas, a big town or a city in the line of view marks where you are. Here, enormous mountains, dark forests, abysses, always leave my mind free to roam. This is Nature emerging from chaos; these are vast solitudes. I have to make an effort to remember, to believe that there is a Paris, that there are other men; and if I encounter some animate being, he always seems to me unique of his kind. And thus I pass whole days wandering in these surroundings of mine, with my dogs, a gun, a book in my pocket that I haven't even taken out, because this kind of existence has occupied me enough by itself; and I assure you that I have rediscovered within myself the seed of that life of the earliest ages. I understand the expression: *content as a savage.* I say to myself then: why all those contortions of politeness, of politics, of duty, of ambition? Why those fine clothes, those elaborate meals; why those furnishings, those liveries, those equipages? Would I not be happier in these comfortable clothes, staff in hand, gathering vegetables according to my appetite, and cooking them by the fire? No one is astonished at how I am dressed, no one pays attention to my comings and goings; the rustics whom I pass say to me: "God keep you," and I say in turn, "God be blessed, He who alone protects me!"—Agnes, this tirade is quite bizarre, but upon my honor, it springs from the very moment, and it is all felt by me just as it is expressed.

I return, then, to the château; it's like a curtain rising when I return to those sweet-voiced women who were afraid of the sun, the humidity, the rough roads, etc. I find myself in a comfortable armchair, and soon the conversation (which is like that of any group of people in the world), the sound of a harpsichord, a few voices ... restore me to ordinary sociability, and my savagery disappears like the backdrop of Armida's cave;[2] or else, as today, I run into my study to leap from the depths of the wilderness to Agnes's knees. I expect you will have experiences like this at Les Marches. You will find overwhelming beauties there which will, I'm certain, produce in you entirely new thoughts; the view of the Alps will transform you, in spite of yourself, into a dryad, a hamadryad, a Diana; you will have a new and unique existence, and perhaps one day you will write me letters yet madder than my own ...

But let's say a little word about what might procure such letters for me. Without infringing the resolution to sue no more, I can send you this letter from the Marquis; by the simplicity of his report, you will judge of the sim-

2. Armida is the enchantress in Torquato Tasso's *Gerusalemme Liberata* (*Jerusalem Delivered*) (1581). Her magical palace collapses into ruins.

plicity of his soul. Cool letters do no harm, but I'm afraid that he is right about Piccolomini. I couldn't resist answering him, "Don't you know that women are cleverer than we are only in what can be dealt with step by step?"

I am horribly distressed at all these obstacles that my dearest friends are encountering, and I find both of you sublime at not being more unreasonable in such circumstances; especially you, divine Agnes, who should never have expected that the Pope would disrupt your fair destiny for even an instant. Pardon me, but I cannot stop these reflections, useless and annoying as they must be for you.

Besides, why shouldn't I speak to you of the Marquis—who is to embrace you some day, and whom I know—, while you speak to me of this painter, whom I do not know, and who, I hope, will never kiss you, in spite your being tempted? You recount this temptation with a grace that is yours alone, like that of your countenance. I take the greatest interest in his enterprise; I also like to see in you that sort of enthusiasm for his work. One is happy in every kind of enthusiasm. But Agnes, that wretched self-seeking, which so degrades man, would make me take more interest in the doings of your celebrated artist if I could flatter myself that the least of the sketches of your likeness was destined for me. Ah! then I too would kiss it! ... You don't tell me whether he is using pastels; I would be sorry to hear it, since they have only a passing brilliance, while one must paint you for posterity; otherwise it's a theft.[3]

Since I have been in Switzerland I have lived only in my woods, and I have enjoyed the pleasure of having no set hours for anything. I hear talk of several Dutch colonies; there are the Bouillier[4] demoiselles who sing your praises; a Mlle Mauclerc whom I had rather disliked at the Hague, whom I had almost liked at Beverwijk because you had (I think) told me good things about her, and whom I don't know how I will like here; your Utrecht abductees who have left again and whom I didn't see at all. No one here knows their story; would you like to tell it to me? It seems to me that people found a certain M. Testas rather amiable, as well as a Mme Abbema; there is also a Count of Nassau—isn't he something of a hothead? He woos all the girls, and attaches himself to the least appealing of them; he gives himself out to be a suitor. Does he have any fortune? I think he's the adoptive child of an uncle, who will leave him no more than his father did. If the Countess of Nassau is behaving scandalously, you do well not to see her any more; I thought that that couldn't last; when a woman is no smarter than she is it's unfortunate if she's given to love-affairs ...

---

3. La Tour was famous as pastelist, and he did use pastels for Belle's portrait. Its beauty seems to have survived.

4. Daughters of a well-known preacher living in Utrecht. In later letters (in the fall of 1767) d'Hermenches and Belle will mock them unmercifully for their playwriting efforts.

The little note from the dear Widow is much too pretty to give me pleasure. A Parisian lady who cared nothing at all about me would have written no differently; these are prescribed, formulaic phrases. I'm not at all pleased; Nevertheless, I will answer her, and with all the affection and attachment that I have for her. And you still believe, Agnes, that a woman who knows how to twine phrases like that wouldn't find herself perfectly happy in France?

They talk a great deal in Lausanne about a Madame Hervey, sister of the Lord Lieutenant of Ireland; she is beautiful and amiable; the Prince of Wurtemberg is enraptured by her. I still haven't seen any of all that. It's a curious thing, this mania that brings to this little hole of a city the most exceptional people from all the corners of Europe.[5] That has to give one a rather bad opinion of the way of life in all the other countries; for this one is full of inconveniences. The daily routine is boring; one must do without many things—and in spite of all that, everyone comes here. Look at Alexandre de Golofkine, back from Berlin, more passionately attached than ever to his country estate.

The King of France has declared that he wants nothing changed in the constitutions of his realm, which exclude Protestants from office;[6] thus, no more talk of a governorship for me. I will follow your advice, and will not pursue it. I also think that for my son's sake, I should not make myself unpleasant in Holland. Please believe that at the Hague I allow myself to say only things that are no worse than what other people say; if I were to change my language, it would be too inconsistent. How fortunate we are, divine Agnes, when someone with more wit than we have deigns to pay attention to our affairs! You make me feel this good fortune very keenly; everything comes together in my heart to chain me forever at your feet.

258. *From Constant d'Hermenches, November 22, 1766*

[*Part of this letter is missing. See Letter 262 for what happened to it.*]

... nor at her ease, but decently, and cordially, with those people, who curse that country themselves, and who go to Paris whenever they can. That poor Widow![1] It was hardly worth waiting so long, doing something extraordinary, and displeasing her family and her whole country to do no better than that!

---

5. In her novel of 1785, *Lettres écrites de Lausanne*, Isabelle de Charrière will use this cosmopolitanism of Lausanne as an essential aspect of her characters' situation.
6. For this use of the term "constitution" see C. B. A. Behrens, *The Ancien Régime* 96–98. It does not refer to any written document but rather to fundamental laws, or "maxims, with which all legislation was supposed to be in accord; from the early seventeenth century on, they were referred to as forming the 'constitution.'"
1. Mme Geelvinck is about to marry the marquis de Chasteler.

I see that this whole letter must be only about marriages; I must tell you then that Count Lolo of Nassau is marrying a young lady who has neither fortune nor beauty nor talents nor birth. I was asked my opinion about it; I said that she has so little to lose that she might as well indulge her fancy and become a Countess. She will be a sensible and orderly wife; poverty will bother her less than it would someone else, and even while she is sharing the lot of that crackpot, at worst she will produce some little beggars who will be related to the Stadholder. He says that he is twenty-six, that he is his own master, that he wants to live here like his wife's parents, with two thousand florins of income.

Good night, Agnes; I only wanted to provide an envelope, and here is a whole volume. Since you have, for all practical purposes, become an Englishwoman, what would I have had to say to you if my lucky star had not sent me those two singular marriages? I think about you continually, and whatever impression you make in that island, believe that no one will ever appreciate you as much as I do, nor with more reason. I am at your feet.

261. *From Constant d'Hermenches, December 12, 1766*

Lausanne

I slip into the Marquis's letter, charming Agnes; like him, I'm telling you that I wish you many amusements and much satisfaction in your journey. But I'm not as good-natured as he is; I'm grumbling furiously at your silence—no, I'm not grumbling, I'm merely moaning. For at heart, I'm sure that you haven't forgotten me; I'm moaning as one does over a privation, not over a theft. Give all your time to the country where you are; there'll be opportunity for you to make it up to me.

I'm leaving for Geneva; I want to see that incensed citizenry,[1] and Voltaire. I'm at your feet.

This is my third letter to England.

᎒ *Belle went to England in November 1766, accompanied by her brother Ditie and her maid, Dorothea Phlügerin. She was first the guest of General and Mrs. Eliott in London, then of her paternal cousin Reiniera and her husband, Johan Bentinck, at their country house in Surrey.*

Belle's expectations about her visit to England were grounded in an idea of England—an Anglophilia—that had come to offer serious competition to the cultural hegemony of France in the European mentality. "Reason is free

1. In the course of the eighteenth century there were power struggles in Geneva between the bourgeois Représentants and the aristocratic Négatifs. The uprising of 1766 gained some concessions for the Représentants.

here and walks her own way," said Voltaire.[2] *In his* Lettres philosophiques
*(1734) he had portrayed England as a country that—unlike France—tole-
rated religious diversity, respected individual freedom, fostered a flourish-
ing commerce, valued its artists and writers, and permitted the kind of un-
trammeled pursuit of the sciences that had produced Newton's work. It was
the land of Pope and Locke; of Shakespeare (whom Voltaire introduced to a
French public that was scarcely aware of him); and of inoculation against
smallpox (of which we will hear more later). These themes resonate in the
discussion between Belle and d'Hermenches about the respective merits of
England and France.*

*Once in England, Belle found it a relief to be unknown and to have left
her reputation as a wit—with all the resentment it had engendered—behind
her in Holland. Her social position gave her access to the highest levels of
English society, and she was presented at court. When she had a minor illness it was the queen's physician who treated her. In the drawing-rooms of
London, men gathered about her, eager to tell her about Shakespeare or the
British system of government.*

262. *To Constant d'Hermenches, January, 2-6, 1767*

Curzon Street, Mayfair

You are quite right not to grumble, my dear d'Hermenches; don't moan,
either—some day I will make up for my omissions. You know what it is to
arrive in a big city that is all new, full of all kinds of novelty; where there
are a thousand things to see, a thousand visits to make, and long letters to
write that one has solemnly promised as one bade farewell to the parental
home. That, it seems to me, is a very good apology; I reserve another to
serve in case of need, if by chance you weren't satisfied by the first.

Still, I want to say it: I didn't know how to write to you. The whole subject of the Marquis is becoming so murky for me that I'm afraid to touch it.
I don't know what to wish for, I don't know what to fear—or rather I sense
that I wish for nothing and that I fear everything—the success of the solicitation as much as its foundering. The Marquis' passivity, your own reflections, the enjoyment—sweeter every day—of my liberty have extinguished
my former wishes. Besides, I haven't seen the Marquis in so long that I
have almost forgotten him; absence has its ordinary effect on me, and there
is no man among those I respect whom I couldn't consider for marriage just
as well as the Marquis. Nothing, then, is so cold as my desires—or rather, I
have no more desires; and I don't think that the laconic assurances of admiration and love that he makes to me in two words—since he finds it unneces-

---

2. Original in English; from a letter Voltaire wrote in April 1728. Quoted in Peter Gay,
Voltaire's Politics: The Poet as Realist 33.

sary to say more—I don't think, I say, that his two words, or even four, will awake what is now asleep. Besides, the influence that my example has apparently had on Mme Geelvinck puts me in a bad humor with myself and my marriage.[1] The original idea—that I would be tranquilly and agreeably happy in that old château, and freer than in any other where I might live as a married woman—still remains with me and combats my coldness and my bad humor; but I am happy and free at present ... I no more know what my own determination will be than I know the Pope's.

Enough on this subject. I can't make up my mind to write to the Marquis; I don't know what to say to him. But just notice, I beg you, that it isn't my fault that M. de Piccolomini has undertaken that unfortunate solicitation; the Marquis's letter remained a long time in my pocket, and presently I think it's in M. Rendorp's desk.

Piccolomini had already been refused before we had even asked him to inquire. I fear the Pope's "Yes," because I don't know what I would like to do; I fear his "No," because it would irrevocably destroy a plan from which I expected my happiness, and which may still be what suits me. I fear everything, then—or rather I would be be afraid if I were willing to think about it—but what good does thinking do? Besides, I don't have the time. I'm enjoying myself very much; I'm receiving a warm welcome—from foreigners, from the English, from everybody—and I am in all respects extremely pleased with my journey. I would have told you about it more definitely before I left if I had had any leisure between the resolution to leave and my actual leaving; but six days before my departure, I still didn't know whether I would leave. You can judge whether the arrangements were rushed and my time precious.

Your long letter addressed to Utrecht was sent to me here; it gave me very great pleasure. The second came directly to me, full of the best reflections on the most ridiculous marriages. Will you scold me? Will you applaud me? I had written to Rendorp everything I could think of to try to break up the unhappy business of Mme Geelvinck; your letter arrives, I read and reread it. I use up my whole inkpot to blot out sentences that might have been displeasing, and in that state I send it to Rendorp,[2] saying that I rely on his judgment and his good faith to use it, if possible, in a way that might be helpful to our friend without being in any way unpleasant for you or for me. I still have no answer. On all sides, they tell me that the Marquis de Chasteler is a self-interested dolt, and that she is committing a wretched blunder. I was not privy to anyone's confidences. I have some hope that the three-month law[3] for these marriages could be salutary for the Widow. Her reason

1. Mme Geelvinck is about to marry a certain marquis de Chasteler, who is regarded as a young fool. Belle and d'Hermenches consider this marriage a disaster for the Widow.
2. This apparently accounts for the missing part of Letter 258.
3. Dutch law required that in the case of a marriage with a Catholic, the three proclamations must extend over three months instead of the three weeks required for an ordinary marriage.

and her friends and her motherly heart will have time to speak. People say that she is often melancholy. —You must not think that I ever take such liberties with your letters without asking for your permission except in this one case. But the case was pressing, and your arguments were so different from mine and so likely to make an impression, that I would have thought myself culpable in your eyes if I hadn't made use of them. If Rendorp shows the letter to my friend, it will be only on condition of secrecy, and she has never broken any promise.

Good night, my dear d'Hermenches. There are fewer words than cross-ings-out in this ugly letter, thanks to a horrible headache and two little girls who have involved me in their games *the whole time* I've been writing. It was too late for the post on Friday; I can only add a few words, my eyes will permit no more. My headache was nothing other than a rheumatism that kept me to my bed for three days; I'm much better and *in very good spirits.*[4]

My compliments to the Marquis. Mme de Welderen asked me to tell you that you had forgotten her *as if she was never be born.*[5] There would be no great harm in that; one could do without her very easily. She is more false, stupid, and crazy than one is allowed to be all at the same time.

You say in your last note, which accompanies the Marquis's letter: *This is the third letter I'm sending to England.* I received one via Utrecht, another directly, and then the note; look to see whether that's all you sent.

At any rate, count on my word that it is impossible to read in your letter what must not be read: it was blotted out with ink, which was then dried, and then with more ink, and dried again; I looked, and tried, and examined; the devil himself couldn't catch a syllable of it.

Tuesday, January 6, 1767

I would have a thousand pretty things to tell you, but I fear for one eye, to which the wrath of rheumatism has fixed itself. I didn't know that one could have such pain in the left eyebrow.

I wanted to talk about you with the Marquis de Fitz-James, but he belonged neither to the Compiègne camp nor to the Villers-Cotterêts cafés.

263. *From Constant d'Hermenches, January 6, 1767*

Lausanne

Although you continue to confound me by a cruel silence since your departure for England, I continue, dear Agnes, to complain to you, and I continue to cherish you and to care about your lot with the warmth that you

---

4. English in the original.

5. Mme de Welderen (née Anne Whitwell) wife of the minister plenipotentiary from the United Provinces to Great Britain. Apparently her French is shaky: Belle's quotation of her is "comme si elle n'avait jamais été naître," which should be "comme si elle n'était jamais née."

alone deserve. The the poor Marquis's sentiments are of such a decency—it touches me to my very soul. He reproaches himself a thousand times over with his perhaps being an obstacle to a beautiful future for you, and his sister laments it. As for me—I continue to believe that he alone is worthy of you, and that one must take all measures to get that dispensation. Not all of England could bring together such qualities as I know the two of them possess to make you happy.

The Cardinal's letter is a great in-folio document written in Italian, in which, with all the elegant turns of that language, he says that one must send him the names of the Marquis and of the *Illustrissime Dame Olandeze,* and he promises all his *szforzo* to obtain this *gratissime* dispensation from the Holy Father.

Agnes, what more can I say? You are indifferent toward this whole continent; is it simply to distress me that you don't write at all? Can it be that you don't have the time? Unfortunately, even that reason cannot come to my aid; I don't know what to think or believe. Shall I speak to you of the uprisings in Geneva, where I have just been? Or of Voltaire's new tragedy,[1] which we are about to perform? It would all seem insipid to you. I must be silent then, assuring you that if you forget your friends you are more cruel than anyone else, because it is impossible for them to do the same to you.

I am at your feet, with ever the same sentiments.

264. *From Constant d'Hermenches, January 23, 1767*

Lausanne

I too was once in England, fair stranger, and I had more business there than you, because a man always has more business than a woman, even for his pleasures! And even if you had as much business as I, you are cleverer: you write more easily than I can think and more quickly than I can read. I am asking, however, whether you received my letters? And whether I was not more concerned with my absent friend than with all those things that distract you? Say, rather, that I do not mean to you what you mean to me; say that someone else—or several others—have taken my place, and then you will be speaking truly, and you will rejoin the circle of ordinary humanity! I will love you none the less, my very lovable friend; I will only be a little less humbled before you, because my kind of friendship will be able to compensate a little for the immensity of advantages and perfections that you have over me. At last, however, I have news from you; I thank you for it as for the keenest pleasure I could receive.

Here is another long Italian letter; since this one is on finer paper, and can

---

1. *Les Scythes* [*The Scythians*], presented in Lausanne in March 1767 in the theatre of Mon-Repos, which belonged to d'Hermenches' sister.

be shared, I send it to you. I tremble for the little note the Marquis sends, if sincerity doesn't make up for the lack of the grandiloquence that perhaps I myself would use in writing to a fiancée such as you. But here is my refrain: it's this Marquis, such as he is, whom I believe to be the husband who will make you the most constantly happy. Besides, if other thoughts occur to you, aren't you still free?

I can't believe that you are really enjoying yourself in London—what *I* would say was enjoying oneself—which would be finding congenial people, light-hearted people, and easy kinds of pleasure. That you are fêted, entertained, immensely distracted and sought-after, I have no doubt; but tell me, in good conscience, are you entirely satisfied with the way you are appreciated? I know Milord Fitz-James very well, but I think that he hasn't been able to tell you anything particular about me; he isn't at all one of those men known to belong to the best circles, and I'm not aware that he belongs to them in Paris.

Since you speak to me so well—or so ill—of Mme de Welderen, I ask you, my dear friend to tell her that as surely as *I am not died,*[1] I wrote to her twice without hearing from her, and at the beginning of 1765 I wrote her a very long letter from Paris, very detailed, on my establishment in France, and my departure from Holland. And while I'm on the subject, would you, charming girl, be so good as to ask Lady Ailesbury quite expressly why she treats me so badly—she who received me so well in England? I had the honor of writing her also in that same year 1765 from Lille in Flanders to compliment her on her husband's post of Secretary of State, and to tell her that I was serving in Flanders; since then, a hundred persons have promised to send her my humble salutations, but I have heard nothing from her.

Do not take it amiss, but I count a little more on the Batavian sluggishness of your confidant Rendorp than on all the ink you have thrown on my letter; what effect do you expect a letter will have on the mind of a woman who is slow and timid, and who has already made her decision?[2] She is going to detest me if she hears that I am criticizing her marriage, and she will be in despair at thinking that she could encounter me in Flanders. I am writing her a little note today, out of sheer politeness, that she will regard as utterly false if that ink-spattered letter is known to her. I had written about her to the Duc d'Arenberg, to introduce her to him, and to repay that good soul what I owe her for the time when we needed her. This is what he answers me: "I am charmed by the news you send me that the languid marquis[3] with the black eyebrow will come back to us escorting an amiable

---

1. D'Hermenches is mimicking the fractured French of Mme de Welderen as Belle did in Letter 262: he has written "je ne suis pas mourir" instead of "je ne suis pas mort."
2. The woman in question is Mme Geelvinck.
3. The marquis de Chasteler, who was regarded as a disastrous match for Mme Geelvinck.

woman; Paris can do without her, and here we have great need of her. If she had wished, she could have made a more brilliant match, but one cannot say that she is committing a blunder. That woman found Holland very tedious; the idea of establishing herself here, where she would be much fêted for a while, influenced her decision at least as much as the charms of the Marquis."

I leave you, Agnes, to go play *Rose et Colas*,[4] and you are going to see *King Lear*.

I think this is the fourth letter I'm sending to England.

265. *To Constant d'Hermenches, January 28-29, 1767*

Wednesday, at midnight

Here, read my letter to the Marquis and send it. Don't tell me that it's long and badly written; I know it. What I like about it is that it isn't dry, nor is it likely to hurt his feelings. I finished writing it yesterday, but I didn't find the time to seal it or to write you. Here as everywhere, I have too much pleasure and too little time; everything amuses me, everything catches my attention, and I can hardly tear myself away from the present pleasure to pass to the next amusement. Really, I find myself quite at ease here, and I am behaving well. I'm not treated as any great intellect, and I keep myself a hundred leagues away from any display of wit; if any one suspects me of it, I interrupt him at once. I have neither any reputation to sustain, nor any annoying prejudice to combat; nothing is known of me except as I speak. I talk to a few foreigners; with the English, usually, I merely ask questions and listen. They seem to find me generally rather pretty, good-natured, and quite sensible.

I have just been to a gathering at Madame de Welderen's; I played a few hands of my game of piquet with her husband. We had two Frenchmen there whose names I have already forgotten, although they were handsome; Madame de Masseran[1] was enchanted; they never stopped talking, and burst into great roars of laughter without knowing why. It was a dreadful din that reduced me to speechlessness; I amused myself by comparing this French group with the tables around us, where people said nothing because they had nothing to say. I'm not sure, but it seems to me that I would prefer the nation that leaves me as I am, and amuses me hardly at all, to the one that pesters me more often than it amuses me.

A little more politeness would do well here. Yesterday I was on the staircase of the Opera, all alone and feeling quite awkward at not being able to follow the lady with whom I had come—her chaise was leaving, and mine

---

4. A comic opera by Sedaine, with music by Monsigny (1764).
1. Wife of the Spanish ambassador to London.

had not come. My distress and anxiety showed in my face. There was a crowd of lackeys and lit torches around me; I saw twenty officers in uniform come down the stairs, all of whom passed by without one of them offering to help me out, and I went back up to ask a man of my acquaintance to help me leave. This behavior is so ordinary that the women get annoyed when they are treated otherwise. The other day General Langlais gave his seat to a woman in a crowded meeting-place; she took it without thanking him. He saw another woman very tired of standing up; he went to find a chair for her; she took it without thanking him. By the way, he knows you, this General Langlais; he says that you have a great deal of wit, and that you are extremely amiable. I see him nearly every day. He speaks as you do of our poor friend's suitor.[2]

Thursday, at midnight

I'm in a foul humor; all my philosophy cannot overcome it; I am in a bad mood like the most commonplace woman, and for the most commonplace reason. I spent all day having my hair done; I got dressed this morning to run errands about town, then had my hair done; and got dressed again for dinner and had my hair done; and dressed once again for the ball this evening and had my hair done. All those people, all that fuss, all that trouble getting me an invitation! I have not yet seen the ball, nor the room in Soho that all Europe speaks of.[3] Mme de Malzan writes me this morning that she will accompany me. While she is a very good woman, at this moment she seems to me quite ridiculous. At eleven o'clock she sends me word that she has no invitation, that she can't go. Then why did the silly woman offer to go with me? I would have found another lady, or else I wouldn't have spent the day getting dressed only to get undressed again without having left my room. I think it would become me to endure this disappointment with an heroic indifference, but—with all due respect to what becomes me—I let things be as they are: I am extremely annoyed.

Now to cheer myself up a little, what shall I tell you? I certainly won't bother to refute your letter and prove that I am not forgetting you at all; I think that is self-evident. Why not talk to me about Geneva? That is certainly always interesting; as for Voltaire and his tragedy, it is true that that would suit my present frame of mind about as well as a blue suit with a green vest. There is a Marquis de Caraccioli, who has a devilish wit and who is not the one who wrote *La Jouissance de soi-même*.[4] He's the only intellect to have impressed me in a long time. He is neither young nor handsome, and he speaks French rather badly, so he is no charmer—you may believe me about that. He has an abstracted and casual air that I like to see

2. Yet another reference to the marquis de Chasteler, suitor of Mme Geelvinck.
3. Probably Carlisle House in Soho Square, famous for its splendid ballroom.
4. There are two different Marquis de Caraccioli: the one Belle has met is an ambassador to London; the other is the author of *La Jouissance de soi-même* [The enjoyment of oneself].

along with wit; he doesn't advertise himself, he makes no ado about his wit, and yet he speaks a great deal. Madame de Welderen said to me the other day: "That Caraccioli is a great chatterer!" "I beg your pardon, Madame," I said. "I told him that just the other day." "You were wrong, Madame." "Yes, that's true, he isn't a chatterer, but he does talk a great deal." She is sometimes jealous of me on her husband's account, to the point of making herself ridiculous in public. I pretend to see nothing; I am polite, and go my way. She gossips about me in a fine correspondence with Madame de Degenfeld, and then comes with a sour smile to tell me all about it; this woman is really too stupid. The Comte de Welderen will take me to Lord Chesterfield's.[5] Hume is in Scotland;[6] I would like to see Milord Chatham,[7] but he is not to be seen. If Madame de Welderen hadn't become bored in the House of Lords on the day after the opening of Parliament, I would have heard two speeches of Lord Chatham; he quarreled with Lord Temple.[8] It was the most curious thing in the world—a unique event for me. But Madame de Welderen, who understood nothing about either the subject or the eloquence, was impatient for her dinner. After hearing three noble lords speak with a kind of affectation particular to that language, and with very little eloquence, we had to leave. The question was interesting; the King had forbidden the export of wheat because of the extreme shortage. The opposition said that this action was illegal, and therefore ought to be censured; the ministers' party called it indispensable and therefore good, although irregular. I would be charmed to see the Queen elsewhere than in a gloomy and tedious drawing-room; of the Princes and Princesses, there isn't one that I'm curious about, but the Queen seems to me very pleasant.[9]

A few days before my little illness, I went to a gathering at Lady Harrington's;[10] she urged me to stay for supper; I accepted; everybody left, and I remained with Milady and her daughter, a middle-aged officer, and the Marquis Fitz-James. Milord March was invited, but he was leaving; I said to him, "Milord, see how out of place a fifth person is here; couldn't I find some pretext to go home?" He said no, and remained. Lord Harrington was having a slight attack of gout and was not with us; I suppose he was taking

5. Philip Dormer Stanhope, earl of Chesterfield (1694–1773), English diplomat and writer. He was the recipient of Samuel Johnson's memorable rebuff: "Is not a Patron, my Lord, one who looks with unconcern on a man struggling for life in the water, and, when he has reached ground, encumbers him with help?"

6. In April, in Letter 271, she will recount a visit with David Hume.

7. William Pitt the Elder (1708–78), created earl of Chatham in 1766, called "The Great Commoner." He was famous as an orator. His leadership during the Seven Years' War contributed much to England's success and to France's embarrassment.

8. Richard Temple Grenville, William Pitt's brother-in-law.

9. The king was George III, and his queen was Charlotte von Mecklenburg.

10. Lady Harrington, one of the beauties of her time, was notorious even by Casanova's standards; he said that she was known as "the stable-yard Messalina." See J. Rives Childs, *Casanova: A Biography Based on New Documents* 178–79.

supper in his room. Lady Amelia, another daughter—I won't say of Milord, but of Lady Harrington—had given a signal to her lover (whom she was to marry the next day, and whom she is no longer going to marry), and they had left together; we heard no more about them. Do you not find that things have already taken on a rather strange air? It was proposed that we go into Milady's chamber for supper; I stop to look for my fan with General Chomly.[11] The others leave. I try to leave; the door has been closed. I'm annoyed; I pull on it; I feel it's being held, and I open it. Not knowing what this ridiculous game may be all about, I take a long look at the cavalier and the lady—and I saw that it was a game that I was having no part in.

We finally arrived in Milady's *dressing-room*.[12] How oddly it was furnished! A great big screen; a worn carpet, old curtains; uncomfortable chairs, two big, heavy, ugly beds; but there were so many pretty candelabra, and clocks, and dolls, and jewelry cases; so many rich little odds and ends on one of the tables! All of these were, no doubt, presents. I sat down on one of the beds; it was hardened by time and frequent use. We waited a long time for supper; supper came, and the conversation became so equivocal—or rather, I should say, so unequivocal—that I didn't know how things stood. No silence I might preserve, I thought, could be deep enough. I rose several times—for my gloves, for a cloak; finally, at two o'clock, I absolutely insisted on leaving; I ran as if fleeing. Milord March ran after me and suggested, even urged, that I let him take me home; he had a carriage, I a chaise, and he assured me very seriously and with honest intentions (I suppose) that I would arrive home more comfortably and quickly. Nothing more would have been needed to complete that revel but for me to accept that ride. The next day, I encountered him, and I told him that such a supper was all very well for one time—but no more.

The women here are very reserved and rather sullen in company; the men are used to that. If you are a little gayer, a little freer, you find that your foot is being pressed, your hand or arm is being squeezed when you least expect it; and this perhaps at the very first meeting. —I'm talking about the dandies, the young fops. There is an infinite variety of manners in London; so far I see only a quarter of it all, and I can only guess at another quarter. Goodbye; I must close.

266. *To Constant d'Hermenches, February 9–10, 1767*

London

Rendorp has had better sense than I; he judged that since advice was useless it was cruel, and he has not shown your letter.

---

11. General James Cholmondeley (1708–75).
12. English in original.

I am just returning from the Princesse de Masseran's with Monsieur and Madame de Welderen. Today she was polite; sometimes she is as jealous as a tiger, and tears me to shreds with her eyes, and says and writes that I am a coquette, that I like married men, that I have no interest in women, and a hundred thousand other stupidities. Other times one might say that she is rather kindhearted; the King joked with her yesterday about the Count's escorting me there and back, and asked her if she wasn't jealous; today she tells me all about it with a laugh. This is all a maze of shabby little banalities that I'm ashamed to recount to you. When I arrived home, I found your letter, which I swallowed in one gulp, and then I turned the sheet over and over, and was vexed that it was only four pages. I will convey your compliments to the fat Countess between two quadrilles, and to Lady Ailesbury between two masked dances. The latter, in spite of the enthusiasm she inspired at the Hague, pays no attention to the Dutch. She may converse at home, but in company all she does is play cards; I don't know why she was so admired. I dined one day, in a rather chill atmosphere, at the home of Lady Holderness, who is a relative of mine; fortunately those civilities are more of a nuisance to me than an amusement, so I'm very glad that people dispense with them. I'm nodding off, I'm dreaming. Goodbye until tomorrow; it's half past one.

Tuesday morning, February 10

Last night I didn't want to open the letter from M. de Bellegarde, for fear of waking myself up and beginning to think again. I have just read it, and it's very good; I'm very pleased with it, and I'll send you a nice letter to forward to him.

You ask me if I am entirely satisfied with the way I'm appreciated here; yes, entirely. I am appreciated just the way I wanted to be, in a manner that I find comfortable. Each person finds in me only as much wit as he wants to find, because I show only as much as I am asked for; that is, I only show the *kind* of wit I am asked to show, and without my needing to hide, no one knows me better than he wants to. It seems to me that nobody dislikes me except Madame de Welderen; at gatherings, all the men who like to talk are clustered around me. They would like to be received at my house in the mornings, but since it isn't the custom, I refuse. The Marquis de Caraccioli especially entreats me every day; in spite of all his wit, I refuse. There are three or four men who dine here very often; one of them is a musician, and we play music together; the other has a perfect understanding of world history, natural history, literary history, and I question him about the government, the products, and the authors of this country. When people want to chat, I chat; sometimes I am as silent as the most "spleenetic" Englishman.[1]

---

1. "Spleenétique" was entering French at this time as the term for a kind of melancholy that the French thought the English were particularly susceptible to. In English, "splenetic" was displacing the older "spleenatic." Belle wrote "spleenatique."

One of the friends of the household knows all the good poets by heart; he's explaining Shakespeare to me. I got sick, and my apothecary fell in love with me; my physician, old Sir John Pringle,[2] talks only of me, to the Queen and to everybody else.

As for the curiosity people displayed at the beginning, it seems to me that that is passing; the duchesses no longer come to see me, and therefore they can't invite me to their gatherings. I still see the foreign women and a few old dowagers; that's quite enough. Tomorrow, I am going to dine with some City merchants in a village near London; there is a subscription ball that people have absolutely insisted I attend. It will be too late for me to return, so I will dine and spend the night there with some respectable people whom I've never seen.

I'm doing just what I meant to do: I'm seeing England as much as a woman can see it in the winter season. You don't think that I am really enjoying myself in London, or that I find *congenial people, lighthearted people, easy kinds of pleasures;* that is extremely well said and rather well surmised—and yet I am enjoying myself. The pleasures here are not at all convenient, and in the computation of what it has cost to go seeking pleasure—in time and trouble, jolting carriages, and hot weather—compared with the pleasure one has actually experienced, the excess is often on the side of the cost. I find few people with whom I am in harmony, but so much the better—I am learning to attune myself to others, just as I speak a foreign language from morning to night. When I see people who are not cheerful, and who would like to be, I cheer them up.

Those are my answers, my dear d'Hermenches; just now I don't have the time to paint you descriptions nor to tell you stories; that will be for another time. Seeing you would be very pleasant and comfortable; I would tell you a hundred thousand things. In spite of our wishes, when we write we have to make choices; that stops us, and we omit a hundred silly things that are worth telling, but would take up too much space. Don't reproach me, and especially not in your thoughts. In Holland, I usually have only one matter on my mind, and I talk about it and write about it. Here, nothing really occupies me, but I see countless things; this dissipation tires me and makes me lazy. I don't know what to write, I don't even care to write; when I am alone for a moment, I take a book to rest myself and concentrate my thoughts. More or fewer letters is not necessarily connected to more or less friendship—don't think it for a minute. Love me, and believe that I am attached to you in a way that deserves all your friendship.

London, Curzon Street, February 10, 1767

I hadn't spoken to the Marquis Fitz-James about you, but only about the camp at Compiègne. He's a handsome fellow; I have become reconciled to his remarks, because he seems to me kind and fairly reasonable.

---

2. The queen's physician.

I have heard Madame de Boufflers talked about here;[3] it seems to me that my curiosity does not flaunt itself as hers does.

CR *Whatever Belle's expectations when she went to England, they did not incapacitate her for judging what she saw. We have, for instance, a portion of a letter to one of her aunts:*

But my dear aunt, would you admire ruins that are new-built? It is so well imitated—the holes, the slits, the color, the crumbling stonework, the real ivy covering half the old battlement; you'd be sure to be taken in—except that you're not. You know that it's all new. I am amazed at the fantasy and I admire the imitation, but I am not able to say that I am pleased with such an ornament ... I will build no ruins in my garden, for fear of being ridiculous ... These ruins are much in fashion; one chooses the century and and the country as one pleases. Some are Gothic, others Greek, others Roman.

[...]

You'd be astonished to see such great beauty with so little grace; such fine figures unable to make a presentable curtsy; virtue of the first rank carried with the air of a grisette. It's a strange country.[4]

269. *To Constant d'Hermenches, March 20, 1767*

Hunger Hill in Surrey

On the eve of my departure from London, I gave your message to Lady Ailesbury; she told me that you were very amiable, that she had the friendliest feelings for you, that she would be very pleased to see you again in England, and that your letter had pleased her very much, but that after a long absence ... when one was so far away ... one didn't know how to express oneself ... but that you were to be persuaded that she had not forgotten you ... but that it was only her laziness that kept her from writing you. As for the Countess of Welderen, she swears by all the gods that she answered you (I could believe she lies, for that's rather a habit with her) without giving too many circumstances; you had given her your address; you had—I have forgotten half of all this detail, but finally she addressed her letter care of Monsieur de Besenval; apparently it got lost; it's no great loss.

The English gazette calls Voltaire's new tragedy *The Scythians*. Please tell me a little about it. I haven't received any letters from you for a long time. I'm well aware that this observation of mine will elicit one from you that is

3. See Belle's Letter 91 of May 1764.
4. Letter 268 in *O.C.* 2: 35.

not greatly to my advantage, but never mind; one is allowed to desire something one does not deserve. Please send your letters to my father in Utrecht; if I'm not yet there, they will keep them for me or send them here.

I have nothing interesting to say today. I am having a quiet visit in the countryside with Mme Bentinck. She is a Tuyll; you say that is a great merit in the eyes of all the Tuylls. She is kind and good-natured; I'm enjoying myself a great deal, and I have the satisfaction of seeing my chambermaid,[1] who had been very sick when I brought her with me from London, recover and get better every day. That is a great relief to me, because I was terribly worried about her, and if she had died I would have believed all my life that the journey, the London air, and the late nights were weapons with which I had killed her.

I have a valet from Paris who is learning English, and whose remarks about this country send me into fits of laughter. Yesterday I sent him off to the theater in Chertsey so that he could bring me back a description; he entertains me every day for at least a half an hour, for he has good sense and wit.

I have a great deal to see in London before I leave. Mr. Hume has arrived from Scotland; I will try to see him, and I will write you about it. The foreigners in London notice my absence, but I don't think that the English know that I have left. I am rather pleased with myself for being able to be at ease among people who pay almost no attention to me. The Chevalier de Saint-Priest and the Chevalier de Pontécoulant left London the same day I did to return to Paris; they were pleasant, and the first, although he talked a great deal, was agreeable and amusing. But there was also M. de Montausier, who was the stupidest creature I have seen in a long time. The last time he was at Court, he said to the Queen that he was in despair at having to leave England since he had had the honor of paying his court to Her Majesty. The Queen was embarrassed, and turned aside to speak to someone else. He said to the Prince regnant of Anhalt,[2] who was returning to Germany: "I beg you, my Lord, to write to me and tell me whether the King of Prussia is setting up camp in Prague." This Prince has been traveling for a long time incognito to avoid expense, and to allow his little state the time to recover from the expenses of war while he and his court were costing his subjects nothing. That is very generous, and they say that he is the best and most honest man in the world; it's a pity that he has all the clumsiness and heaviness that his nation is known for.

It's immensely entertaining to see people of different countries brought together in a random gathering, to hear them judge each other, and to make the comparisons oneself. The Chevalier Saint-Priest was coming from Lisbon, where he is the envoy of the court of Versailles; he was going to Paris.

---

1. Dorothea (Dortie) Phlügerin.
2. Cousin of the count of Anhalt who had briefly courted Belle.

The other chevalier and he, as soon as they were in London, talked only of the fans and moirés and painted linen that they were to buy. I had told them about a certain linen shop, and by chance I ran into them there. They found nothing pretty enough, and were not far wrong; however, I had bought two or three dresses there. They had been told about a fan merchant; I asked them to send her to me; they had each bought one. I bought eleven of them, and gave them one for a Parisian woman whom I had never seen but who is a friend of my brother. As for the moirés, one of them bought a dress, and that was all. Most of the French whom I have seen are magnificent when it comes to words, and very economical in their actions. The English never talk about their expenditures, and most of them are wildly extravagant.

Farewell; send my letter to the Marquis; he is Frenchified, but I'm very glad that he's not French. I love you very much, whatever my long silences might suggest.

270. *From Constant d'Hermenches, April 22, 1767*

Mézières, in Champagne

I have something of a dilemma, charming Agnes; on the one hand, is it worth while to write you only a few words after such a long silence—but on the other, can I risk a long letter that may remain in Utrecht, or else cross the seas and perhaps reach you only when it would no longer mean anything? But seeing that my tender affection signifies in all times (I hope) something real to you, I permit myself to entrust this piece of paper to the post.

Your presence is as vivid in my mind as ever, my dear friend. I have received here a letter from you bearing a great many seals, although it was unsealed; it followed me to Switzerland, to Paris, and finally to Mézières. I sent the enclosed letter to the Marquis. If his pain were not too cruel; if I saw some hope for his ill; if you didn't suffer from it yourself—then I admit to you that I would rather like to see his philosophic calm subjected to distress and tender emotion; but I pity the poor devil. Read this letter; I will send him yours. For a long while now I have been merely the courier of your dispatches, and in good conscience you owe my creditors restitution if I die bankrupt. Bellegarde is right; he alone is to be pitied; you are young, light-hearted, rich, and incomparably attractive; you will not miss him long. But *he* is losing what cannot be found more than once. If he does not face down his King and his family and all circumstances to unite himself with you, or at least to attempt it, you would be wrong to grieve over it: that's the advice I have to give you.

I bless Heaven that you have got over this fantasy of yours about England. More and more do I recognize the excellence of your taste and the accuracy of your judgment. That nation and that country have made the im-

pression on you that I desired they should; and when I say *desired*, it's because I think that it is in just that way that a person of perfect good sense
must see them. I am no longer worried about your prejudices concerning
France and the French; our ideas will agree perfectly when you have seen
for yourself. You were in a state of frightening enthusiasm for the English;
however, you saw them as I have described them to you. It is incredible that
this passion for speaking English did not carry you away; in that, I admire
the marvelous wisdom of your mind. If the French do not charm you, ah
then, you will be a creature more than human! What all this tells me, to my
delight, is that if you were able to spend a year—even a season—in my
country, you would be happy; but as for Paris—Paris will turn your head,
I'm sure of it; or so I judge by your remarks on the French whom you met
in London. Take my word for it—those pretty gallants who displeased you
are more scorned and less regarded in Paris than they are abroad; as for
Montausier, he is recognized as a madman!

As for *The Scythians*, I will tell you that we performed it in Lausanne
much better in all respects than it was performed in Paris; the audience was
moved to tears. I had the audacity to alter my role;[1] whether the author
wanted me to or not, I made it more moving, and that changes the whole
effect of the play. It's a feeble product by the standards of the fifty-year-old
Voltaire, but it's a marvel for a decrepit old man;[2] it would be a masterpiece
for all the tragic dramatists of the century, Lemierre, Saurin, Chateaubrun,
de Belloy, de Laharpe, etc.[3] The play has been published; you will judge of
it better than I can. It's a fine thing for me to defend it, after I have so mercilessly attacked it! I arrived in Paris the day people believed it had failed,
and it was only the author's name that sustained it, for the actors performed
so badly that I don't think they could have succeeded even with *Alzire*.[4]

I stayed in Paris for a few days, and have now returned to the banks of
the Meuse, into which I wanted to leap to come to you. Tell me whether its
waters, mixed with those of the ocean, will bathe some of those pretty villages you still want to see in England, for I have the impression that you are
waiting for your cousin's confinement,[5] and then for the baptism, and then
for her recovery from childbirth, and then . . .

For myself, you will find me here until the end of June; I will set up
camp in July, and if I have the money, and if I get good news from Compiègne, I will go to the Hague in the winter, and that, dear friend, will be to
see you and to see my son!

1. D'Hermenches played the role of Athamare. In letters of February and March of 1767
Voltaire criticized changes d'Hermenches had made in the script when he performed it. See
Voltaire's Correspondence 64: 250–52 and 65: 7–8.
2. In 1767 Voltaire was seventy-three.
3. Minor dramatists of the eighteenth century.
4. A tragedy of Voltaire's (1736), one of his most successful in his time.
5. Her cousin Reiniera Bentinck née van Tuyll, wife of Johan Bentinck.

I saw the Crown Prince[6] again in Paris; he made me offers that I will tell you about when I know where you are; you could even help me a great deal. Our Widow has told me about her marriage; she is perfectly content, and swears perfect friendship to me. I told her that you loved her tenderly as ever. Good night, divine being.

271. *To Constant d'Hermenches, April 22–26, 1767*

London

Am I not a little more intelligent than I was last week? David Hume has come to see me, and a few days later I invited him to dinner. What do you think we talked about? Roast beef and plum pudding![1] But we talked much less than we ate. I am sharing lodgings with my brothers, and dinner was brought to us from the tavern, so the courses were not served in their regularly appointed schedule; the roast chicken came before we had taken our leave of the pudding; it was set next to the fire to await us. A little dog came along, went straight to the chicken, and would undoubtedly have carried it off if David Hume had not gently held it back; for myself, you can well imagine that I would have let it eat both chicken and asparagus—though I am neither a great philosopher nor an historian. I very much liked Mr. Hume's attentiveness, and his honest and straightforward manners. A friend of his who was there at dinner told some very good stories; there was no other attempt at *esprit*. After coffee we played three rubbers of whist, and then we left each other.

It seems to me that I have good sense over here; I hope that it will follow me to Holland. I am waiting for a fine day to see Richmond and Kew, another to see Chelsea and Greenwich: we have had only wind, hail and rain since my return to London. My farewell visits have been made, and I am leaving next week. I leave with regret—not because I enjoy myself a great deal here, but I am free, and am not hated as I am in Holland. It is so restful not to be hated!—to have neither prejudice to tear down, nor imprudences to set right. It seems to me, my dear friend, that I would willingly give the little reputation I have acquired for the convenience of having none at all. The other day someone asked me whether I could write in French. That person at least doesn't slander my letters, and she doesn't tell me that the little tale I wrote three or four years ago[2] is horrible and scandalous. I have not been made an enthusiast by my stay in England; however, if someone proposed that I spend some time in some pretty little rustic spot on the banks of the Thames, with books and people who could explain them to me, I would willingly accept.

6. The future duke of Brunswick.
1. "Du roastbeef et du plum-pudding" in original.
2. *Le Noble.*

Mademoiselle Mauclerc has told me a thousand good things about Switzerland. Where do you get the idea that letters written from Lausanne—letters from you—would not be precious to me! If that were the case I would no longer dare write to you from Zuylen or Utrecht. I often argue with you about your favorite country simply for the amusement of arguing, and because I find you too much the enthusiast. Other times, I defend it with equal warmth. When I see enthusiasm or aversion, I always think I am seeing prejudice and error and a natural subject for disputes.

I would be very happy to go to Paris. If Madame Geelvinck had not married a ridiculous and despotic fool, we could have made a journey there together; I spoke to her about it a long time ago. People tell a thousand ridiculous stories about this husband and this marriage. Self-seeking, they say, has not bothered to mask itself; stupidity performs the office of sincerity, and makes public a thousand faults by absurd conduct and speech. I am greatly vexed that my friend did not profit from the *warnings*[3] that he himself gave from morning to night. If he had given me a tenth of them, I would have broken things off, even if it were at the church during the ceremony.

April 26

I am finishing my letter four days after it should have left. I finish it in a fit of melancholy. A thousand different sensations have been weighing me down all day; I ended in tears. I am so very sorry to be leaving. Why am I so sorry? So sad? My situation is precarious, uncertain, detached from everything. This pleasure of not holding on to anything indissolubly is not without its admixture of pain. By the way, whatever one says to Bellegarde about Rome, he is sure that even in Italy these marriages are performed; perhaps it costs money. How did Monsieur d'Usson manage? Anyway, God bless him! I will speak to my father, but if Bellegarde is still thinking about it, let him write without grumbling.

Miss Conway is going to marry a Mr. Damer, who is prodigiously rich; he is Milord Milton's son. For myself, I have spent my time with my beloved Mrs. Eliott and Mrs. Bentinck, and making much of Mrs. Eliott's little daughter. I amused myself a little with the Marquis de Caraccioli; I amused the Princesse de Masseran a little, as well as two or three old English ladies. As for suitors, I haven't seen a single one. There was one fortune that I knew of by reputation and thought I might like: an old General Pulteney, eighty years old, with an income of thirty thousand pounds; I would have made a conquest of him (old men always take to me), but I didn't see him. Farewell; a fine rhapsody this is.

---

3. English in the original.

272. *To Constant d'Hermenches, May 29–June 1, 1767*

Zuylen

I no longer know what to say, my dear friend, about our old, old subject. I am sorry, however, for myself and for Monsieur de Bellegarde ... I could define this chagrin with subheadings and provisos, but obviously it would be sheer repetition, for haven't I already said everything? I wish that without any more letters, or solicitations, or reasonings, or examinations and disputes, I might wake up tomorrow morning in the Marquis' château and that someone would say to me: "Good morning, Madame de Bellegarde." But I have plodded so far to arrive at that château that I am weary to the point of exhaustion, and since there is so little likelihood that I will ever arrive, I do better to get some rest where I am and enjoy myself. I am not thinking about a better match; I don't know what a good match is. I found your letter at the Hague. Why were you embarrassed to write me? What does it matter whether your letters have to go a little way or a long way, since they are sure to give me a keen pleasure? I receive this pleasure either sooner or later, according to the distance, that's all.

You are pleased with my way of judging England and the English; indeed, what I saw, I saw quite clearly; but there were many things that I was unable to judge. Since the English are less talkative and demonstrative than other people, one needs more time to see them. Besides, since they bother rather less about custom, one does not find as many who are all formed on the same mold. The climate, the government, the public amusements have a universal influence, as they do elsewhere; but the influence of custom is less general, and less absolute. One would be wrong to judge the whole nation by the small number of Englishmen that a woman can see in London in six months. I would be delighted to live freely in the countryside in England, and I can trust that preference of mine because it is not that of an enthusiast. The surroundings are charming, and when one is no vainer than a reasonable person should be, and can live more or less alone with one's thoughts and books, one would be quite content on the banks of the Thames. In Savoie, in Geneva, I have admired views more picturesque and more romantic than those in England, but I have never seen nature so friendly or so beautified. The common people are rich, the public works are admirable, travel is easy. The people are not extremely sociable; they are reserved and *selfish;*[1] one could be a person of merit and yet not be much sought-after—so much the better, perhaps. What would displease me more are the highway robbers, but so many of them have been hanged this winter that I think there are not many left. —Perhaps I am wrong after all; perhaps I would be more affected by the issue of vanity than by that of the robbers. One must not be too positive about judgments of oneself.

---

1. English in the original.

When I arrived at Helvoet and was on the road to the Hague, I found the windowpanes and the streets very clean, but the country was so monotonous! the look of everything was so vapid! At the Hague, I found that ridiculous and vexing remarks were circulating about me; that put me in yet a worse humor than the tedious countryside. "A cow, a meadow, a mill: that's all we see," I said to my brother, but he pointed out to me a Dutch minister of the Gospel, and said that one also can see huge wigs and long dressing gowns.

But to return to the Hague: I was so kindly received by Madame de Voorschoten, by her mother-in-law, by Maclaine,[2] by everyone I care about in the Hague, that I found myself consoled for the unpleasant remarks. I refused to stay longer than two days, however, saying that no doubt people would find some reason to ridicule me if I stayed longer. I had supper at Golofkine's, and I saw everyone I want to see.

Then I came to Utrecht, and my father, my mother and I were very glad to see each other again; at present, I am at Zuylen, and I am very content to be here. I don't look at the mill, or the meadow, or the cow, or the huge wig that enlivens the landscape; but I enjoy myself, I read, I converse, I recount my doings and listen to those of others; I see my Tuyll cousin[3] and his pretty new wife, and I have the pleasure of being equally at ease in the household with the wife and with the husband, which almost never happens to me.

I am so glad when I find I have a little practical merit that is good for ordinary use; I am often afraid that I have it only at a distance, and in my letters. For example, when you praise me and find me more lovable than another, I often wonder whether, from close up, you would say the same thing; whether after two or three months spent peacefully together, a thousand little faults of mine wouldn't efface that preference that your judgment and your heart accord me.

Pope erected a monument to his mother, and engraved an epitaph upon it; one of the most beautiful lines of the *Essay on Man* is in honor of his mother; Pope treated his mother like a dog. Shaftesbury was a brute.[4]

I would be delighted if you came to see your son and me. Tell me about the Prince's proposal,[5] if you can put it in writing; what I have of good sense is not very considerable, but it is at your service. I saw the Prince in

2. Chaplain of the British ambassador and co-pastor of the Presbyterian English church.
3. Her cousin Frederik (Frits), who had once been in love with her.
4. The obelisk Pope erected to his mother bore the words *Ah Editha! / Matrum optima! / Mulierum Amantissima! / Vale!* The lines from the *Essay on Man* are: "Or why so long (in life if long can be) / Lent heav'n a Parent to the poor and me?" Shaftesbury's *Inquiry Concerning Merit and Virtue* had been translated and published by Diderot in 1745 and was immensely influential. He was regarded as one of the most benevolent of philosophers. Belle's comments on these gentlemen would have come as news to her contemporaries.
5. See d'Hermenches' Letter 270 of April 22.

the *drawing-room;* I don't know whether he recognized me, but he didn't speak to me. I have never pleased any great lord. I hope that I will continue to please you always, and I promise always to love you very much.

Write to me; your letter will be sent to me at Rosendaal, where I will be staying. I will be at Amerongen for two or three days. I want to keep these friends. Mademoiselle de Mauclerc is coming here the day after tomorrow; she will spend two days with me. She is enchanted with Switzerland.

June 1, 1767

Have I spoken ill of the Chevalier de Saint-Priest? I would have been wrong, for he was witty, and has amused me on several occasions. When I told him to entertain me, he immediately told me two or three funny stories.

273. *From Constant d'Hermenches, June 18, 1767*

Mézières

At last, my fair and amiable voyager, you are back on our continent, cheerful and content enough, it seems to me, and therefore in good health. As for amiable, that goes without saying—it would be impossible for you not to be; and the proof, moreover, is that this Prince who talks so much to Heiltje de Parc hasn't said a word to you.[1] Certainly not; it is not to amiable and witty people that one has anything to say in that country! As for me, you find me straddling the Meuse where you had left me once; more than ever, I would like to leap into its waters and be carried to the streamsides where you dwell—were it not that just the other day I saw a man who had no wish to go as far down as that drown in the river. Therefore I will restrain myself, and merely order the waves to bear you my homage and my yearnings; for truly, Agnes, I yearn for you, and if I were to drown myself I would yearn no longer, and I flatter myself that that would not please you at all.

As for Bellegarde, I will say nothing. Here is his last scrap of paper. He was in Paris; he was to go to Holland; he was cursing the Pope; and now the rascal has gone off toward the Alps, whence you will no doubt hear from him. You do very well, my dear friend, to accept your situation as it is; besides, it must always come down to Providence, or to destiny, and you are well situated to wait for its decisions, and to enjoy life. You have many years ahead of you for passionate love; you will be very young at thirty, for I am so at forty; and as for a husband, there is none who will not be older

---

1. There is some confusion here that Belle will sort out in a later letter: it was the crown prince (the future Duke of Brunswick) who didn't speak to Belle when they were in the same drawing-room. The prince who is interested in Heiltje van de Parc is the stadholder; in fact, Heiltje de Parc will marry Annebetje's brother-in-law, M. de Reede.

366 LETTER 273: June 18, 1767

than you are at whatever age you take him. You are not one of those ordinary beauties, who play their role for a certain time, and whom one speaks of afterward only in reminiscence. Forever will you reign, forever brilliant. I even dare say that if it were possible to be more interesting, you will become more so. For yourself, there are so many things that you think you have delved into and used up, but to which you will return with pleasure. Thus, of everything that is happening to us, I am only distressed at these days I drag through without seeing you. I lead an execrably vapid life, for you can well imagine that although I am overloaded with business and encumbrances on account of these field exercises at Compiègne—where I am going on the 25th of this month—, and although I am overcome with fatigue, I still find a good half of myself idle. To be living among small-minded superiors or flattering subordinates—never with my equals in anything—is hardly a natural situation. I fear all this will leave me with an extreme indifference for pleasures. Already this winter, I noticed that women no longer aroused my amour-propre; there are few people whose approval interests me, and I catch myself preferring to astonish rather than to please. I have written some rather felicitous verses this winter; I performed extremely well in plays; when I was praised by a person of exacting taste, a true connoisseur, I had a keen moment of joy—and then I fall back again into indifference. Here I do some very distinguished things for my profession; I have composed six delightful marches for my regimental band; I looked forward to a thousand satisfactions. Well now, I already feel that this prestige is extinguished; a trivial comparison, an unjust preference would disgust me more than all the praises of the Court could flatter me. Such is man: it is just as well that he not be too attached to glory—or so it is said; but I think just the opposite: one is happy only by illusion, and only to the degree that one is swept away by some passion. I wish I had that intoxication of poets, musicians, lovers; I would do, and perhaps would have done, fine things. Instead, here I am in a chair, raging when I have to grasp a pen and bend over to write. Finding no one worthy of stirring my feelings, I become a true automaton, and an utter bore for those who have nothing directly to do with me. And half the time those who do have to do with me, lacking any knowledge of me, or judging me by the common measure, are apt to find me harsh and difficult to live with, and to distrust me as they would someone full of guile. —My conclusion, Agnes, is that I think I would do well to return to my first plan: to throw myself into the Meuse.

So I'm going to field maneuvers; address your letters to *Monsieur de Bournonville, bureau chief of the Swiss at Soissons.* I don't know what will become of me next; there is nothing in Holland that might attract me except you, and I probably wouldn't be able to see you. So I will go to Besançon, and from there to Switzerland; come there some time, my dear Agnes. They are writing me many good things about my son, who is at the Hague; I beg you to see him. I am at your feet, my incomparable friend.

275. *To Constant d'Hermenches, July 8, 1767*

Rosendaal

Your letter of June 18 took a long time to reach me, for I received it only four days ago. I have wanted to write you several times since my last letter; I think I even began one, but I have been sick and on the move, and I haven't found a moment of freedom to tell you all the things I wanted to. Before I left Zuylen, Mademoiselle de Mauclerc came to spend two or three days with me. I asked her a thousand questions about her stay in Switzerland; she is enchanted with it. You invited her to your fêtes, she said, with so much politeness and friendliness ... you perform so very well in *The Scythians* ... your house is so well maintained when you are there ... it is so pleasant ... you do the honors with such good grace—she couldn't stop praising you; and as for me, you can well judge that I didn't urge her to stop, so that it took nightfall or dinner to interrupt us—just as in a play.

Apparently I didn't express myself clearly, for you misunderstood me; it's your favorite prince, the Crown Prince, who did not speak to me in the drawing-room at Saint-James. Heiltje de Parc's Prince has been at Het Loo for several days;[1] he runs on foot after the falconers, every day, for several hours, and the whole Court is obliged to run after him, moaning with exhaustion.

So Bellegarde will not stop running about. That business returns to my mind only when someone mentions it to me, and then I have regrets about it, and wish that it could be put on its feet again. I would be married without being too much so; it seems to me that we both love freedom too much for it not to survive between him and me. However, that isn't altogether certain; in a few years, Bellegarde would no longer know what to do with his freedom, and that might then be the end of mine. Let us let things go as Fortune wills it; to force her to do what we wish is perhaps to force her to do us harm.

You praise me in ways I would like to deserve. For some time now, and especially in England, I have seen a great many men either make fun of women who were no longer young or else pity them, and I have reflected a great deal on the subject. Young people who make fun of the elderly make fun of themselves in advance; they ridicule what they will themselves become—what they even hope to become. To fear growing old is to fear a necessary consequence of our existence; it is a weakness. To be distressed at no longer being young is to lament that we began to exist, and that time is a succession. Nevertheless, it is true that a woman no longer young is neglected—often boring and ridiculous, and almost always bored. There would be much wisdom and much happiness in passing through one's whole life with an even step and a serene countenance; to be always just what one should be

1. The stadholder, William V, prince of Orange, not Crown Prince Ferdinand of Brunswick. Het Loo is a seventeenth-century palace built in the middle of a vast hunting terrain.

at each age, without regretting what one has just left behind, and to arrive at the end of this life and leave it as well without agitation and without regret.

No, you really must not throw yourself into the Meuse. When you want to come see me, put yourself in a good solid boat; it isn't romantic, but it's safer, and upon leaving it you would converse much better than if you arrived pell-mell in the current among the fishes of our fair river. If I were sure that there were nymphs, I would fear nothing for you; without a doubt, they would take it upon themselves to carry you. But they might love you too much; they would be jealous of me, and would want to keep you among themselves; so there we are—still back with the ordinary mode of travel. I would like to see you, but I don't know any way; Zuylen is rather inaccessible, and your coming would be a serious matter. It isn't so for everybody; it's very bad of you to be a dangerous character—it's a terrible nuisance.

Reijndert van Randwijck is here; he is very fond of you. Monsieur de Rosendaal and he send their compliments.

I understand very well that one might become indifferent to applause, but is that so unfortunate? In childhood and early youth, one instructs onself out of vanity; then, reason moderates that vanity; the things that one has learned and the habit one has of occupying oneself come to serve one's happiness. One knows and one learns to amuse oneself for oneself, and not to be admired; instead of verses, one does calculations and reflections. One must read as Madame de Rosendaal and I do; we are reading *Antiquity Unveiled through Its Customs*, and in company with the Randwijcks, *The Life of Julian the Apostate*.[2] A friend like her consoles one for many things; she makes me forget a thousand unpleasant remarks, and reconciles me with my country. I read her the part of your letter where you complain about always being with superiors, or with inferiors who flatter, but never with equals. We sympathized with that vexation; only a childish and stupid vanity prefers something other than equals; it is only with them that friendship is at ease, and says what it wishes without praise being taxed with flattery, or sincerity with haughtiness, or a reasonable discourse with pedantry and presumption. *Sweet equality* is sweet and precious in all things.

Near Neuchâtel, in Môtiers-Travers, there lives a Madame Girard, who has a great deal of imagination, little clarity of mind, some insight and taste but no memory, the kindest of hearts, a style à la Rousseau with appalling spelling, a delightful gaiety when she is not overwhelmed with chagrin, and the most tender affection for me—although she hasn't written me for three years. She comes from a very good family in Geneva; her maiden name is Trembley. She was a widow with a child and without any fortune; she came to us and was the governess for my sister and my youngest brother. I was

---

2. Under the name of Nicolas-Antoine Boulanger, d'Holbach published *L'Antiquité dévoilée par ses usages, ou l'examen critique des principales opinions, cérémonies ou institutions religieuses et politiques des différents peuples de la terre* in 1776. *La Vie de l'empereur Julien* was written by J.-P. de La Blèterie in 1735.

thirteen, and it was as if I were *her* governess. After leaving us, she went to Bordeaux, where she was a success with two charming little pupils. About a year ago she returned to Geneva; she planned to settle there with nephews who were to establish a banking house, but government troubles upset commerce, and Madame Girard was obliged to take refuge in Môtiers-Travers until calm returned to her country. I found a letter from her when I returned from England. She is so sad, and without her positively saying so, her situation appears to me so constricted and uncomfortable that I wish someone could offer her a pleasant and easy post in a good household, even if it were only for six months or a year. Might you perhaps know, in Lausanne or thereabout, a rich woman who is alone and who might be glad to have an amiable companion? One would certainly be very pleased with her. I haven't seen her for a long time, but it is easy to see, by several admirable letters to my mother, my sister, and me, that she is still the same person she used to be. It would please me greatly if you could render her this service. I am sure that if you found a position for her it would be a very good one. Write to me if you think of something for her.

Adieu, my dear d'Hermenches. You are in Paris; you are seeing Madame de Chasteler;[3] I have written to her, and I am impatiently waiting for her response. If you see Monsieur Rendorp, do for him everything you possibly can; he is so unhappy, and in such terrible bereavement.[4] When I go to the Hague, I will certainly see your son. I hope he will speak to me. Two years ago he was as serious as he would be with his grandmother.

How silly of me to think you are in Paris, when you are actually in Soissons.

277. *From Constant d'Hermenches, August 11, 1767*

Compiègne

My dear Agnes, your friend counted himself for dead as long as these wretched maneuvers last, and while the Court is deciding what to do; I wanted neither to make you remember him nor to write you from a place where I have the liberty neither to think nor to feel. First of all, I haven't had a day of good health for a month; also, I am occupied only with unpleasant business, and I didn't want you to be mingled with such bad company. But here is a letter from the Marquis, with new propositions; it arouses all my feeling, my energy, and my lively interest in everything that concerns you. I began by answering the Marquis that you would never make such a promise,[1] but that since people are beginning to see reason, he was to write to Rome that you are too honest a person to promise anything blindly,

3. The former Mme Geelvinck, the Widow.
4. He had lost three young children in the space of a month.
1. This promise must be one described in Bellegarde's letter, which we do not have.

and that he begs that no commitment be required of you except *that of receiving instruction*, and to add to that anything he pleases—"be so good as," etc. I think that things can be arranged in that fashion.

I then went to consult with the d'Ussons, who were of my opinion. Madame d'Usson also promised to receive instruction—and then one gets off by being very hard-headed. See for yourself what you think about it, and be good enough to write directly to the Marquis as your heart dictates, and address the letter to me here. I still think that he must passionately desire this union, and all that is needed on your part is honesty and consistency. Please write me here, addressing the envelope to *M. de Bournonville, Head of the Swiss Office.*

I repeat, my dear friend, I lead a wretched existence here. I'm in the midst of the most delightful things, and continual festivities, but I'm dying of fatigue and heat, so my head is in no state to write you a letter with any common sense in it; nevertheless, for business—and especially for yours—my head will always work well enough. Imagine what it is for almost two months never to dine or sup with fewer than a hundred and fifty people unless one claims to be ill; to have to see and command soldiers and horses from morning to evening; to be confined to a tent or a hovel of a room where there isn't space to turn around—and all that surrounded by the whole Court, women, spectacles, parade music; to change one's clothes four or five times a day—all without any purpose, without anything that engages the heart; in addition, to have to be concerned with my fortune, and that of my friends; to be sent packing from one day to the next, and perhaps, in the end, obtain nothing. Fortunate genius, how much better you enjoy life! Because you enjoy yourself, be it with books, or solitude, or shade, or your own idleness! I yearn for a little repose; your letter—which I am so unfit to answer just now—is balm to my heart. You depict everything I feel, and everything I would like to think and do; but I am in the midst of the whirlwind, and although I am not ambitious, I must act as though I were, and exert myself tremendously.

People are perfectly satisfied with me and my corps during these maneuvers, and even prefer us to all the others. I am fêted and praised; but nothing has been done yet; I am told to wait here, and I know that people are busying themselves with my future; success is in the hands of Destiny, and of the hurricanes of the Court. Just now I am going to Enghien, to the Duchesse d'Arenberg; it was arranged during a supper, with women who determine the fortunes of men. People think me very fortunate, and I let that opinion stand. What pleases me in all this is that I will see and give some pleasure to that charming Duchess, who is a friend as Agnes is. Ten days hence, we will be back; from there, I must go to Chantilly, where the Prince de Condé is, and then perhaps to Paris; but certainly by September I will be in Besançon where I am in garrison, and, thank God, on my way to Hermenches.

Ah, if only Mlle Mauclerc had had the talent to persuade you in her travel accounts to do as she does! To go off to Switzerland as you went off to England! I would erect a statue to her; as for you, your altars have long been ready for you there ...

I am at your feet, adorable Agnes!

278. *To Constant d'Hermenches, August 19–20, 1767*

Zuylen

Would you believe that a woman might be neither vain nor curious! I am not curious, for I haven't yet read the Marquis's letter; I'm not vain, for I am genuinely annoyed today at having suitors.

A man who has spent the day here was saying to me every quarter-hour, about another man, "Will you have him?" I've always said I don't know; when all's said and done, I think not. That already made me ill at ease; I receive your letter, and my uneasiness increases. I had thought that the Marquis was forgetting this business, and I said "Amen" to his forgetting; but he is not forgetting, and here I am again not knowing what I want. Yesterday I was much more content. There are two other suitors, and for a few days now I have had a sweetheart.[1] —I'm lying; it's been six weeks. What is a person to do with all this—a person who is not in love and who is getting weary of the mere thought of marriage? I had made two plans for being single—such lovely plans! One for one country, the other for another. I was saying to my father a few days ago that I could hardly resolve to sacrifice my liberty; that with it I was perhaps good for something, and that in a state of dependence I would no longer be good for anything—like those dogs that hunt naturally, who retrieve when they are playing, but who never learn to retrieve when they are forced to. Do you want me to flip a coin for marriage or the single state? If it's heads, I would still have to draw straws for the choice of a husband. Don't expect anything more serious or reasonable from me for the present, and let me drag out my indecisiveness a little longer. The Marquis has wasted a lot of time in his travels; I want to waste a little in turn, for the pleasure of thinking about nothing.

Let's talk about you tomorrow morning, and then I will send this letter. It is very sweet of you to keep liking my letters; that constancy is all the more admirable in that very often they lack both wit and reason. Your letter—except for the fact that it talks of marriage—I find very good; the portrait of your life is excellent; it is better of its kind than the original; for in the original you have the all the fatigue of business while having almost no ambition, and the fatigue of pleasures while finding no pleasure. But wouldn't repose bore you? On that score I don't know you well enough yet.

---

1. One of the suitors is probably the Rhingrave Frederik von Salm-Salm Kyrburg. The "someone in love" is probably Charles-Emmanuel de Charrière.

August 20

After having thought it over, I am chiefly sorry for your being ill-housed and with your health upset. You say you haven't been well for a month. If you were in very good health, one could simply laugh at the tent and the hovel; but at present there is no way to find that amusing. I wish I could lend you my room and my study. When you say you have no ambition, that's a fib; and if I believe you, I'm a dunce. What would one do in your profession without ambition? It's even very praiseworthy, since when one does good, the more one advances and rises, the more good one does. Praise rewards your efforts and your labor while you wait for fortune. I hope that the latter does not delay too long, and that it rewards you generously.

If I make a big win in the lottery, I will go to Paris and Switzerland. I would have as much pleasure in visiting you there as you would have in receiving me: I would see the whole country, and I would make a long stay in Lausanne; it would be lovely.

Madame de Chasteler has been at her mother's since Sunday; she has written me a letter from Paris full of praise for her husband and her lot. He conveys his compliments to me; however, they say that he fears me, and hates me in advance. They would have been able to come see me passing through if they had wanted to—at least I think so, for it's the usual route. I'm still very fond of the Marquise, and I am going to write to her, but it's up to her to come see me, and I will not take a step.

If I marry Bellegarde, people will say that we are two foolish women who wanted to be marquises by any means possible, and at any price. Since my marquisat is older and finer, I would recover and be able to play the great lady, but on the other hand my friend would display a much greater fortune. People would say that one of our marquis was too young, the other not young enough. They would make fun of us, and they would not be wrong; I would laugh along with the others. If we wanted to justify our marriages, we would undoubtedly say: I couldn't bear Amsterdam, I didn't like my country. A fine and honorable excuse! Is one allowed to hate one's own land, a free country, the land of one's friends! When I see the friends I have here, when Madame de Rosendaal and Madame d'Athlone hang on my arms for me to amuse them and make much of them, and when I ramble with them in well-tended fields whose farmers are free and rich, in truth I no longer dare say that I do not love my country, and it ceases to be true. —But keep that romantic little outburst to yourself—notwithstanding that it is a true and natural description of the state of affairs.

I spent six weeks at Rosendaal. Madame d'Athlone came to get me there, I was taken to Amerongen for several days, and then I was brought back here. I do not ever ask to be more loved, more fondly attended to, nor more content than when I was at Rosendaal. Goodbye, my dear d'Hermenches. This whole letter answers nothing and proves nothing; I only wanted to amuse myself and to talk to you.

279. *To Constant d'Hermenches, September 7, 1767*[1]

Zuylen

If you want a quarrel to end, don't quarrel so amusingly, for then I have too much interest in making it last. As I was reading your letter, I was laughing from beginning to end. *My infatuation with my marshes and my bogs* and a thousand and one other things in your letter are priceless, and too funny for words. Two rather tedious women, you say, speaking of Mme de Rosendaal and Lady Athlone. My God, what a terrible vengeance I will wreak, if ever I see those women who make you disdain my friends! I will make it my duty not to let the slightest silliness go unnoticed; I will make a crime of the slightest affectation on their part, the most innocent bit of simpering, a single false thought or gesture, and I will repeat my observations to you a hundred—no, a thousand times.

Meanwhile, just to try your patience, I will tell you that Lady Athlone arrived here yesterday, just after your letter came; that she was charming; that she left her child with us while she took a trip to Overyssel; that I sent Mme de Rosendaal a dress in the English fashion like the ones I wear myself just now, with ribbons and a lot of little details that I enjoyed arranging for her myself; for there is pleasure in adorning such a pretty woman and helping those one is fond of. If I were vain, I would say that these women you find so tedious are delightful when they are with me; that I cheer Mme de Rosendaal, and that I enliven my cousin's mind. Although that's all true, I will say nothing about it; you wouldn't believe me. I'm writing a fairy tale that Mme de Rosendaal asked me for; I have sent her the beginning, where I have portrayed her as the good fairy.[2] Such trifles give us pleasure and amusement, but you would make fun of them: it's all from the country of marshes and bogs; it is, of course, ridiculous to enjoy oneself and to write elsewhere than at Chantilly. I used to have the vapors, and I would curse my country and my compatriots. At present, I am in such good health that I bless everything I see; I am happy, and I am glad to be anywhere as long as I don't have social obligations and wearisome visits to make. Preach to me about boredom all you will; I will enjoy myself in spite of you. I go twice a week to Utrecht; I am reading the English poets with an old Englishman who knows his language well. I have resumed mathematics with Praalder;[3] and to avoid being distracted from it, I have resolved not to go to the Hague all winter if I can avoid it. All I need for perfect contentment is an excellent musician. That's my last word; and if I'm to be madly in love with France, I'll wait until I get there.

1. This letter is in answer to one from d'Hermenches that is not extant.
2. This fairy tale has not been found; however, Belle continued to write in this genre. At the beginning of the Revolution she wrote cryptic warnings to Louis XVI and Marie Antoinette in the form of fairy tales: *Bien Né* and *Aiglonette et Insinuante*.
3. See Letter 87, n. 7.

Why didn't you answer my request on behalf of Mme Girard? That's very bad of you. But there's no longer any need to do anything; she has a position with your brother in Geneva.[4] My brother the sailor[5] left this morning to go to sea, which saddens me; we had spent almost a year together. He had wanted very much to marry Mademoiselle de Reede, Milord Athlone's sister, but she demanded that he quit his naval career, and he refused. We were all of the opinion that a successful career was of more value to him than a marriage, and the affair was broken off.

Have I told you that Mme de Degenfeld had written me the longest and most boring letter imaginable? We get along very well together; but it seems that Mme de Spaen can no longer endure me, which is of no concern to me. It suits M. Reynst and M. de Stokken to be at Bellevue,[6] but not me.

Madame de Chasteler is still at her mother's; I don't think we will see each other, although we would like to.

Monsieur de Welderen, of England, is here; he will be at the Chapter of the Teutonic Knights in a few days.

I am very glad that you are in better health. Drink some Piermont water as I do; it is excellent for the stomach and the nerves; it lifts your spirits and gives you a ravenous appetite all day. I go walking every morning for an hour, before the sun has dispersed the dewdrops. You would think that I was in charge of the Public Works of spiders, so curiously do I examine them. I thought that I didn't love nature, because I take little pleasure in reading the poets' descriptions of dawns and springtimes. Thank God, I was wrong. Nature is greatly superior to descriptions of her; she speaks to the heart a language that poets imitate badly, or that no longer touches them because it has been overused.

Tomorrow morning I would like to see the spiders of Chantilly instead of those of Zuylen—see them with you, that is. Really, you are wrong to say that I disdain what I do not know. I would be delighted to see Paris, Versailles, and Lausanne; but you must not demand that I be discontented with what I have. Isn't boredom a sign of inadequacy? Isn't it a degrading kind of humility to admit that one is bored? This country already has enough gawkers—it doesn't need me—who see nothing good in it, and attest to their scorn by their ridiculous imitations of what our neighbors do. The other day I made a rejoinder to someone who was observing that living in Holland wasn't really *living*, and that there was no pleasure or happiness except in France: I answered that he must bear a grudge against our fathers for having defended this country against Louis XIV, and that it was a pity that we had not become a French province.

---

4. Samuel de Constant. Some years later, Samuel de Constant was to write a popular novel about a miserably henpecked husband, *Le Mari sentimental* [*The sentimental husband*] (1783). As a riposte, Isabelle de Charrière wrote *Lettres de Mistriss Henley* (1784).

5. Ditie.

6. Mme de Spaen's establishment at Cleves.

I can understand very well that the Marquis and I are ruining you;[7] I have no solution for it except for you to give me some commission to perform for you, for one doesn't usually pay me for them. I'm not greatly concerned about settling up accounts with you, but I would be delighted to be of service to you. If you see the Chevalier de Saint-Priest, who has been named the Swedish envoy, send him my greetings. I saw him quite often in London at the Princess de Masseran's. At first, he rather liked me, but by the end I took it into my head to speak ill of his nation, and my chambermaid's sickness made me so morose and so ill-humored that I didn't manage to obtain his forgiveness for my rudeness, no matter what efforts I made. Remind him of all that, and talk about me a little, so that you don't forget me.

281. *From Constant d'Hermenches, September 10, 1767*

Paris

Here, divine person, is the letter that was in Bouillon and that was sent back to me here. I'm glad it wasn't lost, and I hope you will be pleased to receive it. But tell me, charming Agnes, what pens are you writing with? Your last letter is a masterpiece, and I'm sure you don't even realize it![1] It is full of fire and levity, reason and wit; it reached me in the midst of the delights of Chantilly—day after day of continual festivities—where elegance, gaiety and magnificence surpass any idea one might have of such things in other countries. Well now, that letter drew me away from my ecstasies, and rearranged all of them around itself; I would keep taking it from my pocket, and find more pleasure reading it than anything else gave me. You are truly astonishing; there are many people who write charming letters, but no one as sustainedly as you, and I see that you put into them not a shadow of effort or pretentiousness; that is because your imagination is vivid, and gives itself entirely to whatever occupies it at the moment. I'm exactly the opposite; I do nothing without involuntarily thinking of five or six other things, both past and future; I'm always swimming in a cold calculation, uncertain what to choose.

I am presently in Paris, where I have been summoned; my pay is being raised and—were it not for the perfidy of that little toad De Salis[2] (who married in Holland, and knows how to advance himself here)—I would be a brigadier. However, I will be one at the next round of promotions, and arrangements are being made for me to get a regiment; that's all I have to tell you about myself.[3] I am going to Besançon, and I will be traveling a great

---

7. The person receiving the letter paid for the postage.
1. See Letter 87, n. 7.
2. Baron Antoine de Salis de Marschlins, commander of a regiment that bore his name. He seems to have been trying to damage d'Hermenches' reputation with Choiseul.
3. "Brigadier" is not a rank but an assignment as commanding officer of a brigade—an assign-

deal, between the region around my country and the excellent Paris; therefore address your envelopes *Monsieur de Bournonville at Versailles*, and I will be certain to receive your kind letters. I cannot tell you strongly enough that the Marquis de Chasteler is regarded in this country as a madman, and in Brussels as a rather base fellow. Conduct yourself accordingly with them; it's sad for the wife, for people generally found her pleasant.[4]

Tell me then, who are all these suitors being presented to you? I know something of your surroundings, and I don't imagine any great abundance of men who would suit you; and for God's sake don't get taken in by some fine story. Above all beware of Germans; they're all beggars and liars.

Farewell, my kind and lovable friend! I am on my knees in adoration of your beautiful face, your kind heart, and your astonishing mind!

My good friend, do something for my son if you have the occasion; seek him out if you go to the Hague, or recommend him to others, or ask for news of him ... People write me a thousand good things about him, but they are not people I completely trust.

282. *From Constant d'Hermenches, September 19, 1767*

Paris

In enumerating your pleasures, my dear Agnes, what you depict is your boredom! If it requires humility to admit that one is bored, it certainly takes a great deal of wit to know how to enjoy oneself as you do; very few of the things you mention to me would not be a punishment for other women, and—dare I say it?—perhaps for me as well. To get up with the dawn, examine spiders, tend another woman's child, spend hours with an old Englishman, study mathematics, write a story for Mme de Rosendaal who perhaps doesn't understand it, and who certainly doesn't know how to respond to it, make dresses for her, put ribbons on her ... now, Agnes, is there a more insipid, dreary way of spending one's time? Not a single laugh, not one heart-stir, not one triumph, not one illusion, whether through art or through piquant situations. If one says that you are a prodigy, that God has endowed you with a genius more brilliant than that of any of his creatures, that you can suffice unto yourself, that you radiate around you that fire that animates you and adorns, enhances, ignites everything arounds you—one speaks the truth. You have no reason to wreak vengeance on me; when I say, as I believe, that your friends are boring, I am not offering mine as models of perfection. To be boring is by no means a vice; it is a lack of

---

ment frequently given to a colonel. D'Hermenches was not yet expecting a promotion to major general (there was no "brigadier general"). His hope of acquiring his own regiment—which would be quite consistent with his commanding a brigade—was a separate issue.
4. The former Mme Geelvinck.

graces, it is a certain awkwardness, a dreariness. You will find in French-women the general desire to please that is the antidote to this fault; this desire to please puts everyone at ease, and enlivens society. But you will also find in these Frenchwomen haughtiness, effrontery, ridiculous preten-sions; I would be the first to point it out to you, and we would laugh about it together. There are very few women in the world that I do not regard as serving for my amusement (I do not regard *you* as a woman in that sense); I will be only too happy to anticipate you, and offer you the revenge that you threaten me with.

What charms me the most in your letter is what I learn about your health. Even if you had said nothing about it, I would have guessed that it is very good; it is impossible for the mind to be as cheerful and as happy as yours if the body is not perfectly healthy. This is a treasure to be carefully protected. I am a different being altogether, depending on the state of my head and my stomach. There are moments when I sing and laugh all by myself, when it seems to me that I fly as I am walking along; and other times when the most splendid feasts, when the company that pleases me the most, seems to plunge me into a tomb. What makes us happy isn't what we call pleasures; our happiness comes from our contentment of mind, which gives color to everything. That is the moment to seek out pleasures, and then they are ex-quisite; but even without pleasures, if the mind is content, delight springs from everywhere—sunrise, sunset, solitude, the hubbub of society, the com-pany of the simplest, the humblest beings—everything becomes captivating. The sublime discovery is the one that teaches us to arrive at contentment of mind; my own recipe is to learn things, to do good, and to live with people who love me; yours is certainly more complex, but the basis is the same, I am sure.

Don't scold me, Agnes, for my having said nothing to you about Mme Girard; I had written and had learned the state of things. What could I an-swer you before I knew anything? What has turned out very well is that it was one of my close friends who got her the position in my brother's house-hold, without my brother knowing that I had any interest in the matter.

But why, pray tell, have you embarked on a serious correspondence with Mme de Degenfeld? I myself got out of it, and what is curious is that I have never taken any tone with her other than that of pleasantry, without its in-juring her grave respect for me. I think that the poor woman is about to lose in Austria the few satisfactions that her hauteur got for her among us; she will become old, ugly, dismal, haughty, and stiff.[1] Let's forget about her—believe me.

I'm in the country, my dear Agnes, where I have come to spend two days with a friend of mine. She is by no means stylish and she isn't a beauty, but she has a candid heart and a just mind. I brought her *L'Ingénu* and she is

1. Madame de Degenfeld's husband had just been named ambassador to the court of Vienna.

reading it even now, while I am writing to you. Tell me, didn't that bit of foolishness give you immense pleasure?[2] On the way I also read *Eugénie*;[3] it made me weep, which annoys me, because I don't like that play; everything in it is forced, and all its theatrical effects are trite; the valet who goes down on his knees and admits the hoax—that's banal enough by itself to put one off the author . . .

I also read with great pleasure the defense that Loyseau wrote for the Major General de Portes; it created a great sensation in Paris.[4] Read it, and you will see how clever I was to win five lawsuits against these gentlemen. You must also read the letter that the Minister wrote me,[5] and you will see that I have every reason to be pleased with this country. My dear Agnes, even though you write me letters that all deserve to be in print, you will not ever correct the dullness of my own; it's for that very reason that I have established it that dullness is not a vice: it does not keep one from passionately loving and respecting one's friend. I am at your feet.

Continue to address your letters *De Bournonville*. I am leaving for Besançon.

283. *From Constant d'Hermenches, September 22, 1767*

Paris

My dearest friend, as I pass through Paris I find a letter from our suitor; I beg you to answer him, for he thinks that the delay is my fault, and you know how precise I am in these matters. I am going directly to Besançon.

I have had the pleasure of talking about you with a woman worthy of your acquaintance, Madame Necker.[1] Rendorp has often spoken to her about you, and has shown her one of your letters. Your story *The Nobleman* is greatly enjoyed here, and people are asking that it be reprinted. If you would like to rework your comedy, I am sure it would be successful if you entrusted it to

2. A novella by Voltaire (1767), now regarded as one of his best.

3. A sentimental drama by Beaumarchais, produced in 1767—several years before *Le Barbier de Séville* (1775) and *Le Mariage de Figaro* (1781).

4. In 1762 the lawyer Alexandre-Jérôme Loyseau de Mauléon had written an important brochure on behalf of the Calas family (see p. 23). Comte Louis de Portes had served as colonel and chamberlain for the Prince of Orange and had become involved in a lawsuit with the Republic of Berne. Loyseau de Mauléon published a celebrated defense that won de Portes' case. In his letter, d'Hermenches makes a pun on Loyseau's name that just won't work in English: he calls him "l'oiseau," which is pronounced just as the name is, but means "the bird."

5. In this gracious letter Choiseul tells d'Hermenches that the King has been informed of his services, and that he will receive a pension of 2000 livres. (Vissière, *Correspondance* 428.)

1. Suzanne Curchod Necker was the wife of a wealthy banker who became the finance minister of Louis XVI. She was a considerable woman of letters, whose essays and reflections were published by her husband after her death. Her salon was one of the most influential in Paris. Her daughter Germaine became famous as Madame de Staël, whose life was to be intertwined with Isabelle de Charrière's through d'Hermenches's nephew Benjamin Constant.

Madame Necker, who knows every Aristarchus in the country.[2]

I will say nothing more in praise of this country, nor anything against your own, since I see that Holland is spilling over onto the banks of the Seine; and now Mme Huffel is arriving with her faithful Mark as her interpreter. It's really becoming too much! I want to try to see Rendorp for a moment, solely for you, for I haven't yet seen him.

I wish that with all your reputation for infinite wit you were not given out to be eccentric, for you are not. You are too kind, too honest, too natural; find a system that will draw you closer to the accepted forms, and you will be superior to all wits, present and past. —This advice I make so bold as to offer my twenty-six-year-old friend.

Farewell, divine being.

284. *To Constant d'Hermenches, September 28, 1767*

Since the last letter I wrote you, I have received two from you. I am very grateful, dear d'Hermenches, and I am very glad that of all those things that should make you forget me—absence, your business, your triumphs, your pleasures—nothing succeeds. The raise in pay is a very good thing; the praise and the pleasure in feeling that they are deserved is still better, and thus the Minister's letter is delightful to receive; I imagined myself in your place, and I thank you for having sent it to me. I received the packet just last evening, and it is now only morning.

I hasten all the more to write because Madame Girard does not have the position that I thought, and my entire original request to you must be renewed. I don't know what puts her off your brother's household; it's too much for her, I think, both a house to manage and children to be tutored. In any case, I know she has left that position. She wrote about it to my mother, and she would like us to find one for her in this country; but the journey is so long, and it's so unlikely that we could find exactly what would suit her! While we are looking here, I hope you will find something for her in France or in Switzerland. Our ladies here, for the most part, prize orderliness above all else; they are cold and grave in manner. Madame Girard hardly knows that two and two are four, and that there are seven days in the week; she has never clearly understood that there are twelve months in the year. Her entire soul is composed only of imagination and feeling; she is amiable and affectionate, and thus needs to be loved. That is a condition that an old Amsterdam lady who is looking for *een Juffrouw voor geselschap*[1] wouldn't comprehend; she would pay her only with money, and for that money she would want services quite different from those that my friend could render. Thus, I

2. The comedy is probably her play *Justine*, now lost. An "Aristarchus" is a literary critic.
1. A lady companion.

have little hope of finding what she needs, and I beg you to do your best. Your recipe for happiness includes doing good, and therefore this is precisely your business. You will do an essential service to this woman, and you will give me great pleasure. She is asking to stay with a lady as her companion, and that is indeed what would suit her the best, I think; but she would also be well placed with a young girl of twelve to sixteen, and a young girl would certainly profit from her company.

I can't write any longer just now, but this letter is only interrupted, not finished; I will pick it up again, maybe an hour from now, maybe in a day or two. Madame d'Athlone is staying with me, and so my attention is for her. I will no longer talk to you about my amusements, since you think it so admirable that I regard them as such; that would be ridiculous boasting.

I promise to find out exactly how your son is doing. I doubt very much that I will go to the Hague this winter; I am not free enough there. For me to enjoy it, I need a house where I can go and come as I please. Besides, I like being a bluestocking, and staying in my room when everybody is running off to the Hague. Don't worry that I'm paying too much attention to my suitors; if I mention them, it's only because I'm surprised to be thought of as somebody one would want to marry. Farewell. The way you think of me is charming, and I'm very grateful, but why praise my letters? Anyone but you—any man who didn't love me—would only find them carelessly written, and not good at all.

286. *To Constant d'Hermenches, October 26, 1767*

Amerongen

Can it be that I've gone so long without writing you? The last time I wrote, I intended to continue by the following post, and I have let six or eight of them go by, I think. I never do what I meant to do. I'm now at Amerongen; my cousin sent for me, so I came. Monsieur de Reede and the Randwijcks are here too; we are all living like brothers and sisters, and we're enjoying ourselves. You spoke to me about Madame de Degenfeld; I agree with you that she will return from Austria quite dreary. Through all my praises and my politeness, she apparently saw my overwhelming boredom; as I was writing to her, two or three yawns must have slipped into the envelope and I must have sealed them up in it by mistake, for she hasn't answered me. And yet, having nothing better to do, she writes to everyone on earth. I am much obliged to her for singling me out this way, and it's not my fault that we were in correspondence. When she had the smallpox I absolutely had to write to her; it was a ridiculous letter, but unfortunately she found it charming, and so I was urged to write again, and thus a correspondence was launched. It's over now, I think.

I read *L'Ingénu* with pleasure. There are delightful passages in it, which redeem those that are stiff and hackneyed. One mustn't consider the work as a whole, nor ask that it have some purpose—but as you read it you enjoy it, and while you may criticize it when you're done reading, you are still sorry it's over. I haven't been able to find *Eugénie*.

I admit that I'm pleased with the success of *The Nobleman*. As for my comedy, so many things have been said about it, and some of the criticisms have seemed to me so false, that I don't know exactly how to go about re-working it. However, I will do my best as soon as I have some leisure. I have been wanting to write to Bellegarde for a long time. I began a letter even today, but it went all wrong. I will write him tomorrow, and my letter will go directly to Chambéry.

I've found out a great deal about your son. People are very pleased with him. He is intelligent, he is much liked, he does for the service everything required; but he could be doing his duty with yet more pleasure and zeal. I will try to see him at the Hague. I would like to be able to do something to earn the right to give him a casual word of advice now and then, but I won't be there long enough for that. I will try to revive Vernand's interest in him.[1] He speaks of your son in a friendly fashion; but what young man likes advice and exhortations?

Goodbye, the coach is leaving.

287. *From Constant d'Hermenches, October 27, 1767*

Hermenches

I do not know precisely, my most adorable friend, where we have got to in our correspondence; for many months now the letters I have received have been roving as much as I have, which is a great deal. But what I know and feel most keenly is that wherever I may be, my pleasantest thought is of you, and that my eyes and my heart continually turn toward you, just as the needle of the compass turns toward the north; I orient myself with respect to those marshes that I speak of so rudely, but which nonetheless I love, since you live there.

I've received your letter about Madame Girard; my brother was at my house. He thought that she was very content and satisfied; he thinks that she is very competent, and gets along well with her. I think that your friend is somewhat romantic, and therefore it's difficult to find a position that suits her imagination. She has suffered no particular misfortune; she is following the path of a middle-class woman, married without wealth, and who is endowed with no great talents. My brother painted a rather dismal picture of the position he was offering, and yet she persisted in wanting to come to his household, and he is making her life much more comfortable than he had

---

1. An officer who is the owner of a Swiss company in Holland and in a position to look out for d'Hermenches' son.

382 LETTER 287: October 27, 1767

promised her. He's an intelligent fellow, with a great deal of tact; if, between the two of us we can demonstrate our eagerness to help your so-called friend, we will certainly do so; but you must tell us what to do, and how— for what you are asking of me cannot be found. Madame Girard, as you portray her, must not hope to find the felicities she requires in any house or with any lady that one might place her with; to insist on these bonds of sympathy on the part of people who have never seen her, and who would have a position to offer her—that is the search for the philosopher's stone. It distresses me to see my brother reduced to a paid lady companion, a governess for his children; and I advise him to find some sensible girl of his station, of about his age, and remarry. He still misses his wife, and he says that he couldn't think about a second marriage. —That, I think, is an ample response to your request.

I've been in Switzerland for two weeks; I have become acquainted with a new piece of countryside, which I have inherited. There are superb vineyards here, and it's on the lakeshore; but I still return to my rustic Hermenches. I have been hunting here for a week with a few friends, and it wouldn't take much for me to return to my passion for reading and for liberty, which has so often been a source of happiness. But I must return to Besançon; I am more useful there than here. Twelve hundred mortals like me exist there under my orders and by my care; I watch over their welfare, their behavior, their fortune, their preservation—is that not a rather fine vocation? Indeed, that is how one must envisage the military profession, which is so often painted in hideous colors. Write to me in Besançon, my dear friend; I will be there soon. Your letter will be in very suitable company: a magnificent French duke who commands there; a cardinal who is spiritual director; a *parlement*; many noblemen. I think I will spend a very agreeable winter there.

But tell me, my dear Agnes, what vaporish pretensions to wit have addled the brains of your Dutch women? Here are two so-called plays, printed and advertised as products of your country, and they are dreadful. One is *Repsima,* the other *The Self-styled Philosopher* ...[1] The Bouillier ladies have written *Repsima;* it's a monstrous mishmash, an incredible aberration from good sense, a perversion, a hypertrophy of words; and on top of it all they are furious because the public is not marveling, and they are writing idiocies against the censors. These poor girls have lost their minds! Their composition is as contrary to common sense as Sodom and Gomorrha are contrary to nature; and they say that our poor little Mauclerc is involved in it, which drives me to despair; and people implicate you in all this, because these women are acquaintances of yours and pride themselves on letters they have received from you; and indeed, perhaps you do write them letters as charm-

---

1. Lucie and Judith Bouillier were the authors of *Repsima, essai d'une tragédie domestique* (Lausanne, 1767). *Le Philosophe soi-disant* (Maestricht, 1767) is by Mlle A. C. de Kinschott.

ing as the ones to me. It is true that it is impossible for you to write any other way; but why must I always be catching you at these inferior little correspondences? For God's sake, write to Voltaire, to d'Alembert;[2] it would require no greater effort, and *that* would be worth the trouble.

Since I have come here, I have been dealt a blow to the heart: one of my closest friends, a relative whom I loved like a sister, who has every kind of wit and talent, who had acquired and preserved a great deal of respect, has just now—after several years of speculations that have involved her in a thousand deceits and shady dealings—at the age of forty-two, married her lover, who is a young man without any position; noble and good-natured, but without any recognized merit. She didn't dare confront my arguments; she said nothing to me, and she has left for southern France. I renounce my friend because she deceived me; she was in love, and was false.

Farewell, my dear Agnes. I am at your feet, with no falseness at all.

288. *To Constant d'Hermenches, November 8, 1767*

Utrecht

In spite of a thousand things I should be attending to, I must answer your letter, which I've just received. It is good, and funny, and unjust—I love it; I'm putting everything else aside to attend to it. My mother no longer worries about correspondence as she used to: your account of *Repsima* makes her laugh, and she also found your outburst very funny ("For God's sake! Write to Voltaire, to d'Alembert ..."). So you think I write to the Bouillier ladies? They have never received a single word from me as far as I remember—never. I used to see them here once every two years or so. That's the extent of our acquaintance. Their father was a man of great merit, but their mother was arrogant, and our family, who had received them at first, stopped seeing them. If these ladies say that I write to them they are lying; but that lie is a compliment—so let's not punish them for it, but rather let them say what they will. However, if it amused you, you could ask them to show you these letters that they claim to have received ... But could it really be true that they say so? I find it hard to believe that people tell such obvious falsehoods.

Mademoiselle de Mauclerc is so far from having any stake in *Repsima* that she hesitates to have me read it; she thinks that one should spare the authors the fate of becoming a laughingstock in this country as they already are in Switzerland. I'm about to write to her that the work is in print, that there is nothing left to spare, and that she must immediately send me the manuscript. I'm extremely curious about it. Mlle Mauclerc called it a domestic tragedy; she spoke about it as you do. Hume had a letter from Mlle

2. See Letter 85, n. 2.

Bouillier written in a ridiculously romantic style, in which she begged him to mend his relations with Rousseau. We talked about it in London; only the fear of falling into a petty feminine meanness prevented me from urging him to give it to me. I've been told that it's the most ridiculous letter imaginable. As for *The Self-styled Philosopher*, who would have the patience to read it to the end?

So my friend (*your so-called friend*, you say; no, she's my friend) doesn't know what she wants. In a letter of September 16th she writes that she is not going to your brother's; in your letter I see that she is there; so all is well, we need no longer seek a position for her. I hope that he continues to be content with her; it is not so difficult for her to be content. In spite of all your clever remarks, I don't find her aspirations absurd. She inspires the friendship she is looking for quite naturally, because she has the best of hearts and a pleasant spirit. She got along very well in Bordeaux for several years with two little girls and their parents. As long as your brother doesn't remarry, he will not do at all badly with this *paid lady companion.*

You speak of all this lightly, and I forgive you, because I importuned you about it. Besides, we almost never succeed in changing each other's opinions, good or bad, about other people. My friends have never pleased you; if we were living together, that would be a drawback; but as things are, it is of no consequence. Even so, I would much rather see you and quarrel with you than have peace at a distance.

You judge your friend too severely: she's in love, and that's a great folly—but that folly so becomes the heart! Jeanne of Naples, Mary Stuart ...[1] The foolishness of loving greatly is the sweetest pleasure of life. Do not give up your friend. What would you think of me if I gave up Mme de Chasteler? (However, I doubt that she is in love.) Let me say it again: I respect love; loving to the point of madly sacrificing all other interests—it may hardly do honor to the head, but it does great honor to the heart. But you say that your friend is false; —ah, for that vice, I know of no excuse.

Tomorrow I go to the Hague. My dress arrived this morning from Paris; I ordered one for Mme de Rosendaal that will put all the finery of the other guests in the shade. I tried it on myself here; she will receive it today, all ready to wear. She will have all the pleasure of the surprise and none of the nuisance. She will see herself as the prettiest, the most splendid beauty of the Hague. That's what has kept me busy for the last five or six days, since

---

1. The friend is the one d'Hermenches speaks of in Letter 287. Belle has certainly made her point dramatically. Jeanne d'Anjou (1326–82), queen of Naples, was implicated in the death of her first husband. She married four times, and was put to death by the order of her cousin and heir. When Mary Stuart, Queen of Scots, (1542–87) returned to Scotland after the death of her young husband, Francis II of France, her enemies murdered her trusted friend and counsellor, the Italian musician David Rizzio. Her third husband, the earl of Bothwell, was believed to have murdered her second, Lord Darnley. She was beheaded under the orders of her cousin Queen Elizabeth I, but her son succeeded Elizabeth as James I of England.

my return from Amerongen. We gave dinners for the Comtes de Rzewuski, nephews of the one exiled to Siberia.[2] They have a great deal of wit. The younger of them is very young indeed; the elder is self-satisfied and arrogant, but he has seen a great deal and he speaks very well, with all imaginable elegance and grace.

It's said that our Princess is beautiful, charming, and altogether delightful.[3] I will tell you about her when I have seen her. I will see your son, provided he is willing. I will tell Monsieur de Reede to ask him to come see me.

I like and admire your reasons for returning to Besançon: your description is very fine, and I will read it again and again.

You would do me a great favor if you wrote to your brother telling him that Mme Girard's letter was written before she entered his household; that I am very pleased she's there, and that I wish nothing else for her than the continuation of a situation that seems to me very pleasant. Write soon, to undo any harm I may have done to this household: I'm terribly uneasy about it. They might believe that she is unhappy there, and that's not the case at all—she hadn't even arrived yet. Please remember that I am greatly concerned about this woman.

Farewell, my dear d'Hermenches. How sweet of you not to forget me! But by what fate do I get only letters—lovely letters, full of compliments—from our friendship, which would yield me such good company! Letters like yours are to be treasured; but if we could see each other, have conversations, enjoy ourselves together—those would be pleasures even more precious. Let's keep on writing. Perhaps chance will lead your compass to the North Pole, and the needle will be astonished to find itself just where it wanted to be. —So in this metaphor I am a pole; that's a bit awkward, whereas what you said was charming. My embroidery does not improve matters.

Have you ever seen letters as blotted and smeared as mine? I'm constantly wiping away my mistakes with my fingers, and they're covered with ink. Today, out of vanity I think, I tried to scrape those blots away with my penknife, and I've only managed to make them more visible and more unsightly. My letters are displeasing to the eyes; yours are pleasing at the first glance, and the pleasure only increases.

2. Venceslas Rzewuski (1705–79) was a Polish patriot who opposed the powerful Russian intervention in Polish political life.
3. Princess Wilhelmina of Prussia, niece of Frederick the Great, who had married Willem V, Prince of Orange, on October 7, 1767.

290. *From Constant d'Hermenches, December 31, 1767–January 1, 1768*

Besançon

Let us halt this fleeting year! And let me mark its last moments by the best pleasure I have left in this world! Since I cannot see you or hear you or speak to you, my dear Agnes, let me at least write to you. I have been putting it off for a long time, like those voluptuaries who save the most delicious morsel for the end of the meal; but what will happen to me now? I am stuffed with so many coarse, insipid words that I will be stupid. Yes, my incomparable friend, since my return from Switzerland I have been busy with so many tedious but useful tasks, I have written so many necessary letters, paid so many compliments required by protocol, that we can no longer speak the same language. But never mind, your intellect is universal; what my writing lacks in inspiration your reading will make up for. My feeling is always the same: that you are, unchangingly, the friend dearest to my heart and the most admired; a thousand fine phrases, a thousand witty remarks could not give more reality to that statement, and if I were to end my letter here, I claim it would be very presentable.

New Year's Day

You apologize for the erasures in your letter. Ah! they are only too charming; you always leave far behind you those who would claim the least perfection, and I have often reflected that of all the people of superior genius, there is no one who chisels his thoughts as well as you. Nothing is lacking—spelling, prosody, style, characters; I know of no one except Voltaire who has the same concision—a concision that would seem pedantic in anyone else. If I have a complaint, it is (I would say impertinently) that you do not fill up your paper enough; I have copied a few of your pages, and I have put four of yours in less than three of mine.

Agnes, what a good deed you have done! Your remarks about my son have given him concreteness in my mind;[1] I make allowances for your kindness in what you have said, but enough remains to satisfy me, and to make me see him as someone whom I want to treat as a friend, and who must be encouraged. He pleased me very much by the enthusiasm with which he speaks of you; he said to me, among other things: "There are many people here who do not like Mademoiselle de Zuylen, but it is because they don't have enough wit to bear the superiority of hers ..." I encourage him a great deal by indulgence and praise; I have sent him money, and I work at forming his taste by discussing in great detail the things that seem to interest him.

---

1. In her Letter 288 of November 8, Belle had promised to write d'Hermenches after her visit with his son Guillaume-Anne de Constant. Clearly she has done it, but her letter has not been found. There is a letter extant from his son, dated November 12, 1767, describing Belle's graciousness and his own shyness (*O.C.* 2: 521, n. 1).

Here is a letter from poor Bellegarde; he writes me that he doesn't know whether you've returned from England. Write him a few lines, I beg you. I thought that he would go to Holland for the marriage—this illustrious marriage which has excited nobody but a few cloth merchants; for they say that this Princess in no way alters the tedium of the Hague.[2] She is stiff and unsmiling, and neither of them seems to enjoy anything, or anybody—and you will argue with me again whether that is a question of climate! Indifference and bad taste circulate along with scurvy in the blood of your dear country, my dear Agnes. That's a fact, and it is all to your honor that you are not yet afflicted by them.

Speaking of cloth and marriage, I had reason to laugh when, at the same time I got your description of your friend's finery, I received a letter from Paris in which I read, "It was only Mademoiselle de Zuylen who failed to consult me on the choice of her purchases, and they are not in good taste." I must frankly admit to you that I would be more likely to consult you about a poem than about the combination of colors in a dress; you must forgive me. This makes me think of König,[3] who was annoyed when people said that he was a great mathematician, but wanted to fight when he was teased about his grace in dancing the minuet. That bad joke has been on my mind since I received your letter; again, forgive me! It's so easy for you to get even, and, unfortunately for me, on more essential points!

You have not at all upset my brother's household; at least, he has said nothing more to me about your friend. Certainly he is a man of impeccable conduct, and one who appreciates merit. The explanation of the dates clarified all of Mme Girard's apparent inconsistencies.

Well now, have you read *Repsima*? I was inexpressibly relieved when you convinced me of your innocence, and that Mlle Mauclerc is not an accomplice in this crime. Certainly I have always doubted that you could authorize by your correspondence the ridiculous conceit of these literary reptiles; but, when all's said and done, I retract nothing. I regret all the letters you may have written in your whole life to anyone who was not worthy of you—or else I wish that you had written a great many more, so that every one on earth could know you and celebrate you as I do. I wish that you had never written your "Portrait",[4] or that you would write another, or that I were a great enough portraitist to dare undertake it myself! My ambition is limitless for the people I love, and my severity is yet more insupportable. Besides, it is good to swoop down from all sides on the Bouillier imbeciles. If they had been humble and repentant after their adventure, if they had asked forgiveness from God, the printer, and the public, I would have had pity on them;

2. The marriage of the prince of Orange with Princess Wilhelmina.
3. Samuel König (1712–57), a famous German mathematician.
4. Her literary self-portrait, "Portrait de Zélide," which circulated in manuscript. See d'Hermenches' Letter 102.

but they took it all arrogantly, and everyone who might have any connection with them or might be at the place where the crime was committed is honor-bound to shame them so that all Christendom might know the case. I would even be tempted to request a quarantine on anyone who can read and write and who comes from Lausanne.

You are undoubtedly kind enough to want to know how I am living. My dear Agnes, there is nothing very stimulating in my life, but I have a quite pleasant daily routine here, and I think I have already told you on what I base the happiness of my existence. I live here as I intended to, and instead of suffering from the "leave-seeking" disease that afflicts the Dutch, and all the military men in the world, I have made my home with these people who have been entrusted to me. Besides, I have magnificent lodgings; very enjoyable cardgames; a rather elegant household, as well-ordered as my soldiers are; respect and consideration from this entire half-ecclesiastic half-parliamentary city; two extraordinary harpsichords in my apartments; the governor, the Duc de Randon, and the Intendant, who give suppers of twenty-four people every day, and other little suppers; a theater as good as the one in the Hague (except that it doesn't have La Martin). The ladies pay me visits; when one doesn't want to go for supper, one goes to late-night parties in houses; there are rather expensive whist parties everywhere, and you know that, although I don't play a great deal, I do love gambling for high stakes. So that's my Besançon. With all that, I can tell you that there is nothing stimulating for me here, because there are neither intriguing liaisons nor congenial minds; but as for kindness, gentleness, softness, I find all that in a very pretty woman, who is the best thing about this place. Well, all I do is talk to her about morality and reading, and I spend many evenings alone at home, by choice.

I am at your feet, my adorable friend. My respects and best wishes to your worthy parents.

291. *From Constant d'Hermenches, January 4, 1768*

Besançon

By now, my indulgent and most lovable friend, you will have received the letter I had the honor of writing you several days ago. I certainly deserved to be scolded, and yet you aren't scolding me! That's because you know my heart; it is impossible for it to detach itself from you. It is not only my vanity that makes me want to preserve our friendship; if I were to lose you, I would lose the being in all the world who most charms my existence. Now how can that be reconciled with my long silences? I myself have no explanation for it, unless it is that my letters have so far to go, and I have so many things to say to you that I never find the time I would like for answering letters as perfect as yours, nor am I ever as free of mind as I would like to be to sit down and chat with you. I have just received word from Bellegarde again, who begs me to inform him of his fate.[1] To clarify things, I am sending you his letter; you will handle the matter much better between the two of you than by my secondhand explanations. I hope you won't mind my sending him the letter I just received from you.

Ah, my dear Agnes, how fortunate my son is; so he's going to see you and hear you. You'll find him living with the Golofkines, and madly in love with Madame Alexandre;[2] at least, last winter, she did not find him too much of a little boy to be her courtier; she's a nice little woman, who has many good qualities, but who is passionately devoted to pleasure. The present pleasure is never enough for her because she is always preoccupied with a yet greater one that she can imagine; she is young, and experience may teach her to enjoy the present moment.

If only my son were four years older, my dear Agnes, and had a company in the Swiss Guards! I would offer him to you for your husband; since I can't marry you myself, you would at least be my daughter-in-law, and we would spend our lives together, just like the patriarchs. That is always the aim of my wishes and my prayers: to be able to be near you one day, my dear friend!

Why have you and Bentinck fallen out? I have always found all those people a despicable lot.

Farewell, dear Agnes.

○ৱ *Belle has come to the conclusion that it will not be possible to obtain a dispensation for Bellegarde to marry her on terms that she could bring herself to accept.*

293. *To Constant D'Hermenches, January 21, 1768*

Thursday

You have done very well, my dear d'Hermenches, to send me Bellegarde's letter, for it has made up my mind for me. I would already have sent you a letter for him Monday, or else I would have written directly to him Tuesday, if I were not using a little tactic—a permissible one, I think—to give my renunciation some merit in my parents' eyes: I would like them to ask me not to accept the dispensation with its clauses, and not to think of obtaining permission from the King[1] with the intention of satisfying us without a papal dispensation. As a reward for my sacrificing these two

1. The letter from Bellegarde is extant (*O.C.* 1: 522, n. 1). In his inimitable spelling, he tells d'Hermenches that Piccolomini's efforts on his behalf in Rome have met with no success; he is arranging to have other strings pulled, but his tone is not optimistic.
2. A sister-in-law of Gabriel Golofkine.
1. The king of Sardinia, who ruled Savoie.

means we have left (the one sure, but unworthy of the integrity of my character, the other still only an attempt), I would like to obtain more freedom to do as I wish; that would make me enjoy and even prefer the unmarried state.

I have seen many nuptials, but am tempted by none.

said La Fontaine, and I say so too.[2] To say that I am sorry that this marriage is not taking place is not, however, merely a tactical ploy on my part. I have been sad these last few days, and I have wept; but after all, how can I persist? If my father, seeing my regret, and not having seen Monsieur de Bellegarde's letter nor his haste to have matters decided, were to say to me: "Let him try to obtain the King's permission, and I will no longer demand a papal dispensation," I really don't know what I would say or do. Perhaps I would choose to write that to you, and to write to Bellegarde that everything is over; that he may now marry whomever he likes. For to say to him "My father now consents to what he refused for so long; go ask the King for a permission that—because the Pope refuses to give any other dispensation, and I refuse to accept this one—will be very difficult to obtain" —I would not dare to do it, and I absolutely would not want to do it. This is all extremely awkward. My father told me to look for that old Bull of Benedict XIV, so that he can see it again.[3]

Never again speak to me about a husband. If I want one, I will manage to find him myself. All that I would want my friends and my small amount of fame to procure for me would be the good graces of some respectable and distinguished old lady, living in Paris and fairly rich, who might be curious to meet me and might want to show me Paris; if she wrote to me, if she were someone well-known, and if she asked me to come spend three or four months with her, I think I could easily obtain permission to go; that would please me a great deal. But one does not find old ladies like that. Some are too pretentious; others have no eagerness about anything; in this country they are all afraid of going to any trouble. One would have to inspire in them an enthusiasm for me that I hardly deserve—an enthusiasm like yours. But women are rarely enthusiastic about each other. Mme de Chasteler would not, I think, be free to invite me to Brussels, and even less to take me to Paris. What folly! to give up her child, her friends, her liberty![4] We could have gone anywhere together!

If I wanted to crown your horror of the Hague, I would tell you how I was received and treated there, and how they gossiped about me. Because of a ridiculous fear of smallpox, people refused to see me, while they saw

2. From "Le Mal Marié" [The ill-married husband], *Fables* VII, 2.
3. This Bull, dating from the 1740s, specified that marriages not conducted according to the rules of the Council of Trent—that is, before the priest and two witnesses—could nevertheless be valid in Holland and Belgium.
4. Mme de Chasteler had a son by her first husband, Lieve Geelvinck. Her family probably insisted that she give up raising him when she married a Catholic.

others who went into the infected house just as I did. With the others, they forgot that; with me, they remembered. The others they warned to be careful; of me, they asked nothing, and they managed without my company, expressing neither regret nor excuses.

I get along badly with Monsieur Bentinck since I discovered him to be as unkind as he is unamusing.[5] To be both hurtful and boring is too much. He had spoken ill of me, of my relatives—of the most respectable among them; I expressed myself about it freely, he learned of it, and he is getting even any way he can.

For a week or ten days that I spent at the Hague, I went to Mme d'Athlone's every morning and came back every evening; a fiacre brought me back at mealtime, usually in Pope Street, but often at Comte Gabriel's—for he and his wife have very pleasantly stepped forward on my behalf.[6] Because they value seeing me they have calculated the risks and, having found upon reflection that I offered little danger since of the whole Bentinck household I saw only Mme d'Athlone and her child, they asked me to come see them whenever I wished. You would not believe how touched my cousin was by this behavior. I didn't see your son there, although he calls on them often. I never knew in advance when I could go.

Do you think I've told you all the ill I could say about the Hague? No! Not half! but why should I complain about it? I'm not particularly sensitive about it. I haven't been humiliated and I haven't been bored; all is well.

I have often spoken of you with van Monster and with Vernand.[7] I received no men on my third floor. "But," people said, "if Constant were here?" "I would say to him: *niet t'huys*,[8] just as to the others." "But he would not accept *niet t'huys*." I assured them that they were wrong, and that as soon as you saw that it was better for me to receive no one, you would not even dream of seeing me; you would refuse me even if I invited you.

You praise my letters too much. I think I know what they are, and rarely do I find them good. I will learn to put more words on fewer pages. Your first letter, a most delightful one, I was going to answer light-heartedly. The Bouillier sisters with their *Repsima*, the scurvy and the bad taste that run in our veins, your compliments, König—it had all put me in a playful mood, and I intended to avenge my taste and my finery in a spectacular fashion; your other letter, and the one that accompanied it,[9] diverted me to seriousness. I will repeat to you quite flatly that Mme de Rosendaal's dress is charming; it is true that this proves nothing about König's minuet, for it's Monsieur Rendorp, with a whole senate of Parisian women, who chose and

---

5. Anthony Bentinck, married to her cousin Maria Catherina van Tuyll van Serooskerken. D'Hermenches had asked about this falling-out in his Letter 291 of January 4.
6. Gabriel Golofkine had bought d'Hermenches' company.
7. Two officers who have been mentioned a number of times.
8. "Not at home."
9. Bellegarde's letter.

arranged everything. If I were to see you, I would truly have a way to avenge myself: I would dress so very beautifully! I would choose the colors with so much care and so much art that you would be tempted to curse heaven for not having made me more of a philosopher and less of a woman.

Speaking of philosophy, in a week I am beginning a course of speculative and experimental physics. I have been dying to for a long time. Your Besançon sounds very attractive. You speak of your profession in such a way that one hardly knows whom to envy more, you or those you command. Tell me, are they fond of you? Next to the reward of feeling that one is doing good, the affection one receives from others is the sweetest. One day (a long time ago) I was told that the soldiers in your regiment in the Hague did not like you at all. I was surprised and taken aback; how is it possible, I said, to love oneself so little that with all those talents, and a heart that possesses such good qualities, that appreciates generosity and all other virtues, one makes no effort to win the love of others? You will say that the lack of discipline in which their comrades lived made you appear to your own soldiers harsh by comparison; but if you tell me that, I won't believe you. Experience has proved to me over and over again that one can be both strict and benevolent—one can make oneself both loved and obeyed.

I am very pleased to have made you think even better of your son. That's a service to both of you. What I think of him is exactly what I have said to you; I am delighted that our approval is mutual, and that he speaks well of me. I entirely approve of your having sent him some money. At his age, a small amount gives great pleasures; later, vanity pays for luxury with large amounts, and gets little pleasure. Besides, it's at his age or never that one must learn to give. —Look how I enjoy telling you things you know better than I do! You spoil me completely by your prejudice in my favor, and by your praises.

Farewell; perhaps I will add another word this evening. If I don't send you a letter for the Marquis, and if I write him tomorrow, I will write you Monday and tell you what I've said to him.

CR *By late 1767 Belle had been back in touch with James Boswell, who by that time had established himself as a lawyer in Edinburgh, but not yet managed to get himself married. In March 1768 he wrote to his friend Temple, "Do you know, my charming Dutchwoman and I have renewed our correspondence; and upon my soul, Temple, I must have her ..."[10]*

Belle de Zuylen was being talked about in some famous circles in London at this very time—not only as one particular woman, but also as a marker in arguments about women's virtue and intellect. The following conversation with Johnson is recounted in Boswell's journal of March 28, 1768:

10. *Boswell in Holland* 372.

... I told him my objections to the Dutch lady were her superior talents. "O Sir," said he, "you need not be afraid, marry her; before a year goes about you'll find that reason much weaker, and that wit not near so bright." O admirable master of human nature! [11]

However intimidating Boswell found Zélide's superior talents, he hoped to engage them for a French translation of his Account of Corsica—*a book that created such enthusiam in England that one statesman was compelled to remark, "Foolish as we are, we cannot be so foolish as to go to war because Mr. Boswell has been in Corsica . . . ." [12] "I am enchanted with your book, my dear friend," Belle wrote. "I don't know which I like the most in this book: the Corsicans, their leader, or their historian. You show a mind and a heart whose friend I am proud to be." [13]*

Belle had said she would write on the twenty-second or twenty-fifth of January; undoubtedly she did write shortly after that, but the letter is not extant. Apparently it contained some references to Corsica that had been stimulated by her correspondence with Boswell.

296. From Constant d'Hermenches, March 11, 1768

Paris

The letter you told me you were going to write "the following Monday" is what has caused my inexcusable silence: I was waiting for it to arrive before writing to you, and I deprived myself of all my happiness. I had nothing to say about myself, but I had a great deal to say to you about *you* if you had written to me. I love you with passion, emotion, admiration, and veneration; I think of you incessantly; I follow you in all your moments. You can imagine how unhappy I have been at this eclipse of our correspondence; I may seem to be in the wrong, but, fundamentally, it is you who are at fault.

I'm going to Corsica. I could become a brigadier without going there, but I prefer to follow my fortune without forcing anything—to expect from Corsica what I think I will have deserved there; I am experiencing all the reverses, attacks, and infamies that are part of the histories of heroes. May I become one—or at any rate, by the superiority of my patience and the strength of my soul, be one in your eyes.

We have had a considerable advantage; it is most likely that with the means being employed, we will get the better of your dear Paoli; at any rate, I'm going to do my best to—for that's my duty.

When will I be able to converse with you? When will I be able to recount

11. Frank Brady and Frederick Pottle, eds., *Boswell in Search of a Wife* 156.
12. Pottle, *James Boswell: The Earlier Years* 395.
13. By "their leader" Belle means Pasquale Paoli. This letter, dated March 27, 1768, is not in *O.C.* It is quoted in French by Courtney in *Biography* 246.

things to you that will seem wondrous? Send me your news immediately, to Toulon and then to Corsica. Farewell, my divine friend; may you be less ill, less unhappy; may I contribute to your consolation! While I am in Corsica you should still write to me at the address of Monsieur Bournonville—who, by the way, is my enemy. He told Monsieur de Choiseul that I was detested in Holland, that I would not have become a major general,[1] along with any number of such slanders. I laugh at all of it, and I scorn the slanderers. Farewell once more, my excellent friend.

297. *To Constant d'Hermenches, March 27, 1768*

Utrecht

It seemed to me that you were not in a very good humor in your last letter (what you needed was a college of physical sciences), which is why I left you *alone*[1] for some time.[2] Besides, I had nothing new to say except about things you've disdained. When I saw your son in the Hague, I said to him: "We mainly agree, your father and I, about this country; however, I always defend it against him for the pleasure of argument, and because of some remnant of patriotism."

Your remarks on Mlle Kinschott amused me greatly;[3] really, I am vainer about the letters attributed to me than about those that I write.

I was in need of all that foolishness to make me laugh, for the letters of Bellegarde made me weep. Except for that thought, today I am the happiest person in the world. The weather is beautiful, and spring is coming and smiling upon us. My friend Boswell has just sent me his book *An Account of Corsica.* The heroism of this people, the great qualities of their leader, the genius of the author—it's all moving and admirable. I would like to be able to toss it to you, on condition that you toss it back to me quickly, for I want to try to translate it. It contains here and there peculiarities that would seem to you ridiculous and that I myself don't altogether approve of.

Mme de Chasteler is in Amsterdam. I may go to see her tomorrow.

Goodbye; I haven't time to say any more—and what would I say to you? You make fun of my physics, my friends displease you, and my amusements you find pitiable. However, you must at any rate like Plutarch; well now, I

---

1. D'Hermenches' term is "général-major," which was the term used in the Prussian military structure; the corresponding rank in the French military is *maréchal de camp.* The post of brigadier was more a function than a rank, so that the next rank above colonel was that of major general. (Kennett, *The French Armies* 54–55, nn. 3, 4.)

1. English in the original.

2. This seems to be a response not to d'Hermenches' letter of March 11, but rather to an earlier one, because she makes no reference to his departure for Corsica. Her first reaction to that will be in her Letter 302 of June 2.

3. A. C. Kinschott, author of a play called *Le Philosophe soi-disant* [The self-styled philosopher], which d'Hermenches had made fun of in Letter 287.

am reading him with delight in English, in an admirable translation; I had never been able to drag myself through a single one of the *Lives* with that leaden Dacier.[4] Do you find German a beautiful language? I have learned a little these last days. I would like the whole world to be my country.

298. *From Constant d'Hermenches, April 8, 1768*

If it was your intention to mortify me, my dear Agnes, I am frank enough to admit you have succeeded; your silence has done more than distress me, it has humiliated me. I understand how my letters might not please you; that's all very well for my letters, my dear friend! But for my heart, no: there is not the slightest thing in my heart that could displease you—and besides, what makes me tedious is my passionate interest in you! Your fame and my chagrin at finding you eccentric and an enthusiast—that is the subject of all our disagreements! and you ridicule me for exclaiming at your scientific studies by apologizing for reading Plutarch! Plutarch, Agnes! I am having him read to my daughter; I am telling her that Mme Dacier's style lacks taste,[1] that Plutarch was a philosopher, a man of wit—eloquent and sublime—who lived in the flowering of the age of Augustus, who has been rendered better in English than by any Frenchman—even Amyot,[2] whom I prefer to Dacier. It's very good that you're reading the English translation ... and I will be even more pleased if you undertake to translate those Corsican memoirs. I urge you to do it at once—it's a work that will be useful and interesting, and to which your pen will give both grace and fame.

But apropos of writings, do you know about the misfortune of *Repsima*?[3] The unfortunate Lucie Bouillier went to bed the other evening cheerful and in the best of health, and was found dead in her bed the next morning. Madame d'Hermenches is deeply grieved; she was very fond of her. They say that it's the spleen that killed that unhappy woman; the despair of her *Repsima* that she tried to swallow; vanity, pride, vexation, a false sense of reputation—can all that kill a woman? Well, she has died of it; we all have some part in it, and I am sorry for it now; but I cannot help thinking that the decision she made is not altogether unenviable. We said that it would have been much better if she had made a baby instead of *Repsima;* and now the unhappy woman has died in consequence of giving birth to it.

4. Belle is probably reading Sir Thomas North's translation, *The Lives of the Noble Grecians and Romans* (1579), which Shakespeare used. André Dacier's translation was done in 1721.
1. D'Hermenches seems to be confusing André Dacier, the translator of Plutarch, with his wife, Anne Lefebvre Dacier (1647–1720), who translated Homer.
2. Jacques Amyot (1513–93), an influential translator of Plutarch and other writers of antiquity. North's translation was based on his work.
3. In the letters of October and November 1767 Belle and d'Hermenches had ridiculed this domestic tragedy and its authors, Lucie and Judith Bouillier.

I no longer know what I was saying to you about Mlle Kinschott, and so I will not justify myself; the day before, a captain of the Dutch dragoons came by and spoke to me of that Catie,[4] of you, of Maastricht; all that had put me in a bad humor. I wrote to you, and now I see as clear as day that I wrote some nonsense—but that's attributable to the country it came from; please forgive me. If, as you claim, I love neither your friends nor your amusements nor your scientific studies, it is nonetheless true that I love *you* above everything, and that I am as tenderly attached to you as ever. And I convey this to you from a place where I lead the best and most reasonable life imaginable, a place where I have everything that should content a reasonable being. But I have no passions; I judge of things sanely and I enjoy things without being an enthusiast—thus friends such as you lose nothing by it, absent though they be; you are so superior that, short of forgetting you altogether, it is always you that one prefers. And that's how it is with me; you will always be my most beloved friend, charming Agnes, for as long as you are willing to allow it!

Bellegarde is in Holland. Your love-story is certainly a sad one; he is not far from you, and perhaps the two of you can come to some happy resolution—I hope so. But if not, you will have nothing to regret—that's my only consolation—and you will always know how to live happily![5]

Lord, how I would like to have you dine with Mme de La Corée, the wife of the Intendant of Besançon! She would please you immensely! She is French only on the outside; her inner self is English—or Swiss. She is the niece of the famous Madame Guyon.[6] She is full of talents and knowledge; there is a hint of pedantry about her, but she is eager to please; she has few prejudices, and an excellent heart. Farewell, my dear Agnes.

299. *To Constant d'Hermenches, April 28, 1768*

I should have replied sooner to a letter as kind as yours, but I was unable to; I was in Amsterdam, and busy translating. When one is occupied, one puts off writing until the day of mailing, and then, when the day arrives, some unexpected little task makes one put it off again; that's precisely what has been happening since I got your last letter. I received it in bed, where I was so absorbed in Plutarch that I had forgotten to get up; your praises of him could not have come at a better moment. I felt immediately how just

4. "Catie" is a nickname derived from the middle name (Catharina) of Mlle Kinschott.
5. In fact, d'Hermenches already knows that the Bellegarde business is over; he has received a letter from Bellegarde, who says that since "the hope of possessing the charming Agnes is totally lost," he wants to move on to the consideration of the "Widow"—Mme Geelvinck; but she is by now married to the Marquis de Chasteler. (*O.C.* 2: 526.)
6. The seventeenth-century mystic, referred to in another context in d'Hermenches' Letter 65.

they were; and the great Pompey, seeing himself so well and so vividly portrayed in Plutarch, seemed to join us in praising and thanking his author. I had anticipated your advice to translate Boswell; although your approval has encouraged me, I almost regret my commitments to the publisher. I must, however, fulfill them. I would never have believed that it was so difficult and so tedious to translate.

One cannot hear of the tragic end of Lucie Bouillier without being torn between laughter and tears. I would advise young authors to keep that example in mind before they bring their first efforts to the press. It is truly sad, to die so suddenly—so young, so ridiculous! I wish that someone had cried out to her: "Wait! it's not worth dying for! Look at the number of mediocre writers who have perfectly pleasant lives. Do the wise thing—give up writing, and join us in laughing at *Repsima*."

You had said nothing to me about Mlle Kinschott, except that she spoke of me as her intimate friend, and that she was showing my letters around. Since I have never written to her, I merely laughed at that nonsense, that's all; there is nothing to reproach you with in that. I had no intention, I swear to you, of hurting your feelings either by my silence or by my letter. You contradict a little too much, in my opinion, but no matter; that gives me the pleasure of contradicting you, and it all evens out.

My lessons with Monsieur Hahn[1] are quite as interesting as Plutarch, and will not make me more pedantic. On the one hand, we admire the laws of inanimate nature and the use that inventiveness has been able to make of them; on the other, we consider human nature from different points of view, according to how society has disposed it. The knowledge of men is perhaps more useful, but the other is perhaps more curious and more satisfying— why exclude one or the other when both are fascinating?

I also wish I could have supper in Besançon with you and the amiable lady, but not this evening, for I am sullen and sick. Goodbye; the post is about to leave.

I did go to see Mme de Chasteler; she is more amiable and affectionate than ever, and so pleased to be in Holland that you would be scandalized; however, she speaks of Brussels with gratitude, and of Mme d'Arenberg with admiration. Her husband is a nonentity, but I say that to you in a whisper, for I think she would like us to get along well together. He really is a dolt, in the strongest sense of the word.

---

1. Johannes David Hahn (1729–84), professor of physics and medicine at the University of Utrecht and then at the University of Leyden.

Ꮿ *In 1768 d'Hermenches became directly and vitally involved in events that engaged much of Europe: the acquisition of Corsica by France.*[2] *Genoa had possessed Corsica since the Middle Ages, and its occupation had been bloody and acrimonious throughout its history. Through the years, France had needed the friendship of Genoa in order to secure access to commerce with Italy and with the Levant. The Genoese had not had the resources to maintain their hold over Corsica, and had engaged the French, by means of various treaties and sometimes simple payment, to maintain it for them.*

By 1768 there had been organized insurrection in Corsica for some forty years. While the European powers, especially England and France, cast a covetous eye on Corsica on account of its strategic position in the Mediterranean, political thinkers and philosophes saw in the Corsican situation an opportunity to test their theses about the development and the fate of peoples. The Corsicans were regarded as a backward—by some, even a savage—people; the image of their culture, widely associated with the vendetta, made colorful reading in gazettes and memoirs. At the same time, they were admired for their vigor and persistence in their efforts to shake off the Genoese yoke. Corsica had come to be a trope for resistance to tyranny and the struggle for liberty.

From around 1755 the leader—we would now say "charismatic leader"— of Corsican nationalism was Pasquale Paoli (1725–1807). He restructured the army and the system of justice, and revitalized Corsica's economic life. His personality and historic role caught the imagination of the European intellectual community, and he was celebrated as a heroic liberator and legislator. James Boswell, in the course of a two-year European tour, spent five weeks in Corsica in 1765. Armed with a letter of introduction from Rousseau, he presented himself to Paoli, whose fame he helped spread with an idealized portrait in his Account of Corsica, the Journal of a Tour to that Island; and Memoirs of Pascal Paoli *(London, 1768).*

In Europe the structure of national interests and priorities had changed after the Seven Years' War. France's alliances with Austria had become much stronger, and the Austrians' interests had shifted northward to their dealings in central Europe, so that rather than challenging France's position in the Mediterreanean, they were supporting it. Furthermore, France had had the experience of seeing its Mediterranean coast blockaded by English ships operating from Gibraltar and Minorca, and there was now no prospect of dislodging England from either of those positions. France needed Genoa less, while Corsica had become the key to the security of France's Mediterranean commerce: it needed to have at least one, and preferably two, secure stations on the island. Paoli and his forces, while not quite able to drive the Genoese out, could make the positions of the foreign

2. For a compact treatment, see Hall, *The Corsican Question.*

powers insecure, and France was finding it increasingly onerous to keep the peace because the Genoese—for no practical reason that is easy to find— seemed intent on oppressing the Corsicans to the point where revolt was inevitable.

In the spring of 1768 things were at a crisis. The French considered it absolutely vital to have control over Cap Corse—the seven-by-twenty-mile peninsula that juts northward from Corsica—and the ports at the two sides of its base, Saint-Florent and Bastia. Paoli knew that the French possessed and would deploy the resources needed to get that control, and was in negotiations with them. But he also knew that his political position among his countrymen would suffer if he conceded such control to a foreign power: France was perfectly willing to have the Corsicans run their own civil and economic affairs, but Corsican nationalism was intense. The Genoese had concluded that it was simply too costly to keep Corsica, and had offered— for certain guarantees and compensations—to cede it to France, but Louis XV perceived that his accepting it would be provocative to the other European powers.

France's counter-proposal, worked out by its Foreign Minister, the duc de Choiseul, became the Treaty of Versailles that was signed on May 15, 1768. France would control the island and keep peace on it formally on behalf of Genoa; but since Genoa could pay nothing for this service, the compensation would be that France would treat the island as its own property. This control would revert to Genoa upon Genoa's paying France a certain amount plus the expenses of the occupation. Since there was not the remotest prospect for Genoa's ever being able to do that, Corsica effectively became French territory—but technically Louis XV could say that Corsica had not been ceded to him. It has often been said that what Genoa did was not sell Corsica but pawn it.

On the ninth of May, when d'Hermenches wrote the following letter to Belle, Choiseul's offer was still being considered in Genoa, while Choiseul was engaged in negotiations with Paoli in Paris. If Paoli made any concessions to France, he would need French help in controlling splinter groups who might oppose them; if the deal between France and Genoa fell through, he would need help in expelling the recalcitrant Genoese. On the other hand, if Paoli made no concessions, then the French would have to deal with Paoli's forces. As late as June 7, the comte de Marbeuf, commander of French forces in Corsica since 1764, wrote to Choiseul, "We will perhaps have more difficulty preventing them from fighting each other than avoiding war on our own account."[3] It isn't surprising that d'Hermenches said he was embarking "to wage war in Corsica; against whom, I don't yet know." Nobody knew.

3. Hall, *The Corsican Question* 185.

300. *From Constant d'Hermenches, May 9, 1768*

My divine Agnes, it seems that you were inspired when you spoke to me of Corsica, and undertook to translate its history. Imagine, I am going there posthaste! On May 16, the Eptingen regiment is leaving Besançon to go to Toulon, where it will embark with a number of worthy fellows to wage war in Corsica; against whom, I don't yet know. This is a bizarre turn of events, but, fortunately, I'm not displeased; I am exactly in the right state of mind to go running off after adventures. I would not have chosen to be an adventurer, but having embraced a profession out of a liking for it, I cheerfully resign myself to whatever it may bring ... and I would rather be a major fighting in Corsica than a general yawning with boredom on the parade ground in the Hague, with less money and less respect. But Agnes, how I regret going so far from you! Although I will see you no less than I do now, it grieves my heart to put yet greater distance between us. Send me at once, I beg you, everything you know about Corsica that might interest me; the Bournonville address is still the best.

But tell me what news you have of Bellegarde. He wrote me a note when he left Paris, but since then I don't know whether he is dead or alive. Tell me what you are doing.

You are wrong to say that I always contradict you. I am honest, I am frank, I have reflected a great deal, and that's all; I have noticed that when all's said and done, you always admit that I'm right.

I have spent my winter here, without going home even for twenty-four hours; I had counted on going there and staying as long as I liked this summer. But that is not to be—I'm off to Corsica! I have to make a will, put my affairs in order, take leave of my friends—that is expected. But my mind is serene and tranquil, and if I can be useful to those who are with me, I will count my vocation a happy one. Do not think it is ambition that guides me: if I wanted to advance myself, I should be at Versailles, rather than in Corsica—no, Agnes. But the more one encounters obstacles, the more one becomes a man, and I want to die as such, so that you will be yet more flattered by my perfect and inviolable affection. Do not forget me—you would be unfair and ungrateful to do so. And be so good as to read a few pages the less, and write me a few pages the more; those dead people you are reading will not thank you for it, whereas I, being alive, will adore you. I am at your feet, Agnes.

Bournonville will address your letters to me anywhere; send me something rather coherent and detailed about Corsica, addressed to him, *as soon as possible.* You will do me the greatest service; I don't yet know whom we're fighting. It's unfair that the English, from their island, want to command all the islands in the world—admit it![1]

---

1. D'Hermenches is alluding to one of the chief concerns of France and Austria, namely that the English had gained Minorca back from France under the Paris treaty of 1763, and that if

302. *To Constant d'Hermenches, June 2, 1768*

I would have written you a long time ago, because you have been much in my thoughts, had I not been overwhelmed by neuralgia pains aggravated by onsets of violent emotions that came to redouble them, to the point where finally I was only a shadow and a ruin of myself.

It has only been for the last twenty-four hours that I have begun again to be a thing that thinks and speaks. Quickly, I want to speak to you and congratulate you on this little expedition that will bring some variety to your life, introduce you to some new people, and really call you back to your métier. An ugly métier, truth to tell—cruel, destructive; but in spite of all that, I quite feel it that if I were a man of war I would want to wage war, and I would get sick and tired of nothing but garrison duty.

I do not try to choose between Paris and London; but I am against tyrants, and in favor of those men who know how to appreciate their liberty and defend it. My good wishes are with you—but they are against your regiment if you do not wage war on the side of Paoli against the sordid Genoese.

I will be happy to write what you're asking for; it will be a little extract from an interesting book that I do like, but which I'm no longer translating. I had got quite far in it, but I wanted permission to change things that were badly written, and to abridge others that French impatience would find soporifically long-winded. Although the author, at that point, had almost decided to marry me if I had been willing, he refused to sacrifice one syllable of his book to my taste; I wrote to him that I had made up my mind never to marry him, and I abandoned the translation.[1] If I continue not to be completely flattened by sadness and the vapors, I will do for you an abridged portrayal of Corsica and its inhabitants. But first the Prince[2] and Princess must lunch here Saturday, I must see them leave Zuylen, and I must return to my own room in Utrecht. The whole Court, returning from Amsterdam on its way to Soestdijk, is lunching with us—that is to say, dining: for I call it "dining" to eat a meal of soup, roast, and the rest; and it will most likely be at the hour when one usually does dine.

---

they held Corsica as well, they would too tightly command the Mediterranean.

1. Boswell's proposal letter to Belle has been lost, but he gives a resumé of it in his letter to Temple (April 26, 1768): "I have written to her and told her all my perplexity. I have put in the plainest light what conduct I absolutely require of her, and what my father will require. I have bid her be my wife at present and comfort me with a letter in which she shall show at once her wisdom, her spirit, and her regard for me. You shall see it. I tell you, man, she knows me and values me as you do." Apparently she did not, for his journal entry of May 2, 1768, is: "Morning, letter from Zélide: termagant!" (*Boswell in Holland* 373-74.) Their relationship ends at this point. Boswell married his cousin the following year.

Belle's translation would have been redundant: Horace Walpole had sent a copy of the *Account of Corsica* to Madame du Deffand. By July her secretary had finished a translation of it.
2. The stadholder, who was the prince of Orange.

You ask me for news of Bellegarde. He wrote me a polite note from the Hague; I answered it; that's all.

I was so struck by you at the beginning of our acquaintance, I thought you were a sorcerer at the very least—appearing at just the right moment: coming out of the ball, at the entrance to the theatre, on the ugly little staircase at an Italian opera—you, your hand, the headband you wore. I wished for you to be there, and just when I wished it, there you were; if things had gone on that way, I think the sorcerer would have bewitched me. Where do you think these memories, these tender thoughts, are leading me? Simply to tell you that Bellegarde is no sorcerer—or else that he does not want to use his spells on me. He made up a party with Mme de Puente,[3] Mme de Rosendaal, and a dozen men to go to Texel and from there to Amsterdam. Mme d'Athlone, who was at the Hague, was part of the group. With a little skill, Bellegarde could have had me invited. Not at all; he probably thought there was no more room, or else the idea didn't even occur to him.

Mme d'Athlone, who entered into this confederation only by chance, apparently had no say in it. She writes me today: "I wished you were there, we would have enjoyed it more." Which means that they didn't greatly enjoy themselves—I laugh. None of these women knew Amsterdam, which I know very well. Above all, I laugh at your friend's clumsiness; it was the only chance in the world for him to see me freely and talk to me. Perhaps he no longer cares about that at all; in that case, far from being clumsy, he is being very sensible. God bless him!

Will you write to me from that island? You must write me—details, if possible, and (if possible) without modesty, or vanity, or prejudice, so that I may see the truth as in a fine mirror that alters coloring no more than it alters shapes. Goodnight, I'm going to bed. The day the mail leaves is a long way off, but the right moment presented itself, and I seized it. If I can, I will thicken the packet with a little about Corsica. Farewell, my dear d'Hermenches, I wish you pleasure and glory, and I pray Providence to watch over your safety.

303. To Constant d'Hermenches, June 6, 1768

The Prince was here yesterday. Rendorp spent the day with me; my youngest brother left tonight, so you can imagine whether I've had time to write the history of Corsica. I'm beginning to feel completely well again; I flatter myself that I'm going to have a little leisure, and that I will be able to make it valuable to myself by employing it for you.

I saw Lady Athlone; the Texel and Amsterdam party was rather agreeable at times, but so noisy—there was so much gambling and all those gentlemen

3. Wife of the Spanish envoy.

spoke so loudly—that my cousin was glad, after all, that I wasn't there; she said that it would have pained her to see me lost in that crowd, and my voice drowned out by so many voices. Bellegarde acted as major-domo with all possible thoughtfulness and amiability.

ભ *After the signing of the treaty on May 15, 1768, there was a period of negotiations between Choiseul and Paoli. The Comte de Marbeuf had been the French military commander in Corsica since the 1764 Treaty of Com-piègne, under which the role of France was that of mediator between Genoa and Corsica. For the most part, Choiseul had adopted Marbeuf's plan for the island, which was for the French to occupy Bastia, Saint-Florent, and Cap Corse and leave the rest of the island to the Corsicans. If Paoli decided that the Corsicans must have all or nothing, then the French would have to undertake to have it all. A bilateral truce between the French and Corsicans was to run through August 7, 1768—the day after the expiration of the Treaty of Compiègne.*

In any case, the French were increasing their four-battalion "peace keep-ing" force to sixteen battalions, and François-Claude de Chauvelin was to replace Marbeuf. Chauvelin had been a major general in the War of the Austrian Succession, but since 1748 had been a diplomat. He was rather a favorite of Louis XV and had had a hand in political decisions concerning the island, but he was generally regarded as being without relevant military experience.

During the summer of 1768 French troops were moved over to Corsica. In most of the island, they were received with sullen or heated resentment, while in Bastia, crowds cheering "Vive le Roi" greeted the replacing of the Corsican flag with the fleur-de-lis on the city hall, and there was celebration in the streets.

304. *From Constant d'Hermenches, June 13, 1768*

Versailles, June 13

How happy I am, dear Agnes, to receive a letter from you! At a moment when I thought I would be three hundred leagues from you, isolated, aban-doned, I was ordered to come here before going to Corsica, and I find your letter at Versailles, where you are certainly what interests me the most. Your letter is excellent—it's the very genius and spirit of the thing. You speak to me of my lot in the same way I was thinking about it; how fortunate that is for me, and how rare it is to have such friends! No one has written to me as you have about this expedition; no one but you has a mind that moves like the flight of an eagle; you can judge whether I intend to see to it that com-munication between us continues.

Be so good as to continue addressing an envelope to Monsieur de Bournonville, and your letters will safely reach me. You may count on it that, on my side, I shall write regularly; true friendship is not increased or warmed by events, but they give it content and nourishment; I will be more eager to tell you about this new country than about a monotonous garrison. I am to see the Minister[1] today, and I may leave tonight, for I am embarking on the 20th from Toulon. However thickened your packets are with details about Corsica, the couriers and the sailing vessels will bring them to me just as fast.

Haven't I always said that the Marquis was clumsy? Reread my letters, if you still have any of them, and you will find that I have always portrayed him just as he is: I know no human creature who has changed less in all the time I have known him. He would have married with great pleasure; he would have made you very happy, and he would have been happy with you; but his manner of being happy is not altered by his not marrying you. For your part, are you not what you would have been if you had married him? Amiable, free, rich, self-sufficient? In a few years, if you're taken with an urge to marry, you will still be able to find what you have lost in him. I enormously regret the loss of you for his sake, but since he is not dying of regret, he doesn't deserve yours.

Since you know Corsica, I will tell you that I am going to disembark at San Fiorenzo, and from there we will establish communication with Bastia, where our general and a Sovereign Council will be; that we set forth cheerfully and in good company, but that I do not expect great things for my fortune.[2] That will never be the source of my happiness; but I am made happy by your friendship. So preserve it for me, and think of me as always at your feet, and at the foot of that staircase at the opera; my feelings for you will ever be like Bellegarde—that is to say, unchanging.

305. *To Constant d'Hermenches, June 28, 1768*

Zuylen

I have spent two days and two nights under the same roof with Bellegarde at Amerongen.[1] I was surprised; we were both pleased. I was more comfortable with him than I had expected. He doesn't always simply hold forth; he also knows how to respond, or to interject, or to say only two or three words at a time; that put me at my ease, and I chatted away with him. We

1. The duc de Choiseul, minister of war and foreign affairs.
2. The generals in charge of the operation were first the Comte de Marbeuf and then the marquis de Chauvelin. San Fiorenzo (Saint-Florent) and Bastia are at the two sides of the base of Cap Corse—Bastia on the east coast and San Fiorenzo in a bay of the north coast. The first stage of the French strategy was to cut off Cap Corse by occupying the line between them.
1. The chateau of the Athlone family.

had rooms below, at each end of an immense corridor. He escorted me to my room in the evenings, and the thought came to me, although somewhat vaguely, that the Pope didn't want him to stay there; I don't know whether he was thinking about it, but many little things occurred that would have made you laugh. There was a great deal of company in my room: the Comte de Charny (that is, the Prince de Lambesc),[2] Monsieur de Boistel, Monsieur de Reede,[3] Monsieur de Randwijck; there was a little Englishman, the prettiest child in the world, only fifteen, with a great deal of wit and reason, good-hearted, and with a heartfelt courtesy, and polite and charming manners. The Marquis liked him and made much of him; one evening, while we were chatting, the boy hid in my curtains. The others were about leave me, and were looking for him to take him away with them. "Leave him, then!" said Bellegarde. "She will know how to get rid of him." He seemed to be saying, "She is given nothing, at least leave her this child! What cruel care to take everything from her!" Another time, after dinner, I was lying on my bed; Mme d'Athlone was seated near me; Reede came in, and then the others and Bellegarde, who sat on the foot of my bed. The next day he wanted to tell me his dreams, but he was interrupted. If he really wanted me, he would not be amusing himself with dreaming. (That is a worthless remark that means nothing. Sometimes I don't know what I am saying.) You would have been pleased with me if you could have seen how decorous I looked. It is easy to seem decorous with other people; the imagination is silent, and reality leaves the heart quite calm, but ...

What! Am I sending this foolishness to Corsica? What will you say about this letter, you whose life is now made up of long marches, and fatigue, and a soldier's labors? Well then, this letter will be an easy chair where the warrior takes his rest. I'm at Zuylen, it's midnight, my heart is full; and since I'm writing, my heart must speak. Mme d'Athlone said: "Cousin, he began by being about to marry you; he will end up loving you. He is attentive and assiduous; he says charming things to you; I swear he's in love with you."

My father and mother have made me return from Amerongen because of what people might say in public about our being under the same roof, but a few days later he came to Utrecht with the whole troop, and they gave him a fine dinner with very good grace. I played whist cheerfully with Monsieur de Charny, Bellegarde, and my father, who got along splendidly together, and my mother, who was polite and even friendly. I said out loud to the Marquis that if he could find me a square of Indian cloth, I would embroider him a vest from it: in short, I will be his friend in the face of the world, and I will know how to give some grace to the ruins of our plan. I understand very well what you are saying to me, and I think that I am worth quite as much as Bellegarde; but he loses nothing if he doesn't feel that he loses, and

2. Prince Charles-Eugene de Lorraine.
3. Brother of the count of Athlone.

I lose since I think I lose. The only thing that consoles me is that in order to afford his tastes and his travels, one must perhaps be richer than I am. If he wanted to travel alone, I would be lonely in Savoie; but he seems to me so kind, so indulgent, so sensitive to the pains and pleasures of others, that such would probably not be his intention.

They were all in my room in Utrecht; my translations of the Corsican book were right at my hand; they took them off, and they want me to continue or rather to start over, and make an extract rather than a translation. M. de Boistel wrote some pretty verses about it; I have started writing a little in my notebooks again.

Goodnight, I'm going to bed. I agree with you, the Marquis is quite clumsy. Goodnight.

306. *To Constant d'Hermenches, June 30, 1768*[1]

Yesterday we saw the King of Denmark.[1] He resembles the Prince Adolphe de Hesse Philipsthal, but he's a little prettier, and even smaller and slimmer; he looks as though he's fifteen at the most, although he's near twenty; he is excessively blond and pale-skinned; I cannot read his expressions at all—I don't know whether they can be read. He would like to be polite, but he doesn't know what to say. We were walking with him in the Termeer gardens at my aunt Van Lockhorst's; his favorite, the Comte de Bolk, a pretty courtier (a very nimble one), would have liked him to have a talk with me. It had been raining, and I complained laughingly about the fate of my pretty slippers; from then on his Majesty looked only at my slippers and talked to me of nothing else. People say that he has wenches dressed as page boys with him, but that he never drinks wine—apparently because the King his father killed himself with drink. This one would require no great excess to do himself in. The Comte de Bernstorff, who I think is his Prime Minister, seemed to us a person of merit and a man of the world; he has other serious enough persons in his retinue, but it is said that he can't bear them; he loves only this young courtier. His wife and his subjects are very unhappy, and his mistresses are treated no better—for a while ago he had a woman whom he had loved put into prison.[2] And that's what I have seen and learned about his Danish Majesty. I might not dare send you all this nonsense if this letter could reach you at Versailles as the other one did, but at Bastia it may be tolerable. To think that this ill-bred child is all-powerful in his kingdom—that he is a despot! I like seeing with my own eyes these little actors who are charged with the greatest of roles.

1. Christian VII (1749–1808).
2. The king of Denmark did indeed have his mistress Katrine Stovlet sent to a house of correction in Hamburg in 1768.

On the little stage of Corsica you are about to see a character who is truly great: it's too bad that you are made to be his enemy. I could perfectly well send you an excellent map of Corsica, and many descriptions and directions. I could say to you: in such-and-such a place you will find wheat, and meadows; here, a wood; there, a chain of mountains. But against Paoli! No, I will do nothing of the kind. I have mentioned that scruple to Bellegarde, and he approves. I hope that not one of your officers has Boswell's book. (Do these fine Frenchmen understand any language other than their own?) Still, I would not want you to stay in San Fiorenzo, where, according to Boswell, the air is so unhealthy that one is obliged to rotate the garrison personnel every month. The Roman colonies established in the past at Mariana and Aleria were ruined by diseases; that you must avoid. I could console myself for the rest of the troop, but you—for whom I could not console myself—are part of it; so I worry about the bad air. In all the rest of the island except Porto-Vecchio, the air one breathes is pure. Why were you not sent against the Pope instead!

You may ravage the Corsicans, but they cannot be subjugated. Neither the Carthaginians before the Punic Wars, nor the Romans after Scipio's conquest of the island, nor the French when Pepin or Charles Martel seized it, nor the popes to whom the kings of France yielded it, nor the Pisans, nor the Genoese have ever been able to keep tranquil possession of it: *that spirit of liberty which tyrants call rebellion was ever breaking forth.*[3]

In 1729, a Genoese tax-collector tried to make a poor old Corsican woman pay the tax: it was only a *paolo*, but she had nothing. He curses, he threatens, he wants to impound her furniture; she weeps and laments; people hear her, come running, and stand up for her. The tax-collector treats them as rebels to be punished; he's chased off by a pelting with rocks. The Genoese troops come to support their tax-collector; the Corsicans assemble to defend themselves; the war begins and goes on still. Since that time there have been only short intervals of peace.

The leaders who were then designated by the Corsicans were Andrea Ceccaldi and Luigi Giafferi. The Genoese asked for help from the Emperor Charles VI, who sent foreign troops into Corsica commanded by General Wachtendonck. They laid waste the country; it was all they could do; twelve hundred of their men were killed in a single action. But the Prince of Wurtemberg, who was sent with an army of Germans, compelled the Corsicans to sue for peace. The Emperor was the guarantor of the treaty concluded with the Genoese. The Corsican leaders were sent as hostages to Genoa, where they would have been put to death had it not been for the intervention of the Prince of Wurtemberg and Prince Eugene. The Corsicans rose up in rebellion in 1734. Giafferi was again elected general, and he was given as colleague Giacinto Paoli, father of Pascal Paoli, my hero. The Comte de

---

3. English in the original. The quotation is from Boswell, *Account of Corsica* 63.

Rivarola distinguished himself in the cause of liberty, and obtained some help from the King of Sardinia. Around that time appeared poor, ridiculous King Theodore.[4] Since France did not want Corsica to shake off the yoke of Genoa completely, it sent the Comte de Boissieux with a detachment in March 1738. Although he did not act with any great energy, he nonetheless had some successes; he died the following year at Bastia.

The Marquis de Maillebois, a skillful, energetic, fiery general, came to Corsica with sixteen battalions of the best French troops, and a few harquebusiers from Béarn. He burned the villages, laid waste the countryside, had a good many monks hanged, and did such carnage that at the end of the summer of 1739 the brave Corsicans were obliged to lay down their arms. Giafferi and Paoli withdrew to Naples. The French who had been called in departed in 1741, leaving behind a subjugated and peaceful Corsica. *Ubi solitudinem faciunt, pacem appelant.*[5] That quotation is from my author. I am not so clever.

Another time I will continue my anecdotes. My style is horrible, it seems to me. I will write better the next time.

Write to me often; it seems to me that in your heart you will want to write more to me than to anyone else. Be very frank, impartial, unprejudiced; don't let the least exaggeration slip into your praise or your blame. Even the most honest people resort to exaggeration to round out their sentences.

You have surprised and delighted me, finding a way to write to me from Versailles at the very time when you had a conference with the minister, and on the eve of such a departure. That is truly a sign that you love me, and that you deserve to be loved.

I'm very glad that my letter pleased you. When something strikes me, I have only one thought, one impression—sometimes it's right. I wanted to put myself in your place, and fortunately I succeeded: I looked and saw as you did.

Bellegarde thinks very well of your good fortune: he thinks that they are glad to send this regiment in order to have an occasion and a reason to advance its major. I hope so, and I wish the best for you and even for your friends, although I wish no ill at all to the Corsicans.

If you must stay a while in San Fiorenzo, take some precautions, and protect yourself against the bad air: the evening damp is undoubtedly harmful, and one must be careful about the food. Again, next time I will write less badly: your letters will set me the style necessary for talking about the Corsican wars.

---

4. Baron Theodore von Neuhoff, a German adventurer who got himself elected king of Corsica. His rule lasted only a few months in 1736.
5. "Where they make a desert, they call it peace." Belle is quoting Boswell. Tacitus, in his *Life of Agricola,* attributes this to the Caledonian chieftain Galgacus addressing the Britons at the battle of the Grampians.

307. *From Constant d'Hermenches, July 6, 1768*

In the camp of San Fiorenzo

Finally, my dear Agnes, here I am in this island of Corsica—which you were to describe to me in detail and whose inhabitants you have taken under your protection. I spent five dreadful days on the sea, and having survived that, I do believe that nothing more can vex me. Carried toward the coast of Sardinia, pushed back to the islands of Hyères, and brought back to Corsica by a raging sea, I'm now camping here under a soldier's tent, half a league from San Fiorenzo, in the most horrible place in the world, on the edge of the sea, on the pebbles, without the least shade, and at war with—until we can do better—the snakes and the locusts. It is true that I am working on a little summer house that will be of flowering myrtle and rose laurel, of box-wood and olive; I wish that you might be its Annette.[1] You deserve such a punishment for wanting us not to do hurt—justice, rather—to a nation of bandits who do nothing but pillage and murder; who would rather wield a gun and be eaten by vermin than cultivate either the land or any kind of arts; who murder each other from generation to generation, and who cannot see cultivated land, nor a countryman who prospers by his industry, without burning with a desire to lay it waste; who cannot see a man in a decent suit of clothes without coveting the luck of whoever will kill him for the sake of wearing them, and who brazenly come and offer our soldiers ten *sols* for each cartridge they might sell; who refuse to do any kind of work, although they live in wretched poverty, and who coolly reply, "I will have to see if my wife wants to work for that money"—the poor women are their beasts of burden. And your Mr. Boswell wants to make heroes of them, and you want to translate him! And you wish bad luck to our arms! For the honor of humanity, we must exterminate or transplant this abominable race; it would be shameful for an age like ours to let there remain in the bosom of Europe a confederation of such villains, who indict each other—and that very openly; for you must not believe that the celebrated Paoli is universally loved and esteemed by his nation.

The whole country is armed; their pickets are right near ours—though there are no hostilities; that will last until August 8, when the truce expires. There's no longer a Genoese in the island; they said at first that they'd give themselves over to France; today they're starting to say that it's a trick.

This is an arid, feral land, without fruits or vegetables or any sort of for-age—and yet we live well here, and we laugh, because the French laugh and set a good table wherever they are.[2] Tomorrow I am going to Bastia, which I will tell you about some day; I'm still impatiently waiting for news from

1. The heroine of a pastoral play by Marmontel, *Annette et Lubin* (1768).
2. It was well known in military circles that French officers in the field received much higher allowances for their tables than those of other armies. See Kennett, *The French Armies* 67.

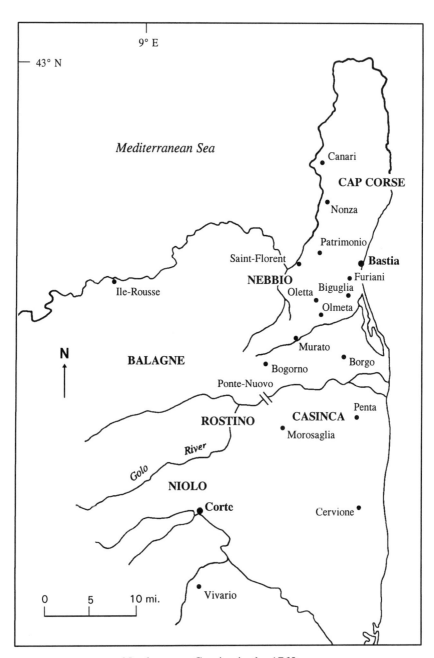

9° E

43° N

Mediterranean Sea

Canari

CAP CORSE

Nonza

Patrimonio

Saint-Florent

NEBBIO

Bastia

Furiani

Oletta Biguglia

Ile-Rousse

Olmeta

N

BALAGNE

Murato

Borgo

Bogorno

Ponte-Nuovo

Penta

ROSTINO

CASINCA

Morosaglia

River

Golo

NIOLO

Corte

Cervione

0   5   10 mi.

Vivario

Northeastern Corsica in the 1760s

you. My dear friend, I am well; I am glad to be here, notwithstanding I am dying of thirst and heat; farewell.

The day before yesterday one of our soldiers, who was wearing a vest, lost his way while he was out gathering wood, and was—undoubtedly—murdered; he was a lad of fifteen. Yesterday we saw a Corsican wearing that same vest, brazenly standing guard a hundred yards from our camp; we wrote to General Barbaggio, Paoli's nephew,[3] to find out the facts of the matter.

308. *To Constant d'Hermenches, July 7, 1768*

Would you have believed me capable of an indiscretion, or an infidelity, or the abuse of a trust? Well now, here is one and here is the occasion of it. I receive Bellegarde's letter for you enclosed in a letter for me; the seal is broken; undoubtedly I had broken it when I opened the envelope. Immediately I was seized by the desire to see whether he speaks of me, and just how; but discretion ... but curiosity ...; perhaps it's the Marquis himself who broke the seal so that I would read the letter. That "perhaps" is so unlikely—it isn't I, it's curiosity that imagines it. Finally, I open the letter, and gently, lightly, as if on tiptoe I look for my name, and I find it, and now I come to confess my fault, in the certainty that confession alone without penance will gain me absolution from you. But if you want a penance, impose it and I will obey. I have unburdened my conscience, and now I am going to bed; I can sleep in peace. But what madness! *He is not worthy of me!* What is so marvelous about me, and what do I require? All he needed was to have a little savoir-faire, and to know how to marry me.[1] I think I would have loved him tenderly in all good faith, for although the imagination is moderated by presence and possibility, I liked very much seeing him seated on my bed.

Midnight, July 7

At midnight, I have no common sense.

309. *To Constant d'Hermenches, July 11, 1768*

You will receive several notes instead of one long letter. When I am interrupted, I stop and I start again later in another mood and on another kind of paper. I think that will amuse you, and give you the impression that we are

---

3. Barbaggio, lieutenant general of Corsica, had married a niece of Paoli.

1. The letter from Bellegarde to d'Hermenches is written from the Hague and dated July 3. Belle is referring to the following sentence: "What consoles me for not marrying her is that I am really not worthy of her; and who is worthy of possessing this treasure?" (*O.C.* 2: 531).

in each other's company, that we are neighbors. People need some such illusion when they would like to be seeing each other, as we would, but instead, Fortune has planted one in the North and sends the other to the South. Today it is impossible for me to continue the Corsican War, and I don't want to make you wait any longer for the letter from the Marquis or for my notes. You had someone at the Hague last year who wrote you all the news—for instance, you knew all about (I know this) what was going on between the virtuous Countess[1] and the great d'Oyenhausen—, but I do not know whether those correspondences are of the kind that nothing can interrupt, and that you invite to follow you all the way to San Fiorenzo. So I'm going to tell you the news; you will see how clumsy I am at it, but you will love my passion for being something and doing something for you that might please you, or rather the passion for being all the things that might please you—even a journalist. Today I will be a journalist.

Monsieur de Boetzelaer, the captain, is finally marrying Mlle de Voshol. These ladies-in-waiting are very pleased when they find a husband, after enduring so much boredom with their princesses. From the financial standpoint this is not a brilliant match, but the one can paint and the other can dance minuets. The mother and the sister are in despair. Mlle Steengracht, daughter of the flirtatious Mme Steengracht, an only daughter, immensely rich and a great coquette, has just married Monsieur de Goltz, adjutant of the King of Prussia. He wanted to direct his attentions to me, but a German slave—I mean a courtier—without any means except a courtier's functions and favors did not suit me at all. It is said that he is a man of wit and merit. I have never seen him.

Mme de Twickel has given birth to a daughter, and Mme de Golofkine to a fine boy whom she continues to nurse, even though she has had an operation for a fistula. She has suffered a great deal, and people feel very sorry for her, for she is much loved. Theirs is really the best household in the Hague, and utterly without ostentation; in my opinion, it's the only house one enjoys being in.

The Prince returns tomorrow from Het Loo, and the day after tomorrow or the following day he will give a ball for the King of Denmark; it is likely that I will take part. They put on a play at Het Loo; they say that the Princess was very good in *Iphigénie*,[2] which she had already played in Berlin. She has a voice and a face that fit the role perfectly. Monsieur de Zoelen had his hand pierced clear through by a fireworks rocket. He was badly hurt, and fainted three times during the first dressing, but they think that he will recover without losing the use of his hand.

The charge of bailiff of Woerden that Monsieur Bentinck had will pass to Monsieur de Hompesch. He wants to stay there winter and summer, for

1. Mme de Degenfeld.
2. A tragedy of Racine.

since he has a fortuneless wife and a child, he needs to be very thrifty. The death of Monsieur de Haren leaves vacant a bailiwick in the mayoralty of Bois-le-Duc; my brother is seeking it.[3] If it were given to someone else (to Monsieur Verelst for example, for it probably would not be given to Madelon and her Monsieur Bouwens, who ask for everything)—that is, if my brother did not obtain the bailiwick—would he ask to be named Minister of the Republic at Brussels? We don't know, but I rather think so. He left this evening for the Hague. The Brussels post is not very lucrative. His taking it would suit *me* very well: whenever I chose, I could be at my brother's, half-way to Paris. I have taken care not to advise him to solicit it. Good night.

One more word. Bellegarde has had a dispute at the dinner table with the King of Prussia over the uprisings in Geneva and their causes. "The government is purely democratic," said His Majesty. "It is *aristodemocratic*," said the Marquis (you know how brilliant he is with words—his language is the most learned imaginable). "I should know something about it, for I have estates in that region—I have lands right at the gates of Geneva where I spend half my life." The Marquis recounted all that to us, and thought that he had done not so badly at paying his court. "The King likes that kind of contradiction," he said. I didn't think so at all. I've been told since then that he could not endure it, and that therefore people let him talk all by himself. People who know him well noticed his impatience during that little scuffle. I couldn't help laughing at our Marquis's mistake; it's just like him. He has so much wit and acquaintance with the world, yet no one could judge less accurately; he never goes deeper than the surface of things.

310. *To Constant d'Hermenches, July 12, 1768*

Every Corsican, according to the gazette, goes against you armed with a gun, a sword, a stiletto, and a dog: these dogs are huge, strong, courageous, and faithful—a terrible weapon. I was saying these past days that if I had a face like two or three women I know, and less of a passion for Paoli than I have, I would enlist in your regiment; but face-to-face with those dogs I would be but a cowardly soldier. You would send me packing. God protect you from the dog, the stiletto, the sword, and the musket! I wish you all the personal glory imaginable, and may that glory lead you pleasantly along to the finest of fortunes.

I'm leaving for the Hague, where I will see Bellegarde. Tomorrow I'm going dancing.

3. Willem René.

313. *From Constant d'Hermenches, August 3, 1768*

San Fiorenzo, August 3

This letter, however short, ought to receive a warm welcome from you, my dear Agnes; I will affix to it the seal of your dear Paoli; but you must be satisfied with that imprint, for I am about to break your heart. We had been languishing for five weeks, sleeping in the open air, in the evening dew, in the sun, on burning sand—four battalions diminished by illness and a few desertions; hemmed in on all sides by gorges and mountains crowned by the fortresses and watchposts of the Corsicans; insulted by them in our camp and massacred whenever we left; receiving goats-milk, rotten pears, and onions only by a passport from Signor Barbaggio, "Tenente Generalle del Regno di Corsica";[1] seeing the sheep that our sutlers had bought and paid for in their own country carried off by these brigands, without compensation. They defied us to the point of saying in our very camp that if we did not begin *la guerra*, they would start it themselves. Pointing their guns at our sentinels; firing cannon on ships flying French colors (which were bringing us your letters); building up their gun emplacements, to the songs and shouts of their women; they would drive us from our camp whenever they wished. Defiantly stationed in an impenetrable gorge called La Bocca di Patrimonio, defended by rocks and steep mountains, of which the only side accessible to scaffolding was guarded at the summit by fortifications, the whole thing defended by all of Corsica and *les bravi di Paoli*—who were confident that it was impossible for us to establish communication between San Fiorenzo and Bastia,[2] these villains, on Sunday the first of August, fell on a detachment that we had rashly sent forward into the Santa Maria gorge. They killed many of our brave men, and among others an officer whom they hanged in full view of his comrades on one of the heights. They inflicted unspeakable torments on the wounded up on the rocks where we could not get help to them, and from which we heard their cries. What's more, they threw them down to us onto their heads from the summit of the rocks. By Sunday evening, our situation was horrible; I had gone as a volunteer and had been a witness to all this, and had come under their "*escopetadas*".[3]

Our communication being closed off by their battery on the gulf and by their entrenchments in the gorges, and the war having started, we were unable to show our noses anywhere without being shot. We were waiting for a move on the part of M. de Marbeuf, the commander at Bastia, to undertake one on our side and to link up forces with him. It was difficult for him to take Monte Bello and move himself up onto the Heights of Barbaggio,[4] a

1. Barbaggio is lieutenant general of the Realm of Corsica and Paoli's nephew by marriage.
2. The first and key component of what Chauvelin had as a strategy. See Letter 304, n. 2.
3. A kind of carbine.
4. "Barbaggio" is not only the name of the Corsican commander, it is a geographical name in the region; there are the Heights of Barbaggio and a village of Barbaggio.

position reputed to be uncapturable from our side—I, who had examined it, thought so too. Four cannon shots were to be M. de Marbeuf's signal if his plan was succeeding. I spent the night observing his movements from the highest rock I could find; I saw that they offered him strong resistance; he had been fighting for two days, and he gave no signal because his cannons, which were carried on the shoulders, could not be gotten into position. All the mountains and their slopes were only a burning brazier—whose heat was directed according to the wind—, which the Corsicans maintained to block the passages, cover all the country with smoke, and in the smoke approach and fire their weapons. We took the signal as having been given.

Monday morning, at break of day, I was given companies of grenadiers and chasseurs and some reserve infantry units. Our whole little camp assembles itself, and I march straight to the mountain in a cloth jacket, a carbine in my hand, a canteen, and a powder-flask over my left shoulder. I climb it in the midst of gunfire, crossing over rolling stones and thorny brush; my troops follow me with inexpressible courage mingled with rage. Halfway up the hill I divide them: I send the troops on my left to flank one of the redoubts, those on my right to attack the other, and in the center I dive into the whole defense system of the mountaintop and the crest between the redoubts. They were covered by two redans that I hadn't expected; I won't even mention other obstacles—slippery rocks, the sheer drop of a ravine under the crest. We take up position on all sides; the enemy fires, flees, or falls into man-traps that were intended for us; everybody defending the redoubts is massacred. There I am in battle with my brave troops on that mountain—six thousand yards up, if you count the detours—and in less than two hours.

During that time, Monsieur de Grandmaison, our general, forces his way through the gorge with cannon; I descend from my battlefield by way of the other side, sweeping up all the blackguards who were still lying in ambush; I had several of them sealed up in caves that they had retreated into. I found I had lost only thirty-five men and one officer. I reach the longed-for plain of Patrimonio, and go directly to the three villages known by that name that are on the opposite side. Terror is everywhere; I disarm everyone there, and I lay siege to the château of Cavelli, the residence and staging area of General Barbaggio. He thought he was perfectly secure there; this château has some little towers that defend a kind of curtain formed from a plateau of rock—steep on all sides, the whole building well crenellated, all the windows masked by enormous stones, on one side a wide vaulted gallery, which makes a blockhouse three stories high with a vaulted roof. I call on him to surrender; he replies with musket fire, and my drummer is mortally wounded. At that juncture I am sent the order (lest I undertake too much) to return to the plain and await Marbeuf's success. I was very angry; I obeyed—partly—and went to M. de Grandmaison and told him that I had his enemy trapped and unable to escape. He was delighted, and said to me: "Go back there then, and I'll have two cannons brought to you."

Barbaggio had three hundred of his *bravi* in that castle, and he had them fire furiously on my troops when I approached. I closed him in; the cannon fired, Barbaggio took fright, threw himself on a horse and escaped from me by a corridor that I had not yet had time to close off. He was followed by half his troops, and by the Most Illustrious Gentile, governor of Capraia and Grand Master of the Treasury for Paoli. He left the command to Sieur Cavelli; he ordered him to defend himself to the death, and ran off in tears as fast as his legs could carry him. All this was a matter of half an hour. The cannon commanded some embrasures; the grenadiers slipped up almost directly under the castle walls, from which a white flag was displayed. I presented myself at the door, which they kept shut, asking us, before they yielded up their arms, to spare their lives. That I promised them: immediately, they presented us their firearms from the windows and from all sides. The door was forced open, and I took a hundred prisoners. Those beggars complained not at all, and were not afraid. To prevent pillage, the women threw themselves into the midst of the soldiers without uttering a cry, and defended room after room, door after door, against all efforts to force them open and search. The general came to bring order, but still, however, the plunder was considerable. Barbaggio had his whole chancellery there: very beautiful silver dishes, furniture, and an immense accumulation of matériel, bread, hams, and very good wine. Our troops made free with it; we left the women everything that they said was theirs, and all the beds. Some of them had been killed, and others gathered around them and spoke to them; a tall man lay stretched out in a chapel, covered with a sheet, a lamp burning nearby, a crucifix on his breast, as if he were dead. This careful arrangement seemed to me suspect; I roused the dead man with a few kicks, and indeed he turned out to be Signor Antònio del Cordetto, one of Paoli's most determined captains, who the day before had ordered so many atrocities committed at the Santa Maria gorge. They were led off to the dungeon—the elite of their brave men; I kept for myself only the national seal, in iron, and an Italian dictionary, along with all the correspondence of Paoli and Barbaggio, which I handed over to M. de Marbeuf. Barbaggio's fortune is a million, they say, and two weeks earlier, when I had gone to see him, his guard had had the insolence to repulse me and to stop me from tying my horse in front of the door of that same castle; you can imagine my chagrin at letting him get away.

However, this third act of the play was not yet the denouement that was to be. We could no longer see or hear M. de Marbeuf's detachments, and we were out of communication that whole day. The extreme heat, our fatigue, and the wine of Patrimonio seemed to make us incapable of any further undertaking. We rallied—satisfaction and successes give one strength. I reassemble my grenadiers and my chasseurs; I request permission to march to the famous post of the village of Barbaggio, which was the difficult link in our joining up. I was told that it was unnecessary, that it was a task reserved for Marbeuf's corps; I was practically forbidden. Stubbornness triumphed; I advanced. A corps from the Bastia side that saw us appear, and that had been fighting a long time, did the same. All of a sudden we saw some Corsican soldiers come out at full speed, firing and hurling themselves in disarray among our chasseurs on our right. They stood firm and returned the fire; meanwhile I go straight up to Barbaggio; the peasants in the first houses cry out and show the white flag; I signal to them to come out to me unarmed; they come and tell me that the village is surrendering, that the troops that have just passed are Paoli's soldiers, whom they have forced to withdraw. I have these rascals march in front of me, threatening to have them massacred if a single shot is fired by them; I enter the village, everybody runs to me crying *misericordia* and kissing my feet; I tell them to go get their weapons immediately, and the women to bring water; I sound the order forbidding pillage, and I send a message to M. de Marbeuf telling him that he is the master of the village, that there are no more enemies, and that he can enter. At the same time his grenadiers arrive; we meet up at seven in the evening, and it is decided to retire our separate ways.

You must admit that this was a day put to rather good use. We pass the night with our weapons at the ready, but nothing happens. The next day the generals make contact; communications are verified, and we return to our camps, dead with fatigue and heat, but relieved to see all those insolent Corsicans—who two days before had been armed to the teeth and had crossed through our camp as though they were sparing us only out of mercy—now passing before us cap in hand, disarmed, and with white flags as their only defense.

I do not know what will happen next; but it is certain that if God has permitted men to make war on each other, this one is the most legitimate one that can be waged—one that aims to destroy cowards, murderers, thieves, traitors, the slothful and the insolent. They say that Paoli is even less of a warrior than Barbaggio, his second; his speeches and his orders have much of the Italian farce about them. He disguises his own ambition behind illusory talk of liberty and disinterestedness, but his people are more wretched, more enslaved under the laws of *la deliberazione della generala Consulta del Regno*[5] than any subject of the princes of the Empire. He goes so far as to force on the women the most arduous labors—they construct fortifications, carry supplies, and wrap and bandage the dead and wounded. I won't even mention the weapons they use: most of the bullets were jagged, or were linked by little chains; I returned with my clothes in shreds, with bruises and scratches from the cliffs, but scarcely wounded.

I have just this moment received your letter, full of news; everything that comes from you is graceful and brilliant. I will read it with delight, for truly, one could hardly be leading a life harder than mine. You don't tell me

5. A Supreme Council elected by provincial assemblies.

whether you received the letter I wrote you when I arrived in Corsica. You were quite right to read Bellegarde's; you are one of those privileged beings who need never repent of their curiosity. You describe him marvelously; keep writing me, I beg you.

But do not go to the trouble of translating Boswell's book: it's the work of an enthusiast who is only a literary fellow and knows nothing of things military—he's a sorry historian and a sorry political thinker. All the facts you present to me have been drawn from bad books of Corsican history, one written by a commissioner, the other by an apothecary. Paoli has neither manuscripts nor archives, and the origins of his authority do him no honor, nor, it follows, is it presented in good faith by Boswell. We undoubtedly have his book here, and I could easily make you blush whenever I wish for giving your admiration to so much inflated prose and hollow rhetoric; and you, my dear Agnes, who spell out for me the long succession of masters that the Corsicans have had and have accepted, you tell me that "for eight hundred years they have fought for their liberty"—how do you reconcile that with sound logic?

I am sending you this account to amuse you; it is very disorderly. All the same, if this beginning of the action causes some stir, may I ask you as a friend to supplement what the Holland gazettes may be able to say about it, since this is very true, and the best and surest report, and—since it came out singularly well for me—to bring to their attention, without affectation, the name of the colonel who commanded the grenadiers and chasseurs during that whole day, who forced the heights and the fortifications, took Patrimonio and the castle of Cavelli, and was the first to enter Barbaggio. I have no wish to write to anyone at all in Holland about this affair—even to Maasdam, to whom I owe a response. M. de Grandmaison and all my comrades have written to France about me in terms that are much too flattering; but, after all, I was lucky to be there and to have been chosen.

A thousand times farewell, my dear Agnes; you are dancing with kings and I am risking a cut throat with brigands! And yet, we love each other and we suit each other! If you write to Bellegarde, give him news of me; he always gives me addresses on his long travels. You will see by the beginning of my letter that I intended to write you only a few lines.

While I have pen in hand, an English frigate, in our full view, is unloading supplies of all kinds for the Corsicans. I forgot to tell you that the Cavelli castle belongs to Signora Catarina Cavelli, Paoli's mistress; that she came here yesterday to ask for her somewhat deranged husband, who was among the prisoners; we have given her asylum at Bastia.[6]

---

6. In a letter to the duc de Richelieu of December 16, 1771, Voltaire had this to say: "A brave Swiss brigadier named M. Constant d'Hermenches, of the Jenner Regiment, who had done good service in Corsica, came to Ferney riding on the horse that had once been Paoli's, and I think that he had ridden his mistress as well. Those are two great claims to fame" (original French in *Voltaire's Correspondence* 80: 200).

314. *From Constant d'Hermenches, September 3, 1768*

San Fiorenzo

Here is a supplement, my dear Agnes, to the history of Corsica. At the time I last wrote, General Barbaggio had withdrawn to Nonza[1]—the best stronghold of Cap Corse—with five hundred men; he had cannon, he had cut off the road, and he was still defended by his gorges and his steep, inaccessible cliffs. He held all of Cap Corse under arms, and Paoli, his dear uncle, had written to him to hold firm—if we were about to attack him, he would come to create a diversion and fall upon our camp. The detachments left the evening of August 23rd, from here and from Bastia. I remained in the camp with only six hundred men. During the night, we heard the cannon from their side and musket-fire right near the camp. It was thought to be Paoli, and we were on the point of running for our arms, when I saw that the fire came from one of their nearest towers; they were firing on a tartan[2] that they had taken from us, and that was escaping very skillfully under cover of night; it made it back to us. At daybreak I was able to reach the detachments; I found them engaged in combat four leagues from the camp. Barbaggio had cut off the Nonza road; the troops, obliged to throw themselves on the right, were caught in a gorge from whose heights the Corsicans had assailed them on three sides. They had had no way to get themselves out of this tight spot except by marching straight on the enemy, which we did with admirable valor. Our grenadiers crawled four by four up to the top and flushed out the Corsicans, rock after rock; it was at that moment that I arrived alone with an adjutant. I had never lived through such a terrible moment; I found myself surrounded by fleeing Corsicans and by dug-in Corsicans who were about to cut off my route and capture me. I made an instant decision; with carbine fire, we drove away those who were pressing on us the closest, and legged it full speed toward our forward units. Once we were masters of the heights, everything collapsed before us, everything was overturned and laid waste. We took Olinetto; we descended upon Nonza where, as we approached, Barbaggio came out with his troops, and Nonza surrendered with good grace.

It's the prettiest place I've seen in Corsica; the inhabitants received us with open arms, cursing Paoli's soldiers, who had been pillaging them and making their life miserable for a month. But Barbaggio had escaped again; we knew that he was withdrawing along the sea towards the extremity of the Cape and that he was trying to reach Canari,[3] an advantageous post. Everyone was exhausted, for the heat and the fatigue we had endured were indescribable. The generals asked me if I felt I had the strength to undertake the venture, and to go capture or attack our man. I undertook it with pleasure; I

1. On the west coast of Cap Corse, about eight miles north of San Fiorenzo.
2. A kind of boat.
3. About four miles north of Nonza.

gathered together the men who were still capable of going, and went after him. He was cut off from Canari, and was hiding out in the bush with two hundred men. As soon as he saw that we were descending on him in force, he signaled that he wanted to parley, and surrendered to the nearest grenadiers. That was a matter of a couple of hours, and I brought back to Nonza in triumph Barbaggio, Franceschetti (Paoli's brother-in-law), thirty chiefs or captains, and a hundred sixty-nine prisoners. As soon as he saw me, Barbaggio stretched out his arms to me; he was wearing a sleeveless black vest so as not to be recognized. He said to me: "It was fated that you were to capture me," and he gave me his parole. I handed him over to the generals, who gave him supper, and I gave him the bed that had been prepared for me. He spoke to us very sensibly; but, with all due respect to you and to Mr. Boswell, he said that Monsieur his Uncle had cheated and swindled him. He was sent to France with his whole unit, and I think he is not displeased to be out of all these entanglements; *hanno salvato il mio honore,*[4] he said.

Two days later, M. de Chauvelin arrived in San Fiorenzo; he published the edict by which the king adopts the Corsicans as his subjects. It is expected that Paoli will do anything he can to sustain the rebellion.[5] He is playing a role; he will stay far away from any gunfire. He has amassed great riches, not a penny of which is in Corsica; if he falls from power, he will go and play the role of the illustrious exile in Leghorn or London, and will worry very little that his country is being laid waste. He has been its tyrant for a long time now; under the fine name of liberty, he confiscates property, he hangs or imprisons everyone who is not of his party. And it is for this fine gentleman that we are going to wage a cruel war, suffer ourselves, and devastate a country that—you must agree—would be happier belonging to France than being at the mercy of the first adventurer who can drum up a handful of partisans.

I had begun to translate the *Account of Corsica,* but already at the dedication I was seized by nausea—what base and fanatic flattery for an Englishman! for a gentleman!—by a second wave of nausea at the comparison of Lycurgus to Paoli and of Corte to Athens—by an urge to vomit at all the pretty little anecdotes, which demonstrate the taste of your protégé Boswell, and the witticisms of his Swiss valet; and then by a continual indignation at the lack of fidelity to historical facts, at the assertions without proof, the words "hero," "bravery," "courage" lavished everywhere without a single example. When Paoli says *La testa mi rompa, allons presto pigliate li pensieri,*[6] that is "sublime." Poor Boswell! That pretty, playful little letter that

4. "They have saved my honor."
5. This and the rest of this paragraph are almost exactly the description of things given by Chauvelin in a letter to Choiseul in June 1768: D'Hermenches' "it is expected ..." may almost be taken to mean "Chauvelin expects ...." See Hall, *The Corsican Question* 193–94.
6. "My head is bursting, quick, record my thoughts" Boswell (*Account of Corsica* 333).

is the only one he cites from his hero and that would be unpardonable in a shopkeeper—all that it proves is that he doesn't like the Genoese, and that he is in fear of being assassinated, insinuating offhandedly: *si seppe che un Capitano genovese cercava compagni par assassinami.*[7]

Ah! my dear Agnes, how I love you, and how much more I respect your good taste for not having wanted either to translate or to marry the fool who dares to have printed "Where shall I find a man greater than Paoli?" (p. 352.)[8] Poor Boswell! Write him that my fingers are itching to give the translation of his book in installments to the *Mercure de France*, with notes—but that out of respect for the friendship you have borne him I am restraining myself. Search his whole book and see if you can find a single passage that demonstrates that Paoli is a great man (which I want neither to grant nor to reject), other than "Having dogs for his attendants is another circumstance about Paoli similar to the heroes of antiquity." As for the charming Buttafuoco,[9] we have him here, and I assure you that he has nothing good to say about Paoli, for all that he made him rich with confiscated goods. I thought I owed you these details, my dear friend, to cure you of a prejudice, which is always unworthy of someone with your superiority of genius.

Love me a little, for I am sick and unhappy. But I am doing my duty, and perhaps I would be bored anywhere else. Farewell.

315. To Constant d'Hermenches, September 7, 1768

Zuylen

You see the use I have made of your report.[1] This same extract has been sent to the Dutch gazetteer of the Hague, and I think he has put the translation of it in his gazette. The gazettes had already pounded this affair into our ears, and if they were to create a sensation with the public once again, they needed to supply some details. You can well imagine that since they are all to your glory, I took an inexpressible pleasure in taking care of this and in publishing them. I was so proud to find myself the friend of a brave warrior, the address-bureau of a military connection, and one of the voices of your renown! However, no one knows that the letter comes from you, nor the extract from me. Another time, when you want me to do the same thing,

---

7. "It was known that a Genoese captain was looking for companions to assassinate me" (Boswell, *Account of Corsica* 380). D'Hermenches had omitted the *r* in "*assassinarmi.*"

8. D'Hermenches is giving this page number and these quotaions from his copy of Boswell's *Account of Corsica*. He gives them in English in his letter.

9. Count Matteo de Buttafuoco, a Corsican who had been in the service of France but who had also been trusted in the role of go-between by both Paoli and Choiseul. In 1764 he had asked Rousseau to write a plan of a constitution for Corsica.

1. Belle had taken extracts from d'Hermenches' Letter 313 of August 3, 1768 to the *Gazette d'Utrecht*, which published them September 2, 1768.

name me some other officer who distinguished himself; that will give yet better grace and a more impartial air to the account. Tell me the sort of style you would like me to use for these extracts, for undoubtedly I go about it rather badly. I have kept as many as I can of your phrases, and I have said nothing insulting about Paoli nor about his nation. We must wait to see how things turn out, and let their conduct be their judge. I must admit that if the others resemble the defenders of Cavelli, or Signori Barbaggio, Gentile and Cardetto, then the enthusiasm that Boswell had inspired in me and in many others was altogether misplaced. I have another book on the Corsicans, where the portrait of them resembles very much what you have seen up to now, but the author knew them only before the time of Paoli, and I thought that their leader and their government had civilized them a little since that time; but on the other hand, I was also persuaded that in his view and portrayal of them, Boswell had been carried away by his own enthusiasm, and for the time being I had placed my opinion precisely between my two authors. I feel myself quite drawn away from Boswell by your letter; however, I still resist, at least as far as Paoli is concerned. I will watch him until the end.

I thanked Providence for having protected you from gunfire, and I would have begun my letter by a compliment expressing my joy if I hadn't thought that you would laugh at my congratulations on something already so old that other exploits and other dangers will almost have made you forget them.

It is sad that our letters are so long en route; we were accustomed to absence, but not to such an immense separation. I hope that this will not last very long; I fear the bad air even more than these random rifle shots. May God make them all pass beside you! All I want for you out of all this is just what is necessary for a fine reputation and for you to be made brigadier, and to find some pleasure again in the monotony of a garrison. This fine reputation is progressing so swiftly that it will soon be achieved, and then I would like to see you re-embark for home. A war cannot be very entertaining, when its greatest successes consist in exterminating a succession of troops of savages perched on a mountain or hidden in the woods.

It seems to me that I am going on and on, and that I am boring you. Let me say again that I love you, that I admire you, that I cherish your successes and your reputation; that you cannot speak to me too much about yourself and everything that you are doing; and that in choosing me for your report you have flattered my pride and touched my friendship beyond anything I can say. Neither Monsieur de Maasdam nor anyone else would have reread your letter oftener or understood it better—or so I think. The gorge, the mountains, the rocks, the Corsicans, the French, and above all your actions, are engraved in my mind, and you stand out in the forefront of this picture as the hero of the affair.

[A portion of this letter is missing.]

... bravely cut off my hair because I couldn't get it dry, and the dampness was unhealthy. "What's my hair," I said, "compared with my health! My hair is not impressive either by its length or by its fullness; its beautiful color will remain, so go ahead, cut! I've made up my mind to it, and it's nothing." Hardly had the fatal scissors cut short its destiny when I find myself like a king who has just abdicated: were it the littlest crown in the world, he would regret it and repent of his action. Today the crownless king has become a philosopher; I no longer think about it. At the Hague people said that I was prettier than ever; I thought, like Mme de Lude, that it was one less thing for people to laugh at, and that was all. One day, seeing that I had an acceptable foot, you too said to me: that's one thing the less for people to laugh at.

Farewell, my dear d'Hermenches. I humbly pay homage to your laurels; I love and embrace your person. My brother has asked to be minister of the Republic at Brussels, but they have sent M. Geelvinck, our friend's brother-in-law.

316. *From Constant d'Hermenches, September 10, 1768*

I do not know, my dear Agnes, whether you are angry with me, whether you aren't receiving my letters, or whether you consider yourself beaten like your protégés, but you are certainly treating me very badly: I haven't had a word from you for a month, and no response to my reports. Are you telling me that you want no more of them? I will venture nonetheless to send you a word or two today; the fifth of this month we attacked the formidable posts of the enemy, Furiani, Biguglia, Oletta, Poggio, Olmeta, and Valincale. The two Paoli brothers were waiting for us with all their forces—Pascal at Olmeta, Clemente at the monastery at Oletta; Rostoria was at Furiani, Giovanni Carlo on the mountain where, with three hundred men, one should be able to stop a whole army. We deployed in several columns: the army of Chauvelin and Marbeuf were to take the heights that divide the island, advancing continually toward the center, and it marched from its side over two other columns, to cut off Furiani and Biguglia and storm the fortress of Maillebois. Grandmaison's army marched in three columns on Oletta, Olmeta, and Valincale; that army being reduced to fifteen hundred men at the most, we pushed ahead across the fire of the Corsicans, who held fast in several posts and killed some of our men. I was at the head of the grenadiers and chasseurs under the orders of M. de Grandmaison; as soon as Pascal heard that we were attacking him, he stood up—he had slept and eaten at Olmeta—and he cried out to his *bravi*, three hundred favorites and twelve hundred mountaineers who never leave him, *"Animo, fillioli,"* [1] mounted his

---

1. "Be brave, my sons."

horse, and fled a quarter of an hour later. Clemente, who was in the monastery, said to the monks, his rosary in his hand, that he was desperately sorry to tell them that he had resolved to bury himself with all his men under the ruins of their convent rather than surrender or withdraw, and that they had to make their own decision. The poor monks, terrified, abandoned their monastery. M. Clemente had made very good entrenchments; he had two thousand ruffians with him; he fired from behind the hedges and wall, and killed some of ours, but when he saw that this did not prevent our advancing on him, he fled also, and our troops, arriving at the monastery, found it abandoned, so that the pillaging was horrible. Clemente said as he left: "You have to admit, the French are brave."

I brought my chasseurs to Poggio, which was also abandoned at my approach, and I found nobody but the parish priest, who still had his pockets full of cartridges, and whom I had garrotted with four or five others of the blackguards. The villages were plundered; that struck terror into all of Nebbio, which came that very day to surrender. The tower of Fornalli, which had worried us a good deal, received the order from Paoli to be blown up, to load the cannons with cartridges, to burn the whole business; but a certain Morel preferred to come hand over everything to me, so he surrendered twenty pieces of artillery and the supplies; the tower of Mortella did the same. These are towers where an Englishman came a month ago to say that they had only to hold fast and that England would send them help before the 20th of September. We suspect Milord Pembroke[2] of that madness.

One cannot imagine more ineptitude and treachery than what Boswell's hero has displayed in all this; to begin with, he and his brother, in the *Consulta* at Oletta, refused to make public the King's edict, and contented themselves by saying, in a contemptuous tone, that it was all deceit.[3] They have threatened, imprisoned, and killed those who talked of surrender; they have spread a thousand lies about our losses, and thereby are bringing about the ruin of their nation to satisfy a lackey's ambition—for there is nothing of the great man about him, not even the bravery; and so the people are opening their eyes. He had assembled his *Generale Consulta* at Casinca; the inhabitants begged him to withdraw, and came to surrender; they say that he doesn't dare go to Corte. If we had troops, I think that in less than two weeks the whole island would be ours; but what we have to suffer is indescribable, and all the military find this war harder that anything they had ever experienced. We are going to set up camp at San Nicolao. I am sick, like everybody else; I am leaving San Fiorenzo, where I didn't want to command, and I am at your feet, my adorable friend.

2. Henry Herbert, earl of Pembroke.
3. In his edict, the king declared the intention to exercise his sovereignty "for the good of this island, our new subjects," and spoke of "the sentiments of his paternal heart" (Hall, *The Corsican Question* 191).

317. *To Constant d'Hermenches, October 3, 1768*

Zuylen

I thank you for your reports, my dear d'Hermenches, with all my heart. Better those than the Corsican spoils and trophies that a paladin of ancient times would have brought to his mistress. Your enemies are so poor and barbarous that it would be a pathetic gift, but the detail of your exploits and your success would please the proudest beauty and soften her heart; you may judge how it is received by your friend! As a reward, I am going to tell you my story.

If I'm not mistaken, I sent you my last letter on the 8th of September.[1] The morning of the 9th we received a letter announcing Prince Henry of Prussia[2] for that very morning—though he didn't arrive until three-thirty. Fortunately, we had an elegant, simple little dinner to offer him, and since he seemed very amiable to me, I wanted to please him: I made myself amusing and chatty, and I succeeded. He talked a great deal, and said a thousand flattering things to me. He speaks very well, with wit and with as much ease as precision.

After dinner, he expressed the desire to see my room, and I led him to it;[3] my table was covered with books; he would have liked to see what was there, but out of civility he didn't dare open them—nor did I, out of modesty. Finally, noticing your long letter, I said to him: "Your Royal Highness would not have guessed that this is an account of the war in Corsica?" "No indeed," he said to me, "I would not have suspected it; but does that interest you?" "Yes, my Lord," I replied, "I take an interest in it because a man who is a friend of mine is doing distinguished service there. But Your Highness will be even more surprised to see the extract of my letter in the gazette." Thereupon I drew the gazette from my pocket and gave it to him. He read the extract, and claimed that it was for the sake of the women of Cavelli's castle that I had made this account public; everyone was greatly amused. The courtiers seized the gazette, and the Prince, continuing to look around at my room, my study, my bath, everything in a dwelling that helps one know the person who lives there, spoke sometimes of me and my amusements, sometimes of Paoli and the Corsicans. He said that Paoli was apparently, like other men, a mixture of good and bad, and that he had regarded him up to this point as a kind of partisan skillful at winning the confidence of the people. (The Prince expresses himself better than that; I am telling you merely the gist of what he said.) I didn't know exactly how to reply to that, and I admitted how hard I found it to make up my mind, because—taking Boswell's word for it—I had regarded Paoli as a great man, as a wise, skillful and generous legislator; but Mr. Boswell's enthusiasm has

1. She refers to Letter 315 dated September 7, 1768.
2. The brother of Frederick the Great.
3. Read, "I led him *and his entourage* to it."

misled us on so many other things—on the bravery of the Corsicans and their other leaders—must one believe him about Paoli? In short, we talked like sensible people who are very much at ease with each other.

Soon it was time to say goodbye, which the Prince was reluctant to do. "Don't you come to the Hague from time to time? May we hope to see you in Berlin?" He expressed over and over his desire to see us again and his regret at leaving us, in a manner that was very flattering because it was obviously sincere. He finally took his leave, and left me enchanted with him and intoxicated with the bit of favor he had shown me—the one augmented the other. Really, to be a great prince, a great and victorious general, and a man of wit and of letters, gentle in conversation, polite and amiable—all this at the same time—that's a great deal. The people in his suite are at ease with him; one sees no constraint in them, and it is claimed that he is beloved in his household. Since I don't think you have ever seen him, I must describe his face: it resembles somewhat that of General Crönstrom (do you know that he has just died, my poor cousin, that good man whom we all loved!). The prince, then, is neither tall nor handsome nor charming to look at; his great eyes, fixed and penetrating, make me lower mine, which are not, after all, especially timid; but the look in them is so candid that it softens his gaze, his countenance is so noble and dignified that it enhances his figure; his clothing seems just to be found there by chance, without any particular care—rich and utterly appropriate; his manners are unstudied, with nothing about them to criticize. Thus, all goes well, and this unimpressive face serves as well as the handsomest.

Upon his return to the Hague, he spoke a great deal of Zuylen and of me. On the twenty-third a fête was given; a few days earlier he said to my sister that he had no doubt that I would come, that he very much hoped so, and that he entreated her to write telling me so and to convey his compliments. By no means could I resist; my mother and I arrived the day before the ball, and since I came to the ball very late, everyone told me that Prince Henry had incessantly asked for me and looked for me. The Prince of Orange led me to him, and he rose from his game and said all the complimentary things imaginable. You should have seen how surprised the ladies of the Hague were, and how inconvenient Mme de Boetzelaer found me when the Prince was speaking to me!

All the seats at the theater for the next day had been taken two weeks before, but the Prince of Prussia made our whole Court of Orange bestir itself to find a pair for my mother and me; even lazy Marcet ran all over until he was out of breath, and finally had us admitted to the loge of the French Ambassador, whom we had never met. So I made the acquaintance of Monsieur de Breteuil at the theater, and I was very pleased—although he was unwilling to visit Prince Henry because the latter is unwilling to reciprocate.

The Ambassador was not even willing to be presented to him during the ball, and when the Prince greeted him with a slight nod of the head as was his custom (he was at the gaming table), M. de Breteuil, who was standing, took care, they say, when he returned the nod, not to bow his head lower than the Prince did. This all seems to me puerile. The Prince seems to me proud, but with a pride that is, so to speak, innate; that one does not adopt, but that one has received along with the rank—a pride that has nothing haughty about it, and that bears no resemblance to arrogance. I think that M. de Breteuil wants to be aloof and austere; as you know, these kinds of intentions are hard to hide. For fear of seeming to be over-friendly or to promise too much, he was severe with me about a modest little request that I made to him, on behalf of a likeable and unfortunate young Frenchman who came to see us five or six times. I wasn't asking anything for him, I was simply telling his story; the Ambassador interrupted it with so many objections, rather harshly expressed, that I blushed with anger and fell silent. He softened, however, and I returned to my subject; at bottom, his intentions were very good, but he had wanted to maintain the forms and air of French politeness. I sent his compatriot to him; all he needs from the Ambassador is some consideration and courtesy that would show the public that he is what he says he is—a gentleman of a recognized family. As it has all turned out, we are now on very good terms, and I know that he has spoken well of me; there is no doubt that he is an intelligent man. "The Ambassador curls his own hair and shaves himself," said the Irishman Onbrourk, a descendant of the kinglets of Ireland. That hair-curling and shaving make a great stir in the Hague, and it is repeated everywhere that it is his major-domo who cuts his hair. You know how people carry on about trivia at the Hague! He neither gambles nor dances. Tell me, who is there for him to talk to? I can think of hardly anyone except Van Monster who knows both how to converse and how to do without gambling.

By the way, do you know that his sweetheart is getting married? Heiltje de Parc is marrying Monsieur de Reede, who is six or seven years younger than she is, and who is the most fickle lover, the most romantic philosopher, the most methodical reasoner, and the most luxury-loving sybarite in the country.[4] This is the sixth time he has been in love since spring, but the tone of this passion suggests nothing but marriage. The guardians are indignant, the public is surprised—Mme d'Athlone more than surprised. My brothers and I are laughing heartily. Well then—it is said that she has an amiable mind and a good heart, and it could well be that in time she will come into an inheritance. One of Prince Henry's courtiers wanted to carry off Mme Huffel, but people say that she is marrying that chatterbox of an envoy, the Comte de Rechteren.

Monsieur de Breteuil has drawn me far from Prince Henry, but I want to return to him. He asked me for news of Corsica. I told him that it was bad

4. M. de Reede is Annebetje's (Mme d'Athlone's) husband's brother. He is marrying the Heiltje de Parc in whom the stadholder had been interested back in Letters 273 and 275.

for Paoli; that his nephew and his brother-in-law spoke ill of him and that he was being represented as the tyrant of those whose liberator he claims to be; I added that I was sorry about it, and that it had given me pleasure to admire him. That is also my answer to you. After having enjoyed being in favor again the day after the theatre, at a long bad concert that was given Sunday at the House in the Woods,[5] I left the Hague on Monday at the same time as the Prince. If I listen to him, I will not get married. "Ah Mademoiselle, stay just as you are!" But if I do marry, I have promised to stipulate in the contract a journey to Berlin.

That's enough of that; let's talk about Corsica. Do you think that I admire all the rhetoric in your letter? By no means. The historical part is truly admirable, but all the insulting epithets that you lavish on Paoli and on the Corsicans are hardly better than Boswell's fanaticism. For a long time now I have refused to argue with you because you would not yield by so much as a period or a comma, and you exaggerate your earlier assertions in proportion as they are contested. That's not good, by the way, and our dear Plutarch doesn't do it. His judgment is an equitable weighing of things; he never praises or blames without putting counterweights on the scale. Even if they are drawn only from his conjectures, or from an obscure tradition, he examines them, discusses them, assesses their merits; and that's why one reads him with so much pleasure and trust. So I haven't argued with you for a long time; I let you heap scorn upon my country and all its inhabitants, and praise all of France and all its Frenchmen; but this time if I were to be silent I would have to be incapable of speech. That Barbaggio should be captured and taken to France is all well and good, if it pleases him; but God forbid that merely on that account, or because of anything you are telling me, I find the war you are waging on the Corsicans a just one! The Corsicans and Barbaggio could leave their country, and see Paris and Versailles, without your going to kill and capture them. Simply because a dwelling-place is bad, I will not go uninvited to set it on fire and burn some fraction of its inhabitants—or if that's my way of being just, the laws' way will be to have me hanged. I was unenthusiastic about Boswell, and much of his book seemed to me in bad taste, but perhaps I did have too much respect for Paoli. You are quite right to cure me of it, and I beg you to continue to instruct me, but in the sentence that you quote: *se seppe che un capitano genovese*, etc., I see nothing ridiculous, nor any proof that he was fearful.[6] A number of passages from his conversations seem to me sublime, as they did to Boswell. The care that he takes to reserve his influence and his credit for important occasions, so that his Corsicans can do without him and get accustomed to obeying laws and magistrates seems to me—if it is true—of a rare, not to say unique, magnanimity; and were you to jeer a hundred times

5. The Huis ten Bosch, a royal villa in the Hague, built in 1645–52.
6. See d'Hermenches' Letter 314.

more, I would say that Paoli is a great man, or else a man of wit who knows how to counterfeit a great man. *La testa mi rompa* is ridiculous, and the prophetic dreams do not impress me—but why make broad judgments? Is a man all of a piece? Isn't one surely wrong whenever one blames or praises immoderately? I admire Prince Henry very much, but if I could spend a whole summer at Reinsberg[7] (as I would like to do), obviously I would not describe him to you the following autumn as a perfect man. Do not use up all your sarcasm and scorn on Paoli; wait, and get to know him well, and judge with moderation.

I speak of you very often, and I quote your judgments. Just the other day, when M. Verelst[8] and M. de Lintorf, Chamberlain of the Queen of Prussia, were having supper here, Corsica was the great subject of the conversation; but you are sometimes suspected of partiality. "One cannot write otherwise of the French army," they said. At such moments I would like to read your letters in their entirety, but I don't dare—the suspicion of partiality would be increased by your style. As for the question of whether the Corsicans would be happier belonging to France—which you are so certain of—, I really know nothing about it. You would not be giving them the climate of France, nor the temperament of the French, which are their great advantages. As for the rest, one must know how they would be treated; whether they would not have judges like those of Toulouse,[9] or a harsh and greedy governor; and whether luxuries for some financier's wife would not devour the product of their sterile land. Not all of France puts on plays at Villers-Cotterêts, nor has exquisite suppers in discreet little villas.[10] In the provinces, they say, people live groaning in poverty. The right of the King of France over Corsica, it seems to me, is simply that of the strongest, just as that of the Spanish over America was that of the cleverest; and from the point of view of morality, one is not more grateful to M. de Chauvelin for having civilized the Corsicans than one is to Don Pedro (was his name Pedro? I no longer remember) for having converted Montezuma.[11] But what does all that have to do with you? Nothing at all. You are not responsible for the war before God or before me, and everything that I'm saying about it is to keep your judgment from going astray, and to urge you to make your commentaries as judicious as they say Caesar's are, and as admirable as your conduct. If you prefer, I will stop contradicting you, for I would not like to anger a friend; when he is so far away, one cannot quickly make peace and embrace.

7. Prince Henry's residence.
8. Minister plenipotentiary from the United Provinces to Berlin.
9. A reference to the Calas Affair.
10. A reference to entertainments offered by the duc d'Orléans, in which d'Hermenches participated.
11. Montezuma II (1466–1520), the Aztec emperor whom Cortés subjugated and placed under house arrest. Father Olmedo tried in vain to convert him to Christianity.

What I care about much more than our political arguments are the things that affect you directly. On the one hand, I am delighted with your wise, bold conduct, which has had such fortunate results and has won you a fine reputation—not to mention the advancements that I hope for and expect; on the other hand, I worry about the extreme fatigue, and I am terribly concerned that you are sick. But what is your illness? If it's a question of nerves, take a cold bath; if it's loss of appetite, a cold bath; if it's too great sensitivity to cold or humidity, a cold bath head first.[12] I'm speaking according to my own experience; I no longer have migraines, or earaches, or toothaches, and I eat like a wolf. Goodbye; I'm leaving you to go take a bath.

Write to me, and love me as a sincere and eternal friend.

318. *To Constant d'Hermenches, October 5, 1768*

Zuylen

What! Paoli too has fled! The coward! And all this time I was wishing you success only with reservations—asking you to have some consideration, and even respect, for his reputation, and to speak of him with moderation! Ah! I abandon him! *Animo, figlioli!* And then to flee himself! Why didn't he let himself be killed while his troops were fleeing? Even if we despised the Corsicans, we would have respected their leader; Boswell could still show his face. But now he can only blush and hide himself forever, with his preface, his dedication, his *Tour of Corsica*, and that whole foolish product of an insane enthusiasm! You must have laughed at my pathetic request of the day before yesterday, when I asked you to suspend your judgment on my former hero. Never mind—when you have laughed at my foolishness, you will still pay attention to the reasonable things that accompany it, and that I will not back down from. The only thing that is misplaced was my asking you to defer your judgment on Paoli; whatever blackguardly things your enemies do, I don't want you to call them *blackguards;* I can't bring myself to pronounce the word, and I want to read and reread your letters aloud—they deserve to be read and shown.

You see that I do not abandon my ground as easily as the Corsicans; it's stubbornness, rather, that is my failing, but you will pardon it. You must be weary of doing nothing but conquering and capturing; everywhere men are surrendering their arms to you, almost without a fight; all you have to do is show yourself. What a fine thing, the capture of the Fornali castle! How fortunate you seem—and worthy of your fortune!

12. See Georges Vigarello, *Concepts of Cleanliness*, on the virtues attributed to cold baths in the 1760s. Voltaire's famous doctor, Théodore Tronchin, is quoted: "As long as the Romans, on leaving the Champs de Mars, went and plunged into the Tiber, they ruled the world. But the hot baths of Agrippa and Nero reduced them gradually to slaves ..." (117).

But why must you be called upon to combat the bad air, the climate, bad food perhaps—enemies against which courage and conduct can do nothing? I wish I could give you, for your evenings, my bath, my supper, and my bed. Are you very sick? In that case, I would stay in my armchair and sleep there. But how can I laugh when you are suffering! Tell me all kinds of details about how you spend the days when you're not fighting. At least, after the victory, the victor should be able to rest in comfort and want for nothing. I'm very glad to see you out of San Fiorenzo. Tell me what diseases this bad air causes, and whether you are better at Saint-Nicolas. Is there nothing you can take to protect you against the sea air and the marshes? Wouldn't quinine be an antidote?

I received your letter this morning, the one dated the 10th of September. You should have mine from the fifth or the eighth,[1] but I am vexed that you have been a month without having news from me, and I reproach myself. I don't know why it's more difficult to write to friends when they are very far away. That will not happen again; I think of you so often that it is very easy to pick up a pen; and your remembering me, so constantly and tenderly, and your letters—such interesting ones—deserve better than anything mine can give you in return. I am ashamed to have nothing worthwhile to say to you; when you see a letter come from so far away, you will probably open it eagerly, but apart from my friendship, you will find only trivial remarks, irrelevant reflections that are already a month old about things that you had written to me two months ago—annoyances, little quarrels that are only of some use when people are close to each other and can interrupt, respond, become heated, get angry, and immediately make peace. I feel all of that when I try to write; to edit out those inconveniences would be even worse: one would be constrained and tedious, and not at all oneself. In spite of distance, in spite of all the risks I run of arriving in Corsica boring and out of date, I will write. I have already said that I will write more often; but *you* must continue to write. Whatever my little criticisms might suggest, your letters increase my respect for you; they do honor to you and to me as well. I speak of them without making myself ridiculous; they are a tribute from your friendship that touches and flatters mine.

Tell me whether you are spending the winter in that ugly country. I hope that at least you will be well housed, and sheltered from everything you are suffering from now. During the siege of Berg-op-Zoom[2] everybody sent *koek* from Amsterdam to the besieged; I would like to send you some *bonbons*. If I remember right, Nebbio is the best cultivated and most fertile canton of Corsica; the army will regain its strength there. I've forgotten where Saint-Nicolas is, but even the most bearable part of the island would make quite bad winter quarters; I hope that you will spend the winter in France or

1. We have only her Letter 315 of September 7, 1768.
2. A city in northern Brabant, besieged by the French in 1747. *Koek* is cake.

in Lausanne. Seeing you here no longer seems to me a possible thing; in three months it will be four years since we have seen each other.

Would you be curious to know how I'm amusing myself? Making knots and laces; I don't know why I have only this insipid handwork to do. My life is a little like my handwork. My three brothers are absent. Yesterday, with my father and the Marquis de Saint-Simon, I made a plan to beautify the grounds and give some variety to the paths. I think I have some good ideas, but I take care not to get too attached to them for fear of being vexed if my father, who listens to me with so much gentleness and even pleasure, were nonetheless, when all's said and done, to leave things as they are. These past days I have read *Richardet;*[3] it's delightful. I'm reading Montaigne and Reid, *On the Human Mind,*[4] and still, Plutarch. Goodbye, my dear friend, I love you very much. I love courage and laurels and merit, and for love of all that, I embrace you with all my heart.

Couldn't you find out why it is that your letters always take so long to reach me? The successes you describe to me have been in all the gazettes for a week. It was the same with your two earlier accounts. If I were the first to receive them, it would be I who would publish them, and there your name would shine. Your letter of the tenth didn't reach me until the fifth—that's a long time. Is Lord Pembroke still in Corsica? Are the English really sending help? Could that little island become the cause of a great war?

There's no news here ...[5]

319. *To Constant d'Hermenches, October 6, 1768*

You see, a letter from Leghorn written the on 16th arrives on the 5th of October, the same time as yours of the 10th. Can it be that they are bothering to hold your letters and read them? I feel sorry for anybody who's doing the same with mine. Could Paoli's flight be the the result of a shrewd political tactic rather than an act of cowardice? Soldiers who only know how to shoot are at a disadvantage when they fight against you; but when they escape into their mountains—which they can climb much better than you—you pursue them, they tire you out, they reappear; their losses are slight, the war goes on, and you expend all your strength. That's what someone was saying yesterday. As for their harshness against those who want to surrender, I'm not at all surprised; they are betraying the fatherland.

A thousand good wishes for your glory and your health.

---

3. She has been reading a French translation of an Italian poem, *Ricciardetto* (1738) by Niccolò Carteromaco (pseudonym of Nicolas Forteguerri).

4. *On the Human Mind: An Inquiry into the Human Mind, or The Principles of Common Sense* (1764), by the Scottish philosopher Thomas Reid (1710–96).

5. There are fragments of a few more lines to this letter, the corner of the paper having been torn off. They apparently contain bits of court gossip.

ভ *Plans are being put in place for Belle's mother to be inoculated against smallpox. The procedure had been introduced into Europe only a few decades earlier, largely through the efforts of Lady Mary Wortley Montagu, wife of the British ambassador to the Ottoman Empire, who had observed the practice in Turkey. The practice spread rapidly in England, but it encountered more resistance on the Continent, where it was viewed as an attempt to circumvent the decisions of Divine Providence. In 1734 Voltaire had treated the subject in his* Lettres philosophiques, *his collection of short essays in praise of England. For him, inoculation represented freedom and intelligence of action for human betterment. Until Edward Jenner discovered the effectiveness of cowpox vaccine in the 1790s, the injected material was taken from actual smallpox lesions, so that inoculation was not without risk, and the patient did experience smallpox symptoms.*[1]

Belle was an advocate of inoculation, and had undergone it herself four times. In a letter to Ditie of November 7, 1768, she describes the "careful, well-conducted preparation" being made for her mother's inoculation. It was to be done by an English physician, Hugh Williamson, who would stay at the house throughout the procedure.

322. To Constant d'Hermenches, October 28, 1768

I'm worried about you, my dear friend. The gazettes talk of nothing but the number of sick in your army. There are also a large number of wounded in the various actions; I find only the names of the leaders. Why don't these wretched gazettes give us news of our friends? Or why don't you yourself send news of a friend who is dear to my heart, whose courage puts him in more danger than most, and whom I see, with anguish, exposed on the one hand to Corsican rifles, on the other to the bad air? I've been waiting for a letter every day. I admit that I haven't deserved to receive any very often, but was it necessary to punish me for a silence that could not have made you doubt my affection? The great distance between us and my being accustomed to receiving an answer from you to each of my letters before I write another—you know perfectly well that those are the only causes of my crime. Today, however, I reproach myself for it as cruelly as if my feeling had been a part of it; I also reproach myself for quarrelling with you, for my strictness on questions that are unimportant when all's said and done. What do I care about the glory of the Corsicans and the way one talks about them? I should have put off our disputes to a more peaceful time; I should have limited myself, while you were in the midst of dangers and fatigues, to simply sending you my good wishes, telling you how warm such wishes are, and urging you by a thousand assurances of affection to send me your

1. See Donald R. Hopkins, *Princes and Peasants: Smallpox in History* 46–81.

news often. Instead of doing that, I have responded to my own mood and the tone of your letters: I believed you were invulnerable, and created to be forever the conqueror. The Corsicans were fleeing, and I thought that they would always flee; it is they who attracted all my pity, and all I feared for you was a few bramble-scratches. My wishes were for your glory, and I saw them being granted; I saw only laurels and advancements, and I still see them—but all these wounded! All these sick! My God! let me learn that you are not among them! If you are well, why not write to me? There may be a letter from you that has been on its way for a long time; I have already told you how slow they are in coming.

I have nothing new to tell you. My mother is getting ready for the inoculation; I tell you about it only because you are at the ends of the earth, for she's making a great secret of it, since she wants to be entirely free to abandon the project the moment she changes her mind, without causing surprise to anybody and without being made fun of. If her resolution holds firm as the time of the operation draws near, we will still be in the country for nearly a month. But if her illness is somewhat serious, I will be all the more uncomfortable because I think I contributed to her deciding to do it. There isn't any real danger at all. However, to put minds at rest, I will talk about it at more length to the inoculator, who is an Englishman—very clever, prudent, and sensible.

Even if I knew some amusing bits of news to relate, I wouldn't tell you, for fear that it come at a wrong time; but I know nothing at all; I see only my books. How I would like to see an envelope arrive written in your hand. If the week goes by without one, I will write to Monsieur de Bournonville and ask him for news of you. Goodbye, I embrace you tenderly; no friend—man or woman—has a heart with more affection for you than mine. Come back from that wretched Corsica. My God, what does that miserable conquest matter to a great king! But if they absolutely insist on subjugating the poor Corsicans—that is to say, exterminating them—let them send other troops, and send you home. I embrace you again, and I love you.

ᗉ *On October 9 the French suffered a humiliating defeat at Borgo, where nearly 200 were killed and the 530-man contingent was forced to surrender. Chauvelin's inexperience and overconfidence had led him to overextend his forces and fail to provide for adequate communication in the field. The affair discredited him altogether, though his long personal friendship with Louis XV kept him in command until December 1768.[1] D'Hermenches recounted this episode in a letter of October 17, which Belle received and read to her family, but which is not extant.*

1. Hall, *The Corsican Question* 193.

323. *From Constant d'Hermenches, November 4, 1768*

San Fiorenzo

I've received both your letters at the same time, my divine friend— treasures of wit, of interesting facts and information. I have just finished the campaign; I am on leave, and I'm about to sail back. There's nothing now to struggle against but the sea and my poor health. I don't believe your remedy of cold baths has any effect against dysentery, or chronic fever, or the *miséréré;*[1] it is easy to see that your ailments are those of a nymph, a muse, a virgin . . .

Today I'm writing you only a couple of words, on the chance that the packet boat will go faster, by way of Antibes, than I will on a ship by way of Toulon. I am going straight to Paris, and it's there that I will receive your letters just as in Corsica, with the same address; from there I will answer these two charming letters that I am carrying for good luck on my voyage. I will quarrel with you no more about Corsica, because when you know it—and Paoli—as I do, we will be in agreement; or so I am vain enough to think. If some of my expressions have wounded your ears, remember that it's a soldier who was writing; and you should not quibble with someone who, in this barbarous country, and considering the life I lead there, should almost be allowed to say *Hell and damnation.*[2]

The story of the Borgo fiasco is this: we were trying with insufficient forces to rescue a place that was being attacked by six thousand men; my brigade was being used only as a diversion. If we had succeeded, and Paoli had been beaten, he had a sailor's clothes all ready and would have been on his way to Switzerland. (That reconciles me a little with him.)

The gazette article that you sent me proves how false and how Paolist the news from Leghorn is. On the 16th of September I was attacked at Oletta by two thousand Corsicans; on the 17th they began again without success. I fell on them with four hundred men; I drove them out, defeated and beaten, as far as Olmeta—precisely the place being discussed. They never captured a single man from me in any action; and the one in question is certainly the best example we'll have of what we're discussing, for the troops were cruelly worn out from the camp in Saint-Nicolas.

If you had married Bellegarde, you would be in mourning; the other day one of his cousins was killed, the Chevalier de Béthisy.

Farewell, Agnes, I will soon be at your feet.

Yes, it is obvious that my letters have been held up, since you get them so late.

---

1. A particularly painful colic.
2. "*Morbleu*" and "*Sacrebleu.*"

326. *To Constant d'Hermenches, November 22, 1768*

Zuylen

No, no—you are wrong to accuse yourself of egotism. Your account is remarkable, wonderful.[1] My father read it with great pleasure; my brother thanked me warmly when he had read it all. At present I am triumphantly displaying the letters from that same man from whom, in the past, the slightest note was such a great crime. My father ought to say to me: "It was very sensible of you to deceive me a little then and not to let yourself be intimidated by my cautious and severe rules of conduct; you have obtained a good friend out of this, and I have an additional resource."

The dark night, the rain, the storm, the mule hurtling down the cliff, the cannon bogged down in the mud—it all left me soaked, chilled, exhausted, and muddied. I felt the heavy blankets on my shoulders. Thank God, you have been neither very sick nor badly wounded. The fatigue will be forgotten in the course of the winter, and the dangers will procure for you, I hope, glorious rewards. In my anxiety I had written to M. de Bournonville; I learned nothing from his response because I had already received your letter. Take care not to offend staff headquarters in what you say. Give up the pleasure of speaking well, of saying the truth, for it will only result in prolonged quarrels; you have done more than your duty, and as for those who forgot or fail to recognize theirs, leave them in peace. The very people who were the most indolent in Corsica might well be quite active of tongue and eager to slander you in the salons of Paris. Besides, even if one gained as much as one generally loses by speaking ill of others, that profit would be *enjoyed*[2] less agreeably than any other by a generous heart.

I hastened to write to your son; I send you his response because I am delighted with it. Send him some friendly words about it, and try to satisfy our desire—his and mine—to see you again. I think he believed, too optimistically, that we were now only separated from you by the sea.

Prince Henry has had some very flattering letters written to me.[3] You know that he is not lavish with them where women are concerned. My mother has been inoculated a second time, and I think the smallpox is finally taking with her. Yesterday I received Sterne's *Sentimental Journey;*[4] I am devouring it. This evening I receive a supply from the London mail. For people who are isolated in the countryside, who see nothing but trees bereft of leaves, and hear nothing but autumn winds, everything becomes a major event. I receive a great many letters, and I am less bored, perhaps, than another woman would be in my situation. Besides, it would be shameful to

1. The lost letter of October 17.
2. English in the original.
3. The brother of Frederick the Great, whose visits to Zuylen and the Hague were described in Letter 317.
4. Laurence Sterne, *A Sentimental Journey through France and Italy* (1768).

complain when you are suffering a thousand times more. But you are acquiring laurels, and I am acquiring nothing; and in spite of all my best intentions, I bother and annoy my father and mother more often than I satisfy them. And yet, in this solitude, what feeling other than a daughter's love offers to enter my heart? None! And when this feeling is disappointed, my heart feels as arid as this bare landscape. Goodbye. Be a good father, and be tender to your son if he loves you.

God protect you from bad air, firearms, and everything that can hurt you.

327. *From Constant d'Hermenches, November 25, 1768*

Toulon

You have a brother in the Navy, dear Agnes; so you have an idea of the pleasure one takes in being back on firm ground. If he hasn't experienced it himself, he has at least seen the effect it has on others. Myself, I feel it to its fullest extent, even in the short distance I had to go; but a ten-days' sail with a pilot fallen overboard has given me all the appetite for dry land that a voyage to the East Indies could do. What joy to disembark at Hyères, and to see oranges, violets, roses—to sleep without fleas, or bedbugs, or scorpions, and to eat cabbage, and turnips, and butter! ... All the same, I am not tired of the Corsican war—I don't know why, for it has yielded me nothing so far; I really think that I must be made for this career. Nothing about it seems difficult to me except looking upon wounded and suffering people; in twenty-three years I haven't been able to become indifferent to the horror of that spectacle. I speak to you a great deal of myself, dear Agnes; but here in Toulon, where nothing seems as delightful as breathing healthy air, drinking, eating, and sleeping, I can think of nothing but earthly things, however attached and involved I am by all the heavenly traits that you comprise.

And you, dear Agnes, what is occupying your mind these days? Do you stay by the fireside, or plunge into the pleasures of society? Do your studies preoccupy you? ... or does a king, a royal prince, a hero, an adoring suitor! ... You can no longer go bathing or walking. Well then, go out into society; go to the ball, find a little pleasure in a good supper; you are so much to be admired everywhere that it is only to your advantage to do what others do. I have recovered my health here; I'm going to Paris. I undertake this journey reluctantly: to turn one's back on the climate of Provence, to throw oneself into the winter sleet and go play the courtier—a sad business! But I have staked so much that I have to see the lottery play itself out.

The tales they tell about Corsica—even here, even in Switzerland where we have often written, and in Paris where the mail arrives every day—compel me to ask you to have this article, of which I'm sending you a copy, inserted into your gazettes. It is true and exact; it's a letter that I found at a merchant's here, and that I'm expanding a little. It was written from Turin;

I have a personal interest in it, and I hope you will forgive my foolishness in asking such a thing; it is to recompense me for what the jealousy of others has cost me in the business of the 17th,[1] which has never been recounted to the Court as it should have been. You are my friend; why would I let you be ignorant of the least of my weaknesses? I am adding the name of my friend d'Arcambal, because he too has been the victim of the harassments that are always inevitable wherever there are men capable of devoting their lives to their own self-interest.[2]

I hasten to Paris to look for your letters; if only I could meet you there! Would it be so impossible, so unreasonable for your rich, beautiful young friends to feel the value and the need of being able to go to the place from which they obtain their bonnets, their coiffures, their manners, their novels, their music, their cook, their plays? Madame Tuyll, Mme d'Athlone, and the rest of them should exercise all the power they have over their husbands, to make that journey, and on their knees implore Agnes to join them. That's my dream for this evening; if it were fulfilled, I would be the happiest of men! For to tell the truth, my respectful passion for you grows stronger with time and habit, and more intense with distance. I am at your feet.

328. *To Constant d'Hermenches, November 27, 1768*

Zuylen

I received your letter of the 4th of November with joy, my dear friend, with the greatest joy. You are now out of that wretched country. I hope that the sea has been calm, and that Aeolus has chained the winds on your behalf. If you haven't been seasick, that's good—one less unpleasantness; if you have been seasick, even better, for that illness is a remedy for more serious ones. Your health will quickly return with rest and good air; but take care of yourself and don't overeat; two extremes are equally dangerous, especially when one follows immediately upon the other. After having lived like a Trappist, now live like a Franciscan, and little by little you will return to the diet of the fat canons. As you see, I want only to rejoice; I imagine the sea calm, and your health returning apace; I see your head crowned with laurels, and the Minister's heart full of rewards. If this mood lasts, in a quarter of an hour I will see you in the Hague, your son on the one side

1. This is the action at Oletta that he recounted in Letter 323.
2. The marquis des Lacs d'Arcambal commanded the regiment of Roverque that penetrated furthest into Corsican-held territory in Casinca on September 8, 1768, and were among the first to be forced back by Paoli's counterattack on the ninth and tenth. D'Hermenches is claiming in November of 1768 that unjust blame was ascribed to d'Arcambal for the rout at Borgo. In December Chauvelin will be replaced by Noël Jourda, comte de Vaux. In the spring of 1769, when the French will rout Paoli's forces, Marbeuf will command the left wing, Vaux himself the center, and Arcambal will be given command of the right wing; Vaux's decision seems to vindicate d'Hermenches' claim.

questioning, me on the other, equally joyful at seeing you.

It is very good of you to take pleasure in my two letters; I apologized for them in a third, which you will receive, I hope, sooner or later; and I wrote yet another one a week ago in response to yours of the 17th of October. My mother has smallpox, but she's hardly sick from it at all: fifty to sixty big pustules.[1] It's only the lesions on her arms that are hurting her very much; but already the pain is diminishing, and we are expecting the pustules to begin to dry up in two days. We are very pleased. Mme de Chasteler also has had the intelligence to have herself inoculated—I know that only by chance, because she is no longer writing to me. Her husband has just been recognized as a descendant of the House of Lorraine, and people say that soon he will be awarded the Golden Fleece.[2] If that consoles her for the tedium of living with a fool, I am very happy for my friend.

Goodbye; I am waiting for news of you. I am extremely pleased with you; no one could be a better or a more loveable friend than you are; and that conviction, along with the gratitude that flows from it and together with my natural inclination, form a solid and tender attachment that you too should be pleased with.

329. To Constant d'Hermenches, December 14, 1768

Utrecht

You ask what I'm doing? Alas! I am weeping for my mother. In the midst of my grief I am running a household, and trying to ease my father's lot, which is dreadful. My brother the sailor coughs incessantly, and we all fear for him; I beg him from morning to night to take care of himself to save his own life.[1] That's what I'm doing, dear d'Hermenches; I envy the lot of everyone else in the world.

The smallpox had come and gone with no ill effect; the pustules had dried up and were falling off; we were rejoicing in her recovery. Then came a sore throat to frustrate our joy; we were concerned but not frightened, since she had no fever. Suddenly on the third of this month, at eight in the evening, a fever came on with such violence, and her breathing became so labored, that all the bleedings, all the blisterings—all kinds of remedies, multiplied one on the other all through the night—did nothing to change her condition. When her strength was exhausted, her anguish diminished; and the next day, at noon, she passed from a peaceful sleep into death.[2]

1. The apology and a discussion of the smallpox inoculation are in Letter 322 of October 28.
2. An honorary order founded by the duke of Burgundy in the fifteenth century.
1. Her favorite brother Diederik (Ditie), to whom she wrote many letters. Her fears were justified; he died of tuberculosis in 1773 at the age of twenty-nine.
2. We don't know whether the throat infection that followed the inoculation of Belle's mother was a separate episode or the result of a vulnerability due to the inoculation itself.

I cannot convey to you the depth of our horror and desolation. Every detail was a dagger to us. My father has lost all his pleasure, his only friend, his company and his consolation. We have all lost; we miss her from morning to night. People pity us, but they spread around a thousand tales accusing us. Fortunately, I don't hear them in all their details; I am able to hide. I see only the people who are our friends, and they come keep us company every evening. Mme d'Athlone comes at all hours, and then I can open my heart. I can neither read nor write; these few lines have cost me infinite pain. When I am alone I do handwork, or I go weep with my mother's old chambermaid. Pity me, my friend; I don't weep the whole day long, but the whole day long my heart grieves, and my mind, which seems to have lost its place, wanders and torments itself in a hundred different ways.

I am happy for you—for the repose, for the abundance, and above all for the health you are recovering on dry land. Why was your pilot thrown into the sea? My brother says he's not familiar with that style of sailoring.

If you want to see me, I think you will have to come her where I am; it doesn't look as though I will be leaving soon. Goodbye. Write to me.

330. *From Constant d'Hermenches, December 25, 1768*

I am made intensely aware of how much you mean to me, my dear friend, by the emotion that your grief causes me. My first wishes are for your health. You are ardent and sensitive; your body will not be as strong as your soul; you will still be ill even after you have recovered from your bereavement. Take care, I beg you, I implore you! Try to distract yourself from your grief. Don't seek too much solitude; avoid somber thoughts; let your heart find its place again. Mourn, but do not despair. Reason, and time, and that fortunate buoyancy that Providence sends to the aid of grieving mortals will restore your soul to its natural seat; but a jolt as violent as this can unsettle your nerves for a long time. You have suffered the cruelest of losses, since your mother was your friend, conducted her household in a firm and orderly way, gave wise advice, and was kind and forgiving. You have suffered an irreparable loss in losing the life companion of your honorable father, whom you cherish. I know of no one as unhappy as a man who, in middle age, loses the only person he loved. Women are much less to be pitied—so many little things compensate them. And then at a certain age they love almost nothing but their own persons; that, again, is a fortunate instinct of nature. As women lose the means to please and to attach others to themselves, they withdraw into themselves, so to speak, and become their own idols. My mother is still alive, dear Agnes; I adored her all my life, and I was unjust enough to prefer her to my father, who was the most excellent of men. Progressively as she gets older, she detaches herself from her children; often she makes enemies of them. Their fortunes and their ills are all becoming indifferent to her; she is concerned only with herself alone and with her own existence.

I feel immensely sorry for your father. At this moment he may not yet feel the full extent of his pain; the condolences, the attentions of others, the very apparatus of grieving can provide a diversion from grief. He finds in you the sweetest comfort, even perhaps a sort of relief; but when he is restored to himself, his state of mind will be sad indeed if he is merely resigned, but not philosophically so. Help him to find, soon, some compensations for his widowhood, and then some comforts in that state. However strong the bond between two people who have lived together for a long time, there are bound to be points of conflict in their tastes and manners; they deprive each other of things they enjoy; they constrain each other. Acquaint him, bit by bit, with the pleasure of no longer constraining himself, of denying himself nothing. Let the things that he did not have before his widowhood fill up, little by little, the emptiness into which he now is plunged. You must have the skill to create a new kind of life for him, rather than trying to make the old life bearable: that's the way to avoid unhappiness for both of you, and it's of the greatest consequence for you. You are dealing with a father who is wise, and superior to the ordinary run of men; that is a great advantage, and a great satisfaction. Avoid all exaggeration, all self-abnegation contrary to your tastes; otherwise, you would begin by simply being a good daughter, but would surely end by appearing ungrateful, and you would be hated. I had a friend who was in your situation; if she had followed my advice, her life and that of her father would not have become a tissue of vexations and reproaches; but she wanted to play the heroine—the victim—and she was finally disinherited. She is not unlike you; she is a woman of immense wit and feeling, and her father was a very gallant man.

I have been in Paris for a week. Neither am I happy nor am I being rewarded. People scarcely want to hear a word about Corsica; the campaign is winning no approval. At present everything is in a state of confusion;[1] I must yield to circumstances. I have been received with kindness and praise, and I must be content with that. My star has never shone but fitfully, and I begin to persuade myself that my career is doomed to mediocrity, for all that I have the attributes that would seem to indicate the opposite: a man of rank, intellect, and talents, and a very good officer. In one of your odd moments, you must give me your thoughts about my situation. The Corsican enterprise will be pursued, it seems to me, so it is very likely that I will set sail again as I did last year. Address your letters care of Monsieur de Besenval; I will spend at least a month here, and I assure you that you do not leave my thoughts.

Your misfortune is a setback for inoculation, but what reason do you have

1. At about this time Chauvelin is being replaced by Vaux as commanding officer in Corsica.

to reproach yourself? Had not your mother wanted it? Was it not properly done? Her hour had come; and that is the only objection I have ever found to inoculation—just that kind of anticipation.

I am at your feet, my adorable, beautiful friend Belle.

331. *To Constant d'Hermenches, January 19, 1769*

Utrecht, Thursday

I have intended to write to you a hundred times, and when the day and the hour of the post come, I'm no longer in the mood: I am lazy, discouraged, downcast, melancholy, and unable to do a thing. I like neither the house, nor my room, nor my books; I run outside to get away from them, and when I arrive at Mme d'Athlone's I am content and my grief is somewhat calmed; I entertain her, and she is tender with me. I spend the morning at her bedside; I return there in the evening; I never leave her without her arranging the time to see me again. Were it not for her, I would die of boredom and sadness; I love her more than anyone. You have never seen two women love each other as we do—never any ill-humor, never any negligence, or forgetfulness, or quarrelling, or the slightest possibility of complaining of each other ... How fortunate for you that I talk to you about Mme d'Athlone—the only thing in my whole heart that is free of horror, anxiety, or regrets!

I thank you for your advice; it is all the better in that it is simple, and that you have not tried, as most advice-givers do, to adorn yourself with an impracticable sublimity that costs nothing to those who preach and that is a heavy burden to those who are preached to. On the contrary—your advice is directed to me, to my happiness, and not to your glory; it calls me back from a high-flown notion of virtue to reason and reality. But, my friend, the best part of what you say is wasted and inappropriate and impossible because of my father's character. *Acquaint him, bit by bit,* you say, *with the pleasure of no longer constraining himself, of denying himself nothing.* Quite—that would all be well and good if he didn't like to constrain himself, if he wanted to deny himself nothing, and if what he required of us were anything other than that very sobriety in everything, that moderation, that simplicity, those privations which he rigorously imposes on himself. He refuses to have a fire in his room; he prefers to go on foot rather than in a carriage, and to sit on a hard chair rather than in an armchair—and he is like that in everything. You see that indulgence and cosseting don't get us very far. Aside from his love of his duties and of order, I know of only one passion of his: that of building. I hope that the chance to satisfy it will present itself. The States-General are considering a building for which he would be chiefly responsible; beyond that, if he listens to my advice, he will buy old houses in order to rebuild and resell them. If there were people in Utrecht who were pleasant company, he would enjoy them, and would form attachments in spite of himself; but our city has no interesting resources to offer.

When Lady Athlone has recovered from childbirth and her husband takes her off to the Hague, I don't know what will become of me from morning to evening. I will tend her son, little Lord Agrim, who is a pretty child of two, gentle and lovable; that will be an amusement for me. "Mourn," you say, "but do not despair." I'm not sure you wouldn't laugh if you could see my mourning garb; I have kept adding to it, and making it blacker and more lugubrious, until everything I wear is black, day and night. It's one sort of superstition that has made me understand other forms of it.

Speaking of superstition, the death rate of our farm animals is becoming a public calamity. Some of our peasants refuse to give medicine to their cows, saying that it would be resisting the hand of God; others receive and follow the prescriptions of our doctors, and their cows die nonetheless. Yesterday I was in a stable near the city. The poor animals were moaning and dying; their masters were weeping, and so was I along with them. Yesterday nine of them died in that stable, the day before yesterday it was twelve.

Don't worry about my health; I'm quite well, except that I am roiled by the least little thing and distraught at the slightest agitation. I bathe in cold water almost every day; that calms my nerves. When I don't bathe, I take walks.

Goodbye. There's someone waiting for me—it is my father. I'll write again on Monday.

332. To Constant d'Hermenches, March 9, 1769

Utrecht

Scold me, I deserve it—but don't hate me, for I love you. I have been to the Hague; I have had great fits of melancholy, I have had all sorts of anxieties and petty vexations, all of which has kept me from writing; I haven't written to anyone else either. But I forgive myself less regarding you than anyone else, for I have not forgotten Corsica, nor that in the midst of combat, sleepless nights, and exhaustion, you have never forgotten me. Ah! I have not forgotten you either—you have no complaint as to that, so don't complain. Forgive me for my letters, so full of myself and my grief—letters that are perhaps not very reasonable, and are certainly not very interesting. Forgive my long silence as well, and write and tell me what you are doing, and what you will do. Will you return to Corsica? —to that ugly little theater of a cruel war that is neither very honorable, it seems to me, nor very just? I would really be very sorry, and you can say to me as much as you please that I'm wrong and that you are not at all sorry to return, I'll still say the same thing. They say that your Minister[1] is a great man; it

1. Choiseul.

seems to me that there are a thousand things for him to do and to reform, in which he would show a noble soul as well as great talents; and I wish that he would leave these poor Corsicans in peace, and be more thrifty with the blood and money of these Frenchmen, who are so brave and so poor. You will not agree with me. Never mind. I have to judge according to my view, and according to where these objects are in my perspective.

I am very sorry that you have not yet received the rewards that, in my opinion, you have so richly deserved. That will come; meanwhile, one must be philosophical, and ask oneself whether we are any happier when Fortune raises us up than when she prevents us from rising in spite of talents that promised another destiny. You must reread Plutarch, as I do, and see whether the most highly-placed men have not always been ambitious for more than they obtained; you must see them suffer and die like others; it makes one reflect and take comfort.

I no longer know where you are, but in any case I'll send this letter to seek you out in Paris. If I return to the Hague, I will certainly see your son. During the week that I spent there six weeks ago I saw only my sister, who was eight months pregnant, and Mlle Fagel, who was sick. My father is in fairly good health. I am no longer in such distress, but I am extremely low in spirits. Goodbye; I am waiting for your news. Two or three of my letters must have arrived in Corsica after you left; I hope they have retraced their steps and gone to Paris, for they should not fall into other hands. If you don't have them, find out what's happened to them.

333. *To Constant d'Hermenches, March 31, 1769*

The Hague, Friday

I didn't want to write you before seeing your son. He had come to see me, but I had gone out. Monday, I asked him to spend the evening with me; Lady Athlone, Mlle Fagel, and Monsieur de Charrière were there. People were very pleased with both him and me; I was as touched by the approval that he elicited as if he had been my own son. I find him much changed for the better, both in appearance and in his wit in conversation; he's everything one might wish for in a young man. In modest tones, easy and unaffected, his remarks, always well-timed, were to the point, perceptive, and polite. He is very well liked, and I hear him spoken of only with praise. All the young men are falling in love with Leentie Bigot;[1] it's his turn now. Mlle Fagel found that he treated her with great courtesy. I can assure you, without flattery, that he is a very likeable young man. If I were to remain here, I would take an interest in his amusements, and inform myself about his tastes; but I'm leaving tomorrow. For two weeks I have been practically

1. Hélène Bigot, maid of honor of the princess of Orange.

locked up with my sister, who is in her confinement; in order to see me, one would have to look for the occasion and take part in my walks with Mme d'Athlone, Charrière, and Rendorp. Your son could hardly have that idea himself; he might have thought he would be under foot, and I myself would not have dared demand that sort of devotion to a friend of his father. He's at an age where a young man has friends and a mistress of his own choosing, and on his own score; and so we weren't able to see each other more often this time.

I should have written you Tuesday, but I was told that the post for France left Thursday. Yesterday, Thursday, they told me Friday, and today I am dying for fear that my letter will arrive too late in Toulon. I am sorry that you are returning to Corsica; I am angry and disgusted by the harassments and villainous slanders that bar your path. To continue to deserve rewards and happiness, that is up to us to do; the rest is in the hands of men and of fate—and the wisest and greatest man is the one who worries the least about it.

I'm leaving my cousin d'Athlone here, and sadly I return to sad Utrecht. I have dark imaginings, with moments of folly that others find more entertaining than I do. People here are very sorry that I am leaving. I would gladly leave to those who miss me the wit that amuses them, if they would give me in exchange a little serenity of soul and an imagination less clouded by phantoms that are as ridiculous as they are distressing. I flatter myself that some day that will all clear up a little. Write to me from Corsica. It was I, surely, who was in the wrong before the last letter, and I have no reason to reproach your friendship.

Tell me what people you are returning to Corsica with, and describe them to me: I love portraits, and it would be pleasant for me to imagine your surroundings and the advantage you might draw from them. You have certainly heard from your son all the anecdotes of the Hague, and the unfortunate miscarriage of our lovely Princess; I hardly need tell you about it, and even less tell you that the people here seem sad and sullen, play for high stakes, have nothing to say, can't amuse themselves, dislike each other—you know all that. I have only had a glimpse of this society, and that's quite enough; I have spent time only with my friends, who are as unsociable as I am.

Farewell, my friend. Never cease to be my friend; we will see each other again one day, and I will always be attached to you.

334. *From Constant d'Hermenches, April 17, 1769*

Hyères

It is my fate, dear friend, to meet with obstacles in all my enterprises. For several days I have sailed against winds and tides, and here I am, thrown back again upon the coast of Provence. I have been leading this life for ten days; Hyères has become my rehabilitation quarters. If only my mind were at rest, it would be the pleasantest of shipwrecks. The garden of Eden could not be more delightful; fruits, flowers and all sorts of vegetables grow under the orange trees and the myrtle; lovely waters, an admirable view ... but I am far more uneasy than I was on the sea. The campaign is about to begin, I am to have my own command, and I can't get there! This campaign is going to decide my fate; it absolutely must change, and my last resort will be to do what I have found so ridiculous in others: after having sacrificed my youth and small fortune to the service, to go end my days in obscurity. But I begin to be persuaded that I do not have what it takes to make one's way in the world. I am neither distressed nor humiliated by that, because I think that if I had wanted to I could have acquired it—that very particular art of winning the favor of those in power.

My dear Agnes, I am talking about myself, and yet it is you I was thinking of when I set about to write. This melancholy of yours isn't natural— you must be ill; take care of yourself! With wit, freedom, and health—even without other advantages—it is impossible to be unhappy. Now as for me, I live the life of a slave, surrounded by envy-ridden scoundrels, abominable creatures who would like to annihilate me—and yet, when my health is good, I am not even blue. And what a distance between your position and mine! The weight of years, children, a wife, nephews, impedimenta of all kinds ... Look after your health; go to the watering places, get a change of air, and your gaiety will be recovered more brilliant than ever. I assure you that even leading my galley-slave's life, I often laugh, sleep, eat, and chat with pleasure. I always wonder, in spite of myself, if one day we won't finish out our lives together. I would like to see you in Switzerland, and I wish that I had a relative or a friend who was worthy of you; with the fortune that you have, I think that your way of being and thinking would be most at home in my country.

I am setting sail today for the third time, and I'll write you from Corsica. My letters will not be as detailed as those of last year, since they are opened and read; but you may be as sure as always that you are one of my chief concerns in all the world. Write to me care of Monsieur de Bournonville, or directly to Corsica if your wish. Let me know whether my son has been fortunate enough to see you, and if he has given you my messages; please send him the news of my sailing. I am at your feet, my divine friend.

CR In December 1768 Chauvelin was replaced in command by Noël Jourda, comte de Vaux, who had been commander in Corsica in 1757 and was a respected military officer. While for all practical purposes, France had never needed anything in Corsica but secure naval bases at a couple of ports, it was now felt that for the sake of the honor of France, nothing less than the total subjugation of the island could erase the Borgo humiliation.

The sixteen battalions would be increased to forty-five battalions of infantry and three cavalry regiments.

D'Hermenches' duties in 1768 had been those of a major. We know he had the rank of colonel, but the circumstances of his transferring over to the French service from the Dutch had entailed his temporarily taking assignments more usually given to majors. Though he had led troops in battle in Corsica, these seemed to be temporary assignments on particular days and in particular battles rather than a regular line command. When he returned to Corsica, his assignment was as colonel of a force of about nine hundred volunteers. While that command was of the size of a regiment, d'Hermenches apparently did not feel it had the status of a regiment of regulars.

335. *From Constant d'Hermenches, May 15, 1769*

From the camp at Lento

I can only repeat to you, my dear Agnes, what I was saying to you last year: Paoli does not merit the respect or admiration that he is accorded. He's a poor charlatan whose reputation was created by us, and whose farce will soon have played itself out. He has retrenched; he has threatened us, and has made Milord Pembroke believe that he would decimate the French before they arrive at Corte. By means of a thousand and one deceits and ruses he has assembled an army. When we marched on him, he heaped insults and invective on us; he had our wounded slaughtered, and in not a single one of his posts did he hold firm. He fled, yelling along the way that Monsieur de Vaux was killed, that all the French were destroyed. He had the *Te Deum* sung at Corte while we were establishing ourselves on the Golo, while the volunteers were taking from him, sword in hand, the posts that Monsieur de Maillebois had been able to have only by capitulation, and while he simply abandoned Borgo, of which he had been so proud.[1]

Nine hundred volunteers, who always march in front, determined all these successes; that was the 5th of May. On the eighth, the Corsicans came to attack us fairly boldly on the Golo. The business lasted from noon to midnight; we lost some brave men there, but the enemy toppled over into the river that it had passed, and suffered great losses.[2] From that point on, a

---

1. The Golo is a river in northern Corsica. The *Te Deum* is ordinarily sung to celebrate a victory, not a series of retreats. The marquis de Maillebois had been in command of the forces charged with the pacification of Corsica under the French-Genoan arrangements in 1739–40. The French wanted to negotiate a peace while the Genoese preferred force; Maillebois managed something between the extremes (Hall, *The Corsican Question* 40–41).

2. Hall's account of the battle: "...[the Corsicans] retreated toward the bridge, where for some inexplicable reason they were fired upon by Prussian and Swiss mercenaries who had been in Genoa's pay but were now serving Paoli and were located on the right bank of the river overlooking the bridge. Whether the mercenaries betrayed their employers or their fire resulted from a misunderstanding has never been resolved" (Hall, *The Corsican Question* 201).

general demoralization: Paoli abandoned by all these people he has been deceiving and tyrannizing for so long, reduced to a hopeless situation with two or three thousand bandits who follow his fortunes and who have nothing to lose. That's our story up to the present. M. de Vaux leads us very wisely; he seems to me a very good general. On the 5th of May I just missed Paoli by fifty or sixty paces; I saw him, I was pursuing him, and I was about to reach him when the people following me, wanting to stop him, fired behind me and put me in great danger. We found all his effects in Murato:[3] the fine English books that Boswell gave him; all his correspondences; my soldiers took the horse he rode, and I took his cockade: *Valor, Virtus, Honor, Libertas,* etc.

You understand that I am not serving in this campaign as part of my corps; I am assigned duty as colonel to the volunteers of the army, always in front, and often on bivouac. I enjoy it, and it does my health no harm. But what you perhaps do not understand is that I am running all these risks with the resolution that after this campaign I will never more expose myself to the caprices of men; I will make way for those who are more fortunate or more clever rather than struggle any longer against envy and deceit. I want to let it be seen that one can be brave without being ambitious, and that one can say what one has done without claiming a reward for it.

Tomorrow, we cross the Golo, and in a few days we can be in Corte. The resources and the resistance that Paoli intends to employ are completely unknown to me, but I have no very high opinion of them. He had Machiavelli on his table with many bookmarks, all in the places that are in the character of a deceiver and a tyrant; but not a single book on military science.

I don't know whether my son is still in Holland; that depends on the review. If the review has not taken place when you receive this letter, please send him a word of my news. I have given him permission to come join me; if the war is over, it will at least be an interesting journey.

I always think of you, my dear Agnes, with feelings I have for no one but you. How I wish I could see you, how I wish I could spend my life with you!

336. *From Constant d'Hermenches, May 22, 1769*

Corte

My dear Agnes, I write to you from Corte, where I was the first to enter, with two hundred volunteers. Paoli had fled during the night; the inhabitants surrendered their arms to me, but there was firing from the castle, and several of my men were wounded; it has just now surrendered to the Comte de Vaux.

On the sixteenth I had had a lively day; after we crossed the Golo, the

3. Paoli's headquarters, halfway between Bastia and Corte.

volunteers attacked Clemente Paoli on the highest rock of the Rostino, and drove hard at him the whole day; meanwhile his brother fled with fifteen hundred men, and abandoned the monastery of Morosaglia, where he had his depot. Corsica has now been subdued, I believe. Paoli has no friends left, and he is greatly discredited in his own nation. His conduct has contributed more to our success than our arms. He found in Monsieur de Vaux a man who was prudent and firm, and that is what was needed. The prisons of Corte were full of evidence to prove Paoli execrable: prisoners who had been there four, eight, or ten years, who have never known what their crime was—a doubt, a vague suspicion was enough to make him treat them as a despot does, and often put them to death.[1]

He is going away—just where, no one knows; but what strikes me as rather gay of him is that when his friend Cafferio reproached him fiercely about his deceitfulness, about all the misfortunes that his trickery had brought down upon the land, he answered with an Italian song that begins *"O detta tante de buggie che il mi conviene d'andar,"*[2] and he got on his horse.

I am at your feet, my dear Agnes. *O creduto che il mi conveneva de voi scrivere de Corte.*[3] Although I'm made of iron, I am dead with fatigue, but content.

337. *From Constant d'Hermenches, June 17–22, 1769*

Santa Maria d'Ornano

This is the third letter I have written you since I have been in Corsica, my dear Agnes, and so far I have received nothing from you. Our undertaking is completed; you will see by the dateline of this letter how far we have come, the volunteers who are following Monsieur de Vaux here. Paoli embarked the morning of the 13th at Porto-Vecchio,[1] with a following of about a hundred thirty people, both men and women, and the most fortunate thing for the people of this country is that the execrable assassin Giovanni Carlo is part of his retinue. That will be a fine present for his protectors in Europe, that rabble of a hundred or so that he drags along with him—it's the scum of the *ladri* and the *banditti* of Corsica. He has ended as he began, with boasts, lies, and lamentations, and never, on any occasion, acting like a hero, or even like a man. Since Corte, he has shown some signs of resistance at Vivaro; he has yelled insults at us, and fired on us repeatedly, from a distance, and then withdrawn to the *altra parte delli monte*. The same thing

1. In one province there was a *junte* that could jail people for "impudent and unlawful words, even though [spoken] without any seditious intent ..." (Hall, *The Corsican Question* 198).
2. "I have told so many lies that I must leave."
3. "I thought that I ought to write you from Corte." Corte was Paoli's capital.
1. A port city in southeastern Corsica.

happened at Bastelica; all that has cost very few lives, but has caused us considerable fatigue, and all the discomfort of marches in these savage lands. The bandits have murdered—and are murdering still—unfortunate travelers on the highways; an artillery major has just lost his life in this way. There are few days in which the volunteers are not involved in some little skirmish. However, Corsica is subjugated, and more so than it has ever been, for there is not a village left that has not accepted its pardon and surrendered its arms. Monsieur de Vaux handles all this very methodically and prudently.

I am finishing this letter on the 22nd of June, upon my return from Cauro and Ajaccio,[2] and I am sending it by the Duke of Lauzun, who is bringing news of the entire submission of this realm. The volunteers will probably still be employed for a while, to go where they are needed; our success is due, apart from the abilities of the General, to the way in which we attacked the most difficult posts. The Corsicans were astonished, terrified; Paoli lost his head, and that was communicated from one end of the island to the other. I don't know what will become of me when I am no longer needed; my desire would be to be nearer to you, and to enjoy the long-desired pleasure of seeing you, hearing you, and telling you all my most ardent and sincere feelings, inspired by my admiration and respect for you, my dear friend.

We leave tomorrow to return to Corte.

Boscognano, the 22nd

338. *To Constant d'Hermenches, June 23, 1769*

I hardly dare write to you any more. How ungrateful, how indolent I am! But I do think about you. I am touched by your friendship and charmed by your letters, but you are so far away! I'm becoming such a stranger to you! The things that concern me are so uninteresting for a man who is fighting the Corsicans, and seizing their capital! However, I wrote you shortly after your departure from Paris, and I addressed my letter to Toulon with a request to the postmasters to send it on to Corsica if you were no longer in Toulon. I don't know whether you received it, but you have not yet responded. I spoke to you a great deal about your son, whom I had just seen, and whom I was extremely pleased with. In order the better to imagine your life in its moments of leisure, I asked you who the people were whom you were living with, and whether you had people of merit—friends—as your comrades; but you really have almost no moments that are without dangers, combats, and triumphs.

---

2. Ajaccio is a port city on the southwestern coast of Corsica and Cauro is a town about ten miles inland from it. One of Paoli's secretaries, Carlo Buonaparte, was blessed with a son, Napoleone, on August 15, 1769 in Ajaccio.

I make no answer to you regarding Paoli: he is unfortunate, and the Corsicans are beaten, that's all I see clearly. As for the song, it would be odious—but you didn't hear him sing it. As for the prisoners, at first they wrenched my heart and made my hair stand on end in horror of your enemy; but then we reflected that in all the countries of Europe, except for Holland, Switzerland and England, one would most likely find in their prisons people angry at being there, who would claim to be ignorant of their crimes, and who would heap insults on those who put them there. Read all the things that have be written in Brittany[1] even at the same time that all the world is saying that the King is the best of men, and that Monsieur de Choiseul is good and humane. Corsica was in a state of turbulence; the Genoans had partisans there—that authorizes or excuses many illegal things. You have, however, succeeded in greatly diminishing the investment the Corsicans and their leader had inspired me to make, and without thinking further, I am very glad to see you successful. I hope that you are even more successful after the end of the campaign; obtain the rewards you deserve, and then come to see me. Were it only to begin to write again with pleasure, we must see each other; but above all, we must for the pleasure of the meeting itself.

My aunt van Tuyll, the General's wife, has been very sick for five weeks of a fever whose name I don't know, and whose outcome no one can yet foresee. My sister also caught the fever at our house and we were very worried for the first days, but it has diminished to the point where she is simply acting like a child in every way possible: she will endure neither noise nor daylight. For myself, I don't want to die of boredom at the bedside of a person who is no longer sick. Thus I see her very little. I have had Mlle Fagel here, whom I like very much. Mme d'Athlone is in Utrecht, and comes very often to Zuylen; she is still *l'idole del cor mio*. Monsieur de Charrière has become a great friend, and after having traveled about, now to Leyden, now to Amsterdam, now to the Hague, he has returned to be with two cousins, and is very well received by them. My youngest brother is still in Germany; he has seen all the maneuvers in Berlin, Magdebourg, and Stettin; the two others are at Zuylen. Two of my sister's children are still here, and (on my account) my cousin's son, and for a few days now, Mme Girard, the woman I wrote to you about and who lived in the household of your brother in Geneva.[2] She says that your nieces are devilishly intelligent, and that M. Constant is a very courtly gentleman, whose way of thinking and acting is the noblest in the world. She is with us only briefly, for she's on her way to Berlin.

---

1. An allusion to a conflict between the *parlement* of Brittany and the governor, concerning the rights of the Breton nobility.
2. Mme Girard was a former governess of Tuyll children. In September 1767, Belle had been seeking d'Hermenches' help in finding a position for her. He had found employment for her in the household of his brother Samuel Constant, but she eventually left. One of the nieces here is Rosalie, whose description of d'Hermenches is given in the Introduction (p. xviii).

I have no news to report. Monsieur de Vernand has gone to Weilbourg with the Prince. Nobody that you know is getting married. Mme Bentinck is still weeping for her husband.[3] You know that Reynst has married a rich widow, not at all young but still pretty. Our Comtesse de Golofkine is becoming a consummate chatterer and busybody, but she is so kindhearted that it's almost a crime to say so. My eldest brother is looking for a wife, but he hasn't yet one amiable enough who is at the same time rich enough and of good enough family and who can be obtained easily enough to please him.[4]

Farewell; don't get tired of writing me, however guilty I may be, and above all don't get tired of loving me.

339. *From Constant d'Hermenches, August 25, 1769*

Pieve del Niolo

There has just occurred a little change in my fortunes, dear Agnes, and I think you would be displeased with me if I didn't tell you about it immediately: I am commander of the Jenner Regiment,[1] that is, lieutenant-colonel of an elderly general officer; and barring very bad luck, I can hope to succeed him. I keep my pensions, and I ought to become brigadier directly. I'm told that my revenues will increase by two thousand francs; since I can't have a regiment right away, it is the most advantageous thing that could be done for me, and they are even providing a good retirement pension for a man who is still young, in order to procure this position for me, and without any cost to me.[2] This was all promised to me before the campaign; I have been waiting for my reward ever since. However, experience teaches me that I should consider myself very pleased and well compensated.

Here I am still waging war in the Niolo, which is the "Assassins' Street" of Corsica.[3] Thirty bandits got together to assassinate as many Frenchmen as they could, with pretty fair success; their priests promised them indulgences for five hundred years. We hunt them down from rock to rock. They

3. Anthony Bentinck had died in 1768.
4. In 1771 Willem René will marry Johanna Catharina Fagel, the "Mlle Fagel" mentioned above.
1. A Swiss regiment in the service of France.
2. D'Hermenches' permanent rank was Colonel. But in the structure of the army, to be Colonel *of a regiment* was to occupy a position in a chain of responsibility to the crown that entailed payment of funds and financial obligations; to "have" a regiment involved a "cost" of some investment. It was not uncommon for the colonel of a regiment to have little military expertise, in which case the actual military command would become the job of the lieutenant colonel. A brigade comprised two or more regiments, and the military command of it did not entail what the proprietorship of a regiment did: a lieutenant colonel often skipped over his colonel in promotion to brigadier. See Kennett, *The French Armies* 55.
3. For "Assassins" d'Hermenches uses the Dutch "Moerdenaers."

drag their wives and children and their herds along with them, which make up a considerable caravan. We always catch at least a few of them; in my last detachment one of them fell into the hands of three of my soldiers. He made as if to surrender his musket, and then shot one of the soldiers in the chest, killing him outright; he immediately picked up some stones and broke the head of another soldier, and was defending himself desperately and furiously when he was finally brought down by a gunshot. With the greatest composure, he said to me in the gentlest voice and with the most touching eloquence and gestures, *"Excelenza, io sono disgratiato, no ho mai sbarato un colpo di schiopetta contro nessuno, io no ho mai portato armi in vita mia, io sempre rifiutata di marchare in tempo di de Paoli ed ora la disgrazzia a voluto chi i banditi mi habiano costretto di prendere l'armi, cito il Cielo in testimonio che non ho fatto per malizia l'homicidio del soldato acui volevo consegnare la mia schiopetta ma solo l'accidento ha fatto che e partita da per se, caspisco che a per i mei peccati passati che I Dio a voluto castigar mi ma non merito punizione per questo evenimento, etc."* [4] I was almost touched; then it was discovered that he was one of the most barbarous of the assassins. He was broken on the wheel; he had his wife and his six little children around him.

It is true that there are some poor wretches who were unwilling to take up arms in Paoli's time, and whom the Corsicans reproached for not being patriots; since that time they have said: "You have reproached us for being *Vittoli;* [5] we're going to show you that we are patriots. There was no merit in marching with Paoli under constraint; today, we are taking up arms against France for ourselves, for the fatherland, etc." How can one judge of men after that!

The anecdote of Paoli's song is absolutely true; I have it from his friend Cafferio, with whom he was singing it the night before his departure from Corte.

I will be staying here until next month; I write you in great haste, but I entreat you to send me your letters. Write care of Bournonville; he will know where to find me. Farewell, my divine friend, I am at your feet.

---

4. "Your Excellency, I am an unfortunate wretch: I have never fired a musket at anybody, I have never carried weapons in my life, I have always refused to march to Paoli's tune, and now misfortune has willed that the bandits have forced me to take up arms. I call heaven to witness that it was not by ill will that I killed the soldier to whom I wanted to surrender my musket, rather it was bad luck that made it go off by itself. I understand that it's for my sins that God wanted to chastise me, but I don't deserve punishment for that incident."
5. "The Corps of Vittoli" was what the Paolists called the Corsican volunteers who fought on the side of the French. The name "Vittoli" is that of a clan who had murdered a Corsican patriot in the sixteenth century (Thrasher, *Pasquale Paoli* 24, 147).

℞ *Paoli had left Corsica in defeat in June. With his brother Clemente and three hundred and forty followers he had embarked in a British ship and proceeded to England by way of Leghorn, Milan, Mantua, and Vienna where he was lionized and greeted by cheering crowds, and as we see in Belle's next letter, by a welcoming stadholder in Holland. He arrived in England in late September. Boswell introduced him into the circle of Samuel Johnson, and England became his home. During the French Revolution, Paoli returned to Corsica as its governor in 1791. He requested the help of the British in ousting the French, and in 1794 The Corsican National Assembly voted to make the island a British protectorate. In 1795 the British ordered Paoli back to England, where he died in 1805. The French recovered Corsica in 1796, and the Congress of Vienna ratified French possession of it in 1815.*

340. *To Constant d'Hermenches, September 18, 1769*

Zuylen

I have received your letters, my dear friend. The last one gave me the keenest pleasure. I see you in an agreeable situation: content with yourself, which is the essential thing; content enough with others; hoping for better in the future, yet not hoping with that over-confidence that makes disappointments painful. You have, according to my count, seven thousand of our florins in salary; you have an occupation, glory, and the approval of those whose approval is worth having. For a philosophical warrior, that's quite good. I'm very glad you're returning, and if one must absolutely destroy the thirty Corsicans who are left out of a poor little nation invaded by a powerful nation, then let them send sixty archers instead of troops and heroes. I can assure you that your style is still that of the friend of Voltaire; it would be well received everywhere, and I would like to be able to chat a little with this man who thinks he has become so uncivilized. Your description of the camp, of all the ambitions, passions, intrigues ... it's one of the strongest and most vivid that I have read in a long time, and your heart is not inferior to your mind, since you are still fond of me and my letters. Lady Athlone finds this constancy so beautiful that she has instructed me to say something pleasant to you on her part. A man who is capable of being the friend of her friend for so long has a claim on her esteem, and becomes interesting to her.

In the name of Heaven, stop talking about *bandits* and *assassins*, and leave off your gibes at Paoli; it's not in good taste. Monsieur de Breteuil also finds it bad that we are welcoming a *rebel* in this country.[1] As for your accounts of assassinations, in all of it I see only what has been recognized

---

1. Breteuil is the French ambassador to the Hague, whom Belle described in Letter 317. Paoli's flight took him to Leghorn, Pisa, and the Hague, where the stadholder invited him to dinner. One sees the diplomatic difficulties.

for a long time, and that is that enemies in war kill each other whenever they can—French as many Corsicans and Corsicans as many French as possible; both of them go at it, and if I wanted absolutely to become indignant, it would not be against the Corsicans. Someone said: "If we hadn't taken Corsica, it would have given itself over to England; that, with Minorca, would have been too much—it would not have suited us to make war on the English over so little." That's the only sensible speech I've heard from your party. You were told to take Corsica; you've taken it; well done. In your view, Boswell exaggerated the merit of Paoli and the Corsicans; I believe you; are you satisfied?

When Paoli came to our city he had to undergo rather stupid questions, stupid speeches, and ridiculous honors, which embarrassed him. Two of my friends who chatted with him found nothing striking about his appearance, his countenance, or his conversation, but everything went well.

I didn't see him; I was at Spa with my cousin Athlone. We had a very good time. I was staying with Mme Thélusson[2] of Paris, my brother's friend; I was free and content. People liked Mme d'Athlone very much; she's beginning to speak these days, and she is very amiable when she likes someone. We were always together, and with our friend M. de Charrière, when we didn't want to be with all the others; thus, not a moment of languor or boredom. I met only two Frenchmen, M. de Serent[3] and Vicomte de Chabot, both of them very amiable in different ways. M. de Serent, seeing that people had told me wonderful things about him, let himself be wished for and sought out; I was about to give up when, finally, he let himself be, ever so slightly, found. The merits of the other had not so grand a reputation, but I liked him better. The English and the Irish made up the majority at Spa, and Madame the Canoness of Blanckart was the divinity of almost everybody, especially our group, and especially of Mme d'Athlone. You must know her because of the admiration that she inspired in the whole French Army. We don't understand why no one has married her and taken her to Paris and showered her with riches and adoration. The Chevalier de Muis was much in love with her. She is sick, languid, unhappy, and all the more charming for it. All these delights of Spa have lasted only thirteen days.

You would like me to leave my household. How I would like to! But how can I leave my father? I must get married, and how can I marry? I wish I could see you, I assure you. We are speaking to each other badly just now; I am not telling you everything I'm thinking, nor my half-plans with their advantages and their drawbacks: it's so pointless from such a distance; we see things so differently! I had my reasons for asking you for a few details about

2. The wife of a famous Parisian banker.
3. Armand-Louis de Serent (1736–1822) a French major general. He was later to become the preceptor of the sons of the comte d'Artois, the future Charles X, and one of the first émigrés after the fall of the Bastille. He was also a friend of M. de Charrière.

the people you had around you, but it's not worth it to describe them and ask questions, because it's all very vague, very uncertain, and not very interesting.[4] Tell me about yourself. Are you going to Switzerland, or must you stay near your new regiment? Talk to me a great deal about yourself, for *you* are interesting to me, and I love you very much.

341. *From Constant d'Hermenches, October 5, 1769*

Toulon

I am torn, my dear Agnes, between the fear of writing you letters too minutely detailed, and the desire to inform you about everything that concerns me. I yield to the latter, because true friendship goes before all, and knows neither glory nor self-love.

Therefore learn that finally I am a brigadier; this rank is the only interesting and difficult one in this service, because before you reach it you hold nothing, and once you have it your path is immediately smoothed before you. So I have it, in spite of jealousies and enmities and entrenched ways. I owe it only to the impartiality of Monsieur le Comte de Vaux, to my own courage, and (I want you to know it) to the excellent exhortations that your friendship often addressed to me; I pay you homage, my very excellent friend!

I had a very bad crossing; I was thrown onto the coast at Nice, where I spoke of you with Bellegarde's uncle and aunt—he is governor there. I am arriving here with lice and scabies, but in better condition than if for the last two years I had been occupied with nothing but cultivating a glow of health and a fine physique. The regiment I am commanding is going to Huningue,[1] which is near the entrance to Switzerland, and I am passing through Lausanne on my way; it's there that I will inquire for news of you.

And now, I can return to the Hague! My vow was not to appear there before winning a cross and a brigade. I am at your feet, dear friend.

344. *To Constant d'Hermenches, November 7, 1769*

Utrecht

Not to tell me about the good fortune that has befallen you, my dear friend, would have been the gravest crime against friendship: thus, you have done well to send me word about the brigade at once. May this good fortune be the beginning of much to come! They can hardly give you greater pleasure than they will give me. Your little compliment about my advice could be quite dangerous; I will give it even more freely in the future, with even

---

4. In her letters of the spring of 1770 Belle clarifies this: one of her last suitors will be the count of Wittgenstein, who served in Corsica.
1. In Alsace.

more pride and confidence. When you come to the Hague, for example, with the brigade and the cross that please me so much, I will absolutely demand such a perfect forgetting of the past—such great indulgence for our peaceable and indolent army—such great modesty in speaking about Corsica and advancements—that people will envy you and miss you without finding any way to backbite, however much they might want to. That will be delightful, and I will be extremely proud. I wish it might be soon.

I wrote to you a few days before receiving your last letter; I flatter myself that my letter reached you, and that there is one from you on its way to tell me your news, and to say that the scabies and the fleas have gone back to Corsica, their native land. I'm very pleased that you are in such good health. For myself, I've had a cold for three weeks, with swollen glands and a little headache that could easily resemble your scabies, although it is given some or other more respectable name; but it's getting better. Nevertheless, I am staying home, and am glad to do so. I have had Mlle Fagel here, who made my room very pleasant. People come to see me from time to time. When no one comes, I do not mind at all. My books, a good warm fire, a very pretty dog, a very comfortable room do not console me for the absence of my best friends, but they do for the absence of company I do not care about.

Goodbye; I know nothing except that I am very glad about your success; that for once I find fortune just and wise; and that I am your friend truly and forever.

355. *To Constant d'Hermenches, March 13, 1770*

Utrecht

What has happened to you, my dear friend? What has happened to your heart, to your friendship for me, which has been so constant, so unswerving until now? If I had deserved your anger or your coldness, I would confess it to you, and without a doubt my confession would be followed by absolution. But I have minutely examined my conscience, and I can recall no sin in word, thought, or action. So tell me where you are, whether you are sick or well, whether you are content, whether you still love me.

I have nothing to say about myself, except that in the last month I have taken up my pastels again, which I had forgotten for twelve years, and have done four portraits that are good likenesses—well drawn, but the coloring is still far from natural. Six weeks of lessons from a skillful painter would make of me a passable painter; it gives me pleasure and keeps me busy.[1] All

1. Of Belle's paintings, there are extant portraits of the countess of Athlone (Annebetje) and Claude de Salgas at the chateau of Amerongen, as well as a self-portrait in a private collection (Courtney, *Biography* 269, n. 32).

that aside, I am as always, gay and sad in turn, with no reason; rather bizarre, but good-natured enough; a little more ignorant than usual; too lazy for the abstract sciences, too reasonable to torment my brain with metaphysics, and quite fed up with what people call "tasteful" books. I get along fairly well with my father, and I have an angora cat and an Italian greyhound who, after Mme d'Athlone, are my dearest loves and my greatest delights.

People say that the King of France had distributed twenty-six regiments. Does the Count of Wittgenstein[2] have one? He's the person I was hoping you would tell me about without my prompting you, and without your knowing that I took any interest in him. I never took more than a very slight interest in him, and I have none at all at present. He was thinking of marrying me; I no longer hear anyone speak of him. Undoubtedly he has some other plan—it doesn't matter. I may very well get married one of these days just to put an end to the uncertainties, the projects, the contradictions; I was born under a strange star! If you were seated at my fireside, I would tell you many things—but how can we really converse from so far away!

Answer me; I will write you without delay. There are loud laments here over the edicts of the King of France.[3] Farewell.

357. *From Constant d'Hermenches, March 25, 1770*

Huningue, in Alsace

I have been in this fort for more than four months, and I have been fool enough to deprive myself of the one thing that could make my existence interesting in all corners of the earth, which is writing to you—charming Agnes!—and receiving your letters. I can give no good reason for it, and I must not excuse myself for it, since it's only myself I have wronged. And I have thought of you very faithfully each day of these four months. But at first I wanted to see how I would find being here; after that, I thought I would not be staying here long, and that I would have a more attractive date line to put than Huningue. I waited for some event, and finally I found that I had waited too long to tell you mere trifles. Today, it is precisely famine that is pressing me—hunger to know what you are doing, and the danger of the mortal grief I would feel if you had forgotten me; and the very natural fear of that quite natural misfortune, of your no longer being the queen, the phoenix of friends!

So here I have been in Huningue for four months now. It's a citadel where I have been shut up all winter. The current affairs of a corps that I

2. Count Georges-Ernest de Sayn-Wittgenstein, a colonel in the French service.
3. The financial situation in France was on the verge of the catastrophic. The Abbé Terray, minister of finance, took drastic measures in the regulation of commerce.

have recently joined, extreme cold, much laziness, little desire to go elsewhere, have confined me here as if I were a state prisoner. Moreover, there has not been a living soul here who could make me take much pleasure in life. I have sustained myself out of my own resources: a lucky light-heartedness; the memory of aversion for places where one is supposed to be supremely happy to live; repose after much action and running about; perhaps a bit of moodiness at seeing that my friends and kinsmen have become quite unaccustomed to me, and that while running after glory I lost my place in their hearts and habits. And then there's my own wife, who, all things considered, is happier when I am absent, because she is old, full of crotchets, much preoccupied with her health—and because my presence gives a more regular and more active cadence to her existence, of which she has lost the habit. You see, Agnes, that I am counting on finding you as I had left you, and so I dare to confide in you all this machinery of my situation; but since I am always the same for you, it doesn't even enter my mind that you could change, and I hope that by these frank confessions of mine I can urge you to let me know where you are with yourself and with all your relations.

My son has come to join me here, and it was high time. He would have become quite used to living without a father, as his mother has without a husband; our bonds grow stronger by our presence. I am doing him a great deal of good; I have a wealth of examples, situations, comparisons that I am passing on to him in a comradely and cheerful tone; I see that he enjoys being with me; besides that, he is taking lessons from the famous Bernoulli at Bâle.[1] He has the musicians of my regiment to practice with, some officers of his own age to cavort with, and some young girls with whom he celebrated carnival and learned to dance the allemande. My books, my horses, my pianoforte are yet more daily resources for him. He sees with amazement and with profit that one can, without displeasure, be busy training soldiers, inventing military maneuvres, instructing young officers. He takes interest in the marches and minuets that I compose for my band practice—and all that will end by making him find the Hague an enchantment when he leaves Huningue, and say: "I am still better off than my father!"

I don't know how I will employ my leisure this year. I have nothing to ask of the Court, and it's possible that I won't go there. I have beautiful countryside, land of my own that I dearly love—but the charm that I counted on finding there one day, when I was beautifying it and planting shade trees, no longer draws me: with whom can I go live there? As I have already said, all my relatives have become unaccustomed to me; they have grown old, they have taken a very different key from the one to which I had pitched them. I am for them—I saw it clearly the last time I was there—an inconvenience and a disruption; for you must know, Agnes, that I still have

---

1. A member of the prodigiously talented Bernoulli family who made fundamental and permanent contributions to mathematics and physics. It could be either Daniel (1700–82) or Johann II (1710–90), who both taught at the University of Bâle.

the same vigor, the same warmth of action and thought that perhaps drew your attention in times past, and that my taste has become more discriminating, my tone perhaps more acerbic. All that—I own up to it—creates continual dissonances with people who have always stayed in one place; whom laziness, age, and the absence of opportunities have rendered prudent and moderate, and who, for lack of being stirred and being called on, have fallen into the habit of loving little, and being contented with tepid things.

I'm thinking of making a journey to Holland. You will be my real magnet; my son will be the pretext. I will go see Bellegarde at his château, which I have liked very much; but I am also afraid that I will find him dull and heavy; at least I know that he has fallen into moralizing. I will go to see Voltaire. If I go to Holland, I will give all the time I can to my friends in Brussels—the Duke and Duchess of Arenberg have changed nothing of their attentiveness and their friendship for me. Would I not be foolish not to enjoy it?

So you see how the prospects that seem best arranged from a distance often present quite distorted shapes when looked at from close up; I had imagined pleasures and enjoyments in the future that I must now design altogether differently. I no longer have any hope of finding a place for myself such as I desire until I find for my son a wife who is amiable, reasonable, and rich, to whom I would hand over the management of my establishments—which really are quite pleasant, even if they were only my theatre, my decorations, my collections, my flowers, my pianoforte, my porcelains, books, etc.

I speak to you, my dear friend, in an outpouring that will seem ridiculous to you, but these are tokens I offer to ensure your treating me likewise. I can no longer bear not knowing what you are doing; and I am at your feet with the most tender and sincere respect.

358. *To Constant d'Hermenches, April 13, 1770*

You speak to me in such a kindly, open, and friendly fashion, that I will tell you my story without fear or reserve. A year and a half ago, or even more, my father and mother spoke to me about M. de Wittgenstein, and showed me one of his letters, written to I know not whom (they wouldn't tell me who it was, nor how this business had been conceived and begun). His letter was honest and simple; in it he spoke of my dowry, and asked that my father make it more ample than originally proposed—which was granted, if I'm not mistaken. People said many good things about his person and his character—but often merit as well as demerit *increases* as it goes *from mouth to mouth*,[1] so that I took only a rather lukewarm interest. There have been

1. Emphasis in the original.

so many prospective German suitors! At that same time, my imagination was attaching itself to a man whom I had seen from time to time, for whom I had always had friendly and affectionate feelings, and who had the same for me. A noble and interesting (though slightly awkward) appearance; a just, upright, and thoroughly enlightened mind; a sensitive, generous, and absolutely honest heart; a firm character; an even, easy-going temper; and a simplicity like that of La Fontaine: such is my lover, in my eyes and in the eyes of all who know him. He's sometimes clumsy in his wit as well as in his manners, for which he is reproached; but one can tease him to one's heart's content—no one has ever been more devoid of vanity! We wrote to each other; the correspondence grew warm: I, alone and idle in the countryside—in the whole land not a single man to arouse my interest ... The correspondence grew yet warmer. My father and mother had a good opinion of M. de Wittgenstein, and spoke about him now and then; business was keeping him in Paris, people said, and he was to come as soon as he was free.

I lost my mother; I no longer thought of marriage; for myself, I construed love as a crime, and I stopped the correspondence.

In February or March, my father had me read a letter from M. de Wittgenstein; he said that he was being sent to Corsica, that he needed beforehand to go outfit himself and that he couldn't come to see me before the campaign, but that he would come immediately afterward if I was not married by then. It seemed to me that for someone going from Paris to Wittgenstein, Utrecht is no great detour: I was put off by this dawdling and the long uncertainty in which he was willing to leave me, and the project lost almost all its appeal for me.

The man of the letters drew closer. Sometimes in Utrecht, sometimes at the Hague, we spent many days together. The withdrawn life I had been living, the trust and freedom I had become accustomed to with him—you can well imagine where all that led us. Don't imagine too much—don't imagine *everything;* you would be wrong, I assure you. I ended where others begin: I fell in love with him, with all my heart. The best of my women friends advised me to marry him. He maintained that it was the worst advice in the world. "I have neither rank nor fortune," he said, "I am only a poor gentleman; my merit is not sufficient to take the place of everything you would be sacrificing. Your attachment is not of a kind that can sustain itself; you desire pleasure, and you don't know how to receive it ... you mistake for love what is merely a fleeting delirium of your imagination ... a few months of marriage would undeceive you; you would be unhappy, you would try to hide it, and I would be still more unhappy than you."

As for M. de Wittgenstein, I heard no more mention of him; he sent me no news of himself. Sometimes in the midst of all my vexations I wanted to write to you and ask you to speak of me to him in such a way as to make him come here after the campaign. I couldn't speak to you without the permission of my father, who had insisted on secrecy; he was willing to let me ask your opinion of M. de Wittgenstein, but his pride forbade me to do anything more; and I—who wanted to marry him in order to leave this place, and not to divert myself by speculatively weighing his merit—I didn't speak to you about him at all. I merely asked you to talk to me about the people whom you were with, thinking that distinguished merit would not go unmentioned. Ambition, intrigues, cabals, jealousies—that, you said, was what surrounded you, and vexed you, and injured you.

The summer passed, and the man I loved went away. As long as I had had him beside me, and had hoped to dare and be able to grant tomorrow what I refused today—content, or, at least, distracted and busy—I had not foreseen what I would suffer from his absence. I found it dreadful. From the other side, my brothers were irritating me. Since the Comte de Wittgenstein did not appear, I thought that his emissaries had told him that I loved another man, and finally I asked that man whether he seriously, absolutely refused to take me as a wife. He spelled out his old objections with a vehemence that often made me accuse him of indifference; he told me that my father would never consent, and that I undoubtedly loved him too much to make him enter a family where he would be looked down on. However, he let me do as I wished. I spoke of it to my father, who answered as predicted, and who then spoke to me again about the Comte de Wittgenstein. He said that he wanted to learn what had become of him and his intentions; I tried to prevent him, fearing a refusal, and fearing too that my father might attribute this refusal to a cause that would bring down upon me his resentment; however, he wrote.

A few weeks after that conversation, another husband was proposed to me, Lord Wemyss[2]—a condemned rebel, and a friend of Milord Marischal.[3] You probably know him. I listened to the proposition, and immediately ran to my father to tell him. "He is richer," I said, "than M. de Wittgenstein. He isn't young; that's an advantage when one isn't loved. Grant me permission to marry a man whom I know and love, and whom you yourself respect, who is surpassed by no one in honor, merit and virtue, whose birth will not make you blush, and whose fortune I will have the pleasure of bettering; or else I will accept and marry Milord Wemyss. Whether he pleases me or not doesn't matter. I am tired of living in a climate that is bad

2. The Scottish baron David Elcho, Lord Wemyss. He had taken part in the Jacobite rebellion of 1745 when Prince Charles Edward Stuart (Bonnie Prince Charlie) tried to reconquer England. After the defeat of the rebels at Culloden, he fled to the continent. He became a citizen of Neuchâtel, and his home was not far from M. de Charrière's manor in Colombier, where Belle came to live in 1771. He died in 1787.

3. George Keith, earl Marischal of Scotland, had participated in the Stuart uprisings of 1715 and 1719. He had been attainted but then pardoned in 1759. He was a counsellor of Frederick the Great of Prussia and became governor of Neuchâtel. He was a friend and protector of Rousseau. He also accompanied Boswell as he left Utrecht to begin his grand tour.

for my nerves and where I am constantly sick and melancholy; I am tired of plans and uncertainties. It is up to you: choose between these two men, and decide which one will be my husband."

This heart-rending declamation left my father unmoved. He spoke to me again calmly about M. de Wittgenstein; but I told him that it was clear that he no longer cared about this marriage; that I didn't want to be refused; that supposing I was still free to have him come, like Lord Wemyss, to be judged by my own eyes, such an inspection would be too ridiculous. He requested that I not commit myself to Lord Wemyss before seeing him, but since he didn't consent to the other marriage, I did get his permission to send word to Lord Wemyss that he could come—that we would both be free, and that the public would not know the reason for his journey. That message was sent off to Lord Wemyss the following day, and he will come in May.

I hastened to inform my friend of all that had happened. The news filled him with fear; he knows Lord Wemyss. This is neither a man I will love nor a man who will give me any freedom; he is debauched, bad-tempered, tyrannical ... "Monsieur de Wittgenstein is surely a better man, you must renew contact with him ..." I answered that it's too late; that, moreover, my mind is made up; that everything he is saying is making no impression on me; that, moreover, I feel so hypochondriac, so full of dark fancies, so incapable of being happy even in the best of circumstances, that I take a certain pleasure in throwing myself into a state as black as my mood—that a person such as I am at present deserves, at best, a Lord Wemyss; for anyone else, I would be too bad an offering.

However, I have written you to learn whether I should be sorry at losing M. de Wittgenstein. I hoped that your answer would allow me to put my friend's mind at rest. A few days ago, I received a letter from him in which he told me that my words and my conduct are absurd and culpable; that there will be no more happiness for him if I make myself irrevocably unhappy. He implores me at least to study Lord Wemyss before marrying him; "Perhaps the public and I do him wrong, but see for yourself, get to know him yourself ..." and he speaks to me again about M. de Wittgenstein.

Yesterday, I received your letter; it is full of praises for this man whom I have lost—or whom I got rid of.[4] What do you think of my lucky star now? I read your reply in my father's presence; I read a few lines aloud; we were interrupted, and he has not brought it up again. I don't know whether he has received a response concerning M. de Wittgenstein. I don't know whether he has written, as I wished, that no answer was required and that everything was said. I neither dare nor wish to question him.

Madame d'Athlone is greatly saddened—and as for me, I laugh, I do my painting, and tears sometimes come to my eyes. You wanted to write to M. de Wittgenstein; that doesn't seem to me possible. If you were to write, you

---

4. The letter in question is not extant; the man is Wittgenstein.

should not pretend to have learned of this plan through others. You should say that I have been your friend for a long time; that having lost sight of me through the Corsican War and that great distance, you asked that I bring you up to date as to my story and my situation; that in response, I told you that there had been mention of a marriage with a Count Wittgenstein, but that seeing that he forgot it, or that he had changed his mind, I had given it up, and that I would probably marry another man; that you are sorry about it, that perhaps there might yet be time . . .

Write to me quickly. If you advise me to procrastinate with the other business,[5] I'll see what I can do . . . However, it seems to me that it's too late, and that I must follow my destiny. If I could still marry the man I love, wouldn't that be the best fortune of all? Mme d'Athlone asked me to send you her best regards; the warm interest and friendship with which you write to me charms and touches her; anyone who is as fond of me as you are has great merit in her eyes.

I hope to see your son. I hope, above all, to see you. You will find me doting on a dog and a cat, like Madame d'Hermenches.[6] I am not very amiable; however, I would be very glad if you came, and I believe as you do that we'd find we got on well together.

Goodbye, it's late. Your first letter is full of the most lively and vivid descriptions; the last one is full of friendship; I love them both very much, and I am obliged to you for them from the depths of my soul.

360. *To Constant d'Hermenches, April 17, 1770*

Utrecht

Hardly had my last letter been sent off when I had some second thoughts—not because of the uncommon sincerity with which I told you my story, since what does not degrade me in my own eyes will not degrade me in yours, and since my secrets are safe with you; but because of the idea of summoning back M. de Wittgenstein, which seems to me a ridiculous weakness and an inconsistency. Was I not running the risk of complicating my future yet further, when my only desire is a resolution? —better an unhappy resolution than one that is endlessly delayed. Monsieur de Wittgenstein may believe that I am trying to bring him back; if he refuses, it's a kind of affront to me; if he comes, will he not believe that I'm obliged to marry him? And then will it be in my power to take advantage of a change of heart on my father's part in favor of my true lover—the one my heart prefers, and whom delicacy of honor also commands me to prefer? That's not all: let's

5. The Wemyss business.
6. In Letter 158 of October 29, 1764, Belle had reported to d'Hermenches rumors that distressed her far more than any tales of libertinage: she had heard that he had mistreated his wife's dog. His reply in Letter 160 had apparently scored no points with Belle.

suppose that M. de Wittgenstein comes, that my father doesn't change his mind at all in favor of the man I love, that Milord Wemyss displeases me, and that I marry M. de Wittgenstein: will you congratulate him, this man that you will have brought back to me? —Will you wholeheartedly congratulate him for having a wife who loves another man, a bizarre, sad, melancholy wife? I find myself only a very mediocre match for a man I dearly love and who has no fortune, because he deserves something much better than me. Milord Wemyss may not deserve better, but M. de Wittgenstein, who has a name and considerable prospects, who is good, amiable and brave—I would pity him, I think, for marrying me.

Here is what my plan was before your last letter, and I think that I must not change it: Lord Wemyss comes in May; I will receive him civilly, and my father will see him. If he says: "This man does not suit you at all; marry whom you wish," then I won't hesitate and that will be that. If, on the other hand, he approves Lord Wemyss's suit, I will marry him immediately, in about the same state of mind that one becomes a nun: I will, I think, take vows of chastity and indifference, but I will also vow to be diligent and useful, if I can.[1]

He was thinking of buying land in Switzerland, and I will approve of that idea. I will establish myself in some ancient castle, in Champvent[2] or somewhere, and will live in an antique style: no potpourris or porcelains on my mantlepieces, no gilt, no armchairs or sofas placed around, but great hearthfires and a table for guests. "You will live," says Mme d'Athlone, "like a medallion." If I have children (I won't have many, I think), I will raise them with care, I will do handwork, I will have girls from poor families work alongside me, I will have books read aloud, I will have music—not operas, but choruses from *Esther* and *Athalie;*[3] I will ask of God a reasonable, gentle, forgiving, charitable devoutness, which will take the place of a lover and of pleasure, and preserve me from a lugubrious fanaticism to which my vapors sometimes seem to dispose me ...

---

1. A few days later Belle writes to Ditie (Letter 362 in *O.C.* 2: 183) about rumors that surround Wemyss: "You ask me what sort of man Lord Wemyss is. Until I have seen him, all I can tell you is that his reputation is not favorable as to his tastes and pleasures and character; but never mind, he probably won't beat me. I don't yet know the history of his exploits nor of the dangers he has met, but in the fury of his rebellious zeal he was of the opinion that all the captured English soldiers should have a finger cut off, and be sent back thus mutilated to their own land. They say that after a battle there was found in the pockets of the slain Scotsmen a proclamation from him and another chieftain to give no quarter to any Englishman. But he was not yet twenty-one at that time, and people are enraged to the point of madness in a civil war; thus these traits say nothing definitive about his heart. My father knows nothing about all that; these are only rumors; besides, this time I don't want anyone else to judge for me. It's my business, and I'm keeping it to myself."
2. Near Yverdon, on Lake Neuchâtel.
3. Plays of Racine: *Esther* had in fact been written at the request of Mme de Maintenon (see Letter 153, n. 2) to be performed by the pupils at her girls' school at Saint-Cyr.

I will let you meditate on this mood of mine and this plan, and I ask you if you don't find, as I do, that we must leave M. de Wittgenstein to his destiny without entangling him in mine. However, do as you please, but remember that even if M. de Wittgenstein comes here, he will not, for all that, be assured of having me; he should not think he is certain of it, for I have a lover whom I love. I think you will not write to M. de Wittgenstein. Farewell.

Better than any assurances, a letter like this one tells you how much I believe you are my friend, and how much I am your friend.

363. *From Constant d'Hermenches, April 27, 1770*

Huningue, via Basel

My very dear friend, you cause me the greatest concern, and you fill my thoughts more painfully than I can express! You are neither happy nor tranquil—you who so deserve to be so, who seem created to make others happy. But, in the name of God, don't let the torment of your situation drive you to some extreme course of action! The advantage over common souls that intellect, reason, philosophy must give you is precisely not to be forced or constrained by circumstances, much less yield to discouragement and vexation!

If, at the time when it was a question of the Comte de Wittgenstein, you had been so kind as to tell me clearly what was at issue, you would have known immediately and from a direct source what you were dealing with. The crime of negligence you ascribe to him may exist; he was very unhappy about going to Corsica, he had very little time to prepare, and his military establishment cost him a great deal. He may still be tending to his affairs, which for any reasonable man must take precedence over courtship proceedings, so that he can then present himself more respectably and more securely. I know nothing about it, but that all seems probable to me. I am writing to him in Paris today; I will ask him his plans and his address, so that I can explain things more clearly to him later.

If you told me the name and the position of the other man who is one of the actors in your story instead of giving me a metaphysical portrait, I could also answer you with all the honesty and frankness of my impassioned interest in your happiness; but it's one of those incredible things about women—they never trust us until they are forced to by necessity. What do you want me to say? Undoubtedly you find him very appealing, this *man you love*, otherwise he would not have charmed you; and so you want to charm me too with your fine portrait of him. His name would decide the question much better, if you think that I'm a good judge and that I am your friend. Mme de Chasteler did the same thing with me ...[1]

---

1. D'Hermenches had hoped in vain to prevent Mme Geelvinck from making what he and Belle regarded as a disastrous marriage with the marquis de Chasteler.

As for Milord,[2] I don't know him at all; I know nothing of his wealth, his position, his residence. If he lives in France, he is not there on a distinguished footing, for I have never heard anyone speak of him. Perhaps he will suit you; but my dear Agnes—dare say it?—my greatest fear and apprehension ever since I have known you has been to see you the prey of some mad Englishman. Now think about it: have you ever seen any of their women happy?

Sooner or later I could have arranged a marriage for you that would have fulfilled most of your wishes.

I am too preoccupied with this subject to talk to you about anything else, and you must believe me, who have myself done so much to be happy in marriage, and yet am not.

Farewell, my adorable friend, I have always said that your epistolomania would lead you farther than you meant to go ... You mean much more to me than I thought: I feel it by the agitation you cause in me. I am at your feet.

I urge you to travel somewhere this year—for instance, come to Plombières!

364. *To Constant d'Hermenches, May 8, 1770*

I think that you speak quite justly, my dear friend, about M. de Wittgenstein and Milord, and about haste and regrets and their long duration. Madame d'Athlone says just about the same things, and begs me with tears not to throw myself rashly into an abyss of troubles and vexations; as for myself, I cannot prevent myself from hoping for a kind of life that will make me calmer, wiser, happier. I imagine that even if I don't draw much satisfaction from the things around me, I would gain by being more satisfied with myself. Apparently we are soon to see Milord. As to whether to say nothing to M. de Wittgenstein, or to say something, you be the judge; tell him anything you please. Knowing my situation and my thoughts as you do, you have too much wit, zeal and friendship to need me to tell you what to say.

There are often slight misunderstandings between us; I don't know where they come from, since we both have a clear style and clear-cut conceptions of things. I have not asked your advice about the man I love; everything I have said to you about that is purely historical; it is from a friend who confides to you her conduct and her heart, and that history itself proves that trust does not always wait for necessity. I no more ask your permission to love my lover and to try to become his wife than I will ask his permission to be your friend as long as I live. I have known him very well for a long time,

2. Wemyss.

and I am very well informed about his situation. You know him only by sight, and if, on the basis of some prejudice or hearsay, you did not speak of him in a manner that accords with my esteem for him, I feel that I would not easily pardon you for it: that's why I stubbornly withhold his name. Had not my father required secrecy, I would not have been so mysterious about the Count of Wittgenstein; but you (let me say in passing) but you— why did you declaim against your comrades without making an exception in favor of this man you respected? It's a kind of justice that one must always demand of oneself, and not sacrifice it to the eloquence of a striking, universal tableau; you would have apprised me about a matter that was of interest to me.

Madame d'Athlone has just given birth to a daughter, and I'm her godmother. The pleasure of seeing her recover so rapidly, the presence of M. de Salgas, who is my friend and hero;[1] and the gaiety and good sense that reign in this childbirth room between Milady, her cousin Mlle de Randwijck, M. de Salgas and me—it all revives my spirits and my courage.

I will write you again as soon as possible; the post is about to leave. I am very glad you love me, whatever pain and agitation it may cost you; that is neither sublime nor generous of me, but it's true and natural.

366. *From Constant d'Hermenches, May 25, 1770*

Bâle, Switzerland

You treat me very badly, my dear Agnes; why do you want to believe that I would speak ill of someone you love? Why do you insist that I was wrong not to except M. de Wittgenstein in my enumeration of the people around me in Corsica? We were at the two opposite ends of the island; we didn't know each other, and we didn't make contact with each other until after the conquest. I found out only a few days ago where he is living; he sends word to me that he is spending the summer in the Palatinate.[1] I asked him a simple question about you, expressing the sentiments that have attached me to you for so long. If not for you, then for my own satisfaction I will learn what his thoughts are. He has just been made brigadier, and certainly he will make his fortune in this service.

Milord Wemyss has lived some time in Switzerland. He is regarded as a rather extraordinary man; very much a libertine, whose fortune, assessed at a thousand louis a year, depends on a brother and a nephew who, from one

---

1. Claude de Narbonne Pelet de Salgas. He was tutor to the Boreel family, first in Holland and then in England. When Jacob Boreel became ambassador to the the court of George III, Salgas was his secretary. Salgas was instrumental in helping negotiate Belle's marriage to Charrière. Belle painted a portrait of him that is at Amerongen.

1. A region in Germany west of the Rhine; at that time an electorate of the Holy Roman Empire.

day to the next, could stop paying it. He had a country home near Neuchâtel; he gave it (or so people believe) to a natural daughter, whom he
married to his valet. People say that he behaved very harshly toward a sister
who had come to see him; perhaps the sister had committed some wrong—
no one knows; but she aroused public opinion against him. He is forty years
old; he has a very handsome appearance; he is a man of wit, and is colonel
in a French regiment with a hundred ducats of living allowance, which leads
to nothing at all once when he leaves the service. That's all I have been able
to learn about him.

I continue to urge you to take no hasty course of action. I would like
more than anything for you to move about a bit in the world. I wish that
you could come to Plombières; I would join you there directly, and we
would chat, and argue, and laugh, I am sure. For I do laugh, I who am not
nearly as tranquil as you, nor as young, nor as rich, nor as witty; but that's
because I am neither an enthusiast nor a romantic, and because I believe that
pains and pleasures are more or less equally apportioned whatever the situation we find ourselves in—except for that class of beings whom fate has put
into the world to give us a horror of life.

You promised me another letter; meanwhile I am at your feet, for the last
ones did not satisfy me.

368. *To Constant d'Hermenches, June 5, 1770*

Utrecht

You are quite right, and I am a bit in the wrong. You could not, indeed,
guess the merit of M. de Wittgenstein, and he was not among those around
you. As for the man I love, if you have seen him it was only in passing, and
in that case either you didn't notice him, or you probably disliked him. The
two of you could only like each other after long acquaintance—I know it,
I'm sure of it; and why should I expose myself to your denunciations of my
choice? I respect your taste too much not to find that prospect unpleasant.

I thank you for having written to M. de Wittgenstein. I accept with gratitude and deference your insistence that I not rush into anything, and I hope I
can follow your advice; but circumstances sometimes leave us so little
choice, so little cool-headedness, so little free will, that one cannot answer
for what one will do. Milord Wemyss must have left Paris today to come to
Utrecht; I will write you my impression of him. What you tell me about him
fits exactly with the account given by the man I do not name. The thousand-
louis income depends neither on his brother nor on his nephew, according to
what people have assured me: it was bequeathed to him by his father, but I
have not been able to learn whether it ceases with his death or passes down
to his heirs. He must have, aside from that, fifteen to sixteen thousand
pounds sterling of capital; his own nephew, M. Charteris, who spent the

winter here, has said so positively. As for the sister: I've been told that he had one, named Lady Mary Hamilton, who had been found in bed with her nephew, the son of another sister, and had left the country immediately after this adventure; it's she, apparently, who went to see her brother, and one can excuse him for having given her a cool welcome.

I will try to put off the decision; send me M. de Wittgenstein's answer as soon as possible. I imagine him to be a younger, more amiable, gentler husband, to whom I would want to *speak my mind*[1] because we would be comrades; and to whom I wouldn't dare *speak my mind* for fear that he might not understand me at all, or that he might yawn or think I was mad. With Lord Wemyss, the question wouldn't even arise; we will never become comrades. My house, my children (if I have any)—that is where I would find my occupation, my pleasures, my marriage bond. The children of M. de Wittgenstein would be proud and poor, as German counts are. I don't have sixteen quarters, nor even eight, so that his daughters could never enter the Chapters.[2] His sons would probably have no resource other than foreign military service. While that is a respected and very noble way of establishing oneself, it seems to me very disagreeable in that one has no fatherland, and one sheds one's blood for the ambition of a sovereign whom one can't respect with the blind enthusiasm that his subjects have for him; since one has no real interest in the cause one is defending, the risks and fatigues have no intrinsic compensation. The children of Lord Wemyss are English, if one can have them born in England. They say that the sons of an *attainted Lord*[3] arouse attention and pity; people seek to compensate them for what they have lost, and favor them more than others. If they are born outside of England, they have the choice of foreign military service or a business house in London or Amsterdam, and they can marry any woman they please without fear of ridicule. That's how I compare these two men from a distance, while "The faults they possess do not leap to my eyes"[4] any more than their good qualities; closer up, I would perhaps use less foresight, and would decide on other bases of comparison.

Yes, I think so too: we would laugh together; I also laugh, but the depth of my soul is doleful. I am, I think, neither an enthusiast nor a romantic, and you are wrong to make fun of me: I am a little crazy, and its quite against my will. It wasn't Pascal's fault that he always saw a brasier beside him, nor Tasso's that he imagined he conversed with a spirit; I am neither more rational nor more culpable than they are. My unhappiness is such that

1. English in the original.
2. That is, they could not have the ecclesiastical title of canoness, which was reserved for the most ancient nobility.
3. English in the original. That is, he was subjected to attainder: he was deprived of all civil rights and made unable to inherit or bequeath any title or property.
4. Adapted from Molière's *Le Misanthrope* (II.iv.698): "Mais les défauts qu'elle a ne frappent point ma vue."

I cannot hope for the return of my reason and my repose except by a change of status, of activities, and of climate. I can only change by getting married, and I have scruples—well-founded, it seems to me, and not romantic at all—about involving a husband in my fate. I am afraid of becoming still more melancholy some day, and perhaps completely mad: so that to give myself a chance of being happier I make the man I marry run the risk of being very unhappy. Lord Wemyss is precisely the one who inspires in me the least scruple because he is the one who has the least merit, apparently the least sensibility, and the least right to a good marriage. If all these *leasts* are what determine me, it will surely be the strangest motive for a decision that anyone has ever seen! As for the man I love, he knows me so well, I have warned him so many times since there has been a question of marriage between us, I have so many times exaggerated to him my failings, my melancholy and the risks that he could run—advising him, so to speak, to give me up—that, since he persists, it's his business. If he were rich, however, I wouldn't dare marry him; but he is poor, he loves me, and I love him. I would receive my father's consent with joy if he gave it without repugnance, but to constrain him to give it by my stubbornness or entreaties or insistence is precisely what I do not want to do. Perhaps I would obtain nothing; but if I were to succeed and then were to see my father sad, discontented, distressed, ill perhaps (and considering his age, there could be yet more to fear), I would hate myself, and would detest any happiness obtained at the cost of his. He doesn't say a word about Lord Wemyss. I don't know whether he has regrets about M. de Wittgenstein and is angry with me for being fed up with that business, or whether the latter displeases him, or whether, when all's said and done, any marriage for me is equally displeasing to him; but the claim that he should keep me at home with him forever would be so unjust that I would nonetheless go my way.

You must know very little about the mood and state of things in our household to propose that I make a journey to Plombières! What trouble I had just to go spend two weeks at Spa! My brother the sailor[5] is in France for his health. That journey was very necessary for him, but his stay in that country is rather expensive. My brother the captain[6] is in France to see the fortresses, garrisons, and maneuvers; the pretext is to learn his métier, while he never opens a book or a map at home. Seeing that he was in great need of getting out of Utrecht, I pressed for his first journey; two years ago, he went to Spa, Aix, Brunswick, Berlin, Stettin, Hamburg, Cassel, and he was gone nearly a year. He was nonetheless taken over by bad company again this winter and he has been no less idle and libertine. Now he has left again; he is riding through the border cities; he's been to Paris, and though he is neither a gambler nor particularly fond of display, his journeys are yet

5. Ditie.
6. Vincent.

another expense. My father has funds in France, and you know how much they have dwindled;[7] you must see that I cannot talk of going to Plombières for my pleasure. And who would accompany me? Besides, I can't leave my father and my brother[8] alone together; they are uncomfortable with each other; they have no relationship with each other—no companionship, no familiarity; I don't know what they will do when I leave them altogether to get married, but to leave them for a whim—that is impossible.

You could not believe how weary I am of this house. My father thinks that I'm quite content here because I go and come as I wish, busy myself as I please, and have horses and servants at my disposal; but believe me, without Mme d'Athlone I would have died long ago of boredom and chagrin, and I would rather be my lover's laundress and live in a hovel than live in all the arid liberty and fine manners of our great houses. My father takes care not to guess that, and when I say it he thinks that I exaggerate, that I am indulging myself in a moment of ill humor, that I am speechifying, that he must let me carry on, and that an hour later, I will be as cheerful and as talkative as ever. He isn't wrong; I talk, I laugh, I play chess, I paint, I never sulk; and it is easier to believe that I am consoled and content than to dig deeper and try to read my soul and my thoughts.

Reread this whole long account. Don't scold me, don't make fun of me; pity me, and write.

You wanted to come to Brussels and then here, but the Duke and Duchess d'Arenberg are in Vienna; where will you spend your summer?

I passed through Amsterdam to see the pour Marquise de Chasteler. She is reduced to a mere skeleton; her collarbones have pierced the skin, and you would think that the same would happen all over her, she is so thin: her bones, her muscles, her veins, are all showing. With her emaciated face, her lifeless eyes, and her long nose, her astonished and yet indifferent gaze made her such a stranger to me that during the whole of my first visit, even though I knew it was she, I failed to recognize her. In the days that followed I became accustomed to this shadow of my friend, and I found her unchanged as to her kindness, easiness, friendship and frivolity. With one foot in the grave, she is still doing errands for everybody in Brussels, and would like to get a male puppy for Mme Royale's[9] female. People thought that she got so terribly thin because she was unhappy, but I am persuaded of the opposite: she is not capable of a great grief, and she seems to me very contented with her husband—although he almost let her die without paying any attention. But that's not his fault; he has no perceptiveness, experience or judgment; and she was letting herself die from the same absentmindedness. His attentions to her are those of a good child: he is careful and avoids making noise, he gives her her drops, he makes much of her doctor, etc.

---

7. See Letter 355, n. 2.
8. Willem René.
9. Anne-Charlotte de Lorraine, sister of the governor-general of the Netherlands.

The air of Brussels (which obviously disagrees with her), in addition to a miscarriage, a whooping cough, smallpox, late hours, an excellent cook, a butcher of a doctor, and terrible accidents that have happened to her since her pregnancy—that's what has put her in this state. She's a little better than she was when she arrived in this country; I hope that she improves considerably during the three or four weeks that she has left here so that she will be strong enough to give birth.

Goodbye, my dear friend; I beg your pardon for the sad and dismal tone of this immense letter.

369. *From Constant d'Hermenches, July 3, 1770*

Huningue

I think, my dear friend, I cannot better inform you about the Count of Wittgenstein's answer than by sending you the answer itself.[1] I know that I never run any risk with you, and whatever assurance I have given him not to compromise him, it seems worthy of you and of me always to entrust each other with the original items. You will judge, without my adding any commentary, of the character and motives and even the mind of this French brigadier, who seems to me to have preserved a great deal of Teutonic frankness. On your side, you will tell me whatever you wish about your interview with the banished Scottish lord; and you will continue to tease me with the secrecy you have so long maintained about the state of your heart; I will nonetheless continue to follow what concerns you, and my existence will be no less intimately tied to your happiness. Do not take offense, however, if I guess the man you love; perhaps what I am about to say is absurd, but I suspect that it's Charrière. That's just the sort of notion someone like you would take into her head, and here and there I've found his name in your letters, which always surprised me. I think he's a fellow of the greatest merit; but this is a union that surely would cause you regrets in the long run, and I don't foresee your parents or your friends ever accepting it. I'm the only one you will always find to be your friend; whatever folly you may want to commit, you may count on that.

But why, in just this moment of turbulence, must you be in such a hurry? You have reached the point in life where a year more or less of being unmarried is of no consequence, and can lead to great changes in your state of mind; whether you marry at twenty-eight or thirty, does it really matter? I beg you, preserve that impression you give of being reflective and hard to please in matters of marriage; and if you marry, let it not be because you are weary of the single state, but to have done with people's forever being after you to get married!

---

1. This letter has not been found.

I have been home to do a little errand, which has delayed this answer. I have returned for the review of the troops, and I am returning to Lausanne, where I have a great many troubles and domestic affairs to attend to; from there I will wait for your news. My wife is in very ill health; they say that she will not live long, which throws a dark cloud over my whole being. I do not want to oppose her in anything, and yet I feel how much a household, a family—when they are abandoned to the vapors of a woman in her decline—are in need of direction. The only trustworthy man I had about me, who conducted my affairs for more than twenty years, is sick, and the doctors have given up on him. That is the situation I have just left, and that I will be returning to at home; you may judge, my dear Agnes, whether I am happy! and even if you are no more so than I am in the midst of your uncertainties, at least you get up and go to bed with no worries except those for yourself, and those are very light for those who are strong of soul!

Inspector Salis[2] has just told me that Mme de Chasteler is quite well again; I was very glad to hear it. Farewell, my dear friend, I am at your feet.

371. *To Constant d'Hermenches, July 14–17, 1770*

I received your letter and that of M. de Wittgenstein the day before yesterday; the post that left yesterday would have brought you my answer if something rather upsetting hadn't prevented me from writing. I'm writing in advance, this evening, since my letter can't leave until the 17th. I'm very pleased that you guessed the man I love, and I smiled with satisfaction reading that whole passage. I especially smiled at this sentence: *That's just the sort of notion someone like you would take into her head.* Whatever meaning you meant to attach to it, I take it as flattering praise. As for the friends that I could lose by this *union*, I assure you that I would not miss them. Moreover, M. de Charrière speaks of this rather as you do when he talks about it; I always wait for his letters; they come rarely. If I were to marry him, it would be neither because I am weary of my present state, nor *to have done with people's forever being after me to get married.* I would not wait two years, nor two months, nor two days, if it were in my power to belong to him right away. If I decide on any other marriage, I have set forth the reasons for it clearly, precisely, and frankly in my last letters.

But whatever weariness I feel, whatever resolution I take, can I accept this Lord,[1] if he displeases me? Will I be able to say, irrevocably, "Yes"? I don't know. From a distance, a man of rank, a gentleman, a handsome man, is an acceptable husband; certain faults, certain vices, even if they can be seen at that distance, do not make one break off the arrangement. But up

2. Baron Antoine de Salis de Marschlins, major of a regiment bearing his name.
1. Wemyss.

close, in detail, when one can foresee the effect of some particular mood or habit in a household, when one foresees the conduct that some fit of temper will lead to in some circumstance or other, who is the man whose eternal companion one would want to become?

The need to love filled me with enthusiasm, and warmed my heart for Bellegarde—from a distance; when I saw him again, I looked in vain for the man I had written to. I would have married him with a cold and deliberate satisfaction, without any emotion of pleasure; but if a marriage with Milord Wemyss does not even inspire in me that cold satisfaction; if—my imagination and memory being filled with another man—I feel on the contrary only distaste and repugnance, what will I do? I don't know.

As for M. de Wittgenstein, it's too much trouble, it seems to me. In order to have him, I would have to expend a great deal of effort and my father a great deal of money—as if I desired him with passion, or as if he were a great match. I haven't spoken about the letter to my father, and I won't show it to him; I will however, keep it in my memory. Milord is retained by some business in Paris. If when I have seen him, some thought for M. de Wittgenstein returns to me, I will let you know, and make use of your zeal on my behalf. I have a very good opinion of this Count ... I am postponing what I would like to say to him until the end of my letter; I will try to place it on my paper in such a way that you can send it to him if it seems appropriate. Good night; I have fallen asleep talking about myself. There's an angora cat purring on my knees, and my dog is waiting for me on my bed. I would not give his place to the banished Lord. I'm falling asleep, I must go to bed. Goodbye. I am not strong of soul.

Tuesday, July 17

I'm sorry about your domestic troubles. Couldn't you make your son come back to be near his mother? She loves him; it would make her situation pleasanter. He received a military lesson from you at Huningue; he would receive a lesson in humanity and gentleness in Lausanne, and he would fulfill a precious duty to nature. Few men know how to feel for others; my father, who is humane and gentle, still thinks that he has done a great deal when he has recommended air and exercise as a remedy for all ills and all sadness.

Were it not for Madame d'Hermenches' ill health and the demands of your affairs, I would urge you to go ahead and take the journey you have so often planned. Already at Landrecies, then in Mézières, and recently in Huningue, you said that you wanted to come see me. You would find me sad and sullen; you would tell me so; I would agree; and then, however, we would talk.

My brother's health is not improving. The day before yesterday, I said a word to my father to the effect of: "I would be very glad to be able to go alone to join him in Languedoc, where he is now, or in Lyon, where he may be going." Yesterday, my father told me that my eldest brother was planning a journey, and spoke of going to visit my brother the commander.[2] I made no reply; it is up to them to do as they please; however, my eldest brother—feeling perhaps that it is detestable to put oneself first, and to have oneself always preferred, and to leave me alone—abandoned to my uncertainties and the tedium of this house—avoids me and doesn't speak a word to me ... Believe me, if you were in my place, and if you had, in spite of yourself, a troubled, vacillating and somber soul, vexed by vapors and melancholy, you would be seized with impatience, and you would not wait two years to get out of here.

Madame d'Athlone has come to Utrecht to be near me. Madame de Reede is with her; M. de Reede is in Zuylen with my cousin de Tuyll. The two brothers and two sisters-in-law and Mlle de Randwijck are leaving on Saturday to spend the rest of the summer together in Amerongen.[3] Monsieur de Reede is considered ruined, both by his crazy expenses and by the means through which he is trying to enrich himself: it's a transaction whose object is still a mystery; he is expecting a hundred percent profit from it. I think that M. de Seryone, one of the satellites of the Comte de Saint-Germain,[4] is the inventor of this scheme, M. Ernst of Berne is one of the associates, and M. de Reede the chief dupe.

What do you think of the escapade of Mlle de Parc and young Van der Duyn?[5] They deserve pity; and yet, they make me laugh. Madame Bouwens—who dreamed it all up and organized it all to avenge herself on her rival and on a lover who was leaving her—is horrible; and yet somehow—I don't know just how—that perfidy elevates the ugly, insipid little rôle I have always seen her play. I was saying so yesterday to M. de Reede; I thought that her vices were limited to clandestine love affairs and cheating at cards; this wickedness had seemed to me beyond her capacities; she is, in my view, a powderpuff who has had the honor of breaking someone's head. She had persuaded that poor girl that M. de Maasdam would not hold out a week against her entreaties and those of his son, so that Bettje is as surprised as she is disconsolate at finding him adamant. A remark is attributed to him that I don't believe at all: he would have warned his son in advance rather than divulge that horrible business, and the beautiful Bettje is too far from resembling all those dark van der Duyn faces.[6]

2. Ditie.

3. The cousin de Tuyll is a male cousin; Mme Athlone is Belle's cousin, Annebetje. M. de Reede is her husband's brother, and Amerongen is the estate of the brothers' family.

4. A famous charlatan, mentioned earlier by d'Hermenches in Letter 134.

5. With the complicity of a relative, Mme Bouwens, Elisabeth van de Parc—"Bettje"—had eloped with Willem van der Duyn, son of Aarnoud van der Duyn, baron van Maasdam. This Bettje is the sister of Mme de Reede—the former Heiltje de Parc—Annebetje's sister-in-law.

6. Belle recounts this whole business better to Ditie: to discourage his son from taking up with Mlle de Parc, Maasdam lets it out that she is his own illegitimate daughter. But Belle can't believe that the "fair-skinned and beautiful Bettje" is related to the all those famously dark van der Duyns (Letter 370 in O.C. 2:198).

Madame de Chasteler has completely recovered from giving birth; her husband gives me the best possible report of her.

You know that M. Reynst is in Middachten, and M. de Golofkine is with his wife in the town hall of Bois-le-Duc. But that's enough of warmed-over bits of old news.

After[7] all the good you have told me about the Comte de Wittgenstein, the interest you take in this affair seems to me a proof of your friendship worthy of your heart. I think that both my fortune and my merit have been exaggerated to your friend. If my dowry were were a hundred twenty thousand Dutch florins, I cannot believe that my hopes for the future are equal to my dowry. A dowry of a hundred thousand French crowns is not above what M. de Wittgenstein should hope and ask for, considering his name, his position and his merit, but it is more than my father could give to all his children; and whether out of pride or out of a proper delicacy, I would not solicit and would not even desire a distinction I have not deserved. My father had a very good opinion of M. de Wittgenstein, and would have wanted this affair to succeed; I too have a very good opinion of him, but I do not have such a good opinion of myself. If we knew each other well; if M. de Wittgenstein had seen me both cheerful and sad, in my best and my worst moments; and if, all things considered, he found me more to his liking than another, I would not have the same scruples. But to come from a long distance either to marry me or not marry me without knowing me well—really, it's not worth the bother. Bear in mind that for a long time now you have known me only by my letters—and who is not reasonable in a letter! It's so easy!

Be discreet—don't speak of Milord if you don't want to make me guilty.

You will ask me perhaps why my humility does not forbid Milord Wemyss to come, and I will reply that, in the case of M. de Wittgenstein, it would be necessary to resume a matter that I thought he was tired of, while in the other I could simply let the matter run its course. Besides, I don't think that there is the same difficulty regarding the fortune—which is just as well for Milord, whom my father is not as predisposed to like as he is the Count; as for me, I take little interest in this circumstance. A little more, a little less of the superfluous touches me little; I am neither vain nor fond of display. I am often melancholy enough to care for no amusement at all, and I always fear the encumbrance and hate the disorder of great houses.

I think I've come to my sixth page; farewell, my dear friend, give me news of your life in Lausanne, with all the details; speak to me also of Mlle de Mauclerc, when you have seen her—and you must go to see her. Farewell.

I haven't spoken to my father about what you are writing to me; about certain matters we speak but little to each other.

7. This is the paragraph that Belle is willing to have sent to Wittgenstein.

I am worried about my brother. Who knows whether his bad health will not bring him to Lausanne to consult Monsieur Tissot?[8] If he does go there, remember that of my sister and three brothers he's the one whom I love best, and who loves me best.

It seems to me that you can send my last page to the Count of Wittgenstein. If he is no longer thinking about it, all well and good; if he came, at least it would not be under false assumptions, and then I would see what I should do.

How did you put it? *That's just the sort of notion someone like you would take into her head.* So much the better, really—so much the better for heads like mine. He is so sick; his eyes hurt him, poor Charrière. If I had told you of this notion I would have annoyed you, and you would have scolded me.

373. *From Constant d'Hermenches, August 8, 1770*

Hermenches, via Lausanne

You must agree, my adorable friend, that even if you had counted me a fool for all the time we have known each other, the shaft of light by which I have revealed my perceptiveness would have rehabilitated me in your mind! You didn't want to say anything to me, for fear of being scolded; and as for me, I held my peace lest I anger you; for I had been tempted for a long time to tell you of my suspicions—or rather my fears.

It's all very well to speak, moralize, philosophize, prudify; a woman's heart is a hearth from which a flame must inevitably dart out on one side or the other; close it off from amorous adventure, seduction, ordinary attacks, and the fire will be kindled by reason, pity, habit … But burn it must! An attraction ought at least to carry some pleasure along with it; and for this one I deplore the ineptitude in which you are like everybody else, for it is without any little advantages—any remedy against boredom, any increase in the enjoyment of the pleasures of society, any comfort or consolation, any scope for whimsy. I think that Charrière is an excellent man, but what pleasure, what amenity could you ever find in this?

When it's a question of happiness, it's a miscalculation to take sentiments into account; can they outweigh the inconveniences and distastes, and annoyances to which these very sentiments would lead? The sum of happiness must be numbered by concrete considerations, and not by sentiments; increase of fortune, agreeable connections, more cheerful habitation, respect, pleasures—delicate feelings may shed a charm over it all, but I do not believe that they can ever charm away the annoyances and regrets and disagreeable things that one must count up in any change of state.

I have seen no examples of people who are completely self-sufficient; and

8. A famous Swiss doctor.

since we have to depend on others, we must be careful not to do anything to give them the advantage over us. Neither have I ever seen any man whose fortune depends on his wife who is more cheerful and content after his marriage than he was before—when he was a bachelor, poor and independent. A man wants to be occupied and free, and must have the preponderance and the authority in his house, whether by right or by fact; and how could you and Charrière sustain any of these relationships? He would be greatly embarrassed by his role, and you would be cruelly surprised not to see him happy, as you imagine him. I repeat: I can see from here this association becoming sad and painful in spite of your reciprocal perfections. I try in vain to imagine a place for you, whether in Holland or in Switzerland.

I don't know whether you will remember that I was complaining of one of my cousins—a rare and respected person, who married—against my advice—a young man who loved her, and who regarded this marriage as a source of well-being and happiness. Well, they are presently at my house on my estate (where I am living like a bachelor). The poor husband is sad, anxious, thin; and he is no longer the man who in the very same château lavished care and attentiveness to deserve this woman, and whose gaiety charmed us all. The woman seems content; she is full of tenderness and attentions for him; she is better than ever in mind and appearance; she listens to him as to an oracle, and even lets herself be dominated by him. One can see that this no longer affects him; now that he is accustomed to this success, the emptiness of inaction and the little cares of the household and the absence of all desires, plans, or occupation make of him a very insipid personage. When all's said and done, he has dwindled into a husband. I saw the Comte d'Usson bored to death by the opulence and the beauty of his wife; he had no peace until he was employed in a German court, and he is much less likeable than he was when he was the Chevalier de Bonnac; and now his wife is back where she was when she was a widow, except for the name and the rank that she has acquired.

And you, Agnes, after a few years, your dearest wish would be to find yourself as you are now: unmarried. Whoever your husband may be, he will count for very little in your satisfactions: those come from the places you live and the relationships you will form—think about that! When I made myself Bellegarde's spokesman, I was sure that you would enjoy living in his château, that his sister would be an inexhaustible resource, and that all his relations would be people you could depend on and whose company you would take pleasure in.

I spell out these things for the sake of discussion with a friend, for, apart from this one point, you can reason and evaluate better than I. But let us always be wary, however perspicacious we may be, of happiness that is a matter of speculation; things that have been experienced and compared are the only ones that prudence and wisdom allow us to count on.

You speak like an angel about your two marriage candidates; what you say for M. de Wittgenstein is too good, too well said for me to send it to him unless he shows ardor and solicitousness of the kind you deserve. He will surely write me once more if he is impatient; besides, I have to know whether, as he feared, he is obliged to return to Corsica, where his regiment is still stationed.

I am singularly touched by your situation, because I find that you deserve a great deal, and that I love you more than anyone in the world. I am racking my brains over you, and the more I reflect the more I conclude that you risk nothing by being in no hurry to change your situation, and that you risk too much—even everything—by throwing yourself into an engagement without more compelling reasons than you have. I feel all your vexations, but believe me, they exist everywhere. You are barely thirty, and you are not one of those people whose age is counted; you still have thirty years to enjoy or deplore the lot that you will have prepared for yourself, and thirty years is a very long time. Bear that in mind, since you find a mere few years of uncertainty and malaise so long. Your mind, your imagination will always be fresh and lively, and even ten years from now you will still not be counted in the ranks of grave and solemn persons. Any moment might present a possibility that would have pleased you much better than the ones that now present themselves. And again, believe me, there is no comparison between putting up with the seriousness, the glumness—even the injustice—of a father, and the tediousness and ill-humor of a husband; and we men, truth to tell, are almost all of us glum and tedious at home. A woman must, as I have already said, find in her situation and her surroundings resources and consolations against all turns of fortune.

You ask me what I am doing? Alas, I am not as happy as I should be; I am not able to enjoy all the things I have done for my prospects, my reputation, my well-being. My wife's mind is so diminished that she is insensible to all that—incapable of managing her household, dangerous for her children by her pusillanimity; so that I am compelled, against my heart, to think and act alone, and to count her for nothing among my pleasures. I am attending to the management of my lands, which require my presence, and I have no plans at all for the winter. Farewell.

381. *To Constant d'Hermenches, October 12, 1770*

Zuylen

I have not answered your last letter because it seemed to me as depressing as a chapter from *Candide*, and quite as unreasonable. Why seek to show that the things that are the most desirable and most desired, once they are obtained, do not give us happiness? If that is so, I want not to know it; I want to hope. If it were so, what good would it do me to be persuaded of it? Would that persuasion be a good guide for our conduct? What conclusion would I draw from it? That we must seek out the things we expect to yield us nothing, and resolve to do what displeases us? No, you will say, you must make for yourself an agreeable situation and surroundings. But is the choice of a situation any more certain, any less subject to miscalculations, than that of a wife or husband? Didn't M. d'Usson and your cousin's husband believe that they were obtaining for themselves an agreeable situation? Are *you* happy, you who have fortune, reputation, pleasures, and a wife who has never offered any obstacles to your desires? There are rumors abroad that you live on very bad terms with her, that you give preference over her to one of your mistresses, and that she is very unhappy. If that is true, I am sorry for you as much as for her. It had been a long time since anyone had spoken ill of you, and I flattered myself that I was seeing everyone come around to my opinion of you.[1]

My eldest brother returned two days ago from the Hague with a nice position that brings in very little money, but that is very honorable when one fills it well. He's very pleased.

I'm interrupting my sentence and crossing out the beginning of it because I must finish. I'm too annoyed with you; I could only scold, and I have no right to scold you—you would say: What business is it of hers? Remember, however, that I am sincerely and constantly your friend, which is precisely the reason for this outburst of mine against you. I have nothing interesting or new or certain to say about myself.

384. *From Constant d'Hermenches, October 24, 1770*

Lausanne

But, my dear Agnes, what a devastating letter! Just at the moment when I expected consolation from you for misfortunes of mine that you should have foreseen for years, you reproach me for the ills that are said of me. You know only too well that I made an unsuitable match, with a woman who is seven years older than I am, without fortune or health, of little intelligence, and the most trivial character—everybody knows it. In spite of all that, I concealed the folly of a young man of twenty and the mistake of parents too little concerned for their son's happiness by making this woman happy, making her shine—by thinking, writing, speaking for her, carrying her from her bed to the ball or the theater, and from there, to society suppers. I loved her because I am loving, and must love; I handled her with tact because I am sensitive and delicate; I put up with her because I was mad enough to believe that I could change her, and that one could show and teach someone to act and think just as one can teach someone to sing and recite. I never let

---

1. A few days later, on October 25 (Letter 385 in *O.C.* 2: 226), Belle describes to Ditie her suspicions, suggested first by her cousin Annebetje, that d'Hermenches' urging her to delay a decision, his comments about Wittgenstein, and his treatment of his wife are all motivated by interests and purposes "into which I certainly would not enter."

anything show, because she was gentle, virtuous and decorous—but for a long time now I had been saying to you: My wife is becoming soured by age; she is raising her children in an unworthy manner; she takes no care of them; she is teaching her daughter to lie and to deceive me; she is making my son effeminate (she prevented him from taking part in the Corsican campaign by culpable ruses); she is careless with my house and my goods; she is ruining me. The more incompetent she is, the more she wants to govern. Then come the deceitful steps she takes to hide the disorder; then the imputations and slanders to drive away those that I had appointed to watch over my affairs in Switzerland while I'm fighting in Corsica.

What could I conclude from all that? —that I was very unfortunate, and that all I could do was arrange the pleasantest possible life for this shadow of a wife and mother; to give her the means to live independent of all the burdens of a great house, to let her lie in bed until noon, and spend the rest of the day petting her dogs, drinking tea with cream, and playing whist, and, for myself, to limit my expenses and put my household economy on a more stable footing. That's what I tried to do in friendly consultation with her; and that is what some ill-informed, malicious people have described to you as "living badly with my wife."

I have no mistress, on my word of honor; I have never had one in this country. The only branch that the rage for slander can clutch at is a merchantwoman who served for seventeen years in the house; she's very ugly, but she has a good head, cleverness, knowledge of all our affairs, and the best proven faithfulness and disinterestedness. Write and ask the Bouilliers, Mlle Mauclerc, whether I am lying!

The frenzy that persecutes me has turned my poor wife's head. People suggest a thousand ridiculous plans, a thousand idiocies to break our agreements. She complains about being separated from me, and she is afraid of seeing me. She asks for lodgings that I prepare for her, and that she then wants to change after a week. My name is bandied about by all the matrons of Lausanne, and Agnes has misjudged me ... am I unhappy enough? And those, Agnes, are the fruits of all unsuitable marriages!

Certainly I could have advanced my fortune in the service better. I ought to have waited until I reached the age of reason to make a marriage in proportion to my hopes, or at least in proportion to reason; to find, if not wealth, then order and economy; if not youth, at least health; if not wit, at least judgment and reason. I was drawn in by the charm of an imaginary happiness, by a sweet voice, by a delicate air, and by a woman who pleased me all the more in that she was already established in the world while I was still a little boy.

I feel that you thundered at me because my letter displeased you; you are furious with me for wanting you to be wiser than I was. But do what you will, Agnes, you have more intellect than the entire universe, and I would be mad to oppose you, or vex you; do what you will, my friendship will at any rate never reproach me for anything. I have risked the greatest of misfortunes for myself—that of displeasing you and seeing you disgusted with me—in order to present these truths to you; I regret it, but I do not repent of it.

I would need four pages more to speak to you of your adorable brother; he isn't a man, he's an angel; he moved me to tears. He adores you; I hope he will live.[1]

389. *From Constant d'Hermenches, December 22, 1770*

Lausanne

Seldom in my life have I felt such pain as I do now, by the silence you maintain with me, and by the state of mind that you have shown me in your last letter. So this is the friendship that was cemented by so many years, by so much openheartedness; that elevated my soul, consoled my heart, made me think that humanity had bonds that no circumstances could destroy, and that made me love humanity once more—all that reduced to nothing![1] For it is clear that if I said nothing more to you, you would simply drop me, and perhaps you would be glad of it. No, Agnes, it isn't possible; it's too bad for you if you have promised more than you could hold to; too bad for you if you have formed so many relationships, intimate friendships, that you find yourself overloaded. As for me, who have never attached myself nor given myself over to anyone the way I have to you, I cannot resign myself to the interruption of our association, and I will at least compel you to tell me that you are like other human beings, I who found you so superior! ...

I want to tell you, although it may be indifferent to you, that during the unhappy crisis in which I found that I had only a simulacrum, a phantom of a wife and mother for my children, I also had a virtuous sister, amiable, beautiful, a worthy wife of a husband who is twenty years older than she is and an excellent mother—who sought to console me and let me taste the intimate and domestic sweetness that I had never found in my own household. The Marquise de Langallerie has a charming establishment at the entrance to Lausanne,[2] which your charming and adorable brother may have mentioned to you (he, in any case, is highly regarded there); I have moved in there and that is where I will spend my winter visits to Switzerland. We live together as a family; her husband is a man of wit, knowledge, probity, gentleness, and cheerfulness; his seventeen-year-old daughter is pretty and very sweet-

---

1. Belle is increasingly preoccupied by Ditie's health; he was suffering from tuberculosis.
1. An echo here of an exchange from their early letters—she wrote that she had been "touched by the passage" in which he had said, "you reconcile me with [...] human society" (Letters 63 and 64).
2. "Mon-Repos," where in earlier years, Voltaire and the Constant family had performed plays together.

natured. My Sophie,[3] whom I have raised myself, is with me; she is fifteen and a half now. She followed me through the two Corsican campaigns; she is an admirable person, who waits on us and amuses us, and we live like the patriarchs, in peace and comfort. If some good actors arrive, we have the theater right at our bedside; if we want music, I have excellent harpsichords; if we want portraits of people we like, Mme de Corcelles does them for us.[4] And I leave my wife with everything she needs to live, with her cats and her serving-woman—who are the only beings she loves, and who are her true family—I leave her to chew her nails with her stupid, foolish relatives, who have never been able to show her duties to her, and who would sue if they had a case. In spite of your cruelties, I wish you the very best, Agnes, and I will adore and respect you all my life.

I have sent my daughter[5] to stay with a relative who is very worthy, and an excellent woman. She is fifteen years old, and has barely had the education of an eight-year-old; she was wasting her time with the daughters of that Mme Blatière who, it seems to me, with all her wit, knowledge, gentleness and honesty, fulfills her role as mother very badly.

My son seems to be doing well at the Hague; I write to him every week, as to a friend; I would like to impart to him solidity and reflectiveness, for he has only flexibility and gentleness. He will have written to you of the distress you are causing me.

392. *To Constant d'Hermenches, January 11, 1771*

Utrecht

How unjust you are, my dear d'Hermenches! I let a few weeks go by without writing to you, and you conclude that I no longer love you. We are, both of us, in a period of crisis and upset. I don't know whether to believe what you say of yourself or what others say of you; I am torn between what I think of myself in the morning, and in the evening, and the next day— and so I keep silent, I wait, I think about you. I have no time to write volumes, and two or three pages would say nothing compared to what I have to say, and so you conclude that if you said nothing to me I would drop you, and perhaps be glad of it! Isn't it true that ever since you were in Valenciennes or Landrecies you always spoke of coming to see me, and yet you didn't come? Isn't it true that after your second return from Corsica, and in your

3. Sophie-Jeanne-Louise Joly Dufey (1753–1841) was born in Savoie and raised at Hermenches. She shared inheritance with d'Hermenches' two legitimate children (Société vaudoise, *Recueil de généalogies vaudoises* 3: 15).

4. Mme de Corcelles, née Louise-Françoise Saussure-Bercher, was d'Hermenches' maternal cousin. Her second husband was in the Jenner Regiment. She will be mentioned later as moving in Belle's circles as well as in d'Hermenches'.

5. His legitimate daughter Constance-Louise, born in 1755.

fortress at Huningue, you were silent for a long time? But did I leap to such hasty and odious conclusions? I forgive your injustice, and I ask your pardon for any harsh expressions that may have escaped me when I spoke of your conduct with Madame d'Hermenches. Let us forgive each other, and love each other as before ... but we have never stopped loving each other.

I am content with what you tell me about your wife; it is more fitting that she stay in your house than it would have been for you to stay there without her. I forgive her indolence, because in that respect we are what nature made us; I forgive her wrongs, because I feel that I too would wrong a husband who is often absent, often unfaithful, and that I would seek consolations in my cats or my dogs, or in other things; but I also find it good that since you cannot live pleasantly with her, you live elsewhere. If she does not know how to raise her daughter, it is right that you put her in other hands; with liberty and with wealth in proportion to the fortune that she brought you when she married you she can console herself for what she is losing, and you must both find yourselves happier than you could be living together. This arrangement seems to me wise and equitable, and I no longer blame you.

If I lived at the Hague, I would watch out for your son's well-being; if I ever have my own household and he can stay with me without being bored, you will send him to me sometimes. I have only been at the Hague for twenty-four hours this winter; I'm not at ease there. To be comfortable, I need a big room, bright and cheerful, where I hear no noise, and where I can receive only the people I want to. I don't find that at my sister's house; she's amiable enough, and she's fond of me, but I neither sleep nor eat when I am there, and I haven't a moment's peace and quiet. Whenever you mention your son to me, I am annoyed and ashamed, remembering that he lives in the same country as I do and yet I can do nothing for him.

We very nearly signed my marriage contract last Tuesday, but I trembled, and shuddered, and drew back; and Monsieur de Charrière didn't dare press me, and protested that he would consider me free, and would respect that freedom, until the moment of the final ceremony. He loves me without illusion, without infatuation; he is sincere and just to the point of offending me and often vexing me; and then I say that he doesn't love me at all, and that I will be unhappy; but I love him, and I cannot resolve to live without him. When I judge him without illusion or infatuation or ardor or rapture, I still find that there is no one superior to him in character or intelligence or temperament. How could one give up such a man!

Goodbye. I will write again as soon as I can.

393. *To Constant d'Hermenches, January 15, 1771*

The other day I didn't say half of what I wanted to say. First, let's talk about my brother. He was enchanted with you. He loved your tone, your speech, your manners, your friendship for me. He told me that he had more than once had the pleasure of accompanying your sister on horseback. But what will interest you yet more is that he wrote from Marseille that his health was infinitely better than it had been for a long time. That gives me great joy. My brother Willem, the eldest, is marrying my friend Mlle Fagel. I had neither foreseen it nor wished for it; however, I approve of it, and I'm very glad. I have never met anyone with a temperament and a mind more likely to please my brother over a long period of time. Sometimes I thought of her for your son, but I thought that she was not pretty enough for his taste, nor sufficiently knowing to suit you. She has the kindest of hearts, and her mind is acute, original, and amiable.

Speaking of marriage, I was engaged yesterday. Many things have gone on in my soul over the last three weeks. I have thought a hundred times that I was never to marry, and that I never wanted to. Monsieur de Charrière did not press me at all and said—and still says—that up until the moment of marriage, I am free; but everyone loves him and I love him more than any-one, and I have never see a man as reasonable, gentle, easy-going, and sin-cere as he is. Besides, my situation is awkward; except by my marrying, it would have been very difficult to change it in a way that would have satis-fied my father, and it would have been detestable to change it in a way that would distress him. In short, the day before yesterday, in the evening, I said that if they wanted to have us sign the contract the next morning and formal-ly engage us, I was disposed to consent. Today, they are sending to Switzer-land the document on which the announcements will be based. I will see you, I will live in a pleasant country, I will live with a man I love and who deserves my love; I will be as free as an honest woman can be. I will retain my friends, my correspondences, the freedom to speak and to write; I will not need to stoop to the least dissimulation. I will not be rich, but I will have in abundance everything that is necessary, and I will feel the pleasure of having bettered my husband's lot in life. If, with all that, I am not happy, I will say to myself that Mme d'Usson, Lady Holderness, Mme de Chasteler are not either . . .

By the way, that poor woman is here. She's a little better.

Goodbye; I embrace you. Goodbye, my dear friend.

ভ *Belle de Zuylen and Charles-Emmanuel de Charrière were married in a Dutch service in the church of Zuylen on February 17, 1771. She described the occasion to her brother Ditie:*

My dress was of a fine white Indian satin; my brother Willem had given it to me .... M. de Charrière joined me in my pew; the minister read the liturgy to us, I listened for both of us in order to guide the "Yes" of M. de Charrière, and I made the promises for myself. Although we got married without ceremony, getting married is a great ceremony .... At half-past midnight *they all went off to bed, some with their wives,*[1] etc. The punch, having no respect for the occasion, made M. de Charrière a bit sick, and my inexorable toothache came to torment me toward morning just as if I had not been a new bride. Since then, I have nearly always been not quite well—just slightly ill; but when I am well it seems to me that nothing is lacking in my happiness.[2]

Belle was plagued off and on by various kinds of ailments, but she expressed contentment with her marriage to a husband who is "the gentlest, the most reasonable, and the most tenderly loved in all the world." "I am hindered neither in thoughts nor words nor actions: I have changed name, and I no longer always sleep alone—that's the only difference." She resorts to her native tongue to describe, with amusement, the permanent temperamental difference between them: "I often find Monsieur de Charrière too ordentlyk [proper], too overleggende [deliberate], and often he finds me too much the opposite."

In the summer the Charrières spent two months of honeymoon in Paris, where Belle took lessons from Maurice Quentin de La Tour, who had done her portrait in pastels at Zuylen, and she sat for a sketch for a new portrait by him. The great sculptor Jean-Antoine Houdon did a bust of her that is now in the Bibliothèque Publique et Universitaire of Neuchâtel. In late September 1771 the couple moved into the Charrière family home Le Pontet in Colombier, near Neuchâtel.

While she was in Paris, in August of 1771, Ditie reported to Belle that he had heard rumors—we don't know how widespread they were nor from whom he heard them—that d'Hermenches had been discussing her marriage and their relationship in compromising ways, and even discussing her letters in company. In the letter where Ditie first mentions these things, he says "I won't send this letter until I've had time to discuss it with someone around here; I don't want to accuse him without being sure of what I'm saying." But he sends the letter anyway, saying, "I have not been able to see anyone to whom I could talk, or whom I could get to talk about the subject of

1. Emphasis in original.
2. This letter and the others quoted here are from *O.C.* 2: 237–39, 242–43, 247.

M. d'Hermenches." This, taken with the suspicions that Annebetje had raised earlier (see Letter 381, n. 1) are so upsetting to Belle that she writes to Ditie, "I was overcome with vexation and embarrassment. His fantasies about my feelings are so absurd that they inspire more pity than anger." She tells Ditie that out of sheer prudence she intends not to break off with d'Hermenches altogether, "because in the past, especially in the time of M. de Bellegarde, I wrote to him with a liberty that he might abuse if he thought he had the right to be nasty." But by October of 1771 Ditie and d'Hermenches seem to be on courteous terms, and in January of 1772 (Letter 413) Belle relays to d'Hermenches that "my brother was very touched by the welcome you gave him and by your kind offers."

405. *From Constant d'Hermenches, October 28, 1771*

Bois-de-Vaux,[1] near Lausanne

Madame, it is an unbearable torment for me to think that you may have arrived in Switzerland and that you might suspect me of knowing it without having, from the very first moment, laid at your feet a thousand good wishes and expressions of tenderness and respect. —No, your judgment is too sound to let you think that I could ever be capable of tepidness or indifference regarding you. Your adorable brother must have told you of how I think about you—about your happiness—and of the vitality of the good wishes that you inspire in me. But perhaps you are still in Paris—Bellegarde writes me that he had the good fortune of seeing you there; thus, it is useless for me to struggle to say to you on paper what you are not yet in a position to read. I will, then limit myself to the question: are you in Switzerland? And what are your thoughts about me? For I am, as I will be all my life, with all the affection and veneration that you deserve, your very humble servant and sincere friend.[2]

408. *From Constant d'Hermenches, November 10, 1771*

Bois-de-Vaux, near Lausanne

My dear Agnes, I have been unable to do anything today, or for several days, except weep, and cherish you all my life, and desire your friendship. I have just lost one of my best friends, a true, tender, enlightened friend, the

---

1. In November 1770, by an arrangement with his wife, d'Hermenches had taken back the property called Bois-de-Vaux, where over the next few years he had several buildings put up, including a farmhouse called "Bellegrange" and a manor house called "Fantaisie."
2. In a letter to Ditie, November 9, 1771, she mentions this one from d'Hermenches: "I received a tender and respectful letter from him; I responded well, I think." But her response seems to be missing (Letter 407 in *O.C.* 2: 253).

only man who is really a man around here—this is De Brenles;[1] he is well known in the region where you live. He died a few days ago, and only a few days earlier we had been laughing and chatting delightfully together; we had read the letters from Cicero to Atticus. We had taken each other's pulse, and I was more feverish than he was! And now he lies in his coffin! . . .

I will always be happy for your happiness, my illustrious and charming friend; thus you could never tell me too much about it, nor too often. There is no happiness without a cloud; you expected it yourself, did you not? You have within yourself an abundance of resources, and I know no one better equipped than you to put yourself above all the little annoyances of life; you will always be fêted everywhere, because to see and hear you is always a celebration. Continue, then, to say with the Roman Vestal: *Moriar nisi nubere dulce est!*[2] She spoke of it only by speculation, and now you are fully aware of what it is. Nature has given the feminine sex a flexibility and suppleness that is often perverted with age, but which makes women more capable of contentment and happiness within the marriage bond than we men are; women usually demand much less than we do.

I do what I can to keep your amiable brother here. I offer him a nice warm little place to stay with a southern exposure; I am prepared to give his horses shelter; he will be the neighbor of an English girl to whom he is said to be very attentive. But he has Naples in his head,[3] and his health is involved: that is too pressing a reason for me to dare to insist.

What do you want me to say about myself? You know my vexations, and you know that they never come alone, and I have them in all varieties. Only De Brenles and another woman friend of mine sustained me and consoled me. Imagine that in all reasonableness—given the circumstances—I must find as much satisfaction in getting unmarried as you can have had in getting married, and in two words you will know my situation.

I know nothing of Mme de Chasteler; if she comes to Lausanne, she has no choice but to stay with me, because all other lodging is taken. Won't you come to see her? I return to Alsace next month, and I plan to spend the winter in Paris. Meanwhile, I live in the country like a hermit.

I am at your feet.

413. *To Constant d'Hermenches, January 12–13, 1772*

Colombier, January 12

I have some news of you, even though our correspondence has been interrupted. One of our young officers often speaks of you to his mother, Mme

1. Jacques Clavel de Brenles, jurisconsult and professor of law at the Academy of Lausanne. He too was a correspondent of Voltaire.
2. "On my life, it is sweet to marry!" Seneca the Elder, *Controversies* VI, chap. 8.
3. Ditie had been charged by the States-General to go to Naples to congratulate the King of Sardinia, Victor-Amédée III, on his accession to the throne.

Chaillet.[1] I know enough to be deeply touched, and to feel for you from the bottom of my heart.[2] And so soon after the loss of a friend! You have always spoken to me of your sister with so much devotion and friendship! You would have no doubts about my heart, my dear d'Hermenches, if you could see the impression made there by your grief.

I have been told about the projects, the solicitations, and the oppositions that were made concerning your regiment, and the conjectures that result from it. What wouldn't I give to see you colonel of the Jenner! It seems to me that that is due to a man who gave up being a major-general in our country to serve the King of France, who underwent so many dangers and ordeals in Corsica, and who has so visibly contributed to the success of that disagreeable war.

I wish that you were so successful in your ambitions that you lost sight of any other plan; so content with those who could help you or harm you that your heart would be softened toward those over whom you have the same power—for I suppose that good fortune softens a heart that is naturally kind. Besides, the more one sees oneself elevated and honorably placed, the more one must feel a repugnance for degrading oneself in the public esteem.

On the occasion of a divorce that was recently granted in Neuchâtel, when I declared my aversion for divorces, people found it excessive, and accused me of being Catholic and of regarding marriage as a sacrament. How I wish I could slip into your soul a little of this prejudice, if it is one! Instead of arguing whether you are in a situation of having to obtain a divorce—an argument in which, it seems to me, no one agrees with you—you would be struck by the unpleasant effects that result even from the most justly obtained divorce: for a wife, to whom her husband's name becomes hateful, to whom the memory of even her children must become hateful; for a husband, especially if he is a father, if he has some delicacy and humanity; for the children, who are embarrassed, who are distressed, who are made to blush every time people speak to them of a father or a mother—every time someone asks them about the most respectable of relationships. Anyone unaware of the misfortunes of their family will speak to them in a way that embarrasses and distresses them. When people do know the situation, they believe that their mother has dishonored herself, or else that their father has been unjust; that is a prejudice that follows them into the world, that torments them and works against them.

Is it worth it, in this short life, to make oneself happy at the expense of others? Can one in fact be happy when one has been willing to be so at the expense of others? You may find me intrusive, but I am your old and true

1. The officer in question is Jean-Frédéric Chaillet, who served in the Jenner Regiment. He is subsequently referred to as "the tall Chaillet."
2. His sister, the marquise de Langallerie, had recently died at the age of forty. Just a year earlier, in Letter 389, he had described how close he and his sister were.

friend—that is my excuse; I have always told you the truth; I have always wanted to see you respected and honored by those whose opinion is a title of honor. If with good grace you were to restore to your wife her position, her fortune, and her peace of mind—if you were to reassure your children, if you were to silence malicious gossip and restore to your friends the pleasure of praising you highly, you would give me—me, particularly—such heartfelt joy that I could hardly describe it to you. Everything that has been said and done for the last year would be regarded as a passing delirium; it would soon be forgotten, and the reconciliation would seem magnanimous. Your own relatives are in mourning; your nephews and your niece no longer have a mother, your family is in a state of distress and confusion. Instead of aggravating the confusion and the distress, try ...

I have taken up the pen, my dear friend, with my heart full of your losses and your pain and—abandoning myself to my fervor—I have written everything that came into my mind on a topic that has already been discussed between us. Suddenly, I have wondered whether my zeal was not indiscreet, and whether you would still want to put up with my outbursts of sincerity as you have in the past. I have stopped. Burn what I have written without reading it, if you have the same doubt; I would not take it amiss. On the contrary, I will thank you for not having wanted to put me in danger of becoming disagreeable to you.

I entreat you to send me news of you. Whose will this regiment be? If only it were mine!

My brother was very touched by the welcome you gave him, and by your kind offers. He is, I hope, in Italy just now. I have received news of him from Nice, where he was waiting for a Dutch ship to go to Livorno. I mean to visit Lausanne in the month of March.

I am in fairly good health, in spite of the snow and the north wind. People here are not too displeased with me, and I am very pleased with them. I do handwork, I play chess, I write and receive a great many letters. Madame de Corcelles will send me some pastels, and then I will paint.[3] Meanwhile, I am cutting out silhouettes—a little talent that I didn't know I had. If I had known of it earlier, I would have in my portfolio all my relatives and friends in Holland. By the way, do you know whether your friend Maasdam is letting his son get married?[4]

Goodbye. My friendship for you is as lively as a new friendship, and as sacred and inviolable as one of long standing. Goodbye, my dear d'Hermenches.

Colombier, January 13, 1772

I am waiting for a letter from you any day now. Let's not fall into those long silences again.

---

3. Mme de Corcelles is d'Hermenches' cousin, mentioned in Letter 389.
4. A reference to the intrigue gossiped about in Letter 371.

414. *From Constant d'Hermenches, January 21, 1772*

Berne

Your friendship and your remembrance of me fill me with gratitude. My dear friend, you owe them to me. They are the very breath of life to me, and yet I thought that I was no longer anything to you. A thousand thanks for your good counsel; the intention is always precious to me; but it makes me think of a physician who proposes trepanning for anemia. You have no knowledge of my ills; thus, your consultation and your prescriptions can hardly be appropriate, in spite of all my trust and my submissiveness to you. I cannot dishonor myself; I am making my children happy, and I am breaking a chain that was corroded, and that could infect us all. Thus, your beautiful words are as unlikely to produce a good effect as the exhortations of a matron who would like to prevent her pregnant daughter from giving birth. Moreover, I am severing connections with the most disgusting relations imaginable, and from the vile citizens of Lausanne, whom you want to go admire during the month of March. I speak crudely, but I am pressed for time, and I want to describe for you in a few broad strokes of caricature my state of mind. I am dying of need and impatience to talk with you; it may well be that one of these days when I go home, and from there to Paris, I will embark at Chevroux,[1] and disembark on the shore of Colombier to spend a couple of hours at your feet. But I will stay at the inn, and await your orders, because I might very well have with me my ward Sophie,[2] that extraordinary person who went through the Corsican war with me, and whom I would have left to your care if I had been killed.

The matter of the regiment has been decided in my favor: Monsieur Jenner has been obliged to give back the money, and keep his regiment; I have triumphed over the cabale, and if I were mean-spirited, I would boast of my triumph over my enemies, the overturned Duc de Choiseul and Salis, for having basely conspired to trick me.[3]

Please receive my respects, divine Agnes.

ᑫ *Isabelle de Charrière and Constant d'Hermenches saw each other only once after she was married. He visited her and her husband in Colombier in January 1772.*

1. A port on Lake Neuchâtel.
2. His natural daughter. See his Letter 389.
3. The Duc de Choiseul had been dismissed as Foreign Minister in 1770.

415. *From Constant d'Hermenches, January 28, 1772*

Lausanne

I count myself fortunate, my adorable friend, for having had the happiness of seeing you. Your esprit, your contentment, your graces, have revivified my very being as if I had never known you possessed them. The water that separates us is no longer the Moerdijk,[1] and in all the agreeable plans I contemplate, I see you as a connection that I will be able to cultivate, and who will have as much indulgence for my gray hair as for my nonsense. I was delighted to make the acquaintance of the husband you have chosen for yourself; it seems to me that when we are all three together we will be able to do without the rest of the ordinary human race; or at any rate, not bother ourselves about it.[2]

My insomnias have turned to fever; I have nothing to do here except to take care of it, and to regret all the moments and all the distance that separates me from you. I will cherish you and respect you all my life. My dear Agnes, give me the greatest portion you possibly can of your friendship and your remembrance.

CR *In this next letter, d'Hermenches seems to be laying before Belle his version of several things about which there was gossip around Lausanne. Of the controversy with his wife that has moved him to publish the inventory of her estate, we learn well enough in the letters; but a couple of other topics need explaining.*

Bénigne Buchet had been a loyal domestic servant in d'Hermenches' household for many years. Her satisfactory performance in that capacity notwithstanding, in 1771 the Consistory of Lausanne took up the question of expelling her from the city for refusing to name the father of her fourth illegitimate child (her first three had been born elsewhere). The bailiff was one Jean-Henri Polier de Vernand,[3] and he seems to have taken her expulsion as his mission. The connections are these: for generations, the Vernand property had been watered by a stream that flowed onto it from the Hermenches' property; Jean-Henri's brother, Georges-Louis, had been d'Hermenches' fellow-officer at the Hague.

When Jean-Henri Polier started proceeding against Bénigne, d'Hermenches built a dam across the stream that fed the Vernand's garden. Polier sued. In court, d'Hermenches claimed that he had come to need the water for his own gardens and that the use by the Vernands had always been a

---

1. That is, she is no longer in Holland but only on the opposite side of Lake Neuchâtel.
2. Back in the early days of the Bellegarde plans, d'Hermenches had entertained a very similar daydream: "... we are going to make a trio of perfect intimacy such as no poet, I think, has ever yet dared imagine" (Letter 118).
3. Our source here is Pierre Morren, *La Vie Lausannoise au XVIIIe siècle* (157–61). Vernand's papers are Morren's source for this episode.

matter of sufferance. Polier claimed it had become a right. In private, Georges was able to report that d'Hermenches had written him that "the lawsuit follows directly from the persecution of Bénigne Buchet, and that if they had left her alone he wouldn't have started anything."

By the end of 1771 Bénigne was pregnant again, and this time, on January 25, 1772, she got married; the marriage lasted six weeks. D'Hermenches' comments to Belle suggest that people were conjecturing about who Sophie's mother was.

416. *From Constant d'Hermenches, February 8, 1772*

Lausanne

I have decided, my divine friend, to let the acknowledgement of the inventory of my wife's fortune be printed, in order to to cut short all the imputations that might make you doubt my frankness. It will be seen, without my having to wear myself out in calculations, that she doesn't have thirty-eight thousand francs in fortune, which, however, I have recognized her to have for the sake of peace.

I told you what I could about Sophie.[1] I love her as my own child; she resembles me very much, but her mother has never held me responsible for her, and she is not baptized under my name. What more can a man of scruples do than to go find her, take her to him, raise her well, and provide for her future? The person who it was given out was her mother, and who is known to claim her—she's a fright![2] Bénigne has been a treasure in my household for eighteen years; she's a modest violet who has been hidden under the other flowers, who has been worth perhaps fifty thousand francs to me by her vigilance, who is sensitive and unselfish, who has loved me passionately since she was fourteen; who resisted me for six years, who yielded for fear of losing me and of seeing me go find some woman to console me for my unhappy association with Madame d'Hermenches—which she had witnessed—and for the futility and distastefulness of our union. I told her that I didn't believe that God would take it ill that, in my situation, I do as little harm as possible; and that a child of hers would please me. Still resistant, still modest, she let herself be persuaded, and yielded herself to me ...

> Et le jour rendant ses mains serviles
> Aux ténébreux plaisirs elle a fait succéder

1. This paragraph might be clearer if we knew what passed between them at his recent visit to Colombier, but we do not.
2. This may be the woman mentioned in Letter 384, who d'Hermenches said might be the subject of scandal-mongers' conjectures; she was, he wrote, "very ugly, but she has ... knowledge of all our affairs, and the best proven faithfulness and disinterestedness."

Les travaux, les bienfaits, les soins les plus utiles,
Sans en vouloir de prix que celui de m'aimer.[3]

She got married, another result of her devotion to me: she wants absolutely, when I get my divorce, for me to find a life's companion who suits me, and she wants to take care of my country estates with her husband ... Is this frankness or not, my dear Agnes? You may be disgusted with me as you read about this, but why do you press me with the reproach that I find the most insulting for true friendship? One must speak of one's weaknesses and vices or else seem to you a deceiver! With you, I can very well accommodate myself to that law; I wish that you could always read inside my heart, if I had the good fortune to interest you enough to give you the curiosity.

O Agnes, how you relieve my soul by showing me such a smooth path to intimacy! Nothing even comes close to your letters; this is an altogether new genre. It isn't the language of men, it's the language of an inventive genius. Reading you, one wishes that you would never do anything but write; seeing you, one is jealous of everyone you write to, and regrets all the moments that you give to paper and to those who are absent!

I was immensely pleased with you: the sort of dignity that the state of a married woman gives you is singularly becoming to you; it is a grace and ease that takes away nothing from the veneration and the Platonic love inspired by the untouched virgin. Am I expressing what I would like to make you understand? I have no idea; but certainly I am struck by finding you as marvellous and adorable a woman as you were a sublime and incomparable girl.

I will do anything I can for your protégé.[4] But you have no need of that to captivate his mother, for I can tell you that you please everyone, and that you have surpassed all the favorable expectations aroused by your prestige. But I beg you, don't prescribe for yourself anything to please people further; you are announcing reforms that I would take for affectation. Why would you show virtues that are not yours? Agnes, that's charlatanism! Give me the satisfaction of knowing your opinion when it is better than other people's; have enough modesty to be willing to make use of everything that is in you to appear perfect, and do not feign modesty in order to show one perfection the more. One must no more disguise the faculties of one's mind and judgment than the features of one's face—and so much the worse for the ill-favored and the stupid who are put off by it.

I am at your feet.

3. "And daybreak restoring her hands to service / The pleasures of darkness she displaced with labors, good deeds, the most useful care, / Wishing no reward save that of loving me."
4. Probably Charles Dapples, a young relative of M. de Charrière whom Belle had recommended to d'Hermenches.

418. *To Constant d'Hermenches, March 11, 1772*

Wednesday evening

Good evening, Monsieur d'Hermenches. I haven't written to you because I have been arranging a corner of the garden, and washing clothes in our beautiful fountain, like a certain princess in the *Odyssey*;[1] but she was a princess, and only washed woolen robes, while I have washed everything. It's one of the keenest pleasures that I know: I have been gardener and laundrymaid with a passion and an excess that have made me slightly sick—which is another cause for my silence; and for the last reason, I offer as excuse an infinite number of indispensable letters to be written. I've received the document that you had printed; the matter is clear.[2] I am very glad to have seen that. As for having had it printed, you know better than I do whether any good can come of it.

Monsieur de Bonstetten and Professor Wilhelmi dined here three weeks ago. They spoke a great deal about you. Monsieur de Bonstetten is very likeable; the other seemed to me to have some wit, but if this man has a true and upright heart then he has certainly fooled me. I no longer value wit enough for it to blind me regarding everything else.

Our coachman was kicked in the head by a horse and has not yet quite recovered from it, and one of our horses has a cold. When both of them are well again, I think we will go as soon as we can to Lausanne. Monsieur de Sévery has written to us about it, very kindly urging us to come. He is sorry that the high season is almost over, and I am very glad of it: aside from the fact that it does't greatly amuse me, it leaves me somewhat sick. What I like to do is take a walk in the morning, do a little handwork or reading, then have a peaceful time for a noon meal and for getting dressed; when I have been allowed to do that, then I can dine as late as you please, and in whatever company. It is less unhealthy for me to wash clothes all day at the fountain than to spend the whole day talking and listening. Will you be in Lausanne? —And by the way, are you in Lausanne now? Will you get my letter? Answer me before I say any more, for it's one thing to write to someone living in Paris, and another thing to write to someone living in Lausanne or Bois-de-Vaux.

Is your fever gone? Write me back, and please tell me (if you know) whether I would find Mlle de Mauclerc in Lausanne in ten or twelve days. I would very much like to. Farewell.

---

1. Nausicaa, who received and cared for the shipwrecked Ulysses.
2. A formal acknowledgement—in four folio pages—of his wife's estate and property.

419. *From Constant d'Hermenches, March 17, 1772*

Bellegrange, Tuesday the 17th, on a heap of stones

That princess in the *Odyssey* didn't have a mind like yours; she didn't have such fine-spun nerves; she was dressed in wool, and you are dressed in gauze and taffeta. I can't bear the thought of your playing washerwoman or nymph of the vegetable patch; you'll do yourself a mischief. Your face will get blotchy; your teeth will fall out, and so will your hair—and I fail to see what profit we shall have from all that! So forgive me if my admiration does not follow you into a garden shed, nor to a fountain that issues forth snow-melt—that is by no means the spring of Hippocrene[1] or the Fountain of Youth. A pretty woman should remain—as long as she can—a pretty woman; and if one is a genius one should take care of one's health, or at least not ruin it for things that others can do as well. You have preached to me so often that I am only too happy to find this occasion to exercise a little severity towards you; really, you don't know the sun of Switzerland, and you will do yourself harm with these rustic excesses. I feel it myself, this sun, and I get sick from it, but I do something sensible about it; I detest Lausanne, and I leave it; I had a house that was a burden to me, and I sell it; I have a well-situated piece of land, and I build on it; I want to go to Paris, and I pack my bags; I have lawsuits, and I win them.

You throw a doubt my way which the faith I have in you makes painful to me: you judge unfavorably the heart of my Professor Wilhelmi. Well now, this is a friend who is devoted to me; he's the best—or at least the most interesting—friend that I have in Switzerland at present! If he were evil or false, I would have expended my friendship very foolishly, and all the more foolishly because it isn't his wit that pleases me, but rather his good-naturedness, cheerfulness and frankness. I don't especially like his joking tone. He thinks that sarcasm and japes are the livery of wit; I don't let him get away with it, but that's the Bernese vice. He wrote to me a great deal about you; he finds you perfect as a woman, and completely lovable in all aspects, and then he utters a few witticisms, as if that true judgment needed spicing: "She seemed to me," he said, "a sylphide who had been deposited at the foot of these mountains, waiting for some sylph to come carry her off."

I'm still here, but I am about to leave, and I have no regret that you won't find me; I would not have had the happiness of seeing you. The people who will surround you are, to me, insipid; nothing but grimaces, squirming, clumsy courtesies—everything in Lausanne is pitched to pride and baseness—, and blandishments so well feigned that I am glad to leave you to enjoy them without undeceiving you; and for that, I have to be a hundred leagues away from you! You won't see there a single man of wit, not one

1. The fount of the Muses.

woman with natural grace or the slightest candor; with all that, you may find them charming, and you will be ridiculed, for that is the fate of all newcomers. In writing this to you I have no fear of making you dislike them; it's rather they who will make you dislike me; but, sooner or later, things will come right again, and I hope to receive you in my salon or in my shack with Monsieur de Charrière and this professor and Bonstetten, if you like. Things will be quite different from what they are in Lausanne: we will have comfort without showiness, luxury without ostentation, music, poetry, and good conversation. If this scribbling of mine reaches you Wednesday, give me your orders for Friday morning: I am leaving for Ferney,[2] Grenoble, and Paris: and I am at your feet, in the midst of my thirty masons.

Mlle Mauclerc is in Lausanne in the same house as the Bouillier family; Hardenbroek has left.

420. *To Constant d'Hermenches, March 18, 1772*

Wednesday

I have so often preached to you, and now you are doing it to me; but I, at least, will docilely follow your advice. You joke about my playing washerwoman; that I will do no more, and as for my gardener's labors, I will try not to overdo them. Someday you will see and admire the work that I'm having done in the garden, and you will find that a bad cold was not too much to pay for my groves and my lawn. I will take better care of myself, and protect myself from the sun and the north wind until my visit to Lausanne, which I think will be at the beginning of next week. On Sunday, although I had a bad cold, I went on foot to Neuchâtel; Monday I stayed in bed; yesterday I went out; today I am quite well, except that my voice still sounds dreadful. When I'm in Lausanne I will avoid dinners and all the fuss of finery and outings that do me a hundred times more harm than water and sun.

You won't be there; so that is decided! You say that you're not sorry about it, and that I shouldn't be either. Very well; I will try to see the matter from that point of view. I promised to tell you everything I think about Lausanne and its inhabitants; I will keep my word, provided that all our pacts of mutual discretion, tacit and otherwise, hold firm on this occasion. For the welcome I will get—even if it were insincere, even if it concealed little hypocrisies, little comments and mocking remarks—will still deserve a kind of gratitude on my part, supposing that I don't clearly see what they intend to hide but merely suspect it; and I would be no better than they are if while accepting their politeness I were to judge them nastily in public. But if my judgments remain in your hands, there is nothing to reproach me with, and I will not have offended a scrupulous good faith. Please, then,

2. The home of Voltaire, just on the French side of the French-Swiss border.

renew your promises of silence, at least regarding those people whom these scruples oblige me to treat with consideration.

I won't recant my conjecture about M. Wilhelmi, but it's only a conjecture. He arrived here late, a long time after M. de Bonstetten, so that we didn't see him for long, and he was unable to get in a great number of his witticisms. He did manage some, but they were good ones, and did not resemble his sylphic inanities—they were satires rather than praises. I'm like you—I'm not especially fond of that style of wit that consists in sarcasm. At first, I find it ingenious, all the more in that I feel myself incapable of the same finesse; but it palls quickly.

Monsieur de Charrière sends his compliments, and wishes you, as I do, a pleasant journey. At the moment I have no errands to be done in Paris. However, since you ask me what my orders are, I will give them to you. Think of me, love me, and write to me.

Farewell, my dear d'Hermenches.

421. *From Constant d'Hermenches, March 23, 1772*

Ferney, March 23

That's a rather better dateline than the last one, is it not, my adorable friend?[1] I wish you were here, rather than in that boring Lausanne where you will arrive just as I am fleeing it; I cannot conceal from you that it nauseates me. What a thing is life! A few years ago I would have walked across burning coals to greet Agnes in Lausanne! But you will console me, you will do me the grace of writing me, and I will certainly be faithful to you.

My stay here is doing me good; this venerable and prodigious old man listens to my miseries, talks to me about my little troubles like a good mother; thus I find him truly great at these moments—rather as Madame de Sévigné found Louis XIV to be a hero after he had danced a minuet with her. You absolutely must come see him; he is worthy of listening to you, and you are infinitely worthy of talking to him, for I always return to the fact that I know no one who has more wit than you—no one whose wit is more agreeable, more natural, nor of a sounder judgment.

I am obliged to leave. I am at your feet, my dear friend.

My address is *care of Messieurs Lullain, bankers, rue Thévenot, Paris.*

Get Mme de Corcelles[2] to talk about me. She will purse up her mouth; and then if you praise me a great deal—as I beg you to do—they will be furious, and say that I am not your friend, or that I am frivolous, or malicious, or perhaps false. You must always maintain that I am an excellent man; when they see that they can't make you budge, they will say that it's true, for fear that you might betray them. I in turn will write and tell you

---

1. D'Hermenches is visiting Voltaire at his estate at Ferney.
2. D'Hermenches' cousin, whose husband was in the Jenner Regiment.

everything that they find wrong with *you*, for I will have very reliable reports.

424. *To Constant d'Hermenches, April 23, 1772*

Colombier

You may well have found that I've been very slow to answer you; I didn't mean to be. In Lausanne I hardly had time to recognize myself. I would get up late because I didn't go to bed until one o'clock in the morning; I would get dressed and go spend an hour with Mademoiselle de Mauclerc, who is still sick and lame. Then we would dine, make visits or receive them; then we would go to someone's reception, and we would have supper in town. During my last days there, I was also invited to breakfast, a fatigue that I cannot bear; but people were so well-intentioned that I could refuse nothing. I left Lausanne well entertained, very grateful, and with a terrible cold.

Once I returned here, I took on the running of the household; here I am, housekeeper and often cook—it keeps me busy and I enjoy it.

I've received a great many letters, containing the best of news: Mme d'Athlone has given birth to a son, and has recovered so fast that she was able to go out after only two weeks. My sister-in-law has also had a son, ten days after my cousin, which is a source of joy in my father's house; she and her son are well. My sailor brother is in better health than usual, and writes me that he intends to be here at the end of May. I had to respond to all that; so you see, my dear d'Hermenches, that I can be excused for having made you wait, and you will pardon me.

Let's talk about the people of Lausanne. I found Mme de Sévery[1] extremely amiable. The first few days, she reminded me of Mme de Degenfeld, and I thought that I would like her no better, but when we became comfortable with each other, I found that she had a great deal of wit and keenness of mind, a fine and engaging cheerfulness—in short, everything that rightly pleases, and she pleased me very much. Her husband is kind, open, easy-going; I was much taken with him. He is, at heart, extremely fond of you; and I met no one who praised you, blamed you—that is to say, talked about you—more eagerly than he did.

I talked a great deal about you and your affairs with your friend M. de Middes; a little with Mme de Chandieu-Vulliens, a little with Mademoiselle de Villardin, who was my favorite in that whole company and the one to whom I had the most to say. She has an appealing, fine, expressive countenance; she is very amiable, and she is the friend of a woman to whom I am much attached. According to what she tells me, her brother has great obligations to you.

1. A cousin of M. de Charrière.

I saw Mme de Corcelles only during my last days there; she was sick, and doing rather poorly. One thing that pleased me when I saw her: a resemblance (a distant one, however, and made yet more distant by a difference of fifteen or twenty years in age)—a resemblance between her and Mme d'Athlone; she has never been as handsome as my cousin (at least, I don't think she has), but she resembles her a little. My cousin's countenance is at times gentler, at times harsher, as her feelings and her circumstances dictate; that of Mme de Corcelles is fashioned by the habit of wanting to please, wanting to be whatever suits others, and therefore hiding her pains, her cares, and her thought. The experience of society has done both good and harm to your cousin; it has done nothing at all to mine, or rather society has given her none of the ordinary social savoir-faire; as my intimate friend, I like her better that way.

I can well imagine how a woman might be foolish enough to fall in love with M. de Corcelles. He has that little art that wins you over if you don't have the luck to see through it, and that subtle silence, and those clever little words that seem to hide all the wit that he is not displaying. I can imagine it all the better since, when I was a child, I loved a man who had that finesse and that sort of charm. The memory of him amused me when I saw M. de Corcelles. The warm and friendly welcome that I received from Mme d'Orges, who is my relative, touched me and gave me great pleasure. Do you know that the man I talked with, and who always placed himself next to me at table, was the Marquis de Gentils?[2] He's a little unkempt, but he's cheerful and knowledgeable and has in all his conversations a sort of good-naturedness and an ease of wit and expression that I like—whereas I detest the precious wits and fine talkers who listen to themselves and want to be listened to and appreciated. I like to have people pursue their thought quickly when they talk; I know how to seize the essential as it flies by ... but I am going on and on, and I'm boring you—enough of this.

There is, however, one more thing I want to tell you, which is that I saw Mme d'Hermenches at the home of Mme de Mézery, and I spoke to her. Since I didn't know for certain whether she had come calling on me or not, I went to her door to pay my respects. If it had been possible to go to her house the day she was receiving, I would have gone, simply to show that you had not turned against her those of your friends who do not know her.

Monsieur Tissot is a man of intelligence.[3] I found him to be just as you have described him to me.

Your last letter was from Ferney; I was very pleased that you thought of me while you were there. You wished that I were there; I don't wish it for myself. He's a malicious man with a great deal of wit. I will read him, but I

2. Philippe de Gentils, marquis de Langallerie, was the husband of d'Hermenches' beloved sister, who had died the year before.
3. The Lausanne doctor who treated Ditie.

will not go worship him.[4] You may well find my letter tedious, my descriptions banal. It's not my fault; I can't speak of something except as I have seen it. I'm not enthusiastic about Lausanne, but I enjoyed myself there. Mme de Sévery is pleasant, Mme de Corcelles interesting, and Mademoiselle de Villardin also.

Write me, please. There are no letters like yours. Goodbye. Count on my affection; my whole life long I will be touched by the constancy of yours. You have, *for me*, a good heart. Your wit is charming; everyone says so.

426. *From Constant d'Hermenches, May 26, 1772*

The Hague

I didn't answer the letter I received from you in Paris from Paris itself, my rare and excellent friend, because you are not well enough disposed toward that country for anything that one might write you from there to affect you very agreeably, and since I was planning a trip to Holland, I thought that at least from here the dateline and the facts would interest you more. Indeed, nothing could interest you more keenly, I think, than the travel preparations of Mme d'Athlone, who is going to spend the summer with you. I sense all the delight that you must find in the visit of this charming cousin; so, whether she wished it or not, I could not keep myself from wanting to have some part in her travel arrangements. I gave her an itinerary—not the shortest, but the most convenient and the most pleasant, and I think I have not done badly with it. It's better to have them arrive at your place pleased with their journey, a little dizzy from everything they have seen, and find all the charms of repose and country life in the bosom of your friendship, more subjects of conversation, fewer plans for things that must be seen. If they follow my advice, they will arrive by the northern end of Switzerland, and will come out through the south; when they arrive at your home they will have passed through Basel, Soleure, and Berne; they will already know Switzerland, and they will only have Lausanne and Berne left to visit. I think that this is better than to have them descend on Colombier in a rush, by some horrible road. I hope that you will forgive my suggesting to them this longer route. Besides, one is always allowed to think of oneself a little: I hope to pay my respects to my friend's cousin when she comes to Huningue around the fifteenth or sixteenth of June.

I found the Hague, as well as its inhabitants, quite unchanged; little in the way of gaiety, its usual bad taste, and men who do not deserve the women they might live with—or rather women who don't require much merit in order be pleased. Dutch women have always pleased me, and (I say it even in

---

4. She does in fact go to see Voltaire five years later and recounts that rather disappointing visit in a letter to her brother Vincent (Letter 472 in *O.C.* 2: 339).

Paris) I prefer them to Frenchwomen. The Princess of Orange seems to me very amiable; the Prince is very kind and quite young. I think that he has the makings of a man; he is polite and cheerful. What a pity that he doesn't have around him amiable and reliable people whom he can trust! I am spending only a few days here, and I am returning to my regiment by way of Paris and Bellegrange. I am content with my travels, although I am bringing back nothing essential; but to see old friends again and cultivate new patrons without undergoing mortifications or abasing oneself is of great value to me.

You speak to me in an marvelously syrupy manner about everything that you have seen in Lausanne. What amiable, witty people! I couldn't help saying to your cousin that for the first time in your life you have descended into insipidity. But since you pride yourself on disdaining Voltaire, it was right that you be enchanted with Lausanne; the one is only a quixotism of the mind, the other comes from kindness of heart. People received you warmly, and you saw everything in its best light—that's only natural. Besides, it's certainly true that the people who want to please us or charm us are always witty; in our eyes, they have already shown a great deal of wit simply by wanting to please us. I am not at all unjust in this respect, and I myself am always the first to be taken in. But what must flatter you is that you please people whom you had no desire to please. In Paris, where I was told that you had done your worst to appear singular, where you affected a disdain for France and the French—well, you got what you deserved! While you were deigning to think of me and I received your letter, I was busy defending you and making you known as you truly are, and I had the satisfaction of hearing one of your critics say: "Even so, I would like to be on good terms with her, and see her often"—it was a woman who was saying this—"Her mind is like none I have ever found anywhere, and you say that she has an excellent and simple heart; so she's a treasure, this woman, whom one would be fortunate to make one's friend; why then didn't I like her?" I answered: "Because she had the little foible of finding it an excellent thing to displease people in France."

I am leaving you, my good friend, to go pay some calls. Be kind enough to send me news of you at Bellegrange the 10th or 11th of June. And please do justice to my affection, and to the admiration and respect with which I am at your feet.

429. *From Constant d'Hermenches, September 30, 1772*

Huningue

I was quite nonplussed when I arrived at Soleure to learn that your cousin had passed through as swiftly as a cat on hot coals; but such is your power, sublime Agnes! When it is a question of you, nothing can be stopped, and people are carried away as if borne on the wind. Bâle and Soleure were, nonetheless, two very good cities to rest in for a few days, and I had made my little arrangements with that idea in mind. In spite of this, I congratulate you on the happiness that you must be enjoying with your closest friend. I would have done the same as she did; I know of no pleasure more delightful that of seeing and hearing you!

All my journeys were very agreeable; I will tell you nothing of Holland, now that Milady is with you. I passed through Ferney again, where neither my friend nor his faults have aged in the slightest, and both still make the same impression on me. I stopped by my country place, which will be superb of its kind, even when I have just seen the splendors of other lands. And now here I am in Huningue, where I must do the honors of host, with the help of Sophie and a good French cook whom I've brought with me; quite airy accommodations, with a great many windowpanes, a great many letters piled up, and a few books; I have the intention of taking up music and even singing again—but you're too busy with your guests for me to chatter away at you any longer.

I am at your feet, Madame, the wittiest and most lovable of women!

PS I beg you to convey my regrets to Milord and Milady, and to thank Milord for his courtesy in telling me of his arrival at your house.

432. *To Constant d'Hermenches, September 30, 1772*

Colombier

Where are you just now? Monsieur Chaillet doesn't know. People in Lausanne have told me that you were expected there any day, but no one knew which day. However, I don't want to put off writing you any longer, and I'll think about the address when my letter is done. You pardoned me for my silence while Lady Athlone was here; you must pardon me for it again, for my brother is visiting me. He is sometimes so sick, and when he is better he is so pleasant to be with, that it's only natural for me to concern myself only with him. That doesn't mean that I'm forgetting you—on the contrary, I think very often about you. I wish that it were always agreeably, and that I might always admire your conduct and your destiny; but it would be asking too much of friends if one needed *only* to rejoice with them, *only* take pride in them. "Everything is mingled with bitterness and charms." [1]

You reproach me for judging *others* too severely; really, you do me wrong. I judge neither rigorously nor indulgently—I don't judge at all. I don't bother about other people's affairs except when I absolutely can't avoid it. The least plant in my garden, the slightest thing to be done around

---

1. Belle had quoted this line from La Fontaine's *Fables* once before back in September of 1765 (Letter 212).

my house, a floorboard or a lock in my new room, occupy me more than all the judgments, all the assessments of conduct, and all the gossip in the world.

I had been slightly put off, I admit, by the display of sentiments and emotion that you made to me about your divorce. I told you frankly what I thought, and since up until now you had never been angered by my sincerity, I was not wrong to do so. But I was wrong in this: since I was very busy when I wrote you, I didn't have the time to soften what I wanted to tell you; I was terse because I was busy, and what is terse can sound harsh when one's mind is unfavorably disposed. I should have put off writing, and should have written only when I was free to do so. I beg your pardon for my dry, hard sentences.

You think that I'm condemning you to spend the rest of your life in sad and sorry reflections! My God! if you are only half as happy as I want you to be, you will be happier than you ever have been! If you take a wife, may you be happy together. I would take so much pleasure in saying: "See, he's a good husband, he's easy-going, gentle, content!"

But here is one thing I require—and my brother, whom you know and respect, and who knows the laws of honor and probity and prudence, requires it also: if you marry, then before your contract is signed you will send me back my letters, *all* of them. A new young wife is the most seductive mistress one can have; next to her, an old friend is nothing. In a word, I require it; and a person who has shown you so much friendship for so long with so much frankness, zeal, and constancy, in spite of absence and distance, in spite of so much opposition and so much gossip, must not demand in vain something on which her peace of mind depends. Goodbye.

PS My brother, whom I'm having read my letter, laughs at my ponderousness at the end: "opposition ...," "on which my peace of mind depends ...," etc. But he finds the rest very good and very necessary and conforming exactly to what he and I had agreed upon. We are not asking for these letters so expressly unless you marry, because we are persuaded that you have taken and will always take—except for that one case—the care necessary to assure that they will never be read by anybody. You know how stupid and ridiculous they would appear.

My brother sends his compliments. He asked me to send him your answer. My husband is slightly ill, but I hope it will be nothing.

435. *To Constant d'Hermenches, November 27, 1772*

Friday after supper

For tomorrow, November 27 or 28

I have received pleasant news of you, my dear d'Hermenches. M. Chaillet ran over here this evening, still in his boots; he had just arrived. He told me that you were very well, that you were in very good spirits, that he had greatly enjoyed himself at your house, that the atmosphere was extremely pleasant, that you were surrounded by three amiable young persons who are fond of each other and who are as content in your château as they could be in the midst of the pleasures of a great city. This picture pleased me, and I dwelt on it a long time. What a joy it is to imagine one's friends happy, and happy in a way that one can feel and share!

I asked M. Chaillet what he had said to you about me; he told you that I went out very little, and that I was often alone with my books and my hand-work. It so happened that he found me alone at just that moment with my chambermaid—she was folding shirts, I was doing embroidery. During the day I am rarely alone, but in the evening it's what I like best. Monsieur de Charrière was playing at tarot at Mme Chaillet's, while her son was over here talking to me about you; then we met up very pleasantly at supper, each of us having spent the evening the way he wished. What you like to do is to hunt from nine or ten until six, then to dine until eight, and to chat un-til midnight. That seems to me quite a sensible way to live. Chaillet said that he refused to leave Hermenches for a ball in Lausanne. It seems to me that he was right; I would have done the same thing. He says that your daughter, Constance, is gentle, docile, a little timid; that she has a very pleasant voice, and that one can see, when she is at all at ease, that she is very intelligent: I was pleased to hear all that; and how good it is that she loves Sophie.

Two months ago someone described to me, with much pathos, Madame d'Hermenches' dying. I was very sorry because of public opinion, and espe-cially because of your own feelings. If that had happened so close upon the divorce, it would have been an unpleasant memory for the rest of your life. Monsieur Tissot came to Colombier some time later and told me that she was neither dead nor dying; I asked for news from M. Chaillet, and it turns out that she is at the theatre from two o'clock until eight. I laughed at my own credulity and fear.[1]

You say you haven't received the letter I had given my brother to give to you; that's very strange! He writes me from Lausanne that you were ex-pected there, and that you would receive my letter when you arrived. Could he have kept it? Could he have put it in unsafe hands? I beg you to find out; it would be most unpleasant if it were to be read by anyone other than you. In it I told you why I was so brusque and terse in my earlier letter, and I asked your pardon. Then I answered a note that you had written me; I wished you a good wife, and for that wife, a good husband, etc., and I told you that if you were to remarry you must send me back all my letters; that this was my brother's opinion, because in such circumstances a wife is the most seductive of mistresses, and in such a case an old friend is nothing, so

1. Mme d'Hermenches had in fact died September 19, 1772.

that these letters would not be safe, and I would have reason to worry; and thereupon I pointed out to you how ridiculous my letters would look in the hands of strangers. It would be inexcusable of my brother, who had read all that, not to have taken care of the packet. I implore you to find out about it—we absolutely must recover it.

Goodbye, my dear friend. I have only old letters from my brother. I have good news from my cousin. Good night.

436. *From Constant d'Hermenches, December 2, 1772*

Bellegrange

I have come here expressly, Madame, to conduct a search for the letter that your brother has taken the trouble to bring. It is here in a desk, securely sealed. It had been so especially brought to the attention of my secretary that he locked it in the desk to which he had the key, waiting for my return. The key had then been sent to me at Hermenches, so that I had to be here for it to be used. Are you now unjust enough to believe that your letters, which will always be my happiness and my admiration, could ever give you cause for anxiety? I have not kept a single one that you could not hand over to the printer. All the others—just as worthy of being printed, but not appropriate for moments other than the time of their writing—I have burned, in accordance with our old agreements.[1] However, everything that I have of your writing will always be subject to your orders, my dear friend, you may rest assured. I am distressed by all these reasonings, motives—threats, almost; but I will no less be ever obedient and adoring. I have more reason to ask you to return my feeble writings; the chaos that reigns in them, the outpouring of trust that you have inspired in me and that often exhibits my worst aspects, the self-examination they would impose on me, would make them useful to me; they are perfectly useless to you.

I'm very grateful to Chaillet for coming to see me, and for having conveyed my respects to you. The proximity that he has the good fortune to enjoy makes him very interesting to me, and I believe that some emanation from your wit and your amiability has exalted him. While he was a very unremarkable man in the regiment, we found him extremely likeable here, and Sophie said triumphantly: "I told you, Monsieur, our tall Chaillet is a man of wit!" He painted for you a favorable portrait of my way of life; you make me love it by your approval, and I found his picture fair enough.

I have even made so bold as to mark out a place for you in this circle in my château, but right away the thought of your connections with the Sublimities of Lausanne thrust me again into the void, where you will always leave me so long as you breathe the atmosphere of the Swiss Welches.[2] I

1. Obviously he did not.
2. "Welches" or "Velches" is the cognate of "Welsh." It was used by German-speaking

have a very beautiful country seat; a place which, I think, would charm you; but never, I'm quite sure of it, will I have the favor of receiving you here into that ease, that cordiality which is the base of my existence, and which I have never been able to communicate to anybody in this finicking country. What a benefit you would be for me—and for Constance! You would give her an aversion to the dissimulation that I fear flows in her veins; you would teach her that a woman's wit does not consist in epigrams, and even less in maxims, and that at a certain age one very much needs to be natural and even to babble a bit. You would perhaps say "How good it is that Sophie loves Constance," because you yourself would not disdain being loved by Sophie.[3] As for me, I would always be as you have always known me—the truest of your partisans, and the most tender, the most sincere, and the most respectful of your friends.

437. *To Constant d'Hermenches, February 14, 1773*

Colombier

They say that your son has been promoted. Although I have no direct news of it, I believe it, because I very much wish it; it was high time that something pleasant happened to you, and that your friends might for once rejoice on your account! This promotion has come at just the right moment to distract your son, and console him for the death of his mother, to whom, I have always heard, he was very attached.[1] I didn't write to you about that, although I was more touched by it than anyone: I didn't know what it was fitting to say.

I have been to Berne; it's a beautiful city, and I was able to do as I pleased there. I liked seeing the prosperity of the people, the abundance of the markets, the cleanliness of the streets, etc. These people manage their households well, and that is a pleasure to see. I am very fond of Mme Stürler, and I often stayed with her; however, I saw the Moderns as well as the Ancients—at any rate, a few Moderns.[2] I was taken to a very fine concert at the home of the Gross ladies; I think it was somewhat in honor of you. Madame Frisching admires you a great deal, and I too have made a conquest of her. I find her as beautiful as a sultan's favorite.

I have often seen M. Wilhelmi, and I have been very pleased.[3] Monsieur

---

peoples to refer to the French and to Latin peoples in general. Voltaire frequently used it as a code word for the French when he wanted to tax them with stupidity, bigotry, and fanaticism.

3. In Letter 435 Belle had said, "How good it is that [Constance] loves Sophie."

1. His mother had died five months earlier.

2. She means she had seen young people as well as the older ones she mentions. This is word-play on a famous literary dispute of the late seventeenth century, the Quarrel of the Ancients and the Moderns: could modern poets and thinkers hope to equal or surpass those of classical antiquity—was progress in creativity possible?

3. There had been discussion of Wilhelmi in Letters 418, 419, and 420.

de Charrière judges of him as I do: each time we have seen him, we have thought better and better of him. I am persuaded that his mind is of the best quality, and that he has a kind and sensitive heart, so that I can now entirely agree with you about him. You told me that he was the most interesting acquaintance that you had in Switzerland; if circumstances were to bring us closer, I think that I would soon say the same. I have seen M. de Bonstetten; he is amiable, and he recounts the slightest things with a very pleasing grace and finesse. Do you know M. Zimmermann, his viola d'amore and his violin? Except for Lolli, I have heard nothing as agreeable.

Speaking of music, my brother is happy to be in Naples; the air suits him, and he's enjoying himself. There is a French theater there for the first time; d'Aufresne is the director. The price of French dictionaries and grammars has risen sharply, and while the public can't yet understand these actors, they get a great deal of applause.

Don't you find that I'm writing like a gazette? Never mind; that's my mood today, and I'll continue.

Now I come to the Netherlands. M. de Chasteler is in Brussels and Madame in Utrecht. He has gambled a great deal and lost a great deal. She has paid out some rather large sums, but she has let it be known that she would no longer cover his debts in the future; according to her marriage contract she can do that. Her health is still fragile; Madame d'Athlone is attached to her and gives her all possible care; my father also takes care of her and her affairs. I am as fond of her as ever, and her troubles distress me. I think about her often, and when I see her surrounded by the people I love the most, and cherished by them, I feel both pity and pleasure. I am hoping that she will be protected from her husband as much as possible, and that she will resign herself to the inevitable unpleasantnesses. She will always be rich, kind, amiable, beloved; she has two sons, so she has many resources and consolations.

It has been extremely cold here; I think it must have been the same where you are. I have a cold; that separates me more than ever from the world and from Neuchâtel. Nevertheless, I went to the theatre; that's the first time that I've seen a society troupe. It isn't bad, but it lacks warmth; the *opéras-comiques* lend themselves a little more to illusion than these comedies in which from one end to the other you see Monsieur and Madame Such-and-Such, rather than the characters of the play. They played *The Unforeseen Wager*.[4] Madame du Peyrou astonished me by the dignity, the finesse, and the ease of her acting; she has a noble countenance and a clear diction, so that she has everything she needs to be an excellent Mme Préville. The tall Chaillet is no longer here; he's in Neuchâtel.

I do a great deal of handwork; I read a little. I read M. de Bougainville with a great deal of pleasure.[5] I have in hand one old book or another; it's

4. *La Gageure imprévue* by Michel-Jean Sedaine (1768).
5. Louis-Antoine de Bougainville (1729–1811) commanded the first French expedition around

an idle amusement. I'm not bored; Monsieur de Charrière is too amiable and I love him too much for me to be bored near him. If it weren't for my nerves, which quite often trouble me, I would be still happier.

I said to you: *How good it is that Constance loves Sophie;* I meant: *How fortunate* ..., and I did not think that the friendship of the one proved more in favor of the other nor did her more honor than the affection of the former would do for the latter. You speak to me of the dissimulation that you fear your daughter is inclined to; you say that I would make her detest it. No doubt; but that would have no effect without your leniency. When the strong are despotic, one can hardly blame the weak for being dissimulating, sly, and cunning. A weak person has a will just as a strong person does, and has desires that are just as keen. To obtain what he desires or prevent what he fears, he resorts to craft: that's only natural. Spiders, children, and women can act neither like lions nor like men. I think that leniency will prevent dissimulation, and that extreme leniency and kindness can destroy it in a young person. After a certain time, I think, the malady becomes incurable—especially with women. They can no longer become truthful; dissembling is their favorite practice, and they often intrigue for the pleasure of intriguing; it fills their leisure and, they think, puts some spice in their life ... but what nonsense I'm talking! The only thing that is true in all this chatter is that if you want your daughter to be truthful with you, you must win her confidence, grant her what she asks for without her needing to be artful to obtain it; and you must correct and demand only with the greatest gentleness. Since she is very young, I think you will succeed with that; without it, never. If you delay, her habits will have taken hold.

Goodbye. This has begun like a gazette and ended like a sermon. How I pity you for receiving such a letter!

439. *To Constant d'Hermenches, March 3, 1773*

I did very well not to write to you about the death of Madame d'Hermenches. If I had congratulated you, you would have been angry; if I had expressed pity, you would make fun of me. I had the wit to remain silent.

In spite of all *your* wit, you are assuredly mistaken on one point. You think that it would be a precious and agreeable thing for you to see me often, and I am convinced of the contrary. I am becoming simple in my conduct and in my speech to the point of insipidity; I set no store by wit either in myself or in others. That brilliant turn you give to whatever you do, that favorable light in which you always place yourself, would first excite my

---

the world (1766–69). His *Voyage autour du monde* was published in 1771. The image of Tahiti presented there was the basis of Diderot's *Supplément au Voyage de Bougainville* (written in 1772, published in 1786).

attention and very often my criticism, and I would seem to you given over to *finickiness;* soon I would no longer say anything, and that would bore you. You often complain of finicky people, yet it seems to me that friendship unavoidably depends on minutiae; nothing escapes it, nothing is indifferent to it. A gesture, a word from my husband, from my brother, or from Mme d'Athlone seems to me an essential thing. If they are wrong in a single word it disturbs me, for it comes from them by some fault or error; they must explain themselves, whether they confess or whether they justify themselves. With those who don't interest me much, I let anything slip by; with my friends, I stop at every little thing; I cannot do without approving of them and respecting them ... but why am I holding forth about myself?

I'm very glad that M. Wilhelmi likes me, because I like him very much. The beautiful Mme Frisching is in Fribourg. She would like to have her husband ask for the divorce that she has desired for a long time; people claim that he will make no move in that direction; people feel sorry for her for being so unhappily married, and pushed by her unhappiness into missteps ... You undoubtedly know all that, for I believe she writes to you. You also know of the death of Mme de Reede[1] and her mother; your son will not have let you remain unaware of these tragic events. A husband left desolate, three little children, a mother who dies of grief—all of that is sad indeed.

Madame d'Athlone was at the Hague. She felt all this keenly.

I came back yesterday from Neuchâtel, where I had spent eight or ten days. There was a very charming performance of *Lucile*, and the *Sylvain* was ravishing.[2]

Goodbye, it's late; I preferred writing you only a dull, grumpy little letter to putting off answering you any longer. I know Mme Cazenove only by sight. Tell me how M. de Voltaire is doing, and whether he is likely to recover.

I have no plan for the spring, except for a few walks and some reading. I read with pleasure what you wrote me about your daughter.

440. *From Constant d'Hermenches, March 12, 1773*

Fantaisie

To hear you, my lovely lady, do you know that one could not doubt that I am—I won't say a coxcomb, but—conceited? And if you assure me that you find me so, do you know that I will not doubt it, such an oracle you are to me! And then there will be nothing for it but for me to try to correct myself.

1. This is Heiltje de Parc, whose marriage to M. de Reede, the brother-in-law of Madame d'Athlone (Annebetje), had been described with amusement in Belle's Letter 317.
2. Both of these are plays by Marmontel.

Speak to me seriously then! To be frank and to have a great deal of wit is not enough; one must also have pity—yes, if I always place myself in a favorable light, you mustn't overlook it, and you must bring me back to what is true and natural; I ask it of you as a favor, and I speak to you very seriously, my dear friend. Within myself I feel that in everything I do I try to do what is best according to my lights; I feel that since what I do is nearly always blamed at first glance, I try to present it not in what I deem its most favorable guise, but in the guise that justifies and explains my intention and my motives. But if you have perceived that I always want to shine, if you have noticed "charlatanism" or ruse in my way of placing myself, then I displease myself, and I wish not to have this fault—just as I do not want, out of some false modesty, to have it said of me that I am modest, or draw an advantage from a feigned ignorance of my advantages ... Don't answer this long litany if it doesn't suit you at the moment. I don't know why I began with that passage of your letter.

It's only today that I'm able to give you reliable news of Voltaire. In Geneva they were giving him out to be dead; Madame Denis[1] wrote to me that he was out of danger. It is certain that he has no more fever, and that there are no more complications, but the great illness remains—that is, his age and that abominable north wind.

How are the delicate nerves of the excellent Agnes managing it? As for me, the wind is killing me; all my arteries have been beating so hard for the last two weeks that they are distinctly visible. It's a springtime nuisance, this double dose of all those particles from the Alps and the lakes that come pounding against us in this rough Swiss climate—which people are mad enough to sing of and to seek out, and which I often curse. All things considered, long live our thick, humid air of the Hague, Utrecht, etc. It's more sociable there: the North Wind doesn't cut the face with biting blades, and the South Wind never shatters the windows with icy shards. The more beautiful I find my place, the more successful "Fantaisie" has been, the more I am furious that one can live in this region neither in summer nor in winter!

Do you find this declamation finicky enough? I defy little Hop or Cazenove Bengale to do better! And there, for example, is something in which you are wrong, perhaps for the first time in your life; I would adore you for your minutiae. My God! It's what I would like to live for—the little daily trifles; the details; the cause of the cause—with someone who has some soul. I am in despair at finding now in the world only free-thinkers or philosophers, who don't pay attention to little things, who don't notice whether it's a little warmer, or a little colder. That's what I quarrel about all day with Constance, with Sophie; I would like them to be alert to the least wrinkle of my brow; because the slightest expression, a gesture, a little change in their voice, a glance that falls a little to one side, makes me think

1. Voltaire's niece, sometimes mistress, and long-term companion.

and disturbs me, and I would like to have a long conversation about it. It's precisely for that sort of thing that I could never leave you! Unless I were carried away, as the post is about to carry away this unfinished letter.

446. *From Constant d'Hermenches, June 12, 1773*

Bitche[1]

It seems quite clear to me, most lovable Agnes, that you no longer care about me, and that our friendship will go its way no better than the other things of this world; still, I go on loving you, and placing you above everything else that I know. I still take care to inquire for news of you wherever I can—from my lieutenant who is your cousin by marriage, and from the tall Chaillet, your neighbor. I'm not gathering much, except that you are becoming very reasonable, for you are dining at half past twelve. They also say you are going to Holland; that's very sensible, I think, for all things considered, once the first enthusiasm has passed—whether for Mount Jura, or the Alps—I think that Neuchâtel, Colombier, etc. (let alone Lausanne, the stupidest place of all!) could not satisfy hearts like ours. Tiresome dialogues, sad little talents, deceptive resources: our country is only good for misers, invalids, or little *beaux esprits*. I can see this all the way from Bitche—which you'd think would be worse, except that here, by my present way of thinking, the absence of all pretension covers a multitude of sins. I prefer these men and women of German Lorraine, who don't have a single book; who eat whatever I give them with a delightful appetite; who laugh at my platitudes; who have fine hair and teeth; who either prove their nobility by the Chapters[2] or else make no claim to it; and who never have pneumonia. My daughter likes it here very well, and is not wasting her time; she is learning the politeness that is absolutely unknown in Welche Switzerland, where everything is sham and haggling. She reads, she does handwork, she takes walks, and in the evenings we choose a few guests from the officer corps. That's the only hour when I find it sad to be alone—I have the use of a big garden where I give my suppers.

I have told you what I have heard of you. You will tell me, if you please, what you have heard about me; if you can't resist it, you may add your censures. I think very often about death; I don't know why. It affects my thoughts on the future, on the demon of ambition, on fortune, on everyday cares, on the falsity of men, on the infirmities of old age. What madness to torment oneself, to write letters, to pay court! ... We must die, and that will be that. If I didn't think that way, I would not be happy without my own regiment. I might be interested in joining up with a woman who was good-natured and unaffected, who had the means to support herself, to

---

1. A garrison town in northern Lorraine.
2. Meetings of the chivalric orders.

whom I would teach all the skills that I'm forgetting; but I want no mistress, and new conquests even less. I would like to make my children happy and philosophical, and get them interested; and when I bore them, let them go their way—I will find someone else to educate. I'll dictate the reflections of my old age to some old friend, take some opium for sleep, and let Atropos do her work ...[3] Why am I writing all this to you? I have no idea. I'm in my garden, I'm about to go and drill my regiment; perhaps this hodgepodge will furnish you with a thousand witty ideas, and I have spent a very pleasant moment with you.

Do me a favor, Madame, if you please! Send me by return mail everything you know of a M. Caneau, a pensioned officer from the regiment of Budé, established near Utrecht, married to a widow Broeckhuysen; he's a sort of adventurer, isn't he? Does he get a fortune from his wife? He is writing to some people here that he has an only daughter whom he wants to marry to their son; that his wife agrees to sell what she has in Holland to transfer the funds into Alsace, and that this son ought to set out right away. The idea of a Dutch marriage always makes people prick up their ears, and these people, who are of solid German nobility, ask me as a favor to give them advice and information. If you can't give me any, please be good enough to ask immediately in Utrecht.

I am at your feet.

℞ *On May 21, 1773, Ditie died of tuberculosis in Naples. In a letter to Vincent a month later, Belle, "If I loved my husband less, if I were less beloved by him, I don't know what would become of me, nor how I could endure what I am suffering. This loss will never be repaired. This bond, now broken, was one of the strongest and dearest that my heart has ever known ... I loved Ditie even more for my own sake than for his, for his pain no longer seems anything to me, and his death is unbearable."*[4]

449. *From Constant d'Hermenches, July 3, 1773*

Bitche

My dear, treasured friend! I am filled with the keenest pain; I shed tears as sincere as yours on the death of this human being who was so touching, so kind, so endearing! He was of a tempering too fine for the world to be worthy of him; he was one of those creatures who vanish quickly and are rarely seen. If he had had to live out the normal course of human nature, he would have had the normal faults and imperfections; we would not have

---

3. Of the three Fates who spin out human life, Atropos is the one who cuts the thread.
4. Letter 448 in *O.C.* 2: 308–9.

loved him as much, and there would have been less reason for your despair. I pity you; such a brother cannot be replaced (being a mere acquaintance, it's not myself I'm thinking of here). But Agnes, it's our teeth, our hair, the freshness of youth, our serenity, our memory—they alone make us find happiness in living, they are our source of pride, and yet we survive them! These losses cannot be repaired; we grow accustomed to them, we're not even distressed by them. I hope that after these first moments, you will return to that point; that is what Providence wills. Instead of sharpening the pain by intensity of feeling, one must dull it by insensitivity—a dreadful maxim! but true and natural. It's a step that we ourselves already take toward annihilation; it's an homage that matter forces from us. Old men no longer know pains other than those of gout or the stone; those of the soul no longer touch them!

Console yourself, my dear Agnes, or rather find some distraction! This poor brother isn't to be pitied; there is certainly more evil than good in our existence, more labor than repose, more tedium than pleasure. Take care of your health, and live; your death would cause much more despair than his, you have more bonds with others than he did, and you are far more cherished. My daughter is literally weeping at my side; Sophie gazes at me and says: "My God, how I pity Madame de Charrière!" She had sometimes talked with your brother.

A thousand thanks to your husband for his letter; it has been burned, and I will make the most prudent use of the information that he has taken the trouble to give me. My humblest compliments to him; I am at your feet, my bereaved friend.

When you write to Monsieur d'Athlone, would you ask him what they know about the fortune of this Caneau?[1]

452. From Constant d'Hermenches, August 5, 1774

Spa

I have known some disappointments in my life, but none more painful than that of learning at Gravelines, through the tall M. Chaillet, that the friend I value the most in the world, and who seems to have forgotten me the most completely, was in Spa! I leave immediately to go there. To explain oneself in a third place, in a neutral country, seems to me in the best taste, and the quickest way to have a quarrel out. I arrive, and no friend! not even an enemy—no Agnes! ... There are only insipid acquaintances; they cry: "Well now! where are you coming from? We haven't seen you in a long time! You haven't changed a bit! Are you here for your health? Whom are you looking for? Delighted to see you again!" But no Agnes! And I— who had just torn myself away from my old and reliable friends in Brus-

---

1. The would-be father-in-law whom d'Hermenches inquired about in the last letter.

sels—I looked toward the door to make my escape, and I didn't know whom or how to ask for Madame de Charrière ... I must now take my chances and write her; let's try Utrecht. Are you going to Switzerland this year, Madame? At what time? What route will you take?

I am here until the twentieth. I'm having my son and daughter come here; they will follow their route through the Ardennes towards "Fantaisie" after having seen Spa, which I am finding delightful. I'm taking the waters so as not to have made a fruitless journey; I've had a vexing time of it this year in Paris, which makes this cure useful to me. I like life less every day, but every day I am gayer; every day I know the human heart a little better—sad knowledge! And every day I am more attached to you, so long as you still have the same mind and the same heart; you will never find any being, man or woman, who better deserves that you treat him as your friend than d'Hermenches.

453. *To Constant d'Hermenches, August 16, 1774*

Zuylen

I would be in Spa right now if my father had wanted to go there. We half thought that was his intention, and perhaps I had spoken of it in the spring as a likely thing; word of it must have got back (I don't know how) to the tall Chaillet, and that's the source of your mistake. If it had made you take a longer or more disagreeable journey than from Brussels to Spa, I would be most distressed; but since it's a very pretty little trip, at the end of which you found baths that are good for you, a charming place to stay, and people delighted to see you again, I'm glad I drew you there even without my being there myself, and I would be even more pleased if I had been. We would not have *explained ourselves*, because we haven't quarreled at all, nor has our friendship cooled.

Your last letter was filled with feeling over the death of my brother; I read it with gratitude. I didn't reply because for a very long time I was in no state to write at all, and since then I have had nothing interesting to tell you. My life has flowed gently and evenly amidst my family, and was hardly troubled or altered except by a neuralgia, the description of which would have made you pity me as much as my amusements would have bored you. I may be presentable enough for tranquil folk who are already fond of me, but it is impossible for me to inspire the slightest interest in the rest of the world. Madame d'Athlone, seeing me read your letter, said to me: "I love Monsieur d'Hermenches for being your eternal admirer." "Yes," I said. "Since we have always been at a distance from each other, what you call admiration has been able to last; but if he were to see me for even two weeks ..." "Ah," she answered, "I agree that he might see things differently; especially now that you are so prodigiously grave and so thoroughly preoccupied with the ailments of your footman and your chambermaid that in order to please you he would have to become their doctor!"

See what a severe presentation of the most thoroughgoing dullness! And that from the lips of the person who, in all the world, is the most prejudiced in my favor. I am dull beyond redemption because I am not sorry to be so. My contempt for mankind is not increasing, but rather my indifference to their approval; that is, I have no desire to occupy their attention, to be noticed or applauded by them, but I am more afraid than ever of wounding them and being reprimanded. You see that all this can hardly result in a way of being that would seem very agreeable to you—you who are always all vivacity, all activity, all ambition. I would divert you as an old man of eighty could divert a lass of twenty.

There are a lot of us here just now—my sister and her husband with all their children, my sister-in-law with her children and her husband, and my youngest brother[1] who as yet has no wife. My father seems very happy to see us all gathered together and getting along so well, all of us content with each other. My husband is respected and cherished by my whole family; everyone applauds my choice and shares my feelings. Madame d'Athlone doesn't let a day pass without seeing me. In the spring she settled in the village of Zuylen, but since she couldn't stay in the house she was living in after the first of August, she returned to Utrecht and has given up the countryside for this year. There are a great many friends, comforts, ties. However, we will soon have to leave: Monsieur de Charrière would like to be home before the grape harvest, and he's right. I don't yet know exactly when we will leave, nor what route we will take. Our servants are not too well; we may do very short days on the road to avoid over-tiring a young man who serves us and whom we are very fond of.

If you want to send me your *Paris vexations*, your plans, your projects, you will still find me discreet as in the old days, and in spite of my indifference " ... *pour la fortune, / Pour ses jeux, pour la pompe et la grandeur des rois* ...,"[2] the vanities that interest you will still interest me. In the past, I used to heap upon you reprimands and advice. Aside from the taste that I had for wit—for *your* wit—, for your letters—the most pleasurable anyone could receive—, I was foolish enough to believe that I would reform you, that I would make you wiser and happier; and that would make me keenly desire to maintain our connection. You said so many good things about me that I thought I was very clever, very eloquent, worthy of having the greatest influence over you. I thought for a long time that I would make you very [...],[3] then that I would at least prevent [...] then that I would persuade you to reduce your expenditures [...] I have learned to value

1. Vincent.
2. "To Fortune, / To its games, to the pomp and grandeur of kings." Adapted from La Fontaine, *Fables*, "Philémon et Baucis."
3. The elisions in this paragraph indicate illegible words crossed out in a different ink in the manuscript, presumably after the letter was received.

myself at my true worth. My zeal may have pleased you, but it has never governed you. It has kept silent since I have been convinced that [...], but my friendship is not extinguished; [...] I no longer have the same keenness in writing you that I once had, but I always have an interest in you.

There is another thing that diminishes my eagerness for our correspondence: I cannot think about writing you without thinking of my letters of the past, and that thought disturbs me. I do not remember ever having had anything dishonorable in my heart, but I know, in a general way, that I used to say everything I was thinking, and that I must have thought a great many foolish things that it was imprudent—and above all ridiculous—to say. That isn't serious enough for me to insist absolutely that you return my letters, and the request would seem to show a distrust of you that I do not feel. But on the other hand, since my marriage, everything that might wound my husband in the slightest has come to have the greatest importance to me, and so I write to you—the less willingly because I cannot write to you without recalling ideas that I would rather put far from me. There you have all the truth of my heart, all the causes of my silence; for my frankness is unchangeable, as is my friendship.

454. *From Constant d'Hermenches, June 18, 1775*

Aire[1]

The Marquis de Bellegarde sends me word, Madame, that he has had the good fortune of seeing you; that you are very amiable, very witty, and that you deigned to talk with him of me; so you are still yourself! And I believed you to be changed; I was in mourning for you ever since I received a certain letter from you when I was in Spa![2] That little servant fellow who prevented you from taking a long journey, ...those letters that you asked to have back and which—if I didn't have them—you should rather have rewritten as precious monuments of your genius and of the respect that our association has always deserved, ... those moralizing aphorisms, the currency with which an expiring friendship thinks it can pay off its debts—everything made me say: Alas, she is no more!... How sweet it would be for me to see you again before I die! New acquaintances mean little to me; besides, I know that I will never again encounter such a treasure of excellent things as your mind and your friendship can furnish. I have not changed in my heart; I am still unchangeably attached to you; I venerate your character, and my sincere wishes for your happiness and that of your husband will always faithfully follow you. But I have gained some philosophic wisdom; I think I now see mortals as they are, and appreciate all the relationships of life. I have fewer illusions, and consequently fewer dissatisfactions.

1. A city about thirty-five miles southeast of Calais.
2. Letter 453 of the previous summer.

I have left my "Fantaisie" retreat and my woods at Hermenches with infinite regret. I think that even if one had no obligations or projects, one would still have enough to do in fulfilling the duties to which an independent being can and must limit himself: to make the people around us as happy as possible; to do one's best not to be too great a burden on them when we reach old age; to enjoy life, and to laugh at everything that presents itself. Finding someone to love would be true happiness, but that is difficult; for loving out of vanity or as a mere dalliance or amusement is not for me. I want to love out of respect and sympathy and a mutual need for companionship. For a long time I have been confining myself to the care I give my daughter; if she has no striking gifts, I hope at least that she will be as free as possible of vices. I'm very glad for her sake that I kept my distance from the customs of Lausanne and from the way things go in novels: all our little ladies go through their fine passions, love letters, etc. So far she has been simply a very good, decent girl.

We are presently in Aire, a place that interested me through the traces of an illustrious origin: Rebecque is near here; my ancestors are known here through the annals of the Crusades. I'm living in the governmental palace, where there is a delightful garden; we play music, we have iced drinks, we read, we laugh, we can daydream under a lovely shade; and I command my soldiers; but the *point* of all this escapes me. Why all this convulsive effort? why go vegetate two hundred leagues from one's own field? Why make new acquaintances every day, new gestures of politeness? ...I am rather struck by the example of my chaplain; he was a robust, cheerful, healthy monk, an exemplary, devout man who preached eloquent sermons. He had some money, and everyone liked to supply him with burgundy, which he drank with pleasure. He read some book or other on suicide; he said that it was *ein verdammtes Buch,*[3] and then he read it again, the other day, without any evident distress. He was found dead on his bed; he had plunged his knife into his heart ... he left a roll of gold pieces on the table, marked *for my monastery* ... If ever I am found dead in that fashion, there will be, I think, on my portfolio: *for Agnes.*

Meanwhile, I am at your feet; please let me hear from you.

I would have some rather banal things to say to you about our old friend,[4] whom I saw again last year with a great deal of pleasure.

455. *To Constant d'Hermenches, July 12 or 13, 1775*

Zuylen

I am very glad that the Marquis de Bellegarde made you think of me, and in a more favorable manner than you were disposed to. I assure you that it

---

3. "A damned book."
4. Mme de Chasteler, formerly Mme Geelvinck—the Widow.

has never yet happened that I forget my friends—I mean *a friend* (the other expression is too vague); I have never yet ceased to take a lively interest in someone who had once interested me. In short, I think I am in all the world the person least guilty of inconstancy, and you are very wrong to be *in mourning* for a heart that is very much alive and for a friendship that will never die. My moralizing displeased you; that is all over, for several reasons; I will no longer bore you with it. You took it ill that I asked to have my letters back. I didn't ask to have them back; I only said to you that I would be more content and my mind more at ease and that I would write to you more willingly if you were willing to return them to me. You do not wish to do that, and you were distressed at what I said to you about it. That too is over now; I will say no more about it, and thus I hope you will be satisfied, that you will believe I still have some common sense, and that I am behaving approximately the same way I did when you honored me with your esteem.

You are fortunate to be so pleased with your daughter; as you describe her to me, she deserves to have you pleased with her. She is precisely what a daughter should be. Moreover, I see, happily, that one can arrive at the same goal by different paths. Here under one roof are we three[1] women whose upbringing and youth have been very different, and yet our husbands have nothing to complain about in any of us; the two others are very good mothers, and I flatter myself that I would be one too if God were to give me children.[2] It may well be that the young women of Lausanne whom you satirize will succeed very well in the end. I still find you a trifle mordant for a philosopher, but I like you that way, and if I saw in you that sweet and benign wisdom that makes one indulgent toward others and oneself and fortune, it would so thoroughly disorient me that your letters would no longer give me the same pleasure. For them to please me, I need still to recognize in them *you*, and find in them that salt that is yours alone—that mixture of gaiety and acerbity that gives all your descriptions such piquancy. When you tell me your opinions—calm, just, full of wisdom—you must still give me your exaggerated impressions in a fiery style; then I recognize you, I read avidly, and the longest letter seems short, much too short.

If you write me soon, address your letter to my father in Utrecht. I may have left for Switzerland; my departure may be very soon, or it may be delayed. In any case, your letter will be sent to me from here, and that will only delay it by a few days.

The story of your chaplain is very grim; I don't have time today to say anything else about it.

I said to Madame de Chasteler that I had received your news; she asked me to convey her compliments. She is more sensible and more amiable than

---

1. Mme d'Athlone (Annebetje) and Mitie are also at Zuylen.
2. It is at about this time that Belle is trying various kinds of remedies for her infertility.

she has ever been; that's all there is to say about her. Goodbye. I'm in a great hurry—I'm even afraid that my letter will arrive too late at the post; I would be greatly annoyed, since I have already delayed too long in answering you. I have seen so many people these days, I have been so taken up with farewells, trunks, etc., that I no longer know how to read or write.

456. *From Constant d'Hermenches, August 9, 1775*

Aire-en-Artois

Your response, Madame, has rekindled my existence, and makes me feel how precious are the bonds of an old friendship. How many fools place these relationships in the ranks of things that can be created or destroyed by circumstances! That's not at all the way I see it. It is as fortunate to have found once in one's lifetime a good and true friend—man or woman—as it is to have been endowed with a just mind or to have sound teeth or good eyes; one must do everything to preserve them. I have never done anything for you, but you have not been unaware of everything that I would have wanted to do. So please believe that if you deign to preserve for me sentiments that are distinct from the conventions of worldly liaisons and proprieties, then I am and will always be for you a friend and servant of such tempering as you will find nowhere else. Friendship, in my view, is like the finest wine; it needs ripening and aging to be its best. I have need of yours, for I no longer trust anyone in the world. Sick and tired of decrepitude and collapse, sick of what is either fickleness or ingratitude, sick of other needs or other motives—even with my many connections I understand how one can find oneself alone on the earth. Father and children, wife and husband stand too close to each other for friendship fully to spread its wings. Friends must be whole and separate entities who turn back, embrace each other again, separate voluntarily; who have something to bring back into the association—the sacrifice of other interests, reflections on other subjects, opposing ways of dealing with society; then, ah then, feeling triumphs, and does its work. I love my daughter tenderly, but why do I find Sophie's company more stimulating? It's because she is a being more like me, at least with respect to the world. Why does my son feel the same thing? If Stance[1] and Sophie were to fall in the water, I would certainly leap in to save Stance first; but if each of them comes to tell me something, on some neutral subject, my first impulse will be, I think, to listen first to Sophie. The bond between these two is a marvel in the history of human relations, and when Villars[2] is there, it's the Trinity.

You stopped me short, Madame, leaving me uncertain as to the place you are staying. It seems to me that it has an enormous influence on what one

1. His daughter Constance.
2. His son.

can write people; if you arrive in Switzerland, you will be an entirely different person. So many duties, recapitulations, concerns, different scenes, at least for a month! Leave my scribbling on your table without opening it. Will you be able to accustom yourself again to a country that is not made for you, or will you be able to put on once again the necessary costume for a completely different theater? I say theater, yes—for my fifty years are teaching me and have taught me well that one does nothing but play-act there; and that when one travels from Geneva passing through Lausanne, Yverdon and Neuchâtel, there aren't three persons to be found who behave naturally. At the moment it's your cousin De Sévery who is the Clairon of the region; as for poor Corcelles, she is now only a Dumesnil on one of her bad days;[3] and in France isn't it the same? There is no longer anyone who says what he thinks, or shows what he is; and as for these reputations that people make for themselves by a sort of concordat—these *honest souls*, these *good characters*, these *sensitive spirits*—, reality has no part in them. Flattery and tactics are the currency; whether yours is in gold ingots or paper, you will pass for whatever suits your society and according to how much you show them you appreciate them. That's also the reason why I'm not even fit to throw to the dogs; it's for that reason too that if you were to introduce me to a good-natured, unaffected woman who might want to keep me company, I would leave tomorrow to go seek her—I would like to attach myself to someone again before I die, and she would find herself in her element with us.

Earlier on I was saying that there's a kind of collapse in most of the people one has been connected with; it is frustrating when we encounter them again. What do you say about good old Bellegarde? Isn't that the story with him? I found he was still the same deep down; but that unhappy soul has been callused by living. Age makes people flaccid; they get used to accommodating to what they find around them, and then all those little points of feeling get worn down. That isn't yet the case with me, and I often suffer for it. Thus it is with rapture and veneration that I receive what comes from you, and that I write to you. I am at your feet.

I must still tell you that I am annoyed with the Chasteler woman, and I have my reasons: collapse indeed! She's just a fool.

℞ *In November 1775 d'Hermenches married Marie Taisne de Removal, a wealthy widow three years younger than Belle. Belle's father died on the first of September, 1776.*

---

3. Clairon and Dumesnil were two famous French actresses. Mme Corcelles, d'Hermenches' cousin, had been active in his and in Belle's circles when she first moved to Colombier.

464. *From Constant d'Hermenches, December 12, 1776*

Fantaisie

Can I inspire in you any sentiment other than pity, Madame, for the ignorance of a wretched garrison-slave who sees only the Paris gazette, and for the grotesque impropriety I committed in sending you bad poetry[1] and talking nonsense at a time when you were plunged into grief, and when my heart should have been torn with regrets over the loss you had just suffered! Only two days ago Monsieur de Penthaz,[2] who was doing me the honor of dining here, told us of your loss, because I asked him for news of you. I was filled with consternation, and I felt just how absurd you must have found me; I hope, however, that my good wishes and condolences, belated though they are, will still find grace with you.

Would it be adding one absurdity to another to propose that you come to distract yourself at "Fantaisie" with Monsieur de Charrière and your friend, with whom I was once acquainted, Monsieur de Salgas?[3] I think I can present to you a friend worthy of you,[4] perhaps a friend such as you have not yet found—except for Madame d'Athlone, of whom you have given me the highest impression. It is so rare that people meet who suit each other, and life is so short, that I thought that such a proposal could not be made too soon. "Fantaisie" is a dwelling where even in winter you will find comforts enough, and hearts eager to meet you and to know you well. Truly I have thought that one in your situation needs to go away for a while: when one is in a place where one has been extremely sad, that is the recipe for restoring one's cheerfulness—that's my experience.

While I await your orders, please receive all the respectful homage of your very humble and faithful servant.

ଓଃ *So far as we know, this was d'Hermenches' last letter to Isabelle de Charrière, and it was never answered. Since her letters to him have come down to us through his estate, we know that he did not comply with her stipulation in Letter 432 that he return them if he ever remarried.*

His second wife bore him a son in 1777 and died in 1779. David-Louis, Baron de Constant de Rebecque, Seigneur d'Hermenches et de Villars-Mendraz, died in Paris in 1785—the year in which Isabelle de Charrière published Lettres écrites de Lausanne.

1. Perhaps a poem entitled "On my Marriage," which he sent to Voltaire. The letter to Belle with which the poem was included is not extant.
2. M. de Charrière's father.
3. Salgas had been instrumental in negotiating Belle's marriage to Charrière.
4. His new wife.

PEOPLE MENTIONED IN THE LETTERS

ANHALT-DESSAU, Friedrich, Count of (1732–94). Aide-de-camp and then adjutant general of King Frederick II of Prussia (Frederick the Great). He was briefly interested in marrying Belle but never came to see her. Eventually he left Prussia and entered the service of Empress Catherine of Russia (Catherine the Great).

ANNEBETJE. See TUYLL VAN SEROOSKERKEN, ANNA ELISABETH CHRISTINA under TUYLL VAN SEROOSKERKEN, Jan Maximiliaan.

D'ARENBERG, Charles-Leopold-Marie-Raymond, Duc (1721–78). Field marshall and colonel; owner of a regiment in the service of the empire. He and his wife, Louise-Marguerite de la Marck (1730–1820), were among the best friends of Constant d'Hermenches and often received him at their chateau in Enghien.

ATHLONE, Count and Countess of. See REEDE, Frederik Christiaan Reinhard.

BELLEGARDE, François-Eugène-Robert Noyel, Marquis de (1720–90). Major general of a regiment in the service of the United Provinces, from a distinguished Savoyard family. He was a close friend of Constant d'Hermenches, who tried to arrange a marriage between him and Belle de Zuylen. The negotiations lasted four years (1764–68). Bellegarde married in 1770 and had three daughters.

BENTINCK VAN RHOON, Antoine or Anthony, Count (1734–68). He was the son of Willem Bentinck, one of the most influential men in Dutch politics. In 1760 Anthony Bentinck married Belle's paternal cousin Marie Catharina van Tuyll van Serooskerken, the sister of Belle's favorite cousin Annebetje.

BENTINCK VAN RHOON, Johan Albert, Count (1737–75). Brother of Anthony. He married another paternal cousin of Belle's, Reiniera, and lived in England, where Belle visited them in 1767.

BOSWELL, James (1740–95). Scottish writer; son of a judge, Lord Auchinleck. Boswell came to Utrecht in 1763 to study law for a year. He became a friend of the Tuylls and a suitor and correspondent of Belle. His *An Account of Corsica* (1768) first brought him fame and influenced the response to the Corsican question all over Europe. He is best known today for his classic of biographical art, *The Life of Samuel Johnson* (1791).

BRÖMBSE, Christian von, Baron (1742–1808). One of Belle's suitors. Her initial impression of him had been fairly favorable; later she received a report about him, the content of which is unknown but which apparently disqualified him utterly. He became burgermeister of Lübeck.

BRUNSWICK-WOLFENBÜTTEL, Ludwig Ernst, Duke of (1718–88). Captain general of the military forces in Holland; guardian and advisor to the Prince of Orange.

CATT, Henri-Alexandre de (1725–95). Tutor to Belle's brothers. When King Frederick II of Prussia visited Holland, he talked to Catt and became interested in Belle's situation. Catt was invited by Frederick to Berlin as a royal lector or reader and tried to arrange a marriage between Belle and the count of Anhalt.

CHARRIÈRE DE PENTHAZ, Charles-Emmanuel de (1735–1808). Born in Colombier near Neuchâtel, he went to Holland and became tutor to Belle's brothers. She married him in 1771 and went to live in his manor-house, Le Pontet, with his father and two unmarried sisters.

CHASTELER. See GEELVINCK, Catherina Elisabeth Hasselaer.

CHOISEUL, Etienne-François de, Duc de (1719–85). One of the most distinguished French political and military figures of his time. After the defeat of France in the Seven Years' War Choiseul undertook a major reform of France's army and marine forces. He was minister of war and foreign affairs during France's acquisition of Corsica in 1768–69. He fell from power in 1770.

CONSTANT, Constance Louise de (1755–1825). Daughter of Constant d'Hermenches by his first wife.

CONSTANT D'HERMENCHES, Louise-Anna-Jeanne-Françoise de, née Seigneux (1715–1772). First wife of Constant d'Hermenches, whom he married in 1744.

CONSTANT D'HERMENCHES, Marie-Catherine-Philippine de, née Taisne de Remonval (d. 1779). Second wife of Constnat d'Hermenches, whom he married in 1776.

CONSTANT DE VILLARS, Guillaume-Anne de (1750–1838). Son of Constant d'Hermenches by his first wife.

DEGENFELD, Louise Suzanne de Nassau, Countess of (1726–1803). The wife of Count Frederick Christian of Degenfeld Schonburg, a major-general in the Dutch army and later minister plenipotentary of the United Provinces at the court of Vienna.

DITIE. See DIEDERIK JACOB, under TUYLL VAN SEROOSKERKEN VAN, Diederik Jacob.

DUFEY, Sophie-Jeanne-Louise Joly (1753–1841). Illegitimate daughter of Constant d'Hermenches; he made her his heir along with his legitimate children.

GEELVINCK, Catherina Elisabeth Hasselaer (1738–92). Often called "the Widow"; a famous beauty, the daughter of a rich Amsterdam merchant family. She was a first cousin of Mme Hasselaer, a close friend of Belle's, and often a go-between in Belle's correspondence with d'Hermenches. Her first husband, Lieve Geelvinck, died in 1757. Ten years later she married the Marquis François de Chasteler, who was six years younger. She was divorced in 1777 and in 1790 married once again.

GOLOFKINE, Gabriel, Count of. Colonel in the Swiss Guards and an adjutant of Prince Willem V. He bought d'Hermenches' regiment in 1764. His brother Pierre was also in the military service in Holland.

HASSELAER, Susanna Hasselaer (1734–1809). First cousin of Mme Geelvinck; wife of a burgomaster of Amsterdam, who was also her cousin, so that her maiden name and married name are the same. Belle made several visits to their country house "Westerhout" in Wijk aan Zee. She later married the lawyer Jan Bost.

LA SARRAZ, Henri de (1709–65). Officer in the Swiss Guards; friend of d'Hermenches.

MAASDAM, Aarnoud van der Duyn, Baron van (1718–85). Lieutenant general of Cavalry and governor of Breda; friend of Constant d'Hermenches and of Belle, who wrote a satirical poem about him.

MITIE. See JOHANNA MARIA, under TUYLL VAN SEROOSKERKEN, Diederik Jacob, Baron van.

OBDAM: see WASSENAER VAN OBDAM, Jacob.

PALLANDT, Adolf Werner Carel Willem van, Baron (1733–1813). Burgomaster of Doesburg. He was one of Belle's two Dutch suitors whom her parents regarded as particularly eligible. He and Belle met at Mme Hasselaer's, where she talked to him late into the night; his indiscretion about that and other matters caused her considerable anxiety. There are extant a dozen letters from her to him (1764–65) but none from him to her.

PAOLI, Pasquale (1726–1807). Corsican nationalist leader. In 1755 he was elected General-in-Chief of the Corsican Nation and made important administrative and educational reforms. He led the opposition against the long-standing Genoese occupation of Corsica and continued the armed struggle for Corsica's independence against the French. He was defeated in 1769 and took refuge in England. In 1790 he was recalled to Corsica as its military governor; with British help he expelled the French. Corsica became a British protectorate, but Paoli was not allowed to be its viceroy. He was ordered back to England, where he died in 1807.

PATER, Albertine, née van Nijvenheim (1743–1805). Friend of d'Hermenches, to whom he wrote verses. She had married Gerard Pater in 1760, and was divorced in 1764. She moved to Paris and joined the circle of the duc de Choiseul; Louis XV was one of her admirers.

PERPONCHER DE SEDLNITZKY, Cornelis de (1733–76). Councillor in the Court of Justice of Holland. He married Belle's sister Johanna Maria (Mitie) in 1763. He died in 1776 in an accidental drowning near Zuylen, leaving five children.

PREVOST, Jeanne-Louise (1721–85). Governess of Belle de Zuylen from 1748 to 1753. In 1750 she took Belle on a journey to Switzerland and France. After she left the service of the Tuyll family she wrote more than fifty letters to Belle between 1753 and 1758; they are the fullest documentation we have of Belle's adolescence.

REEDE, Arent Willem van, Count (1744–1838). Brother of Frederik van Reede, Count of Athlone; brother-in-law of Belle's cousin Annebetje.

REEDE, Frederik Christiaan Reinhard, Count of; also fifth count of Athlone (1743–1808). A principal offier of Utrecht, who had inherited an Irish peerage. In 1765 he married Belle's cousin, Anna Elisabeth Christina (Annebetje) van Tuyll van Serooskerken; they had nine children.

ROSENDAAL. See TORCK, Eusebia Jacoba de Rode van Heeckeren.

SALGAS, Claude de Narbonne-Pelet de (1728–1813). Tutor to the family of the Dutch ambassador to England; friend of Charles-Emmanuel de Charrière, whose marriage to Belle he helped negotiate.

SAYN-WITTGENSTEIN, Georges Ernst, Count of (1735–92). Colonel in the French service; an acquaintance of d'Hermenches in the Corsican campaign. One of Belle's last suitors; they never met.

TORCK, Eusebia Jacoba de Rode van Heeckeren (1739–93). Wife of Assueer Jan Torck, Baron van Rosendaal and Heer van Voorschoten. She is one of Belle's good friends—sometimes called "Mme de Rosendaal" and sometimes "Mme de Voorschoten."

TUYLL VAN SEROOSKERKEN, Diederik Jacob, Baron van, Seigneur of Zuylen and of Westbroek (1707–76). President of the Ridderschap (Council of Nobles) of Utrecht; member of the Admiralty of the Meuse; inspector of dikes and public works, among other offices. In 1739 he married Helena Jacoba de Vicq (1724–68), of the wealthy and powerful Amsterdam bourgeoisie. They had seven children:
—ISABELLA AGNETA ELISABETH, OR BELLE DE ZUYLEN (1740–1805).
—REINOUT GERARD (1741–58). He died in a swimming accident.
—WILLEM RENÉ (1743–1839). He inherited his father's titles and had various important positions as a public official. He married Johanna Catharina Fagel in 1771. They had seven children, the third of whom became the heir of Charles-Emmanuel and Isabelle de Charrière.
—DIEDERIK JACOB, or DITIE (1744–73). Naval commander. He was of fragile health (he probably had tuberculosis) and spent his last years in Switzerland, France, and Italy. He died in Naples, on his way to the Charrières' home in Colombier after having represented the Netherlands at the wedding of the King of Sardinia. He was Belle's favorite brother.

—JOHANNA MARIA, or MITIE (1746-1803). She married Cornelis de Perponcher in 1763, by whom she had six children.

—VINCENT MAXIMILIAAN (1747-94). Lieutenant-colonel in the cavalry. He was wounded in the war between the Dutch Republic and the French Revolutionary forces, was taken prisoner by the French, and died of dysentery in a military hospital at Pont-Sainte-Maxence in France.

—GERTRUDE JACOBA (1749). He died in infancy.

TUYLL VAN SEROOSKERKEN, Hendrik Willem Jacob, Baron van (1713-1800). A paternal uncle of Belle. He was lieutenant general in the cavalry and adjutant general of the Stadholder Willem V. He married Maria-Anna Singendonck in 1759; they had no children. D'Hermenches refers to him in the tale of "the big nightcap" in Letter 134.

TUYLL VAN SEROOSKERKEN, Jan Maximiliaan, Baron van (1710-62). A paternal uncle of Belle; she describes his death in Letter 75. He married twice; his second wife survived him. By his first marriage he is the father of all Belle's paternal cousins. These include:

—ANNA ELISABETH CHRISTINA (Annebetje) (1745-1819). Belle's best friend, who married the count of Reede (Lord Athlone), and is thereafter referred to as Lady Athlone.

—FREDERIK CHRISTIAAN HENDRIK (Frits). He wanted to marry Belle.

—MARIE CATHARINA, who married Anthony Bentinck.

—REINIERA, who married Johan Albert Bentinck.

TWICKEL. See WASSENAER VAN OBDAM, Carel George.

D'USSON, Margaretha Cornelia, née van de Poll. A Dutch Protestant, she was the widow of Cornelis Munter. In 1755 she married a French Catholic, the comte d'Usson, brother of the French ambassador to the Hague. The legal complications attached to this mixed marriage make the case of Mme d'Usson a reference point in the discussions of a marriage between Belle and Bellegarde.

WASSENAER VAN OBDAM, Carel George, Count van, Heer van Twickel (1732-1800). Governor of Franekeradeel; envoy representing the United Provinces at Vienna.

WASSENAER VAN OBDAM, Jacob Jan, Count van (1724-79). Brother of Carel George; administrator and inspector of the dikes. He was one of Belle's unenthusiastic Dutch suitors. Like his brother, he was keenly interested in the French Theater at the Hague.

WEMYSS, David, Lord Elcho (1721-87). A Scottish baron who had been attainted for his part in the failed Jacobite rebellion of 1745, in which he gained a reputation for cruelty. He fled to the Continent and became citizen of Neuchâtel. He was one of the last of Belle's suitors, regarded by her as the least desirable. The two never met.

WITTGENSTEIN. See SAYN-WITTGENSTEIN, Georges Ernst.

SHORT TITLES FOR CITED WORKS

Boswell, *Account of Corsica*   Boswell, James. *An Account of Corsica, the Journal of a Tour to that Island; and Memoirs of Pascal Paoli*. London, 1768.

Boswell in Holland   Pottle, Frederick, ed. *Boswell in Holland (1763–1764), Including His Correspondence with Belle de Zuylen (Zélide)*. New York: McGraw-Hill, 1952.

Courtney, *Biography*   Courtney, C. P. *Isabelle de Charrière (Belle de Zuylen): A Biography*. Oxford: Voltaire Foundation, 1993.

D'Hermenches: Pamphlets   Courtney, C. P., ed. *Constant d'Hermenches: Pamphlets and Occasional Pieces with Replies by Voltaire*. Cambridge: Daemon Press, 1988.

Hall, *The Corsican Question*   Hall, Thadd. *France and the Eighteenth-Century Corsican Question*. New York: New York UP, 1971.

Kennett, *The French Armies*   Kennett, Lee. *The French Armies in the Seven Years' War: A Study in Military Organization and Administration*. Durham, N.C.: Duke UP, 1967.

Nixon, *The Calas Case*   Nixon, Edna. *Voltaire and the Calas Case*. New York: Vanguard, 1961.

O.C.   Charrière, Isabelle de [Belle de Zuylen]. *Oeuvres complètes*. Ed. Jean-Daniel Candaux, C. P. Courtney, Pierre H. Dubois, Simone Dubois-De Bruyn, Patrice Thompson, Jerome Vercruysse, and Dennis Wood. 10 vols. Amsterdam: G. A. van Oorschot, 1979–84.

Vissière, *Correspondance*   Vissière, Isabelle, and Jean-Louis, eds. *Isabelle de Charrière: Une Liaison dangereuse: Correspondance avec Constant d'Hermenches*. Paris: Editions de la Différence, 1991.

Voltaire's Correspondence   Besterman, Theodore, ed. *Voltaire's Correspondence*. 107 vols. Geneva: Institut et Musée Voltaire, 1961.

BIBLIOGRAPHY

COMPLETE WORKS OF ISABELLE DE CHARRIERE

Charrière, Isabelle de [Belle de Zuylen]. *Oeuvres complètes*. Ed. Jean-Daniel Candaux, C. P. Courtney, Pierre H. Dubois, Simone Dubois-De Bruyn, Patrice Thompson, Jerome Vercruysse, and Dennis Wood. 10 vols. Amsterdam: G. A. van Oorschot, 1979–84.

BIBLIOGRAPHIES

Courtney, C. P. *A Preliminary Bibliography of Isabelle de Charrière (Belle de Zuylen)*. Oxford: Voltaire Foundation, 1980.

———. *Isabelle de Charrière: A Secondary Bibliography*. Oxford: Voltaire Foundation, 1982.

EDITIONS OF CORRESPONDENCES

Bergh, Greetje van den, trans. *Ik heb geen talent voor ondergeschiktheid: Belle van Zuylen in briefwisseling met Constant d'Hermenches, James Boswell en Werner C. W. van Pallandt*. Amsterdam: G. A. van Oorschot, 1987.

Candaux, Jean-Daniel, ed. *Benjamin Constant, Isabelle de Charrière: Correspondance (1787–1805)*. Paris: Editions Desjonquères, 1996.

Constant de Rebecque [Wilhelmine-Henriette-Charlotte du Bois], Baronne [Auguste], and Dorine Berthoud, eds. *Les Mariages manqués de Belle de Tuyll (Mme de Charrière), lettres de Constant d'Hermenches*. Lausanne: Payot, 1940.

Godet, Philippe, ed. *Lettres de Belle de Zuylen (Madame de Charrière) à Constant d'Hermenches*. Paris: Plon; Genève: A. Jullien, 1909.

Vissière, Isabelle and Jean-Louis, eds. *Isabelle de Charrière: Une Liaison dangereuse: Correspondance avec Constant d'Hermenches*. Paris: Editions de la Différence, 1991.

ENGLISH TRANSLATIONS OF ISABELLE DE CHARRIERE'S WORKS

Four Tales by Zélide. Trans. S[ybil] M[arjorie] S[cott]. (Includes *The Nobleman*, *Mistress Henley*, *Letters from Lausanne*, and *Letters from Lausanne—Caliste*.) London: Constable, 1925; New York: Scribner's, 1926. Reissued as *Four Tales*. Freeport: Books for Libraries, 1970.

Letters of Mistress Henley Published by Her Friend. Trans. Philip Stewart and Jean Vaché. Introduction, notes, and bibliography by Joan Hinde Stewart and Philip Stewart. New York: Modern Language Association of America, 1993.

Biographies of Isabelle de Charriere

Courtney, C. P. *Isabelle de Charrière (Belle de Zuylen): A Biography.* Oxford: Voltaire Foundation, 1993.

Dubois, Pierre, and Simone Dubois. *Zonder vaandel: Belle de Zuylen: Een biografie.* Amsterdam: Oorschot, 1993.

Farnum, Dorothy. *The Dutch Divinity: A Biography of Madame de Charrière.* London: Jarrolds, 1959.

Godet, Philippe. *Madame de Charrière et ses amis, d'après de nombreux documents inédits (1740–1805).* 2 vols. Genève: A. Jullien, 1906. Rpt., Genève: Slatkine Reprints, 1973.

Scott, Geoffrey. *The Portrait of Zélide.* London: Constable, 1927; New York: Scribner's, 1927. Reissued with introduction by Shirley Hazzard and afterword by Richard Dunn. New York: Turtle Point, 1997.

Trousson, Raymond. *Isabelle de Charrière: Un Destin de femme au XVIIIe siècle.* Paris: Hachette, 1994.

Works on David-Louis Constant d'Hermenches

Courtney, C. P., ed. *Constant d'Hermenches: Pamphlets and Occasional Pieces with Replies by Voltaire.* Cambridge: Daemon Press, 1988.

Roulin, Alfred, ed. [*Voltaire:*] *Lettres inédites à Constant d'Hermenches.* Paris: Corrêa, 1956.

Selected Historical Sources

Besterman, Theodore, ed. *Voltaire's Correspondence.* 107 vols. Geneva: Institut et Musée Voltaire, 1961.

Boswell, James. *An Account of Corsica, the Journal of a Tour to that Island; and Memoirs of Pascal Paoli.* London, 1768.

Brady, Frank, and Frederick Pottle, eds. *Boswell in Search of a Wife.* New York: McGraw-Hill, 1956.

Childs, James Rives. *Casanova: A Biography Based on New Documents.* London: Allen and Unwin, 1961.

Constant, Benjamin. *Ma Vie (Le Cahier rouge).* Ed. C. P. Courtney. Cambridge: Daemon Press, 1991.

Corvisier, André. *L'Armée française de la fin du XVIIe siècle au ministère de Choiseul: Le Soldat.* 2 vols. Paris: Presses universitaires de France, 1964.

Gay, Peter. *Voltaire's Politics: The Poet as Realist.* New York: Vintage, 1959.

Gibbon, Edward. *Le Journal de Gibbon à Lausanne, 17 août 1763–19 avril 1764.* Ed. Georges Bonnard. Lausanne: Libraire de l'Université, 1945.

Hall, Thadd. *France and the Eighteenth-Century Corsican Question.* New York: New York UP, 1971.

Hopkins, Donald R. *Princes and Peasants: Smallpox in History.* Chicago: U of Chicago P, 1983.

Israel, Jonathan. *The Dutch Republic: Its Rise, Greatness, and Fall (1477–1806).* Oxford: Clarendon Press, 1995.

Kennett, Lee. *The French Armies in the Seven Years' War: A Study in Military Organization and Administration.* Durham, N.C.: Duke UP, 1967.

Léonard, Emile. *L'Armée et ses problèmes au XVIIIe siècle.* Paris: Plon, 1958.

Morren, Pierre. *La Vie lausannoise au XVIIIe siècle d'après Jean Henri Polier de Vernand, Lieutenant Baillival.* Genève: Labor et Fides, 1970.

Nixon, Edna. *Voltaire and the Calas Case.* New York: Vanguard, 1961.

Pottle, Frederick. *James Boswell: The Earlier Years (1740–1769).* New York: McGraw-Hill, 1966.

Pottle, Frederick, ed. *Boswell in Holland (1763–1764), Including His Correspondence with Belle de Zuylen (Zélide).* New York: McGraw-Hill, 1952.

Rudler, Gustave. *La Jeunesse de Benjamin Constant, 1767–1794: Le Disciple du XVIIIe siècle, utilitarisme et pessimisme, Mme de Charrière.* Paris: A. Colin, 1908.

Smith, Jay M. *The Culture of Merit: Nobility, Royal Service, and the Making of Absolute Monarchy in France 1600–1787.* Ann Arbor: U of Michigan P, 1996.

Société vaudoise de généalogie. *Recueil de généalogies vaudoises.* 3 vols. Lausanne: Bridel et Payot, 1923–1950.

Thrasher, Peter Adam. *Pasquale Paoli: An Enlightened Hero.* London: Archon Books, 1970.

Vigarello, Georges. *Concepts of Cleanliness: Changing Attitudes in France since the Middle Ages.* Trans. Jean Birrell. Cambridge: Cambridge UP, 1988.

CRITICAL WORKS ON THE
CONSTANT D'HERMENCHES—BELLE DE ZUYLEN
CORRESPONDENCE

Bray, Bernard. "Les Lettres d'Isabelle de Charrière: Apprentissage et culture." *Isabelle de Charrière (Belle de Zuylen): De la correspondance au roman épistolaire.* Ed. Yvette Went-Daoust. Amsterdam–Atlanta: Rodopi, 1995. 7–14.

Diaconoff, Suellen. "Betwixt and Between: Letters and Liminality." *Studies in Voltaire and the Eighteenth Century* 304 (1992): 899–903.

Henriette, Colette. "Isabelle de Charrière, femme de lettres: Etude de la correspondance entre Belle de Zuylen / Isabelle de Charrière et David-Louis Constant d'Hermenches." Diss. U of Maryland, 1995.

———. "'Une Femme vive et sensible': Ce que révèle la correspondance entre Belle de Zuylen et Constant d'Hermenches." *Studies on Voltaire and the Eighteenth Century* 304 (1992): 947–50.

Laden, Marie-Paule Laden. "La Correspondance entre Belle de Zuylen et Constant d'Hermenches, ou comment être soi-même sans sortir de l'ordre." *Literary Generations: A Festschrift in Honor of Edward D. Sullivan.* Lexington, KY: French Forum, 1992. 110–16.

Moser-Verrey, Monique. "L'Oralité dans la correspondance d'Isabelle de Charrière avec Constant d'Hermenches (1760–1776)." *La Lettre au XVIIIe siècle et ses avatars.* Ed. Georges Bérubé and Marie-France Silver. Toronto: Editions du Gref, 1996. 51–65.

———. "L'Oralité dans l'écriture épistolaire d'Isabelle de Charrière." *Une Européenne: Isabelle de Charrière en son siècle. Actes du colloque de Neuchâtel, 11–13 novembre 1993.* Ed. Doris Jakubec and Jean-Daniel Candaux. Neuchâtel: Gilles Attinger, 1994. 271–86.

Pelckmans, Paul. *Isabelle de Charrière: Une Correspondance au seuil du monde moderne.* Amsterdam–Atlanta: Rodopi, 1995.

Thompson, Patrice. "Approches méthodologiques requises par une correspondance: Belle de Zuylen et Constant d'Hermenches." *Zeitschrift für Französische Sprache und Literatur* Supp. vol. 18 (1990). 135–42.

Went-Daoust, Yvette. "La Correspondance Belle de Zuylen-Constant d'Hermenches: enfermement et cosmopolitisme." *Expériences limites de l'épistolaire: Lettres d'exil, d'enfermement, de folie.* Paris: Champion, 1993. 327–39

———. "L'Oeuvre épistolaire de Mme de Charrière." *De Achttiende Eeuw* 27 (1995) 1: 41–54.

———, ed. *Isabelle de Charrière (Belle de Zuylen): De la correspondance au roman épistolaire.* Amsterdam–Atlanta: Rodopi, 1995.

Vissière, Isabelle. "L'Encre et le fiel ou la cruauté souriante de Constant d'Hermenches." *Une Européenne: Isabelle de Charrière en son siècle. Actes du colloque de Neuchâtel, 11–13 novembre 1993.* Ed. Doris Jakubec and Jean-Daniel Candaux. Neuchâtel: Gilles Attinger, 1994. 229–41.

Whatley, Janet. "Letters to a Libertine: The Correspondence of Belle de Zuylen and Constant d'Hermenches." *Women Writers in Pre-Revolutionary France: Strategies of Emancipation.* Ed. Colette H. Winn and Donna Kuizenga. New York and London: Garland, 1997. 335–48.

SELECTED CRITICISM AND COMMENTARY

Allison, Jenene. *Revealing Difference: The Fiction of Isabelle de Charrière.* Newark: U Delaware P, 1995.

Altman, Janet Gurkin. *Epistolarity: Approaches to a Form.* Columbus: Ohio UP, 1982.

Beauvoir, Simone de. *The Second Sex.* Trans. H. M. Parshley. New York: Vintage Books, 1989. Trans. of *Le deuxième sexe.* 2 vols. Paris: Gallimard, 1976.

Bérenguier, Nadine. "From Clarens to Hollow Park: Isabelle de Charrière's Quiet Revolution." *Studies in Eighteenth-Century Culture* 21 (1991): 219–42.

——. "L'Infortune des alliances: Contrat, mariage et fiction au dix-huitième siècle." *Studies on Voltaire and the Eighteenth Century* 329 (1995): 271–417.

Braunrot, Christabel Pendrill. *Madame de Charrière and the Eighteenth-Century Novel: Experiments in Epistolary Technique.* Diss. Yale University, 1973.

Deguise, Alix. *Trois Femmes: Le Monde de Madame de Charrière.* Genève: Editions Slatkine, 1981.

Fink, Beatrice, ed. *Isabelle de Charrière, Belle van Zuylen.* Spec. issue of *Eighteenth-Century Life* 13 (1989).

Goldsmith, Elizabeth C., ed. *Writing the Female Voice: Essays on Epistolary Literature.* Boston: Northeastern UP, 1989.

Jackson, Susan. "The Novels of Isabelle de Charrière; or, A Woman's Work is Never Done." *Studies in Eighteenth-Century Culture* 14 (1985): 299–306.

Jaeger, Kathleen. *Male and Female Roles in the Eighteenth Century: The Challenge of Replacement and Displacement in the Novels of Isabelle de Charrière.* New York: Peter Lang, 1994.

Jakubec, Doris and Jean-Daniel Candaux, eds. *Une Européenne: Isabelle de Charrière en son siècle. Actes du colloque de Neuchâtel, 11–13 novembre 1993.* Neuchâtel: Gilles Attinger, 1994.

Karmarkar, Medha Nirody. *Madame de Charrière et la révolution des idées.* New York: Peter Lang, 1995.

Lacy, Margriet Bruyn. "Madame de Charrière and the Constant Family." *Romance Notes* 23.2 (1982): 154–58.

Letzter, Jacqueline. *Intellectual Tacking: Questions of Education in the Works of Isabelle de Charrière.* Rodopi: Amsterdam – Atlanta, 1998.

MacArthur, Elizabeth J. "Devious Narratives: Refusal of Closure in Two Eighteenth-Century Epistolary Novels." *Eighteenth-Century Studies* 21.1 (1987): 1–20.

Moser-Verrey, Monique. "Isabelle de Charrière: En quête d'une meilleure entente." *Stanford French Review* 11 (spring 1987): 63–76.

Ozouf, Mona. "Madame de Charrière: Isabelle ou le mouvement." *Les Mots des femmes: Essais sur la singularité française.* Paris: Fayard, 1995. 53–83.

Sainte-Beuve, C.-A. "Benjamin Constant et Mme de Charrière." *Portraits littéraires.* Vol. 3. Paris: Garnier, 1862. 184–283.

——. "Madame de Charrière." *Portraits de Femmes.* Paris: Garnier, 1886. 411–57.

Starobinski, Jean. "Les *Lettres écrites de Lausanne* de Madame de Charrière: Inhibition psychique et interdit social." *Roman et lumières au XVIIIe siècle.* Paris: Editions sociales, 1970. 130–51.

Stewart, Joan Hinde. "Designing Women." *A New History of French Literature.* Ed. Denis Hollier. Cambridge, MA: Harvard UP, 1989. 553–58.

——. "Mapping the Quotidian: Isabelle de Charrière." *Gynographs: French Novels by Women of the Late Eighteenth Century.* Lincoln: U of Nebraska P, 1993. 96–117.

Vissière, Isabelle, ed. *Isabelle de Charrière, une aristocrate révolutionnaire: Ecrits 1788–1794.* Paris: Des Femmes, 1988.

Whatley, Janet. "Isabelle de Charrière." *French Women Writers: A Bio-bibliographical Source Book.* Ed. Eva Martin Sartori and Dorothy Wynne Zimmerman. New York: Greenwood, 1991. 35–46.

INDEX